International Trade

International Trade:
Selected Readings

second edition

edited by
Jagdish N. Bhagwati

The MIT Press
Cambridge, Massachusetts
London, England

Second printing, 1988

© 1981, 1987 Massachusetts Institute of Technology

Published 1981. Second Edition 1987.

This book was set in Times New Roman by Asco Trade Typesetting Ltd., Hong Kong, and printed and bound by Halliday Lithograph in the United States of America.

Library of Congress Cataloging-in-Publication Data

International trade.

  Includes bibliographies and index.
  1. Commercial policy.   2. Commerce.   I. Bhagwati,
Jagdish N., 1934–
HF1411.I5185   1987   382   87-2623
ISBN 0-262-02264-8
ISBN 0-262-52119-9 (pbk.)

Contents

II

19

Endogenous Tariff Formation   329
Wolfgang Mayer

VII

Customs Unions   353

20

The Theory of Customs Unions: A General Survey   357
Richard Lipsey

21

**An Elementary Proposition Concerning the Formation of
Customs Unions**   377
Murray Kemp and Henry Wan, Jr.

VIII

Growth and Transfers   381

22

**The Possibility of Income Losses from Increased Efficiency or
Factor Accumulation in the Presence of Tariffs**   385
Harry G. Johnson

23

Tariffs, Foreign Capital, and Immiserizing Growth   389
Richard A. Brecher and Carlos F. Díaz-Alejandro

24

Capital Accumulation in the Open Two-Sector Economy   395
M. Alasdair M. Smith

25

**Investment, the Two-Sector Model, and Trade in Debt and
Capital Goods**   407
Stanley Fischer and Jacob A. Frenkel

26

27

IX

28

29

Editor's Preface

This is the second edition of the earlier set of *Readings* which I had assembled for use in courses on the theory of international trade. Although they had been designed for use primarily with the text by Professor T. N. Srinivasan and myself, *Lectures on International Trade* (MIT Press), they were usable by themselves and were indeed widely used as such.

The original edition was first published in 1981. It went through four reprintings. But by 1986 the first edition was seriously out of date. Two fundamental revolutions had overtaken the field: (1) the theory of imperfect competition, both the large-group case and the small-group "market structure" analysis, had grown exponentially, and (2) the theory of directly unproductive profit-seeking (DUP) and rent-seeking activities had equally expanded dramatically, overwhelming the preoccupations of many theorists of trade and welfare. While the former amounted to outfitting the traditional bicycle with an innovative new motor that outdazzled the older model, the latter amounted to taking the old bicycle down a new road.

The new *Readings* therefore now include four papers in part III on the developments in the theory of imperfect competition and market structure and two papers in part IX on correspondingly new models of multinational direct investment. Equally, they include three papers in part VI on the theory of DUP and rent-seeking activities.

Altogether, twelve papers from the first edition have been dropped, whereas thirteen new papers have been added. In view of the considerable recent revival in interest in two time-honored topics in the theory of international trade, comparative advantage and the transfer problem, three papers on these subjects have been added to the new selection. Ed Leamer's influential work on comparative advantage in the tradition of the factor-content approach of Jaroslav Vanek has now been treated at book-length at MIT Press by him, but the selection here reprints his early, classic paper on the problem in the *Journal of Political Economy*. The renewed interest in the transfer problem has come independently and with explosive force and significant impact in mathematical economics and in international economics. Hence I have reprinted part of Harry Johnson's splendid treatment of the classic Samuelson-initiated analysis of the problem in the two-good, two-country framework, while also including the Bhagwati-Brecher-Hatta generalization of it to the three-country framework. The latter paper has the advantage that it reviews equally other independent contributions in this area, while uniquely managing to integrate the analysis into the general theory of distortions and welfare.

Therefore, although the new selection should bring the student to the edge of all the major new developments in international trade analysis of the last decade, this gain has come at the expense of my having had to drop some excellent papers. This was a hard thing to do, especially as I had to contradict my own sense of what was considered worth including in the first edition! In wielding the axe, I have drawn on the advice of many former students and present colleagues at different universities, going by their experience with trade students over the last few years. Nevertheless, the loss of these earlier papers illustrates anew why economics is important: scarcity is a fact of life.

I must thank David Laster for substantial help with putting the new selection together. He is a splendid student, who was on top of the entire subject and helpful with ideas and suggestions that proved extremely perceptive. I have also benefited from the advice of other students, especially Sunil Gulati and Doug Irwin, and from several economists in the field: Avinash Dixit, Elhanan Helpman, Alan Deardorff, Ronald Findlay, Gene Grossman, Robert Feenstra, Richard Brecher, T. N. Srinivasan, Elias Dinopoulos, Oded Galor, and Kar-yiu Wong. Brian Wesol helped greatly with the proofreading.

I
General Equilibrium

Introduction to Part I

Part I contains five papers on general equilibrium theory and tools. Chapter 1 is Paul Samuelson's classic paper on factor price equalization, which, with its earlier companion paper on the same subject (*Economic Journal*, June 1948), laid the foundation of the modern theory of international trade by casting the Heckscher-Ohlin ideas into a well-defined analytical model. Its precise subject of factor price equalization in this model, now called the Heckscher-Ohlin-Samuelson model, has led to a great body of work on the precise conditions under which factor price equalization will follow from goods-price equalization under free trade, with extensions to the many factors and many goods models by McKenzie, Gale, Nikaido, and others.

Chapter 2, however, which consists of a classic paper by Robert Mundell, turns the problem around and asks whether factor price equalization in a world of international mobility of one of the factors will restore goods price equalization when a tariff has destroyed the goods price equalization directly, and it demonstrates elegantly that indeed the factor price equalization theorem can be turned on its head.

Chapter 3 is a brilliant exploration of the related problem as to whether trade in goods and international factor mobility are substitutes or components. Kar-yin Wong builds on the important work of Samuelson, Mundell, Markusen, and Svennson, distinguishing among alternative definitions of substitution and complementarity, to establish necessary and sufficient conditions under which either outcome will emerge.

Chapter 4 is a beautiful piece by Michael Mussa, which may be viewed as a geometric companion piece to the Samuelson paper insofar as it develops the geometry of the 2×2 model in terms of its dual, thus adding to our pedagogic repertoire. This geometry is particularly helpful in analyzing factor market distortions, and it should be of considerable value insofar as the use of duality theory has become more popular in trade theory as it has in the theory of public finance and elsewhere.

Chapter 5 is an excerpt from a long, important paper by Peter Neary on the analytics of the specific factors model of Ricardo and Viner, independently revived by Paul Samuelson and Ronald Jones. The model has been earlier explored by Michael Mussa and by Wolfgang Mayer, but its properties are more fully dealt with in the Neary paper. The popularity of this model in some of the analytical work on endogenous tariff and foreign investment modeling has made it worth adding to the average student's analytical repertoire.

1

**International
Factor-Price
Equalisation
Once Again**

Paul A. Samuelson

My recent paper attempting to show that free commodity trade will, under certain specified conditions, inevitably lead to complete factor-price equalisation appears to be in need of further amplification.[1] I propose therefore (1) to restate the principal theorem, (2) to expand upon its intuitive demonstration, (3) to settle the matter definitively by a brief but rigorous mathematical demonstration, (4) to make a few extensions to the case of many commodities and factors, and finally (5) to comment briefly upon some realistic qualifications to its simplified assumptions.

I cannot pretend to present a balanced appraisal of the bearing of this analysis upon interpreting the actual world, because my own mind is not made up on this question: on the one hand, I think it would be folly to come to any startling conclusions on the basis of so simplified a model and such abstract reasoning; but on the other hand, strong simple cases often point the way to an element of truth present in a complex situation. Still, at the least, we ought to be clear in our deductive reasoning; and the elucidation of this side of the problem plus the qualifying discussion may contribute towards an ultimate appraisal of the theorem's realism and relevance.

1. Statement of the Theorem

My hypotheses are as follows:

1. There are but two countries, America and Europe.
2. They produce but two commodities, food and clothing.
3. Each commodity is produced with two factors of production, land and labour. The production functions of each commodity show "constant returns to scale," in the sense that changing all inputs in the same proportion

This paper was originally published in *The Economic Journal* (June 1949): 181–197.

changes output in that same proportion, leaving all "productivities" essentially unchanged. In short, all production functions are mathematically "homogeneous of the first order" and subject to Euler's theorem.

4. The law of diminishing marginal productivity holds: as any one input is increased relative to other inputs, its marginal productivity diminishes.

5. The commodities differ in their "labour and land intensities." Thus, food is relatively "land using" or "land intensive," while clothing is relatively "labour intensive." This means that whatever the prevailing ratio of wages to rents, the optimal proportion of labour to land is greater in clothing than in food.

6. Land and labour are assumed to be qualitatively identical inputs in the two countries, and the technological production functions are assumed to be the same in the two countries.

7. All commodities move perfectly freely in international trade, without encountering tariffs or transport costs, and with competition effectively equalising the market price-ratio of food and clothing. No factors of production can move between the countries.

8. Something is being produced in both countries of both commodities with both factors of production. Each country may have moved in the direction of specialising on the commodity for which it has a comparative advantage, but it has not moved so far as to be specialising completely on one commodity.[2]

All of this constitutes the hypothesis of the theorem. The conclusion states:

Under these conditions, real factor prices must be exactly the same in both countries (and indeed the proportion of inputs used in food production in America must equal that in Europe, and similarly for clothing production).

Our problem is from now on a purely logical one. Is "If *H*, then inevitably *C*" a correct statement? The issue is not whether *C* (factor-price equalisation) will actually hold; nor even whether *H* (the hypothesis) is a valid empirical generalisation. It is whether *C* can fail to be true when *H* is assumed true. Being a logical question, it admits of only one answer: either the theorem is true or it is false.

One may wonder why such a definite problem could have given rise to misunderstanding. The answer perhaps lies in the fact that even so simple a setup as this one involves more than a dozen economic variables: at least four inputs for each country, four marginal productivities for each country (marginal productivity of American labour in food, of American land in food ...), two outputs for each country, the prices of the two commodities, the price in each country of the two inputs, the proportions of the inputs in different lines of production, and so forth. It is not always easy for the intellect to move purposefully in a hyperspace of many dimensions.

And the problem is made worse by the fact, insufficiently realised, that constant returns to scale is a very serious limitation on the production functions. A soon as one knows a single "curve" on such a surface, all other magnitudes are frozen into exact quantitative shapes and cannot be chosen at will. Thus, if one knows the returns of total product to labour working on one acre of land, then one already knows everything: the marginal productivity schedule of land, all the iso-product curves, the marginal-rate-of-substitution schedules, and so forth. This means one must use a carefully graduated ruler in drawing the different economic functions, making sure that they are numerically consistent in addition to their having plausible qualitative shapes.

2. Intuitive Proof

In each country there is assumed to be given totals of labour and land. If all resources are devoted to clothing, we get a certain maximum amount of clothing. If all are devoted to food production, we get a certain maximum amount of food. But what will happen if we are willing to devote only part of all land and part of total labour to the production of food, the rest being used in clothing production? Obviously, then we are in effect sacrificing some food in order to get some clothing. The iron law of scarcity tells us that we cannot have all we want of both goods but must ultimately give up something of one good in getting some of another.

In short there is a best "production possibility," or "transformation" curve showing us the maximum obtainable amount of one commodity for each amount of the other. Such a production possibility schedule was drawn up for each country in figure 1.1 of my earlier article. And in each

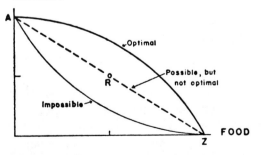

Figure 1.1

case it was made to be a curve *convex* from above, so that the more you want of any good the greater is the cost, at the margin, in terms of the other good. This convexity property is very important and is related to the law of diminishing marginal productivity. Few readers had any qualms about accepting convexity, but perhaps some did not realise its far-reaching implications in showing why the factor-price equalisation theorem had to be true. I propose, therefore, to show why the production possibility curve must obviously be convex (looked at from above).[3]

To show that convexity—or increasing relative marginal costs must hold—it is sufficient for the present purpose to show that concavity, or decreasing marginal costs, involves an impossible contradiction. Now at the very worst, it is easily shown we can move along a straight-line opportunity cost line between the two axes. For suppose we agree to give up half of the maximum obtainable amount of food. How much clothing can we be sure of getting? If we send out the crudest type of order that "half of all labour and half of all land is to be shifted to clothing production," we will (because of the assumption of constant returns to scale) *exactly halve* food production; and we will acquire *exactly half* of the maximum amount of clothing producible with all resources. Therefore, we end up at a point R, exactly half-way between the limiting points A and Z. Similarly, if we decide to give up 10, 20, 30, or 90 percent of the maximum amount of food producible, we can give out crude orders to transfer exactly 10, 20, 30, or 90 percent of *both* inputs from food to clothing. Because of constant returns to scale, it follows that we can be sure of getting 90, 80, 70, or 10 percent of maximum clothing.

In short, by giving such crude down-the-line orders that transfer both resources *always in the same proportion*, we can at worst travel along a straight line between the two limiting intercepts. Any concave curve would necessarily lie inside such a constant-cost straight line and can therefore be ruled out: hence decreasing (marginal, opportunity) costs are incompatible with the assumption of constant returns to scale.

But of course we can usually do even better than the straight-line case. A neophyte bureaucrat might be satisfied to give crude down-the-line orders, but there exist more efficient ways of giving up food for clothing. This is where social-economist (or "welfare economist") can supplement the talents of the mere technician who knows how best to use inputs in the production of any one good and nothing else. There are an infinity of ways of giving up, say, 50 percent of food: we may simply give up labour land, constant percentages of labour and land, or still other proportions. But there will be only one best way to do so, only one best combination of labour and land that is to be transferred. Best in what sense? Best in the sense of getting for us the maximum obtainable amount of clothing, compatible with our preassigned decision to sacrifice a given amount of food.

Intuition tells us that, qualitatively, we should transfer a larger proportion of labour than of land to clothing production. This is because clothing is the labour-intensive commodity by our original hypothesis. This means that the proportion of labour to land is actually declining in the food line as its production declines. What about the proportion of labour to land in clothing production? At first we were able to be generous in sparing labour, which after all was not "too well adapted" for food production. But now, when we come to give up still more food, there is less labour left in food production relative to land; hence, we cannot contrive to be quite so generous in transferring further labour to clothing production. As we expand clothing production further, the proportion of labour to land must also be falling in that line; but the labour-land ratio never falls to as low as the level appropriate for food, the land-intensive commodity.[4]

Intuition tells us that by following an optimal pattern which recognises the difference in factor intensities of the two goods, we can end up on a production possibility curve that is bloated out beyond a constant-cost straight line: in short, on a production possibility curve that is convex, obeying the law of increasing marginal costs of one good as it is expanded at the expense of the other good. Or, to put the same thing in the language of the marketplace, as the production of clothing expands, upward pressure is put on the price of the factor it uses most intensively—on wages relative to land rent. An increase in the ratio of wages to rent must in a competitive market press up the price of the labour-intensive commodity relative to the land-intensive commodity.

This one-directional relationship between relative factor prices and relative commodity prices is an absolute necessity, and it is vital for the recognition of the truth in the main theorem. Let me elaborate therefore upon the market mechanism bringing it about. Under perfect competition everywhere within a domestic market there will be set up a uniform ratio of wages to rents. In the food industry there will be one, and only one, optimal proportion of labour to land; any attempt to combine productive factors in proportions that deviate from the optimum will be penalised by losses, and there will be set up a process of corrective adaptation. The same competitive forces will force an adaptation of the input proportion in clothing production, with equilibrium being attained only when the input proportions are such as to equate exactly the ratio of the physical marginal productivities of the factors (the "marginal rate of substitution" of labour for land in clothing production) to the ratio of factor prices prevailing in the market. The price mechanism has an unconscious wisdom. As if led by an invisible hand, it causes the economic system to move out to the optimal production possibility curve. Through the intermediary of a common market factor-price ratio, the marginal rates of substitution of the factors become the same in both industries. And it is this marginal condition which intuition (as well as geometry and mathematics) tells us prescribes the optimal allocation of resources so as to yield maximum output. Not only does expanding clothing production result in the earlier described qualitative pattern of dilution of the ratio of labour to land in both occupations; more than that, a price system is one way of achieving the exactly optimal quantitative degree of change in proportions.

I have established unequivocally the following facts:

Within any country: (a) an increase in the ratio of wages to rents will cause a definite decrease in the proportion of labour to land in both industries; (b) to each determinate state of factor proportion in the two industries there will correspond one, and only one, commodity price ratio and a unique configuration of wages and rent; and (c) the change in factor proportions incident to an increase in wages/rents must be followed by a one-directional increase in clothing prices relative to food prices.

An acute reader may try to run ahead of the argument and may be tempted to assert: "But all this holds for one country, as of a given total factor endowment. Your established chain of causation is only from factor prices (and factor proportions) to commodity prices. Are you entitled to reverse the causation and to argue that the same commodity-price ratio must—even in countries of quite different total factor endowments—lead back to a common unique factor-price ratio, a common unique way of combining the inputs in the food and clothing industries, and a common set of absolute factor prices and marginal productivities?"

My answer is yes. This line of reasoning is absolutely rigorous. It is only proportions that matter, not scale. In such a perfectly competitive market each small association of factors (or firms, if one prefers that word) feels free to hire as many or as few extra factos as it likes. It neither knows nor cares anything about the totals for society. It is like a group of molecules in a perfect gas which is everywhere in thermal equilibrium. The molecules in any one small region behave in the same way regardless of the size of the room around them. A sample observed in the middle of a huge spherical room would act in the same way as a similar sample observed within a small rectangular room. Similarly, if we observe the behaviour of a representative firm in one country it will be exactly the same in all essentials as a representative firm taken from some other country—regardless of the difference in total factor amounts and relative industrial concentration— provided only that factor-price ratios are really the same in the two markets.[5]

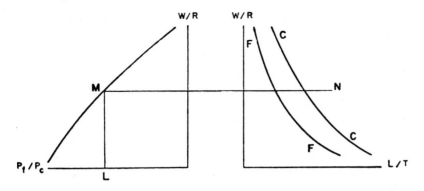

Figure 1.2

All this follows from the italicised conclusion reached just above, especially from (3) taken in conjunction with (1) and (2).

This really completes the intuitive demonstration of the theorem. The same international commodity price ratio, must—so long as both commodities are being produced and priced at marginal costs—enable us to infer backwards a unique factor-price ratio, a unique set of factor proportions, and even a unique set of absolute wages and rents.

All this is summarised in the accompanying chart. On the right-hand side I have simply duplicated figure 1.2 of my earlier paper. On the left-hand side I have added a chart showing the one-directional relation of commodity prices to factor prices.[6] As wages fall relative to rents the price of food is shown to rise relative to clothing in a monotonic fashion. The accompanying chart applies to either country and—so long as neither country is specialising completely—its validity is independent of their differing factor endowments. It follows that when we specify a common price ratio (say at L), we can move backward unambiguously (from M to N, etc.) to a common factor-price ratio and to a common factor proportion setup in the two countries.

3. Mathematical Proof

Now that the theorem has been demonstrated by commonsense reasoning, let me confirm it by more rigorous mathematical proof. The condition of equilibrium can be written in a variety of ways, and can be framed so as to involve more than a dozen equations. For example, let me call America's four marginal physical productivities—of labour in food, of land in food, of labour in clothing, of land in clothing—a, b, c, and d. I use Greek letters—α, β, γ, δ—to designate the corresponding marginal productivities in Europe. Then we can end up with a number of equilibrium expressions of the form

$$\frac{a}{b} = \frac{c}{d}, \quad \frac{\alpha}{\beta} = \frac{\gamma}{\delta}, \quad \frac{a}{c} = \frac{\alpha}{\gamma}, \dots, \text{etc.}$$

A number of economists have tortured themselves trying to manipulate these expressions so as to result in $a = \alpha$, etc., or at least in $a/b = \alpha/\beta$, etc. No proof of this kind is possible. The essential thing is that these numerous marginal productivities are by no means independent. Because proportions rather than scale are important, knowledge of the behaviour of the marginal productivity of labour tells us exactly what to expect of the marginal-productivity schedule of land. This is because increasing the amount of labour with land held constant is equivalent to reducing land with labour held constant.[7]

Mathematically, instead of writing food production, F, as any joint function of labour devoted to it, L_f, and of land, T_f, we can write it as

$$F = F(L_f, T_f) = T_f f\left(\frac{L_f}{T_f}\right), \tag{1}$$

where the function f can be thought of as the returns of food on one unit of land, and where the number of units of land enters as a scale factor. The form of this function is the same for both countries, and there is, of course, a similar type of function holding for cloth production, C, in terms of L_c and T_c namely

$$C = C(L_c, T_c) = T_c c\left(\frac{L_c}{T_c}\right). \tag{2}$$

It is easy to show mathematically, by simple partial differentiation of (1), the following relations among marginal physical productivities:

$$\text{MPP labour in food} = \frac{\partial F}{\partial L_f} = f'\left(\frac{L_f}{T_f}\right),$$

where f' represents the derivative of f and depicts the schedule of marginal product of labour (working on one unit of land). This must be a declining schedule according to our hypothesis of diminishing returns, so that we must have

$$f''\left(\frac{L_f}{T_f}\right) < 0.$$

By direct differentiation of (1), or by use of Euler's theorem, or by use of the fact that the marginal product of land can also be identified as a rent residual, we easily find that

$$\text{MPP land in food} = \frac{\partial F}{\partial T_f} = f\left(\frac{L_f}{T_f}\right) - \frac{L_f}{T_f}f'\left(\frac{L_f}{T_f}\right) = g\left(\frac{L_f}{T_f}\right),$$

where g is the name for the rent residual. It is easy to show that

$$g'\left(\frac{L_f}{T_f}\right) = -\frac{L_f}{T_f}f''\left(\frac{L_f}{T_f}\right)$$

By similar reasoning, we may write the marginal productivity of land in clothing production in its proper relation to that of labour:

$$\text{MPP labour in clothing} = \frac{\partial C}{\partial L_c} = c'\left(\frac{L_c}{T_c}\right)$$

$$\text{MPP land in clothing} = \frac{\partial C}{\partial T_c} = c\left(\frac{L_c}{T_c}\right) - \frac{L_c}{T_c}c'\left(\frac{L_c}{T_c}\right) = h\left(\frac{L_c}{T_c}\right)$$

$$h'\left(\frac{L_c}{T_c}\right) = -\frac{L_c}{T_c}c''\left(\frac{L_c}{T_c}\right)$$

The art of analysis in these problems is to select out the essential variables so as to reduce our equilibrium equations to the simplest form. Without specifying which country we are talking about, we certainly can infer from the fact that something of both goods is being produced with both factors the following conditions:

Real wages (or labour marginal "value" productivities) must be the same in food and clothing production when expressed in terms of a common *measure*, such as clothing; the same is true of real rents (or land marginal "value" productivities). Or

$$\begin{pmatrix}\text{food} \\ \text{price}\end{pmatrix}\begin{pmatrix}\text{MPP labour} \\ \text{in food}\end{pmatrix} = \begin{pmatrix}\text{clothing} \\ \text{price}\end{pmatrix}\begin{pmatrix}\text{MPP labour} \\ \text{in clothing}\end{pmatrix}$$

$$\begin{pmatrix}\text{food} \\ \text{price}\end{pmatrix}\begin{pmatrix}\text{MPP land} \\ \text{in food}\end{pmatrix} = \begin{pmatrix}\text{clothing} \\ \text{price}\end{pmatrix}\begin{pmatrix}\text{MPP land} \\ \text{in clothing}\end{pmatrix},$$

which can be written in terms of previous notation as

$$\left(\frac{P_f}{P_c}\right)f'\left(\frac{L_f}{T_f}\right) - c'\left(\frac{L_c}{T_c}\right) = 0$$

$$\left(\frac{P_f}{P_c}\right)\left[f\left(\frac{L_f}{T_f}\right) - \frac{L_f}{T_f}f'\left(\frac{L_f}{T_f}\right)\right] - \left[c\left(\frac{L_c}{T_c}\right) - \frac{L_c}{T_c}c'\left(\frac{L_c}{T_c}\right)\right] = 0.^8$$

Now these are two equations in the three variables L_f/T_f, L_c/T_c, and P_f/P_c. If we take the latter price ratio as given to us by international-demand conditions, we are left with *two* equations to determine the *two* unknown factor proportions. This is a solvent situation, and we should normally expect the result to be determinate.

But a purist might still have doubts: "How do you know that these two equations or schedules might not twist around and intersect in multiple equilibria?" Fortunately, the answer is simple and definite. On our hypothesis, any equilibrium configuration turns out to be absolutely unique. We may leave to a technical footnote the detailed mathematical proof of this fact.[9]

4. Multiple Commodities and Factors

Adding a third or further commodities does not alter our analysis much. If anything, it increases the likelihood of complete factor-price equalisation. For all that we require is that at least *two* commodities are simultaneously being produced in both countries and then our previous conclusion follows. If we add a third commodity which is very much like either of our present commodities, we are not changing the situation materially. But if we add new commodities which are more extreme in their labour-land intensities, then we greatly increase the chance that two regions with very different factor endowments can still come into complete factor-price equalisation. A "queer" region is not penalised for being queer if there is queer work that needs doing.

I do not wish at this time to go into the technical mathematics of the n commodity, and r factor case. But it can be said that (1) so long as the two regions are sufficiently close together in factor proportions, (2) so long as the goods differ in factor intensities, and (3) so long as the number of goods, n, is greater than the number of factors, r, we can hope to experience complete factor-price equalisation. On the other hand, if complete specialisation takes place it will do so for a whole collection of goods, the dividing line between exports and imports being a variable one depending upon reciprocal international demand (acting on factor prices) as in the classical theory of comparative advantage with multiple commodities.[10]

When we add a third productive factor and retain but two commodities, then the whole presumption towards factor-price equalisation disappears. Suppose American labour and American land have more capital to work with than does European labour and land. It is then quite possible that the marginal physical productivities of labour and land might be double that of Europe in both commodities. Obviously, commodity-price *ratios* would still be equal, production of both commodities will be taking place, but nonetheless absolute factor prices (or relative for that matter) need not be moved towards equality. This is our general expectation wherever the number of factors exceeds the number of commodities.

5. The Conditions of Complete Specialisation

If complete specialisation takes place in one country, then our hypothesis is not fulfilled, and the conclusion does not follow. How important is this empirically, and when can we expect complete specialisation to take place? As discussed earlier, the answer depends upon how disparate are the initial factor endowments of the two regions—how disparate in comparison with the differences in factor intensities of the two commodities.[11]

Unless the two commodities differ extraordinarily in factor intensities, the production possibility curve will be by no means so convex as it is usually drawn in the neoclassical literature of international trade, where it usually resembles a quarter circle whose slope ranges the spectrum from zero to infinity. It should rather have the crescentlike shape of the new moon. Opportunity costs tend to be more nearly constant than I had previously realised. This is a step in the direction of the older classical theory of comparative advantage. But with this important difference: the same causes that tend to produce *constant* costs also tend to produce *uniform* cost ratios between nations, which is not at all in the spirit of classical theory. (Undoubtedly much of the specialisation observed in the real world is due to something different from all this, namely decreasing-cost indivisibilities, tempered and counteracted by the existence of localised resources specifically adapted to particular lines of production.)

A parable may serve the double purpose of showing the range of factor endowment incompatible with complete specialisation and of removing any lingering element of paradox surrounding the view that commodity mobility may be a perfect substitute for factor mobility.

Let us suppose that in the beginning all factors were perfectly mobile, and nationalism had not yet reared its ugly head. Spatial transport costs being of no importance, there would be one world price of food and clothing, one real wage, one real rent, and the world's land and labour would be divided between food and clothing production in a determinate way, with uniform proportions of labour to land being used everywhere in clothing production, and with a much smaller—but uniform—proportion of labour to land being used in production of food.

Now suppose that an angel came down from heaven and notified some fraction of all the labour and land units producing clothing that they were to be called Americans, the rest to be called Europeans; and some different fraction of the food industry that henceforth they were to carry American passports. Obviously, just giving people and areas national labels does not alter anything: it does not change commodity or factor prices or production patterns.

But now turn a recording geographer loose, and what will he report? Two countries with quite different factor proportions, but with identical real wages and rents and identical modes of commodity production (though with different relative importances of food and clothing industries). Depending upon whether the angel makes up America by concentrating primarily on clothing units or on food units, the geographer will report a very high or a very low ratio of labour to land in the newly synthesised "country." But this he will never find: that the ratio of labour to land should ever exceed the proportions characteristic of the most labour-intensive industry (clothing) or ever fall short of the proportions of the least labour-intensive industry. Both countries *must* have factor proportions intermediate between the proportions in the two industries.

The angel can create a country with proportions *not* intermediate between the factor intensities of food and clothing. But he cannot do so by following the above-described procedure, which was calculated to leave prices and production unchanged. If he wrests some labour in food production away from the land it has been working with, "sending" this labour to Europe and keeping it from working with the American land, then a substantive change in production and prices will have been introduced. Unless there are abnormal repercussions on the pattern of effective demand, we can expect one or both of the countries to specialise completely and real wages to fall in Europe relative to America in one or both commodities, with European real rents behaving in an opposite fashion. The extension of this parable to the many-commodities case may be left to the interested reader.

6. Some Qualifications

A number of qualifications to this theoretical argument are in order. In the first place, goods do not move without transport costs; and to the extent that commodity prices are not equalised, it of course follows that factor prices will not tend to be fully equalised. Also, as I indicated in my earlier article, there are many reasons to doubt the usefulness of assuming identical production functions and categories of inputs in the two countries; and consequently, it is dangerous to draw sweeping practical conclusions concerning factor-price equalisation.

What about the propriety of assuming constant returns to scale? In justice to Ohlin, it should be pointed out that he, more than almost any other writer, has followed up the lead of Adam Smith and made *increasing returns* an important cause for trade. It is true that increasing returns *may* at the same time create difficulties for the survival of perfect competition, difficulties which cannot always be sidestepped by pretending that the increasing returns are due primarily to *external* rather than internal economies. But these difficulties do not give us the right to deny or neglect the importance of scale factors.[12] Where scale is important it is obviously possible for real wages to differ greatly between large free-trade areas and small ones, even with the same relative endowments of productive factors. And while it may have been rash of me to draw a moral concerning the worth of emigration from Europe out of an abstract simplified model, I must still record the view that the more realistic deviations from constant returns to scale and the actual production functions encountered in practice are likely to reinforce rather than oppose the view that high standards of life are possible in densely populated areas such as the island of Manhattan or the United Kingdom.

There is no ironclad a priori necessity for the law of diminishing marginal productivity to be valid for either or both commodities.[13] In such cases the usual marginal conditions of equilibrium are replaced by inequalities, and we have a boundary maximum in which we go the limit and use zero of one of the inputs in one industry. If it still could be shown that one commodity is always more labour intensive than the other, then the main theorem would probably still be true. But it is precisely in these pathological cases that factor intensities may become alike or reverse themselves, giving rise to the difficulties discussed in note 6.

In conclusion, some of these qualifications help us to reconcile results of abstract analysis with the obvious facts of life concerning the extreme diversity of productivity and factor prices in different regions of the world. Men receive lower wages in some countries than in others for a variety of reasons: because they are different by birth or training; because their effective know-how is limited and the manner of their being combined with other productive factors is not optimal; because they are confined to areas too small to develop the full economies of scale; because some goods and materials cannot be brought to them freely from other parts of the world, as a result of natural or man-made obstacles; and finally because the technological diversity of commodities with respect to factor intensities is not so great in comparison with the diversity of regional factor endowments to emancipate labourers from the penalty of being confined to regions lacking in natural resources. In the face of these hard facts it would be rash to consider the existing distribution of population to be optimal in any sense, or to regard free trade as a panacea for the present geographical inequalities.

Notes

1. International trade and the equalisation of factor prices, *Economic Journal* 58 (June 1948), pp. 163–184. I learn from Professor Lionel Robbins that A. P. Lerner, while a student at LSE, dealt with this problem. I have had a chance to look over Lerner's mimeographed report, dated December 1933, and it is a masterly, definitive treatment of the question, difficulties and all.

2. Actually we may admit the limiting case of "incipient specialisation," where nothing is being produced of one of the commodities, but where it is a matter of indifference whether an infinitesimal amount is or is not being produced, so that price and marginal costs are equal.

3. I am indebted for this line of reasoning to my colleague at MIT, Professor Robert L. Bishop, who for some years has been using it on beginning students in economics, with no noticeable disastrous effects. This proof is suggestive only, but it could easily be made rigorous.

4. Some readers may find it paradoxical that—with a fixed ratio of total labour to total land—we nevertheless lower the ratio of labour to land *in both industries* as a result of producing more of the labour-intensive good and less of the other. Such readers find it hard to believe that men's wages and women's wages can both go up at the same time that average wages are going down. They forget that there is an inevitable shift in the industries' weights used to compute the average-factor ratio. Really to understand all this, the reader must be referred to the Edgeworth box-diagram depicted in W. F. Stolper and P. A. Samuelson, Protection and real wages, *Review of Economic Studies* 9 (1941): 58–73.

5. The representative firm concept is in the case of homogeneous production functions not subject to the usual difficulties associated with the Marshallian concept; in this case, it should be added, the "scale" of the firm is indeterminate and, fortunately, irrelevant.

6. The left-hand curve is drawn in a qualitatively correct fashion. Actually its exact quantitative shape is determined by the two right-hand curves; but the chart is *not* exact in its quantitative details.

We may easily illustrate the importance of point 5 of our hypothesis, which insists on differences in factor intensities. Consider the depicted pathological case which does not meet the requirements of our hypothesis, and in which factor intensities are for a range identical, and in still other regions food becomes the labour-intensive good. The resulting pattern of commodity prices does *not* necessarily result in factor-price equalisation. Compare figure 1.3 of my earlier article.

7. J. B. Clark recognised in his *Distribution of Wealth* that the "upper triangle" of his labour-marginal-productivity diagram must correspond to the "rectangle" of his other-factors diagram. But his draughtsman did *not* draw the curve accordingly! This is a mistake that Philip Wicksteed in his *Co-ordination of the Laws of Distribution* (London School of Economics Reprint) could not have made. Clark, a believer in Providence, was unaware of the blessing—in the form of Euler's theorem on homogeneous functions—that made his theory possible. Wicksteed, a man of the cloth, appreciated and interpreted the generosity of Nature. Compare also F. H. Knight, *Risk, Uncertainty and Profit*, chap. 4, for a partial treatment of

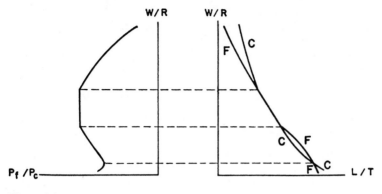

Figure 1.3

these reciprocal relations. G. J. Stigler, *Production and Distribution Theories: The Formative Period*, gives a valuable treatment of Wicksteed's theory as exposited by Flux and others.

8. In terms of our earlier $a, b, \ldots, \alpha, \beta, \ldots$, these equations are of the form

$$\frac{P_f}{P_c} a = c, \quad \frac{P_f}{P_c} b = d, \quad \text{etc.}$$

9. The Implicit Function Theorem tells us that two suitably continuous equations of the form $W_1(y_1, y_2) = 0 = W_2(y_1, y_2)$, possessing a solution (y_1^0, y_2^0), cannot have any other solution provided

$$\Delta = \begin{vmatrix} \dfrac{\partial W_1}{\partial y_1} & \dfrac{\partial W_1}{\partial y_2} \\ \dfrac{\partial W_2}{\partial y_1} & \dfrac{\partial W_2}{\partial y_2} \end{vmatrix} \neq 0.$$

In this case, where $y_1 = L_f/T_f$, etc., it is easy to show that

$$\Delta = \begin{vmatrix} \dfrac{P_f}{P_c} f'' & -c'' \\ -\dfrac{P_f}{P_c}\dfrac{L_f}{T_f} f'' & +\dfrac{L_c}{T_c} c'' \end{vmatrix} = \frac{P_f}{P_c} f'' c'' \left[\frac{L_c}{T_c} - \frac{L_f}{T_f} \right].$$

By hypothesis of diminishing returns, f'' and c'' are negative, and the term in brackets (representing the respective labour intensities in food and clothing) cannot be equal to zero. Hence, the equilibrium is unique. As developed earlier, if the factor intensities become equal, or reverse themselves, the one-to-one relation between commodity and factor prices *must* be ruptured.

10. The real wage of every resource must be the same in every place that it is used, when expressed in a common denominator. This gives us $r(n-1)$ independent equations involving the $(n-1)$ commodity-price ratios and the $n(r-1)$ factor proportions. If $n = r$, we have a determinate system once the goods-price ratios are given. If $n > r$, we have the same result, but now the international price ratios cannot

be presented arbitrarily as there are constant-cost paths on the production possibility locus, with one blade of Marshall's scissors doing most of the cutting, so to speak. If $n < r$, it is quite possible for free commodity trade to exist alongside continuing factor-price differentials. It is never enough simply to count equations and unknowns. In addition we must make sure that there are not multiple solutions: that factor intensities in the different commodities and the laws of returns are such as to lead to a one-to-one relationship between commodity prices and factor prices.

11. The reader may be referred to the earlier paper's discussion of figures 1.1 and 1.2, with respect to "steplike formations" and overlap.

12. Statical increasing returns is related to, but analytically distinct from, these irreversible cost economies induced by expansion and experimentation and which provide the justification for "infant industry" protection. Statical increasing returns might justify permanent judicious protection but not protection all around, since our purpose in bringing about large-scale production is to achieve profitable trade and consumption.

One other point needs stressing. For very small outputs, increasing returns to scale may take place without affecting the above analysis, provided that total demand is large enough to carry production into the realm of constant returns to scale. Increasing the "extent of the market" not only increases specialisation, it also increases the possibility of viable pure competition.

13. A "Pythagorean" production function of the form $F = \sqrt{L^2 + T^2}$ is an example of such a homogeneous function with increasing marginal productivity. So long as neither factor is to have a negative marginal productivity, *average* product must not be rising; but this is quite another thing. Surprisingly enough, the production possibility curve may still be convex with increasing marginal productivity. I have been asked whether any essential difference would be introduced by the assumption that one of the commodities, such as clothing, uses no land at all, or negligible land. Diminishing returns would still affect food as more of the transferable factor is added to the now specific factor of land, but no essential modifications in our conclusions are introduced.

2

International Trade and Factor Mobility

Robert A. Mundell

Commodity movements and factor movements are substitutes. The absence of trade impediments implies *commodity*-price equalization and, even when factors are immobile, a tendency toward *factor*-price equalization. It is equally true that perfect factor mobility results in *factor*-price equalization and, even when commodity movements cannot take place, in a tendency toward *commodity*-price equalization.

There are two extreme cases between which are to be found the conditions in the real world: There may be perfect factor mobility but no trade, or factor immobility with unrestricted trade. The classical economists generally chose the special case where factors of production were internationally immobile.

This paper will describe some of the effects of relaxing the latter assumption, allowing not only commodity movements but also some degree of factor mobility. Specifically it will show that an increase in trade impediments stimulates factor movements and that an increase in restrictions to factor movements stimulates trade.[1] It will also make more specific an old argument for protection.

1. Trade Impediments and Factor Movements

Under certain rigorous assumptions the substitution of commodity for factor movements will be complete. In a two-country, two-commodity, two-factor model, commodity-price equalization is sufficient to ensure factor-price equalization and factor-price equalization is sufficient to ensure commodity-price equalization if (1) production functions are homogeneous of the first degree (that is, if marginal productivities, relatively and absolutely,

This paper was originally published in *American Economic Review* 47 (June 1957): 321–335.

depend only on the proportions in which factors are combined) and are identical in both countries; (2) one commodity requires a greater proportion of one factor than the other commodity at any factor prices at all points on any production function; and (3) factor endowments are such as to exclude specialization.[2]

These assumptions permit us to isolate some important influences determining the pattern of international trade and factor flows and for present purposes will be adhered to. Our first task is to show that an increase in trade impediments encourages factor movements.

Assume two countries, A and B, producing two final commodities, cotton and steel, by means of two factors, labor and capital.[3] Country A is well endowed with labor but poorly endowed with capital relative to country B; cotton is labor intensive relative to steel. For expositional convenience we shall use community indifference curves.

For the moment we shall assume that country B represents the "rest of the world" and that country A is so small in relation to B that its production conditions and factor endowments can have no effect on prices in B.[4]

Let us begin with a situation where factors are immobile between A and B but where impediments to trade are absent. This results in commodity- and factor-price equalization. Country A exports its labor-intensive product, cotton, in exchange for steel. Equilibrium is represented in figure 2.1:

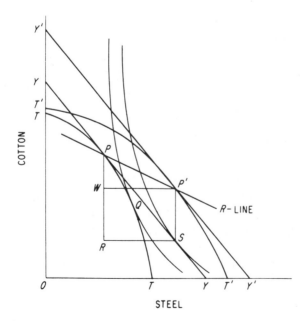

Figure 2.1

TT is A's transformation function (production possibility curve), production is at P, and consumption is at S. Country A is exporting PR of cotton and importing RS of steel. Her income in terms of steel or cotton is OY.

Suppose now that some exogenous factor removes all impediments to the movement of capital. Clearly, since the marginal product of capital is the same in both A and B, no capital movement will take place, and equilibrium will remain where it is. But now assume that A imposes a tariff on steel, and for simplicity make it prohibitive.[5] Initially the price of steel will rise relative to the price of cotton in A, and both production and consumption will move to Q, the autarky (economic self-sufficiency) point. Factors will move out of the cotton into the steel industry, but since cotton is labor intensive and steel is capital intensive, at constant factor prices the production shift creates an excess supply of labor and an excess demand for capital. Consequently the marginal product of labor must fall and the marginal product of capital must rise. This is the familiar *Stolper-Samuelson tariff argument.*[6]

But since capital is mobile, its higher marginal product in A induces a capital movement into A from B, changing factor endowments so as to make A more capital abundant. With more capital, A's transformation curve expands until a new equilibrium is reached.

Some help in determining where this new equilibrium will be is provided by figure 2.2. Country A initially has OC of capital and OL of labor; OO' is the efficiency locus along which marginal products of labor and capital

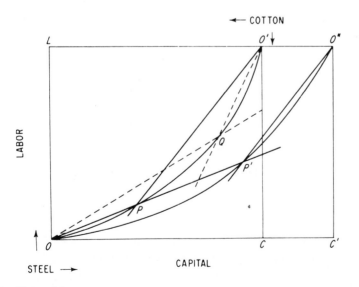

Figure 2.2

are equalized in steel and cotton. Equilibrium is initially at P, which corresponds to P on the production block in figure 2.1. Factor proportions in steel and cotton are given by the slopes of OP and $O'P$, respectively.

After the tariff is imposed, production moves along the efficiency locus to Q, corresponding to the autarky point Q in figure 2.1. The slopes of OQ and $O'Q$ indicate that the ratios of labor to capital in both cotton and steel have risen (that is, the marginal product of capital has risen and the marginal product of labor has fallen). Capital flows in and the cotton origin O' shifts to the right.

With perfect mobility of capital the marginal products of both labor and capital must be equalized in A and B. This follows from the assumption that the production functions are linear, homogeneous, and identical in both countries. Because marginal products in the rest of the world are assumed to be constant, the returns to factors in A will not change. Factor proportions in both steel and cotton in A then must be the same as before the tariff was imposed—so equilibrium must lie along OP-extended at the point where it is cut by a line $O''P'$ parallel to $O'P$, where O'' is the new cotton origin. But this is not yet sufficient to tell us exactly where along OP-extended the point P' will be.

Because marginal products in the new equilibrium are the same as before the tariff, commodity prices in A will not have changed; but if both incomes earned by domestic factors and commodity prices are unchanged, consumption will remain at S (in figure 2.1). Production, however, must be greater than S, because interest payments must be made to country B equal in value to the marginal product of the capital inflow. In figure 2.1, then, production equilibrium must be at some point above or to the northeast of S.

To find the exact point, we must show the effects of a change in capital endowments on the production block. Because steel is capital intensive, we should expect the production block after the capital movement has taken place to be biased in favor of steel at any given price ratio; that this is so has been recently proved by Rybczynski (1955).[7]

Because the same price ratio as at P will prevail, the locus of all tangents to larger and larger production blocks based on larger and larger endowments of capital must have a negative slope. Such a line, which I shall call the R line, is drawn in figure 2.1.

Capital will flow in until its marginal product is equalized in A and B, which will be at the point where A can produce enough steel and cotton for consumption equilibrium at S without trade, and at the same time make the required interest payment abroad. This point is clearly reached at P'

directly above S. At any point along the R line to the northwest of P', country A would have to import steel in order to consume at S (that is, demand conditions in A cannot be satisfied to the northwest of P'). At P' demand conditions in A are satisfied, and the interest payment can be made abroad at the same price ratio as before the tariff was levied. Thus the capital movement need not continue past this point, although any point to the southeast of P' would be consistent with equilibrium.

Production takes place in A at P', consumption is at S, and the transfer of interest payments is the excess of production over consumption in A, SP' of cotton.[8] The value of A's production has increased from OY to OY' in terms of steel, but YY' (which equals in value SP' of cotton) must be transferred abroad, so income is unchanged.

We initially assumed a prohibitive tariff; in face, even the smallest tariff is prohibitive in this model! A small tariff would not prohibit trade immediately: because of the price change some capital would move in and some trade would take place. But as long as trade continues, there must be a difference in prices in A and B equal to the ad valorem rate of tariff —hence a difference in marginal products—so capital imports must continue. Marginal products and prices can only be equalized in A and B when A's imports cease.

The tariff is now no longer necessary! Because marginal products and prices are again equalized, the tariff can be removed without reversing the capital movement. The tariff has eliminated trade, but after the capital movement there is no longer any need for trade.

This is not really such a surprising result when we refer back to the assumptions. Before the tariff was imposed, we assumed both unimpeded trade and perfect capital mobility. We have then two assumptions each of which is sufficient for the equalization of commodity and factor prices. The effect of the tariff is simply to eliminate one of these assumptions— unimpeded trade; the other is still operative.

However, one qualification must be made. If impediments to trade exist in both countries (tariffs in both countries or transport costs on both goods) and it is assumed that capital owners do not move with their capital, the interest payments on foreign-owned capital will be subject to these impediments; this will prevent complete equalization of factor and commodity prices. (This question could have been avoided had we allowed the capitalist to consume his returns in the country where his capital was invested.) The proposition that capital mobility is a perfect substitute for trade still stands, however, if one is wlling to accept the qualification as an imperfection mobility.

2. Effect of Relative Size

The previous section assumed that country A was very small in relation to country B. It turns out, however, that the relative sizes of the two countries make no difference in the model provided complete specialization does not result.

Suppose as before that country A is exporting cotton in exchange for steel. There are no impediments to trade and capital is mobile. But we no longer assume that A is small relative to B. Now A imposes a tariff on steel raising the internal price of steel in relation to cotton, shifting resources out of cotton into steel, raising the marginal product of capital, and lowering the marginal product of labor. A's demand for imports and her supply of exports fall. This decline in demand for B's steel exports and supply of B's cotton imports raises the price of cotton relative to steel in B; labor and capital in B shift out of steel into cotton, raising the marginal product of labor and lowering the marginal product of capital in B. Relative factor returns in A and B move in opposite directions, so the price changes in A which stimulate a capital movement are reinforced by the price changes in B. The marginal product of capital rises in A and falls in B; capital moves from B to A, contracting B's and expanding A's production block.

The assumption that capital is perfectly mobile means that factor and commodity prices must be equalized after the tariff. It is necessary now to show that they also will be unchanged. The price of cotton relative to steel is determined by world demand and supply curves. To prove that prices remain unchanged, it is sufficient to show that these demand and supply curves are unchanged—or that at the pretariff price ratio demand equals supply after the capital movement has taken place. But we know that at the old price ratio marginal products, hence incomes, are unchanged—thus demand is unchanged. All that remains then is to show that at constant prices production changes in one country cancel out production changes in the other country.

This proposition can be proved in the following way: if commodity and factor prices are to be unchanged after the capital movement has taken place, then factor proportions in each industry must be the same as before; then the increment to the capital stock used in A will, at constant prices, increase the output of steel and decrease the output of cotton in A, and the decrement to the capital stock in B wll decrease the output of steel and increase the output of cotton in B. But the increase in A's capital is equal to the decrease in B's capital, and since production expands at constant prices and with the same factor proportions in each country, the increase in resources used in producing steel in A must be exactly equal to the decrease in resources devoted to the production of steel in B. Similarly, the decrease in resources used in producing cotton in A is the same as the increase in resources devoted to cotton production in B. Then, since production functions are linear and homogeneous, the equal changes in resources applied to each industry (in opposite directions) imply equal changes in output. Therefore, the increase in steel output in A is equal to the decrease in steel output in B, and the decrease in cotton output in A is equal to the increase in cotton output in B (that is, world production is not changed, at constant prices, by a movement of capital from one country to another). In the world we are considering it makes no difference in which country a commodity is produced if commodity prices are equalized.

This proposition can perhaps be made clearer by a geometric proof. In figure 2.3a, $T_a T_a$ is A's transformation curve before the tariff, and $T_a' T_a'$ is the transformation curve after the tariff has been imposed and the capital movement has taken place. At constant prices equilibrium moves along A's R line from P_a to P_a', increasing the output of steel by RP_a' and decreasing the output of cotton by RP_a. Similarly, in figure 2.3b, $T_b T_b$ is country B's transformation curve before the capital movement and $T_b' T_b'$ is the transformation curve after capital has left B. At constant prices production in B moves along B's R line to P_b', steel production decreasing by SP_b and cotton production increasing by SP_b'.

To demonstrate the proposition that world supply curves are unchanged, it is necessary to prove that RP_a' equals SP_b and that RP_a equals SP_b'. The proof is given in figure 2.4. OL_a and OC_a are, respectively, A's initial endowments of labor and capital; OL_b and OC_b are the endowments of B. OO_a and OO_b are the efficiency loci of A and B with production taking place

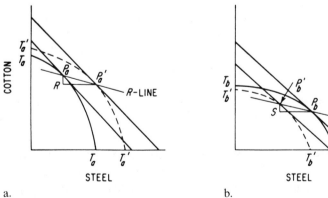

a.   b.

Figure 2.3

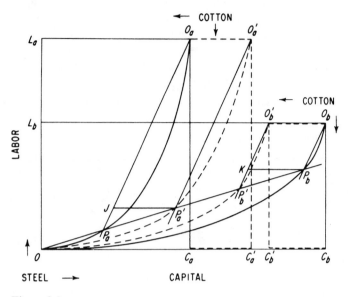

Figure 2.4

along these loci at P_a and P_b, corresponding to the same letters in figures 2.3a and 2.3b.

Now when A imposes a tariff on steel, suppose that $C_b C_b'$ of capital leaves B, shifting B's cotton origin from O_b ro O_b'. At constant prices labor-capital ratios in each industry must be the same as before, so equilibrium must move to P_b', corresponding to P_b' in figure 2.3b. Because the capital outflow from B must equal the capital inflow to A, A's cotton origin must move to the right by just the same amount as B's cotton origin moves to the left (that is, from O_a to O_a'; and A's production equilibrium at constant prices must move from P_a to P_a'). The proof that world supply is unchanged at constant prices is now obvious, since JP_aP_a' and $KP_b'P_b$ are identical triangles. P_aP_a', representing the increase in steel output in A, equals P_bP_b', the decrease in steel output in B, and the decrease in cotton output in A, JP_a, equals the increase in cotton output in B, KP_b'.[9]

This relationship holds at all combinations of commodity and factor prices provided some of each good is produced in both countries. It means that world supply functions are independent of the distribution of factor endowments. More simply it means that it makes no difference to world supply where goods are produced if commodity and factor prices are equalized. Because world supply and demand functions are not changed by the capital movements, so that the new equilibrium must be established at the same prices as before, our earlier assumption that A is very small in relation to B is an unnecessary one.[10]

The general conclusion of this and the preceding is that tariffs will stimulate factor movements. Which factor moves depends, of course, on which factor is more mobile. The assumption used here, that capital is perfectly mobile and that labor is completely immobile, is an extreme one which would have to be relaxed before the argument could be made useful. But a great deal can be learned qualitatively from extreme cases and the rest of the paper will retain this assumption. When only capital is mobile, a labor-abundant country can attract capital by tariffs and a capital-abundant country can encourage foreign investment by tariffs. The same is true for an export tax, because in this model the effect of an export tax is the same as that of a tariff.

The analysis is not restricted to tariffs; it applies as well to changes in transport costs. An increase of transport costs (of commodites) will raise the real return of and thus attract the scarce factor, and lower the real return and thus encourage the export of the abundant factor. The effect of any trade impediment is to increase the scarcity of the scarce factor and hence make more profitable an international redistribution of factors. Later we shall consider, under somewhat more realistic assumptions than those used above, the applicability of this proposition as an argument for protection.

3. Factor Mobility Impediments and Trade

To show that an increase in impediments to factor movements stimulates trade, we shall assume that some capital is foreign owned and illustrate the effects on trade of taxing this capital. Strictly speaking, this is not an impediment to a capital *movement*; but if it were assumed that a steady capital flow was taking place, the tax on foreign-owned capital would operate as an impediment.

We shall use figures 2.1 and 2.2. Begin with equilibrium initially at P' in figure 2.1. No impediments to trade exist, but because factor and commodity prices are already equalized, no trade takes place. We assume that $O'O''$ of capital in figure 2.2 is foreign owned, so a transfer equal in value to YY' in figure 2.1 is made. Consumption equilibrium in A is at S.

If a tax is now levied on all foreign capital, its net return will be decreased, and since factor prices must be equalized in A and B, all of it ($O'O''$) must leave A. As capital leaves A, her production block contracts. At constant prices more cotton and less steel are produced. The price of steel relative to cotton tends to rise, but because there are no impediments to trade, it is prevented from doing so by steel imports and cotton exports.

As all foreign capital leaves A, the final size of A's transformation function is TT, that consistent with domestically owned capital. Production equilibrium moves from P' to P, but consumption equilibrium remains at S because interest payments are no longer made abroad. PR is now exported in exchange for steel imports of RS. The effect of the tax has been to repatriate foreign capital and increase trade. By similar reasoning it could be shown that a subsidy will attract capital and decrease trade, although in the latter case the capital movement will only stop when factor prices change (i.e., specialization takes place).

To achieve efficiency in world production, it is unnecessary that both commodities and factors move freely. As long as the production conditions are satisfied, it is sufficient that *either* commodities *or* factors move freely. But if some restrictions, however small, exist to both commodity and factor movements, factor- and commodity-price equalization cannot take place (except in the trivial case where trade is unnecessary because prices are already equal). This principle applies only to those restrictions that are operative—obviously it does not apply to import tariffs on goods that are exported, transport costs for factors that are immobile anyway, or quotas larger than those required for equalization to take place.

If it were not for the problem of transporting interest payments, referred to earlier, one mobile factor would be sufficient to ensure price equalization. When the labor-abundant country imposes the tariff, equalization will take place as long as the other country continues a free-trade policy and there are no transport costs involved. But if the capital-abundant country imposes a tariff, inducing the export of capital, prices cannot be equalized even if the labor-abundant country maintains free trade unless the transfer of goods constituting interest payments is also tariff free.[11]

4. An Argument for Protection?

The proposition that an increase in trade impediments stimulates factor movements and an increase in impediments to factor movements stimulates trade has implications as an argument for protection. To examine these implications, we shall relax some of the assumptions previously made— first, by introducing trade impediments, then by decreasing the degree of factor mobility, and finally by relaxing the assumption that constant returns to scale apply by taking account of external economies. We shall begin with a model similar to that used earlier, except that we shall assume country A to be considerably smaller than country B.[12]

Take as a starting point the absence of trade impediments; trade is sufficient to ensure commodity- and factor-price equalization. Suppose that, overnight, transport costs come into existence; this raises the price of importables relative to exportables, shifts resources into importables, raises the marginal product of the scarce factor, and lowers that of the abundant factor in each country. Incomes of A-capitalists and B-workers increase, while incomes of A-workers and B-capitalists decrease. These changes in factor returns create the incentive for a capital movement from B to A, a labor movement from A to B, or a combination of both movements. While the final equilibrium will be depends on the degree of factor mobility. I shall assume that labor is immobile between countries but that capital is at least partially mobile.

If we assume that capital is perfectly mobile but that capitalists do not move with their capital, the latter will move from B to A until the return from capital invested in A is the same as from that invested in B; but this implies that marginal physical products cannot be equalized, since transport costs must be paid on the goods constituting interest payments.[13] The introduction of transport costs would, then, reduce world income even if capital were perfectly mobile unless capitalists are willing to consume their income in the country in which their capital is invested.

But we shall not assume that capital is perfectly mobile. Instead suppose that B-capitalists insist on receiving a higher return on any capital they invest in A than on that which they invest in B, perhaps because of political instability, patriotism, risk, or economic uncertainty. Let us assume that B-capitalists require a 10 percent higher return on capital invested in A than on that invested in B, but that if this interest differential rises above 10 percent, capital is perfectly mobile. Suppose further that the return to capital in both countries before introducing transport costs was 12 percent and that the effect of introducing transport costs is to lower the marginal product of capital in B to 11 percent and to raise it in A to 17 percent. Since the interest differential is less than 10 percent, no capital movement will take place.

It is at this point that we shall consider the argument for a tariff in A. Let A impose a tariff, further increasing her relative scarcity of capital and B's relative scarcity of labor. Rates of return on capital change to, let us say, 25 percent in A and 9 percent in B, creating an interest differential of 16 percent. Capital will now move from B to A until this differential is reduced to 10 percent. Obviously the rates of return cannot return to the pretariff rates of 17 percent for A and 11 percent for B, (1) because part of the tariff will be "used up" in bringing the marginal products of capital in A and B to the point where B has an incentive to export capital and (2) because transport costs must be paid on the interest returns.

If capital moves until the return in A falls to 20 percent and in B rises to 10 percent, what can be said about the economic effects of the tariff as far as country A is concerned?

1. A-capitalists are better-off, the tariff increases, and the capital inflow decreases capital scarcity, but the net effect is a higher return than before the tariff.

2. A-workers are worse off in spite of the fact that the total ratio of capital to labor in A has increased. Marginal products are determined not by the total ratio of capital to labor in a country, but by the ratio of capital to labor in each industry. The capital from B is largely absorbed by increasing the output of capital-intensive importables in A; it can never succeed in raising the capital-labor ratio in each industry to its pretariff level. Real wages must be lower than before the tariff.

3. Real national income in A is less than before the tariff; the tariff makes A's scarce factor relatively more scarce, and her abundant factor relatively more abundant, reducing her potential gains from international trade. Even under the most favorable assumptions, with capital perfectly mobile and capitalists moving with their capital, A's income would remain the same; it could not improve.

So far no valid tariff argument has been produced.[14] Capital can be attracted to a capital-scarce country by a tariff, but the capital movement can only alleviate some of the unfavorable effects of the tariff; it cannot eliminate them.

The argument can be rescued if we assume the appropriate nonlinearities of scale.[15] If external economies of scale exist in the production of A-importables,[16] the tariff will encourage more capital to enter than would otherwise be attracted, as the marginal product of capital entering A will not fall as rapidly as it would fall in the absence of economies of scale. The new equilibrium will be established with a higher marginal product of labor, factor returns now being dependent not only on the proportions in which factors are combined but also on the total output of importables. Real wages will be higher in A than without economies of scale, although it is not certain that they will be higher than before the tariff. To demonstrate the latter, it would have to be established that the economies of scale are sufficient to make up for the transport costs which must be paid on the interest returns. If they are sufficient, the tariff would be unequivocally beneficial.[17]

It is easy to see that economies of scale in importables or diseconomies of scale in exportables increase the likelihood that the net effect of the tariff in a labor-abundant country is favorable, and vice versa. To justify an argument for protection on the above grounds, it would have to be established that capital-intensive industries are subject to external economies of scale and/or that labor-intensive industries are subject to external diseconomies of scale, and these nonlinearities are of the required size.[18]

5. Concluding Remarks

A number of questions present themselves. Did increased protection in the late-nineteenth century in North America stimulate the large labor and capital inflows of that period (assuming land to have been the abundant factor)? Did the increased protection in Britain in this century stimulate capital export? Did the breakdown in international factor movements in the interwar period stimulate trade? And to what extent have the high tariff barriers between Canada and the United States contributed to the stimulus of American investment in Canada? It would be interesting to see what help this model offers in finding answers to these questions.

Notes

This paper was originally presented to Professor Meade's seminary at L.S.E. in 1956. I am indebted for helpful comments to W. M. Corden, M. Friedman, A. Harberger, H. G. Johnson, R. Lipsey, J. E. Meade, S. A. Ozga, and T. Rybczynski.

1. This proposition is implied in Ohlin (1935, chap. 9), Iversen (1935, chap. 2), and Meade (1955, chaps. 21 and 22).

2. For the necessity of these assumptions and a fairly complete list of references to the literature on factor-price equalization, see Samuelson (1953–54).

3. It is assumed that capitalists in their role as consuming units do not move with their capital.

4. It will become evident later that the terms of trade and factor prices do not change even when this assumption is dropped.

5. Actually, under the assumed conditions any tariff is prohibitive, as will eventually become clear.

6. Compare Stolper and Samuelson (1941).

7. The proof is easily demonstrated in figure 2.2. At unchanged prices equilibrium must lie along OP-extended. With the larger endowment of capital, $O''P'$ must be shorter than OP. Since these lines have the same slope and constant returns to scale apply, output of cotton at P' must be less than at P. A paper by R. Jones written at the Massachusetts Institute of Technology in the spring of 1955 contained a similar proof.

8. SP' must equal to value the marginal product of the capital inflow at constant prices. In figure 2.2, PP' is the change in output associated with the increase in capital; steel output increases by RS but cotton output decreases by PW. The marginal product of the capital inflow is the value of RS minus the value of PW, which, in terms of cotton, is $P'S$.

9. The R lines in figures 2.3a and 2.3b must be parallel when output expands at the same price ratio in each country, and they must be straight since production changes are compensating.

10. One qualification to the argument must be noted which is not necessary when the other country is very large. A condition for the marginal product of capital in A to rise as a result of the tariff is that the price of steel rise relative to the price of cotton. It is possible, if the foreign offer curve is very inelastic, that the improvement in A's terms of trade in raising the relative price of exports (cotton) will more than offset the effect of the tariff in raising the relative price of imports (steel). The condition that the "normal" case is satisfied requires that the sum of the foreign elasticity of demand and the domestic marginal propensity to import be greater than unity (the marginal propensity to import is relevant because the improvement in the terms of trade increases income). This is Metzler's qualification to the Stolper-Samuelson tariff argument (see Metzler 1949). If this criterion is less than unity, a tariff imposed by a labor-abundant country would stimulate foreign investment rather than attract capital—a result, it should be noted, based on the static assumptions of this model; if dynamic elements were involved, the direction of the capital movement would depend on whether the effects of the tariff on production preceded or followed the effects on the terms of trade.

11. If trade were a perfect substitute for factor movements in the absence of trade impediments, a rough idea of the cost of trade impediments could be acquired by calculating the increase in world income which could take place if capital were redistributed from capital-rich to capital-poor countries until its marginal product throughout the world was equalized. Alternatively, this could be considered the cost of capital immobility. This statement would have to be qualified in the many-factor case.

12. We make this assumption so that the change in the terms of trade resulting from A's tariff is small. In passing, however, it should be noted that the more mobile is capital, the smaller is the change in the terms of trade resulting from a tariff; this means that the optimum tariff will be smaller with, than without, capital mobility; and in the limiting case where capital is perfectly mobile, discussed earlier, the optimum tariff is zero.

Also, in what follows I neglect to discuss the tariff proceeds which are implicitly assumed to be redistributed in such a way as to leave A's indifference map unchanged. Alternatively, to abstract both from changes in the terms of trade and the tariff proceeds, it could be assumed that the tariff is prohibitive.

13. However, interest rates must be the same! Because capital goods—call them machines—can move costlessly from one country to the other, the price of machines in money terms will be the same in both countries; and since machines will move to A until marginal products in money terms are equal, interest rates (the return to a machine as a proportion of the price of a machine) must be the same in both countries. The interest rate, of course, is not commensurable with the marginal product of capital unless the latter is defined as a proportion of the price of machines; in the new equilibrium the two are equal when the marginal product of capital is so defined.

14. It is true that B's national has increased, since the effect of A's tariff is to raise B-wages and stimulate capital investment in A, where B-capitalists receive a higher rate of return than at home; but it cannot be said that B-capitalists are better off, since, *ex hypothesi*, they are indifferent between investment at home and an investment in A in which the rate of return is 10 percent higher. In any case, the purpose of policymakers in A is to raise A's, not B's, income.

15. It may be possible to rescue the argument in other ways by assuming irrational, although possibly not implausible, behavior. For example, after B-capitalists have begun investing in A, they may acquire more confidence and be willing to accept a smaller interest differential. In this case, after the capital movement the marginal product of labor may be higher, and the marginal product of capital lower, than before the tariff, thereby increasing A's national income. Or, whereas some (relatively) capital-scarce countries may fear "exploitation" from foreign investment, others may view the increase in productive capacity resulting from it as desirable in itself (perhaps with the intent of future expropriation!)—in which case this factor would have to be balanced against the reduction in national income.

16. It is sometimes overlooked that internal economies of scale do not constitute an argument for a tariff. An industry must not only be able to compete some years after the tariff, it must also earn a sufficient return to repay the economy for the loss of income resulting from the tariff in the period of the industry's infancy. The investment will them be worthwhile only if future output is sufficient to earn for the firm the current rate of interest on the capital involved. But when economies to scale are internal, the investment will be profitable for private enterprise. Only when divergences between private and social costs due to *external* economies of scale are present is the case for government intervention valid.

17. But if the same nonlinearities of scale exist in B, the argument is weakened; economies of scale in A-importables will cause the marginal product of capital to fall at a slower rate than in their absence, but in this case the marginal product of capital in B will rise at a much faster rate as capital is exported. Similar economies of scale in B, then, may cancel out the effect of economies in A in inducing a larger capital movement, although this effect could be neglected if B were the rest of the world and A were a small country.

18. A possible extension of the model to allow for many goods could be made as follows: all goods could be ordered in terms of their capital intensities (that is, the ratios of capital to labor at any given price ratio); B would export those goods that are most capital intensive, and A those goods that are most labor intensive. In the absence of trade impediments, one of the intermediate commodities would be produced in common, establishing the ratio of factor returns in much the same way as goods produced in common establish the ratio of international values in a Graham model. The effect of a tariff in A (as of any impediment) is to increase the relative price of capital-intensive goods in A and to lower them in B, thus raising in A and lowering in B the marginal product of capital. Thus, not one commodity but a whole series of commodities would be produced in common, A's exports comprising only the most labor-intensive and B's exports only the most capital-intensive goods. In A new capital-intensive industries, and in B new labor-intensive industries, would be created. If some capital were not allowed to move to A, the margin of comparative advantage would be extended to capital-intensive industries in A, thus increasing the number of goods produced in common in both countries.

References

Iversen, Carl. 1935. *Aspects of the Theory of International Capital Movements.* London.

Meade, J. E. 1955. *Trade and Welfare*. London.

Metzler, Lloyd. 1949. Tariffs, the terms of trade and the distribution of the national income. *Journal of Political Economy* 57, 1–29.

Ohlin, Bertil. 1935. *Interregional and International Trade*. Cambridge.

Rybczynski, T. M. 1955. Factor endowment and relative commodity prices. *Economica* 22, 336–341.

Samuelson, P. A. 1953–54. Prices of factors and goods in general equilibrium. *Review of Economic Studies* 21, 1–21.

Stolper, W. F., and P. A. Samuelson. 1941. Protection and real wages. *Review of Economic Studies* 9, 58–73.

3

Are International Trade and Factor Mobility Substitutes?

Kar-yiu Wong

Since Samuelson's (1948, 1949) classic analysis in the Heckscher-Ohlin model of factor-price equalization from free trade in the absence of international factor mobility, and Mundell's (1957) important demonstration of the reverse commodity price equalization from free international factor mobility under protection-induced autarky, the question of the relationship between goods trade and factor flows has continually attracted attention from the theorists of international trade.

The Samuelson-Mundell analysis, of course, demonstrated a full *equivalance* between the two phenomena, with regard to prices and welfare in equilibrium. But, as many analysts, especially Purvis (1972), Markusen (1983), Svensson (1984), and Markusen and Svensson (1985), have demonstrated, this equivalence will not obtain if the Heckscher-Ohlin assumptions such as identity of production functions are relaxed.[1]

The analysis has subsequently been shifted to a related, though different, question: Are factor flows and commodity trade substitutes or complements? That is, does increasing the level of one impact adversely or favorably on the volume of the other?

The present paper is focused precisely on the latter question. Unlike the important earlier contributions, however, the analysis here is not limited to departures from Heckscher-Ohlin assumptions in the specification of precise differences in international techniques or preferences. The analysis that follows develops necessary and sufficient conditions pertaining to the question as to when substitution or complementarity will obtain, thus yielding simultaneously more general insights into the problems at hand.

Section 1 introduces the general equilibrium model that will be used to analyze the problem posed in this paper. Note that the international

This paper was originally published in *Journal of International Economics* 21, no. 1/2 (August 1986): 25–44.

movement of only one factor, with the other factor immobile, is considered; for simplicity, the mobile factor is assumed to be capital though the analysis can easily be extended to the case of labor mobility.[2] Specific properties are established in comparative statics, and simple techniques developed to depict equilibrium in the world. These provide the building blocks for deriving the necessary and sufficient conditions for substitutability and complementarity between goods trade and international capital mobility in section 2. Section 3 then considers these general results in the context of two *special* cases: (1) one country, relative to the other country, is more productive in one sector but equally or less productive in the other sector (the case similar to the one suggested by Bhagwati 1964 as a generalized $2 \times 2 \times 2$ version of the Ricardian theory of comparative advantage), and (2) technology is identical in both sectors across countries, but the countries' factor endowments are different (the Heckscher-Ohlin case).

Since the question of substitution and complementarity between factor flows and goods trade has been dealt with from several viewpoints, as indeed is obvious from the contrast drawn above between the Samuelson-Mundell equivalence question and the Markusen-Svensson substitution-complementarity question, it is thus necessary and appropriate to survey different concepts of substitution and complementarity that have been put in the general literature in this area. This is done in appendix A. Appendix B (not reprinted here) shows in detail the properties of the framework introduced in section 1 when at least one of the countries is completely specialized.

1. The Model

Suppose that the world consists of two countries, each initially endowed with fixed amounts of labor and capital. Call the country in which the rental rate in autarky is higher "the home country," and the other country "the foreign country," implying that, in the absence of goods trade, the home country would be the capital-receiving country if capital mobility were permitted. In autarky both countries produce goods 1 and 2, good 1 being the cheaper good in the home country in the closed-economy situation. The countries are allowed to have different factor endowments, preferences, and technologies, but technologies are those that exhibit constant returns to scale and unique factor-intensity rankings at all prices. Foreign variables are asterisked, and home variables are not.

We start with a discussion of the home country, though a similar analysis can be extended to the foreign country. Arbitrarily, we choose good 1 as the numeraire and define p, w, r, respectively, as the prices of good 2, labor, and capital. It is assumed that when international capital flow occurs, capitalists do not move with capital but repatriate earnings back to their home. Denote K as the amount of foreign capital in the home country (negative for the amount of national capital in the foreign country), and X_i as the production of good i by the (national and foreign) factors in the economy and C_i as the consumption of good i by the nationals ($i = 1, 2$). Assuming that the repatriation is made in good 1,[3] the home's export (import if negative) of good 1 is

$$E(p, K) = X_1(p, K) - C_1(p, I) - r(p, K)K \tag{1}$$

where I is the national income, defined as total domestic output less payments to foreign capitalists.[4] To minimize the use of notation, denote partial derivatives by subscripts; for example, when holding the price p constant, $E_K = \partial E/\partial K$ and $X_{1K} = \partial X_1/\partial K$.

Equation (1) can be simplified as follows. First, suppose that the economy is diversified.[5] Then, in the absence of factor-intensity reversal, a one-to-one correspondence between factor prices and commodity prices exists, and we can write $w = w(p)$, $r = r(p)$, and $I = I(p; \bar{L}, \bar{K}) = w(p)\bar{L} + r(p)\bar{K}$, where $\bar{L}$ and $\bar{K}$ are the given labor and capital endowments of the economy. By substitution, (1) becomes

$$E(p, K) = X_1(p, K) - C_1(p) - r(p)K, \tag{1a}$$

where $\bar{L}$ and $\bar{K}$ are dropped for simplicity.

If the economy is completely specialized, the exact form of equation (1) will depend on which good is produced. Suppose that good 1 is produced and repatriated, then the equation becomes

$$E(p, K) = X_1(K) - C_1(p, I) - r(K)K = I - C_1(p, I), \tag{1b}$$

where $I = (X_1 - rK)$. If good 2 instead is produced, then (1) is replaced by

$$E(p, K) = -C_1(p, I), \tag{1c}$$

where $I = (pX_2 - pr_2K)$ and r_2 is the rental rate in terms of good 2. Note that in both (1b) and (1c), the outputs, X_1 and X_2, and the rental rates, r and r_2, are dependent on K but not on p.

Effects of Capital Flow on the Volume of Trade

We are now ready to develop a framework that depicts the equilibrium of the world's commodity and capital markets and determines the relationship between the volumes of trade and capital movement. The first step is to find out the effects of an increased capital flow on the volume of trade at constant commodity prices. This can be done by making use of the export equations in (1a) to (1c).

PROPOSITION 1   In the case in which

1. the economy is diversified, or
2. the economy is completely specialized in the capital-intensive good and is a capital-receiving country, or
3. the economy is completely specialized in the labor-intensive good and is a capital-sending country,

more investment from abroad will, under constant terms of trade, lead to a smaller export of good 1 (i.e., E_K is negative if and only if good 1 is labor intensive).

Proof   First consider case 1 in which the economy is diversified. Differentiate (1a) with respect to K to get $E_K = X_{1K} - r = -pX_{2K}$, where $r = X_{1K} + pX_{2K}$. By the Rybcyznski theorem, X_{2K} is positive, and thus E_K is negative if and only if good 1 is labor intensive.

In case 3 the economy is completely specialized in the labor-intensive good 1. Differentiate (1b) with respect to K to get $E_K = (1 - c_1')I_K$, where c_1' is the marginal propensity to consume good 1. Now $I_K = X_{1K} - r - K(dr/dK) = -K(dr/dK)$, since $X_{1K} = r$. As $dr/dK < 0$ and if $0 < c_1' < 1$, then $E_K < 0$ if the economy is sending out capital, that is, $K < 0$. Now turn to case 2 in which the economy is completely specialized in the capital-intensive good 2. Then the differentiation of (1c) with respect to K will give $E_K = -c_1'I_K = -c_1'[pX_{2K} - pr_2 - pK(dr_2/dK)] = c_1'pK(dr_2/dK)$, as $pX_{2K} = pr_2$. Thus $E_K < 0$ if the economy is receiving capital. □

Proposition 1 of course implies that in the foregoing cases, E_K is positive if and only if good 1 is capital intensive. In cases not mentioned in the proposition, E_K can be obtained in a similar way, though in general its sign depends not just on the factor intensity of good 1 but also on the technology, preferences, and factor endowments of the economy.

Equilibrium of the World's Commodity Markets

We next make use of proposition 1 to develop a general equilibrium framework for analyzing international goods trade and capital movement. We will first concentrate on the equilibrium of the world's good 1 market in the presence of capital movement. The equilibrium conditions are

$$E(p, K) + E^*(p^*, K^*) = 0, \tag{2}$$

$$K + K^* = 0, \tag{3}$$

$$p = p^*. \tag{4}$$

In (2) and (3), $K(= -K^*)$ is the amount of foreign capital working in the home country. Note that the exact forms of the export functions, $E(p, K)$ and $E^*(p^*, K^*)$, as given in conditions (1a) to (1c), depend on whether the countries are completely specialized. Substitute (3) and (4) into (2) to give

$$E(p, K) + E^*(p, -K) = 0, \tag{2a}$$

which simply says that at any prechosen price level, there may be one or more combinations of home's export of good 1, $E(= -E^*)$, and the amount of foreign capital in the home country, $K(= -K^*)$, that equilibrate the good 1 market of the world. These combinations of equilibrium E for various values of K are plotted as schedule GT in figure 3.1, whose vertical axis represents domestic export (E) and foreign import $(-E^*)$ of good 1 and whose horizontal axis stands for the amount of foreign capital in the home country.[6] Alternatively, schedule GT can be interpreted as the locus of the intersecting points of the domestic Rybczynski lines $E = E(p, K)$ and the foreign Rybczynski lines $-E^* = -E^*(p, -K)$ at the same levels of p. Note that Rybczynski lines of each country are not necessarily parallel to each other. Rybcyznski lines of the two countries corresponding to com-

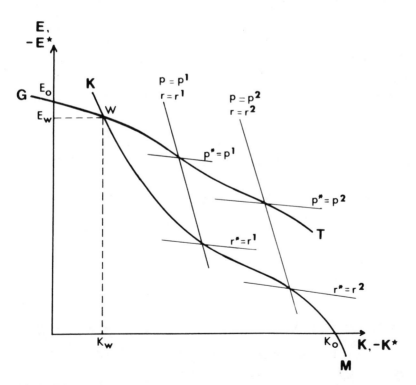

Figure 3.1

modity prices of p^1 and p^2 are shown in figure 3.1 based on the assumption that good 1 is *labor intensive* in both countries and that both countries are diversified. If an economy is completely specialized, the slopes of its Rybczynski curves (not necessarily lines) will vary as the amount of foreign capital inflow, as shown in proposition 1. More details about the Rybczynski curves and schedule GT with complete specialization will be given in appendix B. The vertical intercept, shown as point E_o in the figure, represents the level of domestic export of good 1 under free trade but no capital mobility.

The slope of schedule GT can be obtained by first totally differentiating (2a) and rearranging the terms to give

$$\left.\frac{dp}{dK}\right|_{E+E^*=0} = \frac{E^*_{K^*} - E_K}{E_p + E^*_{p^*}}. \tag{5}$$

The export equation, $E = E(p, K)$ is then totally differentiated and combined with (5) to give the slope of schedule GT:

$$\left.\frac{dE}{dK}\right|_{GT} = \frac{E_p E^*_{K^*} + E^*_{p^*} E_K}{E_p + E^*_{p^*}}. \tag{6}$$

The stability in a Walrasian sense of the international market of good 1 at any level of capital movement requires that $(E_p + E^*_{p^*})$ is less than zero. In those cases described in proposition 1, if both E_p and $E^*_{p^*}$ are negative, or if either of them (but not both) is positive but not of a significant magnitude, then schedule GT is negatively (positively) sloped if good 1 is labor (capital) intensive in *both* countries.[7]

Equilibrium of the World's Capital Market
We now turn to the equilibrium of the world's capital market. We will derive another schedule, called KM, to represent the equilibrium conditions of the capital market. We will concentrate on the case in which both economies are diversified.

First, the equilibrium of the capital market can be described by the following three conditions:

$$E(p(r), K) + E^*(p^*(r^*), K^*) = 0, \tag{2b}$$

$$K + K^* = 0, \tag{3}$$

$$r = r^*. \tag{7}$$

Note that as both countries are diversified, the export functions in (2b) are given by (1a). The three equilibrium conditions can be simplified by substituting (3) and (7) into (2b) to give

$$E(p(r), K) + E^*(p^*(r), -K) = 0, \tag{2c}$$

Equation (2c) gives possible combinations of E and K which equilibrate the international capital market at the indicated rental rate. Graphically, the locus of these combinations at different rental rates is represented by schedule KM in figure 1, which can also be interpreted as the locus of the intersecting points of domestic Rybcyznski lines $E = E(p(r), K)$ and foreign Rybcyznski lines $-E^* = -E^*(p^*(r), -K)$ at the same rental rates.[8] Domestic and foreign Rybcyznski lines corresponding to rental rates of r^1 and r^2 are also shown in the figure. The horizontal intercept of schedule KM, shown as point K_o in the figure, denotes the equilibrium amount of foreign capital in the home country under free capital mobility but autarky in goods trade.[9]

The slope of schedule KM can be obtained in a way similar to the preceding one:

$$\left.\frac{dE}{dK}\right|_{KM} = \frac{E_p p_r E^*_{K^*} + E^*_{p^*} p^*_{r^*} E_K}{E_p p_r + E^*_{p^*} p^*_{r^*}}. \tag{8}$$

Note that as both economies are diversified, E_K and p_r, and $E^*_{K^*}$ and $p^*_{r^*}$, always have opposite signs. Furthermore, if both E_p and $E^*_{p^*}$ are negative, or if one of them is positive but of a small magnitude, then the slope of schedule KM is negative (positive) if sector 1 of both countries is labor (capital) intensive.[10]

We can now make use of schedules GT and KM to analyze simultaneous free goods trade and capital movement. Specifically, the equilibrium of the world's good 1 and capital markets, as described by (2) or (2b), (3), (4), and (7), are depicted as the intersecting point between the two schedules, shown as point W in figure 3.1; because of Walras's law, the good 2 market is also in equilibrium at W.[11] It should be noted that the equilibrium requires the appropriate forms of the export functions of the countries which depend on whether the economies are diversified. An efficient point with diversification is then said to exist if at the final equilibrium point both countries are diversified.

2. Necessary and Sufficient Conditions for Substitutability

This section makes use of the preceding framework to compare the volumes of trade and the amounts of capital movement in the following three different situations: (1) free trade but with no capital mobility, (2) free capital mobility but autarky in trade, and (3) free trade and capital mobility. Specifically, in figure 3.1, this is to compare E_o with W_w, and K_o with K_w. In terms of these four variables, the following definitions can be stated.

DEFINITION 1

1. Capital mobility diminishes (augments) goods trade if and only if the volume of trade under free goods trade and capital mobility is smaller (greater) than the volume of trade under free trade but no capital mobility —that is, if and only if $E_w < (>) E_o$.

2. Goods trade diminishes (augments) capital mobility if and only if the amount of capital transfer under free goods trade and capital mobility is smaller (greater) than the amount of capital transfer under free capital mobility but autarky in trade—that is, if and only if $K_w < (>) K_o$.[12]

DEFINITION 2

1. Goods trade and capital mobility are substitutes if and only if they diminish each other.

2. Goods trade and capital mobility are complements if and only if they augment each other.

Using these definitions, the necessary and sufficient conditions for substitutability and complementarity can be derived as follows. Denote the slope of the (undrawn) line joining points E_o and W by S_G and that joining points K_o and W by S_K. Since $S_G = (E_w - E_o)/K_w$, we have

$$E_w \begin{cases} > \\ = E_0 \\ < \end{cases} \text{ iff } S_G K_w \begin{cases} > \\ = 0 \\ < \end{cases} \text{ or iff } \begin{cases} S_G \text{ and } K_w \text{ have the same sign,} \\ \text{either } S_G \text{ or } K_w \text{ is zero,} \\ S_G \text{ and } K_w \text{ have different signs.} \end{cases}$$

Similar conditions for the change in the equilibrium levels of capital flow are:

$$K_w \begin{cases} > \\ = K_0 \\ < \end{cases} \text{ iff } S_K E_w \begin{cases} > \\ = 0 \\ < \end{cases} \text{ or iff } \begin{cases} S_K \text{ and } E_w \text{ have the same sign,} \\ \text{either } S_K \text{ or } E_w \text{ is zero,} \\ S_K \text{ and } E_w \text{ have different signs.} \end{cases}$$

The preceding conditions can be simplified as follows. First, note that with the assumption about the signs and magnitudes of E_p and E^*_{p*} (see notes 7 and 10), the slopes of schedules GT and KM have the same sign as S_G and S_K, respectively. Second, define r_o and r^*_o, respectively, as the domestic and foreign rental rates under free trade but capital immobility. Then if and only if $r_o > r^*_o$, foreign capital will tend to flow in under free trade and K_w will be positive. In other words, sign $(r_o - r^*_o)$ is equal to sign (K_w). Similarly, if p_o and p^*_o are the relative prices of good 2 in both countries under free capital flow but autarky in trade, then E_w is positive (negative) if and only if $p_o > (<) p^*_o$. Thus the necessary and sufficient conditions for substitutability and complementarity between goods trade and capital mobility are:

PROPOSITION 2

1. Capital mobility diminishes {augments} goods trade if and only if sign (slope of schedule GT) $\neq$ {=} sign (K_w) = sign $(r_o - r^*_o)$.
2. Goods trade diminishes {augments} capital mobility if and only if sign (slope of schedule KM) $\neq$ {=} sign (E_w) = sign $(p_o - p^*_o)$.
3. Goods trade and capital mobility are substitutes if and only if (a) sign (slope of schedule GT) $\neq$ sign (K_w) = sign $(r_o - r^*_o)$, and (b) sign (slope of schedule KM) $\neq$ sign (E_w) = sign $(p_o - p^*_o)$.
4. Goods trade and capital mobility are complements if and only if (a) sign (slope of schedule GT) = sign (K_w) = sign $(r_o - r^*_o)$, and (b) sign (slope of schedule KM) = sign (E_w) = sign $(p_o - p^*_o)$.

COROLLARY   If both countries have the same factor-intensity ranking and if $(r_o - r^*_o)$ and $(p_o - p^*_o)$ have the same sign, then goods trade and capital mobility are either substitutes or complements.

The corollary can be proved easily be making use of proposition 2. An important message brought by proposition 2 is that in general, both the technologies and preferences of the two countries have to be considered simultaneously to determine the relationships between goods trade and capital mobility. Factor intensities of goods in both countries, while affecting the slopes of schedule GT and KM, are not sufficient or necessary for substitutes or complements.

3. Some Specific Examples

This section applies the preceding techniques to examine the relationship between goods trade and capital mobility in some specific models.[†]

Example 1
Suppose that the home country, versus the foreign country, is more productive in sector 1 but equally or less productive in sector 2 as described as follows:

$$F_1(L_1, K_1) > F^*_1(L_1, K_1), \quad \text{for all } L_1, K_1 > 0,$$

$$F_2(L_2, K_2) \leqslant F^*_2(L_2, K_2), \quad \text{for all } L_2, K_2 > 0,$$

[†] *Editor's note*: Only example 1 is reprinted here.

where F_i and F^*_i are respectively the linearly homogeneous production function of sector i in the home and foreign countries. The technological difference can be of any type, but it is assumed that it is not to the extent to cause different factor-intensity rankings of goods in different countries. Further assume that good 1 is labor intensive. In addition to the technological difference, the countries may have different factor endowment and/or preferences so that there may be more than one basis for trade. Note that this is similar to the case suggested by Bhagwati (1964) as a generalized $2 \times 2 \times 2$ version of the Ricardian theory of comparative advantage.

Our analysis will make use of the following lemma which is stated and proved in Findlay and Grubert (1959) and Kemp (1969, chap. 2).

LEMMA   If the economy remains diversified, a technological progress in the capital- (labor-) intensive sector, under constant terms of trade, will raise (lower) the rental rate.[14]

According to the preceding lemma, when both countries are diversified, schedule r^* between the rental rate and the relative price of good 2 can be represented by the r-schedule for the home country and the r^*-schedule for the foreign country in figure 3.2. Each schedule can be divided into three parts: a horizontal one representing the complete specialization in good 1,

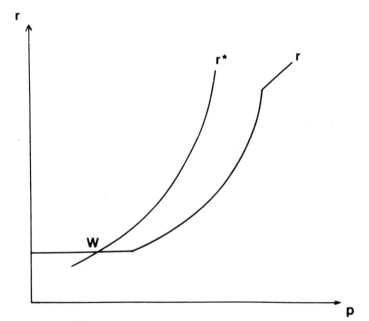

Figure 3.2

a convex-downward curve with production diversification, and a negatively sloped straight line, which points back toward the origin, representing the production of good 2 only.[15] According to the preceding lemma,
when both countries are diversified, schedule r^* must be above schedule r.
This implies that under free trade but no capital mobility and with diversification in both countries, the foreign rental rate is higher than the domestic
one. Thus, if capital movement is then allowed, domestic capital tends to
flow out; or in other words, schedule KM must be below schedule GT, as
shown in figure 3.3. Note that both schedules GT and KM are negatively
sloped because sector 1 is labor intensive in both countries, as explained
in section 1.

However, Uekawa (1972) showed that with such technological difference
across countries, an efficient point with diversification does not exist.[16] In
terms of these figures, as clear from the lemma, schedules r and r^*, and
schedules GT and KM, can never meet as long as both countries are
diversified, implying that the final equilibrium point requires complete

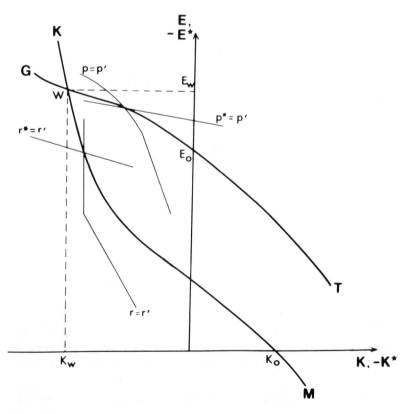

Figure 3.3

specialization in at least one country. The figures show the case in which the home country finally is specialized in good 1.

The relationship between the volume of trade and capital movement can be determined easily from figure 3.3. The figure shows, in terms of the notations in section 2, that (1) $E_w > E_o$ and (2) $K_w < K_o$. Thus we can conclude that (1) capital movement augments good trade, whereas (2) goods trade diminishes capital movement.

The preceding result clearly depends on the assumed technological difference across the countries. Suppose now that we slightly change the assumption: sector 1 is capital intensive in both countries, though the home country (versus the foreign country) is still more productive in sector 1 but equally or less productive in sector 2. By following the preceding line of analysis, we can show that (1) capital movement augments goods trade and (2) goods trade augments capital movement. In other words, goods trade and capital movement are complements.[17]

The general relationship between goods trade and capital mobility in the cases in which a country (versus another country) is more productive in one sector but equally or less productive in the other sector can be summarized by the following proposition:

PROPOSITION 3

1. If the home country is superior in the production of the importable (exportable) good but equally or less productive in the other good, then capital mobility diminishes (augments) goods trade.
2. If the home country is superior in the production of the labor- (capital-) intensive good but equally or less productive in the capital- (labor-) intensive good, then goods trade diminishes (augments) capital mobility.
3. If the home country is superior in the production of the exportable good but equally or less productive in the other good and if the exportable good is capital intensive, then goods trade and capital mobility are complements.
4. If the home country is superior in the production of one good but equally or less productive in the other good and if the exportable is labor intensive, then goods trade and capital mobility are neither substitutes nor complements.

Assumption 1 of proposition 3 confirms the results in Markusen (1983) and Markusen and Svensson (1985) that capital mobility augments goods trade. The former paper assumed that the home country is superior in the production of the *labor-intensive exportable* good but equally productive in the other sector, whereas the latter paper assumed a compensated product-augmenting technological difference across countries that implies that the home country is more productive in one sector but less productive in the other sector. These two papers, however, have not studied the effects of goods trade on capital movement. Such effects, as stated in assumption 2, depend on the factor intensity of the home's more productive sector. Specifically, we can conclude that in the framework of Markusen (1983), goods trade diminishes capital mobility but that no such conclusion can be made in the framework of Markusen and Svensson (1985) as factor intensities of the sectors are not specified.[18]

Appendix A

This appendix briefly surveys different concepts of substitutability and complementarity between goods trade and factor mobility that have appeared in the literature.

(1). *Quantitative-relationship sense.* Goods trade and factor movements are said to be substitutes (or complements) in the quantitative-relationship sense if an increase in the volume of trade will decrease (or increase) the level of factor movements and/or if an increase in the level of factor movements will decrease (or increase) the volume of trade. For example, the terms were used in this sense in Ohlin (1933), Markusen (1983), Svensson (1984), Markusen and Svensson (1985), and Jones and Neary (1984). This concept of the terms is the one used in this paper.

2. *Price-equalization sense.* Mundell (1957, p. 321) stated this concept explicitly: "Commodity movements and factor movements are substitutes. The absence of trade impediments implies commodity-price equalization and, even when factors are immobile, a tendency toward factor-price equalization. It is equally true that perfect factor mobility results in factor-price equalization and, even when commodity movements cannot take place, in a tendency toward commodity-price equalization."

3. *World-efficiency sense.* Meade (1955) had an extensive discussion of the impacts of goods trade and/or factor flows on world efficiency, and Purvis (1972) stated the meaning of the terms in this sense as: "Substitutes here refers to the case where either (trade or factor mobility) is sufficient to establish efficiency in world production, and hence maximise potential world welfare." They are complements if both of them are required to establish world productive efficiency.

4. *National-welfare sense.* This sense of the terms can be found in many papers that analyze the effects of trade, factor mobility, or both, on the welfare of an individual country, though the terms substitutability and complementarity are seldom explicitly stated. Examples are Bhagwati (1973), Brecher and Díaz-Alejandro (1977), Markusen and Melvin (1979), and Bhagwati and Brecher (1980). Specifically, trade and factor mobility

are substitutes if either of them is sufficient to bring maximum welfare to the domestic economy, and complements if both of them are required.

These concepts are closely related but not identical. For example, if goods trade and factor mobility are substitutes in the price-equalization sense, then they must be substitutes in the world-efficiency and national-welfare senses as well. On the other hand, in the Heckscher-Ohlin-Samuelson framework with diversification, they are substitutes in any of these senses.

Notes

1. The relationship between goods trade and factor flow in a Heckscher-Ohlin framework was first analyzed by Ohlin (1933) who argued that they tend to be substitutes. Meade (1955) elaborated Ohlin's argument and provided analysis on the implications of relaxing some of the assumptions of the Heckscher-Ohlin framework on their relationship.

2. One of the main differences between international capital mobility and labor mobility is that whereas capitalists usually repatriate earnings back to the country of source, migrating workers may reside and consume in the country of destination. However, if free trade prevails, it does not matter where the migrating workers consume as far as the final world equilibrium is concerned.

3. In general, if commodity prices are not equalized, the choice of goods for repatriated could affect the equilibrium. See Wong (1983) for an example. However, if free trade exists, which good is repatriated will not matter.

4. An alternative way of defining export, as Kemp (1966, 1969) and Jones (1967) did, is to include the payments to foreign capitalists in the export function, which is then equal to domestic production less national consumption. Whether to include such payments or not is a matter of convenience and would not affect the main results in this paper.

5. For the conditions for diversification in both countries, see Chipman (1971), Uekawa (1972), and Brecher and Feenstra (1983).

6. It is assumed in this paper that schedule GT exists within the relevant range in which K is not smaller than the negative of the capital endowment of the home country but not greater than the capital endowment of the foreign country.

7. The assumption that both E_p and $E^*_{p^*}$ are negative (or if one of them is positive, it is of a small magnitude) is made so that given the same factor intensity of good 1 in both countries is sufficient to know the sign of the slope of schedule GT. One implication is that if goods in both countries have the same factor-intensity ranking at all factor prices, schedule GT is monotonically rising or falling.

8. Again we make the assumption that schedule KM exists within the relevant region defined in note 6.

9. Since an increase in the capital stock in a country tends to lower the rental rate, in the half-space on the right- (left-) hand side of schedule KM, r is smaller (greater) than r^*.

10. See note 7.

11. The Chipman flat (Chipman 1971) can be conveniently illustrated in figure 3.1. The net increase in the world's output of good 1 as one unit of capital is transferred from the foreign country to the domestic country at constant prices is equal to $E_K - E^*_{K^*}$. At the world's equilibrium prices under trade and capital mobility, the net increase in the output of good 1 is represented as the vertical distance between the domestic Rybcyznski line and the foreign Rybcyznski line passing through point W in fgure 3.1 (not shown), and as long as both countries remain diversified, the net increase grows linearly with the amount of capital flow.

12. In definition 1 we are interested in the algebraic but not the absolute values of E_w and E_o and those of K_w and K_o.

13. There are two other possible ways of defining substitutes and complements between goods trade and capital mobility, each with some constraints imposed on the markets. The first one is to check their relationship under *constant terms of trade*, and such relationship is revealed by the slope of the Rybcyznski lines of the countries in figure 3.1. This is the one used by Markusen (1983). The second way is to find out the effects of *an exogenous change* in either the volume of trade or the level of capital movement on one another, and this is, in terms of figure 3.1, to examine the slopes of schedules GT and KM.

14. Findlay and Grubert (1959) and Kemp (1969) showed the effects of the following three types of technological progress: Hicks's neutral, capital saving, and labor saving. In fact, the lemma holds for all types of technological progress as long as the inward shift of the isoquants is not to the extent to reverse the factor-intensity ranking of the sectors. It can be proved qualitatively as follows. Consider a techno-logical progress in the capital-intensive sector, and suppose that the factor alloca-tion and terms of trade are all fixed. Then there will be a rise in the output of the capital-intensive good and the profit of the firms in the sector. As factor flow across the two sectors is then allowed, an excess demand for capital and an excess supply of labor will be created because of the factor intensities of the sectors. At the final equilibrium point the wage-rental ratio must be lowered than before.

15. See Jones and Ruffin (1975) for the details.

16. In fact, what Uekawa (1972) showed is that an efficient point with diversification does not exist if $F_1(L_1, K_1) > F^*_1(L_1, K_1)$ for all L_1, $K_1 > 0$, and $F_2(L_2, K_2) < F^*_2(L_2, K_2)$ for all L_2, $K_2 > 0$. By applying Uekawa's analysis, it is not difficult to show that if one of the inequalities (not both) is replaced by an equality, an efficient point with diversification does not exist either.

17. There is a third case which is not analyzed in this paper: the home country (versus the foreign country) is more productive in sector 2 but equally or less productive in sector 1, and good 1 is labor intensive. For more analysis and the proof of proposition 3, see Wong (1985).

18. Note that goods trade and capital mobility are said to be complements in Markusen (1983) and Markusen and Svensson (1985) if the latter augments the former. In the present paper they are said to be complements if *both* of them augment the other.

References

Bhagwati, J. N. 1964. The pure theory of international trade: A survey. *Economic Journal*, 1–78.

Bhagwati, J. N. 1973. The theory of immiserizing growth: Further applications. In M. B. Connolly and A. K. Swoboda, eds., *International Trade and Money*. Toronto: University of Toronto Press, pp. 45–54.

Bhagwati, J. N., and R. A. Brecher. 1980. National welfare in an open economy in the presence of foriegn-owned factors of production. *Journal of International Economics* 10, 103–115.

Brecher, R. A., and C. F. Díaz-Alejandro. 1977. Tariffs, foreign capital, and immiserizing growth. *Journal of International Economics* 7, 317–322.

Brecher, R. A., and R. C. Feenstra. 1983. International trade and capital mobility between diversified economies. *Journal of International Economic* 14, 321–339.

Chipman, J. S. 1971. International trade with capital mobility: A substitution theorem. In J. N. Bhagwati, *et al.*, eds., *Trade, Balance of Payments and Growth*. pp. 201–237.

Findlay, R., and H. Grubert. 1959. Factor intensities, technological progress and the terms of trade. *Oxford Economic Papers*, 111–121.

Jones, R. W. 1967. International capital movements and the theory of tariffs and trade. *Quarterly Journal of Economics* 81, 1–38.

Jones, R. W., and J. P. Neary. 1984. The positive theory of international trade. In R. W. Jones and P. B. Kenen, eds., *Handbook of International Economics*. Amderstdam: North Holland.

Jones, R. W., and R. Ruffin. 1975. Trade patterns with capital mobility. In M. Parkin and A. R. Nobay, eds., *Current Economic Problems*. Cambridge: Cambridge University Press.

Kemp, M. C. 1966. The gain from international trade and investment: A neo-Heckscher-Ohlin approach. *American Economic Review* 61, 788–809.

Kemp, M. C. 1969. *The Pure Theory of International Trade and Investment*. Englewood Cliffs, N. J.: Prentice-Hall.

Markusen, J. R. 1983. Factor movements and commodity trade as complements. *Journal of International Economics* 14, 341–356.

Markusen, J. R., and J. R. Melvin. 1979. Tariffs, capital mobility and foreign ownership. *Journal of International Economics* 9, 395–410.

Markusen, J. R., and L. E. O. Svensson. 1985. Trade in goods and factors with international differences in technology. *International Economic Review* 26, 175–192.

Meade, J. E. 1955. *Trade and Welfare*. Oxford: Oxford University Press.

Mundell, R. 1957. International trade and factor mobility. *American Economic Review* 67, 321–335.

Ohlin, B. 1933. *International and International Trade*. Cambridge: Harvard University Press.

Purvis, D. D. 1972. Technology, trade and factor mobility. *Economic Journal* 82, 991–999.

Samuelson, P. A. 1948. International trade and equalisation of factor price. *Economic Journal* 58, 163–184.

Samuelson, P. A. 1949. International factor-price equalisation once again. *Economic Journal* 59, 181–197.

Svensson, L. E. O. 1984. Factor Trade and Goods Trade. *Journal of International Economics* 16, 365–378.

Uekawa, Y. 1972. On the existence of incomplete specialization in international trade with capital mobility. *Journal of International Economics* 2, 1–23.

Wong, K. Y. 1983. On choosing among trade in goods and international capital and labor mobility: A theoretical analysis. *Journal of International Economics* 14, 223–250.

Wong, K. Y. 1985. Are international trade and factor mobility substitutes? University of Washington. Mimeo.

4

The Two-Sector Model in Terms of Its Dual: A Geometric Exposition

Michael Mussa

The two-sector model is usually described in terms of the production functions for the economy's two outputs. It is the purpose of this paper to show that for many purposes, particularly for analyzing factor market distortions, it is more convenient to work with the duals of the production functions.[1] This is so because many of the essential features of the two-sector model (e.g., the Stolper-Samuelson theorem and the factor-price equalization theorem) deal with relationships between prices. Production functions, however, focus directly on quantities and only indirectly on prices. In contrast, the duals of the production functions deal directly with prices.

The analysis in this paper is conducted in terms of a simple diagram that is developed in section 1. Sections 2, 3, 4, and 5 show how this diagram may be used to establish the essential properties of the two-sector model: the factor-price equalization theorem, the Rybczynski theorem, the Stolper-Samuelson theorem, and the effects of technological change. Sections 6, 7, and 8 are devoted to the analysis of factor market distortions. Specifically, section 6 shows how to determine the effects of factor market distortions of any degree of complexity on factor prices and factor intensities. This analysis provides a convenient demonstration of the seemingly paradoxical result that a *tax* on a factor in the industry that does not use that factor intensively *increases* the return to that factor in terms of both goods. Section 7 introduces the concept of the 'shadow price' of a factor of production (see Diamond and Mirrlees 1976; Findlay and Wellisz 1976; Bhagwati, Srinivasan, and Wan 1978; and Srinivasan and Bhagwati 1978) and shows how these shadow prices may be used to compare the total distortionary effect of widely divergent factor market distortions. Finally,

This paper was originally published in *Journal of International Economics* 9 no. 4 (November 1979): 513–526.

section 8 considers an economy that is so highly distorted that the shadow price of one factor of production is actually negative, and examines some of the peculiar characteristics of such an economy.[2]

1. The Dual of the Lerner-Pearce Diagram

The basic diagram is shown in figure 4.1.[3] The dual of the production function for commodity X, $\tilde{P}_X(W, R)$, determines the isoprice curve labeled "$\tilde{P}_X = P_X^0$," which indicates the combinations of the wage rate of labor, W, and the rental rate of capital, R, which are consistent with zero profits in producing X, given the price P_X^0. A higher (lower) price of X shifts this curve proportionately outward (inward) along every ray through the origin. The dual of the production function for commodity Z, $\tilde{P}_Z(W, R)$, determines the isoprice curve labeled "$\tilde{P}_Z = P_Z^0$," which indicates the combinations of W and R which are consistent with a given price P_Z^0, for commodity Z. The absolute values of the slopes of the isoprice curves indicate the ratios of labor to capital which will be used in the respective industries.[4] The isoprice curves are convex as viewed from the origin because the labor-capital ratio in each industry is a increasing function of the rental-wage ratio. The curvature of the isoprice curves reflects the elasticity of substitution between labor and capital in the respective industries.[5]

The two isoprice curves shown in figure 4.1 intersect once and only once. This point of intersection, A, determines the wage rate, W^0, and the rental rate, R^0, which are consistent with the production of both commodities at

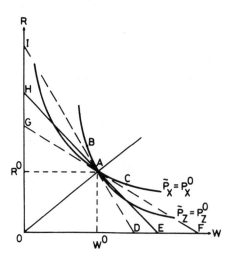

Figure 4.1

the given output prices, P_X^0 and P_Z^0. At this wage-rental combination, the labor-capital ratio in X, l_X^A, is equal to minus the slope of the line FAG; and the labor-capital ratio in Z, l_Z^A, is equal to minus the slope of the line DAI. To indicate the ratio of labor to capital determined by the economy's endowments of these factors (L and K), the line EAH has been constructed with a slope of $-l = -L/K$. In figure 4.1 this line lies between the tangents to the two isoprice cuves at A. In this situation, production of both commodities is consistent with full employment of the economy's factors of production since the labor-intensive industry, Z, uses a labor-capital ratio which is greater than the endowment ratio and the capital-intensive industry, X, uses a labor-capital ratio which is less than the endowment ratio. If l were greater than l_Z^A, the economy would have to specialize in producing Z in order to maintain full employment of both labor and capital. In this situation factor prices would not be determined by the point A, but rather by some point B at which the slope of the isoprice curve for Z is equal to $-l$. At these factor prices, production of X would be unprofitable since the $\tilde{P}_X = P_X^0$ curve lies below B. Conversely, if l were less than l_X^A, the economy would specialize in X and factor prices would be determined by some point such as C.

If, for given prices of X and Z the isoprice curves failed to intersect, the economy would produce only the commodity with the higher isoprice curve. Factor prices would be determined by the point at which the slope of this isoprice curve equaled $-l$. If the isoprice curves intersect more than once, then the relevant point of intersection is the one (there cannot be more than one) at which the slope of the line indicating the endowment ratio lies between the tangents to the two isoprice curves. If no point of intersection satisfies this condition, then the economy will specialize in the commodity which has the higher tangent to its isoprice with a slope of $-l$, and factor prices will be determined by this point of tangency.

2. Factor-Price Equalization

In discussing factor-price equalization, we are concerned with two economies which have identical technologies and face the same *relative* price for their outputs. An equiproportionate change in the nominal prices of X and Z has no effect on the relationships shown in figure 4.1, other than a homogeneous outward or inward shift of the two isoprice curves. Therefore, without loss of generality, we may assume that both countries face the same nominal output prices. Hence, figure 4.1 applies equally to both economies. The only difference between the diagrams for the two countries is that the lines which indicate the endowment ratios will, in general, have different slopes. However, provided both of these lines lie between the tangents to the two isoprice curves at A, both economies will produce both commodities and will have the same factor prices. It follows that the ratios of the two factor prices to each other and to the two commodity prices must be the same for both economies.

This demonstration of factor-price equalization breaks down if the isoprice curves fail to intersect, or if the endowment ratio for either of the economies is such that it specializes. The only circumstance in which factor-price equalization can fail when both economies produce both commodities is if the isoprice curves intersect more than once and if the endowment ratios of the two countries place them at different points of intersection. To preclude this possibility, it is sufficient to impose the "strong factor intensity assumption," which implies that the isoprice curve which is steeper at one wage-rental ratio must be steeper at every other wage-rental ratio.

3. The Rybczynski Effect

From figure 4.1 we may determine the distribution of the economy's capital stock and labor force between X and Z. Adopting Jones's (1965) notation, $\lambda_{KX} = K_X/K$, $\lambda_{KZ} = K_Z/K$, $\lambda_{LX} = L_X/L$, and $\lambda_{LZ} = L_Z/L$ indicate the fractions of the capital stock and the labor force which are used in the production of X and the production of Z. The condition for full employment of the labor force requires that

$$l_X^A \lambda_{KX} + l_Z^A \lambda_{KZ} = l. \tag{1}$$

Using the fact that $\lambda_{KX} + \lambda_{KZ} = 1$, it follows that

$$\lambda_{KX} = \frac{l_Z^A - l}{l_Z^A - l_X^A},$$

$$\lambda_{KZ} = \frac{l - l_X^A}{l_Z^A - l_X^A}. \tag{2}$$

In figure 4.1 the right triangles AR^0G, AR^0H, and AR^0I share a common base and have angles at A for which the tangents are, respectively, l_X^A, l, and l_Z^A. It follows that λ_{KX} is shown by the ratio of the distance HI to the distance GI and that λ_{KZ} is shown by the ratio of the distance GH to the distance GI. A symmetric argument applied to the full employment condition for the capital stock and the right triangles AW^0D, AW^0E, and AW^0F allow us to conclude that

$$\lambda_{KX} = \frac{HI}{GI},$$

$$\lambda_{KZ} = \frac{GH}{GI},$$

$$\lambda_{LX} = \frac{DE}{DF},$$

$$\lambda_{LX} = \frac{EF}{DF}. \tag{3}$$

Using (3), we can determine the effect of a change in the economy's endowment of labor or capital on its outputs of X and Z. An increase in L increases the slope of the line EAH; in particular, the distance $R^0 H$ increases proportionately with the increase in L. It follows that $\lambda_{KZ} = GH/GI$ rises more than proportionately with the increase in L and that $\lambda_{KX} = HI/GI$ falls. Since the capital stock is fixed and since the factor ratios in the two industries remain unchanged, it follows that the output of Z is proportional to λ_{KZ} and the output of X is proportional to λ_{KX}. Hence, the output of Z, the labor-intensive commodity, rises more than proportionately with an increase in L, and the output of X, the capital-intensive commodity, falls. Similarly, by looking at the effect of an increase in the capital stock on the distances DE and EF, we may conclude that the output of X will rise more than proportionately with an increase in K and that the output of Z will fall.

4. The Stolper-Samuelson Theorem

The effects of a change in relative commodity prices may be analyzed with the aid of figure 4.2. An increase in the relative price of X is indicated by a shift of the isoprice curve for X from $\tilde{P}_X = P_X^0$ to $\tilde{P}_X = P_X^1$. This moves the point of intersection between the two isoprice curves from A to B. The wage rate consistent with the production of both commodities falls from W^0 to W^1, and the rental rate rises from R^0 to R^1. Since P_X has risen and P_Z has been held constant, it is clear that the wage rate has fallen relative to the prices of both commodities. Furthermore, since the rental rate associated with the point J is the rental rate which is consistent with a constant ratio of R to P_X, it is clear that the rental rate rises relative to the prices of both commodities. This establishes half of the Stolper-Samuelson theorem: an increase in the price of the capital-intensive commodity increases the return to capital in terms of both commodities and reduces the return to labor in terms of both commodities. Moreover, since both isoprice curves and steeper at B than they are at A, it follows that an increase in the relative

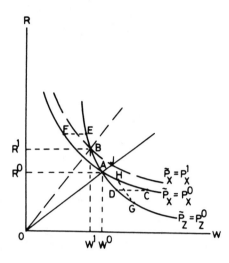

Figure 4.2

price of the capital-intensive commodity induces production of both commodities to become more labor intensive. Combining this fact with the
previous analysis of the distribution of the economy's endowments of labor
and capital, it can be shown that λ_{KX} and λ_{LX} both rise as a result of an
increase in the relative price of X. This, in turn, implies that the output of
X rises and the output of Z declines.

To determine the effects of an increase in the relative price of the labor-
intensive commodity, consider the move from B back to A. We immediately
obtain the other half of the Stolper-Samuelson theorem: the wage rate rises
in terms of both commodities, and the rental rate falls in terms of both
commodities. Moreover production in both industries becomes more capital intensive, and the output of Z rises while the output of X declines.

5. Technological Advance

In terms of the production function, technological advance means that
there is an inward shift of the isoquant; a given level of output can be
produced with lower levels of input. In terms of the dual of the production
function, technological advance means an outward shift of the isoprice
curve; at a given output price, a firm can afford to pay more for its factor
inputs and still maintain zero profits. Specifically, a Hicks neutral technological advance causes a homogeneous outward shift of the isoprice curve
associated with any given output price. In fact, the effect of such a Hicks neutral technological advance in the X industry is precisely what is illustrated

by the outward shift of the $\tilde{P}_X$ curve from $\tilde{P}_X = P_X^0$ to $\tilde{P}_X = P_X^1$ in figure 4.2, except that it is necessary to reinterpret the $\tilde{P}_X = P_X^1$ curve as the isoprice curve corresponding to a higher level of technical efficiency in X, rather than to a higher price of X. With this reinterpretation, it is apparent from figure 4.2 that the effect of a 10 percent Hicks neutral technological advance in X (the capital-intensive industry), at constant output prices, is to increase the rental rate on capital in terms of both goods by more than 10 percent and to reduce the wage of labor in terms of both goods. Similarly, a 10 percent Hicks neutral technological advance in Z (the labor-intensive industry) would shift the $\tilde{P}_Z$ curve homogeneously outward by 10 percent. The effect of such a technological advance in Z would be to increase the wage rate by more than 10 percent and to reduce the rental rate. Moreover it is apparent that this analysis of the effects of technological advance extends to cases where the advance is not Hicks neutral. Any technological advance in X results in a generally nonhomogeneous outward shift of the $\tilde{P}_X$ curve, and hence reduces the wage rate and increases the rental rate. In contrast, any technological advance in Z increases the wage rate and reduces the rental rate.

6. Factor Market Distortions

Figure 4.2 may also be used to determine many of the effects of factor market distortions. Suppose, for instance, that a subsidy is paid to labor used in the production of Z.[6] Given the output prices, P_X^0 and P_Z^0, the equilibrium of the economy must lie at a pair of points like D and C in figure 4.2 for which the rental rate is the same in both industries and for which the wage rate paid by firms in Z (exclusive of subsidy) is below the wage rate paid by firms in X. We see immediately the somewhat paradoxical results that a subsidy to labor in the labor-intensive industry makes both industries become more *capital* intensive and increases the wage paid by firms (exclusive of subsidy) in the subsidized industry. Furthermore, since all workers receive the wage paid in the X industry, all workers gain by more than the rate of subsidy and, hence, the total gain is far in excess of the total subsidy paid.

Next, consider a tax on labor used in the production of X, the capital-intensive commodity. This tax also results in an equilibrium at a pair of points like D and C in figure 4.2. The only difference from the previous case is that workers now receive the wage rate indicated by the point D, rather than the wage rate indicated by the point C. Thus a *tax* on labor in the capital-intensive industry benefits workers, even though it does not benefit them as much as a subsidy to labor in the labor-intensive industry.

A subsidy to labor in X or a tax on labor in Z results in an equilibrium at a pair of points like E and F in figure 4.2. Both the subsidy and the tax benefit the owners of capital by raising the rental rate. The tax on labor in the labor-intensive industry has the most deleterious effect on wages, since under this tax all workers are paid the wage associated with the point F. The more paradoxical result, however, is that a subsidy to labor in the capital-intensive industry actually makes workers worse off than if no subsidy were paid.

Taxes and subsidies on capital used in X or Z can also be analyzed in terms of the diagram. The effect of such distortions is to induce vertical gaps between the two isoprice cuves. The whole analysis is completely symmetric with that for wage distortions. Furthermore the apparatus deals easily with simultaneous distortions of different factor prices. For instance, the pair of points G and H in figure 4.2 represent the equilibrium which would result from any of the following four combinations of distortions: a tax on labor in Z and a subsidy to capital in Z, a tax on labor in Z and a tax on capital in X, a subsidy to labor in X and a subsidy to capital in Z, or a subsidy to labor in X and a tax on capital in X. In each of these four cases the wage rate received by workers is determined by the wage paid in the industry in which labor is not taxed or subsidized and the rental rate received by capital owners is determined by the rental rate paid in the industry in which capital is not taxed or subsidized. For instance, for the case of a tax on labor in Z and a tax on capital in X, the wage rate received by workers is that associated with the point H, and the rental rate received by capital owners is that associated with the point G. Finally, since a tax (subsidy) on an output is equivalent to an equal percentage tax (subsidy) on both inputs used in producing that output, the apparatus of figure 4.2 may be used to analyze the effects of distortions of output prices.

7. Shadow Prices in a Distorted Economy

In an economy free of distortions, the prices of factors measure the marginal social values of these factors. Specifically, the wage rate and the rental rate associated with the undistorted equilibrium point A indicate the amount by which the value of the economy's output would rise if the endowment of labor or capital, respectively, were increased by a unit. The question of what would happen to the value of output, at given output prices, if the supply of a factor were increased remains a meaningful question in a distorted economy. But the answer to this question is not provided by the prices received by factor owners or by the prices paid by factor users. To determine the marginal social values of labor and capital, it is necessary to calculate a shadow wage rate, W^S, and a shadow rental rate, R^S.[7]

Given the prices of the two outputs and the distortions prevailing in the economy, the amounts of labor and capital used to produce a unit of X, a_{LX} and a_{KX}, and the amounts of labor and capital used to produce a unit of Z, a_{LZ} and a_{KZ}, are fixed by the wage rates and rental rates facing the two industries. Given these factor requirements, the appropriate procedure for determining W^S and R^S is to calculate the equilibrium wage rate and rental rate for this fixed-coefficients technology. Specifically, from Jones (1965) it follows that W^S and R^S must satisfy

$$a_{LX} W^S + a_{KX} R^S = P_X^0, \tag{4}$$

$$a_{LZ} W^S + a_{KZ} R^S = P_Z^0. \tag{5}$$

For the set of distortions indicated by the points B and C in figure 4.3, the combinations of W and R which are consistent with (4) are shown by the tangent to the $\tilde{P}_X = P_X^0$ curve at C, and the combinations of W and R which are consistent with (5) are shown by the tangent to the $\tilde{P}_Z = P_Z^0$ curve at B. The point of intersection of these two tangents, S, determines the values of W^S and R^S which jointly satisfy (4) and (5). It is convenient to construct a line through S with a slope equal to -1. The argument of section 3 may be modified to show that the intercepts of this line, relative to the intercepts of the tangents to the two isoprice curves, indicate the distribu-

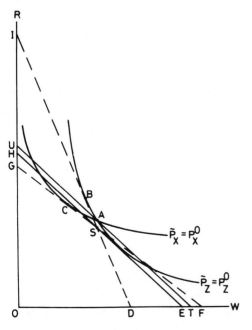

Figure 4.3

tion of labor and capital between X and Z. Specifically, figure 4.3 has been labeled so that (3) continues to hold. By rotating the line which shows the endowment ratio around the point S, it is easily shown that the Rybczynski effect continues to hold in a distorted economy.

One important use for the shadow factor prices is that suggested by Diamond and Mirrlees (1976) and Findlay and Wellisz (1976) and further developed by Bhagwati, Srinivasan, and Wan (1978), Srinivasan and Bhagwati (1978), and Bhagwati and Wan (1979). Suppose that a planning agency is considering the desirability of producing a new commodity and is concerned with how to induce firms to produce it if it is desirable from a social point of view. Given the existing set of distortions, the appropriate social criterion is to produce at least a small amount of a new commodity if the cost of diverting labor and capital (in an optimal fashion) from X and Z is smaller than the value of the new commodity.[8] Graphically, this criterion is satisfied if the isoprice curve for the new commodity lies above the shadow price point, S. From figure 4.3 it is apparent that a commodity could satisfy this criterion and yet not be profitable at the factor prices assoicated with any of the three points, A, B, or C. It follows that in a distorted economy it may be socially desirable to produce some new commodities which would not be socially desirable in an undistorted economy. Furthermore, to ensure that a new commodity which is socially desirable is also privately profitable, and vice versa, it is necessary to tax or subsidize inputs used by producers of new products. The appropriate set of taxes and subsidies is that which makes the factor prices paid by producers of new products equal to the shadow factor prices.

A further use for the shadow factor prices is in determining the total damage done by a given set of distortions and in comparing the damage done by different sets of distortions. The measure of damage is the reduction in the value of the economy's final output, at given output prices. The value of output is given by

$$V = W^S L + R^S K. \tag{6}$$

Dividing V by the economy's labor force yields

$$\frac{V}{L} = W^S + \frac{R^S}{l}. \tag{7}$$

Graphically, V/L is measured by the horizontal intercept of the line through S with a slope of $-l$. Thus, for the distortion analyzed in figure 4.3, V/L is indicated by the distance OE. In comparison, for the nondistorted economy, with shadow factor prices determined by the point A, V/L is indicated by the distance OT. Hence the loss generated by the distortions shown in figure 4.3, relative to the nondistorted situation, is indicated by ET/OT. This loss could be compared with the loss generated by an entirely different set of distortions to determine which set of distortions generates the greatest loss. Finally, it should be noted that the loss measured by the reduction in V/L is the sum of two components. First, as a result of distortions in the factor market, the output transformation curve is generally inside the transformation curve for the undistorted economy; and second, the production point on the new transformation curve does not, in general, correspond to the point at which the value of output is maximized (at given output prices) on the new transformation curve.[9]

8. Negative Shadow Prices and Highly Distorted Economies

When an economy is "highly distorted" by large divergences between required factor returns in different industries, the possibility exists that the shadow price of one of the factors of production (but not both) may be negative. This phenomenon has been explored in recent papers by Srinivasan and Bhagwati (1978) and Bhagwati, Srinivasan, and Wan (1978). For present purposes it is interesting to note that this phenomenon of negative shadow prices is related to other peculiarities that arise in the context of highly distorted economies. Specifically, consider the situation, illustrated in figure 4.4, that arises from either a high tax on the use of capital in Z (the labor-intensive industry) or a high subsidy on the use of capital in X (the capital-intensive industry).

One peculiar aspect of the situation depicted in figure 4.4 is that an increase in the *percentage* rate of tax on capital in Z makes the economy *less* distorted. This is because the ratio of the distance QC to the slope of the line $SFCG$ is greater than the ratio of the distance QB to the slope of the line $SDBI$. As we move a small distance along the two isoprice curves (approximated by their tangents) in the direction of A, the ratio of distance between the curves to the height of the $\tilde{P}_X = P_X^0$ curve rises. Therefore an *increase* in the percentage distortion between the rental rate on capital used in the two industries is associated with a movement *toward* the point A and hence toward a *less* distorted economy. This fact is the source of many counterintuitive results. Normally we would not expect that an increase in the percentage tax on capital employed in Z (or subsidy on capital employed in X) would increase the capital-labor ratios in both industries, increase the wage rate, reduce the return received by capital owners and the rental paid by capital users, and generally reduce the level of distortion in the economy but rather produce the exact opposite of all these results. All of these results make sense once it is recognized that an increase in

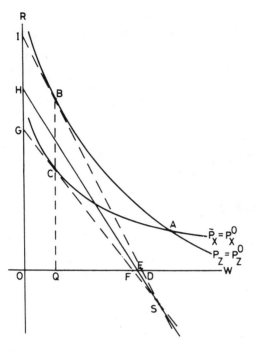

Figure 4.4

percentage distortion means a reduction in the absolute distortion and a move toward the point A.

A second peculiarity of the situation shown in figure 4.4 is that relative factor intensities indicated by physical factor ratios do not correspond to relative factor intensities indicated by relative value shares. This is because the rental rate paid in Z is so much above the rental rate paid in X that it outweighs the fact that X is physically capital intensive and makes the share of capital in the value of Z output greater than the share of capital in the value of X output. Graphically this fact may be seen by noting that the share of capital in X is measured by QF/OF, whereas the share of capital in Z is measured by $QD/OD > QF/OF$. It is apparent, geometrically, that this situation will arise if and only if the tangents to the two isoprice curves intersect below the W-axis.[10]

A third peculiarity associated with figure 4.4 is that an increase in the economy's endowment of capital *reduces* the value of total output. In other words, even holding output prices constant, "growth" that results from capital accumulation is immiserizing.[11] This result may be proved by appealing to equation (6) or by noting that the distance OE in figure 4.4 that measures V/L becomes shorter as K is increased. Initially the finding that an increase in the capital stock reduces the value of output may appear paradoxical. It makes perfect sense once it is recognized that in this highly distorted economy, capital has a negative marginal social value.

A final peculiarity arises in connection with the evaluation of the social benefits of producing new commodities. In a "highly distorted" economy, it is socially beneficial to produce any new commodity with a positive price, provided that it can be produced with a sufficiently high ratio of the factor with a negative shadow price. Since throwing away units of a factor with a negative shadow price improves social welfare, using them to produce something of positive value is exceedingly attractive.

9. Conclusion

The dual of a production function represents technology as a relationship between output price and input prices. For this reason the diagrammatic technique developed in this paper is particularly useful in illustrating the properties of the two-sector model which are essentially concerned with prices: the factor-price equalization theorem, the Stolper-Samuelson theorem, the effects of distortions of factor prices and product prices, and the determination of shadow prices. The behavior of factor ratios is also easily analyzed since these ratios are indicated by the slopes of the respective isoprice curves. It is also possible to use the present diagrammatic technique to ascertain the behavior of quantities of outputs and inputs; however, for this purpose it is probably more convenient to use a diagrammatic technique which is based on the production function representation of technology.

Notes

The initial version of this paper was written while visiting the Center for Monetary and Banking Studies at the Graduate Institute of International Studies in Geneva in the fall of 1976. Financial support for that visit was provided by a grant from the Ford Foundation.

1. See Shepard (1953) and McFadden et al. (1975) for a general discussion of the concept of the dual of a production function and its application. See Amano (1963) and Jones (1965) for the application of this general concept to the two-sector model.

2. The phenomenon of negative shadow prices and its relationship to various peculiarities of highly distorted economies are investigated in recent papers by Srinivasan and Bhagwati (1978) and Bhagwati, Srinivasan, and Wan (1978).

3. Burgess (1976) develops a similar diagram in his analysis of the effects of tariffs. The present diagram was developed while commenting on a paper by Neary and

is used in the final version of that paper (see Neary 1978). The application of this diagram to the exposition of many of the properties of the two-sector model was developed independently by Woodland (1977).

4. The equation that defines the tangent to the $\tilde{P}_X = P_X^0$ curve is given by $a_{LX}W + a_{KX}R = P_X^0$, where a_{LX} and a_{KX} are the amounts of labor and capital, respectively, that are used in producing a unit of X, at the factor price combination indicated by the corresponding point on the isoprice curve.

5. For the case of zero elasticity of substitution between labor and capital, the isoprice curve is a straight line. For the case of infinite elasticity of substitution, the isoprice curve is a right angle.

6. The disposal of tax revenue and the finance of subsidies are neglected in this discussion. The effects of taxes and subsidies on factor owners refer to the effects on them in their role as factor owners, not as general taxpayers or transfer recipients.

7. The concept of shadow prices of factors of production and the application of this concept to diverse issues in international trade theory and in project evaluation has been pursued in a number of recent papers. In particular, see Diamond and Mirrlees (1976), Findlay and Wellisz (1976), and Srinivasan and Bhagwati (1978).

8. This application of shadow prices to project evaluation is consistent with the general principles recommended by Little and Mirrlees (1969). It should be noted that some care is needed in applying this principle to "large" projects, for a large project might well alter the structure of rewards. This is particularly a problem in the context of the standard two-factor model since in this model the introduction of a new output is likely to lead to the cessation of production of one of the economy's existing outputs.

9. Johnson (1966) and later Herberg and Kemp (1971) and Bhagwati and Srinivasan (1971) analyze the effect of factor market distortions on the shape of the transformation curve. It is also generally recognized that factor market distortions lead to a situation in which the tangent to the transformation curve does not necessarily correspond to the projuct price ratio.

10. Jones (1971) and Magee (1973) note that a number of peculiarities of highly distorted economies are associated with a divergence between relative intensities measured by physical factor ratios and relative factor intensities measured by value shares. For the case illustrated in figure 4 the negative shadow rental rate for capital is associated with such a divergence between the two measures of relative factor intensity. More generally, if only wage rates are distorted, or only rental rates are distorted, then a negative shadow price will be associated with a divergence between the two measures of relative factor intensity. However, if both wage rates and rental rates are distorted, there is no necessary relationship between a negative shadow price for one factor of production and a divergence between the two measures of relative factor intensity.

11. It has been recognized for some time that factor market distortions can lead to a situation in which growth in the supplies of factors of production is immiserizing; see Bhagwati (1968) and Bertrand and Flatters (1971). Recently it has been recognized that this possibility is related to the phenomenon of a negative shadow price for a factor of production; see Bhagwati, Srinivasan, and Wan (1978).

References

Amano, A. 1963. Neo-classical models of international trade and economic growth. Ph.D. dissertation. University of Rochester.

Bertrand, T., and F. Flatters. 1971. Tariffs, capital accumulation, and immiserising growth, *Journal of international Economics* 1, 453–460.

Bhagwati, J. 1968. Distortions and immiserising growth: A generalization. *Review of Economic Studies* 35, 481–485.

Bhagwati, J., and T. N. Srinivasan. 1971. The theory of wage differentials: Production response and factor price equalization. *Journal of International Economics* 1, 19–35.

Bhagwati, J., and H. Wan. 1979. The stationarity of shadow prices of factors in project evaluation, with and without distortions, *American Economic Review* 69, 261–273.

Bhagwati, J., T. N. Srinivasan, and H. Wan. 1978. Value subtracted, negative shadow prices of factors in project evaluation, and immiserising growth: Three paradoxes in the presence of trade distortions. *Economic Journal* 88, 121–125.

Burgess, D. 1976. Tariffs and income distribution: Some empirical evidence for the United States. *Journal of Political Economy* 84, 17–46.

Diamond, P., and J. Mirrlees, 1976, Private constant returns and public shadow prices, *Review of Economic Studies* 43, 41–48.

Findlay, R., and S. Wellisz, 1976, Project evaluation, shadow prices, and trade policy. *Journal of Political Economy* 84, 543–552.

Herberg, H., and M. Kemp, 1971, Factor market distortions, the shape of the locus of competitive outputs, and the relation between product prices and equilibrium outputs. In Bhagwati et al., eds., *Trade, Balance of Payments and Growth*. North Holland, Amsterdam.

Johnson, H. G 1966. Factor market distortions and the shape of the transformation curve. *Econometrica* 34, 686–698.

Jones, R. W. 1965. The structure of simple general equilibrium models. *Journal of Political Economy* 73, 557–572.

Jones, R. W. 1971. Distortions in factor markets and the general equilibrium model of production. *Journal of Political Economy* 79, 437–459.

Little, I., and J. Mirrlees, 1969, *Manual for Industrial Project Analysis in Developing Countries*. Vol. 2. OECD, Paris.

Magee, S. P. 1973 Factor market distortions, production, and trade: A survey. *Oxford Economic Papers* 25, 1–43.

McFadden, D. L., et al. 1975. *An Econometric Approach to Production Theory*. North Holland, Amsterdam.

Neary, P. 1978. Short-run capital specificity and the pure theory of international trade. *Economic Journal* 88, 488–510.

Shepard, R. W. 1953. *Cost and Production Functions.* Princeton University Press, Princeton.

Srinivasan, T., and J. Bhagwati. 1978. Shadow prices for project selection in the presence of distortions: Effective rates of protection and domestic resource costs. *Journal of Political Economy* 86, 97–116.

Woodland, A. 1977. A dual approach to equilibrium in the production sector in international trade theory. *Canadian Journal of Economics* 10, 50–68.

5

Short-Run Capital Specificity and the Pure Theory of International Trade

J. Peter Neary

Among its many abstractions from reality, the pure theory of international trade, associated with the names of Heckscher, Ohlin, and Samuelson, assumes that both capital and labour are costlessly and instantaneously transferable between sectors. More recently, however, beginning with articles by Jones (1971b) and Samuelson (1971a, b), a number of writers have returned to an older tradition, traceable in the works of Marshall, Ohlin himself, and Harrod, which assumes that, in the short run at least, capital goods are sector-specific. In the light of this tradition, the Heckscher-Ohlin-Samuelson model is seen as describing positions of long-run equilibrium only. In the short run any disturbance will lead to a reallocation of the labour force between sectors. But capital in each sector is a fixed factor, and so differences emerge between the rentals in the two sectors. Over a longer time-horizon capital will flow between sectors in response to these rental differentials, tending eventually (unless another disturbance intervenes) to a new long-run equilibrium with all capital goods earning the same rental.

This view of the adjustment process, which I propose to call the "short-run capital specificity" hypothesis, is hardly novel; apart from the earlier writers already cited, it is implicit, for example, in Harberger (1962) and Kemp and Jones (1962). However, as formalised in recent work, especially by Mayer (1974) and Mussa (1974), it provides a plausible hypothesis about the economy's response to exogenous disturbances. Moreover these writers have shown that it may be used to explain why there is no necessary contradiction between the somewhat counterintuitive predictions of traditional international trade theory, and the more "commonsensical" views of politicians, businessmen and trade-union leaders.

The aim of this paper is threefold. First, it presents a new diagrammatic

This paper was originally published in *The Economic Journal* 88 (September 1978): 488–510. The present version omits sections 4–7 of the original article.

technique to illustrate the short-run capital specificity adjustment process in a small open economy. This technique is used in sections 1 through 3 to demonstrate the process of adjustment towards long-run equilibrium, following changes in commodity prices, population, and the level of factor market distortions. Sections 1 and 2 expound the findings of Mussa and Mayer on the effects of changes in the terms of trade and in total factor supplies, noting some extensions of these writers' analyses. Section 3 then applies the technique to the consideration of changes in the level of factor market distortions. It is shown that conflicts between long-run and short-run interests may arise in this case: for example, workers in a labour-intensive sector may have an incentive to press for higher wages, despite the fact that in the long run their action will lower wages in both sectors.

Second, the implications of the short-run capital specificity adjustment process are examined in the context of an open economy with preexisting factor market distortions. Much of the recent literature in this area (see especially Jones 1971a and Magee 1976) has been concerned with the elucidation of a number of paradoxes which can arise in the presence of such factor market distortions, of which two of the more notable are a perverse price-output response and a perverse distortion-output response. Section 4 begins by giving a new diagrammatic exposition of these paradoxes, and then shows that, if the economy is assumed to adjust according to the short-run capital specificity hypothesis, then *these paradoxes will never be observed*, because they correspond to *dynamically unstable* long-run equilibria. For devotees of the Heckscher-Ohlin-Samuelson model, this is an encouraging conclusion, since it implies that the long-run predictions of that model in the presence of factor market distortions are much more consistent with simple economic intuition than had been thought. The analysis of this section complements that of a companion paper, Neary (1978b), where the same conclusions are shown to hold under a wider class of disequilibrium adjustment mechanisms.

The third aim of the paper is to point out the central role of the assumption of intersectoral capital mobility in traditional international trade theory. Section 5 surveys a number of cases, additional to those in sections 1 through 3, where this assumption is responsible for "paradoxical" or counterintuitive conclusions. It is argued in section 6 that both common sense and the implications of observed self-interested behaviour on the part of market participants make this assumption inappropriate in the short run, and that the peculiar nature of the primary factor capital which it assumes—a fixed stock of homogeneous, infinitely long-lived, and perfectly mobile machines—makes it suspect in the long run.

1. Short-Run and Long-Run Responses to Changes in the Terms of Trade

We begin by introducing the diagrammatic technique to be used in this paper. Essentially this combines two diagrams: the Edgeworth-Bowley production box, introduced to international trade theory by Stolper and Samuelson (1941), and the sector-specific capital diagram, familiar in writings on economic development and used by Jones (1971b) and Mussa (1974). As shown in figure 5.1, measuring the economy's labour force on the horizontal axis of the Edgeworth-Bowley box enables us to place the two diagrams vertically above one another, and thus to examine simultaneously the short-run and long-run consequences of any exogenous change.

The usual assumptions of the two-sector model of international trade are built into figure 5.1, where the initial equilibrium is indicated by the points A_0 and B_0 in the upper and lower parts of the figure, respectively. The economy produces two goods, X and Y, under perfectly competitive conditions in both commodity and factor markets, using fixed supplies of the two factors, labour and capital, and subject to constant returns to scale. In the long run both factors are completely mobile between sectors. In the short run, however, there are diminishing returns to labour in each sector because of the fixity of capital goods. Hence entrepreneurs in each sector maximise profits by increasing employment until the value marginal product of labour equals the wage. Assuming that the wage rate adjusts to ensure full employment at all times, the initial wage rate and labour force allocation is therefore determined by the intersection of the two value marginal product of labour schedules, V_X^0 and V_Y^0, at A_0 in the upper part of figure 5.1. The location of these schedules depends on the initial commodity prices and on the initial allocation of capital to each sector, with the latter represented by the distances $O_X K_X$ and $O_Y K_Y$ in the lower part of the figure. Finally, the fact that the initial position is one of long-run as well as of short-run equilibrium is shown by the fact that B_0, the point in the lower part of the diagram which corresponds to A_0, lies on the contract curve of the Edgeworth-Bowley box. This contract curve lies below the diagonal of the box, reflecting our last assumption, that X is the relatively labour-intensive sector.

Consider now the effect of a displacement of this initial equilibrium by a once-and-for-all change in the terms of trade, involving an increase in the relative price of X. With capital sector-specific in the short run, we may begin by examining the upper part of figure 5.1. Choosing good Y as numeraire, the value marginal product of labour in Y schedule, V_Y^0, is unaffected, whereas the corresponding schedule for the X sector shifts upwards, from V_X^0 to V_X^1, by the same proportional amount as the price

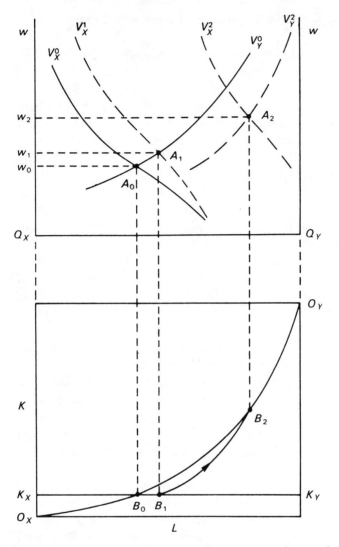

Figure 5.1   Short-run and long-run adjustments to an increase in the relative price of the labour-intensive good X

increase. Therefore the new short-run equilibrium will be that represented by the points A_1 and B_1. (The latter point satisfies the restrictions that it lies vertically below A_1, and on the same capital allocation line, $K_X K_Y$, as B_0.) Labour has moved out of Y into X, and since the amount of capital in X is unchanged, the output of X has increased: thus even in the short run the economy responds to the rise in the relative price of X by expanding its output, to an extent determined by the slopes of the two value marginal product of labour schedules.

The short-run reactions of factor prices to this change have been considered in detail by Mussa (1974). The wage rate increase in terms of Y but falls in terms of X (this may be seen from the fact that the capital-labour ratio rises in sector Y but falls in sector X), so that the effect on the real income of wage earners is not independent of their consumption pattern. As for the rentals on capital, that in the X sector increases in terms of both goods, whereas that in the Y sector falls in terms of both. However, while all of these changes are of interest from the point of view of income distribution, the crucial fact from the point of view of resource allocation is that the capital rental in X has increased relative to that in Y. This may also be seen from the lower part of the diagram: since B_1 lies below the efficiency locus, it follows that the rental wage ratio is relatively higher in X, and since the same wage prevails in each sector this means that the rental must be higher in X than in Y. Given our assumed adjustment process therefore, competitive pressures will lead in the "medium run" to a reallocation of capital from the low to the high rental sector.[1] In the lower part of the diagram, this has the effect of causing the capital allocation line to shift upwards; in the upper part, both the V_X^1 and V_Y^0 schedules shift to the right, since an increase (decrease) in the quantity of capital in a sector must lead the marginal product of labour to rise (fall) at all levels of employment.

To establish the effects of this capital reallocation on factor rewards and on factor usage in each sector, we note first that the transfer of a given amount of capital from Y to X leads the former sector to seek to shed labour and the latter to try to acquire labour.[2] Since X is the relatively labour-intensive sector, the quantity of labour it wishes to acquire will, at the initial factor prices, exceed that which the Y sector is willing to give up. Excess demand for labour in the economy as a whole therefore develops, and so the wage rate is bid up. With both commodity prices constant, the increase in the wage must reduce the rental in each sector. This follows from the fact that the proportional change in the price of each good is a weighted average of the changes in factor prices in each sector, the weights being the share of each factor in the value of output of that sector:

$$\hat{p}_X = \theta_{LX}\hat{w} + \theta_{KX}\hat{r}_X, \tag{1}$$

$$\hat{p}_Y = \theta_{LY}\hat{w} + \theta_{KY}\hat{r}_Y. \tag{2}$$

Since the wage rental ratio rises in each sector as capital reallocates, both capital-labour ratios must also rise. The economy therefore moves away from B_1 in a northeasterly direction, along the path shown by a heavy line, which satisfies the properties that at every point along it the slope of the path is greater than the slope of the ray from O_X to that point, and less than the slope of the ray from O_Y to that point. This path may be called a "*labour-market equilibrium locus*," because although it is characterised throughout by disequilibrium in the capital market, the labour market is in equilibrium at all points along it (in the sense that full employment of labour and a uniform wage rate prevail).

Finally, what happens to the intersectoral rental differential as the economy moves along this locus? The fact that X is the relatively labour-intensive sector means that the distributive share of labour is greater in X than in Y; hence to keep relative commodity prices constant, it is necessary for the rental in X to fall by more than that in Y. This may be seen by setting the proportional changes in price in equations (1) and (2) equal to zero, and manipulating the equations to obtain:

$$\hat{r}_X - \hat{r}_Y = -\frac{\theta}{\theta_{KX}\theta_{KY}}\hat{w}, \tag{3}$$

where θ is the determinant of the matrix of sectoral shares, which is positive in this case, because X is relatively labour intensive.[3] Equation (3) shows that as a result of the transfer of capital between sectors and the consequent increase in the wage, the gap between the rentals in the two sectors has been partially closed. This process of capital reallocation continues until the gap is fully closed; at which time a new long-run equilibrium, corresponding to the points A_2 and B_2, is attained. This new equilibrium is exactly that predicted by Stolper and Samuelson (1941), at which, relative to the initial equilibrium at A_0 and B_0, the wage has risen and the rental common to both sectors has fallen in terms of each good. Thus the short-run effect of the price change in increasing the rental on capital in the X sector is eroded, and eventually reversed, in the course of the adjustment process, as capital flows into the X sector in response to the higher return obtainable there.

Having examined the case where X is relatively labour-intensive, the case where it is relatively capital intensive is straightforward. It is illustrated in figure 5.2. Perhaps the most important feature is that the initial reaction to the increase in the relative price of X is qualitatively identical to that in

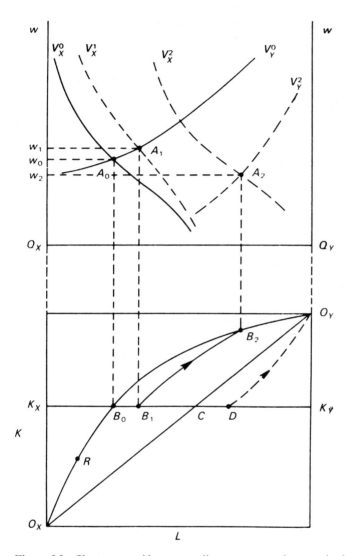

Figure 5.2   Short-run and long-run adjustments to an increase in the relative price of the capital-intensive good X

figure 5.1: as before, the wage rises initially in terms of Y, while the rentals on capital in X and Y rise and fall respectively in terms of both goods. It is only in the course of the adjustment process that relative factor intensities play a role, as the verbal description above will have made clear. In this case, the movement of capital into the relatively capital-intensive sector reduces the demand for labour in the economy; hence the rental in both sectors rises, and the common wage rate falls, throughout the adjustment process. The capital-labour ratio in each sector therefore falls as capital reallocates, and so the path of adjustment from B_1 to B_2 is less steeply sloped at any point than the ray from O_X to that point, and more steeply sloped than the corresponding ray from O_Y. At the new long-run equilibrium (represented by A_2 and B_2) the wage will be lower than its initial value of w_0. But, despite this, it is possible for labour actually to favour the change on completely rational grounds, if its consumption pattern is sufficiently biased towards Y, and if either the speed of capital reallocation is sufficiently slow, or the rate at which labour discounts its future consumption to the present is sufficiently high.

The only additional qualification which must be made to the case where X is initially relatively capital intensive, is that a sufficiently large price increase could cause the new short-run equilibrium point to lie to the right of C in the Edgeworth-Bowley box, thus reversing the initial factor intensity ranking of the two sectors. This possibility was pointed out by Mussa (1974, p. 1200, n. 10), who claimed that such a factor intensity reversal would only be temporary, and that the factor allocation point in the Edgeworth-Bowley box would eventually recross the diagonal. However, this is incorrect: if the new short-run equilibrium occurs at a point such as D, to the right of C in figure 5.2, the factor allocation point will *not* recross the diagonal but will move instead towards O_Y along the labour-market equilibrium locus indicated by the dashed line. The Y industry will eventually be completely eliminated, and the economy will specialise in the production of X. This follows from the fact (already established above) that as capital reallocates, the expansion of the now labour-intensive sector X increases the wage rental ratio in both sectors. Hence the capital-labour ratio in sector Y cannot fall during the adjustment process, as it would have to if the labour-market equilibrium locus were to cross the diagonal.

In summary, this section has illustrated the conclusions of Mayer and Mussa that an increase in the relative price of X under the short-run capital specificity adjustment process will always imply a conflict between the short-run and long-run interests of at least one group of factor income recipients: when X is relatively labour-intensive, this is true of the owners of sector X capital, and when X is relatively capital intensive, it is true of both wage-earners and owners of sector Y capital. In addition it has been shown that contrary to the suggestion of Mussa, a change in the terms of trade can never lead to a temporary reversal of the relative factor intensities of the two sectors, since the price change required to induce a short-run factor intensity reversal is more than sufficient to induce complete specialisation in the long run.

2. Short-Run and Long-Run Responses to Changes in Factor Endowments

The next case to be considered is that of a once-and-for-all increase in population, as examined by Mayer (1974). In figure 5.3 the initial equilibrium is at A_0 and B_0, with X the relatively capital-intensive sector. Suppose now that the labour force (assumed to be identical to the population) increases by an amount equal to the distance $Q_Y^0 Q_Y^1$. With unchanged capital allocations, the V_Y^0 schedule is shifted to the right by the full extent of the population increase, leading to a new short-run equilibrium at A_1, corresponding to the point B_1 in the production box.[4] It is clear from the diagram that the wage falls, and hence at constant (absolute and relative) commodity prices, the rental in each sector must rise. Moreover, from equation (3) it follows that the rental must increase by a greater proportional amount in the relatively labour-intensive sector. Hence, in the "medium run," capital moves along the labour-market equilibrium locus $B_1 B_2$ from the capital-intensive sector X into the labour-intensive sector Y, causing the wage rate to increase steadily, and the rental to fall in each sector, with the gap between the two rentals narrowing and finally being eliminated.

From the Rybczynski theorem (Rybczynski 1955) we know that the final long-run equilibrium must be at B_2 in the production box: with unchanged commodity prices and rentals equalised between sectors, relative factor prices, and hence factor proportions in each sector must be identical to those which prevailed before the population increase. This may also be seen from the upper part of the diagram: the V_X and V_Y schedules have both shifted to the left to intersect at A_2, restoring the original wage w_0. Despite this long-run independence of the wage from the size of population, however, if workers have any positive discount rate, they will, for example, oppose immigration in a small open economy on perfectly rational grounds. Furthermore the strong Rybczynski prediction, that at constant relative commodity prices the output of the capital-intensive sector must fall, is shown to be a long-run result only: with sector-specific capital in the short run, the increased employment in X represented by the move from A_0 to A_1 means that the output of X will initially *rise* as a result of the population growth.

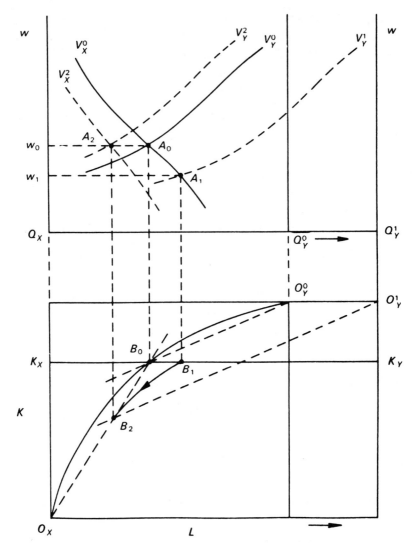

Figure 5.3   Short-run and long-run adjustments to population growth

The case where X is relatively labour-intensive may be examined in the same way. As in section 1, this makes no qualitative difference to the new short-run equilibrium, but from equation (3) the intersectoral differential in capital rentals will be the opposite to the case just considered, leading to the familiar Rybczynski result of a fall in the output of Y in the long (though not in the short) run. Finally, the same diagrammatic technique may also be applied to the case of capital accumulation. Assuming the new capital is initially usable in one sector only, say X, it will displace the value marginal product of labour schedule of that sector to the right. Thus in the short run the wage rate will increase, and so from equation (3) the rental in the relatively capital-intensive sector will increase by more than that in the other sector. Hence, assuming that both the initial and the new capital goods become mobile in the long run, capital will move into the relatively capital-intensive sector, until a new long-run equilibrium is attained where the original factor prices are restored. If X is the relatively capital-intensive sector, its output will increase both in the short and the long run. But if it is relatively labour intensive, its output must fall in the long run. Indeed, in the latter case, not only the proportional, but the absolute amount of capital in use in X will be less in the final long-run equilibrium than that quantity which it used before the initial capital accumulation.

3. Short-Run and Long-Run Adjustments to Changes in Factor Market Distortions[5]

In this section we apply the same framework of analysis to an examination of the process of adjustment to a change in the level of a factor market distortion, such as a trade-union imposed wage differential or a sector-specific factor tax. We continue to assume that the economy has no influence over its terms of trade. Moreover we assume that the factor market distortion is introduced in a situation where factor markets are initially distortion free. This assumption, of no preexisting distortions, is a crucial one, and the consequences of relaxing it are examined in section 4.

We consider first the case of a wage differential, where the high-wage sector is relatively labour-intensive. In figure 5.4 the initial equilibrium is at A_0 and B_0, with the same wage rate prevailing in each sector.[6] Suppose now that workers in Y become unionised, and succeed in obtaining a wage which exceeds that in the X sector by a proportionate amount measured by the distortion parameter α:

$$w_Y = \alpha w_X \quad (\alpha > 1). \tag{4}$$

This change has no immediate effect on the V_X^0 and V_Y^0 schedules in the top half of figure 5.4: with an unchanged capital allocation they continue to

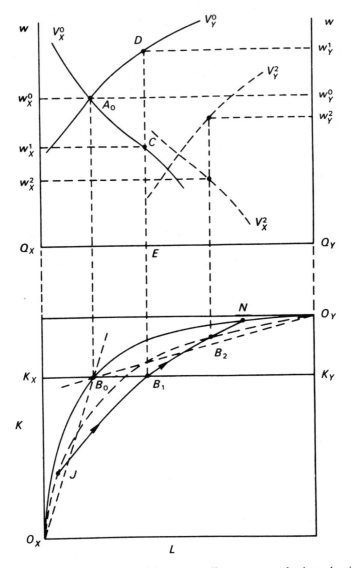

Figure 5.4   Short-run and long-run adjustments to the introduction of a wage differential in favour of the labour-intensive sector Y

represent the value marginal product of labour in each sector. However, the effect of the union action is to drive a wedge between the value marginal products which can prevail in equilibrium in each sector. Faced with the obligation to pay higher wages, entrepreneurs in the Y sector will shed labour, and so a new short-run equilibrium will be established where the ratio between the value marginal product of labour in the two sectors— that is, the ratio between the distance DE and CE—equals the distortion parameter, α. Clearly, the initial impact of the differential is, in qualitative terms, independent of the relative factor intensities of the two sectors: the wage in the unionised sector rises and that in the X sector falls, and each of these changes is less, proportionately, than the change in the differential.

Turning to the lower part of figure 5.4, one effect of the introduction of the wage differential is to shift the contract curve downwards as shown, since in long-run equilibrium the X sector now faces a lower effective wage rental ratio than the Y sector. The new distorted contract curve must therefore cut the initial capital allocation line, $K_X K_Y$, to the right of B_0. However, it cannot cut it at or to the right of the new short-run equilibrium point B_1, because the short-run fall in the X sector wage rate combined with the rise in the Y sector wage rate must at constant output prices lead to an intersectoral rental differential in favour of sector X; hence B_1 must lie below the distorted contract curve. From a similar reasoning to that in section 2, it follows that in the medium run capital will reallocate from the unionised sector Y into the X sector, moving the economy upwards and to the right along the labour market equilibrium locus through B_1; and as capital reallocates into the relatively capital-intensive sector the wage rate is reduced in both sectors, and the intersectoral rental differential is narrowed.

Where will the new long-run equilibrium occur? Evidently it must be at B_2, the intersection of the labour-market equilibrium locus and the distorted contract curve to the northeast of B_1, where the intersectoral rental differential is finally eliminated.[7] (The intersection to the southwest, at J, will be considered in the next section.) Moreover, as Magee (1971) has shown (and as will be demonstrated in the next section), the capital-labour ratio must fall in both sectors between the old and the new long-run equilibria; hence B_2 must lie above the ray $O_Y B_0$. It follows that the long-run effect of unionisation in the labour-intensive sector is to increase the rental and lower the wage in both sectors (implying that nonunion wages must fall by more than the proportional wage differential).[8] This of course is the well-known result, derived in various ways by Harberger (1962), Johnson and Mieszkowski (1970), Jones (1971a), and Magee (1971), that an increase in the differential paid to a factor in the sector which uses it intensively may—and, when commodity prices are constant, must—reduce the factor's reward in both sectors. However, we have shown that this result is a long-run one only, for the short-run effect of the union action was to increase the wage in the Y sector. Hence, contrary to the implication of the result just mentioned, it may be perfectly rational for a union in a relatively labour-intensive sector to press for higher wages, if its discount rate is high enough, and the process of capital reallocation sufficiently slow. Similar results may be derived for the case where the unionised sector is relatively capital intensive: in the long run, labour in both sectors must gain, but once again a conflict between short-run and long-run interests arises, this time in the case of labour in X.

Finally, what can be said of distortions in the capital market, such as a corporate income tax of the kind studied by Harberger (1962)? The imposition of such a tax has no effect on resource allocation in the short run: since capital in the taxed sector is a fixed factor, its income amounts to a Marshallian quasi rent, the taxation of which will have no immediate impact on behaviour.[9] However, the resulting differential between the net rentals in the two sectors will lead eventually to a reallocation of capital away from the taxed sector. This shows an important difference between the short-run consequences of a capital and a labour tax, which follows from our assumption about the relative adjustment speeds of the two factors: the imposition of a capital market distortion has no immediate effect on resource allocation, whereas that of a labour market distortion leads to an immediate contraction of the sector obliged to pay the higher wage. In the long run, on the other hand, there is a basic symmetry between the two types of distortion, at fixed commodity prices, in the sense that qualitatively the same effects will follow the imposition of a tax (or a trade union differential) on labour in sector Y as will follow the granting of a *subsidy* to capital in the other sector.

Notes

1. The timing and speed of this reallocation will depend on a variety of considerations including reallocation costs and entrepreneurial wage and price expectations. For a study which examines these aspects in greater detail, see Mussa (1975).

2. I am very grateful to Alasdair Smith, whose comments suggested a major simplification of the remainder of this section.

3. That is

$$\theta = \begin{vmatrix} \theta_{LX} & \theta_{LY} \\ \theta_{KX} & \theta_{KY} \end{vmatrix} = \begin{vmatrix} \theta_{LX} & \theta_{LY} \\ 1 - \theta_{LX} & 1 - \theta_{LY} \end{vmatrix} = \theta_{LX} - \theta_{LY}.$$

4. The point B_1 is above the new contract curve (not drawn) of the enlarged production box, since at B_1 the wage rental ratio in X exceeds that in Y.

5. Since this section was written, I have found a somewhat similar analysis in Hu (1973).

6. I am very grateful to Dermot McAleese, who pointed out a serious error in an earlier version of this diagram.

7. If the initial move from B_0 to B_1 had been caused by an increase in the relative price of X, the new long-run equilibrium would lie on the original efficiency locus at N. Thus, comparing a price change and a wage differential change, each of which has the same short-run effect, the long-run effect of the price change is greater than that of the wage differential change. This is intuitively plausible, since wage costs are a smaller percentage of variable costs in the long run than in the short run.

8. This is another example of what Jones (1965) has called the "magnification effect" in the two-sector model with intersectoral capital mobility, which does not arise when capital is sector-specific.

9. As is well known, this statement is crucially dependent on the validity of the assumption of profit maximisation.

References

Amano, A. 1977. Specific factors, comparative advantage, and international investment. *Economica* 44, 131–144.

Bhagwati, J. N. 1958. Immiserizing growth: A geometrical note. *Review of Economic Studies* 25, 201–205.

Bhagwati, J. N. 1973. The theory of immiserizing growth: Further applications. In *International Trade and Money*, M. Connolly and A. K. Swobada eds., pp. 45–54. London: Allen and Unwin.

Bhagwati, J. N., and Srinivasan, T. N. 1971. The theory of wage differentials: Production response and factor price equalization. *Journal of International Economics* 1, 19–35.

Brecher, R. A. 1974. Minimum wage rates and the pure theory of international trade. *Quarterly Journal of Economics* 88, 98–116.

Caves, R. E. 1971. International corporations: the industrial economics of foreign investment. *Economica* 38, 1–27.

Corden, W. M., and Findlay, R. 1975. Urban unemployment, intersectoral capital mobility and development policy. *Economica* 42, 59–78.

Ethier, W. 1974. Some of the theorems of international trade with many goods and factors. *Journal of International Economics* 4, 199–206.

Findlay, R., and Grubert, H. 1959. Factor intensities, technological progress and the terms of trade. *Oxford Economic Papers* 11, 111–121.

Hahn, F. H. 1965. On two sector growth models. *Review of Economic Studies* 32, 339–346.

Harberger, A. C. 1962. The incidence of the corporation income tax. *Journal of Political Economy* 70, 215–240.

Harris, J. R., and Todaro, M. P. 1970. Migration, unemployment and development: A two-sector analysis. *American Economic Review* 60, 126–142.

Helpman, E. 1976. Macroeconomic policy in a model of international trade with a wage restriction. *International Economic Review* 17, 262–277.

Hicks, J. R. 1953. An inaugural lecture: 2. The long-run dollar problem. *Oxford Economic Papers* 5, 121–135.

Hu, S. C. 1973. Capital mobility and the effects of unionization. *Southern Economic Journal* 39, 526–534.

Johnson, H. G. 1959. International trade, income distribution and the offer curve. *Manchester School of Economic and Social Studies* 27, 241–260.

Johnson, H. G. 1970. The efficiency and welfare implications of the international corporation. In *The International Corporation: A Symposium* C. P. Kindleberger ed. Cambridge: MIT Press.

Johnson, H. G., and Mieszkowski, P. M. 1970. The effects of unionization on the distribution of income: A general equilibrium approach. *Quarterly Journal of Economics* 84, 539–561.

Jones, R. W. 1965. The structure of simple general equilibrium models. *Journal of Political Economy* 73, 557–572.

Jones, R. W. 1971a. Distortions in factor markets and the general equilibrium model of production. *Journal of Political Economy* 79, 437–459.

Jones, R. W. 1971b. A three-factor model in theory, trade and history. In *Trade, Balance of Payments and Growth: Essays in Honor of C. P. Kindleberger*, ed. J. N. Bhagwati et al. Amsterdam: North Holland.

Jones, R. W. 1975. Income distribution and effective protection in a multi-commodity trade model. *Journal of Economic Theory* 11, 1–15.

Jones, R. W., and Corden, W. M. 1976. Devaluation, non-flexible prices, and the trade balance for a small country, *Canadian Journal of Economics* 9, 150–161.

Kemp, M. C., and Jones, R. W. 1962. Variable labour supply and the theory of international trade. *Journal of Political Economy* 70, 30–36.

Magee, S. P. 1971. Factor market distortions, production, distribution, and the pure theory of international trade. *Quarterly Journal of Economics* 86, 623–643.

Magee, S. P. 1976. *International Trade and Distortions in Factor Markets*. New York: Marcel Dekker.

Magee, S. P. 1977. Three simple tests of the Stolper-Samuelson theorem. The University of Texas at Austin, Graduate School of Business. Working Paper 77-28, February.

Martin, J. P. 1976. Variable factor supplies and the Heckscher-Ohlin-Samuelson model. *Economic Journal* 86, 820–831.

Mayer, W. 1974. Short-run and long-run equilibrium for a small open economy. *Journal of Political Economy* 82, 955–968.

McCulloch, R. 1976. Technology, trade and the interests of labor: A short run analysis of the development and international dissemination of new technology. Harvard Institute of Economic Research, Discussion Paper No. 489, June.

Mussa, M. 1974. Tariffs and the distribution of income: The importance of factor specificity, substitutability, and intensity in the short and long run. *Journal of Political Economy* 82, 1191–1204.

Mussa, M. 1975. Dynamic adjustment to relative price changes in the Heckscher-Ohlin-Samuelson model. University of Rochester, Department of Economics. Discussion Paper No. 75-6, May. *Journal of Political Economy* 86 (1978), 775–791.

Neary, J. P. 1977. On the Harris-Todaro model with intersectoral capital mobility. Nuffield College, Oxford. Mimeo, July. *Economica* 48 (1981), 219–234.

Neary, J. P. 1978a. Capital subsidies and employment in an open economy. *Oxford Economic Papers* 30, 334–356.

Neary, J. P. 1978b. Dynamic stability and the theory of factor market distortions. *American Economic Review* 69, 671–682.

Rybczynski, T. N. 1955. Factor endowments and relative commodity prices, *Economica* 22, 336–341.

Samuelson, P. A. 1971a. An exact Hume-Ricardo-Marshall model of international trade. *Journal of International Economics* 1, 1–18.

Samuelson, P. A. 1971b. Ohlin was right. *Swedish Journal of Economics* 73, 365–384.

Stolper, W. F., and Samuelson, P. A. 1941. Protection and real wages. *Review of Economic Studies* 9, 58–73.

Woodland, A. D. 1977. A dual approach to equilibrium in the production sector in international trade theory. *Canadian Journal of Economics* 10, 50–68.

II
Trade-Pattern Theories

Introduction to Part II

The theory of international trade has addressed, among many "positive" questions, the problem of what determines the pattern of trade of nation states. The traditional one-factor Ricardian theory has long given way to the Heckscher-Ohlin theory, starting with the Samuelsonian formulation noted in part II. The latter explains the trade pattern by reference to factor endowment differences among countries; that is, a labor-abundant country would export labor-intensive goods. Two important questions are raised by this theory.

First, what about the accumulation of capital? If factor endowments change, what happens to comparative advantage a la Heckscher-Ohlin? This is the question most elegantly addressed by Ronald Findlay's piece reprinted in chapter 6. The paper is an important contribution that must be taught as soon as the static Heckscher-Ohlin version has been explained in the classroom.

Second, if there are many commodities introduced into the Heckscher-Ohlin model, can we sustain a Ricardian-type chain proposition, namely, that all of the labor-abundant country's exports will be labor-intensive compared to all of its imports? Jones, in a classic paper (*Review of Economic Studies*, 1956–1957), said yes. I pointed out (*Journal of Political Economy*, September/October 1972) that when factor prices were equalized this need not be so. Alan Deardorff, in chapter 7, has elegantly reexplored these results, proving the Jones proposition carefully for the case when factor prices are not equalized. He also extends the argument to include traded intermediates, thus providing the student with an analytical glimpse into a more realistic model.

Chapter 8, on the other hand, reverts to a more conventional approach to examining comparative advantage, with Ed Leamer's classic paper that utilized the factor-content approach of Jaroslav Vanek to reopen the question of the Leontif paradox.

6

Factor Proportions and Comparative Advantage in the Long Run

Ronald Findlay

The basic model of comparative advantage in the theory of international trade has been that associated with the names of Heckscher and Ohlin. The form in which this model has been analyzed over the last few decades has been in terms of the two-factor, two-good geometry developed by Lerner and Samuelson. All the six papers in the new *Readings in International Economics* (1967) under the section headed "The Theory of Comparative Advantage" are of this type. Recently the model has been extended in some interesting directions. Oniki and Uzawa (1965) have made one of the goods a capital good and studied the effect of accumulation and labor force growth on international equilibrium over time. Komiya (1967) has introduced a third nontraded good into the system and examined the consequences of this for various standard propositions of trade theory within the usual static context. Kenen (1965) has produced an ingenious model in which capital takes the form of augmenting the productivity of labor and land instead of being a separate "factor" in its own right.

The present paper examines a model which combines the Oniki-Uzawa and Komiya features by making the third nontraded good a capital good. The main result is to show how factor proportions, and hence the pattern of comparative advantage, in the long run depend ultimately upon the values of two parameters, the propensity to save and the growth rate of the labor force.

1

The economy produces three types of goods denoted X, Y, and Z. Let X and Y be consumer goods and Z a capital good. Each of the three goods

This paper was originally published in *The Journal of Political Economy* 78 no. 1 (January/February 1970): 27–34.

is produced by the services of labor, which is exogenously given, and capital, which is the stock of goods of type Z available to the economy. The production function for each good is taken to be of the usual neoclassical type with constant returns to scale. The growth rate of labor is also exogenously fixed, and for simplicity it is assumed that capital goods do not depreciate. Capital goods are assumed not to move in international trade, but the consumer goods X and Y can be bought and sold in the world market at fixed prices.

The fixed prices of X and Y in world trade means that the domestic production costs of amounts of X and Y that have the same value at these prices must be the same, assuming perfect competition and the absence of transport costs and tariffs. If the "strong factor-intensity assumption" that one commodity is always more capital intensive than the other at any factor-price ratio is also made, then it is a well-established result that factor prices will be uniquely determined. The capital-labor ratio in the nontraded capital goods sector will hence be determined, along with those for the two consumer goods sectors. The fixed international terms of trade for X and Y therefore fix the capital and labor input coefficients for all three commodities. Physical units can be chosen in such a way that the prices per unit of each commodity are all equal to unity. Taking the initial endowment of capital and labor as given, we have two equations in three unknowns (X, Y, and Z) by the balance conditions that the amount of each factor used in all three sectors must add up to the amount available, the capital and labor input coefficients per unit of each output in these equations being determined by the fixed terms of trade and the production functions. One more equation is needed to close the system, and this is provided by the condition that the proportion of national income saved and invested is a constant. Since investment is nothing but the output of Z, this condition implies that the ratio of the output of Z to the combined output of all three sectors is equal to a constant, which is the average propensity to save.

We, therefore, have the following system of equations:

$$a_{11}X + a_{12}Y + a_{13}Z = L, \tag{1}$$

$$a_{21}X + a_{22}Y + a_{23}Z = K, \tag{2}$$

$$-sX - sY + (1 - s)Z = 0, \tag{3}$$

in which L and K are the initial endowments of labor and capital, the a_{ij} are the technical coefficients determined in the manner explained, and s is the average propensity to save. This system is readily solved for X, Y, and Z, given L and K. For the analysis of growth, however, it is necessary to adjust (1), (2), and (3) by dividing both sides of each equation by K to obtain

$$a_{11}\frac{X}{K} + a_{12}\frac{Y}{K} + a_{13}k = \lambda, \tag{1'}$$

$$a_{21}\frac{X}{K} + a_{22}\frac{Y}{K} + a_{23}k = 1, \tag{2'}$$

$$-s\frac{X}{K} - s\frac{Y}{K} + (1 - s)k = 0, \tag{3'}$$

where $k = Z/K$ and $\lambda = L/K$. Therefore k is the rate of growth of capital since Z represents additions to the capital stock. The solution of this system can give us k, the rate of growth of capital as a function of λ, the labor-capital ratio.

By Cramer's rule we have

$$k = \frac{\lambda s(a_{22} - a_{21}) - s(a_{12} - a_{11})}{\Delta}, \tag{4}$$

where

$$\Delta = (1 - s)(a_{11}a_{22} - a_{21}a_{12}) - s(a_{12}a_{23} - a_{22}a_{13})$$
$$+ s(a_{11}a_{23} - a_{21}a_{13}).$$

The problem that now arises is whether k will converge to the constant growth rate of the labor force, n. If $k > n$ then λ will be falling, and convergence requires $dk/d\lambda > 0$. That is, if the growth rate of capital is faster than labor, the system operates to reduce it, and vice versa, so that the two rates are equal in the limit. Differentiating (4) with respect to λ we obtain

$$\frac{dk}{d\lambda} = \frac{s(a_{22} - a_{21})}{\Delta}. \tag{5}$$

We now investigate the sign of this derivative. A sufficient condition for this derivative to be positive, and hence for the two rates to converge, is easily obtained. If the capital good Z is more capital intensive than X but less capital intensive than Y, it follows that the determinant Δ will be positive. Figure 6.1 shows that under these conditions we must have $a_{22} > a_{21}$. Reversing the relative capital intensities of X and Y will make Δ negative and $a_{22} < a_{21}$, so that the sign of (5) is again positive. Hence a sufficient condition for the convergence of the capital growth rate to that of the labor force is for the capital intensity in the nontraded capital goods sector Z to be between those of the traded consumer goods sectors X and Y.

If Z is either more or less capital intensive than both X and Y, the sign of (5) is indetermine. With the problem of convergence to long-run equili-

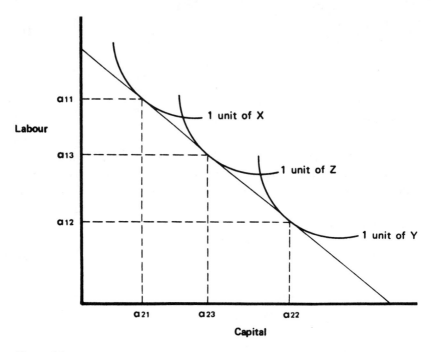

Figure 6.1

brium factor proportions settled, the next section analyzes the pattern of comparative advantage under given demand conditions.

2

The system can also be solved for X/K and Y/K. Division of one by the other will give us the ratio of the outputs of the two consumer goods,

$$\alpha = \frac{X}{Y} = \frac{[(1-s)a_{22} + sa_{23}]\lambda - [(1-s)a_{12} + sa_{13}]}{[(1-s)a_{11} + sa_{13}] - [(1-s)a_{21} + sa_{23}]\lambda}, \tag{6}$$

which gives us the output proportions α as a function of the factor proportions λ.

Demand conditions for X and Y have now to be introduced. As shown by Robinson (1956) and Jones (1956–59), the Heckscher-Ohlin theory requires "homothetic" demand patterns for its logical validity; that is, the proportions of the goods purchased at any price ratio must be independent of the level of income. We thus have

$$\beta = \frac{X}{Y} = f\left(\frac{Px}{Py}\right), \tag{7}$$

where Px/Py is the relative prices or terms of trade and β is the proportion in which the two goods are demanded. Equation (6) can be written as $\alpha = g(\lambda, s, Px/Py)$.

Hence, whether a country exports X or Y, that is to say, whether it has a comparative advantage in X or Y, depends on whether

$$\alpha \gtrless \beta. \tag{8}$$

at the given value of the terms of trade. Since α, depends on λ, which varies over time, there is the possibility that the inequality in (8) can reverse itself in the course of time. The comparative advantage of a country in international trade is thus not something fixed but something changing with the evolution of its factor proportions.

The analysis of relative stability can now be combined with the definition of comparative advantage given in (8), to form the concept of comparative advantage *in the long run*. If the factor-intensity condition is met, we have seen that the system tends to balanced growth of capital and labor at the fixed rate n. Since $k = n$ in the limit, we can solve (4) for the value of λ to which the system tends in terms of x, n, and the technical coefficients.

Denoting the value of λ in the limit by λ^*, this gives

$$\lambda^* = \frac{\Delta n + s(a_{12} - a_{11})}{s(a_{22} - a_{21})}. \tag{9}$$

If α^* denotes the value of α corresponding to λ^*, whether the country has a comparative advantage in the long run in X or Y depends on whether

$$\alpha^* \gtrless \beta. \tag{10}$$

Since α^*, unlike α, is a constant, comparative advantage in the long run does not shift over time at given terms of trade.

The dynamic version of comparative advantage developed above can now be related to the familiar static Heckscher-Ohlin theorem. Equation (6) gives us α^* as a function of λ^*. Differentiating, we obtain

$$\frac{\partial \alpha^*}{\partial \lambda^*} = \frac{(1 - s)\Delta}{D^2}, \tag{11}$$

where D is the denominator of the right-hand side of (6). The sign of this derivative clearly depends on the sign of Δ. If X is more labor intensive than Y, Δ will be positive, meaning that the more labor abundant the country, the greater will be the proportion of the labor-intensive good in production at given terms of trade. If demand conditions are homothetic and the same in all countries, this implies that the labor (capital)-abundant country will have a comparative advantage in the labor (capital)-intensive good. The same result would follow if Y is the labor-intensive good and Δ is negative. The familiar Heckscher-Ohlin theorem is thus derived in a more general setting, including the production of a nontraded capital good. The above analysis can be adapted to the usual case simply by putting Z equal to zero.

3

The Heckscher-Ohlin theorem stops at factor proportions as the fundamental determinant of trade. However, we have shown in (9) that the factor proportion λ ultimately depends on the "dynamic determinants" s and n. The effect of these variables on comparative advantage can be analyzed by differentiation of (9) with respect to each of them:

$$\frac{d\lambda^*}{dn} = \frac{\Delta}{s(a_{22} - a_{21})}. \tag{12}$$

The sign of this expression is positive since both numerator and denominator will be positive if X is more labor intensive, or negative if the opposite is the case. From (11) we have seen that α varies directly with λ so it follows that the greater the rate of growth of labor the greater will be the proportion of the labor-intensive commodity in production in the long run and, therefore, the greater the likelihood that the country will have a comparative advantage in the labor-intensive commodity.

Differentiating (9) with respect to s, we obtain

$$\frac{d\lambda^*}{ds} = \frac{-(a_{22} - a_{21})(a_{11}a_{22} - a_{21}a_{12})n}{[s(a_{22} - a_{21})]^2} \tag{13}$$

From the factor-intensity assumptions the two terms in the numerator of (13) are either both positive or both negative, so that in either case the effect of a higher propensity to save is to reduce the labor-capital ratio toward which the system tends in the long run.

The effect of the propensity to save on comparative advantage is given by differentiating (6) totally with respect to s to obtain

$$\frac{d\alpha^*}{ds} = \frac{\partial \alpha^*}{\partial s}\bigg|_{\lambda^*} + \frac{\partial \alpha^*}{\partial \lambda^*}\frac{d\lambda^*}{ds}. \tag{14}$$

The last two terms have already been obtained in (11) and (13). The first term is given as

$$\frac{\partial \alpha^*}{\partial s}\bigg|_{\lambda^*} = \text{constant} = \frac{(a_{22} - a_{21})a_{23}\lambda^{*2} + (a_{11} - a_{12})a_{23}\lambda^*}{D^2}$$

$$+ \frac{-(a_{22} - a_{21})a_{13}\lambda^* + (a_{12} - a_{11})a_{13}}{D^2}, \tag{15}$$

where D is the denominator of the right-hand side of (6). What (15) shows is the direct effect of the variation in s on α^* through the shift in resources toward the capital goods sector and away from the consumer goods sectors. Obviously, if the resources are withdrawn in the same proportion, α^* will not change directly as a result of the variation in s. This will be the case if the labor-capital ratio in the Z sector is exactly equal to that of the whole economy, so that $\lambda^* = a_{13}/a_{23}$. Inserting this value of λ^* into (15), we observe that the numerator becomes zero, confirming our intuition. If the labor-capital ratio in the Z sector is higher than λ^*, an increase in the output of Z due to a higher s will reduce the labor-capital ratio in the combined X and Y sector, and hence shift α^* in favor of the relatively capital-intensive consumer good, and vice versa in the case where the labor-capital ratio in Z is lower than λ^*. This can again be checked against (15) by differentiating the numerator of this expression with respect to λ^* and evaluating this derivative at the point $\lambda^* = a_{13}/a_{23}$ to obtain

$$\frac{dN}{d\lambda^*} = (a_{22} - a_{21})a_{13} + (a_{11} - a_{12})a_{23}, \tag{16}$$

where N is the numerator of the right-hand side of (15). Each of the expressions in parentheses will be positive if X is more labor intensive than Y, and negative in the opposite case. Thus, if $\lambda^* < a_{13}/a_{23}$ and X is more labor intensive than Y, the sign of (15) will be negative so an increase in s reduces α^* (the output of the capital-intensive good X), and vice versa when $\lambda^* > a_{13}/a_{23}$. If Y is more labor intensive than X, these results will be reversed. If we call the first term of (14) the "direct effect" and the second term the "indirect effect," we observe that both terms either move in the same direction to shift α^* in favor of the capital-intensive good or the direct effect works in the opposite direction, so the result depends on which of the two effects is stronger. If the direct effect were to predominate, a higher s and therefore a lower λ^* or labor-capital ratio, would be associated with a higher ratio of the output of the labor-intensive commodity to that of the capital-intensive one; in other words, the Leontief paradox. It would therefore be of some interest to see whether this case can arise since it would provide another possible explanation of the famous paradox.

If we substitute the right-hand side of (9) for λ^* in (15) and combine the result with the right-hand sides of (11) and (13), we obtain

$$\frac{d\alpha^*}{ds} = \frac{\Delta^2(a_{22} - a_{21})(a_{23}n - 1)n}{[s(a_{22} - a_{21})]^2 D^2}.$$ (17)

The term $(a_{23}n - 1)$ must be negative, since $1/a_{23} = Z/K_z > n = Z/(K_x + K_y + K_z)$, where the K refer to the total capital input in each of the sectors. The last equality holds because the capital growth rate converges to n in the limit. The sign of $(a_{22} - a_{21})$ is positive or negative, depending on whether X or Y is the more labor intensive. Hence the result in either case is that a higher s must be associated with a higher relative output of the capital-intensive good. The Leontief paradox thus cannot arise as the result of the introduction of a nontraded capital goods sector, but only in the long run. A higher s can cause a lower labor-capital ratio to be associated with a higher relative output of the labor-intensive good as a result of the direct effect, but if sufficient time is allowed the higher s will reduce the labor-capital ratio further until the opposite is the case, if n is the same in both cases.

References

Caves, R., and H. G. Johnson, eds. 1967. *Readings in International Economics.* Irwin.

Jones, R. 1956–57. Factor endowment and the Heckscher-Ohlin theorem. *Rev. Econ. Studies* 24: 1–10.

Kenen, P. B. 1965. Nature, capital, and trade, *J.P.E.* 73 (October): 437–460.

Komiya, R. 1967. Non-traded goods and the pure theory of international trade. *Internat. Econ. Rev.* 8 (June): 132–152.

Oniki, H., and H. Uzawa. 1965. Patterns of trade and investment in a dynamic model of international trade." *Rev. Econ. Studies* 32 (January): 15–38.

Robinson, R. 1965. Factor proportions and comparative advantage part I. *Q.J.E.* 70 (May): 169–192.

Note

Attention of the reader should be drawn to a valuable comment by Professor Alan V. Deardorff of the University of Michigan, appearing in the *Journal of Political Economy* 82 (July/August 1974): 829–833. He shows that the sign of the determinant Δ depends only on the relative factor intensities of X and Y. My assumption that the factor intensity of Z is in between those of X and Y is therefore unnecessarily restrictive. He also examines the consequences of relaxing my implicit assumption that both X and Y have positive levels of production.

7

Weak Links in the Chain of Comparative Advantage

Alan V. Deardorff

My purpose in this paper is to investigate the proposition that trade in many commodities can be understood by first ranking the goods in order of factor intensities, then showing that all of a country's exports must lie higher on this list than all of its imports. A similar idea of a chain of comparative advantage was shown by Haberler (1936, p. 137) to be valid in a many-commodity extension of the classical theory of trade, the rankings there being of course in terms of comparative costs. The proposition was also stated for a two-factor, two-country version of the Heckscher-Ohlin model by Jones (1956–57), but was shown by Bhagwati (1972) to be incorrect if factor prices are equalized. Jones and Bhagwati apparently concurred, however, that the proposition would be valid whenever factor prices are not equalized, though neither provided a proof. Since a prime cause of unequal factor prices is the existence of tariffs, and since Travis (1964, 1972) has claimed that protection can account for the Leontief paradox, presumably by altering the pattern of trade, it seems that a consensus has not been reached as to just how general the chain-of-comparative-advantage idea is.[1] In what follows, I explore the matter further and show that these differences of opinion can be reconciled.

Specifically, I show first that Jones and Bhagwati were right, so long as we remain in the model that they were considering, which excludes the possibility of produced goods being used as intermediate factors of production. That is, I will demonstrate the chain proposition in such a model whenever factor prices are unequal, whether that inequality is the result of complete specialization with no impediments to trade (section 1) or of tariffs and transport costs (section 2). Then I will introduce intermediate goods. This modification, it turns out, does not invalidate the chain proposition

This paper was originally published in *Journal of International Economics* 9, no. 2 (May 1979): 197–209.

so long as there are unequal factor prices and free trade (section 3). But when impediments to trade are added as well, the chain proposition collapses. For I show, in section 4, that an increase in a tariff can cause a good that was previously exported to become imported and, at the same time, a good that was previously imported to become exported. It follows that no ranking of the goods is possible, on the basis of factor intensities, autarky prices, or anything else, that will permit separation of exports and imports via a single break in the chain.

It is ironic that Jones, Bhagwati, and others have found comfort in the presence of transport costs and other impediments to trade, which prevent factor-price equalization and thus remove the indeterminacy of production and trade. For the example in section 4 shows that, when there are intermediate goods, these same impediments to trade can invalidate the chain proposition when it would otherwise hold.

In the two-factor world considered here, the chain proposition is related to, but not identical to, the Heckscher-Ohlin theorem. The former merely says that some ranking of goods exists which suffices to determine trade. The latter says that the appropriate ranking is by factor intensities and, furthermore, that relative factor endowments determine which end of the chain contains a country's exports. However, in the cases considered here, the two propositions stand or fall together, so long as the price definition of factor abundance is used in stating the Heckscher-Ohlin theorem. For I will show in sections 1 through 3 that a country in which capital is relatively cheap, with trade, must export more capital-intensive goods than it imports. And it can be shown, if there are only two countries, that relative factor prices must bear the same relationship with trade as without, so long as trade impediments are nonnegative.[2] Thus, these sections also demonstrate the Heckscher-Ohlin theorem: that a country in which capital is relatively cheap in autarky must export relatively capital intensive goods. Also of course the counter example of section 4 shows that both propositions fail when there are both trade impediments and intermediate goods.

While most of the argument will be confined to a two-country world, it is of some interest also to show how the chain idea may extend to a world of many countries. This is not difficult, with the tools available, and, in section 5, I show that the chain of comparative advantage can be broken into several segments, one for each country. With the countries arranged along the chain in the same order as their relative factor endowments, each country will then export only goods within its segment of the chain and will import all others. That is true, however, only if trade is free and factor prices are unequal. Without the need, in this case, for intermediate goods, I will also show that tariffs can cause a rather dramatic rearrangement of the pattern of trade.

Considering the obvious importance, in the real world, of both trade impediments and intermediate goods, the results of this paper may seem to cast doubt on both the Heckscher-Ohlin theory and on the concept of comparative advantage itself. I therefore conclude in section 6 with a discussion of these more fundamental problems.

1. Free Trade

Consider two countries, A and B, producing and trading n goods with no impediments to trade between them, so that the prices of the goods, $p_1, \ldots, p_n$, are the same in both countries. Production of each good requires the use of only two factors of production, capital (K) and labor (L), which are nontraded and available in each country in fixed supply. Production functions are identical between countries and have the usual properties of concavity and homogeneity. Assume further that the goods can be ranked unambiguously in terms of capital intensity, X_1 being the most capital-intensive and X_n, the least. Thus there are no factor-intensity reversals between any pair of goods, and isoquants of different goods can intersect only once. Assume finally that perfect competition prevails in both countries, so that price equals average cost for any good that is produced and is less than or equal to average cost for any good that is not produced.

Suppose now that all that is known about a free trade equilibrium is that particular and unequal factor prices prevail in the two countries. What does this imply about the pattern of trade?

Begin by drawing the unit isocost lines for the two countries. These are shown in figure 7.1 as the lines AA' for country A and BB' for country B, and represent the combinations of capital and labor which would cost, say, one dollar (or other international numeraire) in each of the two countries. They are shown as intersecting at a point M, with country A depicted as having a higher ratio of wage to rental (ω) than country B.[3]

From these isocost lines one can conclude what the free trade prices of each good must be. That is, the price of each good must be such as to place its unit-value isoquant exactly tangent to the outermost of the two unit-isocost lines, as shown by the (solid) isoquants drawn in figure 7.1. For if a unit-value isoquant were to lie wholly outside both AA' and BB', the good would not be produced in either country, whereas if it lay anywhere inside either one of the lines, its production would yield a positive profit in the corresponding country. Furthermore, while it is possible for an isoquant to be tangent to both isocost lines (as good 4 in figure 7.1), this need not happen for any good and, without factor-intensity reversals, cannot happen for more than one.

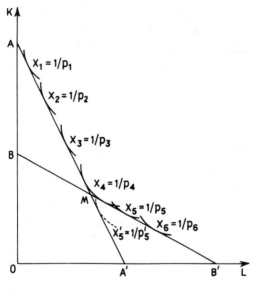

Figure 7.1

It is now immediately evident from figure 7.1 that the pattern of trade must agree with the ranking of the goods by factor intensity. The most capital-intensive goods (1, 2, and 3 in figure 7.1) can only be produced in the high wage country, A, and must therefore be exported by A, while the most labor intensive (5 and 6) must be produced and exported by B. Good 4, in this case, may be produced in both countries and may be exported by either. It therefore constitutes the division of the chain of comparative advantage.

We have already noted that the high relative wage in A implies that it is capital abundant by the price definition.[4] It is also true in this case that A must be capital abundant by the physical definition as well. For we can see in figure 7.1 that all production in A requires a higher ratio of capital to labor than all production in *B*. Thus our result implies that every export of the capital abundant country, by either definition, must be more capital-intensive than every one of its imports.[5]

Before extending this analysis to include tariffs, transport costs, and intermediate goods, it should be pointed out that the technique used here does not derive the trade equilibrium. Rather, it assumes that an equilibrium exists and merely examines a particular property of that equilibrium. Much more information would be needed to determine, for example, what the equilibrium factor prices should be and where, in the chain of comparative advantage, the division between the two countries should be located.

2. Impeded Trade

If tariffs or transport costs permit different prices in the two countries, then the argument as given above is no longer valid, for there will be different unit-value isoquants in the two countries. But the argument can easily be salvaged if direct *subsidies* to trade are not permitted. For then a good will be exported only if its price is at least as high abroad as at home, and imported only if its price is at least as low abroad as at home, to compensate exporters and importers for the additional cost of tariffs and transport.[6]

To see how this works, consider again the two countries whose unit isocost lines, with trade, are those shown in figure 7.1. Suppose that some good, X_i, is exported by country A. To be exported it must be produced, and thus the unit-value isoquant of X_i in A must be tangent to AA'. Suppose it were tangent below the intersection M, like the dotted isoquant X_5' in figure 7.1. For the good to be exported from A, it must also fetch at least as high a price in B (to cover any transport cost or tariff) and this would place B's unit-value isoquant for the same good still closer to the origin than X_5' and certainly inside the line BB'. The good would then yield a positive profit in B, and this is impossible. Thus the unit-value isoquants of all of A's exports must be tangent to AA' above its intersection with BB' exactly as was the case with free trade. Applying a similar argument to exports from B, it follows as before that all of A's exports must be more capital intensive than all of A's imports.

This then validates the Bhagwati-Jones conjecture that a capital abundant country (using the price definition of abundance) will export only goods which are more capital intensive than any of its imports, if there are impediments to trade and unequal factor prices.[7,8]

3. Intermediate Goods and Free Trade

Now suppose that any or all of goods $1, \ldots, n$ can be used as intermediate inputs in production. The argument of section 1 with free trade remains intact if unit-value isoquants are replaced by unit-value-*added* isoquants.

For any good X_i, let the production function be given by

$$X_i = F^i(K_i, L_i, X_{1i}, \ldots, X_{ni}),$$

where X_{ji} are the inputs of goods j into production of good i. Let

$$V_i(K_i, L_i, p_1, \ldots, p_n) = \max_{X_i, X_{ji}} \left[p_i X_i - \sum_{j=1}^{n} p_j X_{ji} \right]$$

$$\text{s.t. } X_i = F^i(K_i, L_i, X_{1i}, \ldots, X_{ni}).$$

For given values of all prices, the functions $V_i(K_i, L_i, \cdot)$ describe, in nominal terms, the maximum net revenue that can be earned and allocated to payment of the primary factors, capital and labor. They can therefore be used to determine the pattern of specilization, in exactly the same way that we earlier used production functions multiplied by prices.[9] That is, unit-value-added isoquants can be defined by setting $V_i = 1$, and production will require tangency between these and the unit-isocost lines.[10]

With free trade, all prices are the same in the two countries, which therefore share identical unit-value-added isoquants. The argument of section 1 can be repeated and the same result obtained. Thus the chain of comparative advantage can still be used when there are intermediate goods, so long as trade is free and the prices of primary factors are not equalized. The factor intensities used in constructing the chain represent only direct capital and labor requirements and do not include factors that are used indirectly by being embodied in intermediate inputs. For as long as inter-mediate inputs are traded freely, they need not be produced within the country in which they are used.

4. Intermediate Goods and Impeded Trade

If trade is not free, however, there is a problem. It arises because the position of a unit-value-added isoquant depends on *all* prices and not just on the price of the corresponding final good. Thus, when a tariff on, say, good 5 in figure 7.1 raises its price in A above that in B, it does, as before, pull A's isoquant toward the origin to a position like X_5'. But it also pushes A's isoquants of other goods that use good 5 as an input out further from the origin than they are in country B. And this makes it impossible to infer individual relative prices from the positions of individual isoquants in the two countries as was done before. The same problem arises if prices differ due to transport costs, though for ease of exposition we will limit attention here to a tariff.

To see what can happen, consider the following special case which will suffice to provide a counterexample to the chain proposition. Suppose there are only three goods, with goods 1 and 2 acting solely as final goods and with good 3 acting only as an intermediate input to production of good 1. Suppose further that country B is so large that we can take its prices as independent of trade with country A and that A is so capital abundant that it produces, in *free* trade, only the most capital-intensive good 1. The free trade situation is depicted as the solid unit-value-added isoquants and isocost lines in figure 7.2. The line AA' represents free trade factor prices in country A, which employs its entire endowment of capital and labor, K^A

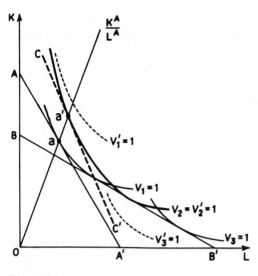

Figure 7.2

and L^A, in the production of good 1 at point a. Country B, with factor prices given by BB', produces all three goods using the unit-value-added isoquants, $V_1 = 1$, $V_2 = 1$, and $V_3 = 1$. Country A exports good 1 and imports goods 2 and 3.

Now suppose that country A levies a tariff on imports of good 3, raising its domestic price. This will pull A's unit-value-added isoquant for good 3 in toward the origin, to a position like $V_3' = 1$. The isoquant for good 2 will not be affected (since good 2 does not use good 3 as an input), but the unit-value-added isoquant of good 1 will be pushed out away from the origin, as additional production is required to cover the increased cost of the input of good 3 and leave a unit left over for value added.[11] If the tariff is large enough and if good 3 is a sufficiently important input into production of good 1, the new unit-value-added isoquant will be $V_1' = 1$ in figure 7.2.[12]

It can now be seen from the figure that country A will specialize completely in production of good 2, at point a', with factor prices given by the line CC', since this is the only pattern of production and factor prices that can both yield zero profits and employ the factors in the ratio K^A/L^A. If both countries consume something of both goods 1 and 2, it follows that country A, with the tariff, will export good 2 and import good 1. The pattern of trade in these two goods has therefore been completely reversed by the tariff on good 3.[13]

The intuition behind this result is straightforward and is reflected in the diagram. When a tariff raises the price of the intermediate good, it also makes the final good more costly to produce, and since the intermediate good is itself very labor intensive, country A cannot reduce that cost by producing it itself. Instead, all production switches to good 2 which does not require the labor-intensive, and now expensive, input of good 3.

Another way of seeing what is going on in this example is to look at effective rates of protection. With a tariff on the intermediate good and none on either final good, the effective rate of protection of industry 1 is negative. Thus, while the explicit effects of tariffs are only to tax trade, the tariff on the intermediate good has the implicit effect of subsidizing imports of, in this case, the capital intensive good.

The counterexample of this section shows that a ranking by capital intensities cannot suffice to determine trade.[14] But more important, it shows that a ranking by *any other criterion* must fail as well. In the example, any ranking that places all of A's exports above all of A's imports with free trade will fail to do so when a tariff is applied. For good 1 has changed from an export to an import, and good 2 has done just the reverse.

5. Many Countries

Analysis of the free trade cases, both with and without intermediate goods, extends readily to the case of many countries, though naturally one cannot expect a single division of the chain of comparative advantage to delineate correctly the trade of all countries. Since the analysis is similar to what has gone before, it will be left to the reader to imagine or draw the appropriate diagrams. Simply insert, as in figure 7.1, the unit isocost lines for all countries. World prices—common to all countries—must then give rise to unit-value (-added) isoquants that are tangent to the outer envelope of all of these isocost lines. Each country will then produce and export only those goods with isoquants tangent to its own isocost line, the intersections of which with adjacent cost lines therefore provide upper and lower limits on the factor intensities of its exports.

Thus the chain of goods ranked by capital intensity is broken into segments, one for each country, and the segments are ordered identically with the relative capital abundance of the countries. As in the two-country case adjacent segments may contain one good in common, if the isoquant for such a borderline good happens to touch two countries' isocost lines in the manner of good 4 in figure 7.1. Otherwise, the division between segments of the chain occurs between goods. Each country must export all goods which appear only in its segment of the chain and must import all goods which do not appear in its segment. Borderline goods may be exported by either or both of the countries in whose segments they appear. It follows that each of a country's exports must be at least as capital intensive as each of the exports of all less capital abundant countries and at least as labor intensive as each of the exports of all less labor-abundant countries.

This conclusion, however, is extremely sensitive to the assumption of free trade. Even without intermediate goods, impediments to trade can drastically alter the pattern of trade.

To see this, return to the two-country configuration of figure 7.1 and add a tiny third country, C, with a factor endowment ratio lying between the ratios employed by A and B in industry 4. With free trade, such a country will specialize completely in production of good 4, exporting it in exchange for imports of all other goods. Now suppose, however, that it levies a large tariff on imports of the most capital-intensive good, 1. The tariff will raise the price of good 1 in C, pulling its unit-value isoquant in toward—and past—C's unit isocost line. Country C will begin production of good 1 and the relative wage in C will fall. However, good 1 is so capital intensive that much of it cannot be produced with the factors available in C and, if demand is also fairly inelastic, imports of good 1 will continue. Thus there is nothing to prevent a further increase in the tariff from raising its price still more, to bring its unit-value isoquant inside BB'. When that happens, a new isocost line must appear in C, tangent only to isoquants of goods 1 and 6. Production of good 4 (C's original export good) ceases entirely and production of good 6 begins instead. And good 6 must also be exported, since good 1 cannot be, and imports of goods 2, 3, 4, and 5 must continue. Thus country C, because of a tariff, has changed from being an exporter of a good of intermediate factor intensity to become an exporter of the most labor-intensive good that there is.

It should perhaps be noted that this extreme response of the trade pattern to a tariff is only possible for a country whose factor abundance is intermediate between those of other countries. This explains why this result was not possible in the two-country case.

6. Conclusion

It would indeed be useful if we could construct some ranking of commodities, by some criterion, which would enable us to predict the pattern of trade, even if only in the sense of saying that each of a country's exports must lie higher on this list than each of its imports. I have shown that such a ranking is possible in certain cases. But it is impossible both in Bhagwati's "not unimportant" case of factor price equalization and in the obviously important case of positive trade impediments and intermediate goods. This does not mean, however, that trade theorists should abandon the Heckscher-Ohlin theorem or the Law of Comparative Advantage. What it does mean is that we should search for alternative statements of these propositions that will retain their validity and still tell us something useful about the pattern of trade in the real world.

One such formulation has been developed, as a statement about the "factor content" of trade. Vanek (1968) showed that, under certain assumptions, the factor content of a country's trade can be inferred from a chain of factor endowment rankings, very much like the chain of comparative advantage in trade of goods discussed here.[15] The assumptions used to prove this result, however, include factor-price equalization. It is therefore not known yet whether the factor content version of the Heckscher-Ohlin theorem can be extended to the troublesome case considered here of trade impediments and intermediate goods.[16] This is an important issue, since it was implicitly the factor content of trade that was the focus of Leontief's (1954) famous calculations.

The result in section 4, in which an export good and an import good exchange roles, is as critical for the theory of comparative advantage as it is for the Heckscher-Ohlin theory. For it implies that no ranking of goods can suffice to determine trade, not even one based on relative autarky prices. Yet this does not mean that comparative advantage plays no role in determining the pattern of trade. Rather, the role that it does play is not as strong as the chain proposition would suggest. I have shown elsewhere that relative autarky prices must be negatively correlated with net exports (Deardorff 1980). The result of section 4 is consistent with such a correlation, so long as the relative autarky price of good 1 is higher than that of good 2.

Finally, I would like to point out a use that has been made of the Bhagwati-Jones proposition of section 2, a use which turns out to be inappropriate in view of the result of section 4. Harkness and Kyle (1975) motivated their use of logit analysis in an empirical test of the Heckscher-Ohlin theorem on the grounds that the theorem predicts only the direction, not the extent, of trade. They acknowledged Bhagwati's (1972) observation that even the prediction of direction fails if factor prices are equalized but argued that transportation costs are such a fact of life that Bhagwati's counterexample cannot arise in the real world. Yet intermediate goods are just as much a fact of life as transportation costs. The counterexample which the two together permit can therefore not be dismissed so easily.

Notes

I would like to thank Jagdish Bhagwati, Ronald Jones, Richard Porter, Robert Stern, and members of the Research Seminar in International Economics, University of Michigan, for their helpful comments.

1. Actually, it is difficult to be sure exactly what Travis was saying. He has never, to my knowledge, provided an example of a tariff that reverses the pattern of trade, though such an example is possible, as I show in section 4. Nor is it clear whether Travis meant his remarks to be valid in a model of only two primary factors. In his (1972) article, he used and vigorously defended the two-factor assumption, but concluded that, if tariffs are high enough, the bulk of trade will be in goods requiring other primary factors.

2. To see this, let t be a vector of ad valorem tariffs cum transport costs for each industry. Given technology, tastes, and factor endowments, the difference between the two countries' factor-price ratios, $\Omega = \omega^A - \omega^B$, must be a continuous function of t, $\Omega(t)$. Let t^0 be a particular vector of nonnegative trade impediments, let t^a be a vector that would prevent trade entirely, and suppose that $\Omega(t^0) > 0$ (as in figure 7.1) yet $\Omega(t^a) < 0$. Then by continuity there exists $t' > 0$ such that $\Omega(t') = 0$ and such that trade takes place. But if $\Omega = 0$, then factor prices are equal and so are commodity prices, and it is impossible for trade to take place over positive trade impediments, $t' > 0$. From this contradiction it follows that $\Omega(t^a) \geqq 0$. Since $\Omega(t^a) = 0$ can also be ruled out as implying that $\Omega(t) = 0$ for all t, it follows that $\Omega(t^0) > 0$ implies $\Omega(t^a) > 0$.

3. Unequal factor prices do not, of course, ensure that the two isocost lines will intersect, as drawn, since one could lie wholly outside the other. In that case, as the analysis below indicates, the chain proposition holds trivially since all goods will be exported by the same country. Were balanced trade assumed, such a situation would of course be excluded.

4. See note 2.

5. Rather remarkably, no assumption has been needed about demand or about relative factor prices in autarky. However, if demand were so biased as to make the autarky relative wage in A less than the autarky relative wage in B, then factor prices would have to be equalized by free trade and the factor prices assumed in figure 7.1 could not arise. This also follows from the argument given in note 2.

6. In another context I have called this the assumption of "natural" trade (see Deardorff 1980). This formulation is consistent with any of a variety of explicit assumptions about the nature of transport costs, so long as these costs are nonnegative. However, the reader may prefer to think of a more explicit assumption, such as that of Samuelson (1954), who let a certain fraction of each good be used up in transport.

7. Note that if trade impediments were positive for all goods, then the qualification that factor prices be unequal would be unnecessary. For equal factor prices would mean equal commodity prices and thus no trade.

8. I have called this a conjecture because I do not regard the argument provided by Bhagwati (1972) to be a proof, though naturally when a proposition is valid there can be some disagreement as to what constitutes proof. Bhagwati (p. 1054) argued that "while a commodity in the middle of a chain of exportables may be priced out of the export market into being a nontraded good by high transportation costs, it is impossible for it to be turned into an imported good." Now it is certainly true that the cost of transporting a given exportable cannot cause *it* to be imported. But I see no a priori reason why the cost of transporting some other good might not cause this to happen. Supose, for example, that the cost of importing eggs were to raise their price so high as to cause substitution away from both bacon and eggs toward oatmeal. Then oatmeal could become imported and bacon exported, even if the reverse would be true if eggs could be imported cheaply. The proof in the text shows that this cannot happen in a two-factor model (where chickens and pigs—or the farmers that raise them—could be employed planting oats), but I see nothing in Bhagwati's remarks to rule this out.

9. Note that since V_i is defined in nominal terms, we do not encounter the problem of defining either a natural unit for value added or a "price" of value added, which has been a source of difficulty in the effective protection literature. In particular, our construction does not require the separability assumption that has been stressed by Bruno (1973) and by Bhagwati and Srinivasan (1973). It should also be mentioned that V_i, as functions of K_i and L_i, possess the same homogeneity and concavity properties that are assumed of the production functions, F_i. See Diewert's (1973) discussion of variable profit functions.

10. In the special case, often assumed, of fixed coefficients between intermediate inputs and final output (so that $X_{ji} = a_{ji} X_i$) the function

$$V_i = \left(p_i - \sum_{j=1}^{n} p_j a_{ji} \right) F^i(K_i, L_i).$$

The isoquants of V_i are then identical to the isoquants of F^i, and the unit-value-added isoquant is that for which

$$X_i = \frac{1}{p_i - \sum_{j=1}^{n} p_j a_{ji}}.$$

11. This may sound like a description of producers who take a loss on every unit but "make it up in volume." This need not be the case since there was initially a positive margin for value added, and hence a small enough input price increase will leave that margin positive. But it does point up the possibility that unit-value-added isoquants may not just move, but may disappear when input prices increase. This is particularly true when there is no possibility of substitution away from intermediate inputs, as in the fixed coefficients case of the preceding note. This possibility makes a counterexample even easier to obtain, however, since it means that a tariff increase can shift all production to good 2.

12. It is essential for the counterexample that the isoquant, $V_1' = 1$, lie outside the line CC', which is tangent to the $V_2 = 1$ isoquant where it crosses the K^A/L^A ray. In the figure this requires a substantial movement of the V_1 isoquant, but this need not be the case. If good 2 were only slightly more labor intensive than good 1, CC' would lie very close to AA' and a small movement of the V_1 isoquant would suffice.

13. I am indebted to Jagdish Bhagwati for suggesting this construction of the counterexample, which is more direct than was used in an earlier version of this paper. The earlier construction drew upon a result of Batra and Casas (1973) who showed that a nontraded intermediate good of extreme factor intensity can cause the Heckscher-Ohlin theorem to be violated. Thus, if we begin, as in this example, with the theorem holding under free trade, a prohibitive tariff on an intermediate good can reverse the pattern of trade.

14. Note that direct-plus-indirect capital intensities do not work either. For when the intermediate good in our example was traded freely, then good 2 was imported even though it may be the most capital intensive on the direct-plus-indirect basis.

15. Melvin (1968) also stated this proposition for the two-factor case. Vanek's demonstration, which has been generalized to bilateral trade by Horiba (1974), allows for any number of factors.

16. Baldwin (1971, p. 130) states in a footnote that "tariffs can weaken the pattern of indirect factor trade in a Heckscher-Ohlin model but cannot alone produce paradoxical results." It is unclear from the context, however, just what model he has in mind and thus whether this is any more than a statement of the (later) Bhagwati-Jones proposition that was proved in section 2.

References

Baldwin, Robert E. 1971. Determinants of the commodity structure of U.S. trade. *American Economic Review* 61, 126–146.

Batra, Raveendra N., and Francisco R. Casas. 1973. Intermediate products and the pure theory of international trade: A neo-Heckscher-Ohlin framework. *American Economic Review* 63, 297–311.

Bhagwati, Jagdish H. 1972. The Heckscher-Ohlin theorem in the multi-commodity case. *Journal of Political Economy* 80, 1052–1055.

Bhagwati, Jagdish H., and T. N. Srinivasan. 1973. The general equilibrium theory of effective protection and resource allocation. *Journal of International Economics* 3, 259–281.

Bruno, M. 1973. Protection and tariff change under general equilibrium. *Journal of International Economics* 3, 205–226.

Deardorff, Alan V. 1980. The general validity of the law of comparative advantage. *Journal of Political Economy* 88, 941–957.

Diewert, W. E. 1973. Functional forms for profit and transformation functions. *Journal of Economic Theory* 6, 284–316.

Haberler, Gottfried von. 1936. *The Theory of International Trade with its Applications to Commercial Policy*. William Hodge, London.

Harkness, Jon, and John F. Kyle. 1975. Factors influencing United States comparative advantage. *Journal of International Economics* 5, 153–165.

Horiba, Y. 1974. General equilibrium and the Heckscher-Ohlin theory of trade: The multicountry case. *International Economic Review* 15, 440–449.

Jones, Ronald W. 1956–57. Factor proportions and the Heckscher-Ohlin theorem. *Review of Economic Studies* 24, 1–10.

Leontief, Wassily. 1954. Domestic production and foreign trade: The American capital position re-examined. *Economia Internazionale* 7, 3–32.

Melvin, James. 1968. Production and trade with two factors and three goods. *American Economic Review* 58, 1249–1268.

Samuelson, Paul A. 1954. The transfer problem and transport costs: Analysis of the effects of trade impediments. *Economic Journal*, 264–289.

Travis, William P. 1964. *The Theory of Trade and Protection* Harvard University Press, Cambridge.

Travis, William P. 1972. Production, trade, and protection when there are many commodities and two factors. *American Economic Review* 62, 87–106.

Vanek, Jaroslav. 1968. The factor proportions theory: The *n*-factor case, *Kyklos* 4, 749–756.

8

The Leontief Paradox, Reconsidered

Edward E. Leamer

The Leontief paradox (1954) rests on a simple conceptual misunderstanding. It makes use of the intuitively appealing, but nonetheless false, proposition that if the capital per man embodied in exports is less than the capital per man embodied in imports, the country is revealed to be poorly endowed in capital relative to labor. This is a true proposition if the net export of labor services is of the opposite sign of the net export of capital services, but when both are positive, as in Leontief's data, the proper comparison is between the capital per man embodied in *net* exports and the capital per man embodied in consumption. Leontief's figures, which produced the so-called paradoxical result that U.S. exports are less capital intensive than U.S. competing imports, can also be used to show that U.S. net exports are more capital intensive than U.S. consumption, which in fact implies that capital is abundant relative to labor. There is no paradox if the conceptually correct calculations are made.

The first section of this paper shows that a country is revealed to be relatively well endowed in capital compared with labor if and only if one of the following three conditions holds, where K_x, K_m, L_x, L_m, K_c, L_c are capital and labor embodied in exports, imports, and consumption:

1. $K_x - K_m > 0$, $L_x - L_m < 0$.

2. $K_x - K_m > 0$, $L_x - L_m > 0$, $(K_x - K_m)/(L_x - L_m) > K_c/L_c$.

3. $K_x - K_m < 0$, $L_x - L_m < 0$, $(K_x - K_m)/(L_x - L_m) < K_c/L_c$.

Although Leontief found that $K_x/L_x < K_m/L_m$, his data are shown in section 2 to satisfy 2, and therefore the United States is revealed to be capital abundant. In a largely overlooked article, Williams (1970) makes a related point.

This paper was originally published in *Journal of Political Economy* 88, no. 3 (1980): 495–503. © 1980, The University of Chicago. All rights reserved.

1. Trade-Revealed Factor Abundance

This reconsideration of the Leontief paradox rests on the Heckscher-Ohlin-Vanek (HOV) theorem (Vanek 1968).

THE HECKSCHER-OHLIN-VANEK THEOREM   *Given:* (1) There are n commodities which are freely mobile internationally. (2) There are n factors which are perfectly immobile internationally. (3) All individuals have identical homothetic preferences. (4) Production functions are the same in all countries and exhibit constant returns to scale. (5) There is perfect competition in the goods and factors markets. (6) Factor prices are equalized across countries.

Then: There exists a set of positive scalars α_i, $i = 1, \ldots, I$, such that the vector of net exports of country i, T_i, the vector of factor endowments of country i, E_i, and the $n \times n$ matrix of total factor requirements A, bear the following relationship to each other:

$$AT_i = E_i - E_w \alpha_i, \quad i = 1, \ldots, I, \tag{1}$$

where E_w is the world's endowment vector, $E_w = \sum_i E_i$.

Proof The proof of this result is straightforward. The equalization of factor prices and constant-returns-to-scale production functions imply the matrix of total factor inputs A, where A_{jk} is the amount of factor j used to produce one unit of commodity k. If Q_i is the vector of outputs of country i, then equilibrium in the factor markets requires factor demand equal to factor supply $AQ_i = E_i$. The summation of this equation over all countries produces $AQ_w = E_w$. Then identical homothetic tastes imply that the consumption vectors C_i of each country are proportional to each other and also proportional to world output Q_w: $C_i = Q_w \alpha_i$. Country i's trade is $T_i = Q_i - C_i$, and the factors embodied in trade are $AT_i = A(Q_i - C_i) = E_i - AQ_w \alpha_i = E_i - E_w \alpha_i$. $\square$

The set of equations (1) serves as a logically sound foundation for a study of trade-revealed factor abundance. Two of these equations describe the relationship between capital and labor endowments and the implicit trade in capital and labor services:

$$K_T = K_i - \alpha_i K_w, \tag{2a}$$

$$L_T = L_i - \alpha_i L_w, \tag{2b}$$

where (K_T, L_T) are capital and labor embodied in net exports, (K_i, L_i) are the factor endowments of country i, and (K_w, L_w) are the world's factor endowments.

We take the following definition of factor abundance.

DEFINITION Capital in country i is said to be abundant in comparison with labor if and only if the share of the world's capital stock located in i exceeds the share of the world's labor force: $K_i/K_w > L_i/L_w$.

Factor abundance is revealed by trade through a comparison of the vector of factors used to produce various vectors of commodities. These vectors may be defined as follows.

DEFINITION The vector of factors embodied in the vector of commodities z is Az, where A is the matrix of total factor requirements.

The following result establishes necessary and sufficient conditions for trade to reveal an abundance of capital.

COROLLARY 1 Capital is revealed by trade to be abundant relative to labor if and only if

$$\frac{K_i}{K_i - K_T} > \frac{L_i}{L_i - L_T}. \tag{3}$$

Proof Equations (2a) and (2b) can be rewritten as

$$K_w = \frac{K_i - K_T}{\alpha_i},$$

$$L_w = \frac{L_i - L_T}{\alpha_i}.$$

Thus

$$\frac{K_i}{K_w} = \frac{\alpha_i K_i}{K_i - K_T},$$

$$\frac{L_i}{L_w} = \frac{\alpha_i L_i}{L_i - L_T},$$

from which (3) is a consequence. □

There are three useful ways of rewriting (3). If K_c is the amount of capital embodied in the commodities used in country i, then $K_i - K_T = K_c$ and, similarly, $L_i - L_T = L_c$. Then (3) is equivalent to

$$\frac{K_i}{L_i} > \frac{K_c}{L_c}, \tag{3a}$$

which means that a country is revealed to be capital abundant if its production is more capital intensive than its consumption.

Another way to rewrite (3) is $K_i(L_i - L_T) > L_i(K_i - K_T)$, or

$$-K_i L_T > -L_i K_T. \tag{3b}$$

If L_T is positive, then this inequality becomes $K_T/L_T > K_i/L_i$, or $K_T/K_i >$ L_T/L_i. Thus a country that is an exporter of both labor services and capital services is revealed by trade to be relatively capital abundant if trade is more capital intensive than production or, equivalently, if the share of capital exported exceeds the share of labor exported. Similarly, if L_T is negative the inequalities are reversed, and a country that is an importer of both labor services and capital services is revealed by trade to be relatively capital aboundant if trade is less capital intensive than production or, equivalently, if the share of capital imported is less than the share of labor imported.

Yet another possibility is to rewrite (3b) as $-(K_c + K_T)L_T > -(L_c + L_T)K_T$, or

$$-K_c L_T > -L_c K_T. \tag{3c}$$

Thus a country that is an exporter of both labor services and capital services is revealed by trade to be relatively capital abundant if the capital intensity of net exports exceeds the capital intensity of consumption, $K_T/L_T > K_c/L_c$, and a country that is an importer of both capital and labor services is revealed by trade to be capital abundant if the capital intensity of net exports is less than the capital intensity of consumption, $K_T/L_T < K_c/L_c$.[1]

Inequalities (3a), (3b), and (3c) identify three equivalent ways of computing trade-revealed factor abundance. Trade even more directly reveals relative capital abundance if the services of one factor are exported and the services of the other are imported, since inequality (3b) is satisfied if $K_T > 0$ and $L_T < 0$ and is violated if $K_T < 0$ and $L_T > 0$. For reference, this will be stated as a corollary.

COROLLARY 2   If the net export of capital services and the net export of labor services are opposite in sign, then the factor with positive net exports is revealed to be the relatively abundant factor.

Corollaries 1 and 2 imply that one should be examining the factor content of *net* exports, but the tradition beginning with Leontief is to distinguish exports from imports. In some cases this is an equivalent procedure.

COROLLARY 3   Given that the net export of capital services and the net export of labor services are opposite in sign, then the capital per man embodied in exports (K_x/L_x) exceeds the capital per man embodied in imports (K_m/L_m) if and only if the country is relatively abundant in capital, $K_i/K_w > L_i/L_w$.

Proof   Suppose first that $K_T > 0$ and $L_T < 0$; then by corollary 2, $K_i/K_w > L_i/L_w$. But $0 < K_T = K_x - K_m$ implies $K_x/K_m > 1$, and $0 > L_T = L_x - L_m$ implies $1 > L_x/L_m$. Thus $K_x/K_m > L_x/L_m$, and $K_x/L_x > K_m/L_m$. Similarly $K_T < 0$ and $L_T > 0$ imply both $K_i/K_w < L_i/L_w$ and $K_x/L_x < K_m/L_m$. □

A substantial practical defect of corollary 3 is that it assumes that K_T and L_T are opposite in sign. In fact, using Leontief's 1947 data, K_T and L_T are both positive: the United States exported both capital services and labor services. In that event the ordering $K_x/L_x < K_m/L_m$ reveals nothing about the relative magnitudes of K_i/K_w and L_i/L_w.

COROLLARY 4   If there are more than two commodities, the ordering of exports and imports by factor intensity, say $K_x/L_x > K_m/L_m$, is compatible with either order of factor abundance, $K_i/K_w < L_i/L_w$ or $K_i/K_w > L_i/L_w$.

Proof   An example of the "paradoxical" case $K_x/L_x < K_m/L_m$ and $K_i/K_w > L_i/L_w$ will suffice. Let the factor requirements matrix be given as

$$A = \begin{bmatrix} 4 & 1 & 1 \\ 3 & 2 & .5 \\ 1 & 0 & 3 \end{bmatrix}$$

where the first row corresponds to capital inputs, the second row to labor inputs, and the third to land inputs. Suppose that the output vectors are given by

$$Q_i = (8, 16, 5)'$$

and

$$Q_w = (12, 68, 52)'.$$

The endowment vectors are then

$$AQ_i = E_i = (53, 58.5, 23)'$$

and

$$AQ_w = E_w = (168, 198, 168)'.$$

If the price vector is $(2, 1, 1)'$, then trade balance, $0 = 1'T_i$, implies

$$\alpha_i = \frac{1'Q_i}{1'Q_w} = \frac{29}{132} = .26.$$

Using this, and the endowment vectors, we can compute the excess factor supplies

$$(E_i - \alpha_i E_w)' = (53, 58.5, 23) - .26(168, 198, 168)$$

$$= (9.32, 7.02, -20.68)'.$$

Therefore country i, on net, exports the services of both capital and labor and imports the services of land. The commodity trade vector implied by the above system is

$$T_i = (4.9, -1.5, -8.4)'.$$

Partitioning this into two vectors, exports (X_i) and imports (M_i), we obtain

$$X_i = (4.9, 0, 0)'$$

and

$$M_i = (0, 1.5, 8.4)'.$$

Computing the factor content of exports and imports separately, we have

$$AX_i = (19.7, 14.8, 4.9)'$$

and

$$AM_i = (9.8, 7.2, 25.1)'.$$

Thus, for example, country i exports 19.7 units of capital and imports 9.8 units. Computing the capital-labor content ratio, we obtain

$$\lambda = \frac{(K_x/L_x)}{(K_m/L_m)} = \frac{1.33}{1.36} = .98,$$

which is less than one. From this we might, as does Leontief, erroneously conclude that capital is scarce relative to labor in this country. However, the true ordering of factor abundance is given by the ratio of country i's endowment to the world's endowment. Computing these ratios for each factor, we obtain

$$\frac{K_i}{K_w} = .315,$$

$$\frac{L_i}{L_w} = .295.$$

This ranking indicates that contrary to the inference based on λ, the country is *abundant* in capital relative to labor. $\square$

Corollary 4 indicates that Leontief's method of computing trade-revealed factor abundance orderings is erroneous. However, in the unlikely world of two commodities, it is a correct method.

COROLLARY 5   If there are only two commodities, and if one is exported and the other is imported, the ordering of exports and imports by capital intensity is the same as the ordering of factor abundance; that is, $K_x/L_x \geqslant K_m/L_m$ if and only if $K_i/K_w \geqslant L_i/L_w$.

Proof   It is necessary to show that a capital-abundant country exports the capital-intensive good, assuming one good is exported and the other is imported. If X and M are the quantity of exports and imports, then equation (1) can be written as

$$A_{Kx}X - A_{Km}M = K_i - \alpha_i K_w,$$

$$A_{Lx}X - A_{Lm}M = L_i - \alpha_i L_w.$$

The ordering $K_i/K_w \geqslant L_i/L_w$ is equivalent to $(A_{Kx}X - A_{Km}M)/K_w \geqslant (A_{Lx}X - A_{Lm}M)/L_w$, which can be rewritten as

$$X\left(\frac{A_{Kx}}{A_{Lx}} - \frac{K_w}{L_w}\right) \geqslant M\left(\frac{A_{Km}}{A_{Lm}} - \frac{K_w}{L_w}\right)\left(\frac{A_{Lm}}{A_{Lx}}\right).$$

The world's capital-labor ratio K_w/L_w must be between the industry-intensity ratios A_{Kx}/A_{Lx} and A_{Km}/A_{Lm}, which implies that the left or right sides of the inequality above are opposite in sign, which is compatible only with $A_{Kx}/A_{Lx} > A_{Km}/A_{Lm}$. Thus $K_i/K_w \geqslant L_i/L_w$ is equivalent to $A_{Kx}/A_{Lx} > A_{Km}/A_{Lm}$.

2. Leontief's Data Reexamined

Tables 8.1, 8.2, and 8.3 contain information extracted from Leontief (1954) and from Travis (1964). Table 8.1 is Leontief's basic summary table, which reveals that $K_x/L_x < K_m/L_m$. But table 8.2 indicates that the United States in 1947 was a net exporter of both capital services and labor services. For this reason, the information contained in table 8.1 does not reveal the relative factor abundance of capital and labor (see corollary 4). The appropriate comparison, as described in corollary 1, is reported in table 8.3. Since net exports are much more capital intensive than consumption, the United States is revealed by its trade to be relatively well endowed in capital compared with labor.[2]

Finally, it is necessary to comment on why the United States had such a large trade surplus according to the data in table 8.2. This is partly due to the fact that "noncompeting" imports, such as coffee, tea, and jute, have been eliminated from the vector of imports. It is difficult to find a theoretically sound justification for this procedure. The HOV theorem uses the

Table 8.1
Domestic capital and labor requirements per million dollars of U.S. exports and of competitiveness import replacements (of average 1947 composition)

	Exports	Imoprts
Capital ($, 1947 prices)	2,550,780	3,091,339
Labor (man-years)	182.313	170.004

Source: Leontief (1954, sec. 6).

Table 8.2
Additional information on trade and endowments

Trade or factor	Value
Exports	$16,678.4 million
Imoprts (competitive)	$ 6,175.7 million
Net exports of capital services (K_T)	$23,450 million
Net exports of labor services (L_T)	1.990 million man-years
Capital-labor intensity of trade (K_T/L_T)	$11,783 /man-year

Source: Leontief (1954, table 2, n.).

Table 8.3
Capital intensity of consumption, production, and trade

	Production	Net exports	Consumption[a]
Capital	$328.519 million	$23,450 million	$305,069 million
Labor	47.273 million man-years	1.99 million man-years	45.28 million man-years
Capital/labor	$6,949/man-year	$11,783/man-year	$6,737/man-year

Source: For production figure, Travis (1964).
a. Uses the identity: Consumption = production − net exports.

factor-price-equalization theorem, which requires incomplete specialization. It is necessary therefore to imagine that the United States in fact produces at least small amounts of coffee, tea, and jute, and so forth. It is natural to suppose that the production of these commodities uses capital, labor, and "tropical land" which is very scarce in the United States. But any capital and labor embodied in the imports of "noncompeting" goods should be included in the above calculations. May we suppose that these products are labor intensive, which works also to explain the Leontief paradox?

Notes

Written with the assistance of Harry P. Bowen and with the support of Ford Foundation Grant 775-0692, Comments from Larry Kotlikoff and a referee are also gratefully acknowledged. The numerical example in the original manuscript has been altered in response to comments from Iraj Heravi to ensure that all commodities are economically produced.

1. It may be observed that Williams (1970) uses (2) to form his equation (23): $(K_w - K_i)/K_i = (1/\alpha_i) - [(K_T + \alpha_i K_i)/\alpha_i K_i]$, which he calls the "plentifulness ratio." This formula suggests erroneously that the consumption share α_i is necessary to infer the relative abundance of capital. Moreover Williams (1970, p. 121) reports that "the percentage of United States net capital, labour and natural resources exported as 7.14, 4.24, and 3.55, respectively. Intuition would suggest that, under these circumstances the United States must be implicitly plentiful in capital." Actually, this is enough (see his eq. 36) to establish the capital abundance of the United States, given $K_T > 0$, $L_T > 0$. This is discussed further below.

2. Baldwin's (1971) finding that the Leontief paradox holds also for 1962 data cannot be explained away so easily. Baldwin reports capital in 1958 dollars embodied in a million (1958) dollars of imports and exports to be $2,132,000 and $1,876,000, respectively. The corresponding man-year figures are 119 and 131. Merchandise exports in millions of 1962 dollars were 20,781 and merchandise imports were 16,260. As in 1947 the United States was a net exporter of both capital services and labor services, $K_T > 0$, $L_T > 0$, but the ratio had fallen to $K_T/L_T =$ $5,579 in 1958 dollars per man-year. This number falls below Travis's estimate of the 1947 capital per man equal to $6,949/man-year and is likely to fall below any estimates for 1962 as well.

References

Baldwin, Robert E. 1971. Determinants of the commodity structure of U.S. trade. *A.E.R.* 61 (March): 126–146.

Leontief, Wassily. 1954. Domestic production and foreign trade: The American capital position re-examined. *Econ. Internazionale* 7 (February): 3–32. Reprinted in *Readings in International Economics*, edited by Richard E. Caves and Harry G. Johnson. Homewood, Ill.: Irwin, 1968.

Travis, William P. 1964. *The Theory of Trade and Protection.* Cambridge: Harvard Univ. Press.

Vanek, Jaroslav. 1968. The factor proportions theory: The N-factor case. *Kyklos* 21 (October): 749–754.

Williams, James R. 1970. The resource content in international trade. *Canadian J. Econ.* 3 (February): 111–122.

III
Imperfect Competition and Market Structure

Introduction to Part III

The theory of international trade has now been extended to include imperfect completion in a systematic fashion, marrying successfully the theory of industrial organization with the theory of international trade. The "large-group" case analysis is associated chiefly with the work of Avinash Dixit, Elhanan Helpman, Paul Krugman, and Kelvin Lancaster. The "small-group" or "market-structure" analysis is largely the work of James Brander, Gene Grossman, Jonathan Eaton, and Barbara Spencer.

Paul Krugman's paper, reprinted in chapter 9, is one of the pioneering contributions to the former set of theoretical innovations. Utilizing a modified version of the Dixit-Stiglitz model of product differentiation with scale economies, he produces trade between identical economies where "comparative advantage" is not the cause of trade, whether that comparative advantage comes from Ricardian or Heckscher-Ohlin factors. Gains from trade also follow. This "new" model of trade is better suited to explain trade in "similar" products between advanced countries, trade that is now called "intraindustry" trade. It also has different implications than the Heckscher-Ohlin model for issues such as the effect of trade policy changes on income distribution. Krugman's work in this area is paralleled by that of Dixit and Norman and also by that of Lancaster, who has indeed pioneered the economic analysis of product quality differences that must lie at the heart of any serious analysis of so-called intraindustry trade. The basic focus on mutual trade in "similar" products, which Lancaster, Krugman, and others seek to model, was essentially provided by Staffan Linder in a classic volume (*An Essay on Trade and Transformation*) in 1961, whose importance was forecast in my 1964 *Economic Journal* survey of trade theory.

The remaining three papers by Brander and Spencer (chapter 10), Eaton and Grossman (chapter 11), and Dixit (chapter 12) address the market-structure issues. Brander and Spencer demonstrate how tariffs can be utilized to extract rents and improve welfare under conditions of monopoly, whereas Eaton and Krugman explore insightfully the broader issues of optimal policy intervention under oligopolistic settings. Dixit provides a splendid early overview of the literature. Since much of this literature is now cited by proponents of protection, though interestingly not by the innovators who remain wedded to advocating freer trade, it is important for the student to appreciate, by careful study of the three papers reprinted here and of associated writings, that the literature primarily suggests that the policy recommendations are extremely sensitive to parametric assumptions and the nature of competition assumed for the oligopolists, ranging sometimes all the way from tariffs to free trade to subsidies for a given market structure, and that therefore the information requirements for a welfare-improving intervention are often mind-boggling.

9

Increasing Returns, Monopolistic Competition, and International Trade

Paul R. Krugman

It has been widely recognized that economies of scale provide an alternative to differences in technology or factor endowments as an explanation of international specialization and trade. The role of "economies of large scale production" is a major subtheme in the work of Ohlin (1933); while some authors, especially Balassa (1967) and Kravis (1971), have argued that scale economies play a crucial role in explaining the postwar growth in trade among the industrial countries. Nonetheless, increasing returns as a cause of trade has received relatively little attention from formal trade theory. The main reason for this neglect seems to be that it has appeared difficult to deal with the implications of increasing returns for market structure.

This paper develops a simple formal model in which trade is caused by economies of scale instead of differences in factor endowments or technology. The approach differs from that of most other formal treatments of trade under increasing returns, which assume that scale economies are external to firms so that markets remain perfectly competitive.[1] Instead, scale economies are here assumed to be internal to firms, with the market structure that emerges being one of Chamberlinian monopolistic competition.[2] The formal treatment of monopolistic competition is borrowed with slight modifications from recent work by Dixit and Stiglitz (1977). A Chamberlinian formulation of the problem turns out to have several advantages. First, it yields a very simple model; the analysis of increasing returns and trade is hardly more complicated than the two-good Ricardian model. Second, the model is free from the multiple equilibria which are the rule when scale economies are external to firms, and which can detract from the main point. Finally, the model's picture of trade in a large number of differentiated products fits in well with the empirical literature on "intraindustry" trade (e.g., Grubel and Lloyd 1975).

This paper was originally published in *Journal of International Economics* 9, no. 4 (November 1979): 469–479.

The paper is organized as follows. Section 1 develops the basic modified Dixit-Stiglitz model of monopolistic competition for a closed economy. Section 2 then examines the effects of opening trade as well as the essentially equivalent effects of population growth and factor mobility. Finally, section 3 summarizes the results and suggests some conclusions.

1. Monopolistic Competition in a Closed Economy

This section develops the basic model of monopolistic competition with which I will work in the next sections. The model is a simplified version of the model developed by Dixit and Stiglitz. Instead of trying to develop a general model, this paper will assume particular forms for utility and cost functions. The functional forms chosen give the model a simplified structure which makes the analysis easier.

Consider then an economy with only one scarce factor of production, labor. The economy is assumed able to produce any of a large number of goods, with the goods indexed by i. We order the goods so that those actually produced range from 1 to n, where n is also assumed to be a large number, although small relative to the number of potential products.

All residents are assumed to share the same utility function, into which all goods enter symmetrically,

$$U = \sum_{i=1}^{n} v(c_i), \quad v' > 0, \quad v'' < 0, \tag{1}$$

where c_i is the consumption of the ith good.

It will be useful to define a variable, ε, where

$$\varepsilon_i = -\frac{v'}{v'' c_i}, \tag{2}$$

and where we assume $\partial \varepsilon_i / \partial c_i < 0$. The variable ε_i will turn out to be the elasticity of demand facing an individual producer; the reasons for assuming that is is decreasing in c_i will become apparent later.

All goods are also assumed to be produced with the same cost function. The labor used in producing each good is a linear function of output,

$$l_i = \alpha + \beta x_i, \quad \alpha, \beta > 0, \tag{3}$$

where l_i is labor used in producing good i, x_i is the output of good i, and α is a fixed cost. In other words, there are decreasing average costs and constant marginal costs.

Production of a good must equal the sum of individual consumptions of the good. If we identify individuals with workers, production must equal the consumption of a representative individual times the labor force:

$$x_i = Lc_i. \tag{4}$$

Finally, we assume full employment so that the total labor force L must be exhausted by employment in production of individual goods:

$$L = \sum_{i=1}^{n} l_i = \sum_{i=1}^{n} (\alpha + \beta x_i). \tag{5}$$

Now there are three variables we want to determine: the price of each good relative to wages, p_i/w; the output of each good, x_i; and the number of goods produced, n. The symmetry of the problem will ensure that all goods actually produced will be produced in the same quantity and at the same price, so we can use the shorthand notation

$$\left. \begin{array}{l} p = p_i \\ x = x_i \end{array} \right\}, \quad \text{for all } i. \tag{6}$$

We can proceed in three stages. First, we analyze the demand curve facing an individual firm; then we derive the pricing policy of firms and relate profitability to output; finally, we use an analysis of profitability and entry to determine the number of firms.

To analyze the demand curve facing the firm producing some particular product, consider the behavior of a representative individual. He will maximize his utility (1) subject to a budget constraint. The first-order conditions from that maximization problem have the form

$$v'(c_i) = \lambda p_i, \quad i = 1, \ldots, n, \tag{7}$$

where λ is the shadow price on the budget constraint, which can be interpreted as the marginal utility of income.

We can substitute the relationship between individual consumption and output into (7) to turn it into an expression for the demand facing an individual firm,

$$p_i = \lambda^{-1} v' \left(\frac{x_i}{L} \right). \tag{8}$$

If the number of goods produced is large, each firm's pricing policy will have a negligible effect on the marginal utility of income, so it can take λ as fixed. In that case the elasticity of demand facing the ith firm will, as already noted, be $\varepsilon_i = -v'/v''c_i$.

Now let us consider profit-maximizing pricing behavior. Each individual firm, being small relative to the economy, can ignore the effects of its decisions on the decisions of other firms. Thus the ith firm will choose its price to maximize its profits,

$$\Pi_i = p_i x_i - (\alpha - \beta x_i)w. \tag{9}$$

The profit-maximizing price will depend on marginal cost and on the elasticity of demand:

$$p_i = \frac{\varepsilon}{\varepsilon - 1} \beta w \tag{10}$$

or $p/w = \beta\varepsilon/(\varepsilon - 1)$.

Now this does not determine the price, since the elasticity of demand depends on output; thus, to find the profit-maximizing price, we would have to derive profit-maximizing output as well. It will be easier, however, to determine output and prices by combining (10) with the condition that profits be zero in equilibrium.

Profits will be driven to zero by entry of new firms. The process is illustrated in figure 9.1. The horizontal axis measures output of a representative firm; the vertical axis revenue and cost expressed in wage units. Total cost is shown by TC, while OR and OR' represent revenue functions. Suppose that given the initial number of firms, the revenue function facing

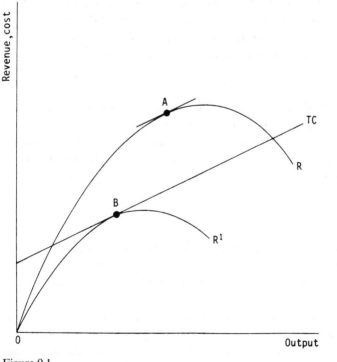

Figure 9.1

each firm is given by OR. The firm will then choose its output so as to set marginal revenue equal to marginal cost, at A. At that point, since price (average revenue) exceeds average cost, firms will make profits. But this will lead entrepreneurs to start new firms. As they do so, the marginal utility of income will rise, and the revenue function will shrink in. Eventually equilibrium will be reached at a point such as B, where it is true both that marginal revenue equals marginal cost and that average revenue equals average cost. This is of course Chamberlin's famous tangency solution (Chamberlin 1962).

To characterize this equilibrium more carefully, we need to show how the price and output of a representative firm can be derived from cost and utility functions. In figure 9.2 the horizontal axis shows *per-capita* consumption of a representative good, whereas the vertical axis shows the price of a representative good in wage units. We have one relationship between c and p/w in the pricing condition (10), which is shown as the curve PP. Price lies everywhere above marginal cost and increases with c because, by assumption, the elasticity of demand falls with c.

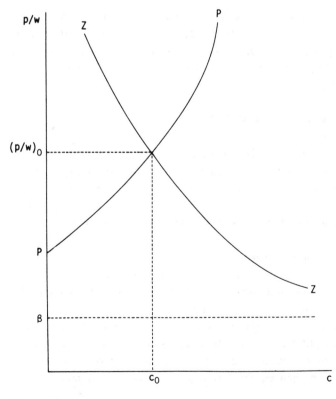

Figure 9.2

A second relationship between p/w and c can be derived from the condition of zero profits in equilibrium. From (9), we have

$$O = px - (\alpha + \beta x)w, \tag{11}$$

which can be rewritten

$$\frac{p}{w} = \beta + \frac{\alpha}{x} = \beta + \frac{\alpha}{Lc}. \tag{12}$$

This is a rectangular hyperbola above the line $p/w = \beta$, and is shown in figure 9.2 as ZZ.

The intersection of the PP and ZZ schedules determines individual consumption of each good and the price of each good. From the consumption of each good we have output per firm, since $x = Lc$. And the assumption of full employment lets us determine the number of goods produced:

$$n = \frac{L}{\alpha + \beta x}. \tag{13}$$

We now have a complete description of equilibrium in the economy. It is indeterminate *which* n goods are produced, but it is also unimportant, since the goods enter into utility and cost symmetrically. We can now use the model to analyze the related questions of the effects of growth, trade, and factor mobility.

2. Growth, Trade, and Factor Mobility

The model developed in the last section was a one-factor model, but one in which there were economies of scale in the use of that factor, so that in a real sense the division of labor was limited by the extent of the market. In this section we consider three ways in which the extent of the market might increase: growth in the labor force, trade, and migration.

Effects of Labor Force Growth

Suppose that an economy of the kind analyzed in the last section were to experience an increase in its labor force. What effect would this have? We can analyze some of the effects by examining figure 9.3. The PP and ZZ schedules have the same definitions as in figure 9.2; before the increase in the labor force, equilibrium is at A. By referring back to equations (10) and (11), we can see that an increase in L has no effect on PP but that it causes ZZ to shift left. The new equilibrium is at B: c falls, and so does p/w. We

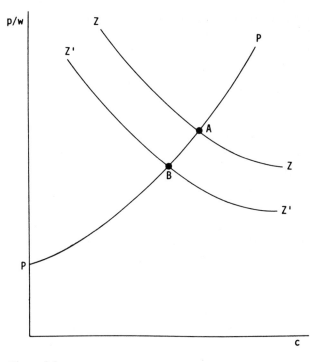

Figure 9.3

can show, however, that both the output of each good and the number of goods produced rise. By rearranging (12), we have

$$x = \frac{\alpha}{p/w - \beta},\tag{14}$$

which shows that output must rise, though, since $n = L/(\alpha + \beta Lc)$, a rise in L and a fall in c imply a rise in n.

Notice that these results depend on the fact that the PP curve slopes upward, which in turn depends on the assumption that the elasticity of demand falls with c. This assumption, which might alternatively be stated as an assumption that the elasticity of demand rises when the price of a good is increased, seems plausible. In any case it seems to be necessary if this model is to yield reasonable results, and I make the assumption without apology.

We can also consider the welfare implications of growth. Comparisons of overall welfare would be illegitimate, but we can look at the welfare of representative individuals. This rises for two reasons: there is a rise in the "real wage" w/p, and there is also a gain from increased choice, as the number of available products increases.

I have considered the case of growth at some length, even though our principal concern is with trade, because the results of the analysis of growth will be useful next, when we turn to the analysis of trade.

Effects of Trade

Suppose there exist two economies of the kind analyzed in section 1, and that they are initially unable to trade. To make the point most strongly, assume that the countries have identical tastes and technologies. (Since this is a one-factor model, we have already ruled out differences in factor endowments.) In a conventional model there would be no reason for trade to occur between these economies, and no potential gains from trade. In this model, however, there will be both trade and gains from trade.

To see this, suppose that trade is opened between these two economies at zero transportation cost. Symmetry will ensure that wage rates in the two countries will be equal and that the price of any good produced in either country will be the same. The effect will be the same as if *each* country had experienced an increase in its labor force. As in the case of growth in a closed economy, there will be an increase in both the scale of production and the range of goods available for consumption. Welfare in both countries will increase, both because of higher w/p and because of increased choice.

The direction of trade—which country exports which goods—is indeterminate; all that we can say is that each good will be produced only in one country, because there is (in this model) no reason for firms to compete for markets. The *volume* of trade, however, is determinate. Each individual will be maximizing his utility function, which may be written

$$U = \sum_{i=1}^{n} v(c_i) + \sum_{i=n+1}^{n+n^*} v(c_i), \tag{15}$$

where goods $1, \ldots, n$ are produced in the home country and $n + 1, \ldots, n + n^*$ in the foreign country. The number of goods produced in each country will be proportional to the labor forces:

$$n = \frac{L}{\alpha + \beta x},$$

$$n^* = \frac{L^*}{\alpha + \beta x}. \tag{16}$$

Since all goods will have the same price, expenditures on each country's goods will be proportional to the country's labor force. The share of imports in home country expenditures, for instance, will be $L^*/(L + L^*)$; the values of imports of each country will be national income times the import share,

$$M = wL\left(\frac{L^*}{L + L^*}\right)$$

$$= \frac{wLL^*}{L + L^*}$$

$$= M^*. \tag{17}$$

Trade is balanced, as it must be, since each individual agent's budget constraint is satisfied. The volume of trade as a fraction of world income is maximized when the economies are of equal size.

We might note that the result that the volume of trade is determinate but the direction of trade is not is very similar to the well-known argument of Linder (1961). This suggests an affinity between this model and Linder's views, although Linder does not explicitly mention economies of scale.

The important point to be gained from this analysis is that economies of scale can be shown to give rise to trade and to gains from trade even when there are no international differences in tastes, technology, or factor endowments.

Effects of Factor Mobility[3]
An interesting extension of the model results when we allow for movement of labor between countries or regions. There is a parallel here with Heckscher-Ohlin theory. Mundell (1957) has shown that in a Heckscher-Ohlin world trade and factor mobility would be substitutes for one another and that factor movements would be induced by impediments to trade such as tariffs or transportation costs. The same kinds of results emerge from this model.

To see this, suppose that there are two regions of the kind we have been discussing and that they have the same tastes and technologies. There is room for mutual gains from trade, because the combined market would allow both greater variety of goods and a greater scale of production. The same gains could be obtained without trade, however, if the population of one region were to migrate to the other. In this model, trade and growth in the labor force are essentially equivalent.

If there are impediments to trade, there will be an incentive for workers to move to the region that already has the larger labor force. This is clearest if we consider the extreme case where no trade in goods is possible, but labor is perfectly mobile. Then the more populous region will offer both a greater real wage w/p and a greater variety of goods, inducing immigration. In equilibrium all workers will have concentrated in one region or the other. Which region ends up with the population depends on initial conditions; in the presence of increasing returns history matters.

Before proceeding further we should ask what aspect of reality, if any, is captured by the story we have just told. In the presence of increasing returns factor mobility appears to produce a process of agglomeration. If we had considered a many-region model the population would still have tended to accumulate in only one region, which we may as well label a city; for this analysis seems to make most sense as an account of the growth of metropolitan areas. The theory of urban growth suggested by this model is of the "city lights" variety: people migrate to the city in part because of the greater variety of consumption goods it offers.

Let us return now to the two-region case to make a final point. We have seen that which region ends up with the population depends on the initial distribution of population. As long as labor productivity is the same in both regions, though, there is no difference in welfare between the two possible outcomes. If there is any difference in the conditions of production between the two regions, however, it does matter which gets the population—and the process of migration can lead to the wrong outcome.

Consider, for example, a case in which both fixed and variable labor costs are higher in one region. Then it is clearly desirable that all labor should move to the other region. But if the inferior region starts with a large enough share of the population, migration may move in the wrong direction.

To summarize: in the model of this paper, as in some more conventional trade models, factor mobility can substitute for trade. If there are impediments to trade, labor will concentrate in a single region; which region depends on the initial distribution of population. Finally, the process of agglomeration may lead population to concentrate in the wrong place.

3. Summary and Conclusions

This paper adapts a Chamberlinian approach to the analysis of trade under conditions of increasing returns to scale. It shows that trade need not be a result of international differences in technology or factor endowments. Instead, trade may simply be a way of extending the market and allowing exploitation of scale economies, with the effects of trade being similar to those of labor force growth and regional agglomeration. This is a view of trade that appears to be useful in understanding trade among the industrial countries.

What is surprising about this analysis is that it is extremely simple. Although the role of economies of scale in causing trade has been known for some time, it has been underemphasized in formal trade theory (and in textbooks). This paper shows that a clear, rigorous, and one hopes persuasive model of trade under conditions of increasing returns can be constructed. Perhaps this will help give economies of scale a more prominent place in trade theory.

Notes

1. Authors who allow for increasing returns in trade by assuming that scale economies are external to firm include Chacoliades (1970), Melvin (1969), Kemp (1964), and Negishi (1969).

2. A Chamberlinian approach to international trade is suggested by Gray (1973). Negishi (1972) develops a full general equilibrium model of scale economies, monopolistic competition, and trade that is smiliar in spirit to this paper, though far more complex. Scale economies and product differentiation are also suggested as causes of trade by Barker (1977) and Grubel (1970).

3. The results in this section bear some resemblance to some nontheoretical accounts of the emergence of backward regions. We might propose the following modification of the model: suppose that the population of each region is divided into a mobile group and an immobile group. Migration would then move all the mobile people to one region, leaving behind an immiserized "Appalachia" of immobile people whose standard of living is depressed by the smallness of the market.

References

Balassa, Bela. 1967. *Trade Liberalization among Industrial Countries*. McGraw-Hill.

Barker, Terry. 1977. International trade and economic growth: An alternative to the neoclassical approach. *Cambridge Journal of Economics* 1, no. 2, 153–172.

Chacoliades, Miltiades. 1970. Increasing returns and the theory of comparative advantage. *Southern Economic Journal* 37, no. 2, 157–162.

Chamberlin, Edward. 1962. *The Theory of Monopolistic Competition*.

Dixit, Avinash, and Joseph Stiglitz. 1977. Monopolistic competition and optimum product diversity. *American Economic Review*, June, 297–308.

Gray, Peter. 1973. Two-way international trade in manufactures: A theoretical underpinning. *Weltwirtschaftliches Archiv* 109, 19–39.

Grubel, Herbert. 1970. The theory of intra-industry trade. In I. A. McDougall and R. H. Snape, eds., *Studies in International Economics*. North Holland, Amsterdam.

Grubel, Herbert, and Peter Lloyd. 1975. *Intra-Industry Trade*. Macmillan, London.

Hufbauer, Gary, and John Chilas. 1974. Specialization by industrial countries: Extent and consequences. In H. Giersch, ed., *The International Division of Labour*. Institut für Weltwirtschaft, Kiel.

Kemp, Murray. 1964. *The Pure Theory of International Trade*. Prentice-Hall.

Kindleberger, Charles. 1973. *International Economics*. Irwin.

Kravis, Irving. 1971. The current case for import limitations, in: Commission on International Trade and Investment Policy. *United States Economic Policy in an Interdependent World*. GPO, Washington, D.C.

Linder, Staffan Burenstam. 1961. *An Essay on Trade and Transformation*. Wiley.

Melvin, James. 1969. Increasing returns to scale as a determinant of trade. *Canadian Journal of Economics and Political Science* 2, no. 3, 389–402.

Mundell, Robert. 1957. International trade and factor mobility. *American Economic Review* 47, 321–335.

Negishi, Takashi. 1969. Marshallian external economies and gains from trade between similar countries. *Review of Economic Studies* 36, 131–135.

Negishi, Takashi. 1972. *General Equilibrium Theory and International Trade*. North Holland, Amsterdam.

Ohlin, Bertil. 1933. *Interregional and International Trade*. Harvard University Press.

10

**Tariffs and
the Extraction of
Foreign Monopoly
Rents under
Potential Entry**

James A. Brander and
Barbara J. Spencer

There seems to be a growing belief that imperfect competition is important in international trade. Although the standard trade models assume perfect competition, there has been work incorporating imperfect competition, including Melvin and Warne (1973), Krugman (1979), and Markusen (1981). One important aspect of imperfect competition is that the price charged for a good exceeds the marginal cost of production. Thus a country importing such a good usually pays a monopoly rent to the exporting firm. Tax policy is the standard instrument for extracting monopoly rents from imperfectly competitive firms in a domestic context. The first point of this paper is that under imperfect competition a country has an incentive to extract rent from foreign exporters by using tariffs.[1]

There is a difficulty with such a tariff policy. Since marginal benefit (price) exceeds marginal cost, an imperfectly competitive good is underconsumed from a world welfare point of view. Even for the domestic country alone, a tariff will drive a wedge between what consumers pay and the price foreign producers are willing to accept. If the foreign firms are concerned about the possibility of entry in the domestic country, however, their behaviour is constrained, and the domestic country will find the policy of using tariffs to extract rents more attractive than otherwise. This is the second point of the paper: potential entry has implications for tariff policy in the presence of imperfect competition.

A sufficiently high tariff will induce entry by a domestic firm. This may be in the interest (although not necessarily) of the domestic country, since rents will be transferred from the foreign firm to the entrant. The new entrant may even find it profitable to export to the foreign market and intra-industry trade could result.[2] A third point of the paper, then, is

This paper was originally published in *Canadian Journal of Economics* 14, no. 3 (August 1981): 371–389.

that imperfect competition can cause intra-industry trade. In addition, if a domestic entrant can earn foreign monopoly rents, protective tariffs become particularly attractive.

An outline of the paper is as follows. A model of entry deterrence in an international setting based on Dixit (1979)[3] is developed. Then the extraction of monopoly rent using tariffs without potential entry is examined. Next, the extraction of monopoly rent with potential entry in the case that a domestic entrant would produce only for its home market is considered, and the welfare implications of an entry-inducing tariff are discussed. Next, the entrant is assumed to consider the possibility of exporting, and it is shown that the type of imperfect competition assumed in the Dixit model can lead to intra-industry trade. We then re-examine rent-extracting tariff policy under the threat of potential entry (by the domestic firm) in both domestic and foreign markets.

1. A Model of Entry Deterrence

We use a slight modification of Dixit's (1979) model of entry barriers.[4] The model used by Dixit is essentially a Stackelberg leader-follower model in which the leader considers producing the "limit" output: that output which prevents entry. This approach was developed by Sylos-Labini (1957) and Bain (1956) and exposited by Modigliani (1958). There are two countries, the domestic (or home) country and the foreign country. In each country demands are assumed to arise from a utility function of the form

$$U = u(z) + m, \tag{1}$$

where z is the level of consumption of good Z, which is produced under imperfect competition, and m is consumption of a competitive numeraire good. Imports of Z are paid for with exports of the competitive good. This utility function is useful for welfare comparisons since there are no income effects and the inverse demand function for Z is simply the derivative of u:[5]

$$p = u'(z). \tag{2}$$

In the initial situation the home country imports all its consumption of Z from a monopolist in the foreign country.[6] There is a potential entrant in the home country but initially the foreign monopolist finds it profitable to deter entry. The potential entrant takes the output of the existing firm as given and, if it enters, will produce the corresponding profit-maximizing output. The existing firm knows that the entrant would follow this Cournot rule and either accepts the Stackelberg leader-follower solution[7] or deters entry, depending on which course is more profitable.

One problem with leader-follower models is that the asymmetry in firms' strategy is often hard to explain. In this model the asymmetry has a natural explanation in that one firm is in the market while the other is not. (See Spence, 1979 for further comments in this vein.) Although the Stackelberg model represents only one specific market structure, it seems a reasonable starting point for analysis of entry deterrence.

Unlike Dixit, we assume that the two firms produce (or would produce) the same product. The total output of the (established) foreign firm is $x + x^*$, where x is the quantity exported to the domestic country and x^* is the quantity sold in the foreign country. (Asterisks will generally denote variables associated with the foreign country.) The output of the domestic entrant (if it enters) is denoted by y. Initially it is assumed that the entrant would sell only in its domestic market. In the absence of a tariff an expression for the profit of the existing firm is

$$\pi^*(x^*, x, y) = V^*(x^*) + V(x, y) - F^* \tag{3}$$

where $V^*(x^*) = x^* p^*(x^*) - c^* x^*$, and $V(x, y) = xp(x + y) - k^* x^*$,

$F^* = $ fixed cost,

$c^* = $ constant marginal cost of production,

$k^* = c^* + $ transport cost,

$V^*(x^*) = $ variable profit from sales in the foreign firm's home market,

$V(x, y) = $ variable profit from exports.

In other words, decreasing costs of a simple form are assumed: fixed cost plus constant marginal cost. The assumption that marginal cost is constant is convenient, since it allows the two markets to be considered independently, and in particular it ensures that the profit maximizing level of sales in the foreign market is unaffected by the values of x and y. It does not affect the nature of our results.

If the home-based firm enters, its profit is

$$\pi(x, y) = yp(x + y) - cy - F, \tag{4}$$

where again for simplicity marginal cost is assumed constant. The entrant chooses its level of output to maximize profit assuming x is fixed. Let $\pi_2(x, y)$ be the partial derivative of π with respect to y. Then the entrant sets

$$\pi_2(x, y) = 0 \tag{5}$$

This implicitly defines the reaction function $y = f(x)$ of the home-based firm, given that it enters. Assuming that the home firm enters only if it anticipates strictly positive profits, the reaction function of the potential domestic firm is

$$y(x) = \begin{cases} f(x), & \text{if } \pi(x, f(x)) > 0, \\ 0, & \text{if } \pi(x, f(x)) \leq 0. \end{cases} \tag{6}$$

To prevent entry, the foreign monopoly must choose a level of exports such that the maximum profit of the entrant is zero. Let $\bar{b}$ be the lowest export level that prevents entry:

$$\pi(\bar{b}, f(\bar{b})) = 0. \tag{7}$$

If the unconstrained monopoly level of exports by the foreign firm, denoted x_m, is greater than or equal to $\bar{b}$, entry is blockaded and the foreign firm does not need to actively consider entry deterrence. We examine the implication of a tariff where entry deterrence is not a consideration in the next section. However, for our purposes the case in which $x_m < \bar{b}$, so that domestic entry is a possibility, is of more interest. In this case the established firm has a maximum profit under entry deterrence of $V^*(x^*_m) + V(\bar{b}, 0) - F^*$, where x^*_m is its profit-maximizing level of sales in its own market (that is, in the foreign country).

The entry deterrence solution is illustrated in figure 10.1 for the case $x_m < \bar{b}$. The curve $f(x)$ is the reaction function of the home-based firm, disregarding fixed costs. Because of fixed costs, the segment of the function $f(x)$ below point d would involve losses for the potential home-based firm, so that it will not enter. The minimum output of the foreign firm which prevents entry is thus $\bar{b}$. The threat of entry prevents the foreign firm from exporting at the monopoly level, x_m.

The foreign firm compares the profitability of the entry deterrence solution with the profitability of the Stackelberg solution that would occur

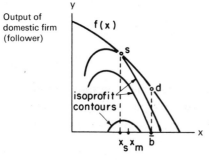

Figure 10.1   Entry deterrence in a Stackelberg leader-follower model

if the domestic firm were to enter. In defining the Stackelberg solution, there are two cases to consider. First, as in figure 10.1, an isoprofit contour can be tangent to $f(x)$ to the left of $\bar{b}$. (The isoprofit contours are combinations of x and y that yield the same variable profit for the foreign firm from its export market.) In this case, which is the interesting case, the Stackelberg solution is easily defined: the foreign firm chooses x to maximize $\pi^*(x^*, x, f(x))$. The output y chosen by the entrant is then positive. The level of exports by the foreign firm, denoted x_s, is the tangency solution and must be strictly less than $\bar{b}$. Lower isoprofit contours correspond to higher levels of profit. Therefore, as drawn, the entry-preventing level of exports, $\bar{b}$, is more profitable than the Stackelberg point, s, for the foreign firm, and it will choose to deter entry. (See Dixit 1979 for a fuller description of the model.)

It is also possible that the tangency between an isoprofit contour and $f(x)$ could occur to the right of $\bar{b}$. However, the possibility that x_s could exceed $\bar{b}$ is an empty box: the domestic firm would not enter. Also, if the tangency does occur to the right of $\bar{b}$, the foreign firm will deter entry, either by selling x_m if $x_m \geq \bar{b}$ or, if $x_m < \bar{b}$ as we assume, by selling $\bar{b}$. (This can be seen from a little experimentation with figure 10.1.) Any tariff that would induce entry must, therefore, first shift the isoprofit contours so that the tangency moves to the left of $\bar{b}$. Consequently, if we assume entry is possible, we can assume $x_s < \bar{b}$ without loss of generality.

We have $y(x_s)$ as the output of the domestic firm given export level x_s by the foreign firm, so the maximum profit of the foreign firm at the Stackelberg solution is

$$\pi^{*s} = V^*(x_m) + V(x_s, y(x_s)) - F^*.$$

We assume that entry deterrence is profitable in the pre-tariff situation so that $V(\bar{b}, 0) > V(x_s, y(x_s))$. For this to be the case it is not necessary that the existing firm have lower costs than the entrant. Even if $c < k^*$, there is some level of fixed cost F at which the existing firm would profit from entry deterrence. Higher levels of F reduce the output $\bar{b}$ required to prevent entry and increase the profit associated with entry deterrence. The level of F does not affect the profit associated with the Stackelberg tangency solution x_s. For some sufficiently high value of F the foreign firm would find entry deterrence more profitable than the Stackelberg solution. The level of F at which entry deterrence is profitable may be less than F^*, which has been incurred by the foreign firm and which is defrayed, at least in part, by variable profits from its home market.[8] Note that there is nothing to rule out the possibility that prices could be different in the two markets, which raises the possibility of arbitrage. We assume that arbitrage is not possible.

Since treating arbitrage explicitly would complicate the algebra and restrict the behaviour of firms in a fairly obvious way without contributing additional insights, it seems appropriate to ignore it.

2. A Rent-Extracting Tariff without Entry

We now consider the effects of a linear tariff placed on imports of good Z from the foreign monopoly firm.[9] Assume, for this section, that domestic entry is not feasible. (Entry is and remains blockaded.) From the demand function (2), the net gain to the home country from imports of Z given tariff t per unit is

$$G_0(t) = u(x(t)) - p(x(t))x(t) + tx(t), \tag{8}$$

where $u - px$ is the consumer surplus[10] from quantity $x(t)$ of good Z imported at tariff t and $tx(t)$ is tariff revenue. From differentiation of (8) and the fact that marginal revenue is set equal to marginal cost, $k^* + t$, by the foreign firm,

$$G_0'(t) = (p - (k^* + t))x'(t) + x(t) + tx'(t), \tag{9}$$

where primes are used to denote derivatives. An increase in the tariff allows an additional $x(t) + tx'(t)$ of the foreign monopoly rent to be extracted as tariff revenue, but consumer surplus is reduced by $(p - (k^* + t))x'(t)$. The home country may gain by charging a tariff to extract some of the foreign monopoly rent, but this gain is at least partially offset by the loss in consumer surplus.

The gains and losses from the tariff are illustrated in figure 10.2 The total tariff revenue is shown by the vertically hatched area and the loss in consumer surplus by the horizontally shaded area, including the double-hatched small triangle.[11]

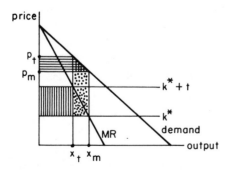

Figure 10.2

This analysis is very similar to the standard analysis in public finance of the effect of a per unit tax on a domestic monopoly. In the case of domestic monopoly the monopoly rent accrues to residents. Since an increase in the tax reduces profits at rate $x(t)$, the marginal gain, $G_0'(t)$ is $(p - k^*)x'(t)$ which is negative. The net loss is shown by the dotted area plus the small hatched triangle in figure 10.2.[12] Such a tax is obviously not an attractive way of collecting revenue in a purely domestic context. In the absence of potential entry, a tariff is attractive only because income is taken from foreigners rather than domestic residents.

3. Extraction of Rent under Potential Entry

The possibility of domestic entry substantially modifies the reaction of the foreign monopoly to the imposition of a tariff. Recall that we are assuming that the entrant would produce for its home market only.

PROPOSITION 1   If the foreign monopoly deters entry, a tariff can extract some monopoly rent at no cost in reduced consumption to the domestic country. The entire tariff revenue is a net gain to the domestic country.

Proposition 1 follows directly from expressions (5) and (7), which imply that the entry-deterring level of exports $\bar{b}$, is unaffected by the tariff.

The amount of monopoly rent that can be extracted is constrained by two requirements. First, the variable profit from exports must remain positive to the foreign firm:

$$0 \leqslant V(\bar{b}, 0; t) \equiv [p(\bar{b}) - k^*]\bar{b} - t\bar{b}. \tag{10}$$

Second, the variable profit from entry deterrence must continue to exceed the variable profit from the Stackelberg leader-follower equilibrium,

$$V(\bar{b}, 0; t) \geqslant V^s(t) \equiv (p(z_s) - k^*)x_s - tx_s, \tag{11}$$

where $z_s = x_s + y(x_s)$: consumption of Z by the domestic country at the Stackelberg equilibrium.

If constraint (11) is never binding, the home country can set the tariff so as to extract the entire monopoly rent from exports at no cost in consumer surplus. Constraint (10) would then hold with equality. Moreover, since x^*_m, the output sold in the foreign firm's home market, is unaffected by the tariff, this transfer of rent is achieved with no reduction in world welfare. (This interesting result still holds in the more general case where maginal costs are not constant.)

On the other hand, if constraint (11) is binding, the total tariff revenue is limited by the requirement that the foreign monopoly earn at least $V^s(t)$

from its policy of entry deterrence. Since proposition 1 ensures that $\bar{b}$ is constant, the tariff revenue increases with the tariff until one of the constraints is binding. This leads to the following remark.

REMARK 1   The optimum tariff in the entry deterrence regime is a tariff just marginally below the minimum tariff that will induce the foreign firm to abandon entry deterrence.

REMARK 2   An increase in the tariff increases the relative attractiveness of the Stackelberg solution to the foreign firm. That is, as t rises, $V(\bar{b}, 0, t) - V^s(t)$ falls.

Proof   An increase in the tariff makes both entry deterrence and the Stackelberg leader-follower solution less profitable for the foreign firm.
By the envelope theorem,[13]

$$dV^s/dt = -x_s,$$

and

$$dV(\bar{b}, 0, t)/dt = -\bar{b}.$$

From the definition of x_s, $x_s < \bar{b}$ so V^s, the variable profit under the Stackelberg solution, falls by less than V, the variable profit under entry deterrence. □

An implication of remark 2 is that a high, but not prohibitive, tariff may induce entry by making the Stackelberg solution more profitable than entry deterrence to the foreign firm.[14] It is of interest to examine the conditions under which a tariff will have this entry-inducing effect.

PROPOSITION 2   The following condition is necessary for the foreign firm to change its policy from entry deterrence to the Stackelberg outcome: $p(z_s) > p(\bar{b})$.

Proof   To accept the Stackelberg outcome the foreign firm requires that

$$V^s(t) \geqslant V(\bar{b}, 0, t),$$

or

$$(p(z_s) - (k^* + t))x_s \geqslant [p(\bar{b}) - (k^* + t)]\bar{b}.$$

Since $\bar{b} > x_s$ and since, for positive variable profit, $p(z_s) > k^* + t$ and $p(\bar{b}) > k^* + t$, it is necessary that $p(z_s)$ exceed $p(b)$ as was to be shown. □

Proposition 2 implies that the domestic country can induce domestic entry only if this action increases the prices of the good.

4. The Entry-Inducing Tariff and Welfare

Since a tariff may induce the Stackelberg solution (and entry), the question immediately arises of whether the domestic country could gain from such a tariff. One would like to compare the optimum tariff under each of the two regimes: entry deterrence and the Stackelberg solution. Unfortunately there is very little that one can say in the general case (without specific functional forms). However, a related question of some interest is whether a marginal increase in the tariff from just below the entry-inducing level to the entry-inducing level will increase or decrease the domestic country's welfare. Although there is perfect information in our model, in a more realistic context policymakers might have only local information about demand and cost and might therefore be interested in this marginal change.

Suppose that at tariff t_0, $V^s(t_0) = V(\bar{b}, 0, t_0) > 0$ so that the foreign monopoly is indifferent between entry deterrence and the Stackelberg solution. As already shown (remark 1) a tariff just marginally below t_0 is the home country's best tariff under the entry deterrence regime. The following proposition indicates the importance of the relative costs of production.

PROPOSITION 3   The following condition is necessary for the welfare of the domestic country to be improved by a slight increase in the tariff from just below the entry-inducing level to the entry-inducing level:

$$cy(x_s(t_0)) + F < k^* y(x_s(t_0)),$$

where t_0 is the entry-inducing tariff and $y(x_s(t_0))$ is the corresponding output of the domestic firm.

Proof   See Appendix. □

From proposition 2, total consumption z_s under entry is always less than $\bar{b}$, the consumption under entry-deterrence. Consequently, the consumer surplus associated with good Z is always less after entry. Furthermore, tariff revenue also declines as imports fall from $\bar{b}$ to $x_s(t_0)$. Therefore a net gain can occur only if the profits earned by the domestic firm more than offset these losses. It transpires that the entrant's profits can be sufficiently high only if the cost condition of proposition 3 holds. If transport costs are low and cost conditions are similar in the two countries so that k^* and c would be similar, significant fixed costs make it unlikely that inducing entry could be welfare improving at the margin for the home country.

Nevertheless, it is possible that a discrete increase in the tariff to some level significantly above t_0 could improve welfare. The additional rent extracted from the foreign firm, if any, and the additional profits earned by the domestic firm would have to be weighed against the loss in consumer surplus from reduced consumption of Z. (See the appendix for further analysis.)

At the extreme, the domestic country could charge a prohibitive tariff so that the domestic entrant would act as a monopolist. Given the assumption that the entrant does not export, such a policy is unlikely to be advantageous for the home country unless domestic costs of production are much lower than foreign costs. Note that a domestic firm may be deterred from entry even if it has lower costs than the foreign firm. The lower its costs, the 'harder' it is for the foreign firm to prevent entry (i.e., $\bar{b}$ is higher), and a sufficiently large decline in domestic costs would, of course, induce domestic entry without the imposition of a tariff.

5. Potential Entry in Both Countries

Intra-Industry Trade

So far we have assumed that the entrant considers producing only for its home market. Another possibility is that the entrant might produce for both markets. This raises the possibility of intra-industry trade: each country may import and export the imperfectly competitive good. We shall see that imperfect competition in itself can cause intra-industry trade. This result is of some interest since trade within commodity groups is now accepted as an important part of world trade. The intra-industry trade result in this paper may seem rather odd, since the good is homogeneous and transport costs exist, but it does follow from the standard, although specific, assumptions made concerning the behaviour of firms.

The extrant is assumed to follow a Cournot strategy in each market, and the existing firm follows a Stackelberg strategy in each market unless it deters entry. If the domestic firm enters its profit is

$$\pi = W(x, y) + W^*(x^*, y^*) - F, \tag{12}$$

where

$$W(x, y) = yp(x + y) - cy \equiv \text{variable profit at home,}$$

$$W^*(x^*, y^*) = y^*p^*(x^* + y^*) - ky^* \equiv \text{variable profit from export,}$$

$$y^* = \text{domestic firm's exports,}$$

$$k = c + \text{transport cost,}$$

$$p^* = \text{foreign inverse demand.}$$

The assumption of constant marginal costs ensures that the variable profit in each market depends only on the sales (of both firms) in that market. The entrant chooses y and y^* to maximize (12) given x and x^*. The first-order conditions require that perceived marginal revenue equal marginal cost in each market:

$$p + yp' = c, \tag{13}$$

$$p^* + y^*p^{*'} = k. \tag{14}$$

Equation (13) is the same as equation (5) and implicitly defines the reaction function $y = f(x)$; similarly, equation (14) defines the reaction function $y^* = f^*(x)$. Corresponding to (6), we define $y(x) = f(x)$, provided π and W are positive, and $y(x) = 0$ otherwise. Similarly $y^*(x^*) = f^*(x^*)$ if π and W^* are positive, and $y^*(x^*) = 0$ otherwise. The maximum profit of the domestic firm (if it decides to enter) is

$$\pi = W(x, y(x)) + W^*(x^*, y^*(x^*)) - F. \tag{15}$$

The possibility of exporting can never reduce the domestic firm's profits. Entry is more likely because the domestic firm can use variable profit from both markets to cover fixed cost.

Under entry the profit of the existing firm is

$$\pi^* = V(x, y; t) + V^*(x^*, y^*) - F^*, \tag{16}$$

where

$$V(x, y; t) = xp(x + y) - (k^* + t)x,$$

and

$$V^*(x^*, y^*) = x^*p^*(x^* + y^*) - c^*x^*.$$

Equation (16) is similar to equation (3). If the existing firm accepts the Stackelberg leader-follower solution, it chooses x_s and x^*_s so as to maximize π^* subject to $y = y(x)$ and $y^* = y^*(x^*)$. The first-order conditions require marginal revenue to be set equal to marginal cost in each market:

$$p + x_sp'[1 + y'(x_s)] = k^* + t, \tag{17}$$

$$p^* + x^*_sp^{*'}[1 + y^*{}'(x^*_s)] = c^*. \tag{18}$$

Equations (13), (14), (17), and (18) are four equations in four unknowns: x_s, x^*_s, y, y^*. Naturally, these equations may or may not have a positive solution, and the solution, if it exists, may or may not be unique. However, for many normal cases there will be a unique strictly positive solution at which profits are non-negative for both firms. This implies intra-industry trade. In a sense, intra-industry trade arises from a kind of discrimination: each firm sees each country as a separate market and tries to set marginal revenue equal to marginal cost in each. A referee suggested that one way of looking at the result is that intra-industry trade occurs because two firms share two national markets, while each firm happens to be located in a different country.

We assume that there is no arbitrage between the two markets. If arbitrage were costless, the difference in prices would be constrained by $p^* \leq p + r$ and $p \leq p^* + r + t$, where r represents per unit transport costs. For many commodities produced under imperfect competition the need for a distribution network would make arbitrage very costly. If arbitrage is regarded as an important possibility, the suggested model of intra-industry trade is less likely to be empirically important.

The type of intra-industry trade arising here is described and analysed more fully in Brander (1981) and Brander and Krugman (1983). It relies on imperfect competition per se as an underlying cause of trade. Competing and perhaps more convincing explanations which rely on product differentiation are in Krugman (1979) and Lancaster (1980). It seems reasonable that actual intra-industry trade might arise from both sources.

Entry Deterrence

The expectation that the entrant will produce for both markets changes the entry deterrence problem faced by the existing firm. The main point is that entry deterrence becomes more difficult; the entry-deterring quantity is greater and the profit is lower than in the case in which the entrant cannot export.

To deter entry, the foreign firm must choose b and b^* such that

$$\pi \equiv W(b, y(b)) + W^*(b^*, y^*(b^*)) - F \leq 0, \tag{19}$$

where

$b = $ entry-deterring output for domestic country,

and

$b^* = $ entry-deterring output for foreign country.

Setting $\pi = 0$ defines b^* as an implicit function of b. We refer to $b^*(b)$ as the bb^* contour:

$$\frac{db^*}{db} = \frac{-dW/db}{dW^*/db^*} < 0. \tag{20}$$

PROPOSITION 4   The possibility of potential entry in both markets cannot cause the entry-deterring firm to sell less in either market. On the contrary, the normal case is for sales to expand in both markets.

Proof   If $b < \bar{b}$ the potential entrant will enter its home market regardless of the export market. Therefore $b \geq \bar{b}$ to deter entry so sales in the domestic market cannot fall. If $W^*[b^*, y^*(b^*)] > 0$, so that the entrant can make some variable profit from exports, then $b > \bar{b}$. Also the foreign firm will never produce less than the monopoly output in its home market.

Extracting Monopoly Rent

The extraction of monopoly rent is more complicated in the case of potential intra-industry trade because the existing firm now has some flexibility. The problem facing the established firm is to maximize its own profit subject to being on the bb^* contour defined in (20) and to compare it with the Stackelberg outcome. The profit of the existing firm under entry deterrence can be written

$$\pi^* = V(b, 0; t) + V^*(b^*, 0) - F^* \tag{21}$$

and, along an isoprofit contour,

$$\frac{db^*}{db} = \frac{-\partial V/\partial b}{\partial V^*/\partial b^*} < 0. \tag{22}$$

The effect of an increase in the tariff is to cause the existing firm to move along the bb^* contour, increasing b^* and reducing b. Its profits are also reduced.

REMARK 3   An increase in the tariff decreases the established firm's exports and lowers the profit obtained under entry deterrence.

$db/dt < 0$ and $d\pi^*/dt < 0$

Proof

1. $db/dt < 0$.

The established firm chooses b to maximize π^* in equation (21). Substituting $b^* = b^*(b)$ the first-order condition is

$d\pi^*/db = 0$

The comparative static result is obtained by totally differentiating the first-order condition with respect to b and t

$db/dt = 1/[d^2\pi^*/db^2] < 0$ by the second-order condition, $d^2\pi^*/db^2 < 0$.

2. $d\pi^*/dt = -b < 0$ by the envelope theorem.

In this case the domestic country cannot extract rent painlessly since the tariff causes a loss in consumer surplus as imports fall. Nevertheless, by proposition 4, for any tariff the domestic country is better off with the threat of entry in both markets than with the threat of entry into the domestic market only.

The possibility of entry in both markets also affects the domestic country's decision about whether to use the tariff to induce entry. As before, inducing entry with a tariff enables the domestic firm to earn profits from its domestic operation and reduces the rents going to the foreign firm. In addition the entrant can earn profits from its foreign operation. If the foreign market is very large, the profits earned there can swamp the welfare losses or gains in the domestic market. Protective tariffs insure that domestic firms can enter and survive, and these firms earn rent from foreign operations.

Finally, a prohibitive tariff is also more attractive in this case. Even though the entrant produces only the monopoly output at home, resulting in a loss of consumer surplus, the entrant can earn rent from overseas which might more than compensate for the domestic welfare losses.

6. Concluding Remarks

As pointed out by a referee, the interest one attaches to this paper depends critically on how one views the limit output model of entry prevention. Since the dominant firm may not produce the limit output if entry should occur, there is some doubt as to whether the limit output is a credible entry-deterring threat. One approach is that the dominant firm 'commit' itself, through capital investment or whatever, to the limit output (see Dixit 1980 and Eaton and Lipsey 1980). This commitment approach seems more realistic. The cost is that the analysis must be made explicitly dynamic. The insights of the analysis in this paper would not seem to be changed by this approach, particularly if one thinks of the government acting ex ante in setting tariffs—before the dominant firm makes a final decision concerning its level of commitment. If commitment is required for entry prevention, then the range of cases in which entry deterrence is possible, and consequently for which the analysis of this paper is relevant, is reduced.

A second caveat, also suggested by a referee, is that different strategies by firms and different tools by government are important possibilities. For example, Katrak (1977) suggests profits taxes and consumption taxes as tools for dealing with foreign monopoly and DeMeza (1979) suggests price controls. See also Just et al. (1979) and Stegemann (1981) on state trading. (Clearly a maximum price equal to marginal cost is the best possible policy, from a national point of view, in a simple deterministic full information world. We would argue that such a policy tool is probably inferior to a tariff in a more realistic world and rarely feasible in any case.) Certainly, different behaviour by firms could lead to different results. There is a large number of competing models of market structure; the model here is a particular type of conjectural variation model. Other possibilities include price-setting models and collusive models. The model we have chosen seems like the natural starting point.

If one is to start considering different possible strategies by the firms and the government(s) involved, the possibility arises of modelling the interaction between agents as a game. Explicit game-theoretic modelling is beyond the scope of this paper, but a few useful preliminary remarks can be made. Consider, first, the simplest case, in which there are only two players: the domestic government and a foreign monopoly. The outcome suggested in the paper is clearly not in the core of a cooperative game with side payments. Specifically, if the monopoly were to set $p = \text{MC}$ the government could pay the monopoly slightly more than it earns under the optimum tariff regime, and in addition the domestic country would be better off. (No wedge would be driven between consumer and producer prices.) In more conventional economic terms, the core contains first-best outcomes while the paper is strictly concerned with a second-best world. Consequently, there is room for direct negotiation between the firm and the government. Thus, by threatening to use a tariff, the government might extract rents more efficiently than by actually using a tariff.

With potential entry there are three players, and sorting out possible outcomes becomes very difficult. However, since the relative bargaining position of the foreign firm is made worse, presumably the domestic country could do better. If there is potential entry in both countries, we should perhaps recognize that there are two tariff-setting jurisdictions, with four players (two governments and two firms); once again it is hard to predict what would happen. At the very least, the prospect of retaliatory tariffs would reduce the ability of any one government to use rent-extracting tariffs. The government-government interaction here is rather like it is in the standard optimum tariff retaliation argument.

There are several points which should be summarized here. Our model is built around the idea that under imperfect competition price exceeds marginal cost, so that countries which import such goods usually pay rent to foreign firms. Some of this rent can be extracted by a tariff, and this kind of tariff policy can be particularly effective under the threat of domestic entry. In the special case in which the foreign firm expects the entrant to produce only for its home market, some rent can be extracted with no additional distortion.

A sufficiently high tariff will force the foreign firm to abandon its strategy of entry deterrence and may therefore induce domestic entry. This is unlikely to be walfare improving for the home country unless the domestic entrant can export and earn rent from its foreign operations. Despite transportation costs and tariffs the domestic entrant may indeed export with the result that intra-industry trade occurs. This is of some interest since intra-industry trade is an important part of world trade that is not well explained by standard competitive models. Furthermore, if the existing firm believes that the domestic firm may enter both domestic and foreign markets, its entry-deterring behaviour is affected. The domestic country can no longer extract rent from the foreign firm in a non-distorting way with a linear tariff. Nevertheless, at any tariff level, the domestic country is better off than it would be if the domestic firm threatened to enter only its home market.

The theme of the paper is that imperfect competition significantly changes the tariff-setting incentives facing a particular country. We are not advocating the use of tariffs to extract foreign rents and do not seriously address the issue of world welfare. We do, however, point out that a country may have an incentive to use tariffs under imperfect competition. Some of the points made seem fairly obvious, yet they rarely emerge in discussions concerning tariffs, perhaps because of the lack of emphasis that imperfect competition has received in international trade theory.

Appendix

PROPOSITION 3   The following condition is necessary for the welfare of the domestic country to be improved by a slight increase in the tariff from just below the entry-inducing level to the entry-inducing level:

$$cy(x_s(t_0)) + F < k^* y(x_s(t_0)),$$

where t_0 is the entry-inducing tariff and $y(x_s(t_0))$ is the output of the domestic firm.

Proof   If there is no entry, the gain to the home country from the consumption of good Z at tariff t_0 is

$$G_1(t_0) = u(\bar{b}) - p(\bar{b})\bar{b} + t_0\bar{b}. \tag{A1}$$

$G_1(t_0)$ is the consumer surplus at t_0 plus the tariff revenue. By adding and subtracting $k^*\bar{b}$,

$$G_1(t_0) = u(\bar{b}) - k^*\bar{b} - V(\bar{b}, 0, t_0). \tag{A2}$$

Similarly, the gain to the home country from the Stackelberg solution at a tariff t, where $t \geq t_0$, is

$$G_2(t) = u(z_s) - p(z_s)z_s + \pi[x_s, y(x_s)] + tx_s, \tag{A3}$$

where, for simplicity, $x_s(t)$ is written as x_s. $G_2(t)$ is the consumer surplus from z_s plus the profit of the domestic entrant and the tariff revenue. This reduces to

$$G_2(t) = u(z_s) - (k^*x_s + cy(x_s) + F) - V^s(t). \tag{A4}$$

The welfare of the domestic country at a tariff just below t_0 exceeds its welfare at the entry inducing tariff if $G_1(t_0) - G_2(t_0) > 0$. From (A2) and (A4), since

$$V(\bar{b}, 0, t_0) = V^s(t_0),$$

$$G_1(t_0) - G_2(t_0) = u(\bar{b}) - u(z_s) - k^*\bar{b} + [k^*x_s + cy(x_s) + F] \tag{A5}$$

$$= [u(\bar{b}) - u(z_s) - k^*(\bar{b} - z_s)] + [cy(x_s) + F - k^*y(x_s)]. \tag{A6}$$

From proposition 2 we know $z_s < \bar{b}$, which implies $u(\bar{b}) > u(z_s)$. Also the value of the additional consumption, $\bar{b} - z_s$, under entry deterrence exceeds its additional cost of production, $k^*(\bar{b} - z_s)$ so that the first term (in square brackets) of (A6) is positive. Therefore $G_1(t_0) - G_2(t_0) > 0$ if $cy(x_s) + F \geq k^*y(x_s)$. Therefore a necessary (but not sufficient) condition for $G_2(t_0)$ to exceed $G_1(t_0)$ is $cy(x_s) + F < k^*y(x_s)$. $\square$

The Marginal Gain from an Increase in the Tariff after Entry
From (A3)

$$G_2(t) = u(z_s) - p(z_s)z_s + \pi[x_s, y(x_s)] + tx_s. \tag{A7}$$

Since marginal revenue to the foreign firm equals $k^* + t$, differentiating (A7) and rearranging terms, we obtain

$$G_2'(t) = [p - (k^* + t)]x_s'(t) + (p - c)y'(x_s)x_s'(t) + tx_s'(t) + x_s(t). \tag{A8}$$

Expression (A8) is the same as expression (9) of the text ($x_s(t)$ replaces $x(t)$) except for the extra term, $(p - c)y'(x_s)x_s'(t)$, which is the marginal net value of the additional output produced by the entrant with an increase in the tariff.

The sum of the first two terms of (A8) represents the net change in consumer surplus and profit earned by the domestic firm from the reduction in imports, x_s, because of a rise in t. This sum could be positive or negative. If it is positive, and if raising the tariff increases tariff revenue, domestic welfare also increases. However, if foreign costs are less than or equal to domestic costs, normally the sum of the first two terms would be negative, since we expect $-1 < y'(x_s) < 0$, which implies that total consumption, $x_s + y(x_s)$, falls as t rises. Even in this case, if x_s is sufficiently inelastic in t, domestic welfare could improve.

Notes

1. It has been suggested, for example, that western nations could use tariffs to extract oil rents from OPEC.

2. Intra-industry trade is trade in which a country imports and exports the same or similar goods. Intra-industry trade is now regarded as an important part of world trade, thanks largely to the work of Herbert Grubel. A standard reference is Grubel and Lloyd (1975). See also Giersch (1979) for some recent contributions on the subject. The inability of the standard models to explain intra-industry trade is one reason for recent interest in models that assume imperfect competition.

3. Entry deterrence is a topic of considerable recent interest. Other recent work includes Schmalensee (1978) and Spence (1979).

4. This paper is not concerned with mathematical generality. We make the 'usual' convenient assumptions about demand functions, profit functions, and reaction functions, except where otherwise noted. Differentiability is assumed where useful, and existence and uniqueness of solutions to maximization problems are also assumed. Although there are dangers in this approach, the pathological properties associated with the models in this paper are well enough understood and sufficiently complicated that further discussion here would be inappropriate.

5. Using a utility function of this form amounts to the partial equilibrium assumptions that the good under consideration uses only a small part of the budget of any particular household, and that cross elasticities of demand are negligible.

6. We are not considering subsidiary investment and multi-national corporations. The entrant must be a different firm from the existing firm.

7. Fellner (1949) remains an excellent reference on simple reaction function models, including the Stacklberg leader-follower model. A more modern discussion can be found in Friedman (1977). A recent paper which uses Stackelberg and Cournot models in an international context in Robson (1980).

8. However, at $F = 0$ and $c \leqslant k^*$, it is not profitable for the established firm to deter entry.

9. Two-part or other non-linear tariffs might be superior for extracting rent. However linear (ad valorem) tariffs are much easier to administer and are so commonly observed in practice that it seems reasonable to restrict attention to them.

10. The inverse demand is $p = u'(z)$ and there are no income effects, so consumer surplus is

$$\int_0^x (u'(z) - p)\, dz$$

which equals $u(x) - p \cdot x$ assuming $u(0) = 0$.

11. These areas are obtained from (8) or alternatively by intergrating the corresponding terms in (9). The optimum tariff is found by setting $G_0'(t) = 0$.

12. Under perfect competition in the domestic country, so that price equals marginal cost, the loss would be the small triangle alone: the familiar deadweight loss triangle.

13. A presentation of the envelope theorem can be found in Varian (1978).

14. This paper does not consider quotas. Nevertheless, an interesting point made by Paul Krugman seems worth reporting. The domestic government can induce entry by setting a quota level slightly below the entry-preventing output $\bar{b}$, but above x_s. The foreign firm's best strategy would then involve producing the Stackelberg output x_s. Thus the quota would appear to be inactive, even though it was having an important effect.

References

Bain, J. S. 1956. *Barriers to New Competition*. Cambridge: Harvard University Press.

Brander, J. A. 1981. Intra-industry trade in identical commodities. *Journal of International Economics* 11, 1–14.

Brander, J. A., and P. Krugman. 1983. A reciprocal dumping model of international trade. *Journal of International Economics* 15, 313–321.

DeMeza, D. 1979. Commerical policy towards multinational monopolies—Reservations on Katrak. *Oxford Economic Papers* 31, 334–337.

Dixit, A. 1979. A model of duopoly suggesting a theory of entry barriers. *Bell Journal of Economics* 10, 20–32.

Dixit, A. 1980. The role of investment in entry-deterrence. *Economic Journal* 90, 95–106.

Eaton, B. C., and R. G. Lipsey. 1981. Capital, commitment and entry equilibrium. *Bell Journal of Economics* 12, 593–604.

Fellner, W. 1949. *Competition among the Few*. New York: Alfred A. Knopf.

Friedman, J. W. 1977. *Oligopoly and the Theory of Games*. Amsterdam: North Holland.

Giersch, H. 1979. *On the Economics of Intra-Industry Trade: Symposium 1978*. Tubingen: Mohr.

Grubel, H. G., and P. J. Lloyd. 1975. *Intra-Industry Trade*. London: Wiley.

Just, R. E., A. Schmitz, and D. Zilberman. 1979. Price controls and optimal export policies under alternative market structures. *American Economic Review* 69, 706–714.

Katrak, H. 1977. Multinational monopolies and commercial policy. *Oxford Economic Papers* 29, 283–291.

Krugman, P. 1979. Increasing returns, monopolistic competition and international trade. *Journal of International Economics* 9, 469–479.

Lancaster, K. 1980. Intra-industry trade under perfect monopolistic competition. *Journal of International Economics* 10, 151–175.

Markusen, J. R. 1981. Trade and the gains from trade with imperfect competition. *Journal of International Economics* 11, 531–551.

Melvin, J. R., and R. Warne. 1973. Monopoly and the theory of international trade. *Journal of International Economics* 3, 117–134.

Modigliani, F. 1958. New developments on the oligopoly front. *Journal of Political Economy* 66, 215–232.

Robson, A. J. 1980. OPEC versus the west: a robust duopoly solution. Working Paper No. 8001. Centre for the Study of International Economic Relations, University of Western Ontario, London, Ontario.

Schmalensee, R. 1979. Entry deterrence in the ready-to-eat breakfast cereal industry. *Bell Journal of Economics* 9, 305–327.

Spence, A. M. 1979. Investment strategy and growth in a new market. *Bell Journal of Economics* 10, 1–19.

Stegemann, K. 1981. State trading and domestic distortions in a mixed world economy. In M. M. Kostecki, ed., *State Trading in International Markets*. London: Macmillan.

Sylos-Labini, P. 1957. *Oligopoly and Technical Progress*. Translated by Elizabeth Henderson, 1962. Cambridge: Harvard University Press.

Varian, H. R. 1978. *Microeconomic Analysis*. New York: Norton.

11

Optimal Trade and Industrial Policy under Oligopoly

Jonathan Eaton and Gene M. Grossman

Implicit in many arguments for interventionist trade or industrial policy that have been advanced recently in popular debate appears to be an assumption that international markets are oligopolistic. It can be argued that international competition among firms in many industries is in fact imperfectly competitive, because the number of firms is few, products are differentiated, or governments themselves have cartelized the national firms engaged in competition. They may do so implicitly through tax policy or explicitly through marketing arrangements.

Government policies that affect the competitiveness of their firms in international markets, as well as the welfare of their consumers, involve not only traditional trade policy (trade taxes and subsidies) but policies that affect other aspects of firms' costs, such as output taxes and subsidies. We refer to intervention of this sort as industrial policy.

Until recently, the theory of commerical policy has considered the implications of intervention only under conditions of perfect competition or, more rarely, pure monopoly. As a consequence, this literature cannot respond to many of the arguments that have been advanced recently in favor of activist government policies. Our purpose in this paper is to extend the theory of nationally optimal policy to situations in which individual firms exercise market power in world markets.

The primary implications of oligopoly for the design of trade policy are (1) that economic profits are not driven to zero, and (2) that a price equal to marginal cost does not generally obtain. The first of these means that government policies that shift the industry equilibrium to the advantage of domestic firms may be socially beneficial from a national perspective. The

This paper was originally published in *The Quarterly Journal of Economics* (May 1986). 383–406. © 1986 by the President and Fellows of Harvard College. Published by John Wiley & Sons, Inc.

second feature of oligopolistic competition suggests that trade policy may be a substitute for antitrust policy if policies can be dervised that shrink the wedge between opportunity cost in production and marginal valuation to consumers.

A number of recent papers have focused on the profit-shifting motive for trade policy under oligopoly. Brander and Spencer (1985) develop a model in which one home firm and one foreign firm produce perfectly substitutable goods and compete in a third-country market. They consider a Cournot-Nash equilibrium and find that if the home country's government can credibly precommit itself to pursue a particular trade policy before firms make production decisions (and if demand is not very convex), then an export subsidy is optimal.[1] Dixit (1984) has extended the Brander-Spencer result to cases with more than two firms and established that an export subsidy in a Cournot oligopoly equilibrium is optimal so long as the number of domestic firms is not too large. Finally, Krugman (1984) shows that under increasing returns to scale, protection of a local firm in one market (e.g., by an import tariff) can shift the equilibrium to the firm's advantage in other markets by lowering its marginal cost of production.

These papers all provide examples in which interventionist trade policy can raise national welfare in imperfectly competitive environments. Yet each makes special assumptions about the form of oligopolistic competition, the substitutability of the goods produced, and the markets in which the goods are sold. It is difficult to extract general principles for trade policy from this analysis. Our purpose here is to provide an integrative treatment of the welfare effects of trade and industrial policy under oligopoly and to characterize the form that optimal intervention takes under a variety of assumptions about the number of firms, their assumptions about rivals' responses to their actions, the substitutability of their products, and the countries where their products are sold.

The paper is organized as follows. In the next section we consider a general conjectural variations model of a duopoly in which a single home firm competes with a foreign firm either in the foreign firm's local market or in a third-country market. We find that the sign of the optimal trade or industrial policy (i.e., whether a tax or subsidy is optimal) depends on the relationship between the home firm's conjectural variation and the actual equilibrium reactions of the foreign firm. We note the form that optimal policy takes in Cournot and Bertrand equilibria and in what Bresnahan (1981) and Perry (1982) have called a "consistent" conjectures equilibrium.

We extend these results to incorporate the interaction between the policies of the home government and an activist foreign government in section 2. Here we consider optimal intervention in a two-stage game in which governments achieve a Nash equilibrium in policies prior to the time that firms engage in product-market competition. In section 3 we further extend the analysis by allowing for oligopoly with arbitrary numbers of firms in each country.

The analysis in sections 1, 2, and 3 assumes a constant, exogenous number of firms. In section 4 we discuss briefly how our results would be modified if firms can enter or exit in response to government policies. Finally, in section 5 we return to the duopoly case and introduce domestic consumption for the first time. This allows us to consider the potential role for trade policy as a (partial) substitute for antitrust policy.

The main findings of the paper are summarized in a concluding section.

1. Optimal Trade Policy and the Role of Conjectural Variations: The Case of Duopoly

In this and subsequent sections we characterize optimal government policy in the presence of oligopolistic competition among domestic and foreign firms in international markets. Each firm produces a single product that may be a perfect or imperfect substitute for the output of its rivals. We specify competition among firms in terms of output quantities with arbitrary conjectural variations.[2] The domestic government can tax (or subsidize) the output of domestic firms, tax (or subsidize) the exports of these firms, and tax (or subsidize) the imports from the foreign rivals of domestic firms. Its objective is to maximize national welfare.

The government acts as a Stackelberg leader vis-à-vis both domestic and foreign firms in setting tax (subsidy) rates.[3] Thus, firms set outputs taking tax and subsidy rates as given. In other words, the government can precommit itself to a specific policy intervention that will not be altered even if it is suboptimal ex post, once firms' outputs are determined. At first we assume the absence of government policy in other countries. We also treat the number of firms as given. The implications of relaxing these assumptions are discussed below.

In this section we consider optimal government policy when oligopolistic competition takes its simplest possible form: a single domestic firm competes with a single foreign firm in a foreign market. In the absence of domestic consumption, government trade policy (export taxes and subsidies) is equivalent to government industrial policy (output taxes and subsidies). We assume that the government places equal weight on the home-firm's profit and government tax revenue in evaluating social welfare. Its objective is therefore one of maximizing national product.

Denote the output (and exports) of the home firm by x, and let $c(x)$ be its total production cost, $c'(x) > 0$. Uppercase letters denote corresponding magnitudes for the foreign firm, with $C'(X) > 0$. Pretax revenue of the home and foreign firms are given by the functions $r(x, X)$ and $R(x, X)$, respectively. These satisfy the conditions that

$$r_2(x, X) \equiv \frac{\partial r(x, X)}{\partial X} \leqslant 0$$

$$R_1(x, X) \equiv \frac{\partial R(x, X)}{\partial x} \leqslant 0,$$

that is, that an increase in the output of the competing product lowers the total revenue of each firm. They are implied by the assumption that the products are substitutes in consumption.[4] Total aftertax profits of the home and foreign firms are given by

$$\pi = (1 - t)r(x, X) - c(x)$$

and

$$\Pi = R(x, X) - C(X),$$

respectively. Here t denotes the ad valorem output (or export) tax.[5] The domestic firm's conjecture about the foreign firm's output response to changes in its own output is given by the parameter γ. The foreign firm's corresponding conjectural variation is Γ.

The Nash equilibrium quantities, given the level of home country policy intervention, are determined by the first-order conditions:

$$(1 - t)[r_1(x, X) + \gamma r_2(x, X)] - c'(x) = 0; \tag{1}$$

$$R_2(x, X) + \Gamma R_1(x, X) - C'(X) = 0. \tag{2}$$

We assume that the second-order conditions for profit maximization and the conditions for stability of the industry equilibrium are satisfied. We now demonstrate

THEOREM 1   A positive (negative) output or export tax can yield higher national welfare than laissez-faire ($t = 0$) if the home firm conjectures a foreign change in output in response to an increase in its own output that is smaller (larger) than the actual response.

Proof   National product generated by the home firm is given by w, where

$$w = (1 - t)r(x, X) - c(x) + tr(x, X)$$

$$= r(x, X) - c(x). \tag{3}$$

The change in welfare resulting from a small change in the tax (or subsidy) rate t is

$$\frac{dw}{dt} = [r_1(x, X) - c'(x)]\frac{dx}{dt} + r_2(x, X)\frac{dX}{dt}. \tag{4}$$

Substituting the first-order condition (1) into (4), we obtain[6]

$$\frac{dw}{dt} = \left[-\gamma r_2 - \frac{tc'}{1-t}\right]\left(\frac{dx}{dt}\right) + r_2\left(\frac{dX}{dt}\right). \tag{5}$$

Expression (2) implicitly defines the output of the foreign firm X as a function of domestic output x. Denote this function $\Psi(x)$. The tax rate t does not appear directly as an argument of this function, since t does not appear in expression (2). Therefore, $dX/dt = \Psi'(x)(dx/dt)$. Define $g \equiv (dX/dt)/(dx/dt) = \Psi'(x)$. The term g measures the slope of the foreign firm's reaction curve, i.e., its *actual* reaction to exogenous changes in x. A first-order condition for maximizing national welfare obtains when $dw/dt = 0$,[7] or, incorporating the definition of g into equation (5),

$$-r_2(g - \gamma) = \frac{tc'}{1-t}. \tag{6}$$

Since $r_2 < 0$, the left-hand and right-hand sides of expression (6) are of the same sign if $1 > t > 0$ and $g > \gamma$, or $t < 0$ and $g < \gamma$. The term $g - \gamma$ is the difference between the actual response of X to a change in x (i.e., $\Psi'(x)$) and the home firm's conjectural variation. When $g > \gamma$, a tax can yield more income than laissez-faire, conversely when $g < \gamma$. $\square$

An intuitive explanation of this result is as follows. Government policy is implemented before the two firms choose their outputs, which they do simultaneously. Intervention consequently allows the domestic firm to achieve the outcome that would obtain if it were able to act as a Stackelberg leader with respect to its competitor. If $g > \gamma$, then the equilibrium output absent policy involves more domestic output than at the Stackelberg point because the home firm cannot or does not fully account for the foreign firm's reaction to an increase in its own quantity in choosing its output level. Conversely, if $g < \gamma$, the home firm's output more than fully reflects the extent of actual reaction by the rival. The sign of the optimal policy is determined accordingly.

We now turn to some specific conjectural variations that are commonly assumed in models of oligopolistic competition.

Cournot Conjectures
Under Cournot behavior, each firm conjectures that when it changes its output the other firm will hold its output fixed. Thus, $\gamma = \Gamma = 0$ in this case, and (6) becomes

$$-gr_2 = \frac{tc'}{1-t}. \tag{7}$$

Totally differentiating the equilibrium conditions (1) and (2) to solve for g, we may write this expression as

$$\frac{r_2 R_{21}}{R_{22} - C''} = \frac{tc'}{1-t}. \tag{8}$$

The second-order condition for the foreign firm's profit maximization ensures that the left-hand side of this expression has the sign of R_{21}. Letting t^* denote the optimal export tax (or subsidy, if negative), we have established

PROPOSITION 1   In a Cournot duopoly with no home consumption, sgn $t^* = $ sgn R_{21}.

Proposition 1 restates the Brander-Spencer (1985) argument for an export subsidy: this policy raises domestic welfare in a Cournot equilibrium by transferring industry profit to the domestic firm. This point is illustrated in figure 11.1. In the figure, representative isoprofit loci for the home firm are depicted in output space by u^0, u^c and u^*. Lower curves correspond to higher levels of profit. The Cournot reaction function for the home firm rr connects the maxima of the isoprofit loci. The direction of its slope is given

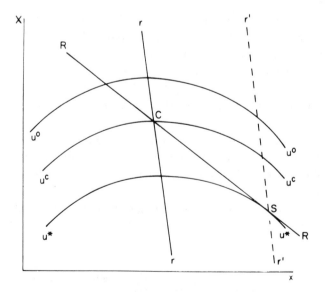

Figure 11.1   Optimal policy with Cournot competition

by the sign of r_{12}. The foreign firm's reaction curve RR is found similarly, and its slope is determined by the sign of R_{21}. Linear demand necessarily implies that $r_{12} < 0$ and $R_{21} < 0$, and many, but not all, specifications of demand imply this sign as well.

The Cournot equilibrium is at point C, where the home firm earns a profit corresponding to u^c. Note that among the points along RR, u^c does not provide the highest level of profit to the home firm and therefore does not yield the highest possible level of home country welfare. Rather, maximum profit corresponds to u^*, which would be the equilibrium if the home firm could credibly precommit its output level and thus act as a Stackelberg leader. Lacking this ability, the home country could nonetheless achieve the outcome at u^* in a Nash equilibrium if the home government were to implement a trade policy that shifted the home firm's reaction locus to intersect RR at S. This is the optimal profit-shifting trade policy; it involves an export subsidy under the Cournot assumptions provided that RR is downward sloping (i.e., $R_{21} < 0$). A downward (upward) sloping foreign reaction curve implies a level of output in the Cournot equilibrium that is less (greater) than that at the point of Stackelberg leadership, thus the sign of the optimal trade policy in this case.[8]

Note that the optimal export subsidy with Cournot competition benefits the home firm (and country) at the expense of the foreign firm. Indeed, the equilibrium with one country pursuing its optimal policy involves smaller (net-of-subsidy) profits for the two firms together than in the laissez-faire equilibrium. Consumers of the product benefit from lower prices when the subsidy is in place, and the net effect on world welfare is positive, since policy pushes prices toward their competitive levels.

Bertrand Conjectures

In a Bertrand equilibrium each firm conjectures that its rival will hold its price fixed in response to any changes in its own price. Define the *direct* demand functions for the output of the home and foreign firms as $d(p, P)$ and $D(p, P)$, respectively. The total profits of the two firms are

$$\pi(p, P) = (1 - t)pd(p, P) - c(d(p, P))$$

and

$$\Pi(p, P) = PD(p, P) - C(D(p, P)).$$

Each firm sets its price to maximize its profit, taking the other firm's price as constant. First-order conditions for a maximum imply that

$$\pi_1 = (1 - t)(d + pd_1) - c'd_1 = 0, \tag{9a}$$

$$\Pi_2 = D + (P - C')D_2 = 0. \tag{9b}$$

The actual and conjectured price responses can be translated into quantity responses by totally differentiating the demand functions to obtain

$$\begin{bmatrix} dx \\ dX \end{bmatrix} = \begin{bmatrix} d_1 d_2 \\ D_1 D_2 \end{bmatrix} \cdot \begin{bmatrix} dp \\ dP \end{bmatrix}.$$

The Bertrand conjecture on the part of the home firm implies a conjectured quantity response given by

$$\gamma = \left(\frac{dX/dp}{dx/dp}\right)\bigg|_{dP=0} = \frac{D_1}{d_1}. \tag{10}$$

The actual response is

$$g = \frac{dX/dp}{dx/dp} = \frac{D_1 - D_2 \Pi_{21}/\Pi_{22}}{d_1 - d_2 \Pi_{21}/\Pi_{22}}.$$

It is straightforward to show, using the conditions for stability of the industry equilibrium, that the term $g - \gamma$ is positive if and only if $\Pi_{21} > 0$ (the foreign firm responds to a price cut by cutting its price). Applying theorem 1, we conclude

PROPOSITION 2   In a Bertrand duopoly with no home consumption, $\text{sgn}\, t^* = \text{sgn}\, \Pi_{21}$.

If the two products are substitutes (i.e., $d_2 > 0$ and $D_1 > 0$) and returns to scale are nonincreasing ($c'' \geqslant 0$, $C'' \geqslant 0$), then $\Pi_{21} > 0$ *unless* an increase in its rival's price has a significantly negative effect on the *slope* of the demand curve facing the home firm. In the special cases of either perfect substitutes or linear demands, this sign necessarily obtains. Presumption regarding the sign of the optimal trade intervention when duopolistic behavior is Bertrand is consequently the opposite of that in the Cournot case; that is, an export *tax* is generally required.

Figure 11.2 illustrates this result. Representative isoprofit loci of the home firm (in price space) are shown as u^0, u^b, and u^*. Higher curves now correspond to higher profit. The Bertrand reaction curves are depicted by rr for the home firm and RR for the foreign firm, and the directions of their slopes correspond to the signs of π_{12} and Π_{21}, respectively.

The Bertrand equilibrium absent policy intervention is the intersection of the two curves, at point B. Here the home firm earns a profit corresponding to u^b. Given RR, a higher profit could be attained at point S, where the home firm charges a higher price than at B. However, unless the home firm can precommit to the higher price or act as a Stackelberg leader, point S is not achievable under laissez-faire. An appropriate output or export tax shifts the home reaction curve to $r'r'$, whence the Nash

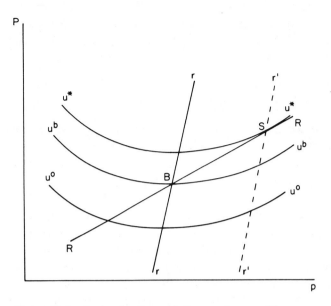

Figure 11.2   Optimal policy with Bertrand competition

equilibrium in the resulting product-market competition yields the superior welfare outcome.[9] Notice that the Bertrand equilibrium for the case in which the foreign reaction curve is upward sloping in price space involves a lower domestic price and therefore a higher domestic output than at the Stackelberg leadership point. This is in contrast to the Cournot outcome and accounts for the qualitative difference in the policy conclusions.[10]

Another contrast with the Cournot outcome is that implementation of the optimal policy by the home government raises profits of the foreign firm. It does so by alleviating oligopolistic rivalry. Of course, the tax affects consumers adversely, and world welfare falls as the equilibrium becomes less competitive.

Consistent Conjectures
The final special case we consider is one in which the home firm's conjecture about its rival's response is "consistent," as is the case if the home firm is a Stackelberg leader vis-à-vis its foreign rival or in a "consistent conjectures equilibrium." This second concept, as defined and analyzed by Bresnahan (1981) and Perry (1982) among others, is an equilibrium in which each firm's conjectural variation is equal to the actual equilibrium responses of its rivals that would result if that firm actually were to change its output by a small amount at the equilibrium point.

The slope of the foreign reaction curve in our model is given by g. Thus, the home firm's conjectures about its rival's response are consistent in the sense of Bresnahan and Perry if $\gamma = g$. The following proposition follows immediately from expression (6):[11]

PROPOSITION 3   In a duopoly with consistent conjectures on the part of the home firm and no home consumption, $t^* = 0$.

The optimality of free trade with consistent conjectures on the part of the home firm emerges because there exists no shift of the home firm's reaction curve that can transfer industry profit to that firm, given the response of its rival.

The duopoly example with no home consumption highlights the profit-shifting motive for trade policy intervention in an imperfectly competitive industry. Under optimal intervention the government uses its first-mover advantage to shift its national firm's reaction function so that it intersects the foreign firm's curve at a point of tangency between the latter curve and a (laissez-faire) isoprofit locus of the home firm. The direction of this shift, and thus the qualitative nature of the optimal policy, depends in general on the sign of the deviation of the home firm's conjectural variation from the slope of the foreign firm's reaction curve.

We now extend the basic result to allow for a foreign policy response, multifirm oligopoly, endogenous market structure, and domestic consumption.

2. Foreign Policy Response

In the analysis up to this point, we have assumed that the foreign rival's government pursues a laissez-faire policy. Imagine now a two-stage game with both governments active in which the governments first arrive at a Nash equilibrium in policy parameters and then duopolistic competition between the firms takes place. For simplicity, we assume no consumption in the rival's country as well. All consumption is elsewhere.

Denoting the foreign ad valorem output or export tax rate as T, the foreign firm's first-order condition for profit maximization, equation (2), becomes

$$(1 - T)[R_2(x, X) - \Gamma R_1(x, X)] - C'(X) = 0. \tag{2'}$$

A Nash equilibrium in policies is a pair of tax-subsidy rates (t, T) such that t maximizes w, given T, and T maximizes $W \equiv R(x, X) - C'(X)$, given t, where equations (1) and (2′) determine x and X.

For $T < 1$, the presence of a foreign tax does not affect the *qualitative* results of the previous section. Theorem 1 is unaffected. For Cournot competition equation (8) is replaced by

$$\frac{r_2(1 - T)R_{21}}{(1 - T)R_{22} - C''} = \frac{tc'}{1 - t}, \tag{8'}$$

so that the sign of t^* remains that of R_{21}. For Bertrand competition the profit of the foreign firm may be written as

$$\Pi(p, P) = (1 - T)PD(p, P) - C(D(p, P)).$$

Appropriate substitution into the previous analysis implies that proposition 2 is unaffected as well. Similarly, proposition 3 remains. Consequently, the *direction* of the optimal policy is unaffected by the possible presence of a foreign export tax or subsidy.

A parallel analysis determines the level of T that maximizes W given t. The following results are immediate.

Under Cournot competition between substitutes with $r_{12} < 0$ and $R_{21} < 0$, the perfect Nash equilibrium is for both governments to subsidize exports. Government interventions together move the product-market equilibrium away from the joint-profit-maximizing outcome toward the competitive equilibrium. Graphically, in terms of figure 11.1, both reaction loci shift outward. Both countries will typically benefit from a mutual agreement to desist from attempts to shift profit homeward via export subsidization. The effect on consumers and on world welfare of such an agreement is, of course, the opposite.

Under Bertrand competition with $\pi_{12} > 0$ and $\Pi_{21} > 0$, the perfect Nash equilibrium is for both governments to tax exports. Intervention moves the equilibrium toward the joint-profit-maximizing point away from the competitive equilibrium. In terms of figure 11.2 both reaction curves shift out. The exporters gain, consumers lose, and world welfare declines.

Finally, if both firms' conjectures are consistent, the perfect Nash equilibrium. is laissez-faire.

3. Optimal Trade Policy: The Case of Multifirm Oligopoly and Consistent Conjectures

In this section we extend our analysis to situations of oligopoly by allowing for the presence of n home firms and m foreign firms in the industry. For analytical convenience we confine our attention to configurations that are *symmetric*, in the sense that (1) each firm, home or foreign, has the same cost function, (2) the revenue functions of any two firms i and j (home or foreign) are identical, except that the arguments x^i and x^j are interchanged, and (3) any two firms producing at the same output level hold the same conjectures about the effect of changes in their own outputs on those of each of their rivals (including each other).

We assume that the conjectures held by all home firms are consistent. We take this as our bench-mark case in order that we may isolate the new implications for trade policy that are introduced when the market structure is oligopolistic rather than duopolistic. When conjectures are other than consistent, the optimal trade policy will incorporate an element of the profit-shifting motive, as discussed in section 1, in addition to the terms-of-trade motive that is the focus of our attention in the present section. We also continue to assume that there is no home consumption of the outputs of the oligopolistic industry. This assumption, too, is dictated by our desire to isolate and discuss a single motive for trade policy at a time. Our basic result is stated in

PROPOSITION 4   In a symmetric, oligopolistic equilibrium with n home firms and m foreign firms and no home consumption, if the domestic firms' conjectures are consistent, then the optimal production or export tax is zero if $n = 1$ and positive if $n > 1$.

Proof   See appendix A. □

The result can be understood intuitively by noting that when home firms' conjectures about the responses of foreign firms are consistent, the profit-shifting motive for government intervention is not present. What remains is the standard terms-of-trade argument for export policy. Whenever there is more than a single home country firm and these firms do not collude perfectly, each home firm imposes a pecuniary externality on other domestic firms when it raises its output. Private incentives lead to socially excessive outputs, since home income includes all home firm profits. The government can enforce the cooperative equilibrium in which the home firms act as a group to maximize the home country's total profit by taxing exports or sales. The externality does not arise when there is only one home firm; consequently, free trade is optimal in that case.

Once we depart from the assumption of consistent conjectures, the profit-shifting and the terms-of-trade motives for trade policy intervention can be present simultaneously. Thus Dixit (1984) finds that for a linear, Cournot, homogeneous-product oligopoly an export subsidy is optimal if the number of domestic firms is not "too large." In this case, the two motives for intervention identified here work in opposition. The two can also be reinforcing, as would generally occur when each of several domestic firms holds Bertrand conjectures.

4. Endogenous Entry and Exit

The analysis up to this point has assumed a fixed, exogenous number of firms. This assumption is reasonable if entry costs are large relative to the effect of policies on total profit or if other government policies determined the number of firms. Otherwise, trade and industrial policies are likely to affect the total number of firms in an industry, both domestically and abroad. A thorough treatment of optimal policies with endogenous market structure lies beyond the scope of this paper. Instead, we discuss how endogenous entry and exit would modify some of our previous results.[12]

The first point to make is that allowing for free entry and exit does not necessarily eliminate the profit-shifting motive for trade or industrial policy. All firms may earn positive profits in a free-entry equilibrium if fixed costs are relatively large compared with market size. Then, despite positive returns to firms present in the market, an additional firm could not enter profitably. Alternatively, heterogeneity among firms could imply zero profit for the marginal entrant but positive profits for inframarginal participants. In either of these cases an incentive remains for governments to use policy to shift profits toward domestic participants in the industry. Only if firms are homogeneous and the market can accommodate a large number of them, so that profits of all firms are identically zero, does the profit-shifting motive for trade or industrial policy vanish.

Two new issues are relevant for the formulation of optimal trade and industrial policy when market structure is endogenous. The first arises because policy alters the total number of firms active in an industry in equilibrium. If governments set their policy parameters before firms choose whether or not to incur their fixed costs of entry, or if firms anticipate policies that will be invoked after entry costs are borne, then export or production subsidies will encourage more firms to be active. This entry can raise industry average cost and cause the addition to national product deriving from profit-shifting to be (more than) dissipated in increased entry fees (see Horstmann and Markusen 1984). Then a tax on exports or production that discourages entry may be called for even when a subsidy would be optimal given an exogenous market structure.

Second, trade and industrial policy alters the relative numbers of domestic and foreign firms. A subsidy to exports or production in the home country causes foreign firms to exit as domestic firms enter. When residual profits exist, the replacement of foreign firms by domestic ones raises national product. Dixit and Kyle (1985) analyze the potential role for trade policy in deterring foreign entry or encouraging domestic entry.[13] In their analysis a subsidy can be optimal even if it entails no profit shifting among a *given* set of firms.

5. Trade and Industrial Policy When Goods Are Consumed Domestically

Thus far we have ruled out domestic consumption of the outputs of the oligopolistic industry under consideration. This has allowed us to focus on the profit-shifting and terms-of-trade motives for trade policy. However, by making this assumption, we have neglected a third way in which interventionist trade or industrial policy might yield welfare gains when markets are imperfectly competitive. Since oligopolistic markets are generally characterized by a difference between the price and the marginal cost of a product, there is a potential second-best role for trade and industrial policy (in the absence of first-best antitrust policy) to reduce this distortion.

When domestic consumption is positive, production taxes or subsidies and export taxes or subsidies are no longer identical. In this section we shall consider the welfare effects of both types of policies in the duopoly model of section 2, recognizing that if we were to allow for the existence of more than one domestic firm, the national-market-power motive for taxation of output or exports would also be present. In addition, in order to focus on the considerations for trade and industrial policy introduced by the presence of domestic consumption, we shall continue to use the consistent-conjectures duopoly model as our benchmark case.

To make our point as simply as possible, we assume that the duopolistic competitors produce a single, homogeneous good. We also assume perfect arbitrage with zero transport costs, so that under a production tax or subsidy consumers at home and abroad face the same price for the product. Thus, we consider the case of an integrated world market, where the potential second-best role for trade policy as a substitute for domestic antitrust policy is greatest.[14]

Production Tax or Subsidy

Let $p(x + X)$ be the inverse world demand function, and let home country direct demand be $h(p)$. The corresponding foreign demand is $H(p)$. If a production tax at rate t is imposed, the profit of the domestic firm is $\pi = (1 - t)p(x + X)x - c(x)$. Consumer surplus at home is $\int_p^\infty h(q)\, dq$.[15] Domestic tax revenue is tpx. Summing these gives total home country welfare from producing, consuming, and taxing the product:

$$w = px - c + \int_p^\infty h(q)\, dq.$$

The change in home welfare resulting from a small change in the output tax is

$$\frac{dw}{dt} = (p + xp' - c')\frac{dx}{dt} + xp'\frac{dX}{dt} - h\frac{dp}{dt}.$$

Upon substitution of the first-order condition for the home firm's profit maximization, this becomes

$$\frac{dw}{dt} = \{xp'(g - \gamma) + t[p + xp'(1 + \gamma)]\}\frac{dx}{dt} - h\frac{dp}{dt}. \tag{12}$$

Evaluating (12) at $t = 0$, and imposing the condition that conjectures are consistent ($g = \gamma$), we find that $dw/dt = -hdp/dt$. The choice between a production tax and a production subsidy hinges on which policy lowers the price faced by domestic consumers, thereby reducing the consumption distortion associated with imperfect competition.

It is easy to calculate $dp/dt = p'(x + X)(dx + dX)/dt$. Applying Cramer's rule to the total differentials of the two firms' first-order conditions, we have

$$\frac{d(x + X)}{dt} = \frac{c'}{\Delta}[(C' - p)X - C''], \tag{13}$$

where Δ is the determinant of the 2×2 Jacobian matrix, and is assumed to be positive for stability. If foreign marginal cost is increasing ($C'' > 0$), then $p > C'$, and the right-hand side of (13) is unambiguously negative. A production subsidy raises world output, and hence lowers world price. Alternatively, if marginal costs at home and abroad are constant ($c'' = 0$ and $C'' = 0$), then the consistent conjectures equilibrium is the Bertrand equilibrium (see Bresnahan 1981), so that $p = C'$ and $d(x + X)/dt = 0$. In this case the optimal industrial policy is laissez-faire.

PROPOSITION 5   In a homogeneous product duopoly with consistent conjectures and nonzero domestic consumption,

1. if $c'' = 0$ and $C'' = 0$, then $t^* = 0$,
2. if $C'' > 0$, then $t^* < 0$.

Trade Tax or Subsidy
Finally, we consider the welfare effects of a small export tax or import subsidy at rate τ.[16] Under this policy domestic consumers pay a price $p(1 - \tau)$ for the good, and home government revenue is $p\tau(x - h)$. The world inverse demand function is now written as $p(x + X, \tau)$, where $p_1 = 1/\{H'(p) + (1 - \tau)h'[p(1 - \tau)]\}$ and $p_2 = ph'[p(1 - \tau)]p_1$. Proceeding as before, we find that

$$\frac{dw}{d\tau}\bigg|_{\tau=0} = hp_1 \frac{d(x + X)}{d\tau} + p_2(x - h).$$

In this case, however, it is no longer possible to sign unambiguously the effect of a small trade tax or subsidy on total world output. In addition, there is a second term that now enters the expression for $dw/d\tau$, which at $\tau = 0$ is unambiguously positive or negative depending upon whether the home country is a net exporter or importer of the product. Given total output, an export tax raises the world price of an export good, while an import tariff lowers the world price of an import good. This standard terms-of-trade effect provides a further motive for an export tax or import tariff, just as it does when the market is competitive.

To recapitulate the arguments of this subsection, a trade policy of either sign may raise domestic welfare in a duopolistic market with domestic consumption. When conjectures are consistent, any profit-shifting motive for policy intervention is absent. What remains is a standard terms-of-trade motive on the consumption side, and what might be termed a "consumption-distortion motive," arising from the gap between price and marginal cost. The former always indicates an export tax or import tariff, while the latter may favor either a tax or a subsidy, depending on the precise forms of the demand and cost functions.

6. Conclusions

We have analyzed the welfare effects of trade policy and industrial policy (production taxes and subsidies) for a range of specifications of an oligopolistic industry. A number of general propositions for optimal policy emerge. First, either trade policy or industrial policy may raise domestic welfare if oligopolistic profits can be shifted to home country firms. Policies that achieve this profit shifting can work only if the government is able to set its policy in advance of firms' production decisions, and if government policy commitments are credible. Furthermore, in the duopoly case, profits can be shifted only if firms' conjectural variations differ from the true equilibrium responses that would result if they were to alter their output levels. The choice between a tax and a subsidy in this case depends on whether home firm's output in the laissez-faire equilibrium exceeds or falls short of the level that would emerge under "consistent" or Stackelberg conjectures.

Second, whenever there is more than one domestic firm, competition among them is detrimental to home-country social welfare. In other words, there exists a pecuniary externality when each domestic firm does not take into account the effect of its own actions on the profits of other domestic competitors. A production or export tax will lead domestic firms to restrict their outputs, shifting them closer to the level that would result with collusion. In this familiar way a production or export tax enables the home country to exploit its monopoly power in trade fully.

These propositions are unaffected by extension of the analysis to cases in which optimal interventions are set simultaneously by two policy-active governments. But allowing for endogenous entry and exit introduces two new considerations. First, policy-induced entry (exit) could raise (lower) the average cost of production. When subsidies engender profit shifting, the gain in national income can be dissipated in additional entry fees. Second, policy alters the relative numbers of domestic and foreign firms in an oligopolistic industry. In the presence of residual profits there is a potential role for trade or industrial policy that serves to deter foreign entry or promote domestic entry.

Finally, when there is domestic consumption of the output of the oligopolistic industry, there are two further motives for policy intervention. First, consumers' marginal valuation of the product will generally differ from domestic marginal cost of production due to the collective exertion of monopoly power by firms in the industry. A welfare-improving policy for this reason should increase domestic consumption. When industrial policy is used, a production subsidy will achieve this result, whereas the appropriate trade policy instrument may be either an export (or import) tax or an export (or import) subsidy. Second, there is the usual externality caused by the multiplicity of small domestic consumers, who do not take into account the effect of their demands on world prices. Industrial policy cannot be used to overcome this externality, but if the country is a net exporter (importer), an export (import) tax will have a favorable impact on the country's terms of trade. The formulation of optimal trade or industrial policy in general requires the weighting of these various influences.

Appendix A: Proof of Proposition 4

The profit of the representative home firm i is

$$\pi^i = (1 - t)r_i(x^1, \ldots, x^n, X^{n+1}, \ldots, X^{n+m}) - c(x^i),$$

where the t denotes the output or export tax imposed on domestic firms. A typical foreign earns

$$\Pi^j = R_j(x^1, \ldots, x^n, X^{n+1}, \ldots, X^{n+m}) - C(X^j).$$

(A foreign policy may be allowed for by defining R^j to be after-tax revenue.) The first-order conditions for profit maximization are

$$(1 - t)r_i^i - c^{i\prime} + (1 - t) \sum_{\substack{j=1 \\ j \neq i}}^{n+m} r_j^i \gamma^{ij} = 0, \quad i = 1, \ldots, n; \tag{A1a}$$

$$R_i^i - C^{i\prime} + \sum_{\substack{j=1 \\ j \neq i}}^{n+m} R_j^i \Gamma^{ij} = 0, \quad i = n+1, \ldots, n+m, \tag{A1b}$$

where $\gamma^{iy}(\Gamma^{ij})$ is the conjecture by the home (foreign) firm i about the output response by firm j, for $j \neq i, j = 1, \ldots, n+m$.

Home-country national product deriving from this industry is

$$w = \sum_{i=1}^{n} (r^i - c^i). \tag{A2}$$

Differentiating (A2) with respect to t at $t = 0$, and imposing the condition of symmetry of the initial (free trade) equilibrium gives

$$\frac{dw}{dt}\bigg|_{t=0} = nr_2^1\left[(n-1)(1-\gamma)\frac{dx^i}{dt} + m\frac{dX^j}{dt} - m\gamma\frac{dx^i}{dt}\right], \tag{A3}$$

where $\gamma = \gamma^{ij}$ for all $j \neq i, i = 1, \ldots, n+m$.

Next we differentiate the first-order conditions (A1a) and (A1b) and again impose symmetry (i.e., $dx^i = dx^k$ for $i, k = 1, \ldots, n$ and $dX^j = dX^l$ for $j, l = n+1, \ldots, n+m$) to derive

$$\begin{bmatrix} \alpha + (n-1)\beta & m\beta \\ n\beta & \alpha + (m-1)\beta \end{bmatrix}\begin{bmatrix} dx^i \\ dX^j \end{bmatrix} = \begin{bmatrix} \lambda dt \\ 0 \end{bmatrix}, \tag{A4}$$

where

$$\alpha \equiv r_{ii}^i - c^{i\prime} + (n+m-1)r_{ij}^i\gamma,$$

$$\beta \equiv r_{ij}^i + r_{jj}^i\gamma + (n+m-2)r_{jk}^i\gamma,$$

$$\gamma \equiv r_j^i + (n+m-1)r_j^i\gamma.$$

Note that the free trade equilibrium has symmetry not only among home firms, but also between home and foreign firms, so that about this point $r_i^i = R_j^j$ and similarly for other derivatives. Using this fact and solving (A4) gives

$$\frac{dx^i}{dt} = \frac{[\alpha + (m-1)\beta]\lambda}{(\alpha - \beta)[\alpha + (n+m-1)\beta]} \tag{A5a}$$

and

$$\frac{dX^j}{dt} = \frac{-n\beta\lambda}{(\alpha - \beta)[(\alpha + (n+m-1)\beta)]}. \tag{A5b}$$

The value of γ determined by imposing the condition that conjectures be consistent is found by perturbing the equilibrium in (A1a) and (A1b) by an exogenous shift in the output of one firm, e.g., x^1, and solving for the full equilibrium response dx^i/dx^1, $i \neq 1$ (see the discussion in Perry (1982), especially footnote 7). Doing so, we find that

$$\gamma = -\frac{\beta}{\alpha + (n + m - 1)\beta}. \tag{A6}$$

Finally, we substitute (A5a), (A5b), and (A6) into (A3), and perform some straightforward algebraic manipulations, which yield

$$\left.\frac{dw}{dt}\right|_{t=0} = \frac{n(n - 1)r_2^1\lambda}{\alpha + (n + m - 2)\beta}. \tag{A7}$$

The denominator of (A7) must be negative for stability of the industry equilibrium (Seade 1980). From the first-order condition (A1a), $\lambda = c^{i\prime}/(1 - t) > 0$. The sign of expression (A7) is consequently opposite to that of r_2^1 if $n > 1$, i.e., positive for goods that are substitutes. For $n = 1$, the expression is zero. $\square$

Notes

1. Spencer and Brander (1983) study a two-stage game in which a capacity or R&D investment is made at a stage prior to production. In such a setting, export subsidies and R&D subsidies are each welfare improving if implemented separately, but an optimal policy package involves an export subsidy and an R&D tax. Brander and Spencer (1984) extend the basic argument for intervention to situations in which duopolistic competition takes place in the home market. In such cases an import tariff often is beneficial.

2. We recognize the serious limitation of the conjectural variations framework in its attempt to collapse the outcome of what is actually a dynamic process into a static formulation. While there exist extensive-form representations of Cournot and Bertrand competition, such is not the case for other conjectural assumptions, including that of consistent conjectures" introduced below. Nevertheless, characterizing the equilibrium in terms of conjectural variations does provide a parsimonious representation of alternative assumptions of firm interaction that includes Cournot and Bertrand equilibria as special cases. In addition, this approach highlights the source of the potential benefit from policy intervention, namely, the deviation between conjectured and actual responses.
Ideally, oligopolistic behavior would be modeled as a truly dynamic, multistage game. Since the development of such models remains, as of now, at a fairly nascent stage, and since existing work on optimal trade policy under oligopoly has been formulated in terms of static models, we choose to pursue the simpler conjectural variations approach.
Note that, within the class of static, conjectural variations models, restricting

attention to those involving output rivalry entails no loss of generality. Kamien and Schwartz (1983) demonstrate that any conjectural variations equilibrium (CVE) in quantities has a corresponding CVE in prices.

3. Analysis of government policy in international markets typically is based on this assumption. See, for example, Spencer and Brander (1983). It may be justified by specifying the political process of establishing policy as time-consuming and costly, or by endowing the government with a reputation for adhering to announced policy.

4. The case of complementary goods can be analyzed similarly. When the two goods are complements ($r_2 > 0$), some of the results reported here (e.g. theorem 1) are reversed.

5. For concreteness, we consider the case of ad valorem taxes and subsidies. Our results would not be affected by the introduction of *specific* taxes and subsidies, as the reader may verify.

6. We henceforth drop the arguments of the revenue and cost functions and their partial derivatives whenever no confusion is created by doing so. The revenue functions and their partial derivatives are understood to be evaluated at the equilibrium value of (x, X), while the cost functions and their derivatives are evaluated at x or X, whichever is appropriate.

7. The second-order condition for a maximum is satisfied locally as long as (1) the home firm's first- and second-order conditions for profit maximization are satisfied and (2) the foreign firm's actual response to a change in x does not differ substantially from the response conjectured by the home firm.

8. If products are complements ($r_2 > 0$), the presumption is also in favor of an export subsidy, since in this case most specifications of demand, including the linear, imply that $R_{21} > 0$: the rival expands output when the domestic firm does, to the benefit of the home firm. The home firm consequently produces less, in Cournot competition, than it would as a Stackelberg leader.

9. When products are complements, $D_2 < 0$. The presumption then is that $\Pi_{21} < 0$: a price increase by the home firm engenders a price cut by its competitor. So, in this case as well, an export tax is optimal. Such a tax causes the foreign firm to lower its price, increasing the home firm's revenue.

10. Our findings for the cases of Cournot and Bertrand competition can be stated concisely using the phraseology suggested by Bulow, Geanokoplos, and Klemperer (1985). They introduce the terms strategic substitutes" and "strategic complements" to denote situations where "more aggressive" behavior on the part of one firm, respectively, lowers and raises the "marginal profitability" of similar moves by its rival. The classification of goods as strategic subsitutes or complements can be made only after the designation of a specific strategy variable, which then gives meaning to the term "more aggressive." For Cournot and Bertrand competition, in which quantity and price are the strategy variables, respectively, their classification hinges on the slope of the reaction curves in the relevant strategy spaces. Accordingly, our propositions 1 and 2 could be rephrased as follows: *for Cournot and Bertrand competition among (ordinary) substitutes, optimal policy involves subsidizing exports if the goods are strategic substitutes and taxing exports otherwise.* If the goods

instead are (ordinary) complements, then the opposite correspondence between strategic substitutes and complements and optimal policy obtains.

11. The second-order condition for a social optimum is satisfied at the free-trade equilibrium if the product-market equilibrium is stable.

12. Horstmann and Markusen (1984) and Venables (1985) analyze the effects of trade policy with free entry for the case of Cournot competition. The first authors assume, as we do in section 5, that world markets are integrated. The second assumes segmented national markets. Both assume large numbers of homogeneous firms, so that all firms' profits are zero.

13. In Venables (1985) the simultaneous exit of foreign firms and entry of an equal number of domestic firms is beneficial because national markets are segmented and transport costs are present. For a given total number of firms, consumer prices at home are lower the greater is the relative number of domestic participants.

14. If world markets are segmented, as has been assumed in a number of the previous studies of trade policy under conditions of oligopoly (e.g., Dixit 1984; Krugman 1984), then trade policy can act as a second-best substitute for domestic antitrust policy only to the extent that marginal cost is not constant, so that the quantities supplied by an oligopolist to the various markets are interdependent.

15. We assume that this integral is bounded.

16. One consequence of our assumption that world markets are integrated is that at most one firm will export. Two-way trade of the sort discussed by Brander (1981) will not emerge as an equilibrium outcome. Thus, our trade policy tool τ, which combines a production tax and a consumption subsidy at equal rates, corresponds to an expert tax or an import subsidy, depending on the direction of net industry trade.

References

Brander, J. A. 1981. Intra-industry trade in identical commodities. *Journal of International Economics* 11, 1–14.

Brander, J. A., and B. J. Spencer. 1984. Tariff protection and imperfect competition. In H. Kierzkowski, ed., *Monopolistic Competition in International Trade*. Oxford: Oxford University Press, pp. 194–206.

Brander, J. A., and B. J. Spencer. 1985 Export subsidies and international market share rivalry. *Journal of International Economics* 18, 83–100.

Bresnahan, T. F. 1981. Duopoly models with consistent conjectures. *American Economic Review* 71, 934–945.

Bulow, J. I., J. D. Geanakoplos, and P. D. Klemperer. 1985. Multimarket oligopoly: strategic subsitutes and complements. *Journal of Political Economy* 93, 488–511.

Dixit, A. K. 1984. International trade policy for oligopolistic industries. *Economic Journal Conference Papers* 94, 1–16.

Dixit, A. K., and A. S. Kyle. 1985. The use of protection and subsidies for entry promotion and deterrence. *American Economic Review* 75, 139–152.

Horstmann, I., and J. R. Markusen. 1984. Up your average cost curve: Inefficient entry and the new protectionism. Mimeographed, November.

Kamien, M. I., and N. L. Schwartz. 1983. Conjectural variations. *Canadian Journal of Economics*, 16, 191–211.

Krugman, P. R. 1984. Import protection as export promotion: International competition in the presence of oligopoly and economies of scale. In H. Kierzkowski, ed., *Monopolistic Competition in International Trade*. Oxford: Oxford University Press, pp. 180–193.

Perry, M. K. 1982. Oligopoly and consistent conjectural variations. *Bell Journal of Economics* 13, 197–205.

Seade, J. K. 1980. On the effects of entry. *Econometrica* 48, 479–489.

Spencer, B. J., and J. A. Brander. 1983. International R&D rivalry and industrial strategy. *Review of Economic Studies* 50, 702–722.

Venables, A. J. 1985 Trade and trade policy with imperfect competition: The case of indentical products and free entry. *Journal of International Economics* 19, 1–20.

12

International Trade Policy for Oligopolistic Industries

Avinash Dixit

Almost all of the received theory of international trade, positive and normative, is based on the model of atomistic competition. All individual consumers and producers are assumed to be price-takers. It is recognized that a country may have monopoly power in trade, but this is supposed to be exercised by its government through the use of tariffs.

In reality, it is becoming increasingly evident that a significant proportion of international trade takes place in imperfectly competitive markets. Here the individual producers and sellers are aware of their monopoly power, and act to profit from it. The resulting markte equilibrium—be it pure monopoly, oligopoly, or monopolistic competition—differs from the textbook Walrasian kind. The determinants and patterns of trade are different, and are differently affected by commerical policy. A new framework of theoretical analysis is therefore required for a proper understanding of many current issues of trade, and of trade policy.

Such research is still in its infancy but is growing rapidly. This lecture is intended to provide a consolidation, and some extension, of the work. I shall begin by describing the new issues that arise when trade is imperfectly competitive, and some new features of the analysis. Then I shall give a brief and somewhat selective review of the literature. Finally, I shall construct a model that synthesises and extends some of the work on trade policy in the context of oligopoly.

1. General Remarks on Imperfectly Competitive Trade

The reasons for the emergence of imperfect competition in international trade are similar to those familiar from the theory of domestic industrial

This paper was originally published in *The Economic Journal* 94, supplement (1983): 1–16. The present version omits section 3 of the original article.

organisation. In both cases we are looking for forces that produce concentrated industries that are sheltered from competition in the relevant market. Of course some new aspects become important in the context of trade.

Let us begin by considering economies of scale and scope, which dictate that firms should have a large scale or product mix. At the level of the production technology, one would expect the importance of this to decrease as international trade enlarges the market. But in some industries, scale economies at the firm's organisation level arise because there are intangible assets such as knowledge or specific managerial skills that cannot be traded in arm's-length markets. This problem is if anything more serious at an international level.[1] Such industries come to consist of few and large multi-national firms, and become oligopolistic.

Next consider entry barriers. These can be innocent consequences of technological features, or erected by incumbents in their strategic interests.[2] With international trade, such strategic behaviour may also occur in a government's actions, i.e. imperfect competition may be a deliberate policy choice.

Third, there is product differentiation, which may be geographic when transport costs are present, or in physical characteristics when tastes differ, or in brand images created by persuasive advertising. In all such cases, the size of the competing market is reduced, and the monopoly power of each firm is increased. Where the product attribute is a non-marketable asset, this interacts with the emergence of large multi-national firms.

Finally, even when production takes place in atomistic units, marketing and trade can be oligopolistic. This can be so when these activities are carried out by a few trading corporations. More important instances are those where collusion among a country's firms for export purposes is encouraged or even arranged by its government. In such cases countries are the units of analysis, and trade is naturally oligopolistic.

The theory of this subject accordingly combines elements from the fields of international trade and industrial organisation, and occasionally goes beyond both.

As regards the technique of analysis, most of the work follows the tradition of industrial organisation in its use of industry analysis or partial equilibrium models. Two aspects of this deserve comment: the neglect of income effects and the exogeneity of factor prices. The former is relatively innocuous in this context. From a comparative static point of view, what is relevant is the extent of the feedback from the profits generated within this industry on the demand for its own product. For most industries, it will be a reasonable approximation to assume this away. As regards welfare, the relevant deadweight losses arise from substitution, not from income effects. The important theoretical advantage of the partial equilibrium formulation is that the profit-maximisation objective of firms can be rigorously justified. In general equilibrium with income effects, consumers' utilities cannot be measured in money terms, and therefore shareholders in monopolistic firms are not agreed about the aim of profit-maximisation.

The neglect of factor price determination may also seem harmless when studying one industry, but this approach clashes with a central concern of trade theory. If factor prices are exogenous to this industry, so is its cost function. This precludes the endogenous determination of international differences in costs, and hence of the pattern of trade itself. More precisely, the pattern of inter-industry trade is kept outside the scope of the analysis. Any two-way trade within this industry is determined as a part of its equilibrium, and that is perhaps as much as we should expect from industry analysis.

The combination of international trade and industrial organisation produces several features of analysis that are novel to the workers in the separate areas. For international economists, there are new aspects of competition, such as quality, advertising research and development, new dimensions of firms' behaviour including strategic moves such as threats and promises, and new equilibrium concepts appropriate to imperfectly competitive markets, for example, Cournot. For industrial economists, there are new reasons for inter-firm cost differences, namely international differences of factor prices, transport costs, taxes, and tariffs.

There are also new aspects on the normative side. In a closed economy, all the effects of a policy instrument would be included in the government's objective function: the surpluses of all consumers, the profits of all firms, and the tax revenues. Trade theorists are used to the idea that one country's objective does not encompass consumers resident in other countries; the optimum tariff that exploits a country's monopoly power in trade is a consequence of this. However, in conventional trade theory with constant returns to scale and perfect competition, there are no pure profits of firms. When there are monopoly profits, each country has an interest in attempting to annexe them for its own residents. If international equity markets are perfect, and ownership of firms' shares is well diversified across countries, this need not have any special implications for trade policy. However, to the extent that the firms located in each country are predominantly owned by its residents, policies that increase homw firms' profits at the expense of foreign firms will have an element of added attraction.

Finally, the fact that different countries' governments are conducting their trade policies simultaneously introduces the dimension of strategic interaction among governments. This exists even when the market equilibrium for any given set of policies is perfectly competitive,[3] but oligopolistic interactions among private producers can significantly alter the ways in which policies interact.

Most of the issues described above have been touched on somewhere in the research that exist in this area. Much of it, however, is directed towards just one policy question, namely the efficacy of trade restrictions under imperfect competition. It is natural that researchers should think of this question, since they come to it from the background of trade policy analysis under atomistic competition, where the role of trade restrictions is known to be minimal. For a small country without domestic distortions and in absence of distributional issues, free trade is optimum even if other countries impose restrictions. Trade restrictions do provide indirect methods for partial correction of domestic distortions and for income redistribution, but these problems are always better handled by other instruments, such as production and consumption taxes or subsidies, that are directly targeted to the problem.[4] The selfish desire of a country possessing monopoly power in trade to improve its commodity terms of trade is the only 'first-best' justification for a policy of departure from free trade. Given these strong results of the perfect competition assumption, it is natural to ask how far they remain valid when competition is imperfect.

Recent research has brought to light some new ways in which trade restrictions can be beneficial to a country in these circumstances. But these results have only compared such policies to complete laissez-faire. There has not yet been any systematic work comparing alternatives to trade policy. Thus we do not yet know whether, or when, trade restrictions are first-best policies, and when other instruments would achieve the same aims more efficiently. This seems an important area of future research. The point should also be borne in mind when interpreting the results of the effects of tariffs discussed in this paper. Any attempts to justify protection on the basis of these results would be, at a minimum, premature.

2. Brief Review of the Literature

There are many forms of imperfect competition, differing in their scope of applicability and methods of analysis. Pure monopoly is the simplest, since it avoids game-theoretic difficulties. Consumers act as price-takers, and their behaviour determines the monopolist's economic environment, i.e. the demand curve. He then maximises profit over this. Thus familiar optimisation methods yield the solution. We can readily extend the analysis to the case of price leadership which is really just pure monopoly exercised over the residual demand curve, obtained by subtracting the supply of the price-taking fringe sellers from total demand. It is therefore natural that cases of pure monopoly or leadership in trade are the most thoroughly studied.

Such models fall into several different categories. The first case is that of a domestic monopolist of price-leader in an import-competing industry. Here trade serves to limit this monopoly power (i.e., acts as an instrument of domestic anti-trust policy). Protection is accordingly especially harmful. The case of tariffs is studied by Corden (1967). Tariffs and quotas are compared by Bhagwati (1965), who finds that quotas are even more conducive to the exercise of domestic monopoly.

Next consider an exporting firm with monopoly in the domestic market. It may or may not have monopoly power in the export markets, but we would typically expect the degree of such monopoly power to be smaller. To the extent that other countries' anti-dumping laws allow, and protection from re-imports is available, the firm would like to charge a higher price in the home market than for exports. The home country's interest, on the other hand, calls for marginal cost pricing at home and exercise of monopoly abroad. Various aspects of this are studied by Katrak (1980), Rieber (1982), Davies and McGuinness (1982), and others. A particularly interesting issue is that of pricing when discrimination across countries is not allowed. Auquier and Caves (1979) examine the second-best policy trading off domestic monopoly welfare losses against the monopoly profits from exports. Jacquemin (1982) shows how the existence of a competitive export opportunity can serve to limit the exercise of domestic monopoly power in such a setting.

In the opposite case, a foreign firm has monopoly or leadership power in the home market, and earns pure profits. Now protection will enable the home country to capture some of this profit, either in the form of tariff revenues or by increasing home firms' profits. This will make some protection desirable from the viewpoint of the home country, although there is a loss of home consumer surplus that must be set against this. The optimum tariff policy in such circumstances is characterised by Katrak (1977) and Brander and Spencer (1981). They do not compare protection with other policies to extract profits from foreign firms, but DeMeza (1979) considers price controls.

International cartels are extensively studied and surveyed (e.g., Caves 1979), so I shall not discuss them here. A producing country's export tax policy to extract some profit from such a cartel is studied in Dixit and Stern (1982).

Next to pure monopoly, the industry structure most amenable to analysis is that of monopolistic competition. This has been thoroughly analysed (e.g., Krugman 1979, 1980; Dixit and Norman 1980; Lancaster 1980; Helpman 1981). The particular attraction of this work is the distinction it draws between intra-industry trade, based on product diversity and scale economies, and inter-industry trade, explained by the usual factor endowment considerations. The result that intra-industry trade would be most prominent among similar economies accords well with recent facts. From a normative viewpoint, such trade has the added mutual benefit of greater product variety. For fairly similar economies, this benefit can be strong enough to outweigh the distributional conflict arising from Stolper-Samuelson effects, making free trade preferable for all with no need for transfers; see Krugman (1981).

The case of oligopoly is conceptually and analytically the most difficult. Work on it so far consists of special models and examples. I shall review them here, and in the next section develop a somewhat more general model that brings together some of their features.

Markusen (1981) is closest to the tradition of trade theory. He has a two-sector general equilibrium model, with a competitives sector Y and an oligopoly sector X. More precisely, there is one producer of X in each country, and they interact as Cournot duopolists. Now country size is a determinant of trade. The larger country imports X, and if its own production of X decreases sufficiently, trade may lower its aggregate welfare.

Brander and Krugman (1980) examine a similar model in partial equilibrium, which brings out a new feature of oligopolistic trade. Firms with different marginal costs can coexist in an imperfectly competitive market for a homogeneous product, if the higher-cost firm perceives an appropriately larger demand elasticity and therefore uses a correspondingly lower mark-up. With Cournot behaviour, the perceived demand elasticity for a firm is the industry elasticity divided by the firm's market share. Thus higher-cost firms have lower market shares in Cournot equilibrium. Brander and Krugman consider identical countries with transport costs between them. Then each country's firm has a cost disadvantage in its export market, so in each market the home firm has a share above 50 percent. But some two-way trade occurs so long as transport costs fall short of each country's monopoly markup. It might seem that such transhipment of identical products is a waste of resources, but there is an offsetting benefit since the duopoly price is below the monopoly price that would prevail under autarky. The net benefit can be positive or negative depending on transport costs and demand elasticities.

Tariff policies in a similar model and analysed by Brander and Spencer (1982a) and Krugman (1982). The former consider optimum tariffs from the point of view of one country, and point out that the existence of a home firm strengthens the profit-extraction role of tariffs by making it possible to divert profits to the home firm. They do not compare tariffs with other instruments, but do recognise that the countries' rivalry in tariff-setting will lead to excessive protection. Krugman allows economies of scale at the margin. Now protection shifts the duopoly equilibrium in the home market so that the home firm's sales there rise and the foreign firm's sales fall. This lowers the home firm's marginal cost and raises that of the foreign firm. Then the equilibrium in the foreign market also shifts in the home firm's favour. Thus import restriction can act as export promotion. It should be emphasised that here, too, other instruments are not considered, and that both countries' pursuit of such policies will be mutually destructive. It should also be noted that the export-promoting effect of tariffs applies only to intra-industry trade; exports of other industries will be discouraged in the usual way through the operation of Lerner symmetry. Brander and Spencer (1982b) consider the strategic use of research and development by a country's government to give its firms an advantage in international competition.

Quite a different strategic use of trade restrictions is pointed out by Krishna (1983). Consider a duopoly where the home and the foreign firm are unable to sustain collusion by themselves. Now let the home government impose an import quota. This makes it profitable for the home firm to raise its price somewhat, with the assurance that the foreign firm will not be able to sell more by undercutting. Then the foreign firm can sell its quota amount at a higher price. This can increase both firms' profits. The effect of the quota is to allow collusion (i.e., it is a "facilitating practice"). The losers are the home consumers who now pay a higher price. This model has special appeal from the viewpoint of the "new political economy," which views trade policy as an outcome of lobbying by concentrated special interest groups.

Finally, Ordover and Willig (1983) study mergers policy with oligopolistic trade. Some of their results will be rederived in the context of the model of the next section.

3. Concluding Comments

We have seen that the policies appropriate when trade occurs in an oligopolistic market differ in significant respects from the ones designed for competitive conditions. The possibility that a partly countervailing duty may be desirable when a foreign country subsidises exports, and that some relaxation of domestic anti-trust activity or some rationalisation may be justifiable, are prominent examples.

However, this conclusion should be qualified in two important ways. As a matter of theoretical analysis, we have not yet seen whether other policies can achieve the same benefits more efficiently than trade restrictions. This must be done, especially in view of the strong presumption in this matter that we have from competitive analysis.

Perhaps even more important is a practical matter. Vested interests want protection, and relaxation of anti-trust activity, for their own selfish reasons. They will be eager to seize upon any theoretical arguments that advance such policies in the general interest. Distortion and misuse of the arguments is likely, and may result in the emergence of policies that cause aggregate welfare loss while providing private gains to powerful special groups.

Perhaps the best way to convey this point is by clarifying my title, "International Trade Policy for Oligopolistic Industries." The dictionary defines several senses of the preposition "for." The one I intend is "with respect to," but there is considerable danger that in the actual use of such policies the operative sense will be "in favour of." Economists should guard against this twist, and strive to prevent it.

Notes

1. See Caves (1982, pp. 3–8) for a fuller discussion of intangible assets in this context.

2. Salop (1979) defines and analyses different kinds of entry barriers.

3. See Mayer (1981) for a recent analysis.

4. See Bhagwati (1971). A more recent survey is in Dixit (1983).

References

Auquier, A., and Caves, R. E. 1979, 'Monopolistic export industries, trade taxes, and optimal competition policy. *Economic Journal* 89, 559–581.

Bhagwati, J. 1965. On the equivalence of tariffs and quotas. In *Trade, Growth and the Balance of Payments*, ed. R. E. Baldwin. Amsterdam: North-Holland.

Bhagwati, J. 1971. The generalized theory of distortions and welfare. In *Trade, Balance of Payments and Growth*, eds. J. Bhagwati et al. Amsterdam: North-Holland.

Brander, J. A. and Krugman, P. R. 1980. A reciprocal dumping model of international trade. Paper presented at the Summer Workshop on International Trade and Finance, Warwick University.

Brander, J. A., and Spencer, B. J. 1981. Tariffs and the extraction of foreign monopoly rents under potential entry. *Canadian Journal of Economics* 14, 371–389.

Brander, J. A., and Spencer, B. J. 1982a. Tariff protection and imperfect competition. In *Monopolistic Competition in International Trade*, ed. H. Kierzkowski. Oxford: Oxford University Press.

Brander, J. A., and Spencer, B. J. 1982b. International R&D rivalry and industrial strategy. *Review of Economic Studies.* Forthcoming.

Caves, R. E. 1979. International cartels and monopolies in international trade. In *International Economic Policy*, eds. R. Dornbusch and J. Frenkel. Baltimore: Johns Hopkins, University Press.

Caves, R. E. 1982. *Multinational Enterprise and Economic Analysis.* Cambridge: Cambridge University Press.

Corden, W. M. 1967. Monopoly, tariffs and subsidies. *Economica* 34, 59–68.

Davies, S. W., and McGuinness, A. J. 1982. Dumping at less than marginal cost. *Journal of International Economics* 12, 169–182.

DeMeza, D. 1979. Commerical policy towards multinational monopolies—Reservations on Katrak. *Oxford Economic Papers* 31, 334–337.

Dixit, A. 1983. Tax policy in open economies. In *The Handbook of Public Economics*, eds. A. Auerbach and M. Feldstein. Amsterdam: North-Holland.

Dixit, A., and Norman. V. 1980. *Theory of International Trade.* Welwyn: Nisbets and Cambridge: Cambridge University Press.

Dixit, A., and Stern, N. 1982. Oligopoly and welfare: A unified presentation with applications to trade and development. *European Economic Review* 19, 123–143.

Hahn, F. H. 1962. The stability of the Cournot oligopoly solution. *Review of Economic Studies* 32, 329–331.

Helpman, E. 1981. International trade in the presence of product differentiation economies of scale, and monopolistic competition. *Journal of International Economics* 11, 305–340.

Jacquemin, A. 1982. Imperfect market structures and international trade: Some recent research. *Kyklos* 35, 75–93.

Katrak, H. 1977. Multi-national monopolies and commerical policy. *Oxford Economic Papers* 29, 283–291.

Katrak, H. 1980. Multi-national monopolies and regulation. *Oxford Economic Papers* 32, 453–466.

Krishna, K. 1983. Trade restrictions as facilitating practices. Manuscript, Princeton University.

Krugman, P. R. 1979. Increasing returns, monopolistic competition, and international trade. *Journal of International Economics* 9, 469–479.

Krugman, P. R. 1980. Scale economies, product differentiation, and the pattern of trade. *American Economic Review* 70, 950–959.

Krugman, P. R. 1981. Intraindustry specialization and the gains from trade. *Journal of Political Economy* 89, 959–973.

Krugman, P. R. 1982. Impoart protection as export promotion: International competition in the presence of oligopoly and economies of scale. In *Monopolistic Competition in International Trade*, ed. H. Kierzkowski. Oxford: Oxford University Press.

Lancaster, K. 1980. Intra-industry trade under perfect monopolistic competition. *Journal of International Economics* 10, 151–175.

Markusen, J. R. 1981. Trade and gains from trade with imperfect competition. *Journal of International Economics* 11, 531–551.

Mayer, W. 1981. Theoretical considerations on negotiated tariff adjustments. *Oxford Economic Papers* 33, 135–153.

Ordover, J. A., and Willig, R. D. 1983. Perspectives on mergers and world competition. Paper presented at NBER conference on Strategic Behavior in International Trade (March).

Rieber, W. J. 1982. Discriminating monopoly and international trade. *Economic Journal* 92, 365–376.

Salop, S. 1979. Strategic entry deterrence. *American Economic Review* 69, Papers and Proceedings, 335–338.

Seade, J. K. 1980. The stability of Cournot revisited. *Journal of Economic Theory* 23, 15–27.

IV
**Quotas and Voluntary
Export Restraints (VERs)**

Introduction to Part IV

Part IV addresses important areas of the "positive" theory of tariffs that have engaged much attention recently.

The first area concerns the question whether tariffs and quotas are equivalent. This question was opened up by my Haberler *Festschrift* paper (in R. Caves, H. G. Johnson, and P. B. Kenen, eds., *Trade, Growth and the Balance of Payments*, Rand McNally, 1965), where I noted that when competitive market-structure assumptions were dropped in a partial-equilibrium framework, the replacement of a tariff by a quota at the level of imports generated by the tariff would not necessarily create an implicit tariff identical to the (explicit) tariff that had been replaced by the quota. The voluminous literature that has followed this paper has then focused on two questions.

First, if tariffs and quotas are equivalent in the sense defined by me, then the real equilibrium and welfare implications of tariffs and (equivalent) quotas are also identical. But suppose that they are *not* equivalent. Then the analyst could well go further and ask which instrument will produce higher welfare, holding *some* target variable (e.g., domestic, import-competing production) constant. This opens up therefore a differently oriented "equivalence" literature. Among important contributions to this type of analysis are the papers of McCulloch and Johnson (*American Economic Review*, September 1973), Fishelson and Flatters (*Journal of International Economics*, November 1975), and Pelcovits (*Journal of International Economics*, November 1976). Next, analysis has proceeded in the direction of exploring equivalence in a general equilibrium framework. Carlos Rodriguez's paper in chapter 13 asks if the Cournot-Johnson analysis of optimum tariffs and retaliation is reexamined by substituting optimum quotas for the optimum tariffs, will the outcome be different? Johnson's analysis allows for the possibility that, despite retaliation, a country exercising its monopoly power could wind up better off than under free trade. By contrast, Rodriguez (and Tower in an independent analysis with similar results in *Review of Economic Studies*, 1975) shows that the optimum quota retaliation relentlessly restricts trade, asymptotically approaching autarky. The differential outcome under tariff and quota retaliation reflects the fact that although a quota and a tariff are equivalent at any one point in the process, they change differently a country's offer curve that the other country faces, hence its response and hence the path characterizing the retaliatory process.

The second area concerns the effects of voluntary export restrictions (VERs). The growing literature on VERs has focused on several issues recently, such as on the transfer of rents to exporters that emerges if VERs replace otherwise equivalent import-country restrictions. The emerging political economy literature focuses on this transfer to theorize about why VERs have proliferated in preference to nondiscriminatory import tariffs.

The Feenstra paper (chapter 14) on the effects of VERs by the United States on autos is focused rather on other aspects of the VER analysis. In particular, it is a brilliant empirical analysis of the quality upgrading of imported autos that the VERs induced. An appendix, invaluable to students, has been specially added on the burgeoning theoretical and econometric literature on quality upgrading that has subsequently emerged.

13

The Non-Equivalence of Tariffs and Quotas under Retaliation

Carlos Alfredo Rodriguez

The standard Marshallian demonstration that, except for revenue effects, tariffs and quotas are equivalent has been reexamined in recent theoretical contributions. Bhagwati (1965) reopened the issue by demonstrating the possibility of non-equivalence in the presence of monopoly, with subsequent contributions by Shibata (1968) and him (1968) distinguishing between alternative ways of defining equivalence but underlining the same basic conclusion that the equivalence proposition could break down in the presence of monopoly. Subsequently, the theoretical analysis of non-equivalence has been extended to the case of U.S. oil-type quotas by McCulloch and Johnson (1973).[1] Yet another theoretical contribution by Fishelson and Flatters (1973) has examined the non-equivalence that would arise under uncertainty.[2]

In this note we extend the theoretical analysis of non-equivalence of tariffs and quotas by introducing the possibility of retaliation. By using a Cournot-Johnson type of retaliation mechanism (such that each country in a two-country system chooses an optimal quota in light of the quota-shifted foreign offer curve facing it and ignoring the consequences of its choice on the quota-level that the foreign country would choose in retaliation), we show that a protective warfare which uses quotas will lead, in general, to a different outcome than when tariffs are the weapons chosen. We also show that, contrary to the case of optimum-tariff retaliation analyzed by Johnson (1953) where the tariff warfare may nontheless improve the welfare of the country which initiated the war, the case of optimal-quota retaliation inexorably leads to elimination of trade and the consequent loss of welfare to each of the trading countries.

We assume two countries, I and II, each producing two goods, X and Y,

This paper was originally published in *Journal of International Economics* 4 (1974): 295–298.

under competitive conditions, Y being exported by country I. When quotas are applied, quota holders are assumed to behave competitively. In figure 13.1, OI and OII represent the offer curves of countries I and II, respectively. Competitive equilibrium in the absence of trade restrictions is attained at point a_0 where OA_0 of good X is imported by country I, a_0A_0 of good Y is imported by country II and the terms of trade are the ratio OA_0/a_0A_0. Following the assumptions and methodology employed by Meade (1952) we can define indifference curves from trade along which each country remains at the same level of utility. $U_0^I U_0^I$ and $U_0^{II} U_0^{II}$ represent the pair of those curves corresponding to the utility levels enjoyed by each country at the unrestricted competitive equilibrium. Since at a_0 both offer curves are less than infinitely elastic, either country could gain by imposing some degree of trade restriction. As is well known, a country will maximize its utility when trading at a point where the foreign offer curve is tangent to an indifference curve from trade.

Assume that country I starts the process and sets an optimal import quota of OA_1 units of good X—it must be $OA_1 < OA_0$ for the quota to be binding—such that the new equilibrium is at point a_1 on OII where the welfare of country I is maximized since the indifference curve $U_1^I U_1^I$ is tangent to the foreign offer curve. The new offer curve of country I which country II is facing becomes the locus $Ob_1 a_1 A_1$ which is the same as the original offer curve until point b_1 where it becomes a vertical line since more imports are not feasible due to the import quota. The response of country II will depend on whether her optimal level of trade falls in the region Oc_1 (on OI) or in the region $c_1 b_1$. If the optimal level of trade for country II falls in the region Oc_1, either an export or an import quota can be used to attain it; if it falls in the region $c_1 b_1$ only an export quota can be used since any point in that region implies more imports and less exports than at the initial equilibrium at a_1. The reader can easily verify that, whatever the initial position, the final result of the retaliation process will be the same; we will thus only illustrate the case where the level of trade that maximizes the utility of country II falls at the kink, b_1, of the new offer curve of country I. To reach point b_1, an export quota in the amount OA_1, equal to the import quota on the same good imposed by country I seems to be necessary. If this quota is imposed, however, the imports of country II are undetermined at any level between $A_1 a_1$ and $A_1 b_1$ and, as such, there is no presumption that trade at b_1 will be reached given the competitive behavior of both suppliers and demanders. It is then reasonable to assume that country II will fix an export quota marginally smaller than OA_1—OA_2 in the figure—which will allow for trade to occur at b_2 (arbitrarily close to b_1). The offer curve of country II now becomes $Oa_2 b_2$

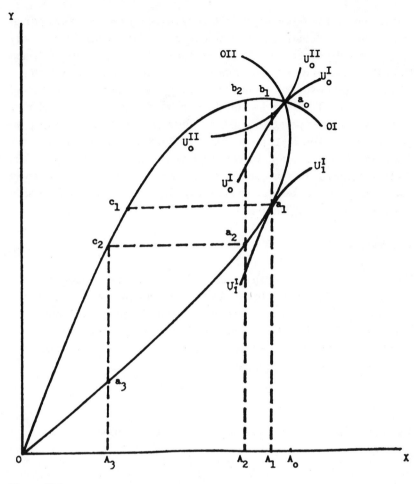

Figure 13.1

which coincides with the original OII only in the region Oa_2. The optimal level of trade for country I must now be at the kink a_2 of the new offer curve of country II. This new level of trade can be unambiguously attained through an export quota in the amount A_3c_2 (the reader can verify that if an import quota slightly smaller than OA_2 is used our final results will be unchanged). To the export quota A_3c_2 of country I, country II now responds with an export quota of OA_3 which shifts trade from point a_2 to point c_2, more favorably to country II. This, however, will bring as response a still smaller export quota by country I in the amount A_3a_3 which shifts trade to point a_3. To this country II responds with a still smaller export quota and, as the reader can easily verify, the process will continue until all trade is completely eliminated.

Conclusions

We can therefore conclude that even in the absence of monopoly, revenue effects, or uncertainty, tariffs and quotas are not equivalent when foreign retaliation is allowed for. Furthermore, we have shown that optimal quota retaliation will lead to the elimination of international trade between the countries involved. Our analysis would seem to strengthen the policy presumption that tariffs are preferable to quotas.

Notes

The author is indebted to Jagdish Bhagwati for his comments and suggestions.

1. I am informed by the editor [Jagdish Bhagwati, for *Journal of International Economics*] that R. Gordon, in an unpublished manuscript, arrived independently (but much later) at similar conclusions to those of McCulloch and Johnson regarding equivalence in the presence of U.S. oil-type quotas.

2. That quotas and tariffs would be non-equivalent under uncertainty seems to be a corollary to the general view that, while a quota may be equivalent to a tariff at one point in time, the equivalence does not hold if supply and demand conditions change; unless, of course, the quota is changed continually to its equivalent tariff value. But, the frequency with which quotas and tariffs can be changed in any economic regime are rarely identical; tariffs frequently can be changed only over a much longer period. Also note that, as Bhagwati (1965) pointed out, industries in some developing countries prefer to have both tariffs and quotas, instead of relying on the latter; the uncertainty of being protected by quotas is rather greater than the uncertainty of holding onto tariff protection, since quotas are also addressed to the balance of payments situation and may well lose their protective effect if the payments situations is improved.

References

Bhagwati, J. 1965. On the equivalence of tariffs and quotas. In Richard Caves et al. (ed.), *Trade, Balance of Payments and Growth*. Amsterdam: North Holland.

Bhagwati, J. 1968. More on the equivalence of tariffs and quotas. *American Economic Review* 58, 142–146.

Fishelson, G., and F. Flatters. 1973. *The (Non) Equivalence of Tariffs and Quotas under Uncertainty*. Unpublished manuscript. University of Chicago.

Johnson, H. G. 1953. Optimum tariffs and retaliation. *The Review of Economic Studies* 21, 142–153.

Meade, J. E. 1952. *A Geometry of International Trade*. Allen and Unwin, London.

McCulloch, R., and H. G. Johnson. 1973. A note on proportionally distributed quotas. *American Economic Review* 63, 726–732.

Shibata, H. 1968. Note on the equivalence of tariffs and quotas. *American Economic Review* 58, 137–142.

Postscript

After his paper reached proof stage, Harry G. Johnson pointed out to me that although the retaliation process seems to lead asymptotically to the elimination of trade, it can never logically eliminate trade completely. It will never pay either country to impose a zero trade quota since this step would always imply a reduction in welfare as compared with some positive amount of trade, however small (see H. G. Johnson, "Quotas and Retaliation: A Note," unpublished manuscript, University of Chicago, 1974). Consequently, the proposition that trade is eliminated should be modified to read that the volume of trade tends asymptotically to zero (although, in fact, never reaches it). It has also been called to my attention that Edward Tower has independently arrived at results which are similar to those presented in this paper.

14

Voluntary Export Restraint in U.S. Autos, 1980–81: Quality, Employment, and Welfare Effects

Robert C. Feenstra

On 1 May 1981 the Japanese agreed to limit their exports of automobiles to the U.S. market. Since the voluntary export restraint (VER) applied to the *number* of autos exported to the U.S. (and not their total value), we expect that Japanese auto producers will shift the composition of exports toward higher price, higher quality cars (Gomez-Ibanez et al. 1983). In this way they are able to maintain the maximum profit per unit sold, while staying within the quantity restraint. Such a response to quota restrictions can be obtained from simple theoretical models (see section 3) and has been observed within the textile and shoe industries (Baldwin 1982).

This quality shift has important implications for the employment and welfare effects of the VER. It is reasonable to assume that consumers demand the *services* of automobiles, where services are measured by automobile size, horsepower, comfort, and so forth, For a single car, the services provided are a measure of quality. Then a change in the price of Japanese automobile services will lead to a welfare loss for consumers and a substitution toward American models. For example, if due to the VER the average price of Japanese auto imports rises by 10 percent, but in addition the average quality of imports improves by 7 percent, then we would conclude that the price of services obtained from these imports has increased by only $10 - 7 = 3$ percent. This 3 percent effective price rise would determine the consumer welfare loss and the extent of substitution away from Japanese models. Clearly, from this example, only looking at the change in purchase price, with no adjustment for quality, can be quite misleading in assessing the impact of the VER. A precise empirical measure of automobile quality is thus essential to our study.

This paper was originally published in Robert E. Baldwin and Anne Krueger, eds., *The Structure and Evolution of Recent U.S. Trade Policies*, University of Chicago Press, 1984.

After reviewing background data on the U.S. auto industry in section 1, a preliminary inspection of the VER is given in section 2. The number of imported Japanese autos met the restriction, and a substantial price increase—quite unprecedented by recent historical standards—occurred following the export restraint. In section 3 we review relevant theory concerning import restrictions and quality shifts. By focusing on the aggregate price of services obtained from Japanese imports, our analysis goes beyond the traditional framework which relates consumer welfare to the purchase price unadjusted for quality. However, like the traditional framework, we relate consumer welfare to the *aggregate* import price. Thus, we do not attempt to measure the consumer loss or gain from a shifting composition of import models within an aggregate level of services. Such an exercise would be beyond the scope of the present study.

To measure the quality shift in imports, we have collected data on retail price and characteristics (length, horsepower, etc.) of twenty-two Japanese models for 1980, 1981, and 1982. The quality of automobiles is measured as the predicted price from hedonic regressions in which model prices are regressed on characteristics (see Griliches 1971). The quality-adjusted or service prices, which determine consumer demand and welfare, are measured by the residuals from the hedonic regressions. Using this method, in section 4 we identify three Japanese models which experienced substantial retail price, quantity, and quality increases following the VER with reductions in quality-adjusted price: Toyota Cressida, Toyota Celica Supra, and Datsun 810 Maxima.

In section 5 we apply hedonic regressions to eleven small and thirty-three large U.S. models for 1980 and 1981. Among the U.S. small cars, there is very little quality change and lower price rises than for other U.S. models. By comparing the results for Japanese imports and U.S. small cars, we conclude that about *two-thirds of the import price rise following the VER is due to quality improvement, with the remaining one-third a de facto price increase.* This is a major conclusion of our study.

In section 6 we apply the results of earlier sections to estimate the U.S. employment and welfare effects of the VER. Since a major part of the import price rise is explained by quality improvement, the employment and welfare effects are both quite small. We estimate that between 1980 and 1981 the welfare loss was approximately 3 percent of revenue spent on Japanese imports. In the first year of the VER, unemployment in U.S. autos was reduced by 5 percent or less of existing layoffs, with the exact magnitude depending on the import elasticity of demand.

1. Recent Experience in U.S. Autos

On 1 May 1981 the Japanese government announced a three-year system of "voluntary export restraints" (VER) on the export of automobiles to the U.S. market. For the period from April 1981 to March 1982 these exports would not exceed 1.68 million units, while for the second year (April 1982 to March 1983) the export ceiling would be raised by 16.5 percent of the growth in the U.S. market. At the end of the second year, a decision about whether to extend the export restraint for a third year would be made. Later the Japanese government announced that the exports of certain "utility" vehicles (e.g., the Subaru Brat, Toyota Land Cruiser and Van) would be limited to 82,500 units over the initial year, and exports to Puerto Rico would not exceed 70,000. Thus, total Japanese exports for all these vehicles in the initial year would not exceed 1,832,500 units. On 29 March 1982 it was announced that the system of VER in place during the first year of the agreement would be extended without change to the second year (presumably because of the lack of growth in the U.S. market). The export limits are administered by the Japanese Ministry of International Trade and Industry (MITI), which allocates fixed proportions of the total export quantity to the Japanese producers; this method of restricting exports does not violate U.S. antitrust law.

These actions were made against a background of falling production and high unemployment in U.S. autos, along with several legislative attempts to curb imports. For example, on 5 February 1981 Senators Danforth and Bentsen introduced a bill (S.396) to impose quotas on the import of automobiles from Japan of 1.6 million units during 1981, 1982, and 1983. Indeed, this bill was scheduled for markup (line-by-line revision) in the Senate Finance Committee on May 12 and no doubt contributed to the specific action announced by the Japanese on May 1. Other outstanding bills include more stringent import quotas and domestic content requirements which specify the minimum content of American-made parts for autos sold in the United States.

An earlier legislative action was the petition for import relief made by the UAW in June 1980 to the U.S. International Trade Commission (ITC). In August 1980 the Commission received a petition for similar import relief from the Ford Motor Company. Under this legislation a recommendation for relief can be given only if the "increased imports of an article are a substantial cause of serious injury, or threat thereof, to the domestic industry." The statute defines the term "substantial cause" as "a cause which is important and not less than any other cause." The ITC determined that, while imports of autos into the United States had increased and the domestic industry was in fact injured, the recession in the United States was a greater cause of injury than the increased imports. Accordingly, import relief was not given. The shift in consumer preferences toward small, fuel-efficient autos (due in part to rising gasoline prices) was also found to be an important cause of injury, but less important than the recessionary conditions.

Recent data on imports of passenger autos (including the "utility" vehicles referred to above) are reported in table 14.1. In the first row, first column it can be seen that actual Japanese imports for April 1981 to March 1982 essentially met the limit of 1,832,500 units. This represents a fall in quantity of 9 percent from the previous year and can be contrasted with an average annual rise of 14 percent in imports over 1978–80. Comparing the April 1981 to March 1982 imports with those of the previous year, and noting that imports had been rising, we certainly expect that the VER restricted imports by *at least* 180 thousand units. The actual extent of restrictions may be significantly higher and will be estimated in section 6.

Data on U.S. factory sales, consumption, and import market shares (ratios of imports to consumption) are also shown in table 14.1. Note that consumption fell continually over the years with a larger fall from 1979 to 1980, whereas import market shares show an abrupt rise in 1979–80 but only small changes in other periods. The rising import market share over 1979–80 is largely attributable to Japanese imports. Despite this larger share, the ITC found that the decline in U.S. consumption over the same period was a more important cause of injury to the domestic industry.[1] As factory sales have been reduced, employment has decreased at a slightly slower rate, resulting in a fall in the average product of labor shown in table 14.1 (eighth row). Along with the reduction in sales, of course, profits of the auto manufacturers have been cut dramatically.

2. Effect of the VER

To determine the employment effect of the VER during its first year of operation, an initial calculation could proceed as follows. Suppose that for each unit of import reduced by the VER, U.S. production rises by one unit. (We shall argue below that this assumption is false, however, due to imperfect substitution and quality change in imports.) Then, if the VER reduced Japanese imports by at least 180 thousand units, as discussed above, this could lead to a rise in U.S. employment of at least $180/9.5 = 19$ thousand workers, where we have used a middle value (9.5) of the average product of labor appearing in table 14.1. The increased employment of 19,000 can be compared with indefinite layoffs in the auto industry approaching 200,000 in late 1981 (see U.S. Department of Transportation 1982). Thus, the VER could affect at least one-tenth of the unemployment in autos during its first year. Of course, additional jobs would also be created in the rest of the economy.[2]

However, the employment impact of the VER may have been less than this estimate due to a shift of Japanese exports toward higher valued cars. Thus, at the bottom of table 14.1 we show the total value of Japanese imports and the average value (or price) obtained as the ratio of value to quantity. Over the period 1978–80 the average price of Japanese auto imports rose at an average rate of 6 percent, below the general rate of inflation. However, in the first year of the VER the price jumped by 17.4 percent as compared with the previous year. Annual inflation over the April 1980 to March 1982 period (as measured by the consumer price index) was 9.6 percent, which leaves a real increase of $17.4 - 9.6 = 7.8$ percent in import prices. Alternatively, we can compare the rise in prices from April 1980 to March 1982 with earlier years and obtain an unexpected increase of $17.4 - 6 = 11.4$ percent in import prices. In any case, it is clear from the data that the rise in average value during the initial year of the VER was quite unprecedented by recent historical standards and can be assumed to be a direct result of the export restraint. The average price of U.S. autos for some periods are shown for comparison; more recent figures will be computed in section 5.

The rise in average import prices may be achieved by (1) a simple rise in prices reflecting scarcity in the market; (2) a shift of Japanese exporters toward higher priced existing models which are larger, heavier, have greater horsepower, and so forth; (3) the introduction of new, or modified, models which are also larger, heavier, and the like. We shall refer to the specific features of a model such as weight and horsepower as "characteristics" and the bundle of characteristics embodied in a particular car as the "quality." With this terminology, the rise in average import price following the VER may be decomposed into a rise in quality (either within or across models) and a residual change in the price after adjusting for quality.

To evaluate the effect of the VER on consumer welfare, we shall have to measure the extent of quality change in Japanese imports. This shall be done in section 4 using hedonic regressions. In the following section we briefly review relevant theory concerning quality shifts in response to quota restrictions.

3. Theory of Import Restrictions and Quality Shifts

The theoretical impact of tariffs and quotas on import quality has been examined in Falvey (1979), Rodriguez (1979), and Santoni and Van Cott

Table 14.1
New passenger automobiles

	April 1981 to March 1982	April 1980 to March 1981	1980	1979	1978
Quantity (thousands of units; thousands of employees)					
Japanese imports	1,833.3	2,012	1,992	1,617	1,563
Total imports	2,840	3,037	3,116	3,006	3,025
U.S. factory sales	5,602[a]	6,220[b]	6,400	8,419	9,165
Apparent U.S. consumption	7,962	8,684	8,904	10,643	11,505
Ratio of Japanese imports to U.S. consumption (percent)	23.0	23.2	22.4	15.2	13.6
Ratio of total imports to U.S. consumption (percent)	35.7	35.0	35.0	28.2	26.3
Average employment[c]	642	662	691	904	922
Ratio of U.S. factory sales to employment	8.7	9.4	9.3	9.3	9.9
Value (millions of dollars) and average price					
Japanese imports	9,421	8,804	8,229	6,471	5,771
Ratio of Jap. import value to quantity	5,139	4,376	4,131	4,002	3,692
Ratio of U.S. production to quantity[d]	—	—	6,097	6,014	5,829

Source: Bureau of Labor Statistics, 1981, *Supplement to Employment and Earnings: Revised Establishment Data*, August and later issues; U.S. International Trade Commission, 1982, *The U.S. Automobile Industry: Monthly Report on Selected Economic Indicators*, Publication 1244, May, Washington, D.C., tables 1, 2, 4; U.S. International Trade Commission, 1981, *Automotive Trade Statistics, 1964–1980*, Publication 1203, December, Washington, D.C., tables 1, 2, 3; U.S. International Trade Commission, 1980, *Certain Motor Vehicle and Certain Chassis and Bodies Therefor*, Publication 1110, December, Washington D.C., table 19.

a. Domestic production, May 1981 to April 1982.

b. Domestic production, May 1981 to April 1981.

c. Employment in SIC 3711 (motor vehicles and car bodies) plus SIC 3714 (motor vehicle parts and accessories).

d. Producer's shipments; 1980 figure is for January to June. Later data were not available.

(1980). Falvey analyzes the case of fixed quality for each imported good but a shifting composition of imports. His analysis can be briefly summarized as follows.

Consider two import goods with unit costs c_1 and c_2, where $c_1 > c_2$ so that good 1 is the higher cost, higher quality item. In the absence of trade restrictions and assuming competition (Falvey also considers the mono-poly case), we have $p_1 = c_1 > p_2 = c_2$, where p_i is the price of good i. In the presence of an ad valorem tariff of rate t, we could have $p_i' = (1 + t)c_i$, for $i = 1$ and 2, which implies $p_1'/p_2' = p_1/p_2$, so the relative price of the goods is unchanged. In this case we expect that the relative quantities imported are also unchanged. However, in the presence of a quota or VER on the *sum* of imports (over both goods), suppliers would ensure that the profits earned per unit imported are equalized in either good. That is, $p_1' - c_1 = p_2' - c_2$, where p_i' are the postquota domestic prices. But an equal increase in the price of each good implies a lower *percentage* increase in the price of good 1, since $p_1 > p_2$ initially. In other words, $p_1'/p_2' < p_1/p_2$, so the relative price has *decreased* for the higher quality good. Correspondingly, we expect a larger relative quantity imported of this good.

Rodriguez, on the other hand, considers a single import good where competitive firms choose the optimal quality. He assumes that the import demand applies to the *services* the good provides, where services equal

$$S = xQ, \tag{1}$$

and S = import demand for services; Q = number of physical units imported; and x = amount of services provided per physical unit, or the unit quality content.

Rodriguez demonstrates that an ad valorem tariff will not affect the quality level x chosen by producers. However, in the presence of a binding quota or VER on imports, the quality content x will be *increased*.

The welfare cost from the VER is shown in figure 14.1. DD' is the import demand curve for services, p denotes the price of services, and the free-trade equilibrium is at E_0. As demonstrated by Rodriguez, the export restraint will lead to a rise in the price of imported services, with a new equilibrium such as E_1. Since the *exporting* country receives the higher price and thus the quota rents, the loss to the importing country is given by the entire shaded region under the import demand curve. This loss is approximately measured by

$$L_S = (p_1 - p_0)S_1 + (\tfrac{1}{2})(p_1 - p_0)(S_0 - S_1). \tag{2}$$

It is interesting to compare the appropriate measure of loss (L_S) with that obtained if the change in quality were not considered. That is, suppose

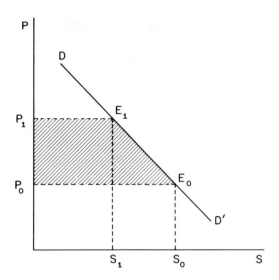

Figure 14.1   Effect of VER on services

we incorrectly measure the loss by the change in physical quantity imported and corresponding price. Since x is the quality content of a physical unit, px is the price per physical unit. Then the quantity measure of loss would be

$$L_Q = (p_1 x_1 - p_0 x_0) Q_1 + \tfrac{1}{2}(p_1 x_1 - p_0 x_0)(Q_0 - Q_1), \tag{3}$$

where the subscript 0 (or 1) refers to pre-(or post-) VER. It can be shown that

$$L_Q - L_S = (\tfrac{1}{2})(x_1 - x_0)(p_0 Q_1 + p_1 Q_0). \tag{4}$$

With unit quality rising after the VER, $x_1 > x_0$, so the physical quantity measure of loss L_Q *overstates* the actual loss L_S. Indeed, relative to the total income spent on importables, the extent of overstatement is approximately equal to the percentage increase in unit quality.

We have been implicitly assuming that the imported good is a perfect substitute for the domestic product. If instead they are *imperfect substitutes*, then the change in the imported services price from p_0 to p_1 will shift the entire domestic demand curve, and a new equilibrium domestic price would be obtained. Let us suppose that the import demand curve DD' in figure 14.1 is drawn while *allowing* the domestic price to adjust to its new equilibrium levels. Then it can be argued (see Tarr 1980, pp. 11–15) that the shaded area in figure 14.1 is still an appropriate measure of welfare loss. This result is obtained essentially because the change in consumer surplus in the domestic market is exactly offset by a change in producer surplus.

Finally, we should mention an important qualification to our measure of welfare loss (L_S). We shall estimate this welfare loss using the *aggregate* price of services from Japanese imports. By this method, we are ignoring any consumer gain or loss from a shifting composition of import models within the aggregate level of services. Measuring the welfare component would be beyond the scope of the present study but could be initiated using the recent theoretical models of monopolistic competition and trade (Helpman 1981; Krugman 1979, 1980; Lancaster 1980). Only recently, however, have these models been extended to incorporate import restrictions (Feenstra and Judd 1982; Lancaster 1982; Venables 1982). One result from these models is that only under very special assumptions will the market equilibrium lead to a socially optimal quantity and range of product varieties (see Feenstra and Judd 1982, sec. 1). It follows that the shift in the composition of import models induced by the VER, holding the aggregate level of services fixed, can raise or lower consumer welfare in general. Thus, by ignoring this welfare component, we may be understating or overstating the actual welfare loss.

4. Model Data and Quality of Japanese Imports

To analyze more closely the impact of the VER, data on twenty-two Japanese models over the calendar years 1980, 1981, and 1982 were obtained from the annual *Automotive News Market Data Book*. These data included quantity imported into the United States (except for 1982), suggested retail price in March or April for the base version (i.e., without options) of each model, and characteristics including length, weight, horsepower, miles per gallon, and others. The twenty-two imported models were comprehensive, except that (1) "utility" vehicles (e.g., the Subaru Brat), referred to in section 1, were omitted and (2) import quantities of individual models included both station wagon and nonwagon quantities (e.g., Toyota Corolla sedan plus wagon), whereas only the price and characteristics of nonwagon imports were obtained.[3]

Summary information for the Japanese imports is shown in table 14.2 (upper portion). The quantity imported fell by 57,000 units from calendar year 1980 to 1981. In addition, the average price (computed as a ratio of total value to quantity) shows a substantial increase of 19.8 percent over this period. Thus, while the calendar year periods do not correspond exactly to those of the VER (i.e., April 1981 to March 1982), the qualitative behavior of the aggregate data is similar to that in table 14.2. Accordingly, we feel that a careful study of the model data will be useful in assessing the impact of the VER.

Table 14.2
Sample of automobiles

	1981	1980	Percent change from 1980 to 1981[a]
Japanese imports			
Quantity (1,000)	1,721	1,778	−3.3
Price ($)[b]	5,950	4,881	19.8
Quality ($)[c]	5,250	4,943	6.0
U.S. small car production			
Quantity (1,000)	1,321	1,449	−9.3
Price ($)	5,673	5,064	11.4
Quality ($)	5,258	5,220	0.7
U.S. large car production			
Quantity (1,000)	2,663	3,010	−12.3
Price ($)	8,233	6,962	16.8
Quality ($)	7,420	7,078	4.7

a. Difference in the natural logarithms.
b. 1982 average price computed using 1981 quantities is $6,306.
c. 1982 quality computed using 1981–82 regression and 1981 quantities is $5,236.

A scatter plot of the quantity change from 1980 to 1981 for individual models is shown in figure 14.2. The greatest percentage increase was obtained by the Toyota Cressida and Datsun 810 Maxima, the second and third most expensive models. (Note that the Toyota Starlet is an outlier, since this model was just introduced in 1980 leading to a high quantity increase in 1981.) The most expensive 1980 model was the Toyota Supra, a luxury sports version of the Celica. While this model experienced an import decline from 1980 to 1981, during the first seven months of 1982 Supra imports had substantially exceeded import sales during all of 1981.[4] Indeed, on an annual basis the import gain from 1981 to 1982 can be computed as 105 percent, placing the Supra up with the Cressida and Maxima as obtaining the largest import gains.

A glance at the other models in figure 14.2 certainly confirms our hypothesis that, due to the VER, the composition of imports shifts toward higher quality models. Next to the Cressida and Maxima, the next highest quantity gain is 30 percent (excluding the Starlet). The great majority of models are priced below $7,000, where there is no discernable trend in quantity changes. The model with the worst quantity decline—the Toyota Corona—will appear as an extreme point in following figures.

In figures 14.3 and 14.4 the price increases for 1980–81 and 1981–82 are shown. Most interestingly, the Cressida and Maxima (for 1980–81) and

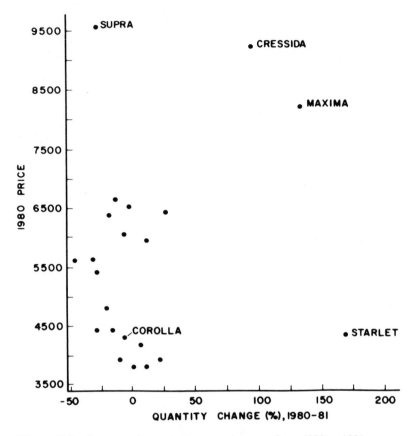

Figure 14.2   Quantity change in Japanese imports, from 1980 to 1981

Supra (for 1981–82) record some of the largest price rises. The question then is how the import gains were accomplished in the face of higher prices. One possibility is that these three models experienced significant quality improvements, making them attractive to buyers despite the price increases. We shall examine this possibility now, using hedonic regressions. (The basic reference on this technique is Griliches 1971; see also Triplett 1975.)

In hedonic regressions we attempt to explain the variation in automobile prices using information on model characteristics. Specifically, we shall regress the natural logarithms of Japanese model prices on their length, weight, horsepower, gas mileage, and dummy variables for five-speed transmission, air-conditioning, and year. The results of these regressions for 1980–81 and 1981–82 are shown in the first two columns of table 14.3.

Since the dependent price variable is measured as a natural log, the coefficients in the regressions can be interpreted as the proportionate

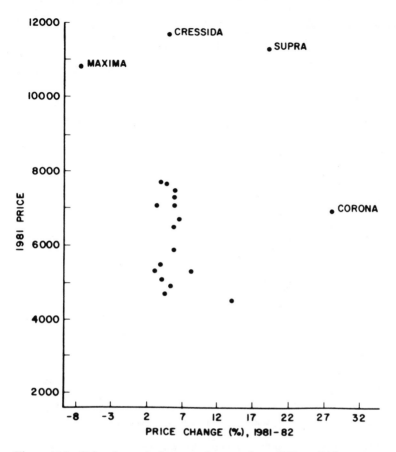

Figure 14.3   Price change in Japanese imports, from 1980 to 1981

change in price from a unit change in the independent variable. For example, in the 1980–81 regression for Japanese imports, an increase in length of one foot reduces the model price by an estimated 16 percent. Similarly, an increase in weight of one ton increases the model price by 77 percent. It can be seen that the presence of a five-speed transmission or air-conditioning as standard features are positively related to price, whereas gas mileage is negatively related. The standard errors of the estimates are shown in parentheses, and the gas mileage coefficient is insignificantly different from zero. Overall, the regression is able to explain 90 percent of the variation in model prices with a total of forty-four observations over the two years.

The regression for Japanese imports in 1981–82 is similar to that of 1980–81. In either case, additional explanatory variables were considered, including interior room area, turning circle, number of doors, hatchback,

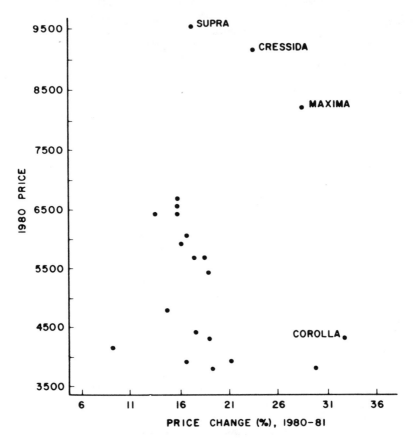

Figure 14.4   Price change in Japanese imports, from 1981 to 1982

and others.[5] However, these variables were generally insignificant and of the "wrong" sign. One useful explanatory variable that was not available is dealer discounts, which were used extensively in 1981 (see U.S. Department of Transportation 1982).

The last variable in each regression is a dummy for the next year. The coefficient of this variable can be interpreted as the average rise in model prices *not* explained by the improvement in characteristics. Thus, for 1980–81 the suggested retail price rose by 19.8 percent, but after adjusting for quality improvements, such as greater horsepower, air-conditioning, and the rest, the residual price rose by only 13 percent. The difference between these two figures is the rise in quality content. More precisely, the total import of Japanese automobile *services* can be measured as the predicted price from the hedonic regression times the quantity, summed over all models.[6] The *quality* of imports is then obtained as the total services divided by total quantity. As shown in table 14.2, we measure the quality content of imports as \$4,943 and \$5,250 in 1980 and 1981, respectively, obtained using the 1980–81 regression. The difference between these figures gives a 6 percent rise in quality.

The sensitivity of this quality measurement to specification of the hedonic regression can be checked by examining the "year 1981" coefficient. For various additional explanatory variables considered, the 1981 dummy coefficient was between 0.126 and 0.136, indicating an average rise in model prices not explained by quality improvement of approximately 13 percent, as found in table 14.3. For example, when variables for roominess, maneuverability, and axle ratio (a measure of durability) are added to the Japanese regression in table 14.3, the year 1981 coefficient is 0.132 for 1980–81. This compares with an estimate of 0.126 for 1980–81 when these three additional variables are excluded. If engine displacement and horsepower/weight are used in place of horsepower and weight, while retaining room, maneuverability, and axle ratio, then the 1981 dummy coefficient is 0.136 for 1980–81. Other combinations and additional explanatory variables result in a coefficient between these bounds. The measure of quality improvement can be approximately obtained as the difference between the retail price increase (19.8 percent) and the year 1981 coefficient (13 percent). Since the latter is not very sensitive to the regression specification, our measure of quality improvement appears to be quite robust.

The scatter plots of the residual, or quality-adjusted, price changes for 1980–81 and 1981–82 are shown in figures 14.5 and 14.6. Comparing figures 14.3 and 14.5, we can see substantial difference in the price changes for the Supra, Cressida, and Maxima, relative to the other models. Thus, while the retail price increases for these models over 1980–81 were well above average, the quality-adjusted price increases were well below average. From the raw data the quality improvement of the Supra can be identified as an increase in horsepower and the introduction of a five-speed transmission; the Cressida became beavier with greater horsepower; and the Maxima increased in weight with air-conditioning and automatic transmission added as standard equipment.

A similar pattern of high retail price increase with much smaller quality-adjusted price change can be seen for the Supra over 1981–82 in figures 14.4 and 14.6. These overall results neatly confirm the hypothesis that the quantity gain in the highest priced Japanese imports was brought about by a significant improvement in the quality content, as expected from the theory. Aside from the Cressida, Maxima, and Supra models, no general pattern of price or quality change is identified.

Table 14.3
Hedonic regressions (dependent variable: natural logarithm of model price)

	Japanese 1980–81	Japanese 1981–82	U.S. small 1980–81	U.S. large 1980–81
	Obs. = 44 $R^2 = 0.90$	Obs. = 44 $R^2 = 0.93$	Obs. = 22 $R^2 = 0.80$	Obs. = 66 $R^2 = 0.95$
Intercept	9.56* (0.82)	9.28* (0.69)	7.96* (0.55)	8.99* (0.44)
Length (feet)	−0.16* (0.069)	−0.10 (0.054)	0.14* (0.040)	−0.16* (0.023)
Weight (tons)	0.77 (0.41)	0.47 (0.30)	−0.48 (0.26)	1.48* (0.16)
Horsepower (100 HP)	0.74* (0.23)	0.54* (0.17)	−0.20 (0.30)	−0.27 (0.093)
Gas mileage (100 MPG)	−0.78 (0.76)	−0.57 (0.64)	−2.29* (1.08)	1.84* (0.80)
Dummy variables:				
Five-speed	0.80 (0.041)	0.15* (0.038)	—	—
Automatic	—	—	—	0.090* (0.040)
Power brakes	—	—	0.12* (0.042)	—
Air-conditioning[a]	0.21* (0.066)	0.26* (0.054)	—	0.43* (0.050)

Year 1981	0.13* (0.034)	—	0.089* (0.035)	0.11* (0.024)
Year 1982	—	0.057* (0.025)	—	—

Note: The * indicates values significant at 5 percent level. Standard errors are in parentheses.
a. For Japanese models this variable indicates air-conditioning and automatic transmission, which were nearly perfectly correlated.

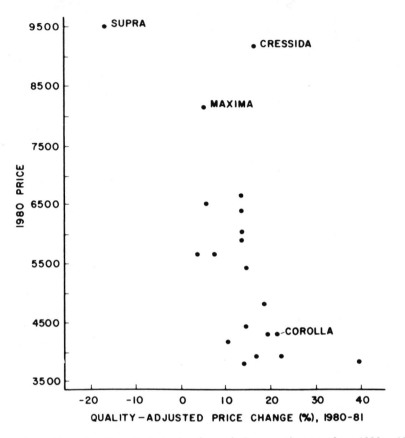

Figure 14.5   Quality-adjusted price change in Japanese imports, from 1980 to 1981

5. Model Data and Quality of U.S. Production

In addition to the data on Japanese imports, data on prices and characteristics of forty-four U.S. models were also obtained from the same source
for the calendar years 1980 and 1981. Station wagons and several other
models were omitted from the sample because of lack of information. The
sample will be used to make comparisons with the Japanese imports and
to establish general conclusions in section 6.

The data for U.S. small cars and large cars are summarized in table 14.2.
(Note that the large car category includes both intermediate and large
models.) The small cars experienced a lower price rise than large cars. This
difference is explained in part by a changing composition *within* the large
car category. In particular, the price of intermediate-sized cars (below

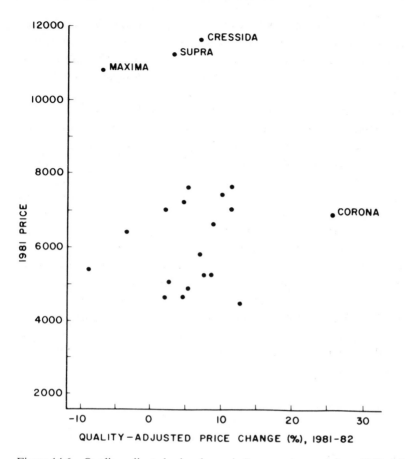

Figure 14.6   Quality-adjusted price change in Japanese imports, from 1981 to 1982

$8,000 in price) rose substantially more in percentabe terms than the price of very large cars (above $8,000 in price). The general price rise, then, partially reflects a quantity shift toward more expensive models within the large car category. Overall, U.S. large cars experienced a greater percentage quantity decline than small cars, as reported in table 14.2.

One conclusion to be drawn from the summary information is that U.S. small car prices do not appear to include a significant monopolistic increase over the 1980–81 period, in contrast to the prediction of traditional theory (see, e.g., Lindert and Kindleberger 1982, app. E). That is, despite the export restriction, those models which compete most directly with Japanese imports—U.S. small cars—experienced lower price increases than intermediate and large cars. One possible explanation for this result is that, faced with limited availability of lower priced, lower quality Japanese imports,

U.S. consumers did not substitute toward small U.S. models. Instead they could have substituted toward intermediate U.S. models, used cars, or they could have decided to defer their purchases.[7] To the extent that substitution did *not* take place toward U.S. cars, the employment impact of the VER is reduced.

Hedonic regressions were also run for U.S. small and large cars, using similar explanatory variables as in the analysis of Japanese imports described in section 4. The results are shown in table 14.3. The U.S. small car regression contains several unusual signs, with less explanatory power than for U.S. large cars.[8] In the latter case, all estimated coefficients are significant at the 5 percent level, with length having a negative and gas mileage a positive relation to price.

As with the Japanese imports, the predicted prices from the hedonic regressions can be used to construct an estimate of total *services* produced (predicted price times quantity, summed over all models). When divided by the quantity of small or large cars, we then obtain a measure of *quality*, as shown in table 14.2. The quality content of U.S. small cars increased only slightly from 1980 to 1981, in contrast to the substantial quality change of Japanese imports. For U.S. large cars, quality increased by 4.7 percent. This is partially explained by the quantity shift from intermediate to very large cars as discussed above.

6. Effects of the VER within the Sample

We shall now derive general conclusions about the effect of the VER within our sample of Japanese imports and U.S. production. In particular, we shall investigate the U.S. employment and welfare impact. Recalling that our sample covers the calendar years 1980 and 1981, whereas the initial year of the VER was April 1981 to March 1982, our quantitative results do not directly measure the effect of the VER in its first year. But we certainly expect that our general conclusions will carry over to other, similar time periods.

Returning to table 14.2, we must first decide what portion of the 19.8 percent rise in retail import prices is a general inflationary effect across producers from cost increases and simple price leadership but not related to the VER. We noted above that the U.S. small car prices do not appear to include a significant monopolistic increase in 1981, rising by less than intermediate and large car prices, so it seems reasonable to regard the 11.4 percent increase in small car prices as the general inflationary effect. It follows that the difference between the retail price increases of Japanese imports and U.S. small cars, or *19.8 − 11.4 = 8.4 percent, is the increase in import prices directly caused by the VER*, after correcting for the inflationary effect across producers. The next question is what portion of this price increase is directly the result of quality improvement. From table 14.2, we see that the quality improvement of the Japanese imports exceeded that of U.S. small cars by 6.0 − 0.7 = 5.3 percent. That is, 5.3/8.4 or about *two-thirds of the rise in import prices can be attributed to quality improvement.* The remaining 8.4 − 5.3 = 3.1 percent, or one-third of the total, is a de facto price increase for which the consumer is not compensated by a change in quality.

To obtain further conclusions, we must begin to introduce some assumptions and parameters. In table 14.4 we give alternative values of the elasticity of U.S. demand for Japanese automobile services, ranging from 2 to 5. Using these elasticities and the 3.1 percent residual price increase obtained above, we can readily compute the value of imported services

Table 14.4
Effects of the VER from 1980 to 1981

	Elasticity of demand for Japanese automobile services		
	2	3	5
Japanese services restricted[a] ($ mill)	560	840	1400
Japanese autos restricted[b] (1,000)	220	277	390
Additional U.S. revenue[c] ($ mill)	317	635	1270
Additional U.S. production[d] (1,000)	53	106	212
Additional U.S. employment[e] (1,000)	5.6	11.1	22.3
Welfare loss:			
L_S ($ mill)[f]	327	332	342
L_Q ($ mill)[g]	915	929	958

a. 0.031 × elasticity × 1981 Japanese services. Services = quality × quantity.
b. (1981 Japanese services + services restricted)/1980 Japanese quality − 1981 Japanese auto imports.
c. 0.031 × (elasticity − 1) × 1981 Japanese import value.
d. Additional U.S. revenue/$6,000.
e. Additional U.S. production/9.5.
f. (0.031 × 1981 Japanese services) + 1/2 × (0.031 × 1981 Japanese service price × Japanese services restricted). Service price = nominal price/quality.
g. (0.084 × 1981 Japanese import value) + 1/2 × (0.084 × 1981 Japanese price × Japanese autos restricted).

restricted by the VER. In the absence of this restraint we would have expected the 1981 Japanese quality to be approximately the same as in 1980. Accordingly, we can compute the extent to which the VER restricted auto imports in the second row of table 14.4. For demand elasticities of 2 and 3, the extent of import restrictions is measured as 220,000 and 277,000 units, respectively.

From the estimates reported in Toder (1978, chap. 3), a value of 1 to 2 for the short-run elasticity of demand for imported autos is expected, while the value of 3 is somewhat high. In assessing the employment impact of the VER during its first year, we shall thus focus on the first two columns of table 14.4. The last column, with an elasticity of 5, would be relevant for periods exceeding one year when consumers show greater adjustment to a price increase.

Let us make the strong assumption that the *overall* U.S. demand elasticity for domestic and Japanese autos is unity. That is, a fixed proportion of total income is spent on these autos, and a reduction of $1 million spent on Japanese imports because of a price change will imply exactly $1 million extra spent on U.S. models. This assumption is supported by the empirical evidence (see Toder 1978, p. 44 and the references cited there) that the price elasticity for *all* cars purchased in the United States is approximately one. By excluding European imports, we may be overstating the income which consumers continue to spend on Japanese and American models after a price rise. The assumption of an overall demand elasticity of unity, combined with specific import elasticities, permits us to model the degree of substitution between Japanese and U.S. models, as follows.

For the various import elasticities in table 14.4 we can readily compute the additional income spent on U.S. autos because of the VER as being equal to the reduced income spent on Japanese imports. Dividing this revenue by an average 1981 price of $6,000 for cars which substitute quite closely with Japanese imports, we obtain the additional U.S. production (fourth row). These production gains can be contrasted to the number of auto imports restricted, with the differences due to imperfect substitution. Further dividing the production gain by the average product of labor, we obtain the additional U.S. employment (fifth row). With import elasticities of 2 and 3, the employment gains are 5,600 and 11,100 workers, respectively. These figures can be compared with indefinite layoffs in the auto industry exceeding 200,000 in early 1982.

Thus, the employment impact of the VER during its first year was 5 percent or less of existing layoffs. Further evidence would be required to assess the employment impact over later years, though the last column of table 14.4 suggests that the reduction in unemployment would be larger.

In the last row of table 14.4 we give the correct welfare loss L_S derived in section 3 and the incorrect loss L_Q which ignores the quality change in imports. These magnitudes can be compared with 1981 expenditures on Japanese imports of $10,240,000. Thus, the correct welfare loss is approximately 3.1 percent of 1981 expenditures, while the incorrect welfare loss is approximately 8.4 percent. These amounts are just the quality-adjusted and unadjusted rise in import prices, respectively, since the welfare loss from the VER is the entire reduction in consumer surplus (see figure 14.1) with quota rents accruing to Japanese producers. The specification of the import elasticity only modestly affects the loss. The correct measure of welfare loss is about one-third of the incorrect measure.

7. Conclusions

Our major conclusion is that two-thirds of the increase in Japanese import prices following the VER was due to quality improvement, with the remaining one-third a de facto price rise for which the consumer is not compensated by a change in quality. This result was found to be quite insensitive to the specification of the hedonic regressions used to measure quality (section 4). It also depends on the general inflationary price increase across producers, not related to the VER. Since U.S. small car prices rose by less than the intermediate or large car prices (section 5), we chose the former as a measure of the general inflationary increase. We then took the *difference* between the Japanese import and U.S. small car price rise and regarded this amount as the increase in import prices directly caused by the VER. Two-thirds of this price increase could be explained by quality improvement in Japanese imports.

The residual import price rise not accounted for by quality change was measured as 3.1 percent. It followed that the loss to American consumers in 1981 from the VER was approximately 3.1 percent of expenditure on Japanese imports. The exact welfare loss depends only slightly on the import demand elasticity, since most of the loss comes from the quota rents obtained by Japanese producers. It is also observed that three Japanese models experienced substantial retail price, quantity, and quality increases following the VER, with reductions in their quality-adjusted prices: the Toyota Cressida, Toyota Celica Supra, and Datsun 810 Maxima. The increased imports of these luxury models neatly confirm the theoretical predictions.

Our conclusions about the effect of the VER on employment in U.S. autos are subject to greater qualification. Clearly, we have not considered the general equilibrium response of wages to unemployment in one industry, or the extent to which decreased U.S. imports would result in lower demand for U.S. exports. More specifically, we have not been able to consider imports from countries other than Japan or the introduction of new U.S. models following the VER. Including European imports into our analysis could decrease the employment impact of the VER because of substitution by U.S. consumers toward these models. On the other hand, introduction of new U.S. models, such as the General Motors J-car (and earlier the Chrysler K-car), could present desirable alternatives for limited Japanese imports. While a consideration of these factors would be useful, our general conclusion that the employment impact of the VER was small during the first year due to quality improvement and imperfect substitution between Japanese and U.S. autos does not seem to be overstated.

Notes

The author would like to thank Joseph Harary for outstanding research assistance and discussions throughout the course of this project, and Mordechai Kreinin and Ronald Jones for their comments as discussants.

1. Thus, suppose the import market share were held *constant* at its 1979 value. Then 1980 factory sales could be estimated as $6,400 + 3,116 - (8,904 \times 0.282) = 7,005$, where the first figure is actual 1980 sales and the next figures are actual and estimated 1980 imports. Factory sales in 1979 were 8,419, so the extent of decline due to falling consumption (i.e., recessionary conditions) is $(8,419 - 7,005)/(8,419 - 6,400) = 70$ percent. The remaining 30 percent of falling sales can be attributed to import competition. Precisely this type of simple calculation was instrumental in leading to the ITC decision.

2. For example, the Council of Economic Advisors (submission to Senate, 3 April 1980) reports that the production of 50 autos creates 10 jobs in the economy, with 2.3 workers employed directly in autos and 7.7 employed elsewhere. These data are from the Department of Labor (apparently based on a study referenced in submission to the House of Representatives, 7, 18 March 1980). However, the average product of labor in autos implicit in these figures is extremely high $(50/2.3 = 22)$. I have been unable to account for the difference between this estimate and those reported in table 14.1.

3. Dealers were contacted to try and separate the station wagon and nonwagon import quantities, but this proved unsuccessful. In addition, note that the imported models include those built for U.S. firms, such as the Chrysler-Mitsubishi Challenger, Champ, and Colt. Imports into Puerto Rico are not included.

4. Imports of the Toyota Celica Supra during 1980, 1981, and the first seven months of 1982 were 21,542 units, 16,146 units, and 19,266 units, respectively. Ward's Communications, Inc., kindly supplied this information. Due to its overall performance, the Supra was chosen as *Moto Trend* magazine's 1982 Import Car of the Year.

5. The occurrence of air-conditioning was very highly correlated with the occurrence of automatic transmissions in the Japanese imports, so these were combined into one dummy variable. Also, the prices were adjusted so that all models excluded a radio.

6. The predicted price used in this calculation does not include that portion of the model price explained by the year dummy in the regression, since the year dummy captures that portion of the price *not* related to the physical characteristics (i.e., services) of the model.

7. Since the 1981 U.S. small and large car prices were collected on April 10, it is of course possible that the small car prices had not responded to the VER simply because it was not announced until May 1. On the other hand, the evidence is quite strong that at least the Japanese had anticipated the VER in setting their prices as of 6 April 1981, which are used in our sample. But whether the VER was anticipated by U.S. producers or not, we still obtain the result that the U.S. small car price rise over 1980–81 does not appear to include a monopolistic increase, and this result will be used in section 6.

8. At a later stage of our research we also pooled the Japanese import and American small car models to test for equality of the regression coefficients. By the usual F-test, the test statistic for the null hypothesis that the regression coefficients were equal, was computed as 1.55. The 95 percent significance point of the F-distribution with degrees of freedom (5, 60) is 2.37, so we cannot reject the null hypothesis. In future research it would be useful to pool these data.

References

Automotive News Market Data Book. 1980, 1981, 1982. Detroit: Automotive News.

Baldwin, Robert E. 1982. The efficacy (or inefficacy) of trade policy. Frank Graham Memorial Lecture, Princeton University.

Falvey, Rodney E. 1979. The composition of trade within import-restricted product categories. *Journal of Political Economy* 87, no. 5 (October): 1105–1114.

Feenstra, Robert C., and Kenneth L. Judd. 1982. Tariffs, technology transfer, and welfare. *Journal of Political Economy* 90, no. 6 (December): 1142–1165.

Gomez-Ibanez, Jose A., Robert A. Leone, and Stephen A. O'Connell. 1983. Restraining auto imports: Does anyone win? *Journal of Policy Analysis and Management* 2: 196–219.

Griliches, Zvi. 1971. Hedonic price indexes for automobiles: An econometric analysis of quality change. In *Price Indexes and Quality Change*, ed. Zvi Griliches. Cambridge: Harvard University Press.

Helpman, Elhanan. 1981. International trade in the presence of product differentiation, economies of scale and monopolistic competition: A Chamberlin-Heckscher-Ohlin approach. *Journal of International Economics* 11 (August): 305–340.

Krugman, Paul R. 1979. Increasing returns, monopolistic competition, and international trade. *Journal of International Economics* 9 (November): 469–479.

Krugman, Paul R. 1980. Scale economies, product differentiation, and the pattern of trade. *American Economic Review* 70 (December): 950–959.

Lancaster, Kelvin J. 1980. Intra-industry trade under perfect monopolistic competition. *Journal of International Economics* 10 (May): 151–175.

Lancaster, Kelvin J. 1982. Protection and product differentiation. Columbia University. Mimeo.

Lindert, Peter H., and Charles P. Kindleberger. 1982. *International Economics.* Homewood, Ill.: Irwin.

Rodriguez, Carlos Alfredo. 1979. The quality of imports and the differential welfare effects of tariffs, quotas, and quality controls as protective devices. *Canadian Journal of Economics* 12, no. 3: 439–449.

Santoni, Gary J., and T. Norman Van Cott. 1980. Import quotas: The quality adjustment problem. *Southern Economic Journal* 46, no. 4 (April): 1206–1211.

Tarr, David. Federal Trade Commission 1980. *Effects of restrictions on United States imports: Five case studies and theory.* Washington, D.C.: GPO.

Toder, Eric J., with Nicholas Scott Cardell, and Ellen Burton. 1978. *Trade Policy and the U.S. Automobile Industry.* Charles River Associates Research Report. New York: Praeger.

Triplett, Jack E. 1975. Consumer demand and characteristics of consumption goods. In *Household Production and Consumption,* ed. Nestor E. Terlecky. Conference on Research in Income and Wealth: Studies in Income and Wealth, vol. 40. New York: Columbia University Press for the National Bureau of Economic Research.

U.S. Congress. Senate. Committee on Banking, Housing, and Urban Affairs. Subcommittee on Economic Stabilization. 1980. *The Effects of Expanding Automobile Imports on the Domestic Economy.* 96th Cong., 2d sess., 3 April.

U.S. Congress. House. Committee on Ways and Means. Subcommittee on Trade. 1980. *World Auto Trade: Current Trends and Structural Problems.* 96th Cong., 2d sess., 7, 18 March. Serial 96-78.

U.S. Department of Transportation. 1982. *The U.S. Automobile Industry, 1981.* May. Washington, D.C.: GPO.

Venables, Anthony J. 1982. Optimal tariffs for trade in monopolistically competitive commodities. *Journal of International Economics* 12 (May): 225–242.

Postscript

Since this paper was written a number of theoretical and empirical papers dealing with quality change in imports have appeared. It is useful to classify these papers according to two approaches. The first approach, which can be labeled neoclassical, treats products as imported in a number of distinct categories, such as types of steel. If more products in a higher priced category are imported, then we say that "quality" has risen or upgrading has occurred. This approach is taken by Falvey (1979). So long as the relative demand for two import types can be written as a function of their relative price (i.e., imports are weakly seperable from other goods), then this approach always leads to upgrading under a quota or specific tariff. This occurs because the quota leads to a *specific* rise in prices, which means a smaller percentage rise for the higher quality product. With an ad valorem tariff no quality change occurs since the relative prices of import products is not affected.

This neoclassical approach has it counterpart in empirical application, where quality change is measured by comparing unit values with true price indexes. If the unit value of imports rises by more than a price index over time, then imports must have shifted toward higher priced categories so that quality has risen. This technique has been applied to U.S. imports of footwear by Aw and Roberts (1986). Anderson (1985) estimates the welfare cost due to the quota system on U.S. cheese imports.

The second approach to modeling quality change, which can be labeled hedonic, treats quality as a variable that can be continuously varied. In this approach goods are identified by their characteristics, as in Lancaster (1979), rather than by discrete categories. The distinction between the neoclassical and hedonic approaches is very similiar to that in monopolistic competition, where Helpman and Krugman (1985) distinguish the "love of variety" and "ideal variety" approaches. The hedonic approach was analyzed by Rosen (1974) under competition and Mussa and Rosen (1978) under monopoly, among others. Rodriguez (1979) focused on trade issues; he found that a quota would lead firms to upgrade quality while an ad valorem tariff would have no effect. However, Rodriguez assumed a rather special form for utility, and more general cases have been analyzed by Das and Donnenfeld (1985, 1986), Krishna (1985a, b), and Feenstra (1986). The general conclusion is that either quotas or ad valorem tariffs have an ambiguous effect on product quality.

To understand this result, consider the case where consumers are choosing over a continuum of products indexed by quality, as in Feenstra (1986) (similiar reasoning applies when only one quality is sold). In a free trade equilibrium there may be either a positive or negative correlation between quality purchases and surplus received by consumers. That is, consumers purchasing the highest quality products may receive the largest surplus, or the lowest (zero) surplus, depending on the utility function assumed. Now suppose a quota is imposed, raising the price for any quality product by the same specific amount (as in Falvey). Then the change in *average* quality will depend on which consumers drop out of the market. If consumers purchasing the lower quality products receive the smallest surplus, then they will drop out, and average quality will rise. But, if consumers purchasing the highest quality products drop out, then average quality will fall instead.

While in theory quality may rise or fall under the quota, there is some presumption that upgrading occurs in practice. Supporting evidence in later years for Japanese car imports is reported in Feenstra (1985, 1986). In contrast, for an ad valoerem tariff there is no presumption as to the sign of quality change, though we might expect the magnitude to be small. This result is confirmed for the case of Japanese truck imports, subject to a 25 percent tariff, where Feenstra (1986) finds no evidence of a sustained quality shift due to the tariff.

References for Postscript

Anderson, James E. (1985). The relative inefficiency of quotas: The cheese case. *American Economic Review* 75, no. 1 (March): 178–190.

Aw, Bee Yan, and Mark J. Roberts. 1986. Measuring quality change in quota-constrained import markets: The case of U.S. footwear. *Journal of International Economics* 21: 45–60.

Das, Satya P., and Shabtai Donnenfeld. 1985. Trade policy and its impact on the quality of imports: A welfare analysis. University of Wisconsin-Milwaukee and New York University, December. Mimeo.

Das, Satya P., and Shabtai Donnenfeld. 1986. Oligopolistic competition and international trade: Quantity and quality restrictions. University of Wisconsin-Milwaukee and New York University, April. Mimeo.

Falvey, Rodney E. 1979. The comparison of trade within import-restricted product categories. *Journal of Political Economy* 87, no. 5 (October): 1105–1114.

Feenstra, Robert C. 1985. Automobile prices and protection: The U.S.-Japan trade restraint. *Journal of Policy Modelling* 7, no. 1 (Spring): 49–68.

Feenstra, Robert C. 1986. Quality change under trade restraints: Theory and evidence from Japanese autos. University of California, Davis. Mimeo.

Helpman, Elhanan, and Paul R. Krugman. 1985. *Market Structure and Foreign Trade.* Cambridge: The MIT Press.

Krishna, Kala. 1985a. Tariffs vs. quotas with endogenous quality. NBER Working Paper no. 1535, January.

Krishna, Kala. 1985b. Protection and the product line: Monopoly and product quality. NBER Working Paper no. 1537, January.

Lancaster, Kelvin J. 1979. *Variety, Equity, and Efficiency.* New York: Columbia University Press.

Mussa, Michael, and Sherwin Rosen. 1978. Monopoly and product quality. *Journal of Economic Theory* 18: 301–317.

Rodriguez, Carlos Alfredo. 1979. The quality of imports and the differential welfare effects of tariffs, quotas, and quality controls as protective devices. *Canadian Journal of Economics* 12; no. 3: 439–449.

Rosen, Sherwin. 1974. Hedonic prices and implicit markets: Product differentiation in pure competition. *Journal of Political Economy* 85: 34–55.

V
Theory of Distortions

Introduction of Part V

The theory of policy intervention in open economies, characterized by distortions, is the centerpiece of postwar developments in the theory of trade and welfare during the 1960s and 1970s. Since then, there has been another major revolution in the theory of trade and welfare, reflecting the incorporation of DUP-theoretic phenomena: part VI addresses that set of developments.

Chapter 15 consists of Harry Johnson's influential restatement of the Bhagwati-Ramaswami (*Journal of Political Economy*, February 1983) propositions that, for domestic distortions, a tariff is not the appropriate first-best policy intervention and that a tariff that fully offsets such a domestic distortion may, in replacing suboptimal *laissez faire* by another suboptimal situation, be immiserizing.

Chapter 16 reprints my Kindleberger *Festschrift* generalization of the theory of distortions and welfare. It goes well beyond the Bhagwati-Ramaswami-Johnson results and synthesizes a substantial body of literature on different types of distortions and ranking of alternative policy interventions designed to deal with them. Chapters 15 and 16 therefore ought to be read in conjunction to get a comprehensive view of the modern theory of commerical policy as it emerged in the years since the 1963 Bhagwati-Ramaswami paper, which, it should be emphasized, was in turn stimulated by the earlier work of Gottfried Haberler (*Economic Journal*, June 1950) and Everrett Hagen (*Quarterly Journal of Economics*, November 1958).

15

Optimal Trade Intervention in the Presence of Domestic Distortions

Harry G. Johnson

In the period since the war, the concern of economists with the problems of the underdeveloped countries and the formulation of policies to stimulate economic development has led to renewed interest in the economic arguments for protection. I use the description 'economic arguments' to distinguish arguments that recommend protection as a means of increasing real income or economic welfare from arguments that recommend protection as a means of achieving such essentially non-economic objectives as increasing self-sufficiency for political and military reasons, diversifying the economy to provide a richer way of life for the citizenry and so strengthening national identity, or preserving a valued traditional way of life. In the first place, writers on economic development have taken over and made considerable use of the theory of the optimum tariff originated by Bickerdike and revived in the 1940s and early 1950s as a by-product of the contemporary debate over the legitimacy of welfare propositions in economics. Second, writers in the economic development area have laid considerable stress on the traditional 'external economies' and 'infant industry' arguments for protection; in recent years they have also developed new, or at least heretofore not much emphasized, arguments for protection based on the alleged fact that in underdeveloped countries wages in manufacturing exceed the opportunity cost of labor in the economy—the marginal productivity of labor in the agricultural sector. Two distinct reasons for the alleged discrepancy between industrial wage rates and the opportunity costs of labor are advanced, it not always being recognized that they are distinct. One, which can be associated with the name of Arthur Lewis (1954, 1958), is that industrial wages are related to earnings in the agricultural sector and that these earnings are determined by the average

This paper was originally published in R. Caves, H. G. Johnson, and P. B. Kenen, eds., *Trade, Growth and the Balance of Payment*, Rand McNally, 1965.

product of labor, which exceeds the marginal product of labor because agricultural labor has familial or traditional claims on the rent of land. The other eason, associated with the name of Everett Hagen (1958) but equally attributable to Lewis (1954, pp. 150–51), is that the industrial wage rate exceeds the agricultural wage rate by a margin larger than can be explained by the economic costs of urban life;[1] this difference Hagen associates with the dynamic need for a growing economy to transfer labor from agriculture to industry, although it can also be explained by social influences on industrial wage determination.

The theory of the optimum tariff rests on the proposition that if a country possesses monopolistic or monopsonistic power in world markets, world market prices for its exports and imports will not correspond to the marginal national revenue from exports or marginal national cost of its imports, and it asserts that by appropriately chosen export and import duties—taxes on trade—the country can equate the relative prices of goods to domestic producers and consumers with their relative opportunity costs in international trade. In other words, the theory of the optimum tariff rests on the existence of a distortion in international markets, viewed from the national standpoint, such that market prices diverge from opportunity costs; and the optimum tariff is recommended as a means of off-setting this distortion. The other economic arguments for protection, with which this paper is concerned, rest on the presence of distortions in the domestic economy, which create a divergence between domestic prices and domestic opportunity costs; in these arguments, protection is recommended as a means of offsetting the distortions that prevent domestic prices from reflecting domestic opportunity costs.

The purpose of this paper is to explain and elaborate on two propositions concerning arguments for protection derived from the existence or alleged existence of domestic distortions. The first proposition is that such distortions do not logically lead to the recommendation of protection, in the sense of taxes on international trade; instead, they lead to the recommendation of other forms of government intervention which do not discriminate between domestic and international trade and which differ according to the nature of the distortion they are intended to correct. The second proposition is that if protection is adopted as a means of correcting domestic distortions, not only will the result be that economic welfare will fall short of the maximum obtainable, but economic welfare may even be reduced below what it would be under a policy of free trade. These two propositions can be combined in the proposition that the only valid argument for protection as a means of maximizing economic welfare is the optimum tariff argument; all other arguments for protection of this kind are in principle arguments for some form of government intervention in the domestic economy, and lead to the recommendation of protection only when supported both by practical considerations that render the appropriate form of intervention unfeasible, and empirical evidence that protection will in fact increase economic welfare.

1. Definitions and Assumptions

As a preliminary to the development of the main theme, it is necessary to comment briefly on certain aspects of the setting of the problem and the definition of terms.

In the first place, it is necessary to define the word "protection." Economists generally use this word in a very loose sense, which carries the connotation of a tariff on imports but also lends itself to extension to any policy that raises the price received by domestic producers of an importable commodity above the world market price. Not only can the effect of a tariff be achieved in the modern world by other devices, such as import restrictions, exchange controls, and multiple exchange rates—devices which may achieve the effect of raising the domestic relative price of importable goods above their relative price in the world market by operating to restrict exports as well as to restrict imports—but the domestic relative price received by producers of importable goods can be raised above the world price by two quite different means—by raising the domestic price to both producers and consumers above the world price, through tariffs or equivalent devices, and by raising the domestic price to producers only above the world price, while leaving consumers free to buy at world prices, through subsidies on production or equivalent taxation of production of alternative products. These two means of raising prices to domestic producers above world prices differ sharply in their economic implications, as will appear from what follows, and the confusion of them in the loose usage of the term 'protection' has been responsible for serious analytical errors in the literature. In this paper, I confine the term "protection" to policies that create a divergence between the relative prices of commodities to domestic consumer and producers, and their relative prices in world markets. This usage does not preclude anyone who wishes to describe policies of subsidizing domestic production by one means or another as protection from doing so, and interpreting my analysis as showing that production by subsidies is economically desirable in certain cases of domestic distortion, provided that he clearly distinguishes protection by subsidy from protection by tariff. It is perhaps worth noting in passing—though this is not part of the subject of this paper—that the identification of protection with the tariff is a potent source of confusion in other contexts than the relation of protection to economic welfare; for example, the degree of protection afforded to a particular industry by a tariff structure depends not only on the tariff rate on its product but on the tariffs and other taxes levied or subsidies paid both on its inputs and on the other goods that could be produced by the resources it uses;[2] and these complications include the effects of overvaluation or undervaluation of the exchange rate.

Second, it is necessary to be precise about the meaning attached to an improvement or deterioration in economic welfare. Disagreement on this question was the foundation of the classic debate between Gottfried Haberler and Thomas Balogh that followed on Haberler's attempt to analyse the issues discussed in this paper with the assistance of a criterion of improvement in welfare that has subsequently been shown to be objectionable (Haberler 1950, 1951; Balogh 1951). This paper employs the concept of welfare in the modern sense of potential welfare, and regards a change in the economic environment as producing a potential improvement in economic welfare if, in the new environment, everyone could be made better off—in the usual sense of enjoying a higher consumption of goods and services—than in the old environment, if income were distributed in accordance with any social welfare function applied consistently in the new and the old environment. This approach permits the use of community indifference curves to represent the potential welfare of the community. One might indeed go further and maintain that the assumption that some social welfare function exists and is implemented is essential to any rational discussion of national economic policy.

Third, it is assumed in this paper, in accordance with the conventions of theoretical analysis of these problems, that government intervention is a costless operation: in other words, there is no cost attached to the choice between a tax and a subsidy. This assumption ignores the empirical consideration, frequently introduced into arguments about protection, that poor countries have considerably greater difficulty in levying taxes to finance subsidies than they have in levying tariffs on imports. This consideration is of practical rather than theoretical consequence, and to constitute a case for tariffs requires supplementation by empirical measurement of both the relative administrative costs and the economic effects of the alternative methods of promoting favored industries—as has already been mentioned. Its relevance to practical policymaking is probably less than is frequently assumed, since, on the one hand, the intent of a protective tariff is not to yield revenue and, on the other hand, the effect of a subsidy on one type of production can be achieved by taxes levied on alternative lines of production. The assumption also ignores the possibility that the income or other taxes levied to finance subsidies to production may have a distorting effect on the supply or allocation of resources. Abandonment of this assumption would also lead to the necessity of empirical assessment of the relative economic costs of alternative methods of promoting favored industries.

Finally, something should be said about the bearing of theoretical analysis of the arguments for protection on practical policymaking and the assessment of actual tariff systems. The demonstration that in certain carefully defined circumstances a tariff levied at a theoretically specified rate would make a country better off than it would be under free trade is not—contrary to the implication of many economic writings on protection—equivalent to a demonstration that past or present tariffs have in fact made the nations imposing them better off than they would have been under free trade, or a justification of whatever tariffs legislators might choose to adopt. Modern economic analysis of the cases in which a tariff or other governmental intervention in the price system would improve economic welfare, in other words, does not constitute a defense of indiscriminate protectionism and a rejection of the market mechanism; rather, it points to a number of respects in which the market mechanism fails to work as it should, and indicates remedies designed to make the market function properly. The usefulness of the exercise depends precisely on the assumption that legislators do not normally know what makes for the improvement of economic welfare, and would be prepared to act on better information if it could be provided. If economists did not customarily accept this assumption, their work on economic policy would have to be oriented entirely differently; in particular, research on commercial policy would—depending on the theory of government adopted—be concerned with inferring from actual tariff structures either the divergences between social and private costs and benefits discovered by the collective wisdom of the legislators to exist in the economy, or the political power of various economic groups in the community, as measured by their capacity to extort transfers of income from their fellow-citizens.

2. The Two Propositions

With the preliminary definitions, assumptions, and observations established, I turn to the main theme of the paper, the two propositions concerning optimal government intervention in the presence of domestic distortions. The first proposition, that the correction of such distortions does not require intervention in the form of taxes on international trade (taxes here include negative taxes or subsidies), follows directly from the well-known first-order marginal conditions of Pareto optimality. These conditions specify that the marginal rate of substitution between goods in consumption should be equal to the marginal rate of transformation between goods in production, and in an open economy include transformation through international exchange as well as transformation through domestic production. It follows that any distortion that prevents market prices from corresponding to marginal social rates of substitution or transformation should be corrected by a tax, a subsidy, or a combination of taxes and subsidies that restores the necessary marginal equalities; for simplicity, it is convenient to consider the simplest remedy, a tax or subsidy imposed at the point where the distortion occurs. Where there is a distortion in foreign markets, owing to imperfectly elastic foreign demand or supply, Pareto optimality requires the imposition of taxes on trade designed to equate the domestic price ratios facing producers and consumers with the marginal rates of transformation between commodities in international trade—that is, the imposition of the optimum taiff structure.[3] In the case of domestic distortions, Pareto optimality requires the imposition of taxes or subsidies on consumption, production, or factor supply, as the situation requires.

Where externalities in consumption make social marginal rates of substitution diverge from private, taxes or subsidies on consumption are required; where external economies in production exist, or where monopolistic influences raise prices above marginal costs, marginal subsidies on production are required; and where external diseconomies are present, marginal taxes on production are required; and where the price of a factor in a particular occupation exceeds its price in other occupations by more than can be accounted for by the nonpecuniary disadvantages of that occupation, a subsidy on the use of that factor in that occupation is required. The point of central importance is that the correction of domestic distortions requires a tax or subsidy on either domestic consumption or domestic production or domestic factor use, not on international trade.

The imposition of any tax or subsidy on international trade, other than what is indicated by the optimum tariff analysis, for the purpose of correcting a domestic distortion itself introduces an inequality between either the marginal rate of substitution in domestic consumption or the marginal rate of transformation in domestic production and the marginal rate of transformation in foreign trade, and so constitutes a violation of Pareto optimality. A tax on luxury imports, for example, designed to discourage an undesirable demonstration effect and therefore to correct an external diseconomy of consumption, permits the marginal rate of transformation of domestic resources into the importable good in question to exceed the marginal rate of transformation through foreign trade. A tax on imports or subsidy to exports of goods subject to external economies or monopolistic pricing in domestic production, designed to offset these distortions, makes the relative marginal cost of these goods to consumers higher than their marginal cost to the economy. Since the offsetting of domestic distortions by taxes or subsidies on trade necessarily removes one distortion at the expense of introducing another, interventions in international trade introduced for this purpose cannot lead to a situation of Pareto optimality. Consequently tariffs and other trade interventions justified on grounds of the existence of domestic distortions cannot lead to the maximization of real income. The only forms of intervention that can do so are interventions that offset the existing distortions without introducing new distortions; such interventions are confined to taxes and subsidies on domestic consumption, production, or factor use.

The second proposition, that taxes or subsidies on international trade designed to offset domestic distortions will not necessarily increase economic welfare by comparison with the free trade situation, is a direct application of the theory of second best developed by Meade (1955), Lipsey and Lancaster (1956–57), and others. One implication of that theory is that it is impossible to predict on *a priori* grounds—that is, without comprehensive empirical information on the tastes and technology of the economy— whether the substitution of one violation of the Pareto optimality conditions for another will worsen or improve economic welfare. Since the use of intervention in trade to offset domestic distortions necessarily involves precisely this kind of substitution, it is impossible to say whether the result will be an improvement in welfare or not. For example, in the consumption externality case mentioned above, free trade produces the result $MRT_d = MRT_f > MRS$; and an import tariff produces the result $MRT_d > MRT_f = MRS$. In the case of external economies in production or monopolistic pricing, free trade produces the result $MRT_d < MRT_f = MRS$, and an import tariff produces the result $MRT_d = MRT_f < MRS$. In the case of a distortion in the market for factors, there are additional violations of the Pareto optimality conditions in the factor markets under both free trade and protection.[4]

The remainder of the paper is concerned with illustrating these propositions by reference to various arguments for protection. For this purpose, it is convenient to follow the general outline of Haberler's classic article (1950), modified to include fuller treatment of the arguments emphasized in the recent literature on underdeveloped countries, and to divide the arguments for protection into four groups. These are arguments derived from immobility of factors and downward rigidity of factor prices, arguments derived from distortions in commodity markets, arguments derived from distortions in factor markets, and the infant industry argument. The first class of argument, to which Haberler devoted considerable space, grew out of the unemployment problem of the 1930s and the associated revival of protectionism. The second includes both the classical problems of external economies and diseconomies and the problem of monopolistic distortions to which considerable attention was devoted in the 1930s following the development of the theory of monopolistic (imperfect) competition. The third involves the essential elements of the new case for protection developed on the basis of the disequilibrium in the labor market alleged to be characteristic of underdeveloped countries. The fourth is, of course, the orthodox accepted exception to the case for free trade.

3. The Standard Trade Model

To provide a frame of reference for the analysis of these arguments, it is convenient to use the standard model of international trade. This model simplifies the problem by assuming that the economy produces two commodities only, by employing only two factors of production, the available quantities of which are assumed to be given; the production functions for the two commodities are assumed to be subject to constant returns to scale, an assumption which eliminates externalities in production; and perfect competition is assumed in the commodity and factor markets, which assumption includes perfect flexibility of prices and mobility of factors between industries. These assumptions permit the production conditions of the economy to be summarized in a community transformation curve between the two commodities, such that at any exchange ratio between the commodities production will be represented by the point on the transformation curve at which the slope of that curve is equal to the exchange ratio. On the demand side, factor owners are assumed to be indifferent between occupations—utility depends only on the quantities of goods consumed— and consumers' welfare is assumed to depend only on personal consumption, which assumption eliminates externalities in consumption. (Such consumption externalities are ignored in the remainder of this paper, since they have not been advanced as an important argument for protection; and the relevant analysis follows directly from the proposition already presented, and from analogy with the cases of production distortion dealt with below.) The individual tastes and distribution of income that determine the demand for the two commodities are assumed to be summarizable in a set of community indifference curves, such that for any given income and exchange ratio the consumption of the two commodities will be that which places the community on the highest attainable indifference curve. Since in a competitive economy the distribution of income depends on the distribution of factor ownership and varies with factor prices, the set of community indifference curves has to be interpreted as embodying either the concept of potential welfare employed in modern welfare economics, or the expression of a particular social welfare function in a particular invariant distribution of income among the members of the community. The conclusions concerning the effects of alternative types of government intervention on economic welfare derived below are to be interpreted as referring to welfare in either of these two senses. Since the concern of the paper is with government intervention in the presence of domestic distortions, it is convenient to exclude distortions in foreign markets by assuming that the opportunity to trade internationally consists in the opportunity to exchange goods in the world market at an exchange ratio different from that which would rule in the economy in the absence of the opportunity to trade, which international exchange ratio is assumed to be independent of the direction or magnitude of the trade of the country under analysis. The two commodities will be referred to as X and Y, and it is assumed throughout that the country's true comparative advantage lies in Y, in the sense that the comparatives cost of Y in the absence of the opportunity to trade is lower than the comparative cost of Y embodied in the international exchange ratio.

This standard model of international trade is represented in the accompanying figure 15.1, where TT is the transformation curve and U_0, U_1, U_2 are the community indifference curves. In the absence of the opportunity

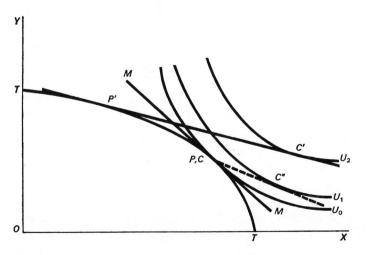

Figure 15.1

to trade, the community would produce and consume at P,C, the closed-economy exchange ratio between the goods being represented by the slope of the common tangent MM to the transformation and indifference curves at that point. The opportunity to trade (represented by the slope $P'C'$) allows the economy to increase its welfare from U_0 to U_2, by shifting from production and consumption at P,C to production at P' and consumption at C'. The gain in welfare resulting from trade can be divided into two components: the increase in welfare from U_0 to U_1 resulting from the opportunity to exchange the goods produced in the absence of trade for the more attractive consumption combination C'' (the consumption or exchange gain) and the increase in welfare from U_1 to U_2 resulting from the opportunity to produce a combination of goods more valuable at the international price ratio than the closed-economy output (the production or specialization gain). The adjustment to the higher international price of Y necessarily involves an increase in the relative price of the factor used relatively intensively in producing that commodity, and a reduction in the relative price of the factor used relatively intensively in producing the importable commodity X.

4. Factor Immobility and Price Rigidity

For the analysis of arguments for protection derived from immobility of factors and downward rigidity of factor prices, it is convenient to pose the problem in terms of whether the opening of the opportunity to trade makes a country worse off when these conditions exist, so that a prohibitive tariff would secure a higher level of welfare than could be attained under free trade, even though in reality the argument for protection on these grounds usually arises when trade is already established and the international price of imports suddenly falls. The difference of assumptions merely simplifies the problem without altering the conclusions.

As Haberler has shown, there is a fundamental difference between the effects of immobility of factors, combined with flexibility of factor prices, and of downward rigidity of factor prices, whether combined with immobility or not. As the analysis of the standard model of trade shows, the country would enjoy a consumption or exchange gain from trade even if production remained at the closed-economy equilibrium point. Production would remain at that point if factors were completely immobile but their prices were perfectly flexible; if factors were partially mobile. production would shift to some point within the transformation curve, but necessarily entailing a higher value of production at world market prices, that is, yielding some production or specialization gain. It follows that so long as factor prices are flexible, immobility of factors cannot prevent the country from being better off under free trade than with protection. The fundamental reason for this is that immobility does not by itself entail a distortion of the first-order conditions of Pareto optimality. So long as factor prices are flexible, and immobility is taken as an immutable fact of life (more is said on this point below), factor prices will reflect the alternative opportunity costs of factors to the economy; hence there is no domestic distortion to be offset by protection, and protection will simply introduce a distortion of the marginal conditions for optimality in foreign trade.

Downward rigidity of factor prices does introduce a distortion, if (as Haberler has carefully pointed out) such rigidity does not reflect a perfectly elastic supply of the factor in question (derived, for example, from an infinite elasticity of substitution between leisure and consumption) but instead reflects institutional limitations on voluntary choice (imposed, for example, by conventional pricing of labor services or collective bargaining).[5] Analysis of the effects of downward rigidity of factor prices requires definition of the terms in which factor prices are rigid downwards, since factor prices may be rigid in terms of one commodity or the other or of the utility level enjoyed, and consideration of various possible combinations of downward price rigidity and immobility.

If factor prices are rigid in terms of X and both factors are immobile, production will remain where it was in the absence of trade (at point P in figure 2). The result will be the same as with factor price flexibility, since the marginal productivities of the factors in the X industry in terms of X are unchanged, while the marginal productivities of the factors in the Y industry are unchanged in terms of Y but greater in terms of X, because the price of X in terms of Y has fallen as a result of trade. If both factor prices are rigid in terms of Y or of constant-utility combinations of X and Y, and both factors are immobile, production of X will cease, and both factors used in producing X will become wholly unemployed (the economy will produce at point A in figure 15.2, level with P, C). This result follows from the fact that the marginal productivities of the factors in the X industry will be unchanged in terms of X but lower in terms of Y or any combination of X and Y, because the price of X in terms of Y has decreased as a result of trade. Since the value of each factor's marginal product is now below its price when the factors are combined in the ratio optimal at these factor prices, and since neither factor price can change to induce factor substitution and raise the marginal productivity of the other factor the cost production of X must exceed its price at any positive level of output.

If both factor prices are rigid (in terms of X or of Y or of a constant-utility combination of X and Y), and both factors are perfectly mobile,

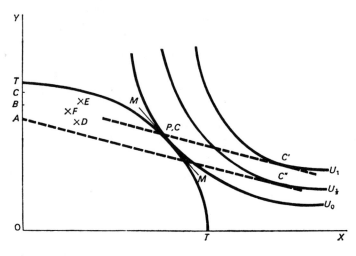

Figure 15.2

production of X will cease and factors will be transferred into production of Y. Some of the factor used intensively in producing X must, however, become unemployed, so that production of Y will be less than the maximum possible production shown by the transformation curve, since full employment of both factors necessitates a reduction of the price of that factor in terms of both commodities, according to the well-known Stolper-Samuelson analysis (1941). The amount of unemployment of the factor in question will be greater, and the increase in production of Y less, if factor prices are rigid in terms of Y than if they are rigid in terms of X, since a given factor price expressed in Y now buys more X, and the marginal productivity of the surplus factor in the Y industry can fall if factor prices are rigid in terms of X but not if they are rigid in terms of Y. (The extremes are represented for illustrative purposes by points B and C in figure 15.2: if factor prices are rigid in terms of utility, production of Y will fall smewhere between these points.)

If both factors are immobile, but the price of one of them is flexible, whereas the price of the other is rigid in terms of Y or of a constant-utility combination of X and Y, production of X will not cease altogether; instead, enough of the rigid-priced factor in that industry will become unemployed to lower its ratio to the other factor to what is consistent with its rigid price. Obviously, the unemployment of that factor and the decrease in production of X will be greater if that factor's price is rigid in terms of Y than if it is rigid in terms of a constant-utility combination of X and Y, and in the latter case will be less the less important is Y in the factor's consumption. (This case is represented in figure 15.2 by the single point D, in the same horizontal line as A and P,C.) If one of the factors is mobile, and its price is rigid in terms of X or of a constant-utility combination of X and Y, whereas the other factor is immobile and flexible-priced, some of the rigid-priced factor will transfer to the Y industry, increasing output there. The transfer will proceed to the point where its effect in raising the ratio of the mobile factor to the other in the Y industry lowers the marginal productivity of the mobile factor in the Y industry to the level set by its price rigidity. (This case is represented by point E in figure 15.2; E may be vertically above D as in the diagram or to the left of it, and must correspond to a higher value of output at world prices than D.) If one of the factors is mobile and flexible-priced, whereas the other factor is immobile and its price is rigid in terms of X or of Y or of a constant-utility combination of X and Y, production of Y will increase and of X decrease as compared with the case of immobility of both factors; production of X may or may not cease entirely depending on the elasticities of substitution between the factors in the two industries and on the terms in which the immobile factor's price is rigid. (This case is represented by point F in the diagram, and may or may not correspond to a higher value of output than at D.)

Whatever the combination of factor immobility and factor price rigidity assumed, production will be altered to some point in the interior of the transformation curve corresponding to production of less X and possibly no more Y than in the closed-economy equilibrium (except for the extreme case of complete immobility and factor price rigidity in terms of X already noted). This does not, however, necessarily imply that free trade makes the country worse off than it would be under the self-sufficiency obtainable by a prohibitive tariff. It may, or it may not. Figure 15.2 illustrates the possibility of the country's being better off with free trade than with a prohibitive tariff even in the extreme case in which production of X ceases altogether, with no consequent increase in the production of Y, owing to a combination of complete factor immobility with factor price rigidity. In this case, as the diagram shows, the country could be made still better off than under free trade by subsidizing production of the initial output of X sufficiently to permit the factors being paid the minimum prices they demand, but trading at the international exchange ratio. In the less extreme cases, more complex forms of subsidy may be necessary to achieve the output combination that has the highest value at the international exchange ratio attainable under the relevant restrictions on factor mobility.

5. Distortions in the Commodity Market

The second group of arguments for protection to be discussed comprises arguments derived from the existence of distortions in the markets for commodities that have the effect or raising the market price of the commodity in which the country has a comparative advantage above its alternative opportunity cost. One possibility is the presence of monopoly or oligopoly conditions in the production of the good, which have the effect of raising the price to consumers above the marginal cost of production. Another is the presence of external economies or diseconomies, which make marginal cost as it appears to producers higher than marginal social cost. The marginal social cost of increased output of a particular commodity may be lower than the marginal private cost because expansion of the industry producing it yields economies of scale external to the individual firm, or because contraction of the industry from which this industry draws its factors of production lowers costs of production in the former because that industry is subject to diseconomies of scale, or because expansion of the one industry lowers the cost of production of the other through any one of a variety of effects.

The result of either type of distortion, in terms of the simple model of international trade, is that the market price ratio at which a particular combination of X and Y will be produced will be less steep than the slope of the transformation curve, reflecting the assumption that the relative price of Y (the good in which the country is assumed to have a comparative advantage) exceeds its social opportunity cost. In the absence of the opportunity to trade, the country will therefore in equilibrium produce more X and less Y than would be socially optimal; the closed-economy equilibrium is represented in figure 15.3 by the point P,C, the slope of MM corresponding to the market price ratio and that of RR to the true comparative

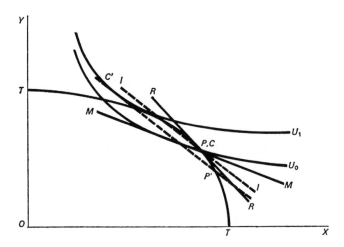

Figure 15.3

cost ratio. The opening of the opportunity to trade at an international price ratio at which the country's true comparative advantage lies in Y has two alternative possible results, according to the relation between the international price ratio and the closed-economy market price ratio: this relation may indicate either an apparent comparative advantage in X, in which case the country specializes in the wrong direction, or an apparent comparative advantage in Y corresponding to the country's true comparative advantage, in which case the country specializes in the right direction but to a suboptimal extent.

The first case is represented in figure 15.3 by the international price ratio II, which leads the country to the production equilibrium P' and the consumption equilibrium C', involving the export of X, in which the country is at a true comparative disadvantage. The point P' necessarily represents a lower value of output at the international price ratio than the closed-economy production point P; but C' may lie on either a lower indifference curve than the closed-economy consumption point C, or a higher one, the latter possibility being illustrated in the diagram. In other words, trade leads to a production loss and a consumption gain, and the latter may or may not offset the former.

The argument for protection in this case is that the country will gain by imposing a tariff on imports to raise their price to consumers above the world price, compensating for the distortion that makes the apparent cost of domestically produced importables exceed their true social cost. (Alternatively, the country could levy a tax on exports to compensate for the distortion that makes their true social cost exceed their apparent cost.) Since the country's true comparative advantage lies in the good it imports, the imposition of an import tariff (or an export duty) at a rate just sufficient to compensate for the distortion would effect a return to self-sufficiency at the production and consumption equilibrium P,C, since a tax on trade cannot reverse the direction of trade. The effect of the tariff would be to increase the value of the country's output at the international price ratio; but, as the diagram exemplifies, the resulting pattern of consumption might yield a lower level of economic welfare than would be attained in the absence of protection. In short, the imposition of the tariff to correct the distortion of domestic prices from opportunity costs achieves a production gain at the expense of a consumption loss, and the net-effect may be a gain or a loss, by comparison with free trade. Thus free trade in the wrong direction may be superior to protection designed to correct a distortion of domestic market prices; which policy is actually superior depends on the magnitudes of the distortion of domestic prices from opportunity costs and the difference between the closed-economy exchange ratio and the inter-

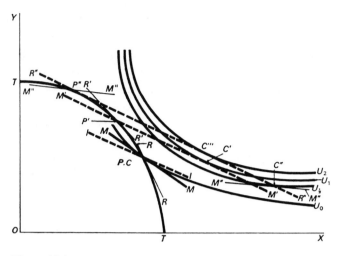

Figure 15.4

national exchange ratio, and the shape of the community's preference system.[6]

The second case is illustrated in figure 15.4, where at the international price ratio II the country's apparent comparative advantage lies in the commodity in which it has a true comparative advantage, and the opportunity to trade leads to the production equilibrium P' and consumption equilibrium C', involving the export of commodity Y. P' necessarily represents a higher value of national output at the international exchange ratio than the closed-economy production point P, so that the country enjoys both a consumption gain and a production gain from trade; but the volume of international trade falls short of the optimum level, owing to the excess of the price of Y over its comparative cost.

In this case, the arguments for intervention in international trade to correct the distortion of domestic prices would indicate an export subsidy on Y (or import subsidy on X). The same policy might be recommended to overcome the inability of the tariff to promote exports in the circumstances of the case previously considered. (In either case, to be effectively a subsidy on trade rather than on production, the export subsidy would have to be accompanied by measures preventing reimportation.) The introduction of such a subsidy at a rate just sufficient to offset the distortion would lead to the production equilibrium P'' and consumption equilibrium C'' shown in figure 15.4, the new domestic price ratio being represented by $M''M''$. The subsidy would necessarily raise the value of output at the international exchange ratio above what it would be under free trade, but, as the diagram illustrates, it might nevertheless lead to a consumption pattern yielding a lower level of welfare than that enjoyed under free trade, owing to the consumption loss induced by the effect of the subsidy in raising the domestic relative price of the exported good Y above the world market price. In order to achieve the maximum attainable economic welfare (C''' in figure 15.4), the country should subsidize production of Y (or tax production of X) at a rate sufficient to compensate for the domestic distortion, without discriminating between domestic and foreign consumers by a tax (in the first case) or subsidy (in the second case) on international trade.[7]

One further comment on arguments for governmental intervention derived from distortions in domestic commodity markets is worth making. The foregoing analysis lumps together distortions originating in external economies and diseconomies, and distortions originating in imperfectly competitive market organization; and it assumes that the distortions are independent of the governmental intervention, so that intervention can be designed to offset them. This assumption is legitimate for the first type of distortion, but of doubtful validity for the second. Monopolistic practices are generally intimately interrelated with commercial policy, and there is reason to believe that producers often collude to exploit the profit opportunities created by protection. Where this is so, the attempt to offset monopolistic distortions by protective interventions in trade (taxes or subsidies on trade) may well be offset by increased distortions, so that intervention generates a consumption loss without a countervailing production gain; the same reaction could render nugatory the attempt to employ optimal intervention in the form of production taxes or subsidies. In these circumstances, the only effective means of achieving maximum economic welfare would be a direct attack on the source of the distortion, through trust-busting policies, although it is worth noting that genuine free trade may be the most effective policy for controlling monopoly.

6. Distortions in the Factor Market

The third group of arguments for protection comprises arguments derived from the existence of distortions in the markets for factors that, by raising the price of a factor used in producing the commodity in which the country has a comparative advantage above the factor's marginal productivity in the rest of the economy, raises the private cost of production of the commodity above its alternative opportunity cost. As mentioned, two reasons for such a distortion are commonly advanced in the literature on economic development, both of which pertain to a distortion in the labor market and are used to favor protection of industry—that earnings of labor in agriculture exceed the marginal productivity of labor there, so that the industrial wage must exceed the alternative opportunity cost of labor, and that industrial wages exceed wages in agriculture by a margin greater than can be accounted for by the disutility or higher cost of urban life.

The effect of such distortions in factor markets is twofold: first, they make the allocation of factors between industries inefficient, so that production is below the maximum attainable—in terms of the model of international trade, the transformation curve is pulled in toward the origin, except at the extreme points of specialization on one or the other commodity. Second, they will normally cause the market exchange ratio between the commodities to differ from the social opportunity cost ratio, the only exception occurring when a distortion in the market for one factor is exactly offset by an opposite distortion in the market for the others. In particular, if the marginal productivity of one particular factor in one industry must exceed its marginal productivity in the other, the price of the commodity produced by the former industry must exceed its opportunity cost. Consequently, in this case the country's economic welfare will be below the maximum attainable, both in the absence of the opportunity to trade and under free trade, for two reasons: first, the country will be on a transformation curve inferior to the transformation curve that would be available to it in the absence of the distortion in the factor market; and second, owing to the discrepancy between private costs of production and social costs in the commodity market resulting from the distortion in the factor market, the country will choose a suboptimal position on the restricted transformation curve available to it.

Given the existence of a distortion in the market for a factor requiring its marginal productivity to be higher in the industry in which the country has a comparative advantage, the opportunity to trade may have either of the two consequences analysed in connection with distortions in the commodity markets; and, as demonstrated in that analysis, the protectionist policy of remedying the effects of the distortion by an export or import duty (if the country specializes on the commodity in which it has a comparative disadvantage) or an export or import subsidy (if the country specializes on the commodity in which it has a comparative advantage) may make the country either worse off or better off than it would be under free trade. A policy of subsidization of production of the commodity overpriced by the distortion, or of taxation of production of the other commodity, would maximize the economic welfare attainable from the restricted transformation curve. The important point, however, is that all of these policies aimed at offsetting the distortion by operating on the prices received by producers of commodities would leave the country on a transformation curve restricted by the inefficiency of factor use induced by the factor market distortion. This particular cause of suboptimal economic welfare could be eliminated in four different ways—by a tax on the use in one industry or subsidy on the use in the other of either factor, the rate of tax or subsidy being chosen to exactly offset the distortion. But only two of these—a subsidy on the use of the factor subject to distortion in the industry in which its marginal productivity is required to be higher, or a tax on its use in the other industry—would simultaneously eliminate the associated distortion of commodity prices from opportunity costs, the other two accentuating the distortion in the commodity market. Thus the attainment of maximum economic welfare in this case requires subsidization or taxation of the use of the factor subject to distortion; taxation or subsidization of commodity production can maximize welfare subject to the inefficiency of factor use but cannot correct that inefficiency; taxation or subsidization of commodity trade not only fails to eliminate inefficiency in factor allocation but may even reduce welfare, given the inefficiency of factor allocation, below what it would be under free trade.

The foregoing argument has accepted the validity of the contention that in underdeveloped countries there is a distortion in the labor market such that the marginal productivity of labor in industry must be higher than the marginal productivity of labor in agriculture (the alternative opportunity cost of labor). Before leaving this group of arguments for protection, it is appropriate to express some doubts about the validity of this contention and its implications for economic policy. As already mentioned, there are two separate arguments supporting this contention—that industrial wages exceed agricultural wags, and that industrial wages are comparable to agricultural earnings but that the latter exceed the marginal productivity of labor in agriculture because agricultural workers claim a share of agricultural rent.

So far as the first argument is concerned, the mere fact that industrial wages exceed agricultural wages is not sufficient to prove a distortion, since the difference may be accounted for by the higher cost of disutility of urban living, the greater skill or stamina required of urban industrial labor, or the economic cost of migration, factors which necessitate compensation in the form of a higher industrial than agricultural wage if allocation of the labor force is to be efficient. An attempt to iron out wage differences due to these factors would involve misallocation of labor. There are, however, two plausible reasons for believing that observed industrial-agricultural wage differences may entail a genuine distortion.[8] The first is that frequently in underdeveloped countries either trade union organization or social legislation and popular sentiment impose industrial wage levels well above the alternative opportunity cost of labor; this possibility is substantiated by the evidence of persistent large-scale urban unemployment, and by the fact that wage levels tend to increase with size of establishment. In so far as trade union organization or political pressure forces industry to page wages above the alternative opportunity cost of labor, however, any attempt to remedy the distortion by subsidization of the use of labor or by protection might be frustrated by the exaction of still higher wages. The second reason is suggested by an interpretation of migration from rural to urban employment as an investment in the formation of human capital, the investment involving both a transportation and an education cost; insofar as the market for capital to finance investment in human beings is imperfect, the marginal rate of return on such investment may be far higher than the social opportunity cost of capital to the economy.

So far as the second reason for distortion is concerned—the excess of agricultural earnings over the marginal productivity of agricultural labor—since this implies that the private return on capital invested in agriculture is less than the social return, the distortion in the labor market may be more than offset by an opposite distortion in the capital market, so that rather than indicating the desirability of subsidization of the use of labor in industry, this argument may in fact indicate the desirability of subsidization of the use of capital in agriculture.

7. The Infant Industry Argument

The fourth type of argument for protection to be considered is the infant industry argument. Although this argument is frequently confused, at least in description, with the "external economies" argument, the two are logically distinct. The external economies argument is static, in the sense that the assumed distortion due to external economies or diseconomies is by implication a permanent characteristic of the technology of production that would require correction by government intervention of a permanent kind. The infant industry argument, by contrast, is explicitly dynamic or more accurately an argument for temporary intervention to correct a transient distortion, the justification for protection being assumed to disappear with the passage of time.

The infant industry argument bases the case for temporary protection on the assertion that the industry in question (or, more commonly in the literature on economic development, manufacturing in general) would eventually be able to compete on equal terms with foreign producers in the domestic or world market if it were given temporary tariff protection to enable it to establish itself, but would be unable to establish itself against free competition from established foreign producers owing to the temporary excessive costs it would have to incur in the initial stages. Since the incurring of costs for a limited period in return for future benefits is a type of investment, the infant industry argument is essentially an assertion that free competition would produce a socially inefficient allocation of investment resources. For the argument to be valid, it is not sufficient to demonstrate that present costs, in the form of losses on production in the infancy of the industry, must be incurred for the sake of future benefits in the form of higher income than would otherwise be earned. For if the higher income accrues to those who incur the costs, and the capital market functions efficiently, the investment will be privately undertaken unless the rate of return on it is below the rate of return available on alternative investments, in which case the investment would be socially as well as privately unprofitable. To provide an argument for government intervention, it must be demonstrated either that the social rate of return exceeds the private rate of return on the investment, or that the private rate of return necessary to induce the investment exceeds the private and social rates of return available on alternative investment, by a wide enough margin to make a socially profitable investment privately unprofitable.

The social rate of return on investment in an infant industry may exceed the private rate of return for a variety of reasons, of which two may be of particular relevance to the problems of underdeveloped countries (Kemp 1960). One relates to the fact that, once created, the product of investment in the acquisition of knowledge, unlike the product of material investments, can be enjoyed by additional users without additional cost of production. In other words, once knowledge of production technique is acquired, it can be applied by others than those who have assumed the cost of acquiring it; the social benefit at least potentially exceeds the private benefit of investment in learning industrial production techniques, and the social use of the results of such learning may even reduce the private reward for undertaking the investment. Where the social benefits of the learning process exceed the private benefits, the most appropriate governmental policy would be to subsidize the learning process itself, through such techniques as financing or sponsoring pilot enterprises on condition that the experience acquired and techniques developed be made available to all would-be producers. The other reason why the social benefit may exceed the private hinges on the facts that much of the technique of production is embodied in the skill of the labor force, and that the institutions of the labor market give the worker the property rights in any skills he acquires at the employer's expense. Consequently, the private rate of return to the employer on the investment in on-the-job training may be lower than the social rate of return, because the trained worker may be hired away by a competitor. The appropriate policy in this case would entail the government either financing on-the-job training or establishing institutions enabling labor to finance its own training out of the higher future income resulting from training.[9] In either of the two cases just described a subsidy on production or on investment in the infant industry would in principle be economically inefficient, since neither type of subsidy would necessarily stimulate the type of investment in knowledge subject to an excess of social over private return.

The private rate of return necessary to induce investment in infant industries may also exceed the private and social rates of return on alternatively investments for a variety of reasons. Entrepreneurs may be excessively pessimistic about the prospects of success, or unwilling to take chances; in this case the most appropriate policy would involve publication of expert estimates of the prospects for the industries in question. Alternatively, imperfections in the capital market may make the cost of finance for investment in new industries excessively high, especially if these industries require an initially large scale for economical production by the firm; in this case, subsidization of provision of capital would be the appropriate policy.

Whatever the distortion in the allocation of investment capital used to support the infant industry argument for protection, it is apparent from the general principles governing optimal governmental intervention in the presence of domestic distortions that the optimal policy entails some sort of subsidy to the infant industries, rather than protection. Where infant industry distortions exist, protection justified by their presence may have the effect of reducing economic welfare rather than raising it. The reason is that protection increases the social cost of the investment in the learning process of the infant industry, by adding to the cost of a transitional subsidy the consumption cost of protection; the additional cost may be sufficient to reduce the social rate of return on the investment below the social rate of return on alternative investments.

It has been mentioned above that, for the infant industry argument to justify government intervention, investment in the learning process of the infant industry must be socially profitable. This requirement implies that the customary formulations of both the infant industry argument and the most potent argument used against it are seriously defective. The customary formulation argues that there is a case for protection on infant industry grounds if the industry could eventually compete in the domestic or world market without protection. This argument is invalid because protection involves a present cost which can only be justified economically by an increase in future income above what it would otherwise be; and a necessary condition for this is that the infant industries should eventually be able to complete while paying higher returns to the factors they employ than those

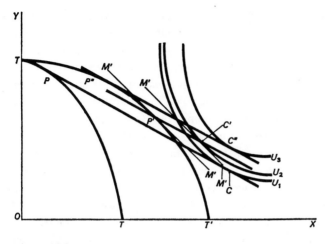

Figure 15.5

factors would have enjoyed if the infant industries had not been assisted to maturity by protection. The most potent argument against infant industry protection is that the infant industries in fact never grow up but instead continue to require protection. The argument overlooks the possibility that, although the continuance of protection is a political fact, it is not always an economic necessity: protection may be continued even though intramarginal firms or units of production do not require it, and the country may gain from infant industry protection even though such protection continues indefinitely. The possibility of such a gain is illustrated in figure 15.5, where as a result of infant industry protection the transformation curve shifts outward from TT to TT', and the community as a consequence enjoys the welfare level U_2 in place of the welfare level U_1 in the long run. If the cost of protection, in terms of a lower welfare level in the period of transition from TT to TT', is low enough, the increase in welfare from U_1 to U_2 great enough, and the social rate of return required to justify the investment low enough, the eventual welfare level U_2 may be superior to the eventual welfare level U_1, even though U_2 is inferior to the welfare level U_3 that could be enjoyed if the infant industry tariff were removed once it had served it purpose.

8. Conclusion: Noneconomic Arguments for Protection

This paper has been concerned with elaborating on two propositions concerning arguments for protection based on the alleged existence of domestic distortions creating a divergence between marginal private and marginal social benefits or costs. These are that welfare maximization requires a correlation of the relevant domestic distortion by an appropriate tax or subsidy on production, consumption, or factor use, and not a tax or subsidy on international trade; and that, given the presence of a domestic distortion, protection designed to offset it may decrease welfare rather than increase it. In conclusion, it is appropriate to comment on two further matters, the reasons why economists who admit the need for correction of domestic distortions are so prone to concede the argument for tariffs in these cases, and the bearing of the analysis on noneconomic arguments for protection.

The explanation for the propensity of economists to concede the argument for protection rather than present the case for more appropriate and theoretically reliable remedies seems to lie in two factors—the tendency of economists when confronted with policy problems to ignore the rather elusive principle of consumers' sovereignty and to adopt the apparently but illusively firmer welfare criterion of an increase in the value of production, and the historical emphasis of the theory of international trade on the real cost approach to economic welfare as contrasted with the opportunity cost approach, an emphasis ultimately derived from the labor theory of value. The latter emphasis has been a major source of weakness in the theoretical analysis of contemporary international trade problems, both in connection with the theory of tariffs and in connection with the more recently evolved theory of customs unions and discriminatory tariff reduction.

While this paper has concentrated on the economic arguments for protection—specifically, on arguments for protection as a means of correcting domestic distortions leading to inequalities between marginal social and marginal private costs or benefits—the analysis does have some important implications for what have been described in the introduction as noneconomic arguments for protection.[10] Such arguments stress the noneconomic value of changes in production and consumption or resource allocation patterns achieved by protection. Conceptually, they can be divided into arguments that stress the noneconomic value of increased *domestic production* of, and arguments that stress the noneconomic value of increased *self-sufficiency* in (a reduced volume of imports of) certain types of commodities that under free trade would be imported. The argument of this paper has shown that where domestic distortions make the production of a commodity lower than it should be, optimal government intervention entails subsidization of production rather than interferences with international trade. The same conclusion can be shown to hold for noneconomic arguments based on the desirability of larger domestic production, such as the national identity and way-of-life arguments mentioned above. On the other hand, it can be shown that for noneconomic arguments based on the desirability of a smaller volume of imports, the method of tariff protection is superior to the method of subsidization. The reason is that in the first case an increase of domestic production achieved by protection, as contrasted with an increase achieved by subsidization, involves an additional cost in the form of a consumption loss. In the second case, however, the reduction in consumption achieved by the tariff is to be regarded as a gain, since it also contributes to the reduction of imports; and since at the margin the production loss from subsidizing production is proportional to the rate of subsidy, and the consumption loss from taxing consumption is proportional to the rate of tax, it follows that a given reduction in imports can be achieved more efficiently by means of the tariff, which subsidizes production and taxes consumption at the same rate, than by means of a production subsidy alone, which subsidy would necessarily be at a higher rate than the required tariff rate.

These propositions are illustrated in figure 15.6, where P' represents the production point and C' the consumption point achieved by the imposition of a tariff that distorts the domestic exchange ratio and transformation ratio from the international exchange ratio $P'C'$ to $M'M'$, It is obvious that the country could reach the consumption point C and the associated higher welfare level U_2, while keeping domestic production at the same level P', by replacing the tariff by a subsidy on production of X (or a tax on production of Y). If, however, the object of policy is not the domestic production pattern shown by P' but the restriction of international trade

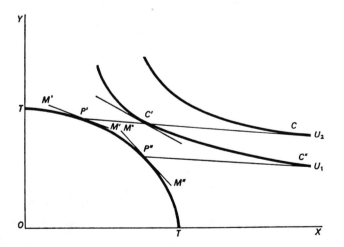

Figure 15.6

to the level represented by the distance $P'C'$, achievement of this object by means of subsidization of domestic production necessarily involves a greater loss of welfare than achievement of it by means of tariff protection. To appreciate this, consider the production subsidy represented by the domestic price ratio $M''M''$, which combined with free trade places the country on the indifference curve U_1 reached with the tariff. It follows from the tangencies of the transformation curve and the indifference curve U_1 to the tariff-distorted domestic exchange ratio at P' and C' that the distance between the production point P'' and consumption point C'' achieved with a subsidy welfare-indifferent to the tariff is greater than that between the production point P' and consumption point C' achieved with the tariff. In short, for a given welfare loss, trade is restricted less by a production subsidy than by a tariff; therefore, the achievement of a given restriction of trade requires a smaller welfare loss if trade is restricted by a tariff than if trade is restricted by a production subsidy.

Notes

This paper originated as a guest lecture at the Claremont Colleges, California, delivered in March 1963. It was originally scheduled for publication in the *Indian Economic Review*, but the editors of that journal have graciously released it for inclusion in this volume (*Trade, Growth and the Balance of Payments*) on the grounds that its contents bear witness to the depth and durability of Gottfried Haberler's contribution to the pure theory of international trade and economic welfare.

The paper represents a condensation of analysis developed in lectures and writings over a period of years. The organization of the argument around the two central propositions of the paper, however, is derived from discussion with Jagdish Bhagwati, and particularly from an early reading of his brilliant joint article with V. K. Ramaswami, "Domestic distortions tariffs and the theory of optimum subsidy," *Journal of Political Economy* 71 (1963): 44–50. To these two authors belongs the credit for reducing a mass of *ad hoc* arguments concerning tariffs to a simple application of second-best welfare theory. The present paper extends their analysis to some arguments for protection not considered by them, elaborates more fully on the infant industry argument, and adds to their results two propositions about noneconomic arguments for protection. I should like also to acknowledge a debt to Erling Olsen, whose comments on an earlier draft prompted improvements in the presentation of the factor-price rigidity case.

1. Hagen (1958, p. 496, n. 2) traces the origins of the argument to Jacob Viner's review of M. Manoilesco's *The Theory of Protection and International Trade*, (P. S. King, 1931), in the *Journal of Political Economy* 40 (1932), pp. 121–125.

2. For an analysis of the protective incidence of a particular tariff structure, see Johnson (1963).

3. It should perhaps be emphasized that the welfare being maximized is the national welfare, and the distortions in question are distortions only from the national point

of view. Also, tariff retaliation by other countries does not necessarily prevent a country from gaining by the imposition of an optimum tariff structure; see Johnson (1953–54).

4. *MRS* symbolizes marginal rate of substitution in domestic consumption. MRT_d marginal rate of transformation in domestic production, MRT_f marginal rate of transformation in foreign trade; all of these are defined in terms of the amount of the export good given up in exchange for a unit increment of the import good.

5. It should be noted that, for analysis with the techniques of trade theory, factor prices must be assumed to be rigid in real terms; if factor prices are rigid in money terms ("money illusion" of the Keynesian type is present), full employment can always be secured by devaluation coupled with an appropriate domestic fiscal-monetary policy. This point is not made explicit in Haberler's analysis; see Haberler (1950), pp. 227–231.

6. Bhagwati and Ramaswami (1963, p. 49) use this demonstration to show that Hagen's analysis errs in concluding that self-sufficiency is necessarily better than free trade in this case.

7. Bhagwati and Ramaswami (1963, p. 47) use this demonstration to show that Haberler was wrong to recommend an export or import subsidy in this case.

8. Bhagwati and Ramaswami (1963) list eight reasons for the existence of a wage differential between the rural and urban sectors, of which four are economic and four (one of which is Hagen's) may involve genuine distortions. They agree with the earlier analysis of Fishlow and David (1961) in regarding Hagen's "dynamic" argument for the existence of a distortion as an illegitimate superimposition of dynamic considerations on static analysis. The same point has been made by Kenen (1963). Fishlow and David's other reasons correspond approximately with those discussed here, although they introduce the interesting case of factory legislation preventing the younger members of the family from working; they do not, however, raise the possibility that there may be a distortion of investment in migration of human capital.

9. The analysis here is incomplete, since in certain circumstances competition would lead to the workers bearing the cost of the nonspecific part of the training received on the job through lower initial wages. On this point see Becker (1962).

10. This paragraph was prompted by the existence of an apparent conflict in the literature on protection. W. M. Corden (1957) shows that the most efficient (least-cost) method of protection is by a subsidy (when the terms of trade are fixed) or by an optimum tariff and a production subsidy (when the terms of trade are variable). J. H. Young (1957) shows that protection by tariff costs less than protection by subsidy. As shown below, both are right. The explanation is that Corden takes the object of protection to be to increased domestic production, whereas Young takes the object to be to replace imports by domestic production.

References

Balogh, T. 1951. Welfare and freer trade—A reply. *Economic Journal* 61 (March): 72–83.

Becker, G. S. 1962. Investment in human capital: A theoretical analysis. *Journal of Political Economy* 70: 9–49.

Bhagwati, J. N., and Ramaswami, V. K. 1963. Domestic distortions, tariffs and the theory of optimum subsidy. *Journal of Political Economy* 71: 44–50.

Corden, W. M. 1957. Tariffs, subsidies and the terms of trade. *Economica* 24: 235–242.

Fishlow, A., and David, P. 1961. Optimal resource allocation in an imperfect market setting. *Journal of Political Economy* 69: 529–546.

Haberler, G. 1950. Some problems in the pure theory of international trade. *Economic Journal* 60 (June): 223–240.

Haberler, G. 1951. Welfare and freer trade—A rejoinder. *Economic Journal* 61 (December): 777–784.

Hagen, E. E. 1958. An economic justification of protectionism. *Quarterly Journal of Economics* 72: 496—514.

Johnson, H. G. 1953—54. Optimum tariffs and retaliation. *Review of Economic Studies* 22: 142–153. Reprinted as chapter 2 in H. G. Johnson, *International Trade and Economic Growth*. Allen and Unwin, 1958.

Johnson, H. G. 1963. The Bladen plan for increased protection of the Canadian automotive industry. *Canadian Journal of Economics and Political Science* 29: 212–238.

Kemp, M. C. 1960. The Mill-Bastable infant industry dogma. *Journal of Political Economy* 68: 65–67.

Kenen, P. B. 1963. Development, mobility and the case for tariffs. *Kyklos* 16: 321–324.

Lewis, W. A. 1954. Economic development with unlimited supplies of labour. *Manchester School of Economic and Social Studies* 22: 139–191.

Lewis, W. A. 1958. Unlimited labour: further notes. *Manchester School of Economic and Political Studies* 26: 1–32.

Lipsey, R. G., and Lancaster, K. 1956–57. The general theory of the second best. *Review of Economic Studies* 24: 11–32.

Manoilesco, M. 1931. *The Theory of Protection and International Trade*. P. S. King.

Meade, J. E. 1955. *Trade and Welfare*. Oxford University Press.

Stopler, W. F., and Samuelson, P. A. 1941. Protection and real wages. *Review of Economic Studies* 9: 58–73. Reprinted as chapter 15 in H.S. Ellis and L. A. Metzler, eds., *Readings in the Theory of International Trade*. Blakiston, 1949.

Viner, J. 1932. Review of M. Manoilesco's *The Theory of Protection and International Trade*. *Journal of Political Economy* 40: 121–125.

Young, J. H. 1957. *Canadian Commercial Policy*, Royal Commission on Canada's Economic Prospects.

Editor's Note

Johnson essentially argues that (1) tariffs are the first-best policy instrument when-ever there is a foreign distortion (in the terminology developed in Bhagwati, chapter 16, in this volume) and that (2) if there is a domestic distortion, offsetting it fully by a tariff (or trade subsidy) will not necessarily improve welfare. These two proposi-tions of Bhagwati and Ramaswami (*Journal of Political Economy*, February 1963) are quite correct.

However, it is incorrect to infer, as Bhagwati and Ramaswami did (and the tenor of Johnson's argumentation implies that Johnson did as well), that a tariff may not exist which *improves* welfare vis-à-vis free trade when there is a domestic distortion. This error was spotted by Kemp and Negishi, and the analysis developed yet further by Bhagwati, Ramaswami, and Srinivasan in their response to Kemp and Negishi (*Journal of Political Economy*, November/December 1969); the correct analysis can be found in Bhagwati, chapter 16.

16
The Generalized Theory of Distortions and Welfare

Jagdish N. Bhagwati

The theory of trade and welfare has recently developed independently in seven areas that have apparently little analytical relationship among themselves:

1. *The suboptimality of laissez-faire under market imperfections*   It has been shown that, when market imperfections exist, laissez-faire (otherwise described as "a policy of unified exchange rates" [5]) will not be the optimal policy. Among the market imperfections for which the suboptimality of laissez-faire has been demonstrated are four key types: (a) factor market imperfection, a wage differential between sectors;[1] (b) product market imperfection, a production externality;[2] (c) consumption imperfection, a consumption externality;[3] and (d) trade imperfection, monopoly power in trade.[4]

2. *Immiserizing growth*   Examples have been produced where a country, after growth (in factor supplies and/or technological know-how), becomes worse off, phenomena described as *immiserizing growth*. I produced an example of such a phenomenon in 1958 [1] (as also did Harry Johnson independently at the time) where growth led to such a deterioration in the country's terms of trade that the loss from the worsened terms of trade outweighted the primary gain from growth. Subsequently, Johnson [19] produced another example of immiserization, in which the country had no ability to influence her terms of trade but there was a tariff (which is necessarily welfare reducing in view of the assumed absence of monopoly power in trade) in both the pregrowth and the postgrowth situations, and growth impoverished the country in certain cases. I later produced yet

This paper was originally published in Jagdish N. Bhagwati, Ronald W. Jones, Robert A. Mundell, and Jaroslav Vanek, eds., *Trade, Balance of Payments, and Growth: Papers in International Economics in Honor of Charles P. Kindleberger*, North Holland Publishing Company, 1971.

other examples of immiserizing growth [6], one in which there was a wage
differential in the factor market, and another in which the country had
monopoly power in trade (as in my original 1958 example), but the country
had an optimum tariff (before growth) which became suboptimal after
growth.

3. *Ranking of alternative policies under market imperfections*   For the four
major imperfections described earlier, the optimal policy intervention has
been analyzed by several economists. Hagen [16] has argued that the
optimal policy for the case of the wage differential would be a factor
tax-cum-subsidy. For the production externality, Bhagwati and Ramaswami [2] have shown that the optimal policy intervention is a production
tax-cum-subsidy. For the consumption externality case, it follows from the
general arguments in Bhagwati and Ramaswami [2] that a consumption
tax-cum-subsidy ought to be used. Finally, for the case of monopoly power
in trade, it has been known since the time of Mill and has been demonstrated rigorously by (among others) Graaff [14] and Johnson [17] that a
tariff is the optimal policy. Recent work of Bhagwati, Ramaswami, and
Srinivasan [8] has then extended the analysis, for each market imperfection, to the ranking of *all* alternative policies: the tariff (trade subsidy)
policy, the production tax-cum-subsidy policy, the consumption tax-cum-
subsidy policy, and the factor tax-cum-subsidy policy.[5]

4. *Ranking of tariffs*   Yet another area of research in trade and welfare has
raised the question of ranking policies that constitute impediments themselves to the attainment of optimality. Thus, for example, Kemp [22] has
analyzed, for a country without monopoly power in trade (and no other
imperfections), the question as to whether a higher tariffs is worse than a
lower tariff. Similarly, Bhagwati and Kemp [10] have analysed the problem
for tariffs around the optimal tariff for a country *with* monopoly power in
trade.

5. *Ranking of free trade and autarky*   A number of trade theorists have
compared free trade with autarky, when there were market imperfections
such as wage differentials (Hagen [16]) and production externality (Haberler [15]), to deduce that free trade was no longer necessarily superior to
self-sufficiency. Melvin [26] and Kemp [23] have recently considered the
comparison between free trade and autarky when there are commodity
taxes.

6. *Ranking of restricted trade and autarky*   Aside from the case in which
trade is tariff restricted (wherein the comparison between restricted trade
and autarky becomes the comparison of tariffs discussed in item 4) Bhagwati [4] has considered the ranking of other policies (e.g., production
tax-cum-subsidies) that restrict trade and autarky.

7. *Noneconomic objectives and ranking of policies*   Finally, a number of economists have addressed themselves to the question of optimal policy intervention when the values of different variables are constrained, as noneconomic objectives, so that full optimality is unattainable. Four key types of noneconomic objectives have been analyzed. Corden [12] has shown that a production tax-cum-subsidy is optimal where the constrained variable is production (for reasons such as defense production). Johnson [18] has shown a tariff to be optimal when imports are constrained instead (in the interest of "self-sufficiency"). Bhagwati and Srinivasan [7] have demonstrated that a factor tax-cum-subsidy is optimal when the constrained variable is employment of a factor in an activity (i.e., in the interest of "national character") and a consumption tax-cum-subsidy when the constrained variable is domestic availability of consumption (i.e., to restrict "luxury consumption"). Bhagwati and Srinivasan have also extended the analysis to the ranking of *all* policy instruments for a number of these noneconomic objectives.

This paper is aimed at putting these diverse analyses into a common analytical framework. This results in the logical unification of a number of interesting and important results, leading in turn to fresh insights while also enabling us to derive remarkable "duality" relationships between the analysis of policy rankings under market imperfections and policy rankings to achieve noneconomic objectives.

1. Alternative Types of Distortions

It can be readily shown, in fact, that the diverse results reviewed so far belong to what might aptly be described as the theory of distortions and welfare.

The theory of distortions is built around the central theorem of trade and welfare: that laissez-faire is Pareto optimal for a perfectly competitive system with no monopoly power in trade.[6] Ruling out the phenomenon of diminishing cost of transformation between any pair of commodities (i.e., the concavity of the production possibility set in the familiar, two-commodity system),[7] the Pareto optimality of the laissez-faire policy follows quite simply from the fact that the economic system will operate with technical efficiency (i.e., on the "best" production possibility curve, if we think again of two commodities for simplicity). The economic system will also satisfy further the (first-order) conditions for an economic maximum: DRT = FRT = DRS (where DRT represents the marginal rate of transformation in domestic production, FRT represents marginal foreign rate of transformation, and DRS represents the marginal rate of substitution in consumption).[8]

The theory of distortions is then concerned with the following four pathologies which may characterize, singly or in combination, the economic system:

Distortion 1: FRT $\neq$ DRT = DRS.
Distortion 2: DRT $\neq$ DRS = FRT.
Distortion 3: DRS $\neq$ DRT = FRT.
Distortion 4: Nonoperation on the efficient production possibility curve.

2. "Endogenous" Distortions

These distortions (implying departures from full optimality) may arise when the economy is characterised by *market imperfections* under a policy of laissez-faire. Thus, the presence of national monopoly power in trade will lead to distortion 1, because foreign prices will not equal FRT. The case of the Meade type of production externality[9] leads to distortion 2. Distortion 3 will follow when sellers of the importable commodity, for example, charge a uniform premium on imported as well as home-produced supplies. Distortion 4 follows when there is a factor market imperfection resulting from a wage differential, for a factor, between the different activities.[10] In these cases, therefore, the resulting distortions (arising from the market imperfections) are appropriately described as "endogenous" distortions.

3. "Policy-Imposed" Distortions

On the other hand, the four varieties of distortions listed earlier may be the result of economic policies, as distinct from endogenous phenomena such as market imperfections. Thus, distortion 1 will arise for a country with no monopoly power in trade if the country has a tariff; it will also arise for a country with monopoly power in trade if the tariff is less or greater than the optimal tariff. Distortion 2 will follow if the government imposes a production tax-cum-subsidy. Distortion 3 will be the consequence similarly of a consumption tax-cum-subsidy policy. Finally, the adoption of a factor tax-cum-subsidy policy will result in distortion 4.[11] These are instances therefore of "policy-imposed" distortions.

But as soon as we probe the reasons for the existence of such policy-imposed distortions, two alternative interpretations are possible. Either we can consider these policies as *autonomous* (i.e., a tariff, which leads to distortion 1, may for example be a historic accident), or we may consider these policies as *instrumental* (a tariff, leading to distortion 1, may be the policy instrument used in order to reduce imports)—as in the case of the theory of noneconomic objectives when distortion 1 is created through the depolyment of a tariff when the objective is to reduce imports in the interest of "self-sufficiency."

We thus have altogether three sets of "causes" for the four varieties of distortions that can be distinguished: *endogenous*; *autonomous, policy imposed*; and *instrumental, policy imposed*. The entire literature that I reviewed earlier can then be given its logical coherence and unity around these alternative classes and causes of distortions.

Before formulating the general theory of distortions and generalizing the theorems discussed in the introduction into other areas, it would be useful to underline the precise manner in which these theorems relate to the different varieties of distortions that we have distinguished so far.

1. The theorems on the suboptimality of different market imperfections clearly relate to the theory of endogenous distortions. Within a static welfare context, they demonstrate that these market imperfections result in the different types of distortions 1–4, thus resulting in the breakdown of the Pareto optimality of laissez-faire in these cases.

2. The theorems on immiserizing growth, on the other hand, relate to the comparative statics of welfare when distortions are present. The theorem developed in this literature involve cases in which growth takes place under given distortions, either endogenous or policy imposed, and the primary improvement in welfare (which would have accrued if fully optimal policies were followed both before and after growth) is outweighed by the accentuation of the loss from the distortion in the postgrowth situation [6].

Thus, in the original Bhagwati example of immiserizing growth, the assumed free trade and hence failure to impose an optimum tariff (to exploit the monopoly power in trade) in both the pregrowth and the postgrowth situations involves welfare-reducing "distortionary" policies in both situations. Immiserization occurs therefore because the gain, which would necessarily accrue from growth if the optimal tariff were imposed in both situations, is smaller than the incremental loss arising from the accentuation (if any) in the postgrowth situation of the welfare loss resulting from the "distortionary" free-trade policy (implying an endogenous distortion 1 in this instance) in both situations.

Harry Johnson's example of immiserization where the country has no monopoly power in trade but a tariff (which thus constitutes an autonomous policy-imposed distortion 1) in both the pregrowth and the postgrowth situations, is to be explained in terms of the same logic. In the absence of monopoly power in trade, the tariff is necessarily "distortionary" and, compared with the fully optimal free-trade policy, causes a loss of welfare in each situation. If the growth were to occur with free trade, there would necessarily be an increment in welfare. However, since growth occurs under a tariff, there arises the possibility that the loss from the tariff may be accentuated after growth, and that this incremental loss may outweigh the gain (that would occur under the optimal, free-trade policy), thus resulting in immiserization. Thus, the policy-imposed distortion (i.e., the tariff) generates the possibility of immiserizing growth.

3. The theorems that rank alternative policies under market imperfections are addressed to a different range of questions. They relate to endogenous distortions, of each of the four varieties we have distinguished, and then seek to rank the different, available policy instruments (extending to the full complement: production, consumption, trade, and factor tax-cum-subsidies) in relation to one another and vis-à-vis laissez-faire itself. The problem has been posed in this fashion by Bhagwati, Ramaswami, and Srinivasan [8] in their recent work.

4. The theorems of Kemp [22] and Bhagwati and Kemp [10], which rank tariffs in relation to one another, however, belong to a yet different genre. They relate to policy-imposed distortions, autonomous in the sense defined in this paper, and aim at ranking different levels at which policy may impose the specified distortion (e.g., distortion 1 in the cases in which tariffs are ranked).

5. The ranking of free trade and autarky under situations involving market imperfections or taxes involves, on the other hand, a comparison of essentially two levels (the zero tariff level and the prohibitive tariff level) at which a policy-imposed distortion (the tariff) is used, in a situation which is itself characterized by another distortion (either endogenous, such as the wage differential in Hagen [16], or policy imposed, such as a tax on consumption of a commodity).

6. The ranking of a situation with trade restricted by a nontariff policy with a situation of autarky (with therefore an implicit, prohibitive tariff) involves an altogether different type of comparison: of one distortion with another, both autonomous policy imposed in Bhagwati's analysis [4].

7. The theory of noneconomic objectives [7], on the other hand, relates to the optimal nature of intervention and the ranking of alternative policies, when certain variables are precluded from specified ranges of values in the interest of "noneconomic" objectives. It is therefore, from an analytical point of view, a theory of how optimally (i.e., at minimum cost) to *introduce* distortions in the economic system, when the attainment of the full optimum is precluded by the noneconomic-objective constraints and also of

what the relative costs of alternative policies or methods of introducing such distortions, in pursuit of the noneconomic objectives, are. It is thus a theory pertaining to the ranking of instrumental, policy-imposed distortions, with each distortion being defined under a common set of economic and noneconomic constraints.

It is clear, therefore, that these diverse theorems relate to different types of distortions and raise a number of diverse questions relating thereto. But as soon as we grasp this central fact, it is possible to unify and extend the entire body of this literature and thus to develop a general theory of distortions and welfare.

4. Distortions and Welfare: General Theory

This generalized theory of distortions and welfare can be developed in terms of seven central propositions.

PROPOSITION 1   There are four principal types of distortions:
1. FRT $\neq$ DRT = DRS.
2. DRT $\neq$ DRS = FRT.
3. DRS $\neq$ DRT = FRT.
4. Nonoperation on the efficient production possibility curve.

These, in turn, can be caused by factors that are
1. Endogenous.
2. Autonomous, policy-imposed.
3. Instrumental, policy-imposed.

This proposition is merely a recapitulation of the concepts and analysis developed in the preceding section and requires no further comment. Note merely, by way of reemphasis, that in each of the $(4 \times 3 = 12)$ distortionary situations, the economic system departs from full Pareto optimality.

PROPOSITION 2

i. Optimal policy intervention, in the presence of distortions, involves a tax-cum-subsidy policy addressed directly to offsetting the source of the distortions, when the causes are endogenous or autonomous, policy imposed. Dual to (i) is the theorem that:
ii. When distortions have to be introduced into the economy, because the values of certain variables (e.g., production or empolyment of a factor in an activity) have to be constrained, the optimal (or least-cost) method of doing this is to choose that policy intervention that creates the distortion affecting directly the constrained variable.

These two propositions, which constitute a remarkable duality of theorems, extend between themselves to all the classes of distortions 1 to 4 and their three possible causes, endogenous, autonomous policy imposed, and instrumental policy imposed. Furthermore, each proposition is readily derived from the theorems on market imperfections and on noneconomic objectives.

Proposition 2(i) was formulated, in essentially similar form, by Bhagwati and Ramaswami [2] and later by Johnson [18], for the case of endogenous distortions. For distortion 1, resulting from monopoly power in trade under laissez-faire, it is well known that the optimal policy intervention is a tariff. For distortion 2, Bhagwati and Ramaswami showed that the optimal policy was a production tax-cum-subsidy. For distortion 3, correspondingly, the optimal policy is a consumption tax-cum-subsidy. Finally, when a wage differential causes distortion 4, Hagen [16] showed that the optimal intervention was through a factor tax-cum-subsidy. In each instance, therefore, the policy required is one that directly attacks the source of the distortion.

It follows equally, and trivially, that if these distortions are autonomous policy imposed, the optimal intervention is to eliminate the policy itself: hence, again the optimal policy intervention is addressed to the source of the distortion itself. Thus, with a suboptimal tariff leading to distortion 1, the optimal policy is to change the tariff to an optimal level (equal to zero, if there is no monopoly power in trade). Similarly, if a consumption tax-cum-subsidy causes distortion 3, the optimal policy is to offset it with an equivalent consumption tax-cum-subsidy (which leaves zero net consumption tax-cum-subsidy and thus restores full optimality).

But the extension of these results, via the "dual" proposition 2(ii), to the class of instrumental, policy-imposed distortions, is far from trivial. And the duality is remarkable. Corden [12] has shown that the optimal policy, if the binding noneconomic constraint relates to production, is a *production* tax-cum-subsidy. Johnson [18] has demonstrated that the optimal policy, if the binding noneconomic constraint relates to import (export) level, is a *tariff or trade subsidy*. Bhagwati and Srinivasan [7] have extended the analysis to show that, if the binding noneconomic constraint relates to the level of employment of a factor of production in a sector, the optimal policy is to use a *factor* tax-cum-subsidy that directly taxes (subsidises) the employment of the factor in the sector where its employment level must be lowered (raised) to the constrained level.[12] They have also demonstrated that the optimal policy for raising (lowering) consumption to a constrained level is a *consumption* tax-cum-subsidy policy.

To put it somewhat differently, a trade-level noneconomic objective is achieved at least cost by introducing a policy-imposed distortion 1 via a trade tariff or subsidy; a production noneconomic objective by introducing a policy-imposed distortion 2 via a production tax-cum-subsidy; a consumption noneconomic objective by introducing a policy-imposed distortion 3 via a consumption tax-cum-subsidy; and a factor-employment (in a sector) noneconomic objective by introducing a policy-imposed distortion 4 via a factor tax-cum-subsidy.

PROPOSITION 3

i. For each distortion, whether endogenous or autonomous, policy-imposed, in origin, it is possible to analyse the welfare ranking of all alternative policies, from the (first best) optimal to the second best and so on.
ii. (a) When distortions have to be introduced into the economy, because the values of certain variables have to be constrained (e.g., production or employment of a factor in an activity), the policy interventions that do this may similarly be welfare ranked. (b) The ranking of these policies is further completely symmetrical with that under the "corresponding" class of endogenous or autonomous policy-imposed distortions (e.g., the ranking of policies for production externality, an endogenous distortion 2, is identical with the ranking of policies when production is constrained as a noneconomic objective).

Since there are four different types of policies (factor, production, consumption, and trade tax-cum-subsidies), the propositions listed here are aimed at ranking *all* of them for each of the (twelve) varieties of distortions and establishing "duality" relations of the kind we discovered for optimal policies alone in proposition 2(ii).

Bhagwati, Ramaswami, and Srinivasan [8] have recently analyzed the welfare ranking of all policies for endogenous distortions and established the following ranking:[13]

Distortion 1: FRT $\neq$ DRT = DRS
This is the case of monopoly power in trade. The ranking of policies then is:

1. First best: Tariff.
2. Second best: Either production or consumption or factor tax-cum-subsidy (all policies are superior to laissez-faire but cannot be ranked uniquely vis-à-vis one another).[14]

Distortion 2: DRT $\neq$ DRS = FRT
This is the case of a pure production externality. The ranking of policies then is:

1. First best: Production tax-cum-subsidy.
2. Second best: Either tariff (trade subsidy) or factor tax-cum-subsidy (both policies are superior to laissez-faire but cannot be ranked uniquely vis-à-vis each other).
3. Consumption tax-cum-subsidy will not help.[15]

Distortion 3: DRS $\neq$ DRT = FRT

This is the case in which, for example, the sellers of a commodity uniform premium to buyers over the cost of supplies, whether imported or domestically produced. The ranking of policies then is:

1. First best: Consumption tax-cum-subsidy.
2. Second best: Tariff.
3. Production or factor tax-cum-subsidy will not help.[16]

Distortion 4: Nonoperation on the Efficient Production Possibility Curve

This is the case in which there is a wage differential, a factor market imperfection. In this case, the ranking of policies is:

1. First best: Factor tax-cum-subsidy.
2. Second best: Production tax-cum-subsidy.
3. Third best: Tariff (trade subsidy).
4. Consumption tax-cum-subsidy will not help.[17]

It is clear that the extension of these rankings to the corresponding cases where the distortions are autonomous policy imposed (e.g., distortion 2 resulting from the autonomous levy of a governmental tax, or distortion 4 resulting from the grant of a governmental subsidy on employment of a factor in one activity) is total and trivial. It is interesting and remarkable, however, that these rankings carry over also to the class of instrumental, policy-imposed distortions.

Thus, for the case of noneconomic objectivies, Bhagwati and Srinivasan [7] have provided the basis for analyzing the rankings of different policies, which I now proceed to develop fully.

Trade Level as a Constraint

The ranking of policies in this case is:

1. First best: Tariff.
2. Second best: Either production tax-cum-subsidy or factor tax-cum-subsidy or consumption tax-cum-subsidy (these policies cannot be ranked vis-à-vis one another).[18]

Note the complete symmetry with the rankings under distortion 1 earlier.

Production Level as a Constraint

The ranking of policies in this case is:

1. First best: Production tax-cum-subsidy.
2. Second best: Either tariff (trade subsidy) or factor tax-cum-subsidy (these policies cannot be ranked vis-à-vis each other).
3. Consumption tax-cum-subsidy will not help.[19]

Note again the complete symmetry with the rankings under distortion 2.

Consumption Level as a Constraint

The ranking of policies in this case is:

1. First best: Consumption tax-cum-subsidy.
2. Second best: Tariff.
3. Production or factor tax-cum-subsidy, when it helps meet the consumption constraint, will be third-best.[20]

Again, the symmetry with the ranking under distortion 3 is total.

Factor Employment (in a Sector) as a Constraint

The ranking of policies in this case is:

1. First best: Factor tax-cum-subsidy.
2. Second best: Production tax-cum-subsidy.
3. Third best: Tariff (trade subsidy).
4. Consumption tax-cum-subsidy will not help.[21]

In this final case as well, the symmetry with the corresponding distortion 4 is complete.

Thus, the duality of the policy rankings, for endogenous and autonomous policy-imposed distortions, on the one hand, and instrumental policy-imposed distortions, on the other hand, is altogether complete and remarkable.

PROPOSITION 4   For each kind of distortion, growth may be immiserizing.

For endogenous and autonomous policy-imposed distortions, belonging to each of the varieties 1 to 4 that we have distinguished, this proposition has already been demonstrated by Bhagwati [6].

Thus, for example, where distortion 1 obtains endogenously under laissez-faire because of monopoly power in trade, Bhagwati's 1958 analysis [1] demonstrates the possibility of immiserization. Where distortions 2 and 4 obtain simultaneously as a result of an endogenous wage differential, the same possibility has again been demonstrated by Bhagwati [6]. Johnson's

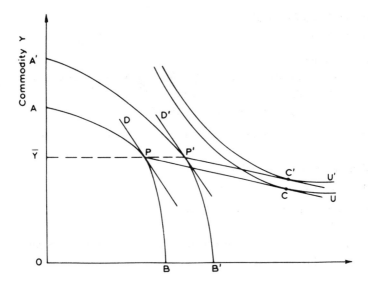

Figure 16.1a AB is the pregrowth production possibility curve; $A'B'$ the post-growth production possibility curve. The international price ratio is given at $PC = P'C'$. Production of y is constrained to level $\bar{y}$. A suitable production tax-cum-subsidy takes production, before growth, to P at domestic, producer price ratio DP. After growth, a suitable production tax-cum-subsidy takes producer price ratio to $D'P'$ and production to P'. Welfare level has increased, after growth, to U' ($> U$).

demonstration [19] of immiserization when a country has no monopoly power in trade but a tariff, illustrate propositon 2 for the case of an autonomous policy-imposed distortion 1.

Note again that the underlying reason for immiserizing growth is that the growth takes place in the presence of a distortion. This distortion produces a loss of welfare from the fully optimal welfare level. Thus, if there is an accentuation in this loss of welfare, when growth has occurred and the distortion has continued, this incremental loss could outweigh the grain that would have accrued if fully optimal policies had been followed in the pregrowth and postgrowth situations [6]. It also follows that such immiserizing growth would be impossible if fully optimal policies were followed in each situation, i.e., if the distortions resulting from the endogenous and policy-imposed cause were offset by optimal policy intervention, as discussed under Proposition 2(i) earlier.[22]

But so far we have discussed only distortions resulting from endogenous and policy-imposed, autonomous factors. However, proposition 4 applies equally, and can be generalized, to *instrumental* policy-imposed distortions as well.

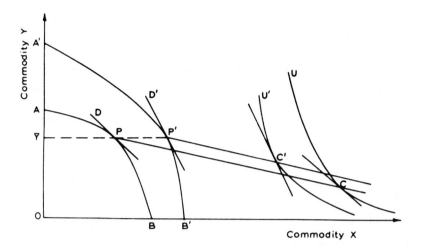

Figure 16.1b   The production possibility curve shifts, after growth, from AB to $A'B'$. In each case, the production of y is constrained to $\bar{y}$ by a tariff. In the pregrowth case, this tariff leads to production at P (with domestic price ratio DP), consumption at C, and welfare at U. After growth, production is at P', consumption at C', and welfare has reduced to U' ($<U$), implying immiserizing growth.

In complete symmetry with the endogenous and autonomous policy-imposed distortions, the phenomenon of immiserizing growth will be precluded when the constrained variable (e.g., production in the case of a production objective) is attained (in the pregrowth and the postgrowth situations) by optimal policy. On the other hand, immiserization becomes possible as soon as any of the second-best (or third-best) policies is adopted to constrain the variable (to a preassigned value in both the pregrowth and postgrowth situations).

This generalization of the theory of immiserizing growth is readily illustrated with reference to production as the constrained variable. Remember that a production tax-cum-subsidy is the optimal policy in this case and a tariff a second best policy. Figure 16.1a then illustrates how it is impossible, after growth, to become "worse off" if the production level of a commodity is constrained to the required level by a suitable production tax-cum-subsidy policy. The y production is constrained to level $\bar{y}$; the production possibility curve shifts our from AP to $A'B'$. With a suitable production tax-cum-subsidy used in both the pregrowth and the postgrowth situations, to constrain y production to $\bar{y}$, it is clear that it is impossible to worsen welfare after growth. Figure 16.1b illustrates, however, the possibility of immiserizing growth when the suboptimal tariff policy is followed instead in each case to constrain y output to level $\bar{y}$. Note that this demonstration, where the welfare level reduces after growth to U' from U, does not require the assumption of inferior goods.

Similar illustrations could be provided for the other three cases, where consumption, factor employment in a sector, and trade level are constrained. In each case, only the pursuit of a suboptimal policy to achieve the specified noneconomic objective could lead to immiserization.

PROPOSITION 5   Reductions in the "degree" of an only distortion are successively welfare increasing until the distortion is fully eliminated.

This theorem holds whether we take endogenous or policy-imposed distortions. However, it needs to be qualified, so as to exclude inferior goods for all cases except where a *consumption* tax-cum-subsidy is relevant.

For autonomous, policy-imposed distortion 1, the Kemp [22] and Bhagwati-Kemp [10] theorems are special cases of proposition 5: Each further requires the exclusion of inferior goods and attendant multiple equilibria if the possibility of the competitive system "choosing" an inferior-welfare equilibrium under the lower degree of distortion is to be ruled out.[23] In point of fact, identical propositions could be derived for alternative forms of autonomous policy-imposed distortions, factor tax-cum-subsidy, production tax-cum-subsidy, and consumption tax-cum-subsidy.[24]

Similarly, we can argue that reduction in the degree of each market imperfection, insofar as it reduces the degree of its consequent distortion, will raise welfare, Thus, for example, a reduction in the degree of production externality will reduce the degree of distortion 2 and increase the level of welfare.[25]

Finally, identical conclusions apply if we reduce the degree of "required" distortion, of the instrumental policy-imposed type, by relaxing the binding constraint on the "noneconomic"-objective variable. Thus, marginally relaxing the constraint on production will suffice to improve welfare. As is clear from figure 16.2a, the relaxation of the constraint on y production, from $\bar{y}$ to $\bar{y}_n$, will necessarily improve welfare by shifting the "availability line" outward—if, in each case, the policy adopted is a production tax-cum-subsidy policy.

If, however, as figure 16.2b illustrates, a (suboptimal) tariff policy is followed instead, to constrain y-production to the required level, the result of a relaxation in the constraint is identical; the only qualification is relating to that arising from inferior goods. Further, an identical conclusion holds, as in the case of a production tax-cum-subsidy, for the case of a factor tax-cum-subsidy instead.

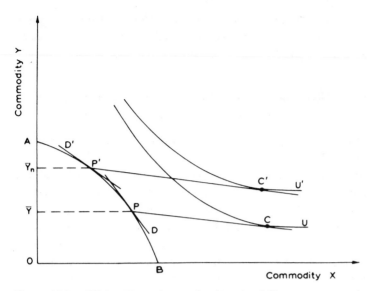

Figure 16.2a With AB as the production possibility curve, $\bar{y}$ and $\bar{y}_n$ are the successive noneconomic constraints on y production, which are met by use of a suitable production subsidy policy in each case. For $\bar{y}$, production then is at P, consumption at C, and welfare level at U. For $\bar{y}_n$, a relaxation in the constraint, production shifts to P' (with producer price ratio at $D'P'$ now), consumption to C', and welfare has increased to U' ($>U$).

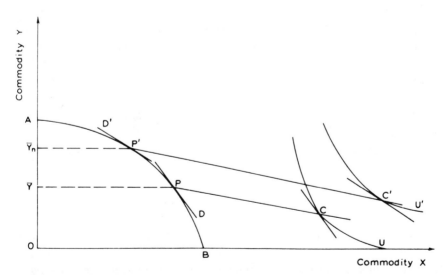

Figure 16.2b With production of y-commodity constrained successively at $\bar{y}$ and $\bar{y}_n$, a tariff used for that purpose, and production possibility curve AB, the production for $\bar{y}$ constraint is at P, consumption at C, and welfare at U. Relaxation in the constraint to $\bar{y}_n$ leads to production at P' and consumption at C' (at price $D'P'$) and welfare increases to U' ($>U$).

Thus, propositon 5 applies in the case of instrumental policy-imposed distortions, no matter *which* policy is considered (in other words, no matter which distortion is introduced in pursuit of the specific noneconomic objective).

PROPOSITION 6   Reductions in the "degree" of a distortion will not necessarily be welfare increasing if there is another distortion in the system.

This proposition is readily established for endogenous or autonomous policy-imposed distortions.

Let us first consider a case in which reductions in one distortion *do* lead to improvement in welfare despite the presence of another distortion in the system. Thus, consider the case in which a production externality, an endogenous distortion 2 where DRT ≠ DRS = FRT, is combined with a consumption tax-cum-subsidy, an autonomous policy-imposed distortion 3 where DRS ≠ FRT = DRT, but there is no monopoly power in trade. Assume further that the two distortions combine so as to yield altogether the initial situation where DRT ≠ DRS ≠ FRT (so that they are not mutually offsetting as far as one inequality is concerned). In this case, successive reductions in the consumption tax-cum-subsidy will necessarily be welfare increasing, given the production externality; and successive reductions in the production externality will improve welfare (except for the complication introduced by inferior goods).[26]

Next, however, consider the case where there is a production externality (endogenous, DRT ≠ DRS = FRT) combined with a tariff without monopoly power in trade (autonomous policy-imposed FRT ≠ DRS = DRT), and assume that the resulting initial situation is characterized by FRT ≠ DRT ≠ DRS. In this case, successive reductions in the tariff will not necessarily improve welfare steadily, if at all, and the gains may turn into losses.[27] The theorems on the possible inferiority of free trade (i.e., zero tariff) to no trade (i.e., prohibitive tariff) when there is a production externality [15] or a wage differential [2] [16] are only special cases of this general theorem that illustrates proposition 6.

It is interesting to note further that this theorem can with equal insight be analyzed in terms of proposition 4 if we recognize that, if optimal policies are followed in *both* the autarkic and the trading "situations," the trade situation must necessarily enable the economy to be "better off"—as is obvious to trade theorists familiar with the Baldwin-envelope technique. If then there is a distortion common to both situations, as with an endogenous wage differential or production externality or with an autonomous policy-imposed production tax-cum-subsidy, the transition to the (free) trading situation may well be immiserizing (i.e., therefore, free trade inferior to autarky) if the loss from this distortion is accentuated and outweighs the primary gain from the shift to (free) trade itself.

PROPOSITION 7   Distortions cannot be ranked (uniquely) vis-à-vis one another.

This is a readily apparent proposition and applies clearly to all the classes of distortions we have discussed.

Bhagwati's demonstration [4] that Kemp's theorem [22] of the superiority of tariff-restricted trade over no trade will not extend to cases where the trade is restricted instead by policies such as consumption and production tax-cum-subsidies becomes intuitively obvious as soon as it is seen that it falls into the class of theorems belonging to proposition 7. For, in this instance, two distortions are being compared: (1) a consumption tax-cum-subsidy leading to distortion 3, $DRS \neq DRT = FRT$, with a situation of autarky and hence implicit prohibitive tariff, thus involving distortion 1, $FRT \neq DRT = DRS$, and (2) a production tax-cum-subsidy leading to distortion 2, $DRT = DRS = FRT$, with autarky involving distortion 1, $FRT \neq DRT = DRS$. In principle, of course, the demonstration of impossibility of unique ranking between autarky and restricted trade could be carried equally into the case where trade restriction occurs via use of a factor tax-cum-subsidy involving distortion 4 along with 2.

5. Concluding Remarks

We have thus succeeded in unifying a considerable body of literature on the welfare economics of trade into a series of major propositions that constitute a generalized theory of distortions and welfare. Aside from the intrinsic elegance of such unification, this has resulted in a number of insights into, and extensions of, the theorems to date in this significant area of economic policy.

Notes

This paper is the result of thinking and research over a period of many years, originating in my 1958 paper on immiserizing growth [1] and developing considerably since my joint paper with the late V. K. Ramaswami in 1963 [2] on domestic distortions. Since 1965, T. N. Srinivasan and I have collaborated on research in related matters, pertaining to the theory of optimal policy intervention when noneconomic objectives are present [7], a subject pioneered by Max Corden's brilliant work [12]. In many ways, therefore, this paper has grown out of the ferment of ideas in Delhi during 1963–1968, when Srinivasan, Ramaswami, and I happened to work together and independently on the diverse subjects which are brought together in this paper. The work of others, particularly Murray Kemp [23], [24] and Harry Johnson [18], has also contributed to the development of my thinking.

1. I assume here that the wage differential is "distortionary" and cannot be attributed to legitimate economic grounds, such as disutility in occupations where the higher wage is charged. For a detailed discussion, see Fishlow and David [13] and Bhagwati and Ramaswami [2].

2. See Kemp [21], Chapter 11, for a fuller discussion of alternative types of production externalities. I have in mind here the case of a "pure" production externality of the Meade variety, as set out in note 9 later.

3. Instead of a consumption externality, one could assume a situation in which sellers charge a uniform premium on a commodity's import and production price.

4. The precise sense in which monopoly power in trade represents a market imperfection, in the trade sector, is that foreign prices will not equal the marginal, foreign rate of transformation (as discussed later in the text).

5. Since the production tax-cum-subsidy policy is equivalent to a tax-cum-subsidy given to *all* factors (used in production) of a equivalent and uniform magnitude, the factor tax-cum-subsidy policy referred to in this paper relates to a tax-cum-subsidy policy that applies in a *discriminatory* fashion between or among factors.

6. The classic proof of this proposition is in Samuelson [28]. For later treatments, see Samuelson [29], Kemp [22], and Bhagwati [4] and [5].

7. The pheonmenon of diminishing marginal cost of transformation can arise either because of increasing returns [21, chap. 8] (which is a purely technological phenomenon) or because of factor market imperfection in the shape of a wage differential [2] [13] [20]. The phenomenon has to be ruled out so as to eliminate certain well-known difficulties that it raises (requiring in particular the distinction between global and local maxima [30] and attention to second-order conditions and possibilities of inefficient specialization [27]).

8. Equalities have been used in stating the first-order conditions, for each pair of commodities, so as to preserve simplicity; they imply, of course, incomplete specialization in production and consumption. Inequalities can be introduced easily, but nothing essential would be gained by way of additional insights. The simplifying assumption of a two-commodity system will also be used through the rest of the paper; this does not critically affect the analysis, although problems associated with devising optimum policy *structures* (e.g., the optimal tariff structure [14] in the case of monopoly power in trade) are neturally not raised in consequence.

9. This externality can be formally stated as follows [21, p. 128]: For linearly homogeneous production functions $x = x(K_x, L_x)$, $y = y(K_y, L_y, x)$, it can be shown that, with y entrepreneurs not having to pay for their "input" of x, the economy will be characterised by distortion 2.

10. A constant wage differential will also lead to distortion 2; in this instance, we have a case of two distortions occurring at the same time. In fact, the wage differential case leads also to the possibility of a nonconvex production possibility set, as we have already noted; furthermore, as Bhagwati and Srinivasan [11] have shown, the response of production to relative commodity price change also becomes

unpredictable, a question, however, of no welfare significance in the context of this paper.

11. A constant rate of factor tax-cum-subsidy will also produce distortion 2, as in the case of a constant wage differential. However, as we shall see later, a variable factor tax-cum-subsidy policy can be devised which produces *only* distortion 4.

12. Unlike the case of a *constant wage* differential, which also leads to distortion 2 in addition to distortion 4, we can devise [7] a variable tax-cum-subsidy that satisfies the constraint on factor employment while creating *only* distortion 4.

13. Their argument is summarized as follows: They use the notation [8]: C_i, X_i denote the consumption and domestic output respectively of commodity i, where $i = 1, 2$. Also, P_c denotes the ratio of the price of the first to that of the second commodity confronting consumers (DRS); P_t denotes DRT $= dX_2/dX_1$; and P_f denotes the ratio of the world price of the first commodity to that of the second commodity, i.e., the *average* terms of trade. The marginal terms of trade FRT $= P_f$ only in the special case in which national monopoly power does not exist.

The welfare function $U(C_1, C_2)$ and the production functions are assumed to be differentiable as required. The U_i denotes the marginal utility of commodity $i (i = 1, 2)$. It is assumed throughout the analysis that under laissez-faire there is nonspecialisation in consumption and production, and that some trade takes place. Then, the following expression, for the change in welfare when there is an infinitesimal movement away from laissez-faire equilibrium, is derived:

$$dU = U_2[dX_1(P_f - P_t) + (X_1 - C_1)dP_f + (P_c - P_f)dC_1].$$

If one uses this expression, the different distortions are easily analyzed for alternate policy rankings. Thus, in the case in which DRT $\neq$ FRT $=$ DRS, which is distortion 2 in the text just following, the expression reduces to $dU = U_2[dX_1(P_f - P_t)]$ because $P_c = P_f$, $dP_f = 0$ and $P_f \neq P_t$. It follows that either a tariff (trade subsidy) or a factor tax-cum-subsidy that increases (reduces) X_1, if $P_f > P_t(P_f < P_t)$, will increase welfare.

14. For finite tax-cum-subsidies, however, the production tax-cum-subsidy will be superior to the factor tax-cum-subsidy.

15. This conclusion holds for infinitesimal tax-cum-subsidy. A finite consumption tax-cum-subsidy will actually be worse than laissez-faire in this instance, as it will impose a "consumption loss" on the economy, over and above the loss it is already suffering from the endogenous distortion 2.

16. This conclusion again holds only for infinitesimal tax-cum-subsidies on production or factor use. For finite tax-cum-subsidies, these policies will necessarily be worse than laissez-faire (unless inferior goods are present).

17. Again, this conclusion concerning the consmption tax-cum-subsidy must be read in the same sense as in note 15.

18. For finite tax-cum-subsidies, however, the factor tax-cum-subsidy policy will be inferior to the production tax-cum-subsidy policy, as Bhagwati and Srinivasan [7] have demonstrated.

19. This statement must again be read in the same sense as in note 5 and note 17 earlier.

20. I am indebted to Dr. Alan Martina for correcting my original error where I argued that a production of factor tax-cum-subsidy would "not help." It *may*, owing to the income effect on consmption as income declines with the use of either of these policy instruments.

21. This statement must be interpreted again in the same sense as in notes 15, 17, and 19 earlier.

22. For phenomena of immiserizing growth arising from reasons other than distortions, see Melvin [25] and Bhagwati [9].

23. On this, see Bhagwati [4], Kemp [23], and Bhagwati-Kemp [10].

24. For the consumption tax-cum-subsidy, the complication arising from inferior goods is not relevant.

25. Note again the *caveat* regarding inferior goods. This will not apply, however, where the consumption distortion is reduced.

26. These conclusions can also be derived by reference to the Bhagwati-Ramaswami-Srinivasan [8] formula, in note 13, which reduces for this case to $dU = U_2[dX_1(P_f - P_t) + (P_c - P_f)dC_1]$.

27. This is seen again by examining the Bhagwati-Ramaswami-Srinivasan formula which reduces, in this instance, to $dU = U_2[dX_1(P_f - P_t) + (P_c - P_f)dC_1]$. It is clear then that a reduction in the tariff, by affecting both X_1 and C_1, may worsen rather than improve welfare and that the welfare effect of successive tariff changes need not be unidirectional.

References

[1] Bhagwati, J. Immiserizing growth: A geometrical note. *Review of Economic Studies* 25 (June 1958).

[2] Bhagwati, J., and Ramaswami, V. K. Domestic distortions tariffs and the theory of optimum subsidy. *Journal of Political Economy* 71 (February 1963).

[3] Bhagwati, J. Non-economic objectives and the efficiency properties of trade. *Journal of Political Economy* 76 (October 1968).

[4] Bhagwati, J. Gain from trade once again. *Oxford Economic Papers* 20 (July 1968).

[5] Bhagwati, J. *The Theory and Practice of Commercial Policy*. Frank Graham Memorial Lecture (1967), Special Papers in International Economics No. 8, Princeton University, 1968.

[6] Bhagwati, J. Distortions and immiserizing growth: A generalization. *Review of Economic Studies* 35 (November 1968).

[7] Bhagwati, J., and Srinivasan, T. N. Optimal intervention to achieve non-economic objectives. *Review of Economic Studies* 36 (January 1969).

[8] Bhagwati, J., Ramaswami, V. K., and Srinivasan, T. N. Domestic distortions, tariffs and the theory of optimum subsidy: Some further results. *Journal of Political Economy* 77 (November/December 1969).

[9] Bhagwati, J. Optimal policies and immiserizing growth. *American Economic Review* 59 (December 1969).

[10] Bhagwati, J., and Kemp, M. C. Ranking of tariffs under monopoly power in trade. *Quarterly Journal of Economics* 83 (May 1969).

[11] Bhagwati, J., and Srinivasan, T. N. The theory of wage differentials: Production response and factor price equalisation. *Journal of International Economic* 1 (February 1971).

[12] Corden, W. M. Tariffs, subsidies and the terms of trade. *Economica* 24 (August 1957).

[13] Fishlow, A. and David, P. Optimal resource allocation in an imperfect market setting. *Journal of Political Economy* 69 (December 1961).

[14] Graaff, J. On optimum tariff structures. *Review of Economic Studies* 17 (1949–1950).

[15] Haberler, G. Some problems in the pure theory of international trade. *Economic Journal* 30 (June 1950).

[16] Hagen, E. An economic justification of protectionism. *Quarterly Journal of Economics* 72 (November 1958).

[17] Johnson, H. G. *International Trade and Economic Growth*, London Allen and Unwin, 1958.

[18] Johnson, H. G. Optimal trade intervention in the presence of domestic distortions. In R. E. Caves, H. G. Johnson, and P. B. Kenen (eds)., *Trade, Growth and the Balance of Payments*. Amsterdam: North Holland, 1965.

[19] Johnson, H. G. The possibility of income losses from increased efficiency or factor accumulation in the presence of tariffs. *Economic Journal* 77 (March 1967).

[20] Johnson, H. G. Factor market distortions and the shape of the transformation curve. *Econometrica* 34 (July 1966).

[21] Kemp, M. C. *The Pure Theory of International Trade*. Englewood Cliffs, N. J.: Prentice-Hall, 1964.

[22] Kemp, M. C. The gain from international trade. *Economic Journal* 72 (December 1962).

[23] Kemp, M. C. Some issues in the analysis of trade gains. *Oxford Economic Papers* 20 (July 1968).

[24] Kemp, M. C., and Negishi, T. Domestic distortions, tariffs and the theory of optimum subsidy, *Journal of Political Economy* 77 (November/December 1969).

[25] Melvin, J. Demand conditions and immiserizing growth. *American Economic Review* 59 (September 1969).

[26] Melvin, J. Commodity taxation as a determinant of trade. University of Western Ontario, 1968. Mimeo.

[27] Matthews R. C. O. Reciprocal demand and increasing returns. *Review of Economic Studies* 17 (1949–1950).

[28] Samuelson, P. A. The gains from international trade. *Canadian Journal of Economics and Political Science* 5 (May 1939).

[29] Samuelson, P. A. The gains from international trade once again. *Economic Journal* 72 (December 1962).

[30] Tinbergen, J. *International Economic Cooperation, Amsterdam:* North Holland, 1946.

VI
Directly Unproductive
Profit-Seeking (DUP)
Activities

Introduction to Part VI

This part reprints three papers that are indicative of the major revolution in the theory of trade and welfare that has been occurring in the last decade, with the incorporation of political economy considerations into the analysis in an essential way.

The theory of DUP (pronounced as "dupe") activities, namely, of ways of making profit or income in ways that do not involve direct or indirect production of goods (items entering the postulated utility functions) but that nevertheless use real resources and hence amount to diverting resources from the production of goods, is what this major development is about. Pareto described such activities as "predation" as distinct from production. Rent seeking, discussed in Anne Krueger's seminal paper (chapter 17), is a classic form of DUP activity, where lobbies chase income in the shape of rents carried by QRs. Equally, the phenomenon of illegal trade or smuggling, analyzed in general equilibrium framework by Bhagwati and Hansen (*Quarterly Journal of Economics*, May 1973) and by many others subsequently, is yet another form of such DUP activity.

The general theory of DUP activities, and its implications for trade theory and for theory generally, are the subject of chapter 18, where Bhagwati, Brecher, and Srinivasan review and synthesize numerous recent contributions to the theory. In particular, they consider the question of what is now called the "determinacy paradox," namely, if policy is made fully endogenous by augmenting the economic model to include political processes that help determine policy, then the economist loses the conventional degree of freedom which permits her to rank-order different economic policies (as in part V, which concerns the traditional theory of trade and welfare). Bhagwati, Brecher, and Srinivasan then propose that the theory of commercial policy must redefine its question away from rank-ordering of policies to asking questions such as: How will welfare be affected if a parametric change occurs, solving for the change in the observed political-economic equilibrium?

Wolfgang Mayer's paper (chapter 19), on the other hand, is a brilliant solution to the "positive" problem of tariff seeking, while the Krueger and Bhagwati-Brecher-Srinivasan papers are primarily directed at examining the normative implications of DUP-theoretic phenomena. It models tariff formation as a function of voting behaviour, linking it to distribution of factor ownership and hence income distribution as affected by trade policy. As such, it complements alternative models of endogenous tariffs built by authors such as Findlay and Wellisz, Feenstra, and Bhagwati, where the coalitions are formed by interests defined by factor classes taken as groups.

17

The Political Economy of the Rent-Seeking Society

Anne O. Krueger

In many market-oriented economies, government restrictions upon economic activity are pervasive facts of life. These restrictions give rise to rents of a variety of forms, and people often compete for the rents. Sometimes, such competition is perfectly legal. In other instances, rent seeking takes other forms, such as bribery, corruption, smuggling, and black markets.

It is the purpose of this paper to show some of the ways in which rent seeking is competitive, and to develop a simple model of competitive rent seeking for the important case when rents originate from quantitative restrictions upon international trade. In such a case (1) competitive rent seeking leads to the operation of the economy inside its transformation curve; (2) the welfare loss associated with quantitative restrictions is unequivcally greater than the loss from the tariff equivalent of those quantitative restrictions; and (3) competitive rent seeking results in a divergence between the private and social costs of certain activities. Although the analysis is general, the model has particular applicability for developing countries, where government interventions are frequently all-embracing.

A preliminary section of the paper is concerned with the competitive nature of rent seeking and the quantitative importance of rents for two countries, India and Turkey. In the second section, a formal model of rent seeking under quantitative restrictions on trade is developed and the propositions indicated above are established. A final section outlines some other forms of rent seeking and suggests some implications of the analysis.

This paper was originally published in *The American Economic Review* 64, no. 3 (June 1974): 291–303. © The American Economic Association.

1. Competitive Rent Seeking

Means of Competition

When quantitative restrictions are imposed upon and effectively constrain imports, an import license is a valuable commodity. It is well known that under some circumstances, one can estimate the tariff equivalents of a set of quantitative restrictions and analyze the effects of those restrictions in the same manner as one would the tariff equivalents. In other circumstances, the resource-allocational effects of import licensing will vary, depending upon who receives the license.[1]

It has always been recognized that there are *some* costs associated with licensing: paperwork, the time spent by entrepreneurs in obtaining their licenses, the cost of the administrative apparatus necessary to issue licenses, and so on. Here, the argument is carried one step further: in many circumstances resources are devoted to competing for those licenses.

The consequences of that rent seeking are examined below. First, however, it will be argued that rent-seeking activities are often competitive and resources are devoted to competing for rents. It is difficult, if not impossible, to find empirically observable measures of the degree to which rent seeking is competitive. Instead, some mechanisms under which rent seeking is almost certain to be competitive are examined. Then other cases are considered in which it is less obvious, but perhaps equally plausible, that competition results.

Consider first the results of an import-licensing mechanism when licenses for imports of intermediate goods are allocated in proportion to firms' capacities. That system is frequently used, and has been analyzed for the Indian case by Jagdish Bhagwati and Padma Desai. When licenses are allocated in proportion to firms' capacities, investment in additional physical plant confers upon the investor a higher expected receipt of import licenses. Even with initial excess capacity (due to quantitative restrictions upon imports of intermediate goods), a rational entrepreneur may still expand his plant if the expected gains from the additional import licenses he will receive, divided by the cost of the investment, equal the returns on investment in other activities.[2] This behavior could be perfectly rational even if, for all entrepreneurs, the total number of import licenses will remain fixed. In fact, if imports are held constant as domestic income grows, one would expect the domestic value of a constant quantity of imports to increase over time, and hence installed capacity would increase while output remained constant. By investing in additional capacity, entrepreneurs devote resources to compete for import licenses.

A second sort of licensing mechanism frequently found in developing countries is used for imports of consumer goods. There, licenses are allocated *pro rata* in proportion to the applications for those licenses from importers-wholesalers. Entry is generally free into importing-wholesaling, and firms usually have U-shaped cost curves. The result is a larger-than-optimal number of firms, operating on the downward sloping portion of their cost curves, yet earning a "normal" rate of return. Each importer-wholesaler receives fewer imports than he would buy at existing prices in the absence of licensing, but realizes a sufficient return on those licenses he does receive to make it profitable to stay in business. In this case, competition for rents occurs through entry into the industry with smaller-than-optimally sized firms, and resources are used in that the same volume of imports could be efficiently distributed with fewer inputs if firms were of optimal size.

A third sort of licensing mechanism is less systematic in that government officials decide on license allocations. Competiton occurs to some extent through both mechanisms already mentioned as businessmen base their decisions on expected values. But, in addition competition can also occur through allocating resources to influencing the probability, or expected size, of license allocations. Some means of influencing the expected allocation—trips to the capital city, locating the firm in the capital, and so on—are straightforward. Others, including bribery, hiring relatives of officials, or employing the officials themselves upon retirement, are less so. In the former case, competition occurs through choice of location, expenditure of resources upon travel, and so on. In the latter case, government officials themselves receive part of the rents.

Bribery has often been treated as a transfer payment. However, there is competition for government jobs, and it is reasonable to believe that expected total remuneration is the relevant decision variable for persons deciding upon careers. Generally, entry into government service requires above-average educational attainments. The human capital literature provides evidence that choices as to how much to invest in human capital are strongly influenced by rates of return upon the investment. For a given level of educational attainment, one would expect the rate of return to be approximately equated among various lines of endeavor. Thus, if there appear to be high official-plus-unofficial incomes accruing to government officials and higher education is a prerequisite for seeking a government job, more individuals will invest in higher education. It is not necessary that government officals earn the same total income as other college graduates. All that is necessary is that there is an excess supply of persons seeking government employment, or that highly educated persons make sustained efforts to enter government services. Competition takes place through attaining the appropriate credentials for entry into government service and through accepting unemployment while making efforts to obtain appointments. Efforts to influence those in charge of making appointments, of course, just carry the argument one step further back.

To argue that competition for entry into government service is, in part, a competition for rents does not imply that all government servants accept bribes nor that they would leave government service in their absence. Successful competitors for government jobs might experience large windfall gains even at their official salaries. However, if the possibility of those gains induces others to expend time, energy, and resources in seeking entry into government services, the activity is competitive for present purposes.

In all these license-allocation cases, there are means, legal and illegal, for competing for rents. If individuals choose their activites on the basis of expected returns, rates of return on alternative activities will be equated, and in that sense, markets will be competitive.[3] In most cases, people do not perceive themselves to be rent seekers, and generally speaking, individuals and firms do not specialize in rent seeking. Rather, rent seeking is one part of an economic activity, such as distribution or production, and part of the firm's resources are devoted to the activity (including, of course, the hiring of expediters). The fact that rent seeking and other economic activities are not generally conducted by separate economic entities provides the motivation for the form of the model developed below.

Are Rents Quantitatively Important?

Granted that rent seeking may be highly competitive, the question remains whether rents are important. Data from two countries, India and Turkey, suggest that they are. Gunnar Myrdal believes India may "...on the balance, be judged to have somewhat less corruption than any other country in South Asia" (p. 943). Nonetheless, it is generally believed that "corruption" has been increasing, and that much of the blame lies with the proliferation of economic controls following independence.[4]

Table 17.1 presents crude estimates, based on fairly conservative assumptions of the value of rents of all sorts in 1964. One important source of rents—investment licensing—is not included for lack of any valid basis on which to estimate its value. Many smaller controls are also excluded. Nonetheless, it is apparent from table 17.1 that import licenses provided the largest source of rents. The total value of rents of Rs. 14.6 billion contrasts with Indian national income of Rs. 201 billion in 1964. At 7.3 percent of national income, rents must be judged large relative to India's problems in attempting to raise her savings rate.

For Turkey, excellent detailed estimates of the value of import licenses

Table 17.1
Estimates of value of rents: India, 1964

Source of rent	Amount of rent (Rs. million)
Public investment	365
Imports	10,271
Controlled commodities	3,000
Credit rationing	407
Railways	602
Total	14,645

Sources:
1. Public investment: The Santhanam Committee, pp. 11–12, placed the loss in public investment at *at least* 5 percent of investment. That figure was multiplied by the average annual public investment in the *Third Five Year Plan.*
2. Imports: The Santhanam Committee, p. 18, stated that import licenses were worth 100 to 500 percent of their face value. Seventy-five percent of the value of 1964 imports was used here as a conservative estimate.
3. Controlled commodities: These commodities include steel, cement, coal, passenger cars, scooters, food, and other price—and/or distribution-controlled commodities—as well as foreign exchange used for illegal imports and other unrecorded transactions. The figure is the lower bound estimate given by John Monteiro, p. 60. Monteiro puts the upper bound estimate at Rs. 30,000 billion, although he rejects the figure on the (dubious) ground that notes in circulation are less than that sum.
4. Credit rationing: The bank rate in 1964 was 6 percent; Rs. 20.3 billion of loans were outstanding. It is assumed that *at least* an 8 percent rate would have been required to clear the market, and that 3 percent of bank loans outstanding would be equivalent to the present value of new loans at 5 percent. Data source: Reserve Bank of India, tables 534 and 544.
5. Railways: Monteiro, p. 45, cites commissions of 20 percent on railway purchases, and extraofficial fees of Rs. 0.15 per wagon and Rs. 1.4 per 100 maunds loaded. These figures were multplied by the 1964 traffic volume; 203 million tons of revenue-paying traffic originated in that year. Third-plan expenditure on railroads was Rs. 13,260 million. There were 350,000 railroad goods wagons in 1964–65. If a wagon was loaded once a week, there were 17,500,000 wagons of freight. At Rs. 0.15 per load, this would be Rs. 2.6 million; 100 maunds equal 8,228 pounds, so at 1.4 Rs. per 100 maunds, Rs. 69 million changed hands; if one-fifth of railroad expenditures were made in 1964–65, Rs. 2652 million was spent in 1964; at 20 percent, this would be Rs. 530 million, for a total of Rs. 602 million.

in 1968 are available.[5] Data on the c.i.f. prices of individual imports, their landed cost (c.i.f. price plus all duties, taxes, and landing charges), and wholesale prices were collected for a sizable sample of commodities representing about 10 percent of total imports in 1968. The c.i.f. value of imports in the sample was TL 547 million, and the landed cost of the imports was TL 1,443 million. The value at the wholesale level of these same imports was TL 3,568 million. Of course, wholesalers incur some handling, storage, and transport costs. The question, therefore, is the amount that can be attributed to normal wholesaling costs. If one assumes that a 50 percent markup would be adequate, then the value of import licenses was TL 1,404 million, or almost three times the c.i.f. value of imports. Imports in 1968 were recorded (c.i.f.) as 6 percent of national income. On the basis of Aker's data, this would imply that rents from import licenses in Turkey in 1968 were about 15 percent of *GNP*.

Both the Indian and the Turkish estimates are necessarily somewhat rough. But they clearly indicate that the value of import licenses to the recipients was sizable. Since means were available of competing for the licenses, it would be surprising if competition did not occur for prizes that large. We turn, therefore, to an examination of the consequences of competitive rent seeking.

2. The Effects of Competitive Rent Seeking

The major proposition of this paper is that competitive rent seeking for import licenses entails a welfare cost in addition to the welfare cost that would be incurred if the same level of imports were achieved through tariffs. The effects of tariffs upon production, trade, and welfare are well known, and attention is focussed here upon the additional cost of competitive rent seeking. A simple model is used to develop the argument. Initially, free trade is assumed. Then, a tariff or equivalent import restriction is introduced. Finally, an equal import restriction with competitive rent seeking is examined.

The Basic Model

Two commodities are consumed by the country under investigation: food and consumption goods. Food is produced domestically and exported. Consumption goods are imported. Distribution is a productive activity whereby food is purchased from the agricultural sector, exported, and the proceeds are used to import consumption goods which are sold in the domestic market. Labor is assumed to be the only domestic factor of production.[6] It is assumed that the country under consideration is small and cannot affect its international terms of trade. Physical units are selected so that the fixed international prices of both goods are unity.

The agricultural production function is

$$A = A(L_A), \quad A' > 0, A'' < 0, \tag{1}$$

where A is the output of food and L_A is the quantity of labor employed in agriculture. The sign of the second derivative reflects a diminishing marginal physical product of labor in agriculture, due, presumably, to fixity in the supply of land.

The level of distribution output, D, is defined to equal the level of consumption-goods imports, M:

$$D = M. \tag{2}$$

One unit of distributive services entails exchanging one unit of imports for food with the agricultural sector at the domestic terms of trade, and exporting the food in exchange for imports at the international terms of trade. Constant returns to scale are assumed for the distribution activity; one unit of distribution requires k units of labor. Total labor employed in distribution, L_D, is

$$L_D = kD. \tag{3}$$

A distribution charge of p_D per unit is added to the international price of imports:

$$p_M = 1 + p_D, \tag{4}$$

where p_M is the domestic price of imports. The domestic price of food is assumed to equal its unit international price.[7]

Society's demand for imports depends upon the domestic price of imports and total income generated in agriculture.[8]

$$M = M(p_M, A), \tag{5}$$

where $\partial M / \partial p_M < 0$ and $\partial M / \partial A > 0$. Demand decreases with increases in the price of imports, and increases with increases in agricultural output (income). Equation (5) is derived from micro utility maximization with the assumption that farmers, distributors, and rent seekers all have the same consumption behavior. Domestic food consumption, F, is simply the quantity not exported:

$$F = A - M. \tag{6}$$

Since the fixed international terms of trade equal unity, food exports equal consumption goods imports.

Finally, it is assumed that the economy under consideration has a fixed labor supply, $\bar{L}$:

$$\bar{L} = L_A + L_D + L_R,\tag{7}$$

where L_R is the quantity of labor engaged in rent seeking.

Free Trade

Under free trade, there is free entry into both agriculture and distribution and competition equates the wage in the two activities:

$$A' = \frac{p_D}{k}.\tag{8}$$

Equations (1) to (8) constitute the free-trade system. These eight equations contain the eight variables A, M, D, F, L_A, L_D, p_M, and p_D. Since there is no rent seeking under free trade, $L_R \equiv 0$.

It is easily established that free trade is optimal in the sense that the domestic price ratio under free trade equals the marginal rate of transformation between food consumption and imports. The consumption possibility locus is obtained by substituting into (6) from (1) and (7)

$$F = A(\bar{L} - kM) - M.$$

The locus has a marginal rate of transformation greater than one:

$$\frac{-dF}{dM} = kA' + 1 > 1,\tag{9}$$

which reflects the positive distribution cost of substituting imports for food consumption. The locus is concave:

$$\frac{d^2 F}{dM^2} = k^2 A'' < 0,$$

since $A'' < 0$, which follows from diminishing returns in food production. Substituting from (8) into (9),

$$\frac{-dF}{dM} = 1 + p_D,$$

which establishes the aforementioned equality.

A free-trade solution is depicted in figure 17.1. Domestic food consumption and import consumption are measured along OF and OM, respectively. The consumption possibility locus is $\hat{F}\hat{M}$. At the point $\hat{F}$ no imports are consumed, and hence there is no distribution. If distribution were costless,

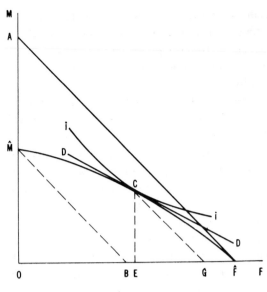

Figure 17.1   Free trade

society could choose its consumption point from the line $\hat{F}A$. However, to consume one unit of import requires exchanging one unit of food *and* withdrawing k workers from agriculture to provide the requisite distributive services. With diminishing marginal product of labor in agriculture, the cost of additional imports in terms of foregone food production rises. Thus, the price of distribution, and hence the domestic price of imports, increases in moving northwest from $\hat{F}$. The consumption point $\hat{M}$ has OB food exchanged for $O\hat{M}$ of imports. The distance $\hat{F}B$ is the agricultural output foregone to distribute $O\hat{M}$ imports.

If society's preferences are given by the indifference curve ii, point C is optimal. The price of distribution is reflected in the difference between the slope of $\hat{F}A$ and the slope of DD at C. At the point C, OG food would be produced, with EG ($= EC$) exported, and the rest domestically consumed.

A Tariff or an Import Restriction without Rent Seeking

Consider now a case in which there is a restriction upon the quantity of imports

$$M = \overline{M}, \tag{10}$$

where $\overline{M}$ is less than the import quantity that would be realized under free trade. Since entry into distribution is now limited, the competitive wage equality (8) will no longer hold. The relevant system contains (1) to (7) and

(10). The variables are the same as in the free-trade case and agan $L_R = 0$. The system may be solved sequentially: given (10), D follows from (2), L_D from (3), L_A from (7), A from (1), F from (6), p_M from (5), and p_D from (4). Since equations (1), (6), and (7) remain intact, the solution for this case is also on the consumption possibility locus.

It is useful to establish the directions of change for the variables following a switch from free trade to import restriction. The reduced import level will reduce the labor employed in distribution and increase the labor force in agriculture. Diminishing returns will reduce the agricultural wage. The domestic price of imports, the distributive margin, and the wage of distributors will increase. Distributors will earn a rent in the sense that their wage will exceed the wage of those engaged in agriculture.

In the absence of rent seeking, a tariff and a quantitative restriction are equivalent[9] aside from the resultant income distribution. Under a quantitative restriction the distributive wage is higher than the agricultural. If instead there were an equivalent tariff with redistribution of the proceeds, the marginal product of labor in agriculture would be unchanged, but agricultural workers would benefit by the amount of tariff proceeds redistributed to them whereas traders' income would be lower. Since the allocation of labor under a tariff and quantitative restriction without rent seeking is the same and domestic prices are the same, the only difference between the two situations lies in income distribution.

The solution under a quantitative restriction is illustrated in figure 17.2, where $\hat{F}\hat{M}$ is again the consumption possibility locus and C the free-trade solution. With a quantitative restriction on imports in the amount $O\overline{M}$, the domestic prices of imports, and hence of distribution, rise from free trade to import restriction. Food output (OJ) and domestic consumption of food increase, and exports decline to HJ ($=O\overline{M}$). The indifference curve $i'i'$ lies below ii (and the point C), and the welfare loss may be described by the consumption and production cost measure given by Harry Johnson.

The wage rate in distribution unequivocally rises for a movement from free trade to a quantitative restriction. The total income of distributors will increase, decrease, or remain unchanged depending upon whether the proportionate increase in p_D is greater than, less than, or equal to the absolute value of the proportionate decrease of imports. For the moment, let p_D, p_M, and M represent free-trade solution values, and let p_D^*, p_M^*, and $\overline{M}$ represent import-restriction solution values. The total arc elasticity of demand for imports for the interval under consideration, η, is

$$\eta = \frac{-(\overline{M} - M)}{\overline{M} + M} \cdot \frac{p_M^* + p_M}{p_M^* - p_M}. \tag{11}$$

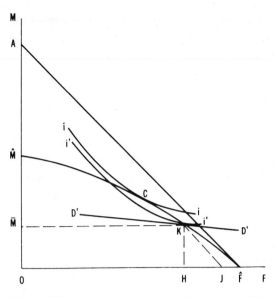

Figure 17.2   Import restriction without rent seeking

Total expenditures on imports will increase, decrease, or remain unchanged as η is less than one, greater than one, or equal to one. The total income of distributors will increase if

$$p_D^* \overline{M} > p_D M.$$

Multiplying both sides of this inequality by $(p_M^* + p_M)/(p_M^* - p_M)$, substituting from (11), and using (4),

$$1 + \frac{2}{(p_D^* + p_D)} > \eta. \tag{12}$$

Hence, distributors' total income can increase even if the demand for imports is price elastic.[10] The smaller is the free-trade distributive markup, the more likely it is that the distributors' total income will increase with a curtailment of imports. The reason is that an increase in the domestic price of imports results in a proportionately greater increase in the price of distribution.

An Import Restriction with Competitive Rent Seeking

In the import-restriction model just presented, the wage in distribution p_D/k exceeds the wage in agriculture A'. Under this circumstance, it would be surprising if people did not endeavor to enter distribution in response to its higher return. Resources can be devoted to rent seeking in all the ways indicated in section 1. This rent-seeking activity can be specified in a number of different ways. A simple and intuitively plausible specification is that people will seek distributive rents until the average wage in distribution and rent seeking equals the agricultural wage:[11]

$$A' = \frac{p_D \overline{M}}{L_D + L_R}. \tag{13}$$

One can regard all distributors and rent seekers as being partially engaged in each activity or one can think of rent seekers as entering in the expectation of receiving import licenses. In the latter case, the final solution classifies the successful seekers in L_D and the unsuccessful ones in L_R. Equation (13) implies risk neutrality in this circumstance.

The model for import restriction with rent seeking contains the same equations, (1) to (7) and (10), and the same variables as the model for import restrictions without rent seeking. In addition, the new model contains (13) and the introduction of L_R as a variable. The essential factor of rent seeking is that L_R becomes positive.

Let us start with a solution for an import restriction without rent seeking and ask what happens to the values of the variables when rent seeking is introduced. By assumption $M = \overline{M}$ is unchanged, so that L_D is unchanged. Therefore, $dL_A = -dL_R$, because the labor that enters rent seeking can only come from agriculture. Substituting into the total differential of (1) and using (6),

$$dF = dA = -A' dL_R < 0. \tag{14}$$

Agricultural production and food consumption are reduced by the introduction of rent seeking. Since the import level remains unchanged, rent seeking entails a welfare loss beyond that for an import restriction without rent seeking. The concavity of the agricultural production function results in a food loss that is less than proportional to decrements in L_A. Differentiating (5) totally,

$$0 = M_1 dp_M + M_2 dA, \tag{15}$$

where M_1 and M_2 are the partial derivatives of (5) with respect to p_M and A, respectively. Solving (15) for dp_M, and substituting from (4) and (14),

$$dp_D = dp_M = \frac{M_2}{M_1} A' dL_R < 0, \tag{16}$$

since $M_1 < 0$ and $M_2 > 0$. The domestic cost of imports will be lower under rent-seeking competition. This follows from the decrease in the consumption of food relative to imports.

The results of (14) land (16) are not dependent upon the particular form of the equilibrium of the labor market. They hold for any specification of competitive rent seeking. Equation (13) serves to determine particular values for L_R and other variables of the system. The mere existence of competitive rent seeking is enough to determine the directions of change of the variables.

The above results are sufficient to indicate that, for any given level of import restrictions, competition among rent seekers is clearly inferior to the tariff equivalent of the restrictions, in that there could be more food consumed with no fewer imports under the latter case than the former. To the extent that rent seeking is competitive, the welfare cost of import restrictions is equal to the welfare cost of the tariff equivalent *plus the additonal cost of rent-seeking activities.* Measurement of that excess cost is considered below.

The tariff-equivalent and rent-seeking equilibria are constrasted in figure 17.3. Equilibrium under rent seeking will be at some point such as L, with the same consumption of imports, but smaller production and consumption of food than occurs under a tariff. The points K and C are the tariff-equivalent and free-trade equilibria, respectively. The line $D'D'$ corresponds to the domestic price of imports in figure 17.2, and the steeper line $D''D''$ corresponds to the lower domestic price of imports under competitive rent seeking.

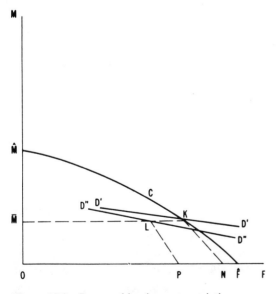

Figure 17.3   Rent-seeking import restriction

So far, it has been shown that for any given level of import restriction, a tariff is Pareto-superior to competitive rent seeking, and the properties of rent-seeking equilibrium have been contrasted with those of the tariff-equivalent case in the absence of competition for the rents. A natural question is whether anything can be said about the properties of rent-seeking equilibrium in contrast to those of a free-trade equilibrium, which is, after all, the optimal solution. It has been seen that the number of persons engaged in distribution declines from free trade to import restriction without rent seeking, and increases as one goes from that situation to competition for import licenses. Likewise, agricultural output increases between free trade and the tariff-equivalent case, and declines between that and rent seeking. The question is whether any unambiguous signs can be placed on the direction of these changes between free trade and rent seeking and, in particular, is it possible that society might produce and consume less of both goods under rent seeking than under free trade?

The answer is that if inequality (12) is satisfied, the absolute number of persons $(L_D + L_R)$ in distribution will increase going from a free-trade to a rent-seeking equilibrium. If import demand is more elastic, the number of persons in distribution will decline. Contrasted with a free-trade equilibrium, there would be less agricultural output *and* fewer imports when inequality (12) holds. If, with import restriction, the income from distribution $p_D^* \overline{M}$ is greater than distributors' income at free trade, more persons will be employed in distribution-cum-rent seeking with import restriction than are employed under free trade.

Measuring the Welfare Loss from Rent Seeking

A tariff has both production and consumption costs, and it has already been shown that rent seeking entails costs in addition to those of a tariff. Many forms of competition for rents, however, are by their nature difficult to observe and quantitify, and one might therefore question the empirical content of the result so far obtained.

Fortunately, there is a way to estimate the production cost of rent seeking. That cost, in fact, is equal to the value of the rents. This can be shown as follows. The rent per import license, r, is

$$r = p_D - kA'. \tag{17}$$

This follows because the labor required to distribute one unit of imports is k, which could be used in agriculture with a return A'. Note that at free trade r equals zero. A distributor could efficiently distribute an import and earn his opportunity cost in agriculture with zero rent. The total value of rents, R, with competitive rent seeking is thus the rent per unit of imports times the amount imported:

$$R = r\overline{M} = (p_D - kA')\overline{M} \tag{18}$$

Using (3) and (13),

$$R = \left(p_D - \frac{k p_D \overline{M}}{L_D + L_R} \right) \overline{M}$$

$$= p_D \left(1 - \frac{L_D}{L_D + L_R} \right) \overline{M}$$

$$= \frac{p_D \overline{M} L_R}{L_D + L_R}. \tag{19}$$

Thus the total value of rents reflects the agricultural wage (A') times the number of rent seekers.

The value of rents reflects the value (at current prices) of the domestic factors of production which could be extracted from the economy with no change in the final goods and services available for society's utilization. Thus, if the value of rents is known, it indicates the volume of resources that could be transferred out of distribution and into other activities, with no loss of distributive services from an initial position of rent-seeking activity. The estimates of rents in India and Turkey, therefore, may be interpreted as the deadweight loss from quantitative restrictions in addition to the welfare cost of their associated tariff equivalents if one believes that there is competition for the rents.

The value of the rents overstates the increase in food output and consumption that could be attained with a tariff to the extent that the marginal product of labor in agriculture is diminishing, since the equilibrium wage will rise between the tariff and the competitive rent-seeking situation. In the case of a constant marginal product of labor in alternative uses, the value of rents will exactly measure foregone output.

The Implications of Rent Seeking for Trade Theory
Recognition of the fact of rent seeking alters a variety of conclusions normally obtained in the trade literature and examination of such cases is well beyond the scope of this paper. A few immediately derivable results are worth brief mention, however.

First, an import prohibition might be preferable to a nonprohibitive quota if there is competition for licenses under the quota. This follows immediately from the fact that a prohibition would relase resources from rent seeking and the excess cost of domestic production might be less than the value of the rents. Second, one could not, in general, rank the tariff-equivalents of two (or more) quotas, since the value of rents is a function of both the amount of rent per unit (the tariff equivalent) and the volume of imports of each item.[12] Third, it has generally been accepted that the more inelastic domestic demand the less is likely to be the welfare cost of a given tariff. For the quota-cum-rents case, the opposite is true: the more price inelastic is demand, the greater will be the value of rents and the greater, therefore, the deadweight loss associated with rent seeking. Fourth, it is usually believed that competition among importers will result in a better allocation of resources than will a monopoly. If rent seeking is a possibility, however, creating a monopoly position for one importer will generally result in a higher real income if not in a preferable income distribution for society. Finally, devaluation under quantitative restrictions may have important allocation effects because it diminishes the value of import licenses, and hence the amount of rent-seeking activity, in addition to its effects upon exports.

3. Conclusions and Implications

In this paper, focus has been on the effects of competition for import licenses under a quantitative restriction of imports. Empirical evidence suggests that the value of rents associated with import licenses can be relatively large, and it has been shown that the welfare cost of quantitative restrictions equals that of their tariff equivalents plus the value of the rents.

While import licenses constitute a large and visible rent resulting from government intervention, the phenomenon of rent seeking is far more general. Fair trade laws result in firms of less-than-optimal size. Minimum wage legislation generates equilibrium levels of unemployment above the optimum with associated deadweight losses, as shown by John Harris and Michael Todaro, and Todaro. Ceilings on interest rates and consequent credit rationing lead to competiton for loans and deposits and/or high-cost banking operations. Regulating taxi fares affects the average waiting time for a taxi and the percent of time taxis are idle, but probably not their owners' incomes, unless taxis are also licensed. Capital gains tax treatment results in overbuilding of apartments and uneconomic oil exploration. And so on.

Each of these and other interventions lead people to compete for the rents although the competitors often do not perceive themselves as such. In each case there is a deadweight loss associated with that competition over and above the traditional triangle. In general, prevention of that loss can be achieved only be restricting entry into the activity for which a rent has been created.

That, in turn, has political implications. First, even if they *can* limit competition for the rents, governments which consider they must impose restrictions are caught on the horns of a dilemma: if they do restrict entry, they are clearly "showing favoritism" to one group in society and are choosing an unequal distribution of income. If, instead, competition for the rents is allowed (or cannot be prevented), income distribution may be less unequal and certainly there will be less appearance of favoring special groups, although the economic costs associated with quantitative restrictions will be higher.

Second, the existence of rent seeking surely affects people's perception of the economic system. If income distribution is viewed as the outcome of a lottery where wealthy individuals are successful (or lucky) rent seekers, whereas the poor are those precluded from or unsuccessful in rent seeking, the market mechanism is bound to be suspect. In the United States, rightly or wrongly, societal consensus has been that high incomes reflect—at least to some degree—high social product. As such, the high American per capita income is seen as a result of a relatively free market mechanism and an unequal distribution is tolerated as a by-product. If, instead, it is believed that few businesses would survive without exerting "influence," even if only to bribe government officials to do what they ought in any event to do, it is difficult to associate pecuniary rewards with social product. The perception of the price system as a mechanism rewarding the rich and well-connected may also be important in influencing political decisions about economic policy. If the market mechanism is suspect, the inevitable temptation is to resort to greater and greater intervention, thereby increasing the amount of economic activity devoted to rent seeking. As such, a political "vicious circle" may develop. People perceive that the market mechanism does not function in a way compatible with socially approved goals because of competitive rent seeking. A political consensus therefore emerges to intervene further in the market, rent seeking increases, and further intervention results. While it is beyond the competence of an economist to evaluate the political impact of rent seeking, the suspicion of the market mechanism so frequently voiced in some developing countries may result from it.

Finally, all market economies have some rent-generating restrictions. One can conceive of a continuum between a system of no restrictions and a perfectly restricted system. With no restrictions, entrepreneurs would seek to achieve windfall gains by adopting new technology, anticipating market shifts correctly, and so on. With perfect restrictions, regulations would be so all-pervasive that rent seeking would be the only route to gain. In such a system, entrepreneurs would devote all their time and resources to capturing windfall rents. While neither of these extreme types could ever exist, one can perhaps ask whether there might be some point along the continuum beyond which the market fails to perform its allocative function to any satisfactory degree. It will remain for further work to formalize these conjectures and to test their significance. It is hoped, however, that énough has been said to stimulate interest and research on the subject.

Notes

I am indebted to James M. Henderson for invaluable advice and discussion on successive drafts. Jagdish Bhagwati and John C. Hause made helpful comments on earlier drafts of this paper.

1. This phenomenon is explored in detail in Bhagwati and Krueger.

2. Note that (1) one would expect to find greater excess capacity in those industries where rents are higher and (2) within an industry, more efficient firms will have greater excess capacity than less efficient firms, since the return on a given amount of investment will be higher will greater efficiency.

3. It may be objected that illegal means of competition may be sufficiently distasteful that perfect competition will not result. Three comments are called for. First, it requires only that enough people at the margin do not incur disutility from engaging in these activities. Second, most lines of economic activity in many countries cannot be entered without some rent-seeking activity. Third, risks of detection (especially when bribery is expected), and the value judgments associated with illegal activities differ from society to society. See Ronald Wraith and Edgar Simpkins.

4. Santhanam Committee, pp. 7–8.

5. I am indebted to Ahmet Aker of Robert College who kindly made his data available to me. Details and a description of the data can be found in my forthcoming book.

6. Labor could be regarded as a composite domestic factor of production. Extensions to two or more factors would complicate the analysis, but would not alter its basic results.

7. These assumptions establish a domestic numeraire. The real analysis would be unaffected by proportional changes in the domestic prices.

8. Food and imports are consumed. But, by choice of food as the numeraire (see equation 6) and the assumed constancy of international prices, agricultural output serves as a measure of income.

9. The change in the price of the import from the free-trade solution is the tariff equivalent of the quantitative restriction described here.

10. Proof of (12) uses the step that $p_D^* \overline{M} > p_D M$ implies $(p_D^* - p_D)/(p_D^* + p_D) > -(\overline{M} - M)/(\overline{M} + M)$. Note that in the continuous case, (12) reduces to $1 + 1/p_D > \eta$.

11. As an alternative, the distributive production function (3) can be altered to treat all persons competing for import licenses as distributors so that L_D also encompasses L_R and $A' = p_D \overline{M}/L_D$. Another alternative is to introduce a rent-seeking

activity distinct from distribution with a wage determined from total rents ($p_D - A'k)\overline{M}/L_R$, and require that this wage equal the wages in distribution and agriculture. These specifications give results equivalent to those that follow from (13).

12. I am indebted to Bhagwati for pointing out this implication.

References

Bhagwati, J. On the equivalence of tariffs and quotas. In *Trade, Tariffs and Growth*. London, 1969.

Bhagwati, J., and P. Desai. *Planning for Industrialization: A Study of India's Trade and Industrial Policies Since 1950*. Cambridge, 1970.

Bhagwati, J., and A. Krueger. *Foreign Trade Regimes and Economic Development: Experience and Analysis*. New York, forthcoming.

Harris, J. R., and M. T. Todaro. Migration, unemployment, and development: A two-sector analysis. *Amer. Econ. Rev.* 60 (March 1970): 126–142.

Johnson, H. G. The cost of protection and the scientific tariff. *J. Polit. Econ.* 68, (August 1960): 327–345.

Krueger, A. *Foreign Trade Regimes and Economic Development: Turkey*. New York, 1974.

Monteiro, J. B. *Corruption*. Bombay, 1966.

Myrdal, G. *Asian Drama*. Vol. 3. New York, 1968.

Todaro, M. P. A model of labor migration and urban employment in less developed countries. *Amer. Econ. Rev.* 59 (March 1969): 138–148.

Wraith, R., and E. Simpkins. *Corruption in Developing Countries*. London, 1963.

Government of India, Planning Commission. *Third Five Year Plan*. New Delhi, August 1961.

Reserve Bank of India. *Report on Currency and Finance*. 1967–68.

Santhanam Committee. *Report on the Committee on Prevention of Corruption*. Government of India, Ministry of Home Affairs. New Delhi, 1964.

18

DUP Activities and Economic Theory

Jagdish N. Bhagwati,
Richard A. Brecher,
and T. N. Srinivasan

Recently, several economists have directed their talents to examining the impact of what have been christened (Bhagwati 1982a) as directly unproductive profit-seeking (DUP) activities. Among the more prominent such contributors, distinguished by different "schools" of thought, are (1) Buchanan, Tullock, and other important members of the public-choice school, with their major work now conveniently collected in Buchanan, Tullock, and Tollison (1980) and reviewed well in Tollison (1982); (2) Bhagwati, Findlay, Hansen, Krueger, Magee, Srinivasan, Wellisz, and other international economists, whose work is reviewed and systematized in Bhagwati (1982a); (3) Becker (1983), Peltzman, Posner, Stigler, and other members of the Chicago school, whose notable work is variously available; and (4) Lindbeck (1976), whose influential work on "endogenous politicians" is widely known.

While considerable progress has been made in formally analyzing individual DUP phenomena (revenue seeking, tariff seeking, monopoly seeking, etc.) in recent works that integrate them into properly specified general equilibrium models, attempts at synthesizing them have begun only recently: among them are Buchanan (1980) and Bhagwati (1982a). In this paper, we propose to examine a somewhat different but equally general and ambitious question: How serious for economic theory, as conventionally practiced, is the systematic integration of DUP phenomena into our analysis?

Section 1 defines DUP activities and lays out a suitable taxonomy of DUP categories or types which will serve our later analysis. Section 2 then considers the implications of different DUP categories for positive analysis. Section 3 addresses welfare or normative implications.

This paper was originally pubished in *European Economic Review* 24 (1984): 291–307. © 1984, Elsevier Science Publishers B. V. (North Holland).

1. DUP Activities: Concept and Taxonomy

The essential characteristic of the phenomena which this volume addresses, and which the many "schools" of thought distinguished above analyze, is that they represent ways of making a profit (i.e., income) by undertaking activities which are directly unproductive; that is, they yield pecuniary returns but produce neither goods and services that enter a conventional utility function directly nor intermediate inputs into such goods and services. Insofar as such activities use real resources, they result in a contraction of the availability set open to the economy. Thus, for example, tariff-seeking lobbying, tariff evasion, and premium seeking for given import licenses are all privately profitable activities. However, their direct output is simply zero in terms of the flow of goods and services entering a conventional utility function. For example, tariff seeking yields pecuniary income by changing the tariff and hence factor rewards; evasion of a tariff yields pecuniary income by exploiting the differential price between legal (tariff-bearing) imports and illegal (tariff-evading) imports; and premium seeking yields pecuniary income from the premia on import licenses. (Krueger's 1974 analysis of what she christened "rent-seeking" activities relates to a subset of the broad class of these DUP activities: she is concerned with the lobbying activities which are triggered by different licensing practices of governments.[1])

From the viewpoint of the analysis presented below, DUP activities can be subdivided into two generic types.[2] The distinction is between introducing policy-related DUP activity in models where the policy itself is *endogenously* determined by the interplay of the DUP activity with the otherwise orthodox economic specification of the "pure" economic system, and where the activity is embedded in a model where the policy is *exogenously* specified while the DUP activity is endogenous to that policy. Examples of the former, using tariff theory, are models where the tariff is endogenously determined; examples of the latter are models where a tariff exogenously specified to be in place leads to seeking for the revenues resulting from the tariff, and models where the tariff is evaded. The former class of DUP activities raises deeper questions for economic analysis than the latter, as we will contend below.

2. DUP Activities and Positive Analysis

Exogenous Policy
When the policy which induces DUP activity is exogenously specified, the implications of such DUP activity for positive analysis are tantamount to

introducing an essentially nontraded sector into the formal model. Thus, depending on the problem and the model, the analytical conclusions derived, on which policy intuitions are based, will change. We illustrate this by briefly considering two recent DUP-theoretic analyses in tariff and transfer theory: revenue seeking in Bhagwati and Srinivasan (1980) and transfer seeking in Bhagwati, Brecher and Hatta (1982).

Revenue Seeking and the Metzler Paradox   Conventional trade theory tells us that, provided suitable convexity assumptions are satisfied, a small country will find that a tariff will necessarily increase the domestic price and hence the output of the protected good. The Metzler paradox is that, for a large country (i.e., one that can influence its terms of trade), the tariff leads to such an improvement in the international terms of trade that the tariff-inclusive domestic price of the importable good falls and hence the importable good is paradoxically deprotected. We thus have the Metzler *price* and hence, what we can christen, the Metzler *production* paradox, in the conventional 2×2 model of trade theory.

But introduce now revenue seeking. Then, as Bhagwati and Srinivasan (1980) have shown, even if the Metzler price paradox were eliminated by assuming a small country, the Metzler production paradox can obtain. Thus, consider figure 18.1. $F_y F_x$ is the production possibility curve. With free trade, this small economy would produce at P^*. With a tariff, production shifts to $\hat{P}$, implying that production of the importable good Y has increased, and consumption is at $\hat{C}$. However, if the tariff leads to DUP lobbying for the tariff revenues, then the production of goods will decline as some resources must be diverted towards revenue seeking. The equilibrium shown must therefore reflect this. If we make the so-called "one-on-one" assumption (i.e., that competitive revenue seeking leads to diversion of one dollar worth of resources for every dollar worth of revenue), then the equilibrium will shift in figure 18.1 such that consumption is at $\hat{C}_y$ on the national-income-at-market-price budget line $\hat{P}\hat{C}_y$, and production is at $\hat{P}_y$ where the world price line $\hat{C}_y \hat{P}_y$ intersects the generalized Rybczynski line $\hat{P}R$ (which reflects successive withdrawals of resources for revenue seeking, at the given tariff-inclusive prices). Trade is defined by $\hat{C}_y$ and $\hat{P}_y$, tariff revenue is equal to the dashed distance $\hat{P}_y Q$ which, in turn, exactly equals (given the one-on-one assumption) the value of resources diverted to revenue seeking since it is equal to the value of reduced output of goods as measured by the difference between $\hat{P}$ and $\hat{P}_y$ at domestic prices. Revenue seeking, in this depiction, takes the form analytically of a nontraded activity that pays market-determined wages and rentals to factors (equal to those in goods production) and whose "output" is simply the revenue that is

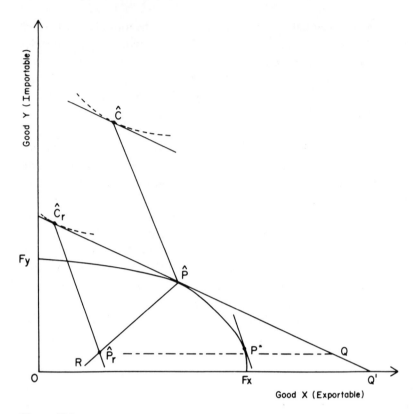

Figure 18.1

"sought" by the lobby. While therefore the value of goods production reduces thanks to it, it is fully offset by the *revenue* in equilibrium, and hence national income/expenditure at domestic market prices is determinate as $\hat{P}\hat{C}_y$, with earned income in goods production being determined at $\hat{P}_y$ and earned income in revenue seeking being equal to the revenue and both adding up to OQ' as the national expenditure or budget.

Note then that figure 18.1 (as drawn) shows the production of the imported good Y at $\hat{P}_y$ as less than at P^*: the Metzler production paradox obtains. The conventional "substitution" effect of the tariff does protect, taking production from P^* to $\hat{P}$; but this is more than offset by the "income" effect of the induced revenue seeking that shifts production again, to $\hat{P}_y$, given that the (generalized) Rybczynski line is positively sloped in the present example.

Transfer Seeking and the Terms-of-Trade Change Criterion   An application of this analysis to the transfer problem can again be shown to change

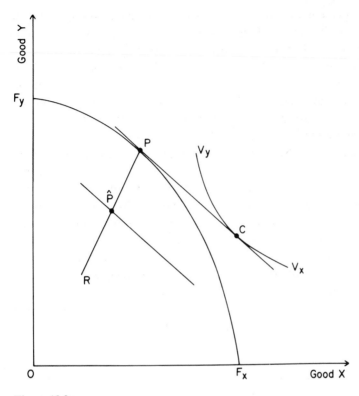

Figure 18.2

dramatically the conventional criterion for change in the terms of trade—
as in the recent work of Bhagwati, Brecher, and Hatta (1982).

Thus, consider the case where the transfer, instead of being received
directly by consumers or given to them as a lump-sum gift as in conventional analysis, goes into the governmental budget and then leads to
transfer-seeking lobbying. (In principle, we could also assume symmetrically that the donor country experiences reduced lobbying when it makes
the transfer: a case we discuss later.) Also consider again the one-on-one
assumption such that the transfer-seeking lobbying uses up a value of
domestic primary factors *equal* in total to the amount of the transfer. This
situation is analyzed in figure 18.2.

Initially, the recipient country produces on its production possibility
frontier $F_y F_x$ at point P, consumes on its social indifference curve $V_y V_x$ at
point C, and trades with the donor country (the rest of the world) along
price line PC from point P to point C. For starters, consider the case where
the terms of trade can not change.

In the small country case, the transfer has of course no impact on the goods-price ratio. The transfer-seeking activity of lobbyists, however, causes output in the recipient to move down the generalized Rybczynski line PR until production reaches $\hat{P}$, where the value of national output has fallen by the amount of the transfer to the level represented by the price line (parallel to PC) through point $\hat{P}$. Since this value of output plus the transfer equals national expenditure, consumption remains at point C. Thus, the transfer has paradoxically failed to enrich the recipient.

In the case of a large country, the recipient's welfare could actually decline, if the marginal propensity to consume good X (along the income-consumption curve) in the donor is less than the (analogous) marginal propensity to produce this good along the (generalized) Rybczynski line PR in the recipient. In this case, the transfer at initial prices would create an excess world demand for good X, and (given stability) the relative price of this commodity would rise to clear world markets. As the equilibrium price line steepens from the initial position PC, the recipient must reach a lower indifference curve, provided that the relative price of X does not rise above the autarkic level (where an indifference curve would touch curve $F_y F_x$). By similar reasoning, the opposite ranking of marginal propensities would lead to a fall in the world price of good X, and hence enrichment of the recipient.

Bhagwati, Brecher, and Hatta (1982) have analyzed also the *symmetric case* where the transfer-seeking DUP activity in the recipient country is matched by identical effects of DUP activity in the donor. To make the symmetry complete, they assume that the donor was initially disbursing domestically a given amount of revenue, resulting in equivalent utilization of resources in competitive subsidy-seeking lobbying, and that the subsequent international transfer payment simply reduces by an equivalent amount the subsidies subject to domestic lobbying and hence also reduces the resource use on such lobbying equivalently. As they then show, given market stability and the above-mentioned proviso about the autarkic level of relative prices, national welfare will then improve (worsen) for the donor and worsen (improve) for the recipient *if and only if* the recipient's marginal propensity to produce its own importable is greater (less) than the donor's marginal propensity to produce this good.

Endogenous Policy

The endogenization of policy *via* DUP activity is also subversive of traditional intuitions. Traditionally, economists are trained to think of governments as "neutral" in positive analysis and of economic agents to compete, perfectly or imperfectly, in alternative types of market environments. Once policy is endogenized, this tradition must necessarily be undermined. For, some or all economic agents may now also operate to have policy defined in their favor; there is a noneconomic, or nontraditional, marketplace, as it were, in which economic agents can simultaneously conduct their profit-making activities.[3] We thus have *two* components of the overall model: the orthodox "economic" specification and the "political" specification where profit motivation may equally extend and where the economic returns accrue through induce policy changes influencing economic returns in the traditionally "economic" sphere of the model.

   While we will deal later with the critical implication of this transformation in modelling policy for othodox welfare-theoretic analysis, we mention here simply that, as with the exogenous-policy DUP activities analyzed earlier, the results in positive analysis are sensitive to this basic change in the way the total economic system is modelled. For example, the customary view is that, given an exogenously specified tariff, an improvement in the terms of trade will reduce the domestic production of the importable good in an economy with given resources, well-behaved technology and perfect markets. But this conclusion need not follow, or may be seriously weakened, if the effect of the terms of trade change is to trigger tariff-seeking lobbying successfully.

   While there is indeed a vast literature on "political economy" models which endogenise policy through DUP activity specification in a variety of contexts, several efforts of a general equilibrium type have emerged recently in trade-theoretic literature in particular. We will give an indication here of the nature of these models by drawing on two of the early papers on tariff seeking:[4] Findlay and Wellisz (1982), and Feenstra and Bhagwati (1982). These papers may be characterized in the following way:

1. Economic *agents* are defined, which will engage in lobbying. In the Findlay-Wellisz model, these are the two specific factors in the two activities in the specific-factors model and their interests are in conflict since goods price changes affect them in an opposite manner. In Feenstra-Bhagwati, there is only one economic agent (that hurt by import competition) which engages in lobbying, in the 2×2 Heckscher-Ohlin-Samuelson model.

2. The agents lobby to have a *policy* adopted or to oppose it. In both Findlay-Wellisz and Feenstra-Bhagwati, that policy is uniquely defined to be a tariff.

3. The "government," as an economic agent, is not explicit in Findlay-Wellisz. The cost-of-lobbying functions which postulate the tariff as a function of the lobbying resources spent in proposing and opposing a tariff

are *implicitly* assuming a government which is subject to these opposing lobbying efforts and whatever preferences the government has are reflected implicitly in the postulated function. On the other hand, in Feenstra-Bhagwati, there is a two-*layer* government: the lobbying process interacts with one branch of government (e.g., the legislature) to enact a *lobbying tariff*, whereas another branch of the government (e.g., the president in the U.S.) then comes into the picture to use the tariff revenues generated by the lobbying tariff to bribe the lobby into accepting a different, welfare-superior *efficient tariff* which yields to the lobby, from both the revenue bribe *plus* the earned income from the market place at the efficient tariff, the same income as from the lobbying tariff.[5]

These papers then define rather well how the theoretical analysis of endogenous policymaking can be approached in the conventional manner of economic theory. By taking a simple set of political-cum-economic assumptions, they manage to get a neat, simple model working. In fact, from a pedagogic viewpoint, the extension of the traditional $2 \times 2 \times 2$ HOS-type trade theory model to an augmented $2 \times 2 \times 2 \times 2$ model, where there are two lobbies and capitalists and workers engage in tariff-seeking lobbying, would be a splendid exercise. It would imply combining, suitably and easily, elements from the Findlay-Wellisz and Feenstra-Bhagwati models.

These models can also be enriched in different directions. Of particular theoretical interest is the role of the government itself. Recall that the Feenstra-Bhagwati model postulates a two-layer view of the government, building in *both* the view (taken exclusively in Findlay-Wellisz) that the government is "acted upon" by political lobbies and that the tariff becomes then a function of the resources expended (presumably in financing re-election) by the respective lobbies, *and* the view that the government acts so as to maximize a conventional social welfare function. Instead, one could well take for example the view, sometimes propounded, that the government will maximize its *revenue*, since that will maximize its patronage. If so, Johnson's classic anslysis of maximum-revenue tariff yields, of course, in a conventional world where other economic agents are not engaged in lobbying, the politically endogenous tariff.

Again, the analysis can be extended instead rather on the dimension of the *policy instruments* for which the economic agents can lobby in response to import competition. Thus, as a supplement to tariffs, one can consider policy instruments in regard to international factor and technological flows. Without formally incorporating them into a model that endogenously yields the equilibrium choice or policy-mix of instruments in response to import competition, Bhagwati (1982a, b), Sapir (1983), and Dinopoulos (1983) have analyzed the *preferences* that different economic agents could have between these instruments when faced by import competition (i.e., improved terms of trade). Such analyses throw light on the incentives for lobbying for different policy adoptions by the government and hence yield the necessary insights into why certain policy options rather than others emerge as actual responses to import competition.

3. DUP Activities and Welfare Analysis

Again, we will consider exogenous and endogenous policies successively.

Exogenous Policies

The welfare effects of specific policies, and of parametric changes in the presence of exogenously specified policies, can be extremely sensitive to whether induced DUP activities are built into the model or not. Again, we take two telling instances:

1. Bhagwati and Srinivasan (1982), following on Foster's (1981) work, have shown that shadow prices for primary factors in a small, tariff-distorted open economy are different, depending on whether the tariff has or has not resulted in revenue seeking. In fact, the shadow prices can be shown to be the market prices when revenue seeking obtains.

2. We will also show here that, while the conventional rank ordering of an arbitrary t percent tariff vis-à-vis a production tax or a consumption tax in a small open economy at the same rate implies that the tariff is inferior to each of the other two policies since the tariff imposes both a production *and* a consumption cost, this rank ordering gets reversed if the different policies also result in revenue seeking!

Shadow Prices in a Tariff-Distorted, Small Economy in Cost-Benefit Analysis

The shadow prices for a small, tariff-distorted economy are known from the cost-benefit literature to be derivable as the duals to the world goods prices at the distorted techniques. On the other hand, it is obvious from the fact that if revenue seeking is present, as in figure 18.1, the economy operates on the national-expediture, social-budget line defined at the market, tariff-inclusive prices. Therefore, a marginal withdrawal of factors from the distorted, DUP equilibrium will evidently imply an opportunity cost reflecting the market prices.[6] To put it another way, with the entire revenue sought away, the consumer expenditure on goods equals income at market prices for factors. And these factor prices and goods prices do not change (as long as incomplete specialization continues), as we vary factor endowments, thanks to the tariff. As such, the value of change in the labour (capital) endowment by a unit is its market reward: hence the shadow factor prices in this DUP-activity-inclusive model are the market prices.[7] The invisible hand strikes again!

Policy Rankings with Revenue Seeking Recall that, for a small economy, a consumption tax on the importable (production tax on the exportable) is welfare superior to a tariff at the same *ad valorem* rate since it avoids the additional production (consumption) loss associated with the tariff. It turns out that once full revenue seeking *à la* Bhagwati and Srinivasan (1980) is unleashed by the imposition of any tax, this welfare ranking is reversed. This is seen as follows.

With tariff at an *ad valorem* rate t, let the output vector of the economy be (X^t, Y^t) under no revenue seeking. Let the free-trade (i.e., zero-tariff) output vector be (X^0, Y^0). With full revenue seeking under the tariff, consumers maximize utility given a relative price of $(1 + t)$ of the importable good Y (with the world relative price normalized at unity) and income Y equal to $[X^t + (1 + t)Y^t]$. They thus derive utility $v(1 + t, X_1^t + (1 + t)Y^t)$ expressed in terms of their indirect utility function $v(p, Y)$. On the other hand, with a consumption tax at an *ad valorem* rate t and full revenue seeking, they face the same price $(1 + t)$ but an income of $(X^0 + Y^0)$, thus obtaining utility: $v(1 + t, X^0 + Y^0)$. From the fact that (X^t, Y^t) maximizes the value of output given the tariff t, we get $\{X^t + (1 + t)Y^t\} \geq \{X^0 + (1 + t)Y^0\} \geq \{X^0 + Y^0\}$. Hence $v(1 + t, X^t + (1 + t)Y^t) > v(1 + t, X^0 + Y^0)$; that is, a tariff with full revenue seeking is superior to a consumption tax with full revenue seeking.

The foregoing argument can be readily illustrated in figure 18.3.[8] Without any seeking and free trade, equilibrium production is at (X^0, Y^0). With a tariff, production shifts at relative price ratio $(1 + t)$ to (X^t, Y^t). With tariff-revenue seeking, consumption is at C_r^t, as shown in figure 18.1 also. Shift, however, to a consumption tax on good Y with attendant revenue seeking. Production then remains at (X^0, Y^0) and the income, measured in terms of good X, is OQ, and is spent at the consumption-tax-inclusive price ratio $(1 + t)$ along QC_r^c, taking consumption to C_r^c. Figure 18.3 also shows production in the consumption-tax-cum-seeking equilibrium. It is given at P_r^c by the intersection of the world price line from C_r^c and the R-line which is the Rybczynski line for the world price ratio (unity) at (X^0, Y^0). Evidently, welfare at C_r^t dominates that at C_r^c: the tariff is superior to the consumption tax.

Consider now a comparison between a tariff at rate t and a production

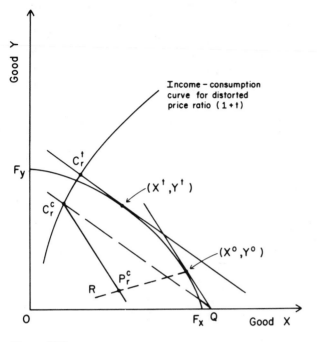

Figure 18.3

tax on good X yielding the same domestic relative good price as the tariff, both with attendant full revenue seeking. Under the tariff, equilibrium consumption is then at C_r^t in figure 18.4. But shift now to the production tax. Income, in terms of good Y, will then be OQ as with the tariff, but consumers will face the world price ratio (unity) and consumption will be at C_r^p. The production equilibrium will then be at P_r^p, the intersection between the expenditure line QC_r^p and the R-line from (X^t, Y^t) at the tax-distorted price $(1 + t)$. Evidently, C_r^t dominates C_r^p: welfare under the tariff exceeds that under an indentical production tax, when full revenue seeking obtains in each case.

The intuitive explanation of these results is evidently that, with no revenue seeking, a consumption (production) tax generates more revenue than a tariff at the same rate,[9] the reason being that the offsetting production (consumption) subsidy effect of a tariff is absent. In effect, what we are getting into is a situation where there are *two* distortions, rather than one, associated with each of the policies being ranked: the direct distortion implied by the policy itself and the indirect distortion implied by the (induced) DUP activity. What is interesting in the specific policy rankings

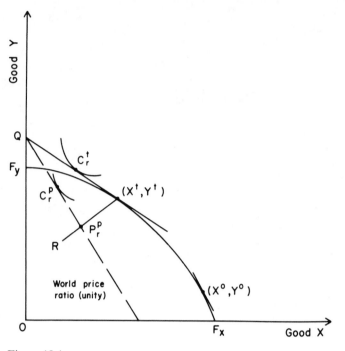

Figure 18.4

considered here is that these rankings are still possible, and in fact get reversed, when the indirect DUP effect is considered!

From a welfare-theoretic viewpoint, therefore, the analyst has to be alerted to the possibly critical role that (policy-induced) DUP activities can play in analyzing policies and hence in determining desirable policy intervention. This conclusion is also dramatically highlighted by the welfare-theoretic analysis of transfers. Thus, revert to our discussion of the DUP-theoretic transfer problem in section 2 and to figure 18.2. Recall that, in the traditional 2×2 (non-DUP) framework, exacting a reparation payment will always be enriching for the recipient of the resulting transfer in a Walras-stable market. Once, however, full transfer seeking is permitted, this is no longer so! Thus, take the case of a "large" recipient country, as discussed above in figure 18.2. If the terms of trade worsen in this DUP-activity-inclusive 2×2 model, that is *sufficient* to immiserize the recipient in a Walras-stable market, whereas by contrast such deterioration in the terms of trade cannot ever be large enough to offset the primary gain from the transfer in a Walras-stable market in the orthodox non-DUP-activity 2×2 model.

We therefore need to re-examine a number of policy intuitions if policies induce DUP activities in the real world, as they indeed do. The world lies somewhere along the continuum defined by two end points: one where no DUP activity is induced and the other where DUP activity is induced fully (on a one-to-one basis).[10] But while we have charted reasonably in depth the former end, we are only beginning to understand and sketch the latter end. An agenda for research to map out the latter landscape clearly awaits a new generation of researchers in all branches of economic theory.

Endogenous Policy and the "Determinacy Paradox"

A far more critical question is raised, however, once you fully endogenize policy in DUP-theoretic models. Exploiting our comparative advantage, we may consider again a trade-theoretic example to raise and probe this issue.

Take a tariff-seeking model of any species that you prefer. The endogenous tariff that emerges then in such a model may be illustrated in figure 18.5. $F^{ex}F^{ex}$ is the production possibility curve when all resources are

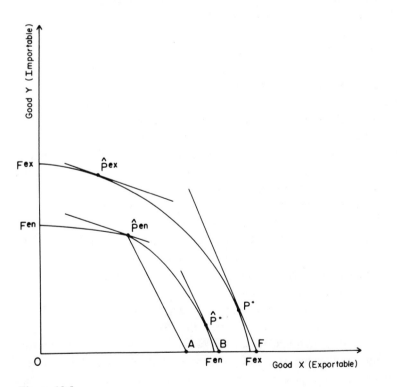

Figure 18.5

deployed for producing X and Y, and an *exogenous* tariff leads this small economy from P^* at given world prices to $\hat{P}^{ex}$ under protection. But now the model is augmented to endogenize the tariff, and in equilibrium, resources are used up in tariff-seeking DUP activity and the tariff-inclusive equilibrium is at $\hat{P}^{en}$. The production possibility curve $F^{en}F^{en}$ is a hypothetical construct, taking the endowment of factors as *net* of those used up in tariff-seeking *equilibrium:* the tariff-inclusive goods-price ratio must therefore be tangent to it at $\hat{P}^{en}$. It is assumed, of course, that revenue-seeking induced-DUP activity is not simultaneously present here.[11]

Now, as Bhagwati (1980) has shown, if we wish to measure the cost of protection in this endogenous tariff model, the appropriate way to do it would be to put the world price ratio tangent to $F^{en}F^{en}$ at $\hat{P}^*$ and then, using the Hicksian equivalent-variational measure, to take the move from $\hat{P}^{en}$ to $\hat{P}^*$ as the standard production cost of protection (reflecting the distortion of prices faced by producers), and the further move from $\hat{P}^*$ to P^* as the added cost of tariff-seeking lobbying (reflecting the loss due to resource diversion to lobbying). Hence the *total* cost of protection in an endogenous tariff model would be AF, reflecting the comparison between the free-trade equilibrium position at P^* and the endogenous tariff equilibrium position at $\hat{P}^{en}$. In turn, it is decomposed then into AB, the conventional "cost of protection," and BF, the "lobbying cost." It might be appropriate perhaps to christen the total cost as the cost of the "protectionist process," to avoid confusion between AF and AB.[12]

While this analytical innovation to extend the traditional cost-of-protection analysis to the case where the tariff is endogenous may be applauded, it raises the deeper question that we now wish to address.

Once the tariff is endogenized, it will generally be determined uniquely as at $\hat{P}^{en}$ (though, of course, multiple equilibria can be introduced as readily as in conventional "strictly economic" models). To compare this outcome with a hypothetical free-trade policy leading to P^* is to compare a policy choice that is made as a solution to the entire, augmented economic-cum-policy-choice system with a wholly hypothetical policy that descends like manna from heaven! Such a comparison makes obvious sense, of course, when we take policies as exogenous: we are then simply varying them, given the conventional economic system, and reading off their welfare consequences. But, with only one policy outcome determined endogenously, we simply cannot compare policies as in orthodox economic analysis: this is the *determinacy paradox.* Comparison between the observed, endogenized policy and another hypothetical policy arrived at by exogenous specification, while of course possible, is not compelling. It is virtually as if we had wiped out one (the "political") side of our model for our point of reference!

It would appear therefore that we need to *change* the way we pose welfare-theoretic questions once policies are endogenized critically, as in the foregoing analysis. Thus, it is not particularly meaningful to rank-order policies as in traditional analysis, once policies are endogenous. Nor is it appropriate to compare them vis-à-vis a reference point (such as P^* in figure 18.3) which reflects an exogenously specified policy.

Rather, it would appear that the analyst must now shift focus and concentrate on *variations around the endogenous equilibrium* itself (i.e., around $\hat{P}^{en}$ in figure 18.3). Thus, it is customary to ask what happens, given a policy, to welfare when accumulation comes about, or when technical know-how changes, etc. We can rephrase these questions as follows, keeping in mind that there are now two parts of the overall economic system, "economic" and "political": What will happen to welfare if, on the economic side of the model, these changes such as accumulation, technical progress, etc., occur; and what happens if changes occur instead on the political side such as an increased cost of lobbying for a tariff if there is an exogenous shift in attitudes against protection?[13] In short, the overall system must be solved for endogenous policy change and for final welfare impact for parametic changes that can occur now *either* in the "economic" *or* equally in the "political" side of the overall, augmented system. An interesting way to decompose the overall welfare impact of such parametic changes in either the "economic" or the "political" side of the system could be to assume first that policy does remain exogenous and then, in the next stage, to allow it to change to its endogenous value. The first stage should capture the essence of what we have come to think of as the customary impact of a parametic change in the system; the second stage can be taken to correspond to the fact that policy is endogenous.

4. Concluding Remark

Evidently, therefore, the integration of DUP activities into theoretic analysis is a serious business. We hope that we have raised the issues sufficiently sharply to stimulate the response of our fellow economists in the shape of future research on what promises to be an extremely important innovation in economic theorizing.

Notes

Bhagwati's research has been supported by the National Science Foundation. This paper was presented, in an earlier version, at a conference at Middlebury College, and will appear in selected proceedings of the conference: David Colander, ed.,

Neoclassical Political Economy: The Analysis of Rent-Seeking and DUP Activities (Ballinger, Cambridge, Mass.) in Fall 1984.

1. Her focus is on licensing/quantity restrictions and the rents thereon, and her generic set of rent-seeking activities excludes from its scope other DUP activities such as price-distortion-triggered DUP activities or distortion-triggering DUP activities. For a fuller analysis of the relationship, analytical and terminological, between DUP and "rent seeking" activities, the reader should consult Bhagwati (1983).

2. Other classifications, addressed better to other purposes, are also possible, as in Bhagwati's (1982a) synthesis of the welfare effects of DUP activities.

3. Of course, this is also true of DUP lobbying and policy-evading models we considered in the case where the policy *causing* the DUP activity was specified exogenously.

4. The earliest, pioneering work is that of Brock and Magee (1978, 1980).

5. Feenstra and Bhagwati note that the efficient tariff may pardoxically exceed the lobbying tariff if the shadow price of lobbying activity is negative.

6. Thus, as Anam (1982) has shown, Johnson's (1967) type of immiserizing growth in the presence of a tariff is impossible when all tariff revenues are sought.

7. If not all of the tariff revenues are subject to seeking, the shadow prices would be differently defined, as noted by Anam (1982).

8. For an important diagrammatic analysis of a consumption tax with revenue seeking, see Anam (1982), who showed that such a tax might be welfare-inferior to a tariff in achieving a given level of consumption for one good.

9. See also Anam (1982) on this point.

10. The latter end point may even be more drastic if, as Tullock (1981) has suggested, seeking leads to more resources being spent on chasing a prize than the value of the prize itself, depending on how you model the terms and conditions of such a chase.

11. See Tullock (1981) and Bhagwati (1982b) for analysis of the case where however this DUP activity is simultaneously present.

12. Bhagwati (1980) also shows that it is incorrect to argue that the cost of an endogenous tariff at t percent always exceeds the cost of an exogenous tariff at t percent. This proposition involves comparing $\hat{P}^{ex}$ with $\hat{P}^{en}$; and, since this is a second-best comparison, the endogenous tariff can be less harmful than the exogenous one. This is also at the heart of the problem with the Buchanan-Tollison definition of DUP activities, as discussed in Bhagwati (1983).

13. On this point, see Brecher (1982).

References

Anam, Mahmudul. 1982. Distortion-triggered lobbying and welfare: A contribution to the theory of directly-unproductive profit-seeking activities. *Journal of International Economics* 13, no. 1/2 (August): 15–32.

Becker, Gary S. 1983. A theory of competition among pressure groups for political influence. *Quarterly Journal of Economics* 93 (August): 371–400.

Bhagwati, J. N. 1980. Lobbying and welfare. *Journal of Public Economics* 14 (December): 355–363.

Bhagwati, J. N. 1982a. Directly-unproductive, profit-seeking (DUP) activities. *Journal of Political Economy* 90 (October): 988–1002.

Bhagwati, J. N. 1982b. Lobbying, DUP activities and welfare: A response to Tullock. *Journal of Public Economics* 19 (December): 395–401.

Bhagwati, J. N. 1983. DUP activities and rent seeking. Working paper, Columbia University. Abbreviated version in *Kyklos* 36: 634–637.

Bhagwati, J. N., and T. N. Srinivasan. 1980. Revenue seeking: A generalization of the theory of tariffs. *Journal of Political Economy* 88 (December): 1069–1087.

Bhagwati, J. N., and T. N. Srinivasan. 1982. The welfare consequences of directly-unproductive profit-seeking (DUP) lobbying activities: Prices versus quantity distortions. *Journal of International Economics* 13: 33–44.

Bhagwati, J. N., R. A. Brecher, and T. Hatta. 1982. The generalized theory of transfers and welfare: Exogenous (policy-imposed) and endogenous (transfer-induced) distortions. Mimeo., July. *Quarterly Journal of Economics*, forthcoming.

Brecher, Richard A. 1982. Comment. In Jagdish N. Bhagwati, ed., *Import competition and Response*. University of Chicago Press.

Brock, William, and Steven P. Magee. 1978. The economics of special interest politics: The case of tariff. *American Economic Review* 68 (May): 246–250.

Brock, William, A., and Steven P. Magee. 1980. Tariff formation in a democracy. In J. Black and B. Hindley, eds., *Current Issues in International Commercial Policy and Diplomacy*. Macmillan, New York, pp. 1–9.

Buchanan, J. 1980. Rent seeking and profit seeking. In J. Buchanan, G. Tullock, and R. Tollison, eds., *Towards a General Theory of the Rent-Seeking Society*. Texas A & M University Press, College Station.

Buchanan, J., G. Tullock, and R. Tollison, eds. 1980. *Towards a General Theory of the Rent-Seeking Society*. Texas A & M University Press, College Station.

Dinopoulos, E. 1983. Import competition, international factor mobility and lobbying responses: The Schumpeterian industry. *Journal of International Economics* 14 (May).

Feenstra, R., and J. N. Bhagwati. 1982. Tariff seeking and the efficient tariff. In J. N. Bhagwati, ed., *Import Competition and Response*. University of Chicago Press, pp. 245–258.

Findlay, R., and S. Wellisz. 1982. Endogenous tariffs, the political economy of trade restrictions, and welfare. In J. N. Bhagwati, ed., *Import Competition and Response*. University of Chicago Press, pp. 223–233.

Foster, E. 1981. The treatment of rents in cost-benefit analysis. *American Economic Review* 71 (March): 171–178.

Johnson, Harry G. 1967. The possibility of income losses from increased efficiency or factor accumulation in the presence of tariffs. *Economic Journal* 77 (March): 151–154.

Krueger, A. O. 1974. The political economy of the rent-seeking society. *American Economic Review* 64 (June): 291–303.

Lindbeck, Assar. 1976. Stabilization policies in open economies with endogenous politicians. Richard Ely Lecture. *American Economic Review* 66 (May): 1–19.

Sapir, Andre. 1983. Foreign competition, immigration and structural adjustment. *Journal of International Economics* 14 (May): 381–394.

Tollison, R. D. 1982. Rent seeking: A survey. *Kyklos* 35: 575–602.

Tullock, Gordon. 1981. Lobbying and welfare: A comment. *Journal of Public Economics* 16: 391–394.

19

Endogenous Tariff Formation

Wolfgang Mayer

Interest in the process of tariff formation has grown considerably during the last decade. Robert Baldwin (1976, 1982), William Brock and Stephen Magee (1978, 1980), as well as Ronald Findlay and Stanislaw Wellisz (1982) have suggested alternative models for studying the economic and political forces that interact in determining a country's actual tariff structure.[1] The underlying premise of these studies is that political decisions on tariff rates are reflections of the selfish economic interests of voters, lobbying groups, politicians, or other decision makers in trade policy matters.[2,3]

Brock and Magee, as well as Findlay and Wellisz, treat tariff formation as a noncooperative game among competing economic interest groups.[4] In Brock and Magee's papers, the tariff positions of opposing political parties are explained, where each party maximizes its chances of being elected, and the probability of reelection hinges on contributions from tariff-sensitive lobbying groups. In Findlay and Wellisz, the economic interests of land and capital owners are opposed, with labor standing on the sidelines. Baldwin, on the other hand, postulates majority voting by owners of productive factors. Hence, Baldwin introduces a collective decision rule to tariff determination which plays a major role in the public choice literature.[5] Specifically, he argues that accepted optimal trade policy prescriptions, such as free trade for a small country, would be voted in by factor owners if voters' tastes were homothetic and there were no restrictions on income redistributions, no voting and information costs, and no possibilities for logrolling. However, when these ideal assumptions are gradually removed, Baldwin (1976, p. 71) suggests that actual tariff rates are decisively affected by economic groups which are large in size and whose potential gains or losses are substantial.

This paper was originally published in *The American Economic Review* 74, no. 5 (December): 970–985.

Baldwin's discussion is rich in detail and offers many valuable insights. Most important, it breaks new ground in suggesting determinants of actual tariffs, such as the distribution of factors of production, the existence of voting costs, and the specific nature of the underlying economic and political system. The purpose of this paper is to study some of these alternative determinants of tariff rates in a rigorously formulated general equilibrium model. In particular, the paper attempts to evaluate the dependence of actual tariff rates on factor-ownership distribution, voter eligibility and participation rules, and the degrees of factor mobility and industry diversification in the economy.

The standard assumption on factor ownership, which also is adopted by Baldwin (1982, p. 268), states that each person owns one factor of production only. This implies that all owners of a given factor form a well-defined interest group whose membership is independent of the prevailing tariff rate. Accordingly, voter allegiances are exogenously imposed rather than endogenously determined. Baldwin's correct observations, that majority voting could eliminate all trade of a capital-abundant country if there were more workers than capitalists, suggests that this standard assumption on factor ownership has limited appeal in explaining actual tariff structures under majority voting. This paper changes the standard assumption by allowing a person to own more than one factor of production. Also, factor-ownership shares may differ among people. As a result, the number of factor owners voting for or against a given tariff change will no longer be fixed, but will depend on the prevailing tariff rate. Under shifting voter allegiances, a tariff equilibrium is attained when no majority can be found to push for either an increase or a reduction in the existing tariff rate. Whether such an equilibrium tariff is positive, zero, or negative crucially hinges on the underlying factor-ownership distribution. I demonstrate that each factor owner has an optimal tariff rate whose value is uniquely related to the individual's factor ownership. In the special case of majority voting with no voting costs, it is the median factor owner's optimal tariff rate that will be chosen to become the actual tariff rate.

Given a country's distribution of factor ownership, tariff equilibria are affected by voter eligibility rules and participation costs. Some factor owners may not be eligible to participate in the voting process. Others are eligible but have no incentive to participate as voting costs are high relative to benefits from enacting or preventing a proposed tariff change.[6] Over the last century, most countries have undergone drastic liberalizations with respect to voter eligibility rules. But even today there are many factor owners, such as young people or foreign workers, who are not permitted to vote. This paper also relates actual tariff structures to voter eligibility rules and, more importantly, to the existence of significant voting costs on the part of factor owners.

Tariff formation is discussed under two alternative assumptions about the underlying production structure. First, I employ the common two-by-two Heckscher-Ohlin model, later a multisectoral factor-specific model is introduced. The advantage of the former is that it is sufficiently simple to illustrate the tariff formation process and it offers a plausible explanation for long-run tariff adjustments as factor-ownership distribution, voting costs, or voter eligibility rules change. Its main shortcoming is its failure to explain the frequently observed phenomenon that a relatively small industry, that does not have support from the majority of eligible voters, succeeds in gaining tariff protection. The factor-specific multisector model is more appropriate for studying such industry-specific efforts to raise a given tariff. In such a model, higher tariffs on a given import good lead to significant welfare gains for the average specific-factor owner in the protected industry but to rather small welfare losses for average specific-factor owners in all other industries. The small number of big potential gainers, therefore, has much greater incentives to participate in the political process than the large number of small potential losers, whenever there exist significant voting costs. Hence, I am proving rigorously what Baldwin (1976, p. 71) hypothesizes and Anthony Downs suggested, namely that small important producer groups can be quite successful in securing import protection.

In addition to studying the determinants of actual tariff rates, I will ask whether there exist factor-ownership distributions under which the majority of voters would support a free-trade policy for a small country. Stated differently, I am in search of those factor-ownership distributions that, given the assumed production structure, result in Pareto-efficient resource allocations.

Section 1 states general assumptions about consumer preferences, factor distributions, and tariff revenue redistributions in a Heckscher-Ohlin model, and describes what tariff rate is optimal for a given person with predetermined factor ownership. Section 2 deals with the impact of tariff changes on the individual's economic interests, as measured by real income changes, and demonstrates how the actual tariff rate is chosen under majority voting. The relationship between the chosen tariff rate and changing voting costs is emphasized in this context. Section 3 introduces a multisector, factor-specific production model, as discussed in Ronald Jones (1975) and expanded in Roy Ruffin and Jones (1977). My aim is to demonstrate that, under rather neutral assumptions, there is a very strong presumption that a small industry will succeed in gaining import protection even though all other industries are hurt.

1. Optimal Tariff Rates in a Heckscher-Ohlin Model

Assumptions

Consider a small open economy in which capital and labor are employed to produce two commodities, X_1 and X_2. Each inhabitant of this country possesses one unit of labor and no or some positive amount of capital; that is, $L^i = 1$ and $K^i \geqq 0$, where $L^i(K^i)$ denotes labor (capital) owned by individual i, $i = 1, \ldots, I$. Both factors are perfectly mobile between the two industries, all markets are competitive, and the firms' production functions are homogeneous of degree one.

Preferences of the country's inhabitants are assumed to be homothetic and identical,[7] such that a redistribution of income will affect neither the country's aggregate demand nor imports, as long as total income remains unchanged. Preferences of individual i are described by an indirect utility function,

$$U^i = U^i(p, y^i), \quad i = 1, \ldots, I, \tag{1}$$

where U^i denotes maximum utility attainable by individual i, given the price of the first in terms of the second commodity, p, and income of individual i, y^i, measured in terms of the second commodity. There are three potential sources of income: ownership of labor, ownership of capital, and redistributions from tariff revenues. Total income of individual i is

$$y^i = w + rK^i + T^i, \tag{2}$$

where w and r denote the returns on labor and capital, respectively, T^i represents tariff revenues received by individual i, and $L^i = 1$. Concerning the redistribution of tariff revenues, it is assumed that there are predetermined rules that are not voted on in conjunction with the tariff issue, and that are neutral with respect to the overall distribution of income. Neutrality means that the ith individual's share of total tariff revenues is identical to the ith person's income share from factor ownership, ϕ^i; that is,

$$T^i = \phi^i T, \tag{3}$$

where T represents total tariff revenues and

$$\phi^i = \frac{w + rK^i}{wL + rK}. \tag{4}$$

In equation (4), L is the total labor supply or number of inhabitants and $K = \sum_i^I K^i$. Also, it should be noted that $\sum_i^I \phi^i = 1$. Substituting (3) and (4) in (2) yields

$$y^i = \phi^i(wL + rK + T) = \phi^i Y, \tag{2'}$$

where Y denotes the economy's total income in terms of the second commodity.

Finally, it is assumed that, for all relevant tariff rates, incomplete specialization in production prevails and the first commodity is imported. Total tariff revenues are expressed as

$$T = t\pi M, \tag{5}$$

where t is the tariff rate, π the world price, and M the imported quantity of the first commodity.

Optimal Tariff Rates for Individuals

When factor ownership differs among a country's people, their welfare is not affected uniformly by a tariff increase, as can be seen by substituting (2′) in (1):

$$U^i = U^i(p, \phi^i Y), \quad i = 1, \ldots, I. \tag{1′}$$

The ith person's maximum attainable utility depends on its own income share, in addition to domestic prices and aggregate income as faced by all individuals. If a tariff rate is changed, all people are confronted with identical price and aggregate income changes, but in general with different effects on their income share. Consequently, a given tariff change benefits some and hurts others, whereby the magnitude of welfare changes may vary greatly among gainers and losers. Inequality in the factor-ownership distribution is responsible for this differentiation in welfare effects.

To see the impact of a tariff increase on a given individual's welfare, let us substitute $p = \pi(1 + t)$ in (1′) and differentiate (1′) with respect to t:

$$\frac{\partial U^i}{\partial t} = \left(\frac{\partial U^i}{\partial y^i}\right)\left[-\phi^i \pi D_1 + \phi^i\left(\frac{\partial Y}{\partial t}\right) + Y\left(\frac{\partial \phi^i}{\partial t}\right)\right], \tag{6}$$

where D_1 denotes aggregate demand for the first commodity. In deriving (6), use is made of Roy's identity and of the property of homothetic utility functions that the ith person's demand for a commodity equals the product of its income share and aggregate demand for the same commodity.

The economy's aggregate income is given by

$$Y = wL + rK + T = pX_1 + X_2 + t\pi M, \tag{7}$$

where X_j indicates industry output of commodity $j, j = 1, 2$. Differentiating (7) with respect to t yields

$$\frac{\partial Y}{\partial t} = \pi D_1 + t\pi\left(\frac{\partial M}{\partial t}\right), \tag{8}$$

where $\partial M/\partial t < 0$. After substitution of (8), equation (6) can be rewritten as

$$\frac{\partial U^i}{\partial t} = \left(\frac{\partial U^i}{\partial y^i}\right)\left[\phi^i t\pi\left(\frac{\partial M}{\partial t}\right) + Y\left(\frac{\partial \phi^i}{\partial t}\right)\right]. \tag{6'}$$

There are two channels through which individual welfare is altered by a tariff increase: changes in the tariff-weighted value of imports, $t\pi(\partial M/\partial t)$, and changes in the individual's income share, $(\partial \phi^i/\partial t)$. While imports always decline as import tariffs rise,[8] the direction of change of a person's income share depends on individual factor endowments relative to the nation as a whole, on the one hand, and on the relative factor intensity of the import industry, on the other hand. More will be said on this point shortly.

A tariff rate is optimal for individual i if $(\partial U^i/\partial t) = 0$ in (6') and U^i is strictly concave in t.[9] Assuming the concavity property is satisfied, the optimal tariff rate for individual i, $\tilde{t}^i$, is given by

$$\tilde{t}^i = -\left(\frac{Y}{\pi\partial M/\partial t}\right)\left(\frac{\partial \phi^i/\partial t}{\phi^i}\right). \tag{9}$$

Since $-(\partial M/\partial t) > 0$, a person's optimal tariff rate is positive, zero, or negative as a higher tariff raises, keeps constant, or lowers the person's income share.

The relationship between a tariff and a given person's income share, in turn, depends on that person's endowments, as well as on the production structure through which factor returns and commodity prices are linked. For example, in the present section, the economy's production side is described by a Heckscher-Ohlin model. Differentiating the income-share expression of (4) with respect to t, we obtain

$$\frac{\partial \phi^i}{\partial t} = \left[\frac{wL}{(wL + rK)^2(1 + t)}\right]\left[\frac{r(k - k^i)(\hat{w} - \hat{r})}{\hat{p}}\right], \tag{10}$$

where $k = K/L$ and $k^i = K^i/L^i = K^i$. The "hat" indicates percentage changes, and $(\hat{w} - \hat{r})/\hat{p}$ is positive (negative) as the first or import commodity is relatively labor-(capital) intensive in production. Equation (10) reveals that a tariff increase results in a higher (lower) income share for the ith individual if the individual, compared to the nation as a whole, is relatively well (poorly) endowed with the import good's intensively used factor of production; that is, $\partial \phi^i/\partial t > 0$ if either $k^i < k$ and $k_1 < k_2$ or $k^i > k$ and $k_1 > k_2$, where k_j is the capital-labor ratio in industry j and good one is imported.

In light of this relationship between income shares and tariffs, the following conclusions can now be drawn about individually optimal tariff rates, as stated in (9):

1. The optimal import tariff is positive (negative) for people who are relatively well (poorly) endowed with the import good's intensively used factor.

2. The greater the difference between individual and national endowment ratios, the greater the deviation of individually optimal tariff or subsidy rates from free-trade policy.[10]

3. The optimal tariff rate is zero for each person whose personal capital-labor ownership ratio equals the national capital-labor endowment ratio.

2. Tariff Determination under Majority Voting

Actual tariffs are assumed to be the result of majority voting, where votes reflect the economic interests of those that are eligible and willing to participate in the tariff formation process. This section starts with a description of the relationship between a person's economic interests, on one side, and actual tariff rates, as well as personal factor endowments, on the other side. It is followed by an analysis of tariff equilibria under alternative majority voting rules.

Real Income Effects of Tariff Changes

Changes in real income indicate to what extent a person's economic interests are affected. Measured in units of the second commodity, the real income change of individual i brought about by a tariff increase can be expressed as

$$B^i(k^i, t) = \frac{\partial U^i/\partial t}{\partial U^i/\partial y^i},$$ (11)

where $\partial B^i/\partial k^i > 0$ (<0) if the imported good is relatively capital (labor) intensive and $\partial B^i/\partial t < 0$ always.

In order to show that $\partial B^i/\partial k^i > 0$ for a capital-intensive import good, let us first determine the value of the individual endowment ratio, $\tilde{k}^j$, at which the prevailing tariff rate t would be optimal. Using (9) and (10), the value of $\tilde{k}^j$ must be such that

$$t = -\left[\frac{Y}{\pi(\partial M/\partial t)}\right]\left[\frac{wL(\hat{w} - \hat{r})}{(wL + rK)\hat{p}(1 + t)}\right]\left[\frac{r(k - \tilde{k}^j)}{w + r\tilde{k}^j}\right].$$ (9')

Next, we return to the definition of B^i and employ (6') to obtain

$$B^i(k^i, t) = \phi^i\left[t\pi\left(\frac{\partial M}{\partial t}\right) + \frac{Y(\partial\phi^i/\partial t)}{\phi^i}\right].$$ (11')

Substitution of (9') for t and of (10) for $(\partial\phi^i/\partial t)$, as well as some manipulations, yield

$$B^i = -\left[\frac{(\hat{w} - \hat{r})}{\hat{p}(1 + t)}\right]\left[\frac{Ywr}{(w + r\tilde{k}^j)(wL + rK)}\right](k^i - \tilde{k}^j), \tag{11''}$$

where $-[(\hat{w} - \hat{r})/\hat{p}] > 0$ for a capital-intensive import good. Equation (11'') expresses that a given tariff increase raises (lowers) the ith person's real income if the ith person's capital-labor endowment ratio, k^i, exceeds (falls short of) the capital-labor endowment ratio, $\tilde{k}^j$, of the person for whom the prevailing tariff rate is optimal. Furthermore, $(\partial B^i/\partial k^i)$ must be positive since, at a given tariff rate, no term inside the first two brackets of (11'') will change as k^i varies.

The negative sign of $(\partial B^i/\partial t)$, on the other hand, immediately follows from the utility function's properties of strict concavity in tariff rates and homogeneity of degree one in commodities.

The relationship between B^i, on the one hand, and k^i and t, on the other hand, is depicted in figure 19.1 for an economy whose import industry is relatively capital intesive. The $B_0 B_0$ locus is drawn under the assumption that there is free trade. Since $t = 0$ when $\tilde{k}^j = k$, it follows from (11') that $B^i \gtreqless 0$ as $k^i \gtreqless k$. The $B_0 B_0$ locus is upward sloping as real income gains from tariff increases rise with the magnitude of a person's capital ownership. The $B_1 B_1$ locus, on the other hand, is drawn under the assumption that the actual tariff rate is positive, that is, $t > 0$. This tariff rate would be optimal for a person with endowment ratio $\tilde{k}^j$. Only those individuals gain from further tariff increases for whom $k^i > \tilde{k}^j$, while all others lose. Consequently, if the level of tariffs is raised, the number of people who gain from

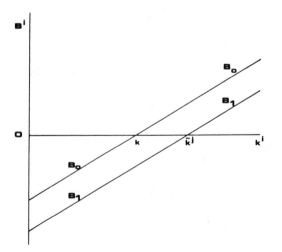

Figure 19.1

further tariff increases becomes smaller, while the number of people who lose becomes larger.

Majority Voting without Restrictions

A tariff rate is called an equilibrium tariff rate when no majority of voters can be formed to alter that rate. Duncan Black (1948a) demonstrated that, in the absence of voting costs, such an equilibrium exists if voters possess "single-peaked" preferences and that the adopted policy is determined by the median voter's peak preference. Black's equilibrium condition is indeed satisfied in my tariff choice model, as each factor owner has a unique optimal tariff rate. Accordingly, the median voter's optimal tariff rate, denoted by $\tilde{t}^m$, becomes the equilibrium tariff rate under majority voting.

Who the median voter is depends on voter eligibility rules and the distribution of factor ownership. Concerning eligibility, assume at this point that there are no restrictions; each factor owner has one vote and participates in voting. Concerning factor ownership, it is assumed that capital is unevenly distributed, ranging from no capital ownership, $k^i = 0$, to maximum capital ownership, $k^i = k^{max}$. It is convenient to describe capital-labor ownership ratios by $k(e)$, where e is an index such that $0 \leq e \leq 1$. All people with no capital ownership are indexed with $e = 0$, and e rises as the capital-labor ownership ratio rises; that is, $k(0) = 0$, $\partial k/\partial e > 0$, and $k(1) = k^{max}$. The proportion of factor owners with the same factor ownership is defined as $f[k(e)] \geq 0$, where $\int_0^1 f[k(e)]\,de = 1$. As

$$\int_0^1 k(e)f[k(e)]\,de = \frac{K}{L} = k, \tag{12}$$

the economy's capital-labor endowment ratio is the mean of the factor-ownership distribution. Equations (9) and (10) revealed that a given person's optimal tariff rate hinges on the relation between its own and the whole economy's capital-labor ratio. Applied to the median voter whose preferences are crucial for the actual choice of tariff rates, one can evaluate the *sign* of the economy's equilibrium tariff rate, t^*, by comparing the *median* with the *mean* of the factor-ownership distribution. Provided the distribution is unimodal,

$$t^* = \tilde{t}^m \gtreqless 0, \tag{13}$$

as the distribution is skewed to the left, symmetric, or skewed to the right. A tariff (subsidy) on capital-intensive imports will be voted in if the majority of people has capital-labor ownership ratios that exceed (fall short of) the capital-labor endowment ratio of the country. And a small country will choose free trade as its policy in the special case of a symmetric distribution.[11,12]

For most nonsocialist countries there is strong evidence that capital-labor ownership distributions are not symmetric, but skewed to the right. Accordingly, one would expect a built-in tendency towards protection of labor's interests, through subsidies on capital-intensive imports or tariffs on labor-intensive imports. However, this intrinsic bias in favor of labor may not translate into prolabor tariff legislation if it is negated by voter eligibility and participation restrictions, as discussed next.

Majority Voting under Restrictions

Downs, Buchanan and Tullock, Baldwin, Peltzman, and many others, have emphasized that there are considerable costs to participants in the voting process.[13] Voter participation costs imply that some eligible voters may choose not to exercise their voting rights. If participation costs exceed the gains from a proposed tariff change, an individual is best off not to vote at all. But even if gains from proposed tariff actions exceed voting costs, voter participation is not certain. Following Peltzman, this paper assumes that the probability of a person voting (or the fraction of people with identical factor ownership which will participate) is directly related to the magnitude of "net" gains.[14]

A person with capital-labor ownership index e will enjoy a net gain from a tariff increase if, for a given t,

$$B[k(e), t] - c(e) > 0, \tag{14}$$

where $c(e)$ denotes the real income loss from voting, or simply voter participation costs, for people with factor-ownership ratio $k(e)$. The fraction of people with $k(e)$ that will vote for a tariff increase, $\rho(e)$, is

$$\rho(e) = \rho\{B[k(e), t] - c(e)]\}, \tag{15}$$

where $0 \leq \rho < 1$ and $\rho' \geq 0$. Since the total number of people with factor ownership $k(e)$ equals $f[k(e)]L$, the total number of votes for a *tariff increase*, E, is

$$E = L \int_{\tilde{e}}^{1} \rho(e) f[k(e)] \, de, \tag{16}$$

where $\tilde{e}$ is the factor-ownership index for persons with zero net gains from the tariff rise; that is, for those with $B[k(\tilde{e}), t] = c(\tilde{e})$.

Similarly, a person will enjoy a net gain from a tariff *decrease*, if

$$D[k(e), t] - c(e) = -B[k(e), t] - c(e) > 0, \tag{17}$$

where D is the real income gain from a tariff decrease. The fraction of people with factor-ownership ratio $k(e)$ that votes for the tariff decrease is denoted by $0 \leq \sigma(e) < 1$, where σ is positively related to the left-hand expression in (17). The total number of votes cast for a tariff decrease, A, is

$$A = L \int_0^{\tilde{\tilde{e}}} \sigma(e) f[k(e)] \, de, \tag{18}$$

where $\tilde{\tilde{e}}$ is the factor-ownership index for persons with zero net gains from the tariff decline; that is, for those with $D[k(\tilde{\tilde{e}}), t] = c(\tilde{\tilde{e}})$.

If, at a given tariff rate, $E > A$, a majority will vote for higher tariffs. As the tariff is raised, the voting strength of proponents (E) for a tariff increase will decline while opponents (A) increase their votes. This follows from (16) and (18), as σ, $\tilde{e}$, and $\tilde{\tilde{e}}$ are directly and ρ is inversely related to t. An equilibrium tariff finally is established, when $E = A$, or[15]

$$\int_{\tilde{e}}^1 \rho(e) f[k(e)] \, de = \int_0^{\tilde{\tilde{e}}} \sigma(e) f[k(e)] \, de. \tag{19}$$

It is clear that the equilibrium tariff depends on the factor distribution at both tails, that is, for people with indexes $e \geq \tilde{e}$ and $e \leq \tilde{\tilde{e}}$, as well as on voting probabilities on the part of winners, $\rho(e)$, and losers, $\sigma(e)$. Whether a person is going to vote at all and with what probability, in turn, depends on the person's factor-ownership ratio, voting costs, and actual tariff rate.

It is relatively easy to see that the equilibrium tariff rate with voting costs, t^*, is less than the optimal tariff rate of the marginal gainer from a tariff increase, $\tilde{t}(\tilde{e})$, and larger than the optimal tariff rate of the marginal gainer from a tariff decrease, $\tilde{t}(\tilde{\tilde{e}})$.[16] Hence, the equilibrium tariff will be the optimal tariff of a nonvoting factor owner.

Depending on the specifically made assumptions on factor-ownership distributions and voting probabilities, different hypotheses on tariff determination can be developed. Here, it only should be noted that free trade would be adopted if factor-ownership distribution, voting costs, and voting probabilities were symmetric.[17]

Earlier I mentioned the role of voter eligibility restrictions as a possible determinant of actual tariff rates. Even today, every country excludes some factor owners from voting. Major restrictions result from age, residency, and citizenship criteria. Young factor owners, as well as migrant and alien workers, are generally not eligible to vote. In the past, women and poor people, including small property owners and small taxpayers, were excluded as well. Such eligibility restrictions are really a special form of prohibitive voter participation costs. Their major effect is that the factor-ownership distribution of voters is no longer identical to that of the population. In most instances these restrictions tend to cut off, or at least flatten, the left tail of the factor-owner distribution. With the exclusion of many "capital poor" people, eligible voters are more likely to protect the interests of capital owners; if the factor-ownership distribution of all people is symmetric, a tariff on the capital-intensive import good will be voted in as the factor-ownership ratio of the median voter exceeds the endowment ratio; and even if there is positive skewness, as suggested before, it still is possible that the median voter's optimal tariff is positive.

Changing voting rules affects the identity of the median voter and thereby tariff policy. If it is accepted that past voting restrictions were directed against workers and small capital owners, one should observe that the gradual dismantling of voting restrictions has been associated with or followed by declining tariffs on capital-intensive imports and rising tariffs on labor-intensive imports. Empirical support for this hypothesis, as presented by Bennett Baak and Edward Ray (1982) for the United States, is not fully conclusive.

3. Protection of Industry-Specific Interests[18]

The discussion of tariff formation in a Heckscher-Ohlin type economy emphasized the role of factor-ownership distributions, voting costs, and voter eligibility in determining tariffs. Where a given factor is employed (i.e., its association with a given industry) was irrelevant. This framework seems most suitable in explaining long-run tariff trends, especially in relationship to changes in voter eligibility rules, voting costs, or overall factor-ownership distributions. It is much less suitable, however, in explaining more short-term attempts by individual industries to gain tariff protection. In particular, it sheds no light on the frequently observed phenomenon that a single industry succeeds in raising tariffs on its product, even though the vast majority of eligible voters does not benefit from such a policy. In the following, I introduce a many-industries model with specific factors to show how majority voting can result in tariff protection of a small industry. First, I lay out the model and discuss the impact of a tariff increase on a person's income share. Later, I demonstrate how a small minority of gaining factor owners can become a majority of actual voters for a tariff increase on a given commodity.

The Model
The production structure of this section is described by Jones' (1975) multicommodity model with specific factors. There are $n > 2$ industries, each of which employs a fixed amount of a factor specific to that industry,

$V_j, j = 1, \ldots, n$, and a variable amount of a mobile factor, V_N. The mobile factor is employed in all industries. Since we are again concerned with the implications of tariffs for income shares of different individuals, the main interest lies in the relationships between commodity and factor prices in such a model. When needed, I will take these relationships from the Jones paper, using the same notation where appropriate.

With many commodities, the ith individual's indirect utility function is stated as

$$U^i = U^i(p_1, 1, p_3, \ldots, p_N; \phi^i Y), \tag{20}$$

where p_j is the domestic price of commodity j in terms of the second commodity. The ith person's income share in the presence of n specific factors is

$$\phi^i = \frac{R_N V_N^i + \sum_{j=1}^{n} R_j V_j^i}{R_N V_N + \sum_{j=1}^{n} R_j V_j}, \tag{21}$$

where $R_j, j = 1, \ldots, n$, and R_N denote returns on the jth specific and the mobile factor, respectively, V_j^i and V_N^i are the ith person's ownership of the jth specific and mobile factor, and V_j and V_N are the corresponding factor endowments of the country. Let us consider the mobile factor to be labor and assume, as before, that each individual owns one unit; that is, $V_N^i = 1$.

Total income, Y, consists again of domestic factor income and tariff revenues. It is assumed that the first m commodities are imported and the other $(n - m)$ commodities are exported in the relevant range of tariff rates. Denoting imports (exports) of the jth commodity by M_j (E_j) and the corresponding import (export) tariff by t_j (τ_j), the economy's income is

$$Y = \sum_{j=1}^{n} p_j X_j + \sum_{j=1}^{m} t_j \pi_j M_j + \sum_{j=m+1}^{n} \tau_j p_j E_j. \tag{22}$$

As was the case in the two-by-two Heckscher-Ohlin model, it is again asked how the ith individual's welfare is affected by a given tariff change, say on the gth commodity. Differentiation of (20) with respect to t_g and some manipulations yield:

$$\frac{\partial U^i}{\partial t_g} = \left(\frac{\partial U^i}{\partial y^i}\right) \left\{ Y\left(\frac{\partial \phi^i}{\partial t_g}\right) + \phi^i \left[\sum_{j=1}^{m} t_j \pi_j \left(\frac{\partial M_j}{\partial t_g}\right) + \sum_{m+1}^{n} \tau_j p_j \left(\frac{\partial E_j}{\partial t_g}\right) \right] \right\}, \tag{23}$$

indicating that personal welfare effects depend on how a given tariff change affects a person's income share, on the one hand, and the tariff-weighted value of imports plus exports, on the other hand. Note that the direction of the change in the tariff-weighted value of imports and exports is generally not known without further restrictions; but it will be zero under the restriction that initially there is free trade. Corresponding to the analysis in section 2, it would be possible to utilize (23) for all $g = 1, \ldots, n$ and derive an optimal tariff vector for individual i. As shown by Murray Kemp (1969, p. 298) for multicommodity optimal tariff structures of a country, such an optimal tariff vector is one-dimensionally indeterminate. And, without imposing severe restrictions, relatively little can be said about the precise structure of the tariff vector. Fortunately, for the issue under consideration, namely how a single industry can succeed in gaining tariff protection, knowledge of the optimal tariff vector is not crucial.

Tariff-Induced Changes in Income Shares
An individual associates with the interests of a given industry if his or her specific factor ownership is concentrated in that industry. In order to emphasize this association between an individual's and a given industry's interests in describing voting behavior, assume now that each person possesses at most one *type* of specific factor in addition to one unit of the mobile factor. The income share of individual i with specific factor ownership in industry h, $h = 1, \ldots, n$, therefore, is defined as

$$\phi_h^i = \frac{R_N + R_h V_h^i}{R_N V_N + \sum_{j=1}^n R_j V_j}. \tag{21'}$$

Differentiation of (21') with respect to t_g indicates how a tariff increase on commodity g affects the ith individual's income share:

$$\frac{(1 + t_g)\partial \phi_h^i}{\partial t_g} = \left(\frac{R_h V_h^i}{R_N V_N + \sum_{j=1}^n R_j V_j} \right) \left(\frac{\hat{R}_h - \hat{R}_N}{\hat{p}_g} \right)$$
$$- \phi_h^i \left[\sum_{j=1}^n \alpha^j \left(\frac{\hat{R}_j - \hat{R}_N}{\hat{p}_g} \right) \right], \tag{24}$$

where $\alpha^j = R_j V_j / (R_N V_N + \sum_{j=1}^n R_j V_j)$ is the jth specific factor's distributive share in national factor income,

$$\sum_{j=1}^n \alpha^j = 1 - \alpha^N,$$

and

$$\alpha^N = \frac{R_N V_N}{(R_N V_N + \sum_{j=1}^n R_j V_j)}.$$

The term in brackets on the right-hand side of (24) can be interpreted as the "gth commodity's bias with respect to the mobile factor." Ruffin and Jones (calling the mobile factor labor and denoting its return by w_L instead of our R_N) define "commodity j to be unbiased with respect to labor if the relative change in the wage rate (w_L) brought about by an increase in p_j is precisely the average for the changes in all factor prices" (p. 339). And the average of all factor price changes is obtained by weighting each factor's relative price change by the factor's share in national income. Hence, one can define commodity g to be biased against, unbiased, or biased toward the mobile factor as

$$b_g = \sum_{j=1}^{n} \alpha^j \left(\frac{\hat{R}_j - \hat{R}_N}{\hat{p}_g} \right)$$

$$= \frac{\sum_{j=1}^{n} \alpha^j \hat{R}_j + \alpha_N \hat{R}_N - \hat{R}_N}{\hat{p}_g} \gtreqless 0. \tag{25}$$

The sign of the first term on the right-hand side of (24) crucially depends on the ith individual's association with a given industry. If an individual's specific factor ownership is in the industry whose tariff rate is raised (i.e., $g = h$), one can show that

$$\frac{\hat{R}_g - \hat{R}_N}{\hat{p}_g} = \sum_{\substack{h=1 \\ h \neq g}}^{n} \frac{\beta_h}{\theta_{gg}} > 0, \tag{26}$$

where I utilized equations (13) and (14) of the Jones (1975) paper, $\beta_g > 0$ indicates the relative change in the mobile factor's return as the gth commodity's price rises by 1 percent and $\theta_{gg} = (R_g V_g)/(p_g X_g)$ denotes the cost share of the specific factor in the production of commodity g. Substitution of (26) in (24) reveals that an individual's income share will definitely rise if commodity g is biased towards labor or not biased at all. If, on the other hand, an individual's specific ownership is in an industry whose tariff rate is not changed (i.e., $g \neq h$), then one can show that

$$\frac{\hat{R}_h - \hat{R}_N}{\hat{p}_g} = -\frac{\beta_g}{\theta_{hh}} < 0. \tag{27}$$

Consequently, the individual's income share will definitely decline, if commodity g is biased against labor or not biased at all. Finally, it should be noted that the first term on the right-hand side of (24) is zero for people with only labor but no specific factor ownership. Their income shares rise, remain unchanged, or fall, as commodity g is biased towards, unbiased, or biased against labor.

In the special case where the above-stated bias is zero (i.e., $b_g = 0$ in equation 25), Ruffin and Jones (pp. 339–340) prove that β_g also represents the fraction of total factor income generated in industry g; that is, if $b_g = 0$, then

$$\beta_g = \frac{p_g X_g}{R_N V_N + \sum_{j=1}^{n} R_j V_j}.$$ (28)

Furthermore, it should be noted that under all circumstances—whether commodity g is labor biased or not, it must hold that $\sum_{h=1}^{n} \beta_h = 1$.

In the next subsection, the assumption that the commodity on which the tariff is imposed is unbiased towards labor is used. Under this assumption, only the income shares of specific factor owners in the "protected" industry will rise. Specific factor owners in all other industries will suffer a decline in their income shares, and income shares of people who are workers only will not be affected.

Industry Protection under Majority Voting

Factor owners are assumed to vote their economic interests. Equation (23) above revealed that a given tariff increase affects a person's welfare through two forces: changes in the person's income share and changes in the tariff-weighted value of exports and imports. One could easily construct a scenario such that the latter change is positive and one could conclude that it is, at least, conceivable that a majority of voters gain from a given tariff increase, even though owners of the specific factor in the protected industry are a minority. While this possibility has to be recognized, the intent here is not to adopt a set of unusual assumptions for demonstrating that a small industry can gain tariff protection under majority voting. Instead, the objective is to postulate a rather neutral set of plausible assumptions to substantiate my contention. These assumptions are:

1. Initially, free trade is prevailing and only one industry, namely industry g, tries to gain tariff protection.[19]
2. Commodity g is unbiased with respect to the mobile factor (i.e., $b_g = 0$).
3. There are voter participation costs and these costs are the same for every voter, whether voting for a tariff or a subsidy.

In the presence of voting costs, the decision to participate in voting is based on an individual's assessment of tariff-induced real income changes relative to voting costs. The real income change from leaving free trade and imposing a tariff on commodity g, as experienced by the ith individual with specific factor ownership in industry h, is given by

$$B_{hg}^i = Y \left(\frac{\partial \phi_h^i}{\partial t_g} \right)$$

$$= Y \left(\frac{R_h V_h^i}{R_N V_N + \sum_{j=1}^{n} R_j V_j} \right) \times \left(\frac{\hat{R}_h - \hat{R}_N}{\hat{p}_g} \right),$$ (29)

where the assumptions above and equations (23) and (24) were employed. If individual i owns a specific factor in the industry where the tariff increase takes place, then

$$B_{gg}^i = Y(1 - \beta_g)\beta_g\lambda_g^i > 0, \tag{30}$$

where $\lambda_g^i = (V_g^i/V_g)$ denotes the ith individual's ownership share of specific factor g, and where we used (26) and (28), the property $\sum_{h=1;h \neq g}^n \beta_h = (1 - \beta_g)$, and the definition of θ_{gg} in reducing (29) to (30). Alternatively, if individual i owns a specific factor employed in any other, not protected industry h, then

$$B_{hg}^i = -Y\beta_h\beta_g\lambda_h^i < 0, \tag{31}$$

using (27). Finally, for all those people who do not own any specific factor, as $V_g^i = V_h^i = 0$, there is no real income change in the small neighborhood of the initial free-trade equilibrium.[20]

An assessment of real income changes of people owning specific factors in either the protected or one of the many other industries reveals that the former will gain while the latter will lose. Accordingly, only a small fraction of all factor owners would favor such a tariff increase and it would not be voted in by a majority if all factor owners participated in voting. In fact, the majority of people would gain from a subsidy on importing commodity g. In the presence of voting costs, however, the *magnitude of gains or losses* relative to voting costs must be considered as well. Equations (30) and (31) state that the magnitude of real income changes depends on the value of national income, Y, and a person's specific factor-ownership share, λ_h^i. But, most important, it depends on the relative sizes of the protected industry and of the industry whose specific factor is owned, as β_g and β_h measure the respective industries' shares in national income. The industry-size element in affecting real income is most significant since it introduces an asymmetry between the magnitude of gains and losses for people with identical specific factor-ownership shares held in the protected and non-protected sectors, respectively. More precisely, for all $\lambda_g^i = \lambda_h^i$, where $h = 1, \ldots, n$ and $h \neq g$,

$$B_{gg}^i > -B_{hg}^i, \tag{32}$$

as $(1 - \beta_g) > \beta_h$ always, if there are more than two industries. As shown next, this asymmetry between the size of gains and losses implies that, with voting costs, a minority of factor owners may become a majority of participating voters.[21]

Per capita voting costs c were assumed to be the same for both supporters and opponents of the tariff increase. A factor owner definitely will refrain from voting if real income gains from a tariff or subsidy increase do not exceed voting costs. Hence, a person will not participate in voting for a tariff increase if

$$B^i_{gg} = Y\beta_g(1 - \beta_g)\lambda^i_g \leqq c. \tag{33a}$$

And a person will not participate in voting for a tariff decrease or subsidy if

$$D^i_{hg} = -B^i_{hg} = Y\beta_g\beta_h\lambda^i_h \leqq c, \tag{33b}$$

where D^i_{hg} is the subsidy-induced real income gain to person i owning some of specific factor h. People with factor ownership shares $\lambda^i_g \leq \tilde{\lambda}^i_g$ and $\lambda^i_h \leq \tilde{\tilde{\lambda}}^i_h$ definitely will not participate in voting, where

$$\tilde{\lambda}^i_g = \frac{c}{Y\beta_g(1 - \beta_g)} \tag{34}$$

and

$$\tilde{\tilde{\lambda}}^i_h = \frac{c}{Y\beta_g\beta_h}, \quad h \neq g; h = 1, \ldots, n,$$

can be called the specific factor-ownership share of the marginal voter for a tariff and subsidy, respectively. Comparing these ownership shares of marginal nonparticipants in voting, one can see that

$$\tilde{\tilde{\lambda}}^i_h > \tilde{\lambda}^i_g \tag{35}$$

as $[(1 - \beta_g)/\beta_h] > 1$ always. The separation between definite nonvoters and potential voters occurs at a much higher endowment share in the many nonprotected industries than in the single protected industry. Hence, it is quite possible that only a few large specific factor owners in each losing industry remain potential resisters to the tariff increase, while a large number of factor owners in the gaining industry tend to support it. In fact, it is quite possible that losers will pose no active resistance at all to the proposed departure from free trade.

A simple example will illustrate the magnitudes by which the marginal nonparticipants' factor-ownership ratios may differ between gainers and losers. First, assume there are 10 industries: for each industry $\beta_h = .1$, and voting costs and income are such that $\tilde{\lambda}^i_g = 1/10,000$. Then $(1 - \beta_g)/\beta_h = 9$ and $\tilde{\tilde{\lambda}}^i_h = 9/10,000$. Second, assume there are 100 industries $\beta_h = .01$ for each industry, and again $\tilde{\lambda}^i_g = 1/10,000$. In this case, $\tilde{\tilde{\lambda}}^i_h = 99/10,000$. The examples illustrate that the marginal nonparticipant's factor-ownership share is far greater among losers than gainers, and that it tends to rise the more diversified the economy is (i.e., the more sectors it has).

So far, I have only tried to describe the separation line between definite nonvoters and potential voters among factor owners in both protected and nonprotected industries. The number of potential voters in the two opposing camps crucially depends on the height of voting costs, the distribution of specific factor ownerships in the various sectors, and the degree of diversification of the economy. As mentioned above, it is quite possible that a minority of factor owners gaining from a tariff increase becomes a majority of potential voters. However, even if losing factor owners maintain a majority of potential voters, it still is quite possible that the gaining industry's factor owners will succeed in obtaining tariff protection. What matters for tariff policy formation are actual votes rather than potential votes, and the minority of potential votes among gainers could easily become a majority of actual votes as will be shown next.

The probabilities of potential voters' participation in voting depend, as mentioned in section 2, on the magnitude of net gains from a certain outcome. Denoting the probability of a specific factor owner in industry g to vote for the tariff increase by ρ_g and the probability of a specific factor owner in industry h to vote for a subsidy or tariff decrease by σ_h, we have

$$\rho_g = \rho[B_{gg} - c] \quad \text{and} \quad \sigma_h = \sigma[D_{hg} - c], \tag{36}$$

where $\rho_g = 0$ for $(B_{gg} - c) \leq 0$, $\sigma_h = 0$ for $(D_{hg} - c) \leq 0$ and $\rho'_g > 0$, $\sigma'_h > 0$ in the range of positive net gains. Unrestricted comparisons of ρ_g with σ_h are, of course, not possible. If, however, it is assumed that the voting probabilities for given values of net gains are the same, then we can compare the voting probabilities of factor owners in different industries with the same specific factor ownership shares. Assuming that $\lambda_g = \lambda_h$, one can see that

$$\rho_g = \rho[B_{gg} - c] > \sigma_h$$

$$= \sigma[(B_{gg} - c) - (B_{gg} - D_{hg})], \tag{37}$$

since $B_{gg} > D_{hg}$, using (32) and (33b). Potential voters with identical factor ownership shares are more likely to vote if they are gainers than if they are losers from a tariff increase. Hence, it is quite possible that a majority of potential voters against a tariff increase becomes a minority of actual voters once voting probabilities are accounted for.

I have demonstrated that the existence of voting costs can be most instrumental in helping a small industry gain tariff protection. The push for protection is, however, not unlimited since resistance to tariff increases will rise and the forces for tariff increases will weaken as the tariff rate, t_g, further departs from zero. This can be seen from (23) which for $t_g > 0$ and all other $t_j = \tau_j = 0$, becomes

$$\frac{\partial U^i}{\partial t_g} = \left(\frac{\partial U^i}{\partial y^i}\right)\left[Y\left(\frac{\partial \phi^i}{\partial t_g}\right) + \phi^i t_g \pi_g \left(\frac{\partial M_g}{\partial t_g}\right)\right]. \tag{23'}$$

Since $(\partial M_g/\partial t_g) < 0$, each person's real income change is affected by a negative force in addition to the income share change. The higher t_g, the less the gainers will gain and the more the losers will lose. Hence, the drive for a further increase in t_g will eventually stall as no majority can be formed to keep raising the tariff rate.

My findings support Baldwin's conjecture that a small group of big gainers may succeed in obtaining tariff protection. Crucial for this occurrence is that each person's specific factor ownership is relatively concentrated in one industry and that there are voting costs. In this case, a large number of losers from a tariff increase becomes a much smaller number of potential voters which, in turn, becomes an even smaller number of actual voters. Among gaining factor owners, there also will not be full voter participation, but the shrinkage tends to be much less. In the end, the gainers may be successful in gaining tariff protection through a majority vote.

5. Concluding Remarks

This paper argues that a country's actual tariff policy is the result of its underlying factor-ownership distribution. There are two links in the chain of causality between factor-ownership distribution and tariff policy. The first link describes how the economic interests of people in a given tariff policy are related to the factor-ownership distribution. One may call it the "economic link" since the economy's production structure is the main determinant of the process through which a person's real income is affected. I deal with two alternative production structures. The two-by-two Heckscher-Ohlin model, that is highly aggregated and frequently associated with long-run portrayals of production structures, seems most useful in explaining long-run changes in the overall tariff structure. The many-commodity model, with specific factors, on the other hand, seems more appropriate in explaining day-to-day attempts by individual industries or interest groups in gaining tariff protection. Irrespective of the production structure, each person is shown to have an optimal tariff policy that generally differs from the actual policy. The second link between factor-ownership distribution and tariff policy may be called the "political link" as it refers to the political process through which economic interests are translated into actual tariff policy. My analysis emphasizes the sensitivity of tariff policies to changing voter eligibility rules and voter participation costs under majority voting. In particular, it is demonstrated how a small minority of factor owners can succeed in gaining tariff protection for its industry under majority voting provided voting costs are significant.

This paper's assumptions concerning both the economic structure and political process were deliberately chosen to allow tracing of the path from factor-ownership distributions to tariff policies. Although the assumptions are quite standard in the trade-theoretic and public choice literature, it would be most desirable to relax some of the restrictions. Concerning the economic link, future research should explore more general descriptions of factor-ownership distributions, imperfect information of factor owners on real income effects of tariff changes, and nonhomothetic tastes. Concerning the political link, one should try to account for multiple-issue voting and logrolling, policy formation in a representative democracy, and the working of a multiparty system.

Notes

1. In addition to the literature on endogenous tariff formation, there are a number of authors (e.g., Bhagwati 1982; Hillman 1982; and Dinopoulos 1983) who discuss endogenous tariff adjustments in response to exogenous changes in the international terms of trade. How the initial tariff rate was selected is, however, not part of their decision problem. Also there is a growing empirical literature on changing tariff structures of various countries, such as the works by Pincus (1975), Caves (1976), Helleiner (1977), as well as Marvel and Ray (1983).

2. The relationship between public policymaking and economic interests is widely discussed in the public choice literature, such as in Downs (1957), Buchanan and Tullock (1962), and Mueller (1979).

3. A quite different approach at explaining tariff structures has been used by Ray (1974).

4. For extensions of these models, see Young and Magee (1983), Wellisz and Findlay (1983), and Wellisz and Wilson (1983).

5. For a thorough discussion of majority voting rules, see Black (1948a, b) and Mueller.

6. In the tariff formation literature, voting costs have been emphasized by Baldwin. More generally, they play an important role in discussions of the voter's calculus; for example, Downs, Riker, and Ordeshook (1968), or Mueller (pp. 121–124). Sam Peltzman (1976) incorporates voting costs into his general theory of regulation.

7. Furthermore, the ith individual's direct utility function is assumed to be homogeneous of degree one in the two commodities.

8. For a precise expression, see Jones (1969).

9. Implicitly it is assumed that the import tariff is the only instrument to alter a person's welfare. Hence, the question of what the first-best instrument would be to redistribute income is not addressed in this paper.

10. If each person owned only labor or only capital, as usually assumed, there would be just one optimal trade policy for the "worker" and another one for the "capitalist," irrespective of individual persons' factor-ownership shares.

11. Hence, if the capital-labor ownership distribution is symmetric and there are no voting restrictions, majority voting results in a Pareto-efficient allocation of resources.

12. Under the assumptions of this model—one issue, all individuals vote, symmetric, unimodal factor distribution—free trade would also be chosen in a two-party representative democracy.

13. The terms "voting" and "voter participation costs" have a broader meaning than marking a ballot and incurring costs in going to the voting booth. Voting can be interpreted as any form of communicating a person's response to a given policy proposal whether through the ballot, letters to political representatives, participation in political meetings, or public demonstrations. Since a politician in a two-party representative democracy will also choose the median-voter's optimal tariff, informing politicians of one's attidues is a form of voting. Voting costs include all expenses incurred in transmitting this information. In parts of the public choice literature, voting costs also include information-gathering costs. Strictly speaking, this is legitimate only if B^i is independent of such information-gathering costs.

14. Peltzman's formulation of voting probabilities as related to net income changes is a convenient way of accounting for the free-rider problem associated with voting on tariff policies. On the problem of free riding and political participation, see Olson (1965).

15. Adjustment to such an equilibrium implies the possibility of repeated voting on the same tariff issue. While repeated voting in the sense of going again and again to the voting booth is quite unrealistic, repeated voting through other forms of communications from the public to the politician is far more realistic.

16. At the equilibrium tariff, t^*, there exists a marginal voter among net gainers from a tariff increase for whom $B[k(\tilde{e}), t^*] = c(\tilde{e})$. Without voting costs, the marginal gainer's optimal tariff $\tilde{t}(\tilde{e})$ is such that $B[k(\tilde{e}), t] = 0$. Since $(\partial B/\partial t) < 0$ and $c(\tilde{e}) > 0$, it must be that $t^* < \tilde{t}(\tilde{e})$. Similarly, one can show that $t^* > \tilde{t}(\tilde{\tilde{e}})$.

17. Symmetric voting probabilities mean that, for all $(B - c) > 0$, $\rho = \sigma$ if $(B - c) = (D - c)$.

18. The association of tariffs with the economic interest of sector-specific groups is one of three models tested by Caves.

19. If several industries try to obtain tariff protection more or less at the same time, the possibility of logrolling must be allowed for. In this case, a unique equilibrium generally will not exist.

20. This is the same conclusion as the one obtained by Ruffin and Jones for the case when tariff proceeds are redistributed (see their p. 344).

21. One can show that, in the small neighborhood of the initial free-trade point, the sum of total real income gains is exactly equal to the sum of real income losses when all factor owners are accounted for.

References

Baak, Bennett D., and Ray, Edward John. The political economy of tariff policy: A case study of the United States. Ohio State University, February 1982. Mimeo.

Baldwin, Robert E. The political economy of postwar U.S. trade policy. *The Bulletin.* Graduate School of Business Administration, New York University, 1976.

Baldwin, Robert, E. The political economy of protection. In J. N. Bhagwati, ed., *Import Competition and Response.* Chicago: University of Chicago Press, 1982, pp. 263–286.

Bhagwati, Jagdish N. Shifting comparative advantage, protectionist demands, and policy response. In J. N. Bhagwati, ed., *Import Competition and Response.* Chicago: University of Chicago Press, 1982, pp. 153–184.

Black, Duncan. 1948a. On the rationale of group decision making. *Journal of Political Economy* 56 (February 1948): 23–34.

Black, Duncan. 1948b. The decision of a committee using a special majority. *Econometrica* 16 (July 1948): 245–261.

Brock, William A., and Magee, Stephen P. The economics of special interest politics: The case of the tariff. *American Economic Review Proceedings* 68 (May 1978): 246–250.

Brock, William A., and Magee, Stephen P. Tariff formation in a democracy. In J. Black and B. Hindley, eds., *Current Issues in International Commercial Policy and Diplomacy.* London: Macmillan, 1980, pp. 1–9.

Buchanan, James M., and Tullock, Gordon. *The Calculus of Consent.* Ann Arbor: University of Michigan Press, 1962.

Caves, Richard E. Economic models of political choice: Canada's tariff structure. *Canadian Journal of Economics* 9 (May 1976): 278–300.

Dinopoulos, Elias. Import Competition, international factor mobility and lobbying response: The Schumpeterian industry case. *Journal of International Economics* 14 (May 1983): 395–410.

Downs, Anthony. *An Economic Theory of Democracy.* New York: Harper and Row, 1957.

Findlay, Ronald, and Wellisz, Stanislaw, Endogenous tariffs, the political economy of trade restrictions, and welfare. In J. N. Bhagwati, ed., *Import Competition and Response.* Chicago: University of Chicago Press, 1982, pp. 223–234.

Helleiner, G. K. The political economy of Canada's tariff structure: An alternative model. *Canadian Journal of Economics* 10 (May 1977): 318–326.

Hillman, Arye L. Declining industries and political-support protectionist motives. *American Economic Review* 72 (December 1982): 1180–1187.

Jones, Ronald W. Tariffs and trade in general equilibrium: Comment. *American Economic Review* 59 (June 1969): 418–424.

Jones, Ronald W. Income distribution and effective protection in a multicommodity trade model. *Journal of Economic Theory* 11 (August 1975): 1–15.

Kemp, Murray C. *The Pure Theory of International Trade and Investment*. Englewood Cliffs: Prentice-Hall, 1969.

Marvel, Howard P., and Ray, Edward J., The Kennedy round: Evidence on the regulation of international trade in the United States. *American Economic Review* 13 (March 1983): 190–97.

Mueller, Dennis C. *Public Choice*. Cambridge: Cambridge University Press, 1979.

Olson, Mancur. *The Logic of Collective Action*. Cambridge: Harvard University Press, 1965.

Peltzman, Sam. Toward a more general theory of regulations. *Journal of Law and Economics* 19 (August 1976): 211–240.

Pincus, Jonathan J. Pressure groups and the pattern of tariffs. *Journal of Political Economy* 83 (August 1975): 757–778.

Ray, Edward J. The optimum commodity tariff rates in developed and less developed countries. *Review of Economics and Statistics* 56 (August 1974): 369–377.

Riker, William H., and Ordeshook, Peter C. A theory of the calculus of voting. *American Political Science Review* 62 (March 1968): 25–42.

Ruffin, Roy, and Jones, Ronald W. Protection and real wages: The neoclassical ambiguity. *Journal of Economic Theory* 14 (April 1977): 337–348.

Wellisz, Stanislaw, and Findlay, Ronald. Some thoughts on protection and rent-seeking in developing countries. International Economics Research Center Paper No. 30, Columbia University, June 1983.

Wellisz, Stanislaw, and Wilson, John D. A theory of tariff formation. Columbia University, August 1983. Mimeo.

Young, Leslie, and Magee, Stephen P. Factor returns and resource allocation in the political economy of trade distortions. Presented at the North American Summer Meeting of the Econometric Society, Northwestern University, June 1983.

VII
Customs Unions

Introduction to Part VII

Part VII singles out two important papers that represent divergent analytical approaches to the theory of preferential tariff reduction.* Chapter 20, a paper by Lipsey, represents a review of the major analytical contributions, beginning with Viner's classic work and then encompassing the important contributions of Lipsey, Lancaster, Meade, and others, where the analysis is predicated on a country reducing its tariff down to zero for another member country but retaining it at the initial level for the "outside" non-member country. Following Viner, the analysis then distinguishes between unions that will then lead to reduced, and those that will lead to increased, welfare for country and establishes conditions for these differential outcomes.

Kemp and Wan, on the other hand, in their paper presented in chapter 21, take an altogether different approach. They argue that it is always possible for any subset of countries in the world economy to abolish tariffs on one another, choose an external tariff that maintains trade with the outside world (and hence the outside world's welfare as well) unchanged, and improve the welfare of some member(s) of the union without hurting any other member's welfare by using lump-sum transfers. In short, their approach, by making the common external tariff a policy variable, enables them to resurrect the pre-Vinerian intuition that a *partial* move to free trade by any subset of countries could be made welfare improving for them and for the world as a whole.

* Yet another approach to customs union theory, not represented here, is represented by the Brecher-Bhagwati (*Journal of Political Economy*, June 1981), analysis of multi-agent models in trade theory. That analysis is explicitly noted by these authors as applicable to analyzing the welfare impact, on specific member countries of a customs union with free trade *and* factor mobility, as in the EEC, when policy and parametric changes in the union as a whole or in other member countries occur.

20

The Theory of
Customs Unions:
A General Survey

Richard Lipsey

This paper is devoted mainly to a survey of the development of customs-union theory from Viner to date; since, however, the theory must be meant at least as an aid in interpreting real-world data, some space is devoted to a summary of empirical evidence relating to the gains from European Economic Union. It is necessary first to define customs-union theory. In general, the tariff system of any country may discriminate between commodities and/or between countries. Commodity discrimination occurs when different rates of duty are levied on different commodities, while country discrimination occurs when the same commodity is subject to different rates of duty, the rate varying according to the country of origin. The theory of customs unions may be defined as that branch of tariff theory which deals with the effects of geographically discriminatory changes in trade barriers.

Next we must turn our attention to the scope of the existing theory. The theory has been confined mainly to a study of the effects of customs unions on welfare rather than, for example, on the level of economic activity, the balance of payments or the rate of inflation. These welfare gains and losses, which are the subject of the theory, may arise from a number of different sources: (1) the specialization of production according to comparative advantage which is the basis of the classical case for the gains from trade; (2) economies of scale; (3) changes in the terms of trade; (4) forced changes in efficiency due to increased foreign competition; and (5) a change in the rate of economic growth.[1] The theory of customs unions has been almost completely confined to an investigation of (1) above, with some slight attention to (2) and (3), (5) not being dealt with at all, while (4) is ruled out of traditional theory by the assumption (often contradicted by the facts) that production is carried out by processes which are technically efficient.

This paper was originally published in *The Economic Journal* 70 (1960): 496–513.

Table 20.1
Money prices (at existing exchange rates) of a single commodity (X) in three countries

Country	A	B	C
Price	35s.	26s.	20s.

Throughout the development of the theory of customs unions we will find an oscillation between the belief that it is possible to produce a general conclusion of the sort: "Customs unions will always, or nearly always, raise welfare," and the belief that, depending on the particular circumstances present, a customs union may have any imaginable effect on welfare. The earliest customs-union theory was largely embodied in the oral tradition, for it hardly seemed worthwhile to state it explicitly, and was an example of an attempt to produce the former sort of conclusion. It may be summarized quite briefly. Free trade maximizes world welfare; a customs union reduces tariffs and is therefore a movement towards free trade; a customs union will, therefore, *increase* world welfare even if it does not lead to a world-welfare *maximum*.

Viner showed this argument to be incorrect. He introduced the now familiar concepts of trade creation and trade diversion (Viner 1950, chap. 4) which are probably best recalled in terms of an example. Consider the figures in table 20.1. A tariff of 100 percent levied by country A will be sufficient to protect A's domestic industry producing commodity X.[2] If A forms a customs union with either country B or country C, she will be better off; if the union is with B, she will get a unit of commodity X at an opportunity cost of 26 shillings-worth of exports instead of at the cost of 35 shillings-worth of other goods entailed by domestic production.[3] This is an example of trade creation. If A had been levying a somewhat lower tariff, a 50 percent tariff, for example, she would already have been buying X from abroad before the formation of any customs union. If A is buying a commodity from abroad, and if her tariff is nondiscriminatory, then she will be buying it from the lowest-cost source—in this case country C. Now consider a customs union with country B. B's X, now exempt from the tariff, sells for 26s., while C's X, which must still pay the 50 percent tariff, must be sold for 30s. A will now buy X from B at a price, in terms of the value of exports, of 26s., whereas she was formerly buying it from C at a price of only 20s. This is a case of Viner's trade diversion, and since it entails a movement from lower to higher real cost sources of supply, it represents a movement from a more to a less efficient allocation of resources.

This analysis is an example of what Mr. Lancaster and I have called *the general theory of second best* (Lipsey and Lancaster 1956–57): "if it is impossible to satisfy *all* the optimum conditions (in this case to make all relative prices equal to all rates of transformation in production), then a change which brings about the satisfaction of *some* of the optimum conditions (in this case making some relative prices equal to some rates of transformation in production) may make things better or worse."[4]

Viner's analysis leads to the following classification of the possibilities that arise from a customs union between two countries, A and B:

1. Neither A nor B may be producing a given commodity. In this case they will both be importing this commodity from some third country, and the removal of tariffs on trade between A and B can cause no change in the pattern of trade in this commodity; both countries will continue to import it from the cheapest possible source outside of the union.

2. One of the two countries may be producing the commodity inefficiently under tariff protection while the second country is a nonproducer. If country A is producing commodity X under tariff protection this means that her tariff is sufficient to eliminate competition from the cheapest possible source. Thus, if A's tariff on X is adopted by the union, the tariff will be high enough to secure B's market for A's inefficient industry.

3. Both countries may be producing the commodity inefficiently under tariff protection. In this case the customs union removes tariffs between country A and B and ensures that the least inefficient of the two will capture the union market.[5]

In case 2 above any change must be a trade-diverting one, while in case 3 any change must be a trade-creating one. If one wishes to predict the welfare effects of a customs union, it is necessary to predict the relative strengths of the forces causing trade creation and trade diversion.

This analysis leads to the conclusion that customs unions are likely to cause losses when the countries involved are complementary *in the range of commodities that are protected by tariffs*. Consider the class of commodities produced under tariff protection in each of the two countries. If these classes overlap to a large extent, then the most efficient of the two countries will capture the union market and there will be a reallocation of resources in a more efficient direction. If these two classes do not overlap to any great extent, then the protected industry in one country is likely to capture the whole of the union market when the union is formed, and there is likely to be a reallocation of resources in a less efficient direction. This point of Viner's has often been misunderstood and read to say that, in some general sense, the economies of the two countries should be competitive and not complementary. A precise way of making the point is to say that the customs union is more likely to bring gain, the greater is the degree of overlapping between the class of commodities produced under tariff protection in the two countries.

A subsequent analysis of the conditions affecting the gains from union through trade creation and trade diversion was made by Drs. Makower and Morton (1953). They pointed out that, *given that trade creation was going to occur*, the gains would be larger the more dissimilar were the cost ratios in the two countries. (Clearly, if two countries have almost identical cost ratios, the gains from trade will be small.) They then defined competitive economies to be ones with similar cost ratios and complementary economies to be ones with dissimilar ratios, and were able to conclude that unions between complementary economies would, if they brought gain at all, bring large gains. The conclusions of Viner and Makower and Morton are in no sense contradictory. Stated in the simplest possible language, Viner showed that gains will arise from unions if both countries are producing the same commodity; Makower and Morton showed that these gains will be larger, the larger is the difference between the costs at which the same commodity is produced in the two countries.[6]

We now come to the second major development in customs-union theory—the analysis of the welfare effects of *the substitution between commodities* resulting from the changes in relative prices which necessarily accompany a custom union. Viner's analysis implicitly assumed that commodities are consumed in some fixed proportion which is independent of the structure of relative prices. Having ruled out substitution between commodities, he was left to analyse only bodily shifts of trade from one country to another. The way in which Viner's conclusion that trade diversion necessarily lowers welfare depends on his implicit demand assumption is illustrated in figure 20.1. Consider the case of a small country, A, specialized in the production of a single commodity, Y, and importing one commodity, X, at terms of trade independent of any taxes or tariffs levied in A. The fixed proportion in which commodities are consumed is shown by the slope of the line OZ, which is the income- and price-consumption line for all (finite) prices and incomes, OA indicates country A's total production of commodity Y, and the slope of the line AC shows the terms of trade offered by country C, the lowest cost producer of X. Under conditions of free trade, country A's equilibrium will be at e, the point of intersection between OZ and AC. A will consume Og of Y, exporting Ag in return for ge of X. Now a tariff which does not affect A's terms of trade and is not high enough to protect a domestic industry producing Y will leave her equilibrium position unchanged at e.[7] The tariff changes relative prices, but consumers' purchases are completely insensitive to this change, and if

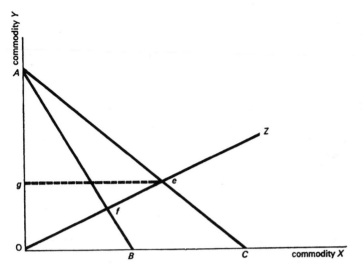

Figure 20.1

foreign trade continues at terms indicated by the slope of the line AC, the community must remain in equilibrium at e. Now consider a case where country A forms a trade-diverting customs union with country B. This means that A must buy her imports of X at a price in terms of Y higher than she was paying before the union was formed. An example of this is shown in figure 20.1 by the line AB. A's equilibrium is now at f, the point of intersection between AB and OZ; less of both commodities are consumed, and A's welfare has unambiguously diminished. We conclude therefore that, under the assumed demand conditions, trade diversion (which necessarily entails a deterioration in A's terms of trade) *necessarily* lowers A's welfare.

   Viner's implicit assumption that commodities are consumed in fixed proportions independent of the structure of relative prices is indeed a very special one. A customs union necessarily changes relative prices, and in general, we should expect this to lead to some substitution between commodities, there being a tendency to change the volume of already existing trade with more of the now cheaper goods being bought and less of the now more expensive. This would tend to increase the volume of imports from a country's union partner and to diminish both the volume of imports obtained from the outside world and the consumption of home-produced commodities. The importance of this subsitution effect in consumption seems to have been discovered independently by at least three people, Professor Meade (1956), Professor Gehrels (1956–57), and myself (1957).

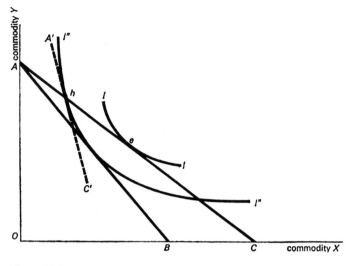

Figure 20.2

In order to show the importance of the effects of substitutions in consumption, we merely drop the assumption that commodities are consumed in fixed proportions. I shall take Mr. Gehrels's presentation of this analysis because it illustrates a number of important factors. In figure 20.2 OA is again country A's total production of Y, and the slope of the line AC indicates the terms of trade between X and Y when A is trading with country C. The free-trade equilibrium position is again at e, where an indifference curve is tangent to AC. In this case, however, the imposition of a tariff on imports of X, even if it does not shift the source of country A's imports, will cause a reduction in the quantity of these imports and an increase in the consumption of the domestic commodity Y. A tariff which changes the relative price in A's domestic market to, say, that indicated by the slope of the line $A'C'$ will move A's equilibrium position to point h. At this point an indifference curve cuts AC with a slope equal to the line $A'C'$; consumers are thus adjusting their purchases to the market rate of transformation and the tariff has had the effect of reducing imports of X and increasing consumption of the home good Y. In these circumstances it is clearly possible for country A to form a trade-diverting customs union and yet gain an increase in its welfare. To show this, construct a line through A tangent to the indifference curve I'' to cut the X axis at some point B. If A forms a trade-diverting customs union with country B and buys her imports of X from B at terms of trade indicated by the slope of the line AB, her welfare will be unchanged. If, therefore, the terms of trade with B are

worse than those given by C, but better than those indicated by the slope
of the line AB, A's welfare will be increased by the trade-diverting customs
union. A's welfare will be diminished by this trade-diverting union with B
only if B's terms of trade are worse than those indicated by the slope of AB.

The commonsense reason for this conclusion may be stated as follows:

The possibility stems from the fact that whenever imports are subject to a
tariff, the position of equilibrium must be one where an indifference curve
[surface or hyper-surface as the case may be] cuts (not is tangent to) the
international price line. From this it follows that there will exist an area
where indifference curves higher than the one achieved at equilibrium lie
below the international price line. In Figure 2 this is the area above I'' but
below AC. As long as the final equilibrium position lies within this area,
trade carried on in the absence of tariffs at terms of trade worse than those
indicated by AC, will increase welfare. In a verbal statement this possibility
may be explained by referring to the two opposing effects of a trade-
diverting customs union. First, A shifts her purchases from a lower to a
higher cost source of supply. It now becomes necessary to export a larger
quantity of goods in order to obtain any given quantity of imports. Secondly,
the divergence between domestic and international price is eliminated when
the union is formed. The removal of the tariff has the effect of allowing ...
consumer[s] in A to adjust ... purchases to a domestic price ratio which
now is equal to the rate at which [Y] can be transformed into ... [X] by
means of international trade. The final welfare effect of the trade-diverting
customs union must be the net effect of these two opposing tendencies; the
first working to lower welfare and the second to raise it.[8]

On this much there is general agreement. Professor Gehrels, however,
concluded that his analysis established a general presumption in favour of
gains from union rather than losses. He argued that "to examine customs
unions in the light only of *production* effects, as Viner does, will give a biased
judgement of their effect on countries joining them" (Gehrels 1956–57,
p. 61), and he went on to say that the analysis given above established a
general presumption in favour of gains from union. Now we seemed to be
back in the pre-Viner world, where economic analysis established a general
case in favour of customs unions. In Lipsey (1956–57) I attempted to point
out the mistake involved. The key is that Gehrels model contains only two
commodities: one domestic good and one import. There is thus only one
optimum condition for consumption: that the relative price between X and
Y equals the real rate of transformation (in domestic production or international trade, whichever is relevant) between these two commodities. The
general problems raised by customs unions must, however, be analysed in
a model containing a minimum of three types of commodities: domestic
commodities (A), imports from the union partner (B), and imports from the
outside world (C). When this change is made Gehrels's general presumption
for gain from union disappears. Table 20.2 shows the three optimum con-

Table 20.2

Free trade (1)	Uniform ad valorem tariff on all imports (2)	Customs union with country B (3)
$\dfrac{P_{Ad}}{P_{Bd}} = \dfrac{P_{Ai}}{P_{Bi}}$	$\dfrac{P_{Ad}}{P_{Bd}} < \dfrac{P_{Ai}}{P_{Bi}}$	$\dfrac{P_{Ad}}{P_{Bd}} = \dfrac{P_{Ai}}{P_{Bi}}$
$\dfrac{P_{Ad}}{P_{Cd}} = \dfrac{P_{Ai}}{P_{Ci}}$	$\dfrac{P_{Ad}}{P_{Cd}} < \dfrac{P_{Ai}}{P_{Ci}}$	$\dfrac{P_{Ad}}{P_{Cd}} < \dfrac{P_{Ai}}{P_{Ci}}$
$\dfrac{P_{Bd}}{P_{Cd}} = \dfrac{P_{Bi}}{P_{Ci}}$	$\dfrac{P_{Bd}}{P_{Cd}} = \dfrac{P_{Bi}}{P_{Ci}}$	$\dfrac{P_{Bd}}{P_{Cd}} < \dfrac{P_{Bi}}{P_{Ci}}$

Note: Subscripts A, B, and C refer to countries of origin, d to prices in A's domestic market, and i to prices in the international market.

ditions that domestic prices and international prices bear the same relationship to each other for the three groups of commodities, A, B, and C.[9] In free trade all three optimum conditions will be fulfilled. If a uniform tariff is placed on both impots, then the relations shown in column 2 will obtain, for the price of goods from both B and C will be higher in A's domestic market than in the international market. When a customs union is formed, however, the prices of imports from the union partner, B, are reduced so that the first optimum condition is fulfilled, but the tariff remains on imports from abroad (C) so that the third optimum condition is no longer satisfied. The customs union thus moves country A from one nonoptimal position to another, and in general, it is impossible to say whether welfare will increase or diminish as a result. We are thus back to a position where the theory tells us that welfare may rise or fall, and a much more detailed study is necessary in order to establish the conditions under which one or the other result might obtain.

The above analysis has led both Mr. Gehrels and myself to distinguish between *production effects* and *consumption effects* of customs unions (Gehrels 1956–57, p. 61; Lipsey 1957, pp. 40–41). The reason for attempting this is not hard to find. Viner's analysis rules out substitution in consumption and looks to shifts in the location of production as the cause of welfare changes in customs unions. The analysis just completed emphasizes the effects of substitution in consumption. The distinction on this basis, however, is not fully satisfactory, for consumption effects will themselves cause changes in production. A more satisfactory distinction would seem to be one between *inter-country substitution* and *inter-commodity substitution*. Inter-country substitution would be Viner's trade creation and trade diversion, when one country is substituted for another as the source of supply for some commodity. Inter-commodity substitution occurs when one commodity is substituted, at least at the margin, for some other commodity as a result of

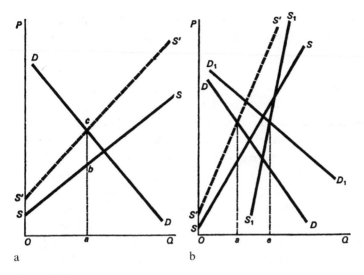

Figure 20.3

a relative price shift. This is the type of subsitution we have just been analysing. In general, either of these changes will cause shifts in both consumption and production.

Now we come to Professor Meade's analysis. His approach is taxonomic in that he attempts to classify a large number of possible cases, showing the factors which would tend to cause welfare to increase when a union is formed and to isolate these from the factors which would tend to cause welfare to diminish.[10] Figure 20.3a shows a demand and a supply curve for any imported commodity. Meade observes that a tariff, like any tax, shifts the supply curve to the left (to $S'S'$ in figure 20.3a) and raises the price of the imported commodity. At the new equilibrium the demand price differs from the supply price by the amount of the tariff. If the supply price indicates the utility of the commodity to the suppliers and the demand price its utility to the purchasers, it follows that the utility of the taxed import is higher to purchasers than to suppliers, and the money value of this difference in utility is the value of the tariff. Now assume that the marginal utility of money is the same for buyers and for sellers. It follows that if one more *unit of expenditure* were devoted to the purchase of this commodity, there would be a net gain to society equal to the proportion of the selling price of the commodity composed of the tariff. In figure 3a the rate of tariff is cb/ab percent, the supply price is ab and the demand price is ac, so that the money value of the "gain" ("loss") to society resulting from a marginal increase (decrease) in expenditure on this commodity is bc.

Now assume that the same *ad valorem* rate of tariff is imposed on all imports so that the tariff will be the same proportion of the market price of each import. Then the gain to society from a marginal increase in expenditure (say one more "dollar" is spent) on any import is the same for all imports, and this gain is equal to the loss resulting from a marginal reduction in expenditure (one less "dollar" spent) on any import. Now consider *a marginal reduction* in the tariff on one commodity. This will cause a readjustment of expenditure, in the various possible ways analysed by Meade, so that in general more of some imports and less of others will be purchased. Since, *at the margin*, the gain from devoting one more unit of expenditure to the purchase of any import is equal to the loss from devoting one less unit of expenditure to the purchase of any import, the welfare consequences of this discriminatory tariff reduction may be calculated by comparing the increase in the volume of imports (trade expansion) with the decrease in the volume of other imports (trade contraction). If there is a net increase in the volume of trade the customs union will have raised economic welfare. A study of the welfare consequences of customs unions can, therefore, be devoted to the factors which will increase or decrease the volume of international trade. If the influences which tend to cause trade expansion are found to predominate it may be predicted that a customs union will raise welfare. The main body of Meade's analysis is in fact devoted to a study of those factors which would tend to increase, and to those which would tend to decrease, the volume of trade. Complications can, of course, be introduced, but they do not affecte the main drift of the argument.[11]

Meade's analysis, which makes use of demand and supply curves, suffers from one very serious, possibly crippling, limitation. It will be noted that we were careful to consider only *marginal reductions* in tariffs. For such changes Meade's analysis is undoubtedly correct. When, however, there are *large* changes in many tariffs, as there will be with most of the customs unions in which we are likely to be interested, it can no longer be assumed that the demand and supply curves will remain fixed; the *ceteris paribus* assumptions on which they are based will no longer hold, so that both demand and supply curves are likely to shift. When this happens it is no longer obvious how much welfare weight should be given to any particular change in the volume of trade (even if we are prepared to make all of the other assumptions necessary for the use of this type of classical welfare analysis). In figure 20.3b for example, if the demand curve shifts to $D_1 D_1$ and the supply curve to $S_1 S_1$, what are we to say about the welfare gains or losses when trade changes from Oa to Oe?

There is not time to go through a great deal of Professor Meade's or my own analysis which attempts to discover the particular circumstances in which it is likely that a geographically discriminatory reduction in tariffs will raise welfare. I shall, therefore, take two of the general conclusions that emerge from various analyses and present these in order to illustrate the type of generalization that it is possible to make in customs-union theory.

The first generalization is one that emerges from Professor Meade's analysis and from my own. I choose it, first, because there seems to be general agreement on it and, second, although Professor Meade does not make this point, because it is an absolutely general proposition in the theory of second best; it applies to all suboptimal positions, and customs-union theory only provides a particular example of its application. Stated in terms of customs unions, this generalization runs as follows: when only some tariffs are to be changed, welfare is more likely to be raised if these tariffs are merely *reduced* than if they are completely *removed*. Proofs of this theorem can be found in both Meade (1956, pp. 50–51) and Lipsey and Lancaster (1956–57, sec. 5), and we shall content ourselves here with an intuitive argument for the theorem in its most general context. Assume that there exist many taxes, subsidies, monopolies, etc., which prevent the satisfaction of optimum conditions. Further assume that all but one of these, say one tax, are fixed, and inquire into the second-best level for the tax that is allowed to vary. Finally, assume that there exists a unique second-best level for this tax.[12] Now a change in this one tax will either move the economy towards or away from a second-best optimum position. If it moves the economy away from a second-best position, then, no matter how large is the change in the tax, welfare will be lowered. If it moves the economy in the direction of the second-best optimum, it may move it part of the way, all of the way or past it. If the economy is moved sufficiently far past the second-best optimum welfare will be lowered by the change. From this it follows that, if there is a unique second-best level for the tax being varied, a small variation is more likely to raise welfare than is a large variation.[13]

The next generalization concerns the size of expenditure on the three classes of goods—those purchased domestically, from the union partner, and from the outside world—and is related to the gains from inter-commodity substitution. This generalization follows from the analysis in my own thesis (Lipsey 1958, pp. 97–99 and appendix to chap. 6) and does not seem to have been stated in any of the existing customs-union literature. Consider what happens to the optimum conditions, which we discussed earlier, when the customs union is formed (see table 20.2). On the one hand, the tariff is taken off imports from the country's union partner, and the relative price between these imports and domestic goods is brought into conformity with the real rates of transformation. This, by itself, tends to increase welfare. On the other hand, the relative price between imports from the union partner and imports from the outside world are moved away from equality with real rates of transformation. This by itself tends to reduce welfare. Now consider both of these changes. As far as the prices of the goods from a country's union partner are concerned, they are brought into equality with rates of transformation *vis-à-vis* domestic goods, but they are moved away from equality with rates of transformation *vis-à-vis* imports from the outside world. These imports from the union partner are thus involved in both a gain and a loss and their size is *per se* unimportant. What matters is the relation between imports from the outside world and expenditure on domestic commodities: the larger are purchases of domestic commodities and the smaller are purchases from the outside world, the more likely is it that the union will bring gain. Consider a simple example in which a country purchases from its union partner only eggs while it purchases from the outside world only shoes, all other commodities being produced and consumed at home. Now when the union is formed the "correct" price ratio (i.e., the one which conforms with the real rate of transformation) between eggs and shoes will be disturbed, but, on the other hand, eggs will be brought into the "correct" price relationship with all other commodities— bacon, butter, cheese, meat, etc., and in these circumstances a customs union is very likely to bring gain, for the loss in distorting the price ratio between eggs and shoes will be small relative to the gain in establishing the correct price ratio between eggs and all other commodities. Now, however, let us reverse the position of domestic trade and imports from the outside world, making shoes the only commodity produced and consumed at home, eggs still being imported from the union partner, while everything else is now bought from the outside world. In these circumstances the customs union is most likely to bring a loss; the gains in establishing the correct price ratio between eggs and shoes are indeed likely to be very small compared with the losses of distorting the price ratio between eggs and all other commodities. If, to take a third example, eggs are produced at home, shoes imported from the outside world, while everything else is obtained from the union partner, the union may bring neither gain nor loss; for the union disturbs the "correct" ratio between shoes and everything else except eggs, and establishes the "correct" one between eggs and everything else except shoes. This example serves to show that the size of trade with a union partner is not the important variable; it is the relation between imports from the outside world and purchases of domestic goods that matters.

This argument gives rise to two general conclusions, one of them appealing immediately to common sense, one of them slightly surprising. The first is that *given a country's volume of international trade*, a customs union is more likely to raise welfare the higher is the proportion of trade with the country's union partner and the lower the proportion with the outside world. The second is that a customs union is more likely to raise welfare, the lower is the total volume of foreign trade, for the lower is foreign trade, the lower must be purchases from the outside world relative to purchases of domestic commodities. This means that the sort of countries who ought to form customs unions are those doing a high proportion of their foreign trade with their union partner, and making a high proportion of their total expenditure on domestic trade. Countries which are likely to lose from a customs union, on the other hand, are those countries in which a low proportion of total trade is domestic, especially if the customs union does not include a high proportion of their foreign trade.

We may now pass to a very brief consideration of some of the empirical work. Undoubtedly a serious attempt to predict and measure the possible effects of a customs union is a very difficult task. Making all allowances for this, however, a surprisingly large proportion of the voluminous literature on the subject is devoted to guess and suspicion, and a very small proportion to serious attempts to measure. Let us consider what empirical work has been done on the European Common Market and the Free Trade Area, looking first at attempts to measure possible gains from specialization. The theoretical analysis underlying these measurements is of the sort developed by Professor Meade and outlined previously.

The first study which we will mention is that made by the Dutch economist Verdoorn, subsequently quoted and used by Scitovsky (1958, pp. 64–78). The analysis assumes an elasticity of subsitution between domestic goods and imports of minus one half, and an elasticity of substitution between different imports of minus two. These estimates are based on some empirical measurements of an aggregate sort, and the extremely radical assumption is made that the same elasticities apply to all commodities. The general assumption, then, is that one import is fairly easily substituted for another, while imports and domestic commodities are not particularly good substitutes for each other.[14]

Using this assumption, an estimate was made of the changes in trade when tariffs are reduced between the six Common Market countries, the United Kingdom and Scandinavia. The estimate is that intra-European trade will increase by approximately 17 percent, and, when this increase is weighted by the proportion of the purchase price of each commodity that is made up of tariff and estimates for the reduction in trade in other directions are also made, the final figure for the gains from trade to the European countries is equal to about one-twentieth of 1 percent of their annual incomes. In considering this figure, the crude estimate of elasticities of substitution must cause some concern. The estimate of an increase in European trade of 17 percent is possibly rather small in the face of the known fact that Benelux trade increased by approximately 50 percent after the formation of that customs union. A possible check on the accuracy of the Verdoorn method would have been to apply it to the pre-customs union situation in the Benelux countries, to use the method to predict what would happen to Benelux trade and then to compare the prediction with what we actually know to have happened. Whatever allowances are made, however, Scitovsky's conclusion is not likely to be seriously challenged:

The most surprising feature of these estimates is their smallness.... As estimates of the total increase in intra-European trade contingent upon economic union, Verdoorn's figures are probably under-estimates; but if, by way of correction, we should raise them five- or even twenty-fivefold, that would still leave unchanged our basic conclusion that the gain from increased intra-European specialization is likely to be insignificant. (Scitovsky 1958a, p. 67)

A second empirical investigation into the possible gains from trade, this time relating only to the United Kingdom, has been made by Professor Johnson (1958). Johnson bases his study on the estimates made by *The Economist* Intelligence Unit of the increases in the value of British trade which would result by 1970, first, if there were only the Common Market and, second, if there were the Common Market and the Free Trade Area. Professor Johnson then asks what will be the size of the possible gains to Britain of participation in the Free Trade Area? His theory is slightly different from that of Professor Meade, but since it arrives at the same answer, namely that the gain is equal to the increased quantity of trade times the proportion of the purchase price made up of tariff, we do not need to consider the details. From these estimates Johnson arrives at the answer that the possible gain to Britain from joining the Free Trade Area would be, *as an absolute maximum*, 1 percent of the national income of the United Kingdom.

Most people seem to be surprised at the size of these estimates, finding them smaller than expected. This leads us to ask: might there not be some inherent bias in this sort of estimate? And, might not a totally different approach yield quite different answers? One possible approach is to consider the proportion of British factors of production engaged in foreign trade. This can be taken to be roughly the percentage contribution made by trade to the value of the national product, which can be estimated to be roughly the value of total trade as a proportion of GNP, first subtracting the import content from the GNP. This produces a rough estimate of 18 percent of Britain's total resources engaged in foreign trade. The next step would be to ask how much increase in efficiency of utilization for these resources could we expect: (1) as a result of their reallocation in the direction of their comparative advantage, and (2) as a result of a reallocation among possible consumers of the commodities produced by these resources. Here is an outline for a possible study, but, in the absence of such a study, what would we guess? Would a 10 percent increase in efficiency not be a rather conservative estimate? Such a gain in efficiency would give a net increase in the national income of 1.8 percent. If the resources had a 20 percent increase in efficiency, then an increase in the national income of 3.6 percent would be possible. At this stage these figures can give nothing more than a commonsense check on the more detailed estimates of economists such as Verdoorn and Johnson. Until further detailed work has been done, it must be accepted that the best present estimates give figures of the net gain from trade amounting to something less than 1 percent of the national income (although we may not, of course, have a very high degree of confidence in these estimates).[15]

When we move on from the possible gains from new trade to the question of the economic benefits arising from other causes, such as economies of scale or enforced efficiency, we leave behind even such halting attempts at measurement as we have just considered. Some economists see considerable economies of scale emerging from European union. Others are sceptical. In what follows, I will confine my attention mainly to the arguments advanced by Professor H. G. Johnson.[16] His first argument runs as follows:

It is extremely difficult to believe that British industry offers substantial potential savings in cost which cannot be exploited in a densely-populated market of 51 million people with a G.N.P. of £18 billion, especially when account is taken of the much larger markets abroad in which British industry, in spite of restrictions of various kinds, has been able to sell its products. (Johnson 1957, p. 35)[17]

Let us make only two points about Professor Johnson's observation. First, many markets will be very much less than the total population. What, for example, can we say about a product sold mainly to upper middle-class males living more than 20 miles away from an urban centre? Might there not be economies of scale remaining in the production of a commodity for such a market? Second, in the absence of some theory that tells us the statement is true for 51 and, say, 31, but not 21, million people, the argument must remain nothing more than an unsupported personal opinion. As another argument, Professor Johnson asks, "Why are these economies of scale, if they do exist, not already being exploited?" (Johnson 1958b, p. 10; 1957, p. 35.) It is, of course, well known that unexhausted economies of scale are incompatible with the existence of perfect competition, but it is equally well known that unexhausted economies of scale are compatible with the existence of imperfect competition as long as long-run marginal cost is declining faster than marginal revenue. Here it is worth while making a distinction, mentioned by Scitovsky (1958, pp. 42ff), between the long-run marginal cost of producing more goods, to which the economist is usually referring when he speaks of scale effects, and the marginal cost of making and selling more goods (which must include selling costs). This leads to a distinction between increasing sales when the whole market is expanding and increasing sales when the market is static, and thus increasing them at the expense of one's competitors. The former is undoubtedly very much easier than the latter. It is quite possible for the marginal costs of *production* to be declining while the marginal costs of *selling* in a static market are rising steeply. This would mean that production economies would not be exploited by the firms competing in the market but that, if the market were to expand so that *all* firms in a given industry could grow, then these economies would be realized.

Let us also consider an argument put forward in favour of economies of scale. Gehrels and Johnson (1955) argue that very large gains from economies of scale can be expected. In evidence of this they quote the following facts: American productivity (i.e., output per man) is higher than United Kingdom productivity for most commodities; the differential is, however, greatest in those industries which use mass-production methods. From this they conclude that there are unexploited economies of mass production in the United Kingdom. Now this may well be so, but before accepting the conclusion, we should be careful in interpreting this meagre piece of evidence. What else might it mean? Might it not mean, for example, that the ratios of capital to labour differed in the two countries so that, if we calculate the productivity of a factor by dividing total production by the quantity of one factor employed, we will necessarily find these differences? Second, would we not be very surprised if we did not find such differences in comparative costs between the two countries? Are we surprised when we find America's comparative advantage centred in the mass-producing industries, and if this is the case, must we conclude that vast economies of mass production exist for Europe?

Finally, we come to the possible gains through forced efficiency. Business firms may not be adopting methods known to be technically more efficient than those now in use due to inertia, a dislike of risk taking, a willingness to be content with moderate profits, or a whole host of other reasons. If these firms are thrown into competition with a number of firms in other countries who are not adopting this conservative policy, then the efficiency of the use of resources may incerease because technically more efficient production methods are forced on the businessman now facing fierce foreign competition. Here no evidence has as yet been gathered, and rather than report the opinions of others, I will close by recording the personal guess that this is a very large potential source of gain, that an increase in competition with foreign countries who are prepared to adopt new methods might have a most salutary effect on the efficiency of a very large number of British and European manufacturing concerns.[18]

Notes

An earlier version of this paper was read before the Conference of the Association of University Teachers of Economics at Southampton, January 1959.

1. Points (1) and (2) are clearly related, for the existence of (1) is a *necessary* condition for (2), but they are more conveniently treated as separate points, since (1) is not a *sufficient* condition for the existence of (2).

2. In everything that follows the "home country" will be labelled A, the "union partner" B and the rest of the world C.

3. This argument presumes that relative prices in each country reflect real rates of transformation. It follows that the resouces used to produce a unit of X in country A could produce any other good to the value of 35s., and since a unit of X can be had from B by exporting goods to the value of only 26s., there will be a surplus of goods valued at 9s. accruing to A from the transfer of resources out of X when trade is opened with country B.

4. The point may be made slightly more formally as follows: the conditions necessary for the maximizing of *any* function do not, in general, provide conditions sufficient for an increase in the value of the function when the maximum value is not to be obtained by the change.

5. One of the two countries might be an efficient producer of this commodity needing no tariff protection, in which case, *a fortiori*, there is gain.

6. Care must be taken to distinguish between complementarity and competitiveness in costs and in tasts, both being possible. In the Makower-Morton model these relations exist only on the cost side. An example of the confusion which may arise when this distinction is not made can be seen (Meyer 1956). Meyer's definitions, if they are to mean anything, must refer to the demand side. Hence he is not entitled to contrast his results with those of Makower and Morton, or of Viner, all of whom were concerned with cost complementarity and competitiveness.

7. It is assumed throughout all the subsequent analysis that the tariff revenue collected by the government is either returned to individuals by means of lump-sum subsidies or spent by the government on the same bundle of goods that consumers would have purchased.

8. Lipsey (1957, pp. 43–44). The changes made in the quotation are minor ones necessary to make the notation in the example comparable to the one used in the present text.

9. If we assume that consumers adjust their purchases to the relative prices ruling in their domestic markets, then the optimum conditions that rates of substitution in consumption should equal rates of transformation in trade can be stated in terms of equality between relative prices ruling in the domestic markets and those ruling in the international market.

10. The point of his taxonomy or of any taxonomy of this sort, it seems to me, must be merely to illustrate how the model works. Once one has mastered the analysis, it is possible to work through any particular case that may arise, and there would seem to be no need to work out all possible cases beforehand.

11. For example, the same rate of tariff might not be charged on all imports. In this case it is only necessary to weight each dollar's increase or decrease in trade by the proportion of this value that is made up by tariff—the greater is the rate of tariff the greater is the gain or loss. It is also possible, if one wishes to make inter-country comparisons, to weight a dollar's trade in one direction by a different amount than a dollar's trade in some other direction. These complications, however, do not affect the essence of Meade's analysis, which is to make a *small change* in some tariffs and then to observe that the welfare consequences depend on the net change in the volume of trade and to continue the study in order to discover in what circumstances an increase or a decrease in the net volume of trade is likely.

12. A unique second-best level (i.e., the level which maximizes welfare subject to the existence and invariability of all the other taxes, tariffs, etc.) for any one variable factor can be shown to exist in a large number of cases (see, e.g., Lipsey and Lancaster 1956, sec. 5 and 6) but cannot be proved to exist in general (ibid., sec. 8).

13. This may be given a more formal statement. Consider the direction of the change—towards or away from the second-best optimum position—caused by the change in the tax. Moving away from the second-best optimum is a *sufficient*, but not a necessary, condition for a reduction in welfare. Moving towards the second-best optimum is a *necessary*, but not a sufficient, condition for an increase in welfare.

14. Note also that everything is assumed to be a substitute for everything else; there are no relations of complementarity.

15. Perhaps a more intuitively appealing argument as to why these estimates probably do not over estimate the order of magnitude of the gain is as follows:

Typical European tariffs on manufactured goods are in the order of 20 per cent. This means that industries from 1 to 20 per cent less efficient than foreign competitors will be protected by these tariffs. If the costs of different industries are spread out evenly, then some tariff-protected industries would be 20 per cent less efficient than foreign competitors, but others would be only 1 per cent less efficient, and their average inefficiency would be in the order of half the tariff rate, which is 10 per cent less efficient than foreign competitors. Typically, not much more than 10 per cent of a country's resources would be devoted to producing behind tariff walls. This means that 10 per cent of a country's resources would be producing 10 per cent less efficiently than if there were no tariffs, which makes a reduction in national income of something in the order of 1 per cent." (See Lipsey 1968, p. 772.)

16. In singling out Professor Johnson, I do not wish to imply that he is alone in practising the sort of economies which I am criticizing. On the contrary, he is typical of a very large number of economists who have attempted to obtain quantitative conclusions from qualitative arguments.

17. See also Johnson (1958b) for a similar argument.

18. Milton Friedman's argument (1953) that survival of the fittest proves profit maximization notwithstanding. What seems to me to be a conclusive refutation of the Friedman argument is to be found in Archibald (1959).

I have since changed my mind in respect to this belief. See the more detailed arguments in Lipsey (1967, p. 12). The following quotation should indicate the nature of my present disagreement with the argument in the text:

Before you accept this argument which is usually thrown about quite uncritically ask yourself what the text books all say about the argument that a poor, low productivity country cannot trade profitably with a rich, high productivity one. "Nonsense," say the books, "it is comparative not absolute advantage that determines the flow of trade and the gains from it." Assume, for example, that everybody in Britain is absolutely 20 per cent less efficient than everybody on the Continent. If we go into the Common Market on an exchange rate which will yield an external balance, then there will be *no* effect on overall efficiency: some industries will have a comparative advantage, some will not, and payments will be balanced at the given levels of efficiency. The only way in which increased efficiency could be forced on Britain would be if we went in at an over-valued exchange rate. This means that very few industries would be able to export and that imports would flood in from the continent. We would then be hoping that the domestic level of efficiency would react so that the overall level of costs and prices would fall in Britain, *vis-à-vis* Europe, and that a balance of payments would be achieved at the formerly over-valued rate once the increase in efficiency had occurred. But there is no reason to think that a rise in efficiency with a constant price level which is the equivalent to a temporary increase in the rate of economic growth would improve the balance of payments. Certainly there is little in our recent history to suggest that it would cause a deflation. Probably the best we could hope for would be a parallel rise in wages and no change in the price level. Thus, even if the gain were realized, we would have to contemplate a subsequent devaluation of the pound. This is itself would be no disaster but it is not easy to devalue a single currency within the rules of the Common Market nor is there any evidence that the Six would contemplate allowing us to enter on an over-valued rate. We would also be taking the chance—in my opinion a very outside one in light of evidence of the 1920s—that an overvalued exchange rate would produce a rise in efficiency rather than a decline in employment and in national income.

References

Archibald, G. C. 1959. The state of economic science. *British Journal of the Philosophy of Science*, June.

Friedman, M. (1953). *Essays in Positive Economics*. University of Chicage Press.

Gehrels, F. (1956–57). Customs unions from a single country viewpoint. *Review of Economic Studies* 24.

Gehrels, F., and Johnson, H. G. 1955. The economic gains from European integration. *Journal of Political Economy* (August).

Johnson, H. G. 1957. The criteria of economic advantage. *Bulletin of the Oxford University Institute of Statistics* 19.

Johnson, H. G. 1958a. The gains from free trade with European: An estimate. *Manchester School of Economic and Social Studies* 26.

Johnson, H. G. 1958b. The economic gains from free trade with Europe. *Three Banks Review* (September).

Lipsey, R. G. 1958. The theory of customs unions: A general equilibrium analysis. Ph.D. thesis. University of London. Published by Weidenfeld and Nicolson, London, 1972.

Lipsey, R. G. 1956–57. Mr. Gehrels on customs unions. *Review of Economic Studies* 24: 211–14.

Lipsey, R. G. 1957. The theory of customs unions: Trade diversion and welfare. *Economica* 24.

Lipsey, R. G. 1967. The balance of payments and the Common Market. *Economics: The Journal of the Economics Association* (Autumn).

Lipsey, R. G. 1968. *An Introduction to Positive Economics*. Weidenfeld and Nicolson.

Lipsey, R. G., and Lancaster, K. J. 1956–57. The general theory of second best. *Review of Economic Studies* 24.

Makower, H., and Morton, G. 1953. A contribution towards a theory of customs unions. *Economic Journal* 62: 33–49.

Meade, J. E. 1956. *The Theory of Customs Unions*. North Holland.

Meyer, F. V. 1956. Complementarily and the lowering of tariffs. *American Economic Review* 46.

Scitovsky, T. de. 1958. *Economic Theory and Western European Integration*. Allen and Unwin.

Viner, J. 1950. *The Customs Unions Issue*. Carnegie Endowment for International Peace.

21

An Elementary Proposition Concerning the Formation of Customs Unions

Murray Kemp and Henry Wan, Jr.

In the welter of inconclusive debate concerning the implications of customs unions the following elementary yet basic proposition seems to have been almost lost to sight.[1]

1. Proposition

Consider any competitive world trading equilibrium, with any number of countries and commodities and with no restrictions whatever on the tariffs and other commodity taxes of individual countries and with costs of transport fully recognized. Now let any subset of the countries form a customs union. Then there exists a common tariff vector and a system of lump-sum compensatory payments involving only members of the union, such that each individual, whether a member of the union or not, is not worse off than before the formation of the union.

A detailed list of assumptions, and a relatively formal proof, may be found in section 2. Here we merely note that there exists a common tariff vector which leaves world prices, and therefore the trade and welfare of non-members, at their pre-union levels. If the net trade vector of the union is viewed as a (constant) endowment, it is then plausible that both the union as a whole and (after appropriate internal transfers) each member must be left not worse off by the removal of internal barriers to trade.

The proposition is interesting in that it contains no qualifications whatever concerning the size or number of the countries which are contemplating union, that pre or post-union trading relationships, their relative states of development or levels of average income, and their propinquities in terms of geography or costs of transportation.

This paper was originally published in Murray Kemp, *Three Topics in the Theory of International Trade: Distribution, Welfare and Uncertainty*, North Holland Publishing Company, 1976.

The proposition is also interesting because it implies that an incentive to form and enlarge customs unions persists until the world becomes one big customs union, that is, until world free trade prevails. More precisely, given any initial trading equilibrium, there exist finite sequences of steps, at each step new customs unions being created or old unions enlarged, such that at each step no individual is made worse off and such that after the last step the world is free trading. (In general, at each step some individual actually benefits.) Indeed, on the basis of these observations one might attempt to rehabilitate the vague pre-Vinerian view that to form a customs union is to move in the direction of free trade.

Evidently the incentive is insufficiently strong; tariffs and other artificial obstacles to trade persist. That the real world is not free trading must be explained in terms of

1. the game theoretic problems of choosing partners, dividing the spoils and enforcing agreements, and
2. the noneconomic objectives of nations.

A role may be found also for

3. inertia and ignorance concerning the implications of possible unions (in particular, concerning the long list of lump-sum compensatory payments required), and, in the short run, for
4. the restraint exercised by international agreements to limit tariffs.

However topic 4 can form no part of an explanation of the persistence of trading blocks in the long run.

Topics 1 through 3 form a possible agenda for the further study of customs unions. For a preliminary analysis of 1, the reader may consult Caves (1971); and for suggestive work in 2, he is referred to Cooper and Massell (1965), Johnson (1965), and Bhagwati (1968).

2. Proof of the Proposition

Suppose that

1. (a) the consumption set of each individual is closed, convex and bounded below; (b) the preferences of each individual are convex and representable by a continuous ordinal utility function; (c) each individual can survive with a consumption bundle each component of which is somewhat less than his pre-union consumption bundle;
2. the production set of each economy is closed, convex, contains the origin and is such that positive output requires at least one positive input (impossibility of free production).

Consider a fictitious economy composed of the member economies but with a net endowment equal to the sum of the member endowments plus the equilibrium pre-union net excess supply of the rest of the world. In view of 1 and 2, the economy possesses an optimum, and any optimum can be supported by at least one internal price vector (Debreu 1959, pp. 92–93, 95–96). Either the pre-union equilibrium of the member countries is a Pareto-optimal equilibrium of the fictitious economy (i.e., corresponds to a maximal point of the utility possibility set), or it is not; in the latter case, a preferred Pareto-optimal equilibrium can be attained by means of lump-sum transfers among individuals in the fictitious economy. That essentially completes the proof. It only remains to note that the required vector of common tariffs may be computed as the difference between the vector of pre-union world prices and the vector of internal union prices.

Commodities can be indexed by location. Hence the resource-using activity of moving commodities from one country to another is accommodated in the several production sets; no special treatment of cost of transportation is needed.

Note

1. The proposition together with an indication of the lines along which a proof may be constructed, may be found in Kemp (1964, p. 176). A geometric proof for the canonical three-countries, two-commodities case has been furnished by Vanek (1965, pp. 160–165).

References

Bhagwati, J. 1968. Trade liberalization among LDCs, trade theory, and GATT rules. In J. N. Wolfe ed., *Value, Capital, and Growth, Papers in honour of Sir John Hicks.* Edinburgh University Press, Edinburgh, pp. 21–43.

Caves, R. E. 1971. The economics of reciprocity: Theory and evidence on bilateral trading arrangements. Harvard Institute of Economic Research, Discussion Paper No. 166.

Cooper, C. A., and B. F. Massell. 1965. Towards a general theory of customs unions for developing countries. *Journal of Political Economy* 73, 461–476.

Debreu, G. 1959. *Theory of Value.* Wiley, New York.

Johnson, H. G. 1965. An economic theory of protectionism, tariff bargaining, and the formation of customs unions. *Journal of Political Economy* 73, 256–283.

Kemp, M. C. 1964. *The Pure Theory of International Trade.* Prentice-Hall, Englewood Cliffs, N. J.

Vanek, J. 1965. *General Equilibrium of International Discrimination. The Case of Customs Unions.* Harvard University Press, Cambridge.

Postscript

For clarification of the conditions needed for the proof, see M. C. Kemp and H. Wan, Jr., The Comparison of Second-Best Equilibria: The Case of Customs Unions, *Zeitschrift für Nationalokonomie*, forthcoming.

Editor's Note

In the Kemp-Wan proposition, the phrase "and other commodity taxes" should be eliminated. Alternatively, as Kemp and Wan have noted in correspondence, a customs union may be *defined* to be free of commodity taxes other than tariffs, in which case the phrase "and other commodity taxes" can be retained.

VIII
Growth and Transfers

Introduction to Part VIII

Part VIII deals with a number of topics, and influential papers on them, relating to the broad rubric of growth and transfers.

Chapter 22 is a classic note of Harry Johnson, discovering an important new example of immiserizing growth. In my earlier model of immiserizing growth (*Review of Economic Studies*, June 1958) I had shown how a decline in the growth-induced terms of trade may lead to a secondary loss that outweighs the primary gain from growth, whereas chapter 22 by Johnson shows immiserization as a possibility when growth takes place subject to a tariff in a small economy. Both paradoxes can be explained of course as arising because growth is taking place subject to a distortion whose cost is accentuated by the growth sufficiently to outweigh the gain that would arise if growth were to occur with optimal policies in place, as I subsequently noted (*Review of Economic Studies*, November 1968). Thus, in my 1958 paper, the distortion arises from the failure to use an optimal tariff when the country is large, and in chapter 22 it arises from the fact that a tariff is distortionary for a small country.

Chapter 23 utilizes the approach of chapter 22 to analyze the question whether the inflow of foreign capital is immiserizing if a small economy is tariff distorted, a question of great interest as many countries have used tariffs to *induce* capital inflow. Brecher and Díaz-Alejandro, as Uzawa had done previously and independently in Japanese, show that if the importable good is capital intensive, foreign capital inflow will be necessarily immiserizing. Their analysis is then extended to embrace the earlier analyses of the welfare impact of foreign inflows in the presence of tariffs, including the classic Mundell analysis in chapter 2.

Whereas chapters 22 and 23 are contributions that are essentially comparative-static in nature, chapter 24 contains a comprehensive survey by Smith of recent contributions to the dynamic theory of growth and trade. It should help the student to get a quick and firm grasp of the central findings of this area of research and then be better prepared to confront the welfare-theoretic issues that have been raised by Emmanuel, Steedman, and others, in one way or another, alleging the possible suboptimality of free trade vis-à-vis autarky in growing economies. The student who wishes to pursue these questions is advised to consult Smith (*Journal of International Economics*, May 1979), Samuelson (*Journal of International Economics*, November 1975 and February 1978), Emmanuel versus Samuelson (*Journal of International Economics*, February 1978), and Srinivasan and Bhagwati (in Chipman and Kindleberger, eds., *Essays in International Economics*, Memorial Volume for Sohmen, North Holland, 1980).

A relatively different approach to growth-theoretic issues is associated with the work of Frenkel, Onitsuka, and Fischer. Chapter 25 is an abbreviated version of a paper by Fischer and Frenkel, which presents a two-sector model of a small growing economy that trades in both investment goods and securities as well as consumption goods. While the two-sector model had frequently been used in analyzing the growth process of open economies, it was usually assumed that there was trade in consumption goods and in either securities or investment goods but not both. The main difficulty in modeling trade in both investment goods and securities when the terms of trade are fixed is that a country's income will be the same whether it acquires income streams from abroad by buying securities paying the world interest rate or whether it obtains income by investing in capital that yields the same rate of return. By specifying a demand function for investment goods, based on an adjustment cost formulation in which more rapid rates of investment reduce the rate of return to capital, the authors allow for trade in both investment goods and securities and are also able to break the familiar link between the stability of the two-sector model and relative factor intensities in production. The model is used to study the dynamics of capital accumulation and the various trade accounts for a small open economy.

Chapters 26 and 27, by Harry Johnson and by Richard Brecher, Tatsuo Hatta, and myself, respectively, address the transfer problem which has always interested major writers in the theory of international trade.

The Johnson excerpt restates elegantly the central results established by Paul Samuelson in one of his famous paired articles, in the two-good, two-country, general equilibrium framework.

One of his central results was the demonstration that the possibility of a welfare paradox (originally noted by Wassity Leontief), such that the donor would be enriched and the recipient immiserized by the transfer, would be ruled out by assuming Walras stability. The three-agent (or three-country) analysis in the Bhagwati-Brecher-Hatta paper, and independently by other economists such as Harry Johnson, Ryutaro Komiya, and David Gale, shows that this is no longer so: the presence of a third agent in the marketplace, outside of the bilateral transfer process, can amplify the possibly perverse secondary effect through change in the terms of trade so as to bring about these transfer paradoxes despite Walras stability. Aside from the several alternative ways in which this result is explained, a key distinguishing characteristic of chapter 27 is the integration of this result with the theory of distortions and welfare (as stated in part V).

22

The Possibility of Income Losses from Increased Efficiency or Factor Accumulation in the Presence of Tariffs

Harry G. Johnson

The adoption of more efficient technology and the accumulation of factors of production are generally assumed to increase the real income available to an economy. But when a country is following a protective policy improved efficiency in the protected industry or accumulation of the factor used intensively in that industry will actually reduce the country's real income, over a range of change set by the degree of protection. This possibility of income-reducing growth is relevant to the fact that countries industrialising by means of protectionist and import-substitution policies are frequently dissatisfied with the results. This note presents a formal demonstration of the possibility, in terms of the standard Heckscher-Ohlin model of international trade.

Figure 22.1 depicts production and consumption equilibrium with the initial technology and factor supplies and the tariff. TT' is the transformation curve, deduced from the standard box-diagram, II is the international price ratio, MM and $M'M'$ are the internal price ratio (which differs from the international price ratio to an extent determined by the rate of protection of Y), and P and C are the production and consumption equilibrium points.

Now suppose that neutral technical progress occurs in the protected Y industry, and in that industry only. As a result, the transformation curve will shift outward except at point T (where no Y is produced) to TT''; and the new equilibrium production point P' must lie to the northwest of P.[1] P' may lie either to the left or to the right of II, depending on the tariff rate, the extent of the technical improvement, and the elasticities of substitution between the factors in the two production functions. The new utility level of the country is given by the community indifference curve that intersects a new II curve through P' with a slope equal to that of $M'M'$. It is obvious,

This paper was originally published in *The Economic Journal* (March 1967): 151–154.

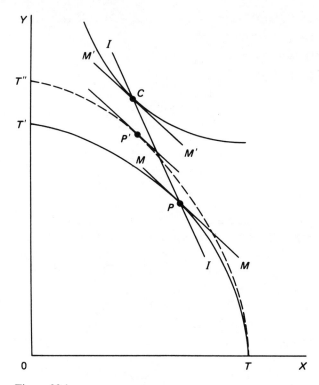

Figure 22.1

on the usual assumption that neither good is inferior, that the new utility level will be higher if P' lies to the right of II, and lower if P' lies to the left of II. In the latter case the country is made worse off by technical progress in its protected industry. Moreover, it is obvious that for a small enough degree of technical progress in that industry the country must be made worse off, while with a large enough degree of progress it must be made better off, by technical improvement.

If, instead of neutral technical progress in the protected industry, there were an increase in the stock of the factor used intensively in producing the protected product, the transformation curve would shift outward throughout its length; but (by the Rybczynski theorem) the new equilibrium production point P' would in this case also have to be to the northwest of P, again entailing the possibility of loss or gain of real income, the necessity of loss if the factor increment is small enough, and the necessity of gain if the factor increment exceeds some initial minimum quantity.

The analytical results just presented may be understood in the light of the following considerations. Technical progress increases efficiency and therefore potential output per head; but it also shifts resources toward the industry in which progress occurs. If this is the export industry, there is an additional gain from the reduction of waste implicit in the excess cost of protected production; but if it is the import-substitute industry, there is an offsetting loss from increased waste through the excess cost of additional protected production, which may more than absorb the increase in potential output per head. Similarly, an increase in the supply of a factor increases potential real output but also reallocates production towards the industry using that factor intensively; and if that industry is protected and so wastes resources through excess production costs, the shift again involves increased waste of resources, which may more than absorb the increase in potential output per head.

It is an interesting reflection on policy that protectionists usually demand increased protection when comparative advantage shifts against the protected industries, in effect claiming that part of the increased productive potential inherent in such a shift should be spent on the increased support of these industries.

In conclusion, it should be noted that the possibility of income-reducing growth demonstrated here is quite different from the possibility of "immiserizing growth" developed by Jagdish Bhagwati.[2] The latter is associated with the adverse effects of growth on the terms of trade; the former is associated with the presence of protection, under conditions in which any terms-of-trade effects of growth are excluded by assumption.

Notes

The possibility of income losses from increased efficiency or factor accumulation in the presence of tariffs was first pointed out to the author by J. H. Dales of the University of Toronto, who developed it in connection with his study of the effects of Canadian "National Policy" of industrial protection. The formal demonstration presented here was provoked by the disbelief of H. S. Houthakker.

1. For proof, see Harry G. Johnson, International trade and economic growth—A supplementary analysis, *Arthaniti* 5, 1–13. The same result will follow from non-neutral technical progress in the protected industry, unless it is sufficiently strongly biased toward saving the factor used intensively in the export industry.

2. Jagdish Bhagwati, Immiserizing growth: A geometrical note. *Review of Economic Studies* 25, no. 3, (June 1958), 201–205.

23

Tariffs, Foreign Capital, and Immiserizing Growth
Richard A. Brecher and Carlos F. Díaz-Alejandro

Within the standard two-commodity two-factor model of international trade Bhagwati (1973) has demonstrated the possibility of immiserizing growth caused by a tariff-induced inflow of capital from abroad, assuming that the host country is small and continues to import the capital-intensive good while remaining incompletely specialized. The deterioration in welfare may be decomposed (for comparative-static purposes) into the following three contributing effects: (1) the well-known loss due to tariff-created distortions in consumption and production, given only the initial factor endowments; (2) the loss or gain that would result even from accumulation of nationally owned capital in the presence of a tariff, for reasons expounded by Johnson (1967) and further explored by Bertrand and Flatters (1971) and Tan (1969); and (3) the loss arising when foreign profits are subtracted to determine national income.

Assuming that foreign capital receives the full (untaxed) value of its marginal product, the present paper shows that the ambiguous effect 2 plus the negative effect 3 necessarily yield a net loss. Therefore, national reduction in welfare must result on balance, even before the negative effect 1 is added to the "net inflow-impact," which here denotes the combined impact of effects 2 plus 3. In other words, Bhagwati's (1973) possibility (immiseration) is in fact the only outcome that can result from a tariff-induced inflow of untaxed capital from abroad. Of course, if taxation of foreign profits were taken into account as suggested by Bhagwati (1973), host-country deterioration in welfare could be avoided.

Since the inclusion of (negative) effect 1 would serve merely to reinforce the following argument, the analysis will restrict itself only to effects 2 and 3, by starting from the tariff-inclusive but pre-inflow situation. This

This paper was originally published in *Journal of International Economics* 7 (1977): 317–322.

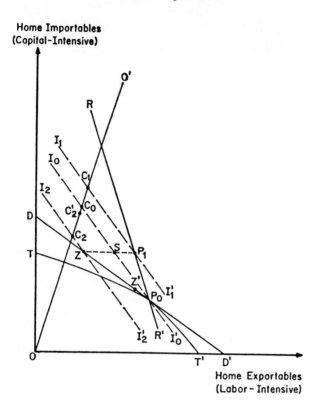

Figure 23.1

approach helps not only to simplify the exposition but also to emphasize that, once protection has been granted, further reduction in welfare would result from any exogenous (as well as tariff-induced) inflows of capital from abroad.

In figure 23.1, the small protectionist country produces (with constant returns to scale) initially at P_0, using only the national endowments of capital and labor which generate the home production possibility frontier labelled TT'. The domestic (tariff-inclusive) price ratio is given by the slope of line DD', tangent to TT' at P_0; whereas the world price ratio, as fixed by the small-country assumption, is given by the slope of line I_0I_0'. Consumption is at C_0, where I_0I_0' intersects line OO', which is the income-consumption curve corresponding to domestic prices. Linearity of OO' simplifies the diagram but is not required for the analysis. To avoid cluttering the geometry, the diagram omits the community indifference curves, one of which passes through C_0 with a slope equal to that of DD'.

Effect 2 will first be examined in isolation. The once-for-all increase in the capital stock shifts out the production possibility frontier (not shown in its new position), and at constant prices, production moves from P_0 to P_1. Point P_1 lies northwest of P_0, according to the Rybczynski theorem, and both of these points lie on RR', which is the familiar Rybczynski line corresponding to the (fixed) ratio of domestic prices. Since RR' is steeper than the world-price line in the particular case illustrated, the real value of total output increases at international prices, as the world-price line shifts from $I_0 I_0'$ to $I_1 I_1'$. Therefore, consumption increases from C_0 to C_1 and welfare improves. Alternatively, if the world-price line had been drawn steeper than RR', welfare would have decreased by similar reasoning, and the following analysis clearly would go through *a fortiori* because effect 2 would be negative.

Now effect 3 also will be incorporated, by subtracting foreign profits to leave only national income. Assuming that capital from abroad receives the full (tax-free) value of its marginal product, foreign profits absorb the entire increase in total output valued at domestic prices, by reasoning similar to Mundell's (1957). Expressed in terms of the exportable good, these profits are therefore represented by $P_1 Z$, which is the horizontal distance between point P_1 and line DD'. Supposing that foreign profits are repatriated in terms of home exportables, the home country is left with commodity bundle Z, which can be exchanged internationally along the world-price line $I_2 I_2'$ to achieve consumption at C_2. Since C_2 must lie southwest of C_0, the capital inflow clearly reduces the host country's welfare.

Thus, even though capital accumulation could increase national welfare in the absence of foreign profits, the host country must suffer from foreign investment which receives its market rate of return. By way of extension, the following four observations could be substantiated readily. First, the analysis (qualitatively speaking) depends neither upon the type of goods used to repatriate foreign profits, nor upon the assumption that foreigners consume these profits abroad rather than locally.[1] Second, if host-country taxes were levied to reduce the repatriation of foreign profits from $P_1 Z$ to $P_1 S$ or less, the net inflow-impact (combining effects 2 plus 3) would be zero or positive, respectively. Third, if home importables were instead labor intensive—in which case effect 2 is known to be positive—the net inflow-impact necessarily would be positive. Fourth, in the alternative situation of a trade subsidy (i.e., a negative tariff), the net inflow-impact would be positive, assuming that host-country importables are capital intensive (but negative if these goods were labor intensive). Of course, if the net inflow-impact were positive for either of these three reasons, effect 1 might be outweighed and tariff-induced inflows of capital from abroad clearly need not be immiserizing.

In figure 23.1, the inflow of capital reduces home imports of capital-intensive goods, because output of these commodities increases (as production shifts from P_0 to P_1) while consumption of these goods decreases (from the level at C_0 to the level at C_2). Also, the capital inflow shifts the pattern of output in favor of capital-intensive goods at the expense of labor-intensive commodities, as production moves northwestwardly (from P_0 to P_1) along RR'. Until this stage in the discussion, however, the inflow of capital is not large enough to extinguish home-country imports or achieve complete specialization in production. The implications of larger inflows will now be considered briefly.

As Minabe (1974) observes, host-country welfare rises above its tariff-inclusive pre-inflow level if the capital inflow is large enough to achieve Mundell's (1957) tariff-induced equilibrium, involving incomplete specialization with no home imports of commodities and with no divergence between domestic and foreign prices. In present terminology, the net inflow-impact in this case is positive. Effect 2 is now augmented to incorporate the familiar gains due to the disappearance of distortions in production and consumption, as domestic prices become equal to international prices. Under these circumstances, however, clearly the net inflow-impact is exactly offset by effect 1, since Mundell's (1957) tariff-induced (post-inflow) equilibrium yields precisely the same level of host-country welfare as does his free-trade (pre-inflow) situation. Therefore, this case does not provide an argument in favor of using tariffs to attract capital from abroad.

If the capital inflow then proceeds even further, initially it has no additional consequences for home welfare, by reasoning similar to Mundell's (1957), as long as specialization remains incomplete. Eventually, however, the inflow leads to extra host-country gains, by reasoning similar to MacDougall's (1960) (cited also by Hamada 1974) or Minabe's (1974), once specialization becomes complete in the capital-intensive good. Although such further inflows of capital would not be induced by the original tariff (imposed selectively on the good no longer imported), they could be exogenously determined.

The analysis of the present paper may be summarized in figure 23.2. The free-trade pre-inflow position is at point F. The distance FT represents the welfare loss due to imposing a tariff in the absence of capital inflows from abroad. Given the tariff, the welfare effects of (untaxed) capital inflows are illustrated by the curve $TAMM'D$ (whose lowest point is A), assuming that home importables are capital intensive along FT. Segment TA shows

Home Welfare

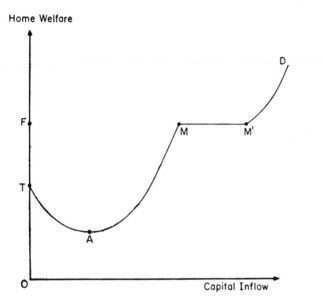

Figure 23.2

the type of welfare loss analyzed in the previous diagram. Segment AM (in figure 23.2) shows the welfare path to the Mundell (1957) equilibrium at point M, which has the same height as F.[2] The home country remains incompletely specialized with no capital-intensive imports along the horizontal segment MM', until complete specialization in capital-intensive goods is reached at point M'. This pattern of specialization with home imports of labor-intensive goods is maintained throughout the segment $M'D$, which represents the region in which MacDougall's (1960) reasoning applies. Alternatively, if home importables were labor intensive (instead of capital intensive) along FT, $TAMM'D$ would be replaced by a continuously upward-sloping curve (not drawn) through T, according to a similar line of argument.

Notes

The authors are grateful to Jagdish N. Bhagwati, Christopher J. Heady, and Vahid F. Nowshirvani for helpful comments. The authors alone are responsible for any remaining errors or shortcomings. Carlos F. Díaz-Alejandro thanks the National Science Foundation for financially supporting his research under NSF grant SOC 75–04518.
    After this research was completed for the case of capital inflows not large enough to extinguish host-country imports or achieve complete specialization in production, the editor of this journal drew the authors' attention to independent work

by Hamada (1974) and Minabe (1974), who present (among other things) analysis similar to that offered here and who cite a related contribution by Uzawa (1969). This literature also considers cases with zero imports or complete specialization, which subsequently were taken into account here as well, by including some additional discussion.

1. If foreign profits were repatriated in terms of home importables (instead of exportables), the host country would be left with bundle Z' (instead of Z), and home consumption would be at point C_2' (instead of C_2); where point Z' (on line DD') lies directly below P_1, line $Z'C_2'$ (not drawn) has a slope given by the world price ratio, and C_2' (like C_2) lies necessarily southwest of C_0. In general, if foreign profits were repatriated in terms of both goods, the host country would be left with a bundle on line segment ZZ', and home consumption would be at the corresponding point on line segment C_2C_2'. A particular case of interest would arise if foreign profits were repatriated by withdrawing the two goods in the proportion given by the slope of line OO', since this case is analytically similar to having these profits consumed in the host country by the foreigners according to the home pattern of demand.

2. Point A corresponds to the capital inflow just large enough to extinguish home imports, because Mundell's (1957) analysis shows that a tariff-imposing country with zero imports gains from a capital inflow as the domestic product-price ratio approaches the international ratio of commodity prices.

References

Bertrand, T. J., and F. Flatters. 1971. Tariffs, capital accumulation, and immiserizing growth. *Journal of International Economics* 1, 453–460.

Bhagwati, Jagdish N. 1973. The theory of immiserizing growth: Further applications. In Michael B. Connolly and Alexander K. Swoboda, eds., *International Trade and Money*. University of Toronto Press, 45–54.

Hamada, Koichi. 1974. An economic analysis of the duty-free zone. *Journal of International Economics* 4, 225–241.

Johnson, Harry G. 1967. The possibility of income losses from increased efficiency or factor accumulation in the presence of tariffs. *Economic Journal* 77, 151–154.

MacDougall, G. D. A. 1960. The benefits and costs of private investment from abroad: A theoretical approach. *Economic Record* 36, 13–35.

Minabe, Nobuo. 1974. Capital and technology movements and economic welfare. *American Economic Review* 64, 1088–1100.

Mundell, Robert A. 1957. International trade and factor mobility. *American Economic Review* 47, 321–335.

Tan, Augustine H. H. 1969. Immiserizing tariff-induced capital accumulation and technical change. *Malayan Economic Review* 13, 1–7.

Uzawa, H. 1969. Shihon Jiyuka to Kokumin Keizai (Liberalization of foreign investments and the national economy). *Economisuto* 23, 106–122 (in Japanese).

24

Capital Accumulation in the Open Two-Sector Economy

M. Alasdair M. Smith

1. The Basic Model

The model is the standard two-sector model, with one of the outputs being a pure investment good, the other being a pure consumption good.

Production levels of the goods are, respectively, Q_I and Q_C; and I and C denote domestic absorption levels. The investment good is taken as the numeraire, and the price of the consumption good is p. The capital and labour inputs available are K and L; the rental rate on capital is r and the wage rate is w.

A full-employment, perfectly competitive open economy with balanced trade satisfies the following relations:

$$K = a_{KI}Q_I + a_{KC}Q_C, \tag{1}$$

$$L = a_{LI}Q_I + a_{LC}Q_C, \tag{2}$$

$$1 \leqslant ra_{KI} + wa_{LI} \tag{3}$$

with equality if $Q_I > 0$,

$$p \leqslant ra_{KC} + wa_{LC} \tag{4}$$

with equality if $Q_C > 0$,

$$p(C - Q_C) + I - Q_I = 0. \tag{5}$$

Equations (1) and (2) are full-employment conditions; perfect competition requires (3) and (4); and (5) is the statement of balance-of-trade equilibrium. The coefficients a_{MN} measure the amount of input M required in the production of one unit of output Q_N. They are chosen so as to mini-

This paper was originally published in *The Economic Journal* 87, no. 346 (June 1977): 273–282.

mise the cost of production; that is, they minimise $ra_{KN} + wa_{LN}$ subject to $f^N(a_{KN}, a_{LN}) = 1$, where f^N is the constant-returns-to-scale production function of Q_N. Optimal choice of technique is easily shown to give rise to the equations

$$0 = rda_{KN} + wda_{LN}(N = I, C) \tag{6}$$

(which hold trivially in the case of no choice of technique), so that changes in p, r and w must satisfy

$$0 = dra_{KI} + dwa_{LI} \tag{7}$$

if $Q_I > 0$, and

$$dp = dra_{KC} + dwa_{LC} \tag{8}$$

if $Q_C > 0$, these equations being obtained from the total differentiation of (3) and (4) and from (6).

The value of national income is

$$Y = I + pC \tag{9}$$

$$= Q_I + pQ_C \tag{10}$$

$$= rK + wL, \tag{11}$$

where (10) follows from (5), and (11) from (1)–(4). The labour force grows exogenously at the rate n, so steady state requires investment at a level which makes the capital stock grow at the rate n also:

$$I = nK, \tag{12}$$

and from (9), (11) and (12) we have

$$pC = (r - n)K + wL. \tag{13}$$

Taking the total differential of (13) with L constant enables us to compare steady states with different saving rates and different relative prices. Equations (1), (2), (7), and (8) allow the elimination of the input prices:

$$dpC + dpC = (r - n)dK + drK + dwL \tag{14}$$

$$= (r - n)dK + dpQ_C, \tag{15}$$

which implies

$$pdC = (r - n)dK + dp(Q_C - C). \tag{16}$$

This equation plays a central role throughout the paper.

In a closed economy $Q_C = C$, and in an open economy which is so small as to have no influence on its terms of trade $dp/dK = 0$. In either case, (16) implies that across steady states dC/dK has the sign of $(r - n)$, which is the standard "golden rule" result on the effect of capital accumulation on steady state consumption.

In a large open economy, however, a rise in K will lead to an increased net export of the more capital-intensive product, implying an endogenous change in p, so that dC/dK depends not only on $(r - n)$ but also on the "terms of trade effect" $(Q_C - C)dp/dK$.

This fact seems first to have been noted by Bertrand (1975). It may seem paradoxical, for the golden rule is accepted as a result of complete generality. There is, however, an interpretation of the apparent paradox as a standard second-best proposition. Free trade is not the optimal trade policy for a large country. If the optimal trading rule is not applied, there is no reason to suppose that the usual rule for optimal savings will continue to be valid. (Negishi 1972, pp. 174–177, has demonstrated in the case of a small country the converse proposition that in the absence of optimal savings, the free-trade rule for optimal trade no longer holds.) What we should expect, however, is that with an optimum tariff, the standard relationship between consumption and capital accumulation will be restored.

The formal argument is as follows. (The derivation of the optimum tariff follows the lines of the analysis in Caves and Jones 1973, pp. 244–247.) Let net exports of the consumption good be $E_C = Q_C - C$, and let the domestic price of the consumption good be π, which will, in general, be different from the world price p. Relationships (1), (2), (3), (5), (6), and (7) continue to apply, but (4) and (8) hold with p replaced by π, which modified relationships are denoted by (4′) and (8′) below. The value of national income at domestic prices is

$$Y = I + \pi C \tag{17}$$

$$= Q_I + \pi Q_C + (p - \pi)E_C \tag{18}$$

$$= rK + wL + (p - \pi)E_C, \tag{19}$$

using (5), (3), (4′), (1), and (2). Taking differentials for constant K and L and using (7), (8′), (1), and (2) gives

$$dI + \pi dC = -d\pi C + drK + dwL + (dp - d\pi)E_C + (p - \pi)dE_C \tag{20}$$

$$= -d\pi C + d\pi Q_C + (dp - d\pi)E_C + (p - \pi)dE_C \tag{21}$$

$$= dpE_C + (p - \pi)dE_C. \tag{22}$$

The tariff is at its optimal level if the value of income is maximised at domestic prices, which implies $dI + \pi dC = 0$, so that

$$dpE_C + (p - \pi)dE_C = 0, \tag{23}$$

an optimum tariff formula which may be more familiar in the form

$$\pi = p + E_C \frac{dp}{dE_C} = \frac{d(pE_C)}{dE_C}, \tag{24}$$

showing the equality of the domestic price ratio and the slope of the foreign offer curve.

In steady state (12) continues to hold, but (17) and (19) imply that (13) is replaced by

$$\pi C = (r - n)K + wL + (p - \pi)E_C \tag{25}$$

so that across steady states

$$\pi dC = -d\pi C + drK + dwL + dpE_C - d\pi E_C + (r - n)dK$$
$$+ (p - \pi)dE_C \tag{26}$$
$$= (r - n)dK \tag{27}$$

from (21), (22), and (23).

Recalling that the optimum tariff in a small economy is zero, (27) allows us to state a general result that in the comparison of steady states in a open economy *imposing an optimum tariff*, dC/dK has the sign of $(r - n)$.

2. Comparative Dynamics: Capital-Labour Ratio Constant

The equation (16) can form the basis of an analysis of the effects of trade in a two-sector economy under alternative assumptions about capital accumulation. In this section I assume that the capital-labour ratio is the same in trade as in autarky.

In the short run, the inputs K and L are in fixed supply. It is a standard proposition of the two-sector model of production that a rise in the relative price of one good induces an increase in its production. This is usually shown as a shift along the transformation curve. A formal proof uses (1)–(4) and the fact that input coefficients are chosen to minimise costs to establish the inequality

$$(p^1 - p^2)(Q_C^1 - Q_C^2) \geqslant 0, \tag{28}$$

which is the desired result, where 1 denotes the situation before and 2 the situation after the relative price change.

Let the world price of the consumption good be p^T and the autarky price be p^A. If initially $p^T > p^A$, so the country has a comparative advantage in the consumption good, then Q_C rises above Q_C^A and Q_I falls below Q_I^A. But if we wish the economy to remain in steady state with the same K/L ratio, (12) requires that I remains the same, so that $Q_I - I$ becomes negative and $Q_C - C$ positive, from (5). Hence (16) with $dK = 0$ shows that as p rises from p^A to p^T, *if* the economy invests just enough to remain in steady state, then consumption is increased by trade. This case is illustrated in figure 24.1.

The same is true, *a fortiori*, if the economy were to impose an optimum tariff. For, if π^0 and p^0 are the domestic and foreign prices when the optimum tariff is imposed, then if the country is a net exporter of consumption goods, it must be the case that $p^0 > \pi^0 > p^A$, as illustrated in figure 24.2. Equation (26) implies that with K and L constant

$$\pi dC = dpE_C + (p - \pi)dE_C \tag{29}$$

and in the movement from autarky to the optimum tariff equilibrium p rises, E_C rises, and $p - \pi$ becomes positive, so that the economy attains steady state with a permanently increased level of consumption.

The fact that these new equilibria, attainable immediately as a result of trade, are steady states and therefore sustainable into the future is a clear

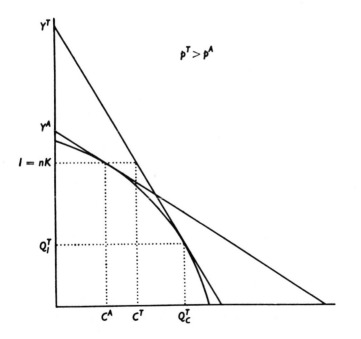

Figure 24.1

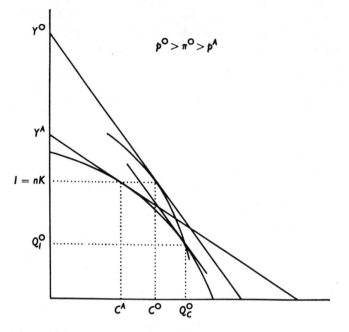

Figure 24.2

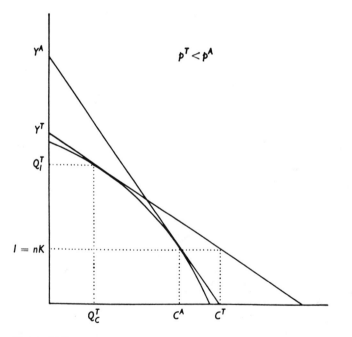

Figure 24.3

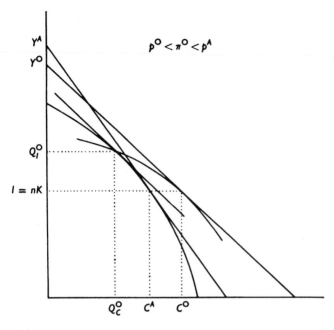

Figure 24.4

indication of the existence of gains from trade. Consumption at every point in time will be higher than on the autarky steady state path.

The alternative case in which $p^T < p^A$ can be analysed similarly. The comparative advantage in the investment good leads Q_C to fall below Q_C^A and Q_I to rise above Q_I^A. $Q_C - C$ becomes negative because $Q_I - I$ becomes positive. Again equation (16) with $dK = 0$ shows that if the economy is to remain in steady state, consumption will rise, and, again consumption rises also in the case of an optimum tariff being imposed. These two cases are shown in figures 24.3 and 24.4.

3. Comparative Dynamics: Saving Rate Constant

The effect of trade on steady state consumption if the saving rate is the same in trade as in autarky is easy to deduce from the results of the previous section. Again equation (16) is the key, though now it is used in a different way. What I do here is make more precise the argument sketched out in Smith (1976, sec. 7) and extend it to the case of a large economy. The first step is to compare the steady state analysed in the previous section with the steady state with the same saving rate as the autarky equilibrium.

In contrast with the previous section, the direction of comparative advantage is important. If $p^T > p^A$, then, in the obvious notation, for fixed K and L

$$Y^A = I^A + p^A C^A < I^A + p^T C^A < r^T K + w^T L = I^T + p^T C^T = Y^T, \quad (30)$$

where (30) follows from the same type of argument as establishes (28). The fact that $Y^A < Y^T$ means that if, as in section 2, I were to be held constant, the saving rate would be reduced from $s = I^A/Y^A = nK^A/Y^A$ to $s' = nK^A/Y^T$. The free trade steady state with the same capital-labour ratio as the autarky steady state has a lower saving rate.

If, therefore, when trade opens up the saving rate is kept at s, capital will accumulate faster than the labour growth rate. The economy will move towards a steady state with a higher value of K/L than the steady state of section 2.

When an optimum tariff is imposed, $(p^0 - \pi^0)E_C$ is positive. If $\pi^0 > p^A$, (17)–(19), and the type of argument used to establish (30) imply, in the obvious notation, that

$$Y^A < I^A + \pi^0 C^A < r^0 K + w^0 L < r^0 K + w^0 L + (p^0 - \pi^0)E_C = Y^0. \quad (31)$$

Now, equation (16) (or in the case of the optimum tariff, equation 27) can be used to compare the open steady state with saving rate s' with the open steady state with saving rate s. Accumulation will raise consumption if r exceeds n, in a small economy or in a large economy imposing an optimum tariff. Consumption falls if r is less than n.

In a large open economy with free trade, there is a terms-of-trade effect that must be taken into account, and its sign will depend on which good is the more capital intensive.

Conversely, if $p^T < p^A$, $Y^T < Y^A$ in the short run, and there will be decumulation, which in a small country equation (16) tells us will lower or raise consumption as $(r - n)$ is positive or negative. In a large free trade economy, there is again a terms-of-trade effect to be taken additionally into account.

In a large economy imposing an optimum tariff for which $\pi^0 < p^A$, Y^0 may be larger or smaller than Y^A. The gain from the tariff may outweigh the effect on the value of income of the shift along the transformation curve. Then, (27) shows that dC/dK depends only on $(r - n)$, but we cannot tell whether K will rise or fall.

Figures 24.1 through 24.4 show the effect of trade on the value of income under the assumption about saving made in section 2. The corresponding diagrams for the case of fixed saving rates would be slightly different but would show qualitatively similar changes in Y.

What I have done so far is to compare the steady state with the same saving rate as in autarky and the steady state with the same capital-labour ratio as in autarky. To compare the autarky steady state with saving rate s and the trade steady state with the same saving rate, we have to put the above argument together with the analysis of section 2.

Before listing the results, one more observation must be made. The terms of trade effect may obviously outweigh the effect of capital accumulation or decumulation, especially if $(r - n)$ is close to zero. But it cannot outweigh the effect, analysed in section 2, of the initial opening up of trade. This is because, as Deardorff (1974) has shown, if the autarky steady state is stable (a necessary condition for this type of comparative dynamics to be meaningful), then the direction of comparative advantage will not reversed by capital accumulation or decumulation. Equation (16) implies that when we compare p^A and the *final* value of p^T the second term must be positive.

Thus we obtain the following results:

1. In a small economy with initial comparative advantage in the consumption good, the initial gain in consumption represented by the possibility of immediately attaining steady state with saving rate s' is reinforced by the subsequent effects of capital accumulation if r exceeds n throughout the transition towards the asymptotic steady state.
2. In a small economy with initial comparative advantage in the investment good, the initial consumption gain may, if r exceeds n, be counteracted by the effects of capital decumulation.
3. In a large free trade economy, the effects of terms of trade changes may reinforce or counteract the effects of capital accumulation or decumulation, but, if the autarky steady state was stable, the total effect is as in 1 or 2 above.
4. In a large open economy imposing an optimum tariff, with initial comparative advantage in the consumption good, the effects are as in 1 above.
5. In a large open economy imposing an optimum tariff, with initial comparative advantage in the investment good, the initial consumption gain may be followed by either capital accumulation or decumulation, the effects of this depending on the sign of $(r - n)$.

These results extend somewhat the results of Johnson (1971), Vanek (1971), Deardorff (1973), Togan (1975), and Bertrand (1975).

4. Comparative Dynamics: Profit Rate Constant

I turn now to the final comparison: trade and autarky steady states which have the same profit rate. One special feature of this case is that, because of the factor price equalisation theorem, complete specialisation is likely to occur, but the basic relations of the model, we have seen, continue to apply.

Suppose that when trade opens up the country has a comparative advantage in the more capital-intensive product. (I assume no factor-intensity reversals.) We have seen that one short-run effect is to change the value of income, but there will also be a change in factor prices: the profit rate will rise and the wage rate fall. This is the Stolper-Samuelson theorem, which is easily confirmed from (7) and (8). To move from this steady state to a steady state with the lower, autarky, profit rate, a rise in the capital-labour ratio is required. If the country is small so that the world price is given, the Rybczynski theorem (which follows from equations 1 and 2) implies that there will be increased production of the more capital-intensive good (and it is clear from equations 3 and 4 that there will be complete specialisation if the rest of the world has the same technology).

If the country is large and does not impose an optimum tariff, the eventual equilibrium price will be different from the initial world price, but the direction of comparative advantage must be the same and the above argument still holds.

The final effect on consumption levels is deduced by using (16) to compare the autarky steady state and the free trade steady state with the same profit rate. The second term in (16) must be positive: it encompasses the initial effect of the opening-up of trade and the terms of trade effect, if any. The first term has the sign of $(r - n)$.

The optimum tariff case is rather like the small-country case. From (29) we have seen that the opening-up of trade with the imposition of an optimum tariff raises the level of C. If the domestic price π^0 is such as to induce increased production of the capital-intensive product, then, as above, there will be capital accumulation, and from (27), its effect has the sign of $(r - n)$.

Thus, if the target profit rate satisfies $r \geq n$, both the free trade steady state and the optimum tariff steady state have higher consumption levels than the autarky steady state with the same profit rate. If $r < n$, the total effect on consumption is ambiguous.

A similar argument applies to the case where the country has its comparative advantage in the more labour-intensive product, but now trade leads to decumulation so that it is when $r \leq n$ that trade leads to increased steady state consumption, while if $r > n$, the total effect is of ambiguous sign.

In Smith (1976, sec. 6), I drew a distinction between the "static" and "intertemporal" effects of trade—the "static" effects being the effects associated with the price changes between autarky and trade, the "intertemporal" effects being the effects of changes in the capital stock. In the model presented here, this distinction is neatly illustrated in equation (16) where the first term is the "intertemporal" effect, the second is the "static" effect. This model also shows the possibility of an alternative dichotomy, between the short-run effect analysed in section 2 and the capital accumulation effects analysed above.

5. Two Comments

1. Since at several points in sections 3 and 4 the possibility arises of trade reducing steady state consumption, even when $r \geqslant n$ and when trade policy is optimal, it should be emphasised that this is not to be taken as contradicting the usual gains from trade propositions. Section 2 has shown us that trade always implies a potential Pareto improvement in the sense that consumption at each point in time is increased. Section 3 and 4 show that depending on the saving objective, actual consumption may be unequally distributed over time. It is easy to confirm that when $r \geqslant n$, trade can reduce steady state consumption only by boosting consumption in the short run. We have the usual result that trade benefits some and harms others: here the "some" are the early time periods of the open economy, the "others" are the later time periods.

2. The basic model of section 1 is easy to generalise to more than two sectors, and the result of section 2 is also clearly a general result; but the comparative dynamics results of sections 3 and 4 do not generalise. (In Smith 1976, I have shown how some fundamental aspects of this model carry over to input-output and vintage technologies, but how, similarly, only the simplest forms of such technologies give determinate comparative dynamic results.) The model is therefore to be taken as providing illustrative and, perhaps, instructive examples of how trade may affect the intertemporal allocation of consumption rather than precise predictions about the real world.

6. Conclusions

A glance at sections 3 and 4 will show the impossibility of giving a brief summary of results, and even there a complete list of possible cases is not given. The fact is that there is, in a way typical of trade theory, a range of different cases to be considered. My aim here has not been to attempt to present a simple and memorable taxonomy of results. It has been to present methods by which results can be obtained and thereby make the theory of trade and growth more accessible. There are several features of those methods worth recalling in conclusion:

1. The equation (16) is a crucial relationship, allowing one to discuss the effects of price changes, both exogenous and endogenous, and of capital accumulation, under alternative saving assumptions.
2. The steady state which is immediately attainable on the opening up of trade is an important benchmark in the analysis.
3. Although the terms of trade effect of capital accumulation in large economies seems at first likely to complicate the analysis, it turns out that this effect is always dominated by the effects of the initial price change resulting from the opening up of trade, and also that the analysis is easily extended to the case of the imposition of an optimum tariff, in which case the terms of trade effect is eliminated.

Note

I am grateful for helpful comments on an earlier version of this paper from John Black and John Martin.

References

Bertrand, T. J. 1975. The gains from trade: An analysis of steady state solutions in an open economy. *Quarterly Journal of Economics* 89 (4), 556–568.

Caves, R. E., and Jones, R. W. 1973. *World Trade and Payments*. Boston: Little Brown.

Deardorff, A. V. 1973. The gains from trade in and out of steady-state growth. *Oxford Economic Papers*, N. S., 25 (2), 173–191.

Deardorff, A. V. 1974. Trade reversals and growth stability. *Journal of International Economics* 4 (1), 83–90.

Johnson, H. G. 1971. Trade and growth: A geometrical exposition. *Journal of International Economics* 1 (1), 83–102.

Jones, R. W. 1965. The structure of simple general equilibrium models. *Journal of Political Economy* 73 (6), 557–572.

Negishi, T. 1972. *General Equilibrium Theory and International Trade*. Amsterdam: North Holland.

Smith, M.A.M. 1976. Trade, growth and consumption in alternative models of capital accumulation. *Journal of International Economics* 6 (4), 371–384.

Togan, S. 1975. The gains from international trade in the context of a growing economy. *Journal of International Economics* 5 (3), 229–238.

Vanek, J. 1971. Economic growth and international trade in pure theory. *Quarterly Journal of Economics* 85 (3), 377–390.

25

**Investment, the
Two-Sector Model,
and Trade in Debt
and Capital Goods**

Stanley Fischer and
Jacob A. Frenkel

The two-sector model of economic growth has frequently been used to analyze the growth process of an open economy. Two different sets of assumptions have been made about the structure of trade. One specification allows for trade in both consumption and investment goods (e.g., Oniki and Uzawa 1965 and Johnson 1971). The alternative specification allows for the existence of international financial markets and assumes that there is trade in consumption goods and securities, but not in investment goods themselves (e.g., Frenkel and Fischer 1972 and Fischer and Frenkel 1974a, 1974b).

The main difficulty in modeling trade in both investment goods *and* securities using a two-sector model of an economy for which the terms of trade are fixed is that if a country can trade in both securities and investment goods, then it is a matter of indifference what its capital stock is. Its income will be the same at all times—so long as it is not specialized—whether it acquires income streams from abroad by buying securities or whether it owns physical capital.

This paper presents a two-sector model of a small growing economy that trades in both investment goods and securities as well as consumption goods. The key innovation is the specification of a demand function for investment goods, based on an adjustment cost formulation in which more rapid rates of investment reduce the rate of return to capital. The introduction of the investment demand function not only allows for simultaneous trade in investment goods and securities but also breaks the familiar link between the stability of the model and relative factor intensities in production: the model introduced here is not unstable even if investment goods are more capital intensive in production than consumption goods.

This paper was originally published in *Journal of International Economics* 2 (August 1972): 211–233. The present version includes a shorter introduction and omits section 6 of the original article, which analyzes the composition of the trade account.

The model is used to study the dynamics of capital accumulation and the various balance of payments accounts. Particular stress is laid on the interaction of foreign borrowing, debt service, and domestic capital accumulation.

The relationship we posit between the rate of investment and the production possibilities of the economy is introduced informally in section 1. In section 2 we discuss the production technology and derive the demand function for investment goods; the complete model is presented in section 3; the steady state of the system is considered in section 4; the dynamics of the capital stock and trade accounts are discussed in section 5, with concluding remarks in section 6.

1. Investment and the Transformation Frontier

The basic innovation of this paper is the positing of a relationship between the rate of investment at each instant and the position of the production possibility frontier at that instant. Since the nature of this relationship is not immediately obvious from our formulation of the production functions for the two sectors (in section 2), we provide an informal discussion of it in this section.

We distinguish between investment—the installaton of capital goods—and the production of investment goods. Denote gross investment per capita by $(\dot{k} + nk)$, the production of investment goods by Q_I, and that of consumption goods by Q_c. Given the capital stock at any moment of time, and neoclassical production functions in each sector, we obtain a concave-to-the origin production possibility frontier (PPF), such as any of the frontiers shown in figure 25.1.

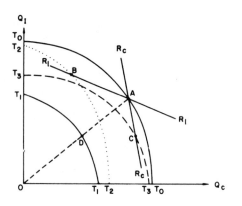

Figure 25.1

We assume that the position of the PPF in figure 25.1 depends on the rate of gross investment per capita in the economy. In particular, let $T_0 T_0$ be the frontier, at a given level of the capital stock, at which there is zero gross investment. At any higher level of investment, the PPF will lie inside $T_0 T_0$, and the more rapid is investment, the closer to the origin is the PPF assumed to be. The basic notion these shifts reflect is that the process of investment disturbs the regular production processes.[1]

Our formulation is, however, specific: the PPF map, as a function of the rate of investment, is assumed to be homothetic. That is, as between any rates of investment, corresponding to, say, $T_0 T_0$ and $T_1 T_1$, the ratio of the distance of the two frontiers from the origin along every ray through the origin is assumed to be the same. For obvious reasons, we call this "Hicks' neutral adjustment costs."[2]

2. The Rate of Return on Capital and the Demand for Investment Goods

The production functions in the two sectors are

$$Q_c = \alpha F_c(K_c, L_c), \tag{1}$$

$$Q_I = \alpha F_I(K_I, L_I) \tag{2}$$

where K_i and L_i are the inputs of capital and labor in each sector, and α is an efficiency factor, which determines the shrinking of the PPF. The production function is linearly homogeneous in its arguments, with diminishing marginal returns to each factor. The same production functions, with $\alpha = 1$, exist in the rest of the world, although in fact nothing substantive in the paper depends on having the same production functions.

In per capita terms,

$$q_c = \frac{k - k_I}{k_c - k_I} f_c(k_c), \tag{3}$$

$$q_I = \alpha \frac{k_c - k}{k_c - k_I} f_I(k_I), \tag{4}$$

where $q_i \equiv Q_i/L$, $k_i \equiv K_i/L_i$, $k \equiv K/L$, and $f_i \equiv F_i/L_i$. The small country assumption implies that p_k, the relative price of capital goods, is given to this economy, as is i, the world interest rate. This interest rate is taken to be the return on equities issued abroad and is equal to the world rental rate on capital, $r(p_k)$, divided by p_k. The rental rate on capital is determined by the world production technology, which is given by (3) and (4) with $\alpha = 1$.

We consider now the rate of return on capital in the domestic economy, ρ, as a function of α, the efficiency factor, and k, the per capita capital stock, leaving aside for the moment the consequences of any differences between the domestic and world rates of return. The relationship between ρ, α, and k depends on whether the economy is producing both goods or whether it is specialized in the production of only one of the goods. In the nonspecialized region, we shall compare a situation where α is greater than unity (in the domestic economy) with a situation where α is equal to unity (in the world economy). The higher is α, the greater the *effective* amounts of capital and labor in the economy though the overall capital—labor ratio is unaffected by changes in α. Thus capital-labor ratios in each industry will be the same as they are in the world economy, and factor payments per *effective* unit of capital and labor will be the same as they are in the world economy. However, the rental rate per *physical* until of capital and the wage rate per *physical* unit of labor will be higher in the domestic than in the world economy. Accordingly, the rental rate per physical unit of capital will be higher the greater is α. The return to be obtained by investing domestically one unit of capital, costing p_k in the world market, will be an increasing function of α and will exceed i, the world interest rate, so long as α exceeds unity.

Thus ρ is an increasing function of α in the nonspecialized region; it is also clear that ρ does not depend on k, so long as the economy is not specialized, since the economy is free to adjust the scale of operation of the two sectors by moving along a Rybczynski line.

The relationship between ρ, α and k is slightly different in regions of specialization. Suppose that only the investment good is being produced. Then the per capita output of the investment good is

$$q_1 = \alpha f_1(k) \tag{5}$$

with the rate of return on physical capital

$$\frac{\partial q_1}{\partial k} = \alpha f_1'(k). \tag{6}$$

By differentiating (6) will respect to α and k, we obtain the effects of changes in these variables on the rate of return:

$$\frac{\partial^2 q_1}{\partial k \partial \alpha} = f_1'(k) > 0, \tag{7}$$

$$\frac{\partial^2 q_1}{\partial k^2} = \alpha f_1''(k) < 0. \tag{8}$$

Thus increases in the efficiency factor increase the rate of return on physical capital, while increases in the capital stock reduce the return. Similar relationships hold where only the consumption good is produced.

Summarizing the above discussion, we have the domestic rate of return on physical capital, ρ, as a function of α and k:

$$\rho = \rho(\alpha, k), \quad \rho_1 > 0, \quad \rho_2 = 0, \quad \underline{k} \leqslant k \leqslant \bar{k},$$

$$\rho_1 > 0, \quad \rho_2 < 0 \quad \text{otherwise,}$$

$$(9)$$

where ρ_i is the partial derivative of $\rho(\ )$ with respect to its ith argument and $\underline{k}$ and $\bar{k}$ are the lower and upper specialization points, respectively.

Further, in the nonspecialized region, when $\alpha = 1$ and accordingly the efficiency of domestic and foreign factors is the same, equation (10) must be satisifed:

$$\rho(1, k) = i, \quad \underline{k} \leqslant k \leqslant \bar{k}. \tag{10}$$

As discussed in section 1 above, the efficiency factor, α, is assumed to be a decreasing function of the per capita rate of gross investment:

$$\alpha = \alpha(\dot{k} + nk), \quad \alpha' < 0. \tag{11}$$

We assume further that there are positive values of per capita investment at which α exceeds unity.

The demand for investment goods is now readily derived. So long as the domestic rate of return on capital exceeds the world interest rate, i, there will be an incentive to borrow to finance purchase and installation of investment goods. At each instant, investment will be desired at that rate which makes the domestic return on capital equal to the world return. In the nonspecialized region this will be achieved when α is unity (from (10)). In general, we have

$$\rho(\alpha(\dot{k} + nk), k) = i \tag{12}$$

So that the demand for gross investment per capita—which, given access to the world securities market, it assumed always to be satisfied—is

$$\dot{k} + nk = \phi(k, i), \quad \phi_1 = 0, \quad \phi_2 < 0, \quad \underline{k} \leqslant k \leqslant \bar{k},$$

$$\phi_1 < 0, \quad \phi_2 < 0 \quad \text{otherwise,}$$

$$(13)$$

where ϕ_i is the partial derivative of $\phi(\ )$ with respect to its ith argument.

From the gross investment demand function we obtain the equation describing the behavior of the capital stock through time:

$$\dot{k} = \phi(k, i) - nk. \tag{14}$$

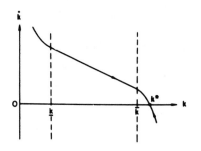

Figure 25.2

This function is illustrated in figure 25.2. Within the nonspecialized region, α is constant at unity, and the locus relating $\dot{k}$ to k is linear with a slope of $(-n)$. Outside this region the locus is steeper as diminishing returns on capital force continuously increases in α, the efficiency factor, to maintain the rate of return on capital constant. We have indicated k^*, the steady state capital stock, as being in the region $k > \bar{k}$ purely for expositional reason—there is no reason why k^* should not lie in either of the other regions.

Notice that the differential equation for $\dot{k}$, (14), is qualitatively a special case of the differential equation for $\dot{k}$ in the closed two-sector model with consumption goods more capital intensive (or the open two-sector model with no trade in capital goods and the usual factor intensity assumption)—but the link between investment and the output of investment goods has been broken. In particular, the derivative $\partial \dot{k}/\partial k$, so crucial to stability, does not depend on the factor intensity assumption.

3. The Model

We now set out the supply and demand functions and the balance of payments accounts for this economy. The production and supply relations depend on the capital stock, on α, and on the (fixed) relative price of capital.

Given that α is unity in the nonspecialized region, the per capita supply functions in that region can be written as they are in the standard two-sector model:

$$q_c = q_c(k, p_k), \quad (k_c - k_1)\frac{\partial q_c}{\partial k} > 0, \quad \frac{\partial q_c}{\partial p_k} < 0 \tag{15}$$

$$\underline{k} \leqslant k \leqslant \bar{k}.$$

$$q_1 = q_1(k, p_k), \quad (k_c - k_1)\frac{\partial q_1}{\partial k} < 0, \quad \frac{\partial q_1}{\partial p_k} > 0 \tag{16}$$

The effects of increases in the capital stock on the outputs of the two sectors depend on the factor intensities (the Rybczynski theorem).

In the specialized regions, the supply functions are

$$q_c = \alpha f_c(k), \quad if (k_c - k_l)(k - \bar{k}) > 0,$$

$$= 0, \qquad if (k_c - k_l)(k - \bar{k}) < 0, \tag{17}$$

$$q_l = \alpha f_l(k) \quad if (k_l - k_c)(k - \bar{k}) > 0,$$

$$= 0, \qquad if (k_l - k_c)(k - \bar{k}) < 0, \tag{18}$$

subject to

$$\frac{\partial q_c}{\partial k} = \alpha f_c'(k) = r, \quad \text{if } q_c > 0 \text{ and } q_l = 0, \tag{19}$$

$$\frac{\partial q_l}{\partial k} = \alpha f_l'(k) = i, \quad \text{if } q_l > 0 \text{ and } q_c = 0, \tag{20}$$

so that

$$q_c = \frac{p_k i}{f_c'(k)} f_c(k), \quad \text{if } q_c > 0 \text{ and } q_l = 0, \tag{21}$$

$$q_l = \frac{i}{f_l'(k)} f_l(k), \quad \text{if } q_l > 0 \text{ and } q_c = 0. \tag{22}$$

The expressions on the right-hand side of (17) and (18) indicate that when the overall capital labor ratio is below $\underline{k}$, the entire capital stock is employed in whichever sector has the lower capital intensity, and similarly when $k > \bar{k}$, the capital stock is employed in the industry with the greater capital intensity. Equations (19) and (20) provide a relationship between α and k which must be satisfied if there is specialization—it is the requirement that the domestic rate of return on capital be the same as the world return—and substitution into (17) and (18) gives the "reduced form" production functions (21)–(22) in the specialized regions.

Our basic production and supply relations are thus (15) and (16) in the nonspecialized region and (21) and (22) in the specialized regions.[3]

The wage is the residual of output per capita after payments to capital. It is clear from (21) and (22) that as capital increases over time and α is appropriately adjusted through investment behavior, the output of the good produced increases. In addition, the wage rate in the specialized region, which is

$$v = p_j \alpha [f_j(k) - k f_j'(k)], \quad j = I, c,$$

$$p_l = p_k, p_c = 1, \tag{23}$$

is an increasing function of k. Thus outside the nonspecialized region, in which the wage rate is constant at the world rate, the real wage increases with the capital stock.

On the demand side we assume, for convenience, a constant savings ratio:

$$c^d = (1 - s)y, \tag{24}$$

where y is per capita income. Investment demand is given by (13), repeated here:

$$(\dot{k} + nk)^d = \phi(k, i). \tag{13}$$

Income in turn consists of payments to factors located in the economy, plus interest payments (in terms of the consumption good) on net ownership of foreign securities, iz:

$$y = rk + v(k) + iz, \tag{25}$$

where r is the rental rate on capital and v is the wage rate.

Saving is equal to the value of the accumulation of assets per capita, so that

$$sy = p_k(\dot{k} + nk)^d + (\dot{z} + nz)^d, \tag{26}$$

where $\dot{z} + nz = \dot{Z}/L$ is the rate of accumulation of foreign securities, per capita. It is assumed that all demands are satisfied at each instant. The trade balance surplus per capita, b_T, is given by

$$b_T = q_c - c^d + p_k[q_1 - (\dot{k} + nk)]$$
$$= q_c + p_k q_1 - [c + p_k(\dot{k} + nk)]. \tag{27}$$

It is the difference between the value of domestic output and the value of domestic demand for commodities (consumption plus investment).

The service account surplus, b_s, is earnings on net holdings of foreign securities:

$$b_s = iz. \tag{28}$$

The capital account deficit, b_c, must be equal to the surplus in the current account, and is accordingly

$$b_c = b_T + b_s$$
$$= q_c + p_k q_1 + iz - [c + p_k(\dot{k} + nk)]$$
$$= sy - p_k(\dot{k} + nk),$$

so, using (26),

$$b_c = \dot{z} + nz. \tag{29}$$

That is, the capital account deficit is the difference between saving and investment and is equal to net imports of foreign securities

4. The Steady State

In the steady state the capital stock is constant at a level k^*, determined by investment behavior (equation 14). Corresponding to that level of the capital stock is the steady state wage rate. If the steady state capital stock is within the nonspecialized region, the wage rate will be the same as the world wage rate. Outside the nonspecialized region the steady state wage rate is given by (23).

In the steady state, savings is just sufficient to maintain the stock of nonhuman assets per capita constant. Thus, from (26),

$$s[rk^* + v(k^*) + iz^*] = n[p_k k^* + z^*],$$

$$p_k k^* + z^* = \frac{sv(k^*)}{n - is}. \tag{30}$$

Thus a necessary and sufficient condition for steady state wealth and income to be positive is that $n - is > 0$.

The steady state level of net holdings of foreign securities, in turn, is

$$z^* = \frac{sv(k^*)}{n - is} - p_k k^*$$

or

$$z^* = \frac{s[v(k^*) + rk^*] - np_k k^*}{n - is} \tag{31}$$

Thus, if savings out of steady state *output* exceed steady state investment, net holdings of foreign securities will be positive, and conversely.

In the steady state the capital account deficit is nz^*, and the service account surplus is iz^*. The trade account surplus is, therefore, $(n - i)z^*$. According, whether the capital account will be in deficit or surplus (and the service account correspondingly in surplus or deficit) in the steady state depents solely on whether savings out of steady state *output* exceed or fall short of steady state investment. If, in the steady state, the savings out of domestic output exceed domestic investment, the country will be a net creditor with a capital account deficit and service account surplus. If the country is a creditor, then the steady state of the trade account depends on the relationship between i and n; if, as we assume henceforth, $i > n$, a creditor country will have a deficit on trade account.

5. Dynamics of the Capital Stock and International Accounts

Figure 25.3 is the basic diagram used in analyzing the behavior of the trade account, the service account, the capital account, and the balance of indebtedness through time. In figure 25.3 we show the loci in (z, k) space along which the various accounts balance.

The Net Creditor Position
From equations (13), (25), and (26) we derive equation (32) for the change in per capita holdings of foreign securities:

$$\dot{z} = s(rk + v) - p_k \phi(k, i) - (n - is)z. \tag{32}$$

The rate of change of holdings of securities, per capita, $(\dot{Z}/L)$ is equal to savings minus investment; (32) follows by recognizing that $(\dot{Z}/L = \dot{z} + nz)$. Since, given p_k and i, $\dot{z}$ is a function only of z and k, we can draw the locus on which $(\dot{z} = 0)$—per capita holdings of foreign securities are constant—in figure 25.3. The slope of that locus is

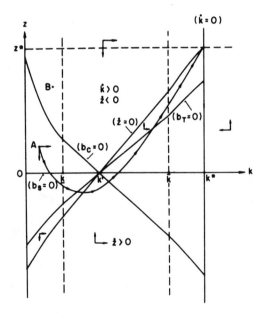

Figure 25.3

$$\left. \frac{dz}{dk} \right|_{\dot{z}=0} = -\frac{\partial \dot{z}/\partial k}{\partial \dot{z}/\partial z} = \frac{s[r + (dv/dk)] - p_k(\partial \phi/\partial k)}{n - is} > 0. \tag{33}$$

The slope is positive, since dv/dk and $(-\partial \phi/\partial k)$ are both nonnegative, while the existence of a steady state implies $n - is > 0$.

Note that in the nonspecialized region both dv/dk and $\partial \phi/\partial k$ are zero, and thus, the $(\dot{z} = 0)$ locus is linear with a slope of $sr/(n - is)$. From (32) it is seen that the intersection of the $(\dot{z} = 0)$ locus with the k axis occurs at that k—call it k'—for which $s(rk' + v) = p_k\phi(k', i)$. At any point above the $(\dot{z} = 0)$ locus, $\dot{z} < 0$, and below the $(\dot{z} = 0)$ locus, $\dot{z} > 0$. Note that k' is not necessarily in the nonspecialized region.

The Trade Account
The trade account is balanced when the value of output $(rk + v)$ equals the the sum of consumption demand $[(1 - s)y]$ and investment demand $(p_k\phi)$. Thus (using equation 25) the condition for a balanced trade account is

$$(1 - s)iz = s(rk + v) - p_k\phi(k, i). \tag{34}$$

Accordingly, the slope of the $(b_T = 0)$ locus—the locus on which the trade account is balanced—is

$$\left. \frac{dz}{dk} \right|_{b_T=0} = \frac{s[r + (dv/dk)] - p_k(\partial \phi/\partial k)}{(1 - s)i} > 0. \tag{35}$$

By considerations similar to those involved in the discussion of the $(\dot{z} = 0)$ locus, the $(b_T = 0)$ locus is linear in the nonspecialized region with a slope of $sr/(1 - s)i > 0$. Under the assumption that $i > n$, the $(b_T = 0)$ locus is flatter than the $(\dot{z} = 0)$ locus. Note also that its intersection with the k axis occurs at the same value of k ($k = k'$) for which the $(\dot{z} = 0)$ locus intersects the k axis. Since in the specialized regions dv/dk and $[-(\partial \phi/\partial k)]$ are positive, both the $(\dot{z} = 0)$ and $(b_T = 0)$ loci are steeper in those regions than they are in the nonspecialized region.

At any point above the trade balance locus, $(b_T = 0)$ income is higher than it is on the locus, and consumption demand is increased, causing a trade balance deficit. Thus above the $(b_T = 0)$ locus, $b_T < 0$, and below that locus, $b_T > 0$.

While the path of the balance of trade does not depend on the relative factor intensities in production, the *composition* of the trade account as between consumption and investments goods does depend on the relative factor intensities. (For details see Fischer and Frenkel 1972, sec. 6.)

The Capital Account

The deficit in the capital account is the excess of savings over investment. The capital account accordingly balances when

$$s(rk + v + iz) - p_k\phi(k, i) = 0. \tag{36}$$

We can now show the locus on which there is balance in the capital account in figure 25.3. It has the slope

$$\frac{dz}{dk}\bigg|_{b_c=0} = -\frac{s[r + (dv/dk)] - p_k(\partial\phi/\partial k)}{is} < 0. \tag{37}$$

This locus has a negative slope because increases in the capital stock tend to increase the excess of savings over investment; decreases in z are required to reduce savings to maintain balance in the capital account when k rises.

In the nonspecialized region the ($b_c = 0$) locus is linear with a slope of $-r/i = -p_k$; its slope is steeper in the specialized regions. Its intersection with the k axis also occurs at the point k'. For any point above the ($b_c = 0$) locus, saving exceeds investment, and there is a capital account deficit, while below the locus, $b_c < 0$.

The Service Account

The surplus in the service account is simply iz, and thus the ($b_s = 0$) locus is the k axis along which $z = 0$. Obviously there is a service account surplus above the k axis and a deficit below it.

The Accumulation of Capital

We have already discussed the $\dot{k}$ equation (14). There is a unique value of k, k^*, at which the per capita capital stock is stationary. In terms of figure 25.3, k^* may be anywhere on the k axis—in particular it could be either less than or greater than k'. If k^* exceeds k'—which is the case we study— the country will be a net creditor in the steady state.

Since, from (14) and (32), $\partial\dot{k}/\partial k < 0$ and $\partial\dot{z}/\partial z < 0$ (and also $\partial\dot{k}/\partial z = 0$), the system is stable in k and z. Hence, the directions of the arrows in figure 25.3.

Consider now a time path for the economy starting from initial conditions A. At point A, the economy is a net creditor, the trade account is in deficit, and the capital and service accounts are in surplus. Savings fall short of investment so that the economy exports securities, reaching a point where its net creditor position is zero. At that point of time, the service account is balanced, and the surplus in the capital account equals the deficit in the trade account. As the process continues, the economy becomes a net debtor. The cumulative debt increases, and the deficit in the trade account

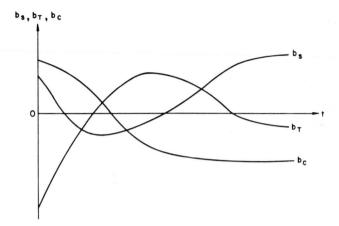

Figure 25.4

decreases monotonically. When the trade account balances, the deficit in the service account equals the surplus in the capital account, and the country's net debtor position continues to rise until it reaches its maximum —the point in time at which $\dot{z} = 0$—and the deficit in the service account also reaches a maximum.[4] From then onward the capital account surplus decreases and eventually (in the case shown) becomes a deficit. Similarly, the service account eventually switches back to, and remains in, surplus.

In the path starting at A the trade account is shown switching only twice, and the economy reaches a steady state with a trade account deficit. In general, although the trade account cannot switch more than twice in the nonspecialized region, it may switch from surplus to deficit and vice versa several times in the specialized regions, unless there are restrictions on the production functions and the $\alpha(\ )$ function.[5] For example, given Cobb-Douglas production functions and $\alpha'' \geqslant 0$ (see equation 11), there can in fact be no more than two switches, as in path A. Figure 25.4 describes the time path of the various accounts as implied by path A of figure 25.3.

6. Concluding Remarks

The purpose of the present paper has been to construct a simple model of a small open two-sector economy which includes, on the one hand, trade in both consumption and investment goods and, on the other, trade in securities. Models, including trade in both consumption and investment goods but not in securities, exist (see, e.g., Oniki and Uzawa 1965 and Johnson 1971), as do models with trade in consumption goods and securities (see Frenkel 1971; Frenkel and Fischer 1972; and Fischer and Frenkel 1974a, 1974b).

The basic difficulty in constructing a model with trade in both types of goods and securities arises from the indeterminacy of the rate of investment, and consequently the capital stock, in the usual two-sector small country model when there is access to a world securities market. The model becomes determinate once a demand for investment goods is introduced. This demand is derived, in the present paper, from considerations of the effects of the rate of investment on the efficiency of production.

Given our formulation of the investment demand function, the stability of the model and the time pattern of the major international accounts do not depend on factor intensities. The time pattern of the major accounts depends on saving and the demand for investment and not on details of the technology; under reasonable specifications of the behavioral functions, these accounts behave in a manner consistent with the well-known stages-of-development hypothesis (e.g., Kindleberger 1968, p. 484). The only economy which depends crucially on factor intensities is the composition of the trade account. Our formulation also permits an analysis of the behavior of the economy in specialized regions which is symmetric with the analysis for the nonspecialized region.

In principle, the demand for investment goods could be derived from portfolio considerations without appealing to technological factors such as adjustment costs. In the absence of uncertainty, however, appeals to xenophobia or national pride are necessary to generate determinate portfolio demand functions in a model as simple as the two-sector small country model (see Bardhan 1967).

The model developed can, of course, be used to investigate the effects of various policy measures on the steady state values of endogenous variables and on their time paths. Such policy measures would include taxes and/or subsidies on production, on consumption, on factor markets, on trade in goods, or on trade in securities.

Finally, the analysis is confined to a barter economy. It could be extended to a monetary economy by adding portfolio relationships determining the demands for money and other assets; part of the flow of savings manifests itself as a flow demand for money, while the behavior of the monetary authority determines the flow supply. The essentials of the analysis are, however, unaffected.

Notes

We are indebted to Harry G. Johnson for providing much of the stimulus for this paper and for his subsequent comments. Thanks are also due to Rudiger Dornbusch and other members of the International Economics Workshop at the University of Chicago.

1. Although we do not, in this paper, consider situations in which there is gross disinvestment, it would seem appropriate to assume that increases in the rate of disinvestment also move the PPF toward the origin. We note that our specification of the per capita rate of gross investment as the determinant of the shrinkage of the PPF is only one possibility; for example, others are the rate of gross investment per unit of output or per unit capital. Each of these has different consequences for the stability of the system; our specification is—as we repeat later—chosen in large part for its simplicity.

2. In principle, other assumptions about the nature of the shifts are, of course, possible. For example, if the adjustment costs of investment affect only the efficiency of labor ("Harrod neutral adjustment costs"), and the production of consumption goods is labor intensive, then investment would shift $T_0 T_0$ to $T_2 T_2$ and the new production point—at the given terms of trade—would be at point B on the Rybczynski line $(R_1 R_1)$. Similarly, in the case of "Solow neutral adjustment costs," where only the efficiency of capital is affected, the transformation frontier shifts to $T_3 T_3$; and the new production point would be at C on the Rybczynski line $(R_c R_c)$. Our specification is motivated by the desire to present the argument in its most simplified form.

3. It will be found, differentiating (21)–(22) with respect to k, that the value of the "marginal product" of k so obtained exceeds r, the rental rate on capital. This is because there is a relationship between α and k which is satisfied at every instant as a result of aggregate investment behavior. It is, however, assumed that the economy is made up of numerous investors, each of whom takes α as given, and that accordingly capital receives the world rental rate, r. This corresponds to an assumption of competition in the rental and investment markets. The discrepancy between the private and social returns to capital entails a distortion—similar to those arising in models of learning by doing—which could be corrected by taxing investment.

4. At the point for which the deficit in the service account equals the surplus in the capital account, $iz = \dot{z} + nz$. Since $z < 0$, $\dot{z} = (i - n)z < 0$ (since $i > n$) and thus the net debtor position rises.

5. The slope of the growth path increases monotonically with k; since the $(b_T = 0)$ locus is linear in the nonspecialized region, there cannot be more than two intersections (at one of which the path has a negative slope) between them in the nonspecialized region. In the specialized regions, the behavior of the slope of the $(b_T = 0)$ locus depends on elasticities of substitution and also α''.

References

Bardhan, Pranab K. 1967. Optimum foreign borrowing. In K. Shell, ed., *Essays on the Theory of Optimal Growth*. Cambridge: MIT Press, pp. 117–128.

Fischer, Stanley, and Frenkel, Jacob A. 1972. Investment, the Two-Sector Model and Trade in Debt and Capital Goods. *Journal of International Economics* 2 (August 1972): 211–233.

Fischer, Stanley, and Frenkel, Jacob A. 1974a. Economic growth and stages of the balance of payments: A theoretical model. In G. Horwich and P. A. Samuelson, eds., *Trade Stability and Macroeconomics: Essays in Honor of Lloyd A. Metzler*. New York: Academic Press, pp. 503–521.

Fischer, Stanley, and Frenkel, Jacob A. 1974b. Interest rate equalization, patterns of production, trade and consumption in a two-country growth model. *Economic Record* 50 (December 1974b): 555–580; and Errata. *Economic Record* 51 (September 1975).

Frenkel, Jacob A. 1971. A theory of money, trade and the balance of payments in a model of accumulation. *Journal of International Economics* 1, 2: 159–187.

Frenkel, Jacob A., and Fischer, Stanley. 1972. International capital movements along balanced growth paths: Comments and extensions. *Economic Record* 48 (June 1972): 266–271.

Johnson, Harry G. 1971. Trade and growth: A geometrical exposition. *Journal of International Economics* 1, 1: 83–101.

Kindelberger, Charles P. 1968. *International Economics*. 4th ed. Homewood, Ill.: Irwin.

Oniki, H., and Uzawa, H. 1965. Patterns of Trade and Investment in a Dynamic Model of International Trade . *Review of Economic Studies* 32 (1): 15–38.

26

The Transfer Problem and Exchange Stability

Harry G. Johnson

The transfer problem bulks large in the literature of international trade theory, both because international economic relations have abounded in transfer problems of various kinds and because the problem offers an attractive opportunity for the application of new theoretical techniques.[1] My purpose here is not to survey the literature,[2] but to offer a straight-forward and (it is hoped) simplified exposition of the theory of transfers in modern terms, based largely on recent literature but extending and unifying it in certain respects. In addition, it will be argued that transfer theory has a wider application than might appear at first sight and that, in particular, it can be applied directly to the problem of exchange stability.

In the context of modern international trade theory, the transfer problem can be posed in either of two ways—as a *real* problem or as a *monetary* problem. More precisely, it can be approached either on the classical assumption that the economic system works so as to maintain equality between income and expenditure at the level corresponding to full employment of resources in each country, or on the Keynesian assumption that the economy of each country is characterized by a perfectly elastic supply of labour and commodities at a fixed wage and price level,[3] so that output and income are determined by aggregate effective demand. In this paper the problem will be discussed from both approaches.

On either set of assumptions, classical or Keynesian, the transfer problem can be separated into two problems for analysis. The first is whether the process by which the transfer is financed in the transferor country and disposed of in the transferee will affect each country's demand for imports (at unchanged prices) sufficiently to create the trade surplus and deficit

This paper was originally published in *The Journal of Political Economy* 64, no. 3 (June 1956): 212–225. © 1956, The University of Chicago. All rights reserved. The present version reprints only section 1 of the original article.

necessary to effect the transfer. The financing and disposal of the transfer will tend to reduce the transferor's demand for goods and increase the transferee's demand for goods; both effects will tend to improve the balance of trade of the transferor and worsen that of the transferee, and the changes may fall short of, or exceed, the amount of the transfer. Unless the changes in trade balances are exactly equal to the amount of the transfer, there will remain a balance-of-payments disequilibrium which must be corrected by some adjustment mechanism. In the classical model the adjustment mechanism is assumed to be a change in the terms of trade of the countries, brought about by price deflation and inflation;[4] in the Keynesian model the adjustment mechanism may be assumed to be either deflation and inflation of effective demand or a terms-of-trade change brought about by devaluation. In either model an alternative method of adjustment would be the tightening and relaxation of trade restrictions.

The second part of the transfer problem is whether the adjustment mechanism will be effective in restoring equilibrium. This problem really raises two subsidiary questions, one of direction and one of magnitude of influence. Taking the classical mechanism of a change in the terms of trade as an example, there is, first, the question whether a small deterioration in a country's terms of trade will tend to improve or to worsen its trade balance—the stability problem. Second, on the assumption that the balance would be improved by a small deterioration in ther terms of trade, there is the question whether the trade balance can be improved sufficiently by this means to achieve a surplus of a given size. The same two questions arisè with respect to the Keynesian mechanism of demand deflation and inflation, and also with respect to the use of trade controls of various kinds. It is obvious that the second question is an empirical one on which theory can render little assistance, since it would always be possible to specify a surplus too large to be achieved by any method of adjustment. The question of direction of effect is, however, susceptible of theoretical analysis, and conditions for the mechanism to work in the right direction can be established.

To summarize, the transfer problem has two theoretical facets: whether the transfer will be undereffected or overeffected as a consequence of the process by which it is financed and disposed of (i.e., the direction in which the adjustment mechanism will be required to operate) and whether the adjustment mechanism will operate in the direction of restoring equilibrium. This chapter is concerned mainly with the first of these problems, and the argument will assume that the adjustment mechanism will suffice. A large part of the answer to the second problem will, however, be provided by applying the results of the argument on the first problem to the general problem of exchange stability, and to the problem of the effect of various kinds of governmental intervention in trade on the trade balance.

The argument which follows makes the usual simplifying assumptions, namely, that the world consists of two countries, A and B, producing two commodities or commodity bundles, A-goods and B-goods, these being the commodities exported by A and B, respectively. It is assumed that A is the transferor and B the transferee.

1. The Classical Transfer Problem[5]

On classical assumptions, the question whether the transfer would be undereffected or overeffected at constant prices is extremely simple to deal with, since the assumption of automatic full employment implies that the transfer must be financed and disposed of in such a way as to reduce aggregate expenditure by the transferor and increase aggregate expenditure by the transferee by the amount of the transfer and thus rules out any multiplier effects. The transferor's balance of trade is improved by both the reduction in its expenditure on imports and the increase in the transferee's demand for its exports. The total improvement, expressed as a proportion of the transfer, will be equal to the sum of the proportions of the expenditure changes in the two countries which fall on imports—more precisely, the sum of the proportions of the expenditure changes by which the receipts of the exporting country change. The transfer will be undereffected or overeffected, and the terms of trade will be required to change against, or in favour of, the transferor, according to whether the sum of these proportions is less or greater than unity. This general rule may be translated into several equivalent forms, by use of the fact that the proportion of the expenditure change which does not fall on imports must fall on exportable goods. The most convenient of these forms to work with is that the transfer will be undereffected or overeffected according to whether the sum of the proportions of expenditure change falling on the countries' export goods is greater or less than unity.

This rule, however, does not establish anything very interesting (beyond the demonstration that either result is possible), since nothing has been said about what determines the proportions of expenditure change. In general, these would depend on the nature of the transfer and the assumed conditions of international trade; as there is no reason for identifying the effects of the financing and disposal of a transfer with the effects of any other kind of economic change, nothing more can, in strictest generality, be said. Nevertheless, it is customary in the literature (and defensible in many cases) to identify the effects of the transfer on expenditure with those of an income tax and a subsidy. On this assumption the proportions of expenditure change can be related to the countries' marginal propensities to spend on exportables or importables, the precise relation depending on the assumed conditions of international trade. Three cases may be distinguished:

1. *Free trade, no transport costs*   In this case all expenditure on imports constitutes receipts for the exporting country, and the proportions of expenditure change are equal to the marginal propensities to spend. The transfer criterion is therefore whether the sum of the marginal popensities to spend on exportables is greater or less than unity.

2. *Tariffs, no transport costs*   Tariffs introduce a difference between the price paid by residents of a country for imports and the receipts of the foreign exporters. In conformity with classical assumptions, the tariff proceeds cannot be allowed to disappear from circulation but must be assumed to be spent by someone. The simplest assumption is that they are redistributed as an income subsidy and spent like any other increment of income, in which case part of the initial change in expenditure on imports associated with the transfer will wind up as a change in expenditure on exportables (out of redistributed tax proceeds). Consequently, the proportions of expenditure change falling on exportables will be larger than the marginal propensities to spend on exportables, and the transfer criterion is accordingly whether the sum of the marginal propensities to spend on exportables is greater or less than a critical value which will be less than unity.[6]

3. *Transport costs, no tariffs*   In this case also there will be a difference between the price paid by residents for imports and the price received by the exporters, the difference representing the transport costs. To the extent that transport of exports utilizes the exported good, the transport costs will constitute receipts for the exporting country. In the extreme case where transport utilizes only the exported good, all expenditure on imports will be (direct, or indirect) receipts for the exporting country, the proportions of expenditure change will be equal to the marginal propensities to spend, and the transfer criterion will be the same as in the no-impediments case (case 1 above). But to the extent that transport utilizes the exportable good of the importing country, transport costs constitute an indirect demand for that good; consequently, the proportions of expenditure change falling on exportables will be larger than the (direct) marginal propensities to spend on exportables, and the critical value for the transfer criterion will be something less than unity, as in the previous case.[7]

The transfer criteria derived in the three cases just examined suggest a reference to a question which has concerned many writers on the transfer problem, namely, whether, even though the classical proposition that the terms of trade *must* turn against the transferring country is erroneous, there nonetheless remains a presumption in favour of this conclusion. Fundamentally, this is a meaningless question, since only ignorance can come from ignorance and no satisfactory basis exists for assessing the likely magnitudes of the marginal propensities to spend which enter into the criteria, short of measuring them in particular cases, when no question of presumption would arise.[8] An argument from "equal ignorance" might, however, be drawn on the following lines: given only that the sum of the marginal propensities to spend on imports and exportables is unity, equal ignorance would suggest no presumption that the average marginal propensity to spend on exportables is either greater or less than one-half. Thus in the no-impediments case there would be no presumption in favour of the classical conclusion; but there would be such a presumption in the cases of tariffs and of transport costs incurred in the exportable good of the importing country, since in these cases the transfer would be undereffected if the average marginal propensity to spend on exportables were exactly one-half. In the latter case the presumption would be reinforced by the fact that, if these transport costs absorbed half the delivered price of imports on the average, the transfer would necessarily be undereffected for any positive values of the marginal propensities to spend on exportables.[9]

A less controversial, more "positive," approach to the classical presumption is to examine what it implies about the countries involved in the transfer. For this purpose it is convenient to use an alternative form of the transfer criterion, namely, that the transfer will be undereffected if the extra physical quantity of A-goods purchased (directly or indirectly) out of an increase in income in A is greater than it is in B;[10] that is, the transfer will be undereffected if the countries are biased (at the margin) toward the purchase of their exportables.

In the free-trade, no-transport-cost case the prices facing consumers are the same in both countries. Consequently, the classical presumption requires either that the countries differ in tastes and are biased toward consumption of their exportables or that, tastes being identical, the goods differ in degree of necessity and the country with the higher income per head produces the more "luxurious" good for export. In the case of tariffs and of transport costs the relative prices facing consumers differ, each commodity being relatively cheaper in the exporting than in the importing country. Consequently, if the economies were on identical consumption indifference curves before the transfer, each would have the marginal bias *in direct consumption* toward the purchase of its exportable commodity required by the classical presumption. To put it another way, so far as *direct* consumption is concerned, tastes must be biased toward imported goods or the country with the higher income per head must produce the more necessary commodity if the classical presumption is to be invalid. But indirect consumption must also be considered. In the case of tariffs without transport costs, indirect consumption out of tariff proceeds is assumed to behave in the same way as direct consumption, leaving the foregoing argument unaffected. In the case of transport costs and free trade, the bias toward direct consumption of exportables induced by the difference in prices is reinforced if transport costs are incurred entirely in the exportable good of the importing country and mitigated—perhaps outweighed—if transport costs are incurred entirely in the imported good. The effects of transport costs incurred in both goods are too complex to be analysed here, though analogy with the tariff case indicates that, in the case of identical pretransfer indifference curves, a necessary condition for invalidation of the classical presumption is that transport is more "import intensive" than is marginal consumption expenditure in the importing country.

Before concluding this section, it is appropriate to consider briefly the effects of relaxing some of the simplifying assumptions. The possibility of varying home production of the imported good makes no difference, since this is conditional on the price ratio between the goods changing, which in turn depends on the criteria derived previously. The introduction of non-traded goods does alter the criteria, since changes in demand for such goods must be classed either as changes in (virtual) demand for exportables or as changes in (virtual) demand for imports, according to whether they are more substitutable in production and consumption for one or the other.[11] In both these cases, however, the direction of change of the commodity terms of trade is not uniquely determined by whether the transfer is undereffected or overeffected at constant prices. The introduction of more countries also alters the criterion, since the balances of payments of the two countries are no longer equal and opposite in sign. From the transferor's point of view, the transfer will be undereffected or overeffected (at pretransfer prices) according to whether the sum of the proportions of the transfer by which the transferor's expenditure on imports is reduced, and the transferee's expenditure *on the transferor's exports* (not on imports in general) is less or greater than unity. Again, the movement of the commodity terms of trade is not decided by whether the transfer is undereffected or overeffected.

Notes

This chapter was drafted during my tenure of a visiting professorship at Northwestern University; it has benefited greatly, though perhaps insufficiently, from criticisms of colleagues there and elsewhere in the United States and the United Kingdom.

1. The argument has been extended to include the application of transfer theory to trade intervention.

2. For such surveys see Jacob Viner, *Studies in the Theory of International Trade* (New York, 1937), chap. 6; Paul A. Samuelson, The transfer problem and transport costs, *Economic Journal* 62, no. 246 (June 1952), 278–304, and 64, no. 254 (June 1954), 264–289; and Gottfried Haberler, *A Survey of International Trade Theory* (Princeton, 1955).

3. It is possible, but unnecessarily complicating, to assume a perfectly elastic supply of labour at a fixed money wage and an imperfectly elastic supply of output, as Keynes did in the *General Theory*. An analysis of this case may be found in James E. Meade, *The Balance of Payments* (London, 1951), and its *Mathematical Supplement*.

4. Strictly speaking, what must change is the double-factoral rather than the commodity terms of trade, since with nontraded goods the commodity terms of trade can change in either direction as the price level changes.

5. This section reproduces, in a somewhat simpler form, the argument of my note, The transfer problem: A note on criteria for changes in the terms of trade, *Economica*, N.S., 22, no. 86 (May 1955), 113–21. That note and some of the additional argument of the present section owe much to Samuelson's two masterly *Economic Journal* articles cited in note 2.

6. Let C and M be the marginal propensities to spend on exportables and imports and t be the proportion of the final price of imports taken in taxes. Then total expenditure at market prices will change by

$$1 + tM + (tM)^2 + \cdots = \frac{1}{1 - tM}$$

times the amount of the transfer, and the proportion of the transfer by which expenditure on exportables changes will be

$$\frac{C}{1 - tM} = \left(1 + \frac{tM}{1 - tM}\right)C.$$

Since the transfer will be undereffected or overeffected according to whether the sum of these proportions is greater or less than unity, that is, according to whether

$$\left(1 + \frac{t_a M_a}{1 - t_a M_a}\right)C_a + \left(1 + \frac{t_b M_b}{1 - t_b M_b}\right)C_b \gtreqless 1,$$

the critical value of the transfer criterion will be

$$C_a + C_b = 1 - \frac{t_a M_a C_a}{1 - t_a M_a} - \frac{t_b M_b C_b}{1 - t_b M_b}.$$

The right-hand side of this expression must be less than unity, since t, M, and C are all positive fractions.

7. Let k be the proportion of the price of imports representing transport cost incurred in the importer's exportable commodity; then the proportion of the

transfer by which expenditure on exportables changes is $C + kM$, and the critical value of the transfer criterion is

$$1 - k_a M_a - k_b M_b,$$

which is less than unity.

8. Statistical estimates of marginal propensities to import in the interwar period (1924–38) have produced results for some countries well above the average of one-half required by the criteria. For example, T. C. Chang (*Cyclical Movements in the Balance of Payments*, Cambridge, 1951, p. 37) found six agricultural countries with marginal propensities to import ranging from 0.52 to 0.73, though in all but one case (Denmark, 0.54) the estimates are based on relatively short series. More recently J. J. Polak (*An International Economic System*, London, 1954, Summary of results, opposite p. 156) has obtained the following estimates: for the whole period, Denmark, 0.73; Norway, 0.67; for the 1920s Finland, 0.93; New Zealand, 0.65; Indonesia, 0.62; Union of South Africa, 0.57. While these estimates do not correspond very precisely with the theoretical concepts employed here (imports generally being valued c.i.f., which excluded tariffs but may include invisible receipts of the exporting country) and their application is complicated by the presence of many countries and many commodities, they are not inconsistent with the possibility that in some cases a transfer might be overeffected.

9. On the assumption that $k_a + k_b = 1$, the criterion of note 7 becomes $k_a C_a + k_b C_b$, which is necessarily less than $C_a + C_b$.

10. One formulation of the rule developed in the first paragraph of this section is that the transfer will be undereffected or overeffected according to whether the proportion of expenditure change in the transferor which falls on exportables is greater or less than the proportion of expenditure change in the transferee which falls on the transferor's exportables. Since the latter deducts tariffs and transport costs from the delivered price and adds back in transport cost incurred in the exported good, which amounts to measurement at factor cost in the transferor, deflation by factor cost gives the criterion stated in the text. Further, it follows that, since the sum of the proportions of expenditure change measured in this way must equal unity for each country, the condition respecting A-goods, as stated previously, implies the reverse for B-goods.

11. If it can be assumed that nontraded goods are substitutes for exports, this strengthens the classical presumption that the terms of trade turn against the transferor; but contrary cases are conceivable (Samuelson 1954, pp. 288–289).

The Generalized Theory of Transfers and Welfare: Bilateral Transfers in a Multilateral World

Jagdish N. Bhagwati, Richard A. Brecher, and Tatsuo Hatta

Paul Samuelson's (1952, 1954) classic papers on the transfer problem addressed two separate analytical issues: the "positive" effect of a transfer on the terms of trade, and the welfare effect of the transfer on the donor and the recipient.

Since then, a considerable body of literature has grown up on the positive analysis. While Samuelson (1954) himself had extended the 2 × 2 × 2 free trade analysis to allow for tariffs and transport costs, subsequent writers have analyzed other extensions of the model: for example, to allow for nontraded goods as with leisure in Samuelson (1971), or general nontraded goods in John Chipman (1974) and Ronald Jones (1970, 1975).

Remarkably, however, the welfare analysis of transfers has not paralleled these developments. Since Wassily Leontief (1936) produced an example of immiserizing transfer from abroad and Samuelson (1947) argued that the example required market instability, the proposition that has monopolized attention has been that a transfer in the conventional 2 × 2 × 2 model in its free trade version cannot immiserize the recipient or enrich the donor as long as world markets are stable (in the Walras sense). Interestingly, Samuelson (1954), who did extend the positive analysis to include tariffs, did not go on to ask whether immiserization of the transfer recipient (and hence symmetrically enrichment of the donor in a two-country model) could now arise consistent with market stability.

Recently, the welfare analysis of transfers has been extended in two different directions, both apparently unconnected, and both yielding the conclusion that transfers from abroad can be immiserizing (and that the donor may improve its welfare) despite market stability. One route to this conclusion has been the introduction of a third economic agent (or country)

This paper was originally published in *The American Economic Review* 73, no. 4 (September 1983): 606–618. © The American Economic Association.

that is outside of the transfer process. In the appendix of his 1960 paper analyzing the interaction between trade policy and income distribution, Harry Johnson discussed the possibility of welfare-paradoxical redistribution between two factor-income classes (capital and labor) in an open economy, thereby providing what can be interpreted as a treatment of the three-agent transfer problem for the case in which donor and recipient are both completely specialized in the ownership of a single different factor.[1] An independent analysis of the three-agent transfer problem, using a restrictive model with given endowments of goods and fixed coefficients in consumption, was also undertaken in an important paper by David Gale (1974).[2] Brecher and Bhagwati (1981) also independently pioneered this analysis in the context of a three-agent model where the recipient country is split into one subset of "national" factors and another of "foreign" factors, and the conditions for the immiserization of the national factors after receiving a transfer from abroad are analyzed and shown explicitly to be consistent with market stability.

Another route has been to consider transfers in the presence of exogenously specified domestic distortions. Thus, Brecher and Bhagwati (1982) have analyzed the case of a transfer in the presence of a production distortion in the recipient country and shown that the recipient can get immiserized despite market stability if the recipient's "overproduced" good is inferior in the donor's consumption. Hatta, in an early unpublished paper (1973a), has also demonstrated for a closed economy with constant-cost production that a transfer between two agents, when there is a distortionary wedge between producer and consumer prices, could immiserize the recipient consistent with market stability. Peter Diamond (1978) has also recently considered the welfare impact of transfers when a price distortion exists in an economy with convex technology, and he gives comparative-static results that are consistent with paradoxes.

This recent proliferation of paradoxical cases of immiserizing transfers (and enriching transfer payments) is reminiscent of the earlier multiplication of cases involving immiserizing growth, with Bhagwati's (1958) analysis of the case of a large country in free trade being followed by Harry Johnson's (1967) analysis of the case of a small country with a tariff.[3] The latter proliferation led to the generalized theory of immiserizing growth (Bhagwati 1968b) whose major, influential proposition is that growth, in the presence of a distortion implying departure from full optimality, can be immiserizing since the primary gain from growth at optimal policies may be outweighed by an accentuation of the loss from the distortion vis-à-vis the optimal policies.

Can a similar, striking generalization be developed in regard to the transfer-induced paradoxes? It is the general conclusion of our analysis in this paper that, indeed, it can. We demonstrate that the phenomenon of immiserizing transfers from abroad (and the analytically symmetric phenomenon of enriching transfer payments) in the presence of market stability can arise only if there is a distortion characterizing the economy in question.

This general conclusion is critically dependent on our demonstration below that the three-agent case, which appears prima facie to involve no distortion while producing the noted paradoxes, is indeed characterized by what Bhagwati (1971) has called a *foreign* distortion, since the country is not using an optimal tariff. Moreover, the exercise of their joint monopoly power by the recipient and donor (viewed as members of a customs union) vis-à-vis the nonparticipant agent will be shown to eliminate the paradoxes in question.

Thus, in section 1, we developed the basic analysis of transfers when there are two economic agents (countries) engaged in the transfer process, but there is an added agent *outside* the transfer process so that we have a bilateral transfer in a multilateral context. Conditions are established for immiserization of the recipient, for enrichment of the donor and for the "double perversity" when these two paradoxical outcomes arise simultaneously. Economically intuitive explanations of these results are derived in a number of alternative ways.

In section 2, yet further intuition on these results, in consonance with the theory of immiserizing growth, is arrived at, and suitable geometry of the three-agent transfer problem is simultaneously developed. Importantly, the role of inferiority in consumption or inelastic foreign demand is established in making feasible the perverse outcomes, which are shown to involve a foreign distortion (correctable by a uniform optimal tariff policy applied jointly by the donor and the recipient against the nonparticipant). In turn, this establishes an interesting parallel between the conditions for the immiserizing-transfer paradox in the three-agent, foreign-distortion case and the conditions established in Bhagwati's (1958) immiserizing-growth case which also involves a similar foreign distortion (i.e., growth for a large country that is failing to use an optimal tariff because of its free trade policy).

Section 3 then presents the implications of our results for some important theoretical and policy problems in both international and closed-economy contexts.

1. Transfers with Three Agents: Model and Analysis

We begin with a formal analysis of the three-agent transfer problem, drawing on duality theory in terms of compensated demand functions, which have been introduced into the welfare-theoretic analysis of international trade by Hatta (1973b, 1977), Hatta and Takashi Fukushima (1979), and most notably and comprehensively by Avinash Dixit and V. Norman (1980), although earlier applications such as indirect utility functions are to be found also in the work of Chipman (1972).

The Model

Consider a world economy consisting of three countries: α, β, and γ. (While the analysis is couched in terms of three countries, it is applicable immediately to a closed-economy context with three agents within the economy, or to a two-country international economy where one country is disaggregated into two groups as in Brecher-Bhagwati, 1981.) Each country produces and consumes two goods, X and Y. Free trade and perfect competition prevail.

Now, suppose that country α makes a transfer to country γ. Country β does not participate in the transfer process. We will call α the *donor*, γ the *recipient*, and β the *nonparticipant* "outside" country. The objective of the analysis will be to determine the effect of the transfer on the welfare levels of the three countries.

The following notation will be used in presenting our model:

$q = $ the relative price of good X,

$u^i = $ the welfare level of country i,

$T = $ the value of the transfer in terms of good Y,

$e^i(q, u^i) = $ the expenditure function of country i,

$r^i(q) = $ the revenue function of country i,

$x^i(q, u^i) = $ the compensated import-demand function for good X by
country i, for $i = \alpha, \beta, \gamma$.

We then define an *overspending function* c^i as follows:

$$c^i(q, u^i) \equiv e^i(q, u^i) - r^i(q), \quad i = \alpha, \beta, \gamma.$$

Evidently, the value of this overspending function represents the difference between the expenditure necessary to achieve the utility level u^i when the goods-price ratio is q *and* the revenue of the producers of country i at the same price ratio. Thus, c^i is the amount of added revenue (i.e., transfer income) that is necessary for this country to sustain u^i when the price ratio is q.

Using this notation, we can write our model as follows:

$$c^\alpha(q, u^\alpha) + T = 0, \tag{1}$$

$$c^\beta(q, u^\beta) = 0, \tag{2}$$

$$c^{\gamma}(q, u^{\gamma}) - T = 0, \tag{3}$$

$$x^{\alpha}(q, u^{\alpha}) + x^{\beta}(q, u^{\beta}) + x^{\gamma}(q, u^{\gamma}) = 0. \tag{4}$$

This model of four equations contains four variables: u^{α}, u^{β}, u^{γ}, and q. Equations (1)–(3) are the budget equations for the respective countries, while equation (4) is the market equilibrium condition for good X. (In view of Walras's law, the market-clearing equation for good Y has been omitted.)

Comparative Statics

We now examine the impact of an exogenous increase in T upon the variables of the model above. Throughout the paper, subscripts always indicate partial differentiation with respect to a particular variable; for example, $c_u^{\alpha} \equiv \partial c^{\alpha}/\partial u^{\alpha}$ and $x_q^{\gamma} \equiv \partial x^{\gamma}/\partial q$. The following theorem can now be derived.

THEOREM 1　*Assume (without loss of generality) that $e_u^{\alpha} = e_u^{\beta} = e_u^{\gamma} = 1$ initially; and let $\Delta \equiv x^{\alpha}x_u^{\alpha} + x^{\beta}x_u^{\beta} + x^{\gamma}x_u^{\gamma} - x_q$, where $x_q \equiv x_q^{\alpha} + x_q^{\beta} + x_q^{\gamma}$. Then*

$$\frac{dq}{dT} = \frac{x_u^{\gamma} - x_u^{\alpha}}{\Delta}, \tag{5}$$

$$\frac{du^{\alpha}}{dT} = \frac{x_q - x^{\beta}(x_u^{\beta} - x_u^{\gamma})}{\Delta}, \tag{6}$$

$$\frac{du^{\beta}}{dT} = \frac{-x^{\beta}(x_u^{\gamma} - x_u^{\alpha})}{\Delta}, \tag{7}$$

$$\frac{du^{\gamma}}{dT} = \frac{-x_q - x^{\beta}(x_u^{\beta} - x_u^{\alpha})}{\Delta}. \tag{8}$$

Proof　Taking the total differential of (1) through (4), applying the assumptions of the theorem, and using the well-known property that $c_q^i = x^i$ (for $i = \alpha, \beta, \gamma$), we obtain

$$\begin{bmatrix} 1 & 0 & 0 & x^{\alpha} \\ 0 & 1 & 0 & x^{\beta} \\ 0 & 0 & 1 & x^{\gamma} \\ x_u^{\alpha} & x_u^{\beta} & x_u^{\gamma} & x_q \end{bmatrix} \begin{bmatrix} du^{\alpha} \\ du^{\beta} \\ du^{\gamma} \\ dq \end{bmatrix} = \begin{bmatrix} -1 \\ 0 \\ 1 \\ 0 \end{bmatrix} dT.$$

Applying Cramer's rule to this system and taking notice of (4), we immediately obtain the theorem. □

It is readily shown that Δ equals (minus) the slope of the general equilibrium, excess-demand schedule of good X for the world as a whole.[4] Thus, the Marshall-Lerner condition for (Walrasian) stability implies that $\Delta > 0$.

Note also that equations (5) and (7) yield $du^\beta/dT > 0$ if and only if $-x^\beta dq/dT > 0$. Thus, the welfare of the country not involved in the transfer improves if and only if the price of its export good goes up as a result of the transfer—as is indeed immediately evident.

Paradoxes: Enrichment of Donor and Immiserization of Recipient

The welfare impacts of a transfer upon the donor and the recipient, however, are not as simple as this. In the remainder of this section, therefore, we will give various interpretations of theorem 1, to shed more light on the conditions under which the paradoxes of immiserized recipient and enriched donor arise. Note immediately, however, that if either $x^\beta = 0$ or $(x_u^\beta - x_u^\gamma) = 0$, that is, if either β's net trade is zero or β and γ share an identical marginal propensity to consume X,[5] the second term in the numerator of the right-hand side of (6) is zero. In this case, equation (6) reduces to $du^\alpha/dT = x_q/\Delta$, which is, of course, the familiar expression for the welfare effect on the donor in the two-country analysis. With $\Delta > 0$ and $x_q < 0$, du^α/dT must be negative; that is, the donor must be immiserized. When the only trade partner of the donor is the recipient, or when the recipient and the nonparticipant share an identical marginal propensity, therefore, the welfare impact on the donor is *as if* we were in a two-country world, and the donor paradox never arises. A symmetric conclusion can be derived for the welfare effect on the recipient from equation (8).

Generally, however, the second term in the numerator of the right-hand side of (6) or (8) can cause paradoxical welfare effects, and we have the following necessary conditions for the paradoxes:

$$\frac{du^\alpha}{dT} > 0 \quad \text{implies that } x^\beta(x_u^\beta - x_u^\gamma) < 0, \tag{9}$$

$$\frac{du^\gamma}{dT} < 0 \quad \text{implies that } x^\beta(x_u^\beta - x_u^\alpha) < 0. \tag{10}$$

In fact, (6) and (8) make it clear that when $x_q = 0$ (i.e., when substitution effects are assumed away), the second inequalities in (9) and (10) are not merely necessary but also sufficient conditions for the paradoxes. And it is equally clear that if x_q is sufficiently negative (i.e., if X and Y are readily substitutable in production and consumption), the paradoxes are unlikely to occur.[6]

Decomposition of Welfare Changes

In further understanding our results in theorem 1, note first that the right-hand sides of (6)–(8) contain the x_u^i terms for all countries $i (= \alpha, \beta, \gamma)$, *except* for the one whose welfare is stated by the equation in question. Let us now examine why this curious fact holds; it leads us into an insightful way of looking at our results.[7]

For this purpose we may conceptually decompose the transfer from α to γ into two stages. At the *first* stage, α gives transfers to both β and γ in proportion to their initial import demand for X.[8] At the *second* stage, β gives γ what it received from α in the first stage, with the final situation ending up therefore as equivalent to the actual transfer going exclusively from α to γ. The welfare effect on the donor α can then be decomposed into two effects corresponding to these two stages.

Rewriting (6), we have[9]

$$\frac{du}{dT} = \frac{x_q}{\Delta} - \frac{x^\beta}{(x^\beta + x^\gamma)} \frac{(x^\beta + x^\gamma)(x_u^\beta - x_u^\gamma)}{\Delta}. \tag{11}$$

Now it is possible to show that the first stage leads to the first term on the right-hand side of (11).[10] Making transfers to every other country in the world economy in proportion to its initial import demand for X is therefore tantamount to making a transfer to the other country in a two-country context! This process therefore results in a negatively signed term; the paradox of donor enrichment cannot come from this stage.

On the other hand, the second stage leads to the second term on the right-hand side of (11).[11] The sign of this term depends exclusively on the direction of the price change caused by the second-stage transfer. We already know from (9) that $x^\beta(x_u^\beta - x_u^\gamma) < 0$ is a necessary condition for the paradox of donor enrichment, and why this occurs is readily seen from (11) and the second-stage argumentation.

Alternative Necessary Conditions for Paradoxes

We now turn to an alternative, equally insightful way of looking at theorem 1. We first establish a set of necessary conditions for the paradoxes of donor enrichment and recipient immiserization. Then, it will be shown how these conditions are also necessary for price amplification effects which further help to explain the paradoxical possibilities.

Take again the case of donor welfare, and apply the Slutsky equation to (6) to get[12]

$$\frac{du^\alpha}{dT} = \frac{(x_q^\alpha + x_q^\gamma + \tilde{x}_q^\beta + x^\beta x_u^\gamma)}{\Delta}, \tag{12}$$

where $\tilde{x}^\beta(q)$ is the uncompensated import-demand function for country β. Now, given $\Delta > 0$, and assuming throughout the rest of this section without loss of generality that $x^\beta < 0$ (i.e., country β exports good X), we see immediately that the donor can be enriched only if either $x_u^\gamma < 0$, or $\tilde{x}_q^\beta > 0$, or both. That is, if a transfer enriches donor α, then *either* X is an inferior good to the recipient γ *or* the offer curve of the nonparticipant outside country β is inelastic (such that the export supply of X by β falls as the relative price of X rises).

Similarly, for the immiserization of the recipient, we must have $du^\gamma/dT < 0$, and this can be shown to imply that $x_u^\alpha < 0$ *or* $\tilde{x}_q^\beta > 0$, or both.

To understand more fully why these conditions are necessary for the paradox of (say) donor enrichment, the Slutsky equation and (4) may be used straightforwardly to rewrite the stability condition as $\Delta = x^\alpha(x_u^\alpha - x_u^\gamma) - x_q^\alpha - x_q^\gamma - (\tilde{x}_q^\beta + x^\beta x_u^\gamma) > 0$. If $(\tilde{x}_q^\beta + x^\beta x_u^\gamma) > 0$—which can happen only if either $\tilde{x}_q^\beta > 0$ or $x_u^\gamma < 0$ (given still that $x^\beta < 0$)—Δ will be smaller than in the two-country case (in which $\tilde{x}_q^\beta = x^\beta = 0$), *ceteris paribus*. Therefore, the price change measured by equation (5) is amplified by the presence of the third (nonparticipant) country β. If this price-amplification effect applies to an improvement in the terms of trade for α, the donor may be paradoxically enriched by the transfer, even though the (smaller) terms-of-trade improvement in the two-country case cannot be great enough for the paradox of donor enrichment. By similar reasoning,[13] if β's offer curve is inelastic or good X is inferior for α, an amplified deterioration in γ's terms of trade may be great enough for the paradox of recipient immiserization.

These necessary conditions for an international transfer paradox are, interestingly, analogous to those established by Bhagwati (1958) for immiserization due to domestic growth (in the form of factor-endowment expansion or technological improvement). As he showed, the paradoxical possibility of immiserizing growth requires that *either* growth be ultra-biased against production of the importable (i.e., the importable be an "inferior" good in production) *or* the foreign offer curve be inelastic. This analogy suggests immediately that if immiserizing growth paradoxes are attributable to the presence of distortions, as shown in Bhagwati (1968b), it should be possible to interpret the present transfer analysis in the three-agent context also as one where the paradoxes of immiserized recipient and enriched donor arise only when a distortion is present. The distortion here, as in Bhagwati (1958), must again arise as a foreign distortion in the sense of Bhagwati (1971), that is, the failure to exploit monopoly power in trade. Indeed, this can be demonstrated, as in section 2 below.

2. Viewing Three-Agent Paradoxes as Resulting from Foreign Distortion

We now proceed to demonstrate that the perverse welfare responses to bilateral transfers in the multilateral framework of three agents are attributable to the presence of a foreign distortion, and that the introduction of a suitable optimal tariff that eliminates this distortion will rule out the paradoxes. We first demonstrate this geometrically, using a technique that is suitable for "large" (as well as "small") transfers.

The Geometry of the Free Trade Case

We begin by illustrating in figure 27.1 the possibility of a perverse welfare response to bilateral transfer in the three-agent case. For convenience of exposition without loss of generality, the diagram treats countries α and γ as partners of a customs union engaged in (free) trade with country β. (This treatment takes on more than expositional importance below, when α and γ uniformly impose an optimal tariff policy against β.) In the initial pre-transfer equilibrium, the union produces on its production possibility frontier $Q_y Q_x$ at point Q, consumes on its Scitovsky (1942) frontier $S_y S_x$ at point S, and trades with country β from point Q to point S along the price line QS.[14] To avoid cluttering the diagram, we have not drawn country β's offer curve, which starts at point Q and passes through point S. For the sake of concreteness only, let country β be again an exporter of commodity X (i.e., $x^\beta < 0$) while country α imports this good (with $x^\alpha > 0$).

Now, with country α making a transfer to country γ, suppose that the former's terms of trade consequently improve because the marginal propensity to consume good X is greater for country α than for its union partner. Figure 27.1 illustrates the broderline case in which the terms-of-trade improvement is exactly enough to leave country α's welfare un-

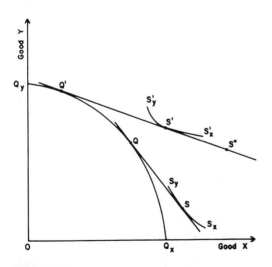

Figure 27.1

changed, despite the transfer. The union shifts in production to point Q' on curve $Q_y Q_x$, and moves in consumption to point S' on curve $S'_y S'_x$, which is another Scitovsky frontier in the map corresponding to a constant level of country α's welfare. Country β's offer curve (still not drawn) now starts at point Q' and passes through point S'.

In figure 27.1 as drawn, good X is clearly inferior for the union as a whole. This inferiority, moreover, must characterize country γ in particular, since country α's welfare is constant throughout the entire Scitovsky map. By contrast, no such inferiority would be implied if curve $S'_y S'_x$ were redrawn to touch line $Q'S'$ at point S'' (lying east of point S), while country β's offer curve (not shown) were redrawn to pass through point S'' when starting at point Q'. In this alternative case, however, the offer curve of country β must be inelastic, because a deterioration in this country's terms of trade is now associated with a rise in exports to the union. (These two alternative conditions are, of course, those already established in section 1, for the paradox of donor enrichment.)

By similar reasoning, an actual rise in country α's welfare, in response to a transfer to country γ, might occur provided that *either* good X is inferior in the latter country *or* the offer curve of country β is inelastic. This paradoxical possibility would occur in figure 27.1 if country β's offer curve (not drawn) were respecified to cross line $Q'S'$ southeast of the consumption point S' (or alternatively S'') after starting at the production point Q'. In this case, after the transfer, there would remain a world excess supply of good X if q fell only enough to leave u^α constant at the initial (pretransfer) level. Thus, given stability, country α's terms of trade would ultimately have to improve still further, thereby leading to the paradox of donor enrichment.[15]

Essentially the same argument shows that country γ might incur a welfare loss from receiving the transfer, provided that either good X is inferior in country α, or (as before) the offer curve of counry β is inelastic. If the required conditions for a perverse response in welfare hold simultaneously for both partners of the union, the transfer from country α to country γ could raise the former's welfare and lower the latter's, implying a double perversity of outcomes.

Optimal Tariff against a Nonparticipant Country
Consider now the following alternative ways of demonstrating how the use of an optimal tariff by the union rules out the paradoxes at issue:

1. *A geometric analysis* Consider the extension of the preceding analysis to the case where the union of α and γ always maintains a uniform, optimal tariff vis-à-vis β, the nonparticipant country. Thus, for each value of the

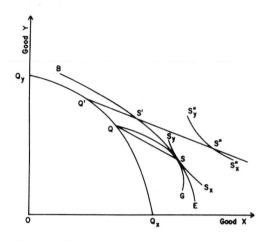

Figure 27.2

domestic goods-price ratio in figure 27.2, the union adjusts the tariff to set the world-price ratio at the level consistent with the Robert Baldwin (1948) envelope BE, given the union's production possibility frontier $Q_y Q_x$ and the offer curve QG of country β. To avoid cluttering the diagram, we have drawn this offer curve with its origin in only one of the many possible positions. Alternatively, if this origin were placed at point Q' (instead of Q) for example, the offer curve would touch curve BE at point S' (rather than S). Following a common convention, tariff revenues collected by each union member are returned to its consumers in lump sum fashion.

This optimal-tariff policy must result in the union consuming along its Baldwin envelope BE of figure 27.2 in equilibrium. Initially, the union produces on its production possibility frontier $Q_y Q_x$ at point Q, consumes on its Scitovsky frontier $S_y S_x$ at point S, trades with country β along the external-price line QS from point Q to point S, and imposes a tariff to create the proportional wedge between this price line and the (parallel) domestic-price lines (not drawn) tangent to curve $Q_y Q_x$ at point Q and to curve $S_y S_x$ at point S.

Now let the transfer take place from country α to country γ, and imagine what would hypothetically happen if the domestic relative price of good X within the union fell exactly enough to leave the donor country α's welfare constant, despite the transfer. Under these circumstances, the union would move to point Q' in production, trade along the external-price line $Q'S''$ with the rest of the world, and plan to consume at point S'' on the Scitovsky frontier $S_y'' S_x''$ drawn for the initial level of country α's welfare. (For well-known reasons, the slope of curve $S_y'' S_x''$ at point S'' equals the union's internal product-price ratio, given by the common slope of curves $Q_y Q_x$ and BE at points Q' and S', respectively.) In this way, an excess demand (represented by the length $S'S''$) for good X for the world as a whole would necessarily emerge,[16] and the relative price of this good would have to rise to clear world markets under stable conditions.

This implies that country α, the donor, cannot enjoy enrichment since the initial fall in the price of X which exactly offset the primary loss from the transfer would now be reduced, leaving α worse off. Similarly, we could establish that the recipient, γ, cannot be immiserized.

It follows, therefore, that the paradoxes of donor enrichment and recipient immiserization cannot arise if the union of the donor and the recipient follows the policy of adopting an optimal tariff that equates their domestic rates of (producer) transformation and (consumer) substitution to the foreign rate of transformation, such that $DRS^\alpha = DRS^\gamma = DRT^\alpha = DRT^\gamma = FRT$. Under free trade, however, the paradoxes become possible since the situation suffers from a foreign distortion such that $DRS^\alpha = DRS^\gamma = DRT^\alpha = DRT^\gamma \neq FRT$.

2. *Algebraic analysis*   The preceding geometric analysis immediately suggests an approach to a formal proof of the proposition that the union of α and γ, utilizing an optimal tariff against β, would not admit of the paradoxes in question. Thus we should be able to show that, if such a tariff were in place, the paradoxes would be ruled out. This can indeed be done as follows.

Utilizing the model so far, we now distinguish between q as the domestic relative price of X and p as the external price. Then, we write the foreign-offer curve function as $\tilde{x}^\beta(p)$. Now, define the function ρ by

$$\rho(q, p) \equiv (q - p)[-\tilde{x}^\beta(p)]. \tag{13}$$

If q and p take on their equilibrium values, then $\rho(q, p)$ gives the tariff revenue of the union of α and γ. Also, let $p^*(q)$ represent the value of p that maximizes $\rho(q, p)$, given q, and define the function ρ^* by

$$\rho^*(q) \equiv \rho[q, p^*(q)]. \tag{14}$$

Now, if the international market is in equilibrium with $p = p^*(q)$, so that $\rho(q, p)$ takes on its maximized value $\rho^*(q)$ for the prevailing q, then it can be readily observed that the union must be operating on its Baldwin envelope at the point where FRT equals that q. In this case, therefore, $q - p^*(q)$ is equal to the union's optimal tariff rate. Of course, there is no a priori guarantee that any arbitrary q and the corresponding $p^*(q)$ are equilibrium values; in general, they are not. But the observation above implies that if the union always sets the tariff rate equal to $q - p^*(q)$ for the prevailing q, then this rate coincides with the optimal tariff rate when equilibrium is reached. The following result can now be established:

LEMMA 1   If $p = p^*(q)$, then $(q - p)\tilde{x}_p^\beta = \tilde{x}^\beta$.

Proof   Recalling that the optimal tariff maximizes ρ given q, we have $\partial \rho[q, p^*(q)]/\partial p = 0$, from which the lemma follows immediately. $\square$

Now, reformulate the model of this paper to allow for the union always imposing the tariff rate $q - p^*(q)$. Also assume that countries α and γ collect tariff revenues equal to $[q - p^*(q)]x^\alpha(q, u^\alpha)$ and $[q - p^*(q)] \, x^\gamma(q, u^\gamma)$, respectively. (Thus, we implicitly assume that both union members import good X from country β, although the results of the analysis would be essentially unaffected if one member received all of the tariff revenues because the partner imported nothing from β.) The overspending functions c^α and c^γ are now given by

$$c^\alpha(q, u^\alpha) \equiv e^\alpha(q, u^\alpha) - r^\alpha(q) - [q - p^*(q)]x^\alpha(q, u^\alpha), \tag{15}$$

$$c^\gamma(q, u^\gamma) \equiv e^\alpha(q, u^\gamma) - r^\gamma(q) - [q - p^*(q)]x^\gamma(q, u^\gamma), \tag{16}$$

Then, our full revised model is given by

$$c^\alpha(q, u^\alpha) + T = 0, \tag{17}$$

$$c^\gamma(q, u^\gamma) - T = 0, \tag{18}$$

$$x^\alpha(q, u^\alpha) + \tilde{x}^\beta[p^*(q)] + x^\gamma(q, u^\gamma) = 0. \tag{19}$$

This three-equation model has three variables: u^α, u^γ, and q.

The following theorem can be derived:

THEOREM 2   If (17)–(19) hold and (by normalization) initially $e_u^\alpha = e_u^\gamma = 1$, then

$$\frac{dq}{dT} = \frac{x_u^\gamma - x_u^\alpha}{\Delta^t c_u^\alpha c_u^\gamma}, \tag{20}$$

$$\frac{du^\alpha}{dT} = \frac{x_q^t}{\Delta^t c_u^\alpha c_u^\gamma}, \tag{21}$$

$$\frac{du^\gamma}{dT} = -\frac{x_q^t}{\Delta^t c_u^\alpha c_u^\gamma}, \tag{22}$$

where $\Delta^t \equiv -x_q^t + (c_q^\alpha x_u^\alpha/c_u^\alpha) + (c_q^\gamma x_u^\gamma/c_u^\gamma)$ and $x_q^t \equiv x_q^\alpha + \tilde{x}_p^\beta p_q^* + x_q^\gamma$.

Proof   Taking the total differential of (17)–(19), we get

$$
\begin{bmatrix} c_u^\alpha & 0 & c_q^\alpha \\ 0 & c_u^\gamma & c_q^\gamma \\ x_u^\alpha & x_u^\gamma & x_q^t \end{bmatrix} \begin{bmatrix} du^\alpha \\ du^\gamma \\ dq \end{bmatrix} = \begin{bmatrix} -1 \\ 1 \\ 0 \end{bmatrix} dT.
$$

We thus obtain

$$
\frac{du^\alpha}{dT} = \frac{[c_u^\gamma x_q^t - (c_q^\alpha + c_q^\gamma)x_u^\gamma]}{\Delta^t c_u^\alpha c_u^\gamma}. \tag{23}
$$

From (15) and (16), we get

$$
c_q^\alpha + c_q^\gamma = p_q^*(x^\alpha + x^\gamma) - (q - p^*)(x_q^\alpha + x_q^\gamma),
$$

and

$$
c_u^\gamma = 1 - (q - p^*)x_u^\gamma.
$$

Thus, we have

$$
[c_u^\gamma x_q^t - (c_q^\alpha + c_q^\gamma)x_u^\gamma] = [x_q^t - (q - p^*)x_u^\gamma(x_q^\alpha + \tilde{x}_p^\beta p_q^* + x_q^\gamma)]
$$
$$
- [p_q^*(x^\alpha + x^\gamma) - (q - p^*)(x_q^\alpha + x_q^\gamma)]x_u^\gamma
$$
$$
= x_q^t - x_u^\gamma p_q^*[(q - p^*)\tilde{x}_p^\beta - x^\beta] = x_q^t, \tag{24}
$$

where the last expression follows from lemma 1 and equation (19). Substituting (24) into (23) immediately yields (21). The other equations in theorem 2 are derived similarly. $\square$

It is evident then from (21) and (22) that, with $\Delta^t c_u^\alpha c_u^\gamma > 0$ owing to market stability,[17] and with $x_q^t < 0$,[18] we necessarily get $du^\alpha/dT < 0$ and $du^\gamma/dT > 0$. That is, the donor must be immiserized and the recipient must be enriched. Paradoxes cannot arise.

3. *A general proposition* Now that we have demonstrated that the pursuit of an optimal tariff policy by the (union of the) donor and recipient jointly vis-à-vis the nonparticipant agent will rule out transfer paradoxes, in a Walras-stable context, we are able to see that the presence of a *suitably interpreted* (foreign) distortion is required in the three-agent case if the paradoxes are to arise.[19] At the same time, for the case of two agents, we know that *exogenously imposed* price distortions (e.g., tax-cum-subsidies on production, consumption or trade) can also generate the transfer paradoxes (in the presence of inferior goods), as established by Brecher and Bhagwati (1982) and ourselves (1982a). We also known from the former paper, which analyzes transfer-induced distortions in the context of additionality requirements, and from the latter paper which analyses transfer-seeking *DUP* activities by domestic and foreign lobbyists, that *endogenous*

(i.e., transfer-induced) distortions can also generate transfer paradoxes, consistent with Walrasian stability. We can therefore now state the following general proposition:

PROPOSITION   *The paradoxes of enriched donor and immiserized recipient cannot arise unless a distortion is present in the system.*

3. Conclusion: Implications for Analytical and Policy Problems

The foregoing analysis has important implications in a number of areas of theoretical and policy concern.

International
(1) Our analysis of the three-agent problem does modify the earlier theoretical presumption against the possibility of stability-compatible paradoxes. (2) Since, in the international context, reparations and aid are never given by one country to the "rest of the world" but are always bilateral transactions in a multilateral context, policymakers should be alert to the possibility that their intentions may be frustrated by paradoxical outcomes. (3) As noted by Brecher and Bhagwati (1981), the three-agent transfer problem has an immediate counterpart in the analysis of customs unions with full mobility of factors within the union. Thus, for instance, it is possible for Italy to be immiserized within the EEC by receiving an aid inflow from the non-EEC world, under conditions established by us, consistent with market stability.

Domestic
(1) Internal redistribution from the rich to the poor may also be counterproductive under the conditions established here. Thus, if the poor receive the transfer from the rich while the not-so-poor outside group is a net exporter of food and the rich also have a lower marginal propensity to consume food than the not-so-poor, then we know that the conditions are satisfied to make it possible for the poor to be immiserized by receipt of the transfer. (2) The three-agent analysis also brings into sharp focus problems raised by the "basic needs" prescription that the targeted poor be given purchasing power to buy their nourishment, etc. If this purchasing power is taken from the rich, the nonparticipant not-so-poor may well find that their real income is diminished by a transfer-induced deterioration in their terms of trade (under an appropriate ranking of marginal propensities to consume) so that the poor become not-so-poor, whereas the not-so-poor are reduced to the ranks of the poor! Indeed, our three-agent analysis similarly implies a certain caution in treating famine relief through transfers

of puchasing power to the distressed income groups. Unless a similar security net is available elsewhere, you may then be pushing the malnourished not-so-obviously-starving poor (who are not receiving this purchasing power) below the line so that *they* are now ravaged by the famine.

The Invisible Shakedown

Our analysis also suggests a generalization of the idea underlying Gale's (1974) example where both the donor and the recipient are enriched by a transfer, at the expense of the nonparticipant outside agent. What is implied here is a seemingly innocuous process that involves enrichment at the expense of an unsuspecting agent. Through this process, the outside agent is hurt, for the benefit of the transfer-process agents, in a fashion that is by no means perceived as such, unlike in overt and visible instances, such as where an optimal tariff may be levied against that agent.

Gale's example is, however, only one such instance: where the transfer is between the two agents (α and γ), with the third agent (β) remaining outside of the transfer process. But it is easy to see that one of the two agents (say α) could equally exploit the third agent (β) by making a *direct* transfer to it—immiserizing it while enriching itself (and even, if need be, the other agent, γ)—the conditions for this being readily established from equations (6)–(8) above. This is a clear case where a gift horse does need to be looked at in the mouth since, to mix metaphors ever so slightly, it turns out to be a Trojan horse.

The class of cases where (seemingly innocuous) transfers can improve the donor's welfare at the expense of either the direct recipient or an agent outside of the transfer process, or both, may then be christened generically as phenomena involving an *invisible shakedown*.

Notes

Bhagwati: Department of Economics, Columbia University, New York, NY 10027; Brecher: Department of Economics, Carleton University, Ottawa, ON K1S 5B6; Hatta: Department of Political Economy, The Johns Hopkins University, Baltimore, MD 21218. We thank the National Science Foundation, grant no. 5-24718, for partial financial support of the research underlying this paper. The paper was written when Brecher and Hatta were visiting Columbia University, 1981–82. Gratefully acknowledged are helpful comments and suggestions from John Chipman, Avinash Dixit, Jacques Drèze, Robert Feenstra, Jacob Frenkel, Ronald Jones, Murray Kemp, Andreu Mas-Colell, Michael Mussa, John Riley, Lars Svensson, and Robert Willig, from anonymous referees, and from seminar participants at Berkeley, Harvard, Minnesota, Rochester, Chicago and the University of California-Los Angeles.

1. After the present paper was submitted for publication, and following its presentation at Rochester, our attention was drawn to this appendix, which was noticed by a student of Ronald Jones. Subsequently, we learned from Makoto Yano that Motoshige Itoh had pointed out an important related paper by Ryuotaro Komiya and T. Shizuki (1967), whose condition (11) for the Johnson case anticipated our equation (12) below. We are grateful for having both of these references brought to our attention.

2. Gale constructs an example in which the donor is enriched along with the recipient. Furthermore, this immediately implies that a reverse transfer will immiserize the (new) recipient. A simple calculation, moreover, shows that the Gale example is Walras-stable. Gale's work has stimulated a number of papers, most of which assume fixed commodity endowments and/or fixed consumption coefficients. A notable exception is an analysis of the three-agent transfer problem by Makoto Yano (1981), who introduces substitutability in both production and consumption. (We are grateful to Ronald Jones and Peter Neary for drawing our attention to Yano's work, after the research for the present paper was virtually completed.) A fuller discussion of these and related papers, in an evidently growing and important literature, is provided by us (1982b) elsewhere.

3. Robert Aumann and B. Peleg (1974) have rediscovered, in a restrictive model with no substitution in production, the immiserizing growth case of Bhagwati (1958). See also Bhagwati (1982).

4. First use equations (1), (2), and (3) to write $u^\alpha = v^\alpha(q, T)$, $u^\beta = v^\beta(q)$, and $u^\gamma = v^\gamma(q, T)$, respectively. Then define $x^\alpha[q, v^\alpha(q, T)] + x^\beta[q, v^\beta(q)] + x^\gamma[q, v^\gamma(q, T)] \equiv \tilde{x}(q, T)$, which is the world's uncompensated excess-demand function for good X. Now, we have $\tilde{x}_q = x_q^\alpha + x_u^\alpha v_q^\alpha + x_q^\beta + x_u^\beta v_q^\beta + x_q^\gamma + x_u^\gamma v_q^\gamma = -x^\alpha x_u^\alpha - x^\beta x_u^\beta - x^\gamma x_u^\gamma + x_q \equiv -\Delta$.

5. As may be readily verified, the marginal propensity to consume good X in country i equals qx_u^i/e_u^i for $i = \alpha, \beta, \gamma$. Therefore, if β and γ share an identical marginal propensity to consume X, this implies that $x_u^\alpha = x_u^\gamma$ (recalling the normalization that $e_u^\alpha = e_u^\beta = e_u^\gamma = 1$).

6. This might explain why Gale (1974), who tried to construct an example of donor enrichment, wound up assuming fixed coefficients in consumption (with fixed coefficients in production also implied by his exchange model), and confessed his inability to admit "smooth preferences." Interestingly, the absence of smooth preferences also characterizes the examples that Gale attributes to other major mathematical economists such as Drezè and McFadden. Just recently, Daniel Leonard and Richard Manning (1982) provided a paradoxical example involving smooth preferences within an exchange model.

7. In section 2 and in note 15 below, we spell out an alternative way of seeing why the income terms of only the two "other" countries appear in equations (6) and (8).

8. That is, when α gives out a transfer of one unit of Y, β receives $x^\beta/(x^\beta + x^\gamma)$ units of Y and γ receives $x^\gamma/(x^\beta + x^\gamma)$ units of Y. If these ratios are positive, both countries receive positive amounts of transfer. If $x^\beta/(x^\beta + x^\gamma)$ is negative, β receives a negative transfer, viz, it gives a transfer of $-x^\beta/(x^\beta + x^\gamma)$ to α. In this situation, γ receives one plus $-x^\beta/(x^\beta + x^\gamma)$ units of Y, since $x^\gamma/(x^\beta + x^\gamma) = 1 - x^\beta/(x^\beta + x^\gamma)$. Similarly, γ gives a positive transfer to α when $x^\gamma/(x^\beta + x^\gamma)$ is negative.

9. The reader can similarly rewrite (8) for the welfare effect on the recipient, γ.

10. To see this, appropriately exploit the essence of the result in (6). A unit transfer from α to β implies

$$\frac{du^\alpha}{dT^{\alpha\beta}} = \frac{x_q - x^\gamma(x_u^\gamma - x_u^\beta)}{\Delta}, \tag{a}$$

and from α to γ implies

$$\frac{du^\alpha}{dT^{\alpha\gamma}} = \frac{x_q - x^\beta(x_u^\beta - x_u^\gamma)}{\Delta}. \tag{b}$$

With actual transfers in the first stage divided according to the ratios $x^\beta/(x^\beta + x^\gamma)$ and $x^\gamma/(x^\beta + x^\gamma)$ between β and γ, these ratios should be multiplied into (a) and (b), respectively. Adding the resulting equations yields x_q/Δ.

11. This readily follows from appropriately using the essence of the result in (7) and the fact that $x^\beta/(x^\beta + x^\gamma)$ represents the share of the transfer β received at the first stage and hands out to γ in the second stage. Equation (7) applies since, when β makes a transfer to γ, the welfare effect on α is as if α is the nonparticipant, outside country; the resulting welfare impact on α per unit transfer from β to γ is

$$\frac{du^\alpha}{dT^{\beta\gamma}} = -\frac{x^\alpha(x_u^\gamma - x_u^\beta)}{\Delta} = -\frac{(x^\beta + x^\gamma)(x_u^\beta - x_u^\gamma)}{\Delta}.$$

12. Substituting $\tilde{x}_q^\beta = x_q^\beta - x^\beta x_u^\beta$ into (6) and recalling $x_q = x_q^\alpha + x_q^\beta + x_q^\gamma$ yields (12).

13. In this case, the Slutsky equation and (4) should be used to rewrite the stability condition as

$$\Delta = x^\gamma(x_u^\gamma - x_u^\alpha) - x_q^\alpha - x_q^\gamma - \tilde{x}_q^\beta - x_q^\beta x_u^\alpha > 0.$$

14. For further details on the use of production possibility and Scitovsky frontiers corresponding to a pair of countries involved directly in a bilateral transfer, see Brecher and Bhagwati (1982).

15. In determining whether there remains a world excess supply of good X when q is adjusted to keep u^α constant after the transfer, clearly the substitution effect but not the income effect plays a role in (the unchanged-welfare) country α, whereas both of these effects are relevant in countries β (as u^β varies with q) and γ (as u^γ varies between Scitovsky frontiers). Thus, we have additional insight into why the income effects x_u^β and x_u^γ but not x_u^α enter the necessary condition (9). Similar reasoning sheds extra light on (10).

Two further remarks are in order. First, the use of the Scitovsky technique to analyze *welfare* changes here is only a natural counterpart to the two-stage derivation technique used by trade theorists in *positive* analyses. Thus, if the impact of a parametric change on the terms of trade is analyzed, one can hold the terms of trade constant, compute excess demand for one of the two goods, and then use the stability condition to determine the direction of the terms-of-trade change, a procedure introduced by Johnson, Mundell, and many other trade theorists in the 1950s. Identically, if one is interested instead in welfare change (of say the donor), one can equally hold welfare (of the donor) constant, compute excess demand, use the stability condition to determine the terms-of-trade change and then immediately the welfare change. This was, in fact, the procedure utilized in the analysis of immiserizing growth in Bhagwati (1958); and for the transfer problem, it leads naturally to the resurrection of the Scitovsky curves, as in the text above. Second, the use of Scitovsky curves in analyzing the transfer paradoxes was introduced earlier in Brecher and Bhagwati (1982). Whereas our Scitovsky technique easily handles large changes, the use of the two-stage holding-welfare-constant technique for small changes has also been introduced in Yano (1981) who credits Ronald Jones for the idea.

16. Note that point S'' in consumption must lie outside the curve BE, assuming that good Y is not sufficiently inferior to violate the Vanek (1965)-Bhagwati (1968a)-Kemp (1968) condition (discussed in more detail by us elsewhere, 1982a) for stability in the presence of tariffs. See also note 17 below.

17. By reasoning similar to that of note 4 above, $\Delta^t = \tilde{x}_q^t$, where $\tilde{x}^t(q, T) \equiv x^\alpha[q, v^\alpha(q, T)] + \tilde{x}^\beta[p^*(q)] + x^\gamma[q, v^\gamma(q, T)]$, while the indirect utility functions v^α and v^γ now come respectively from equations (17) and (18). Thus, Walrasian stability requires that $0 < \Delta^t$. Also, as explained by us elsewhere (1982a), c_u^α and c_u^γ must both be positive to satisfy the Vanek-Bhagwati-Kemp condition assumed in note 16 above.

18. As we move along the Baldwin envelope, $p_q^* > 0$ and $\tilde{x}_p^\beta < 0$ are well-known properties of economic efficiency. Thus, $x_q^\alpha + \tilde{x}_p^\beta p_q^* + x_q^\gamma < 0$.

19. While our analysis can be viewed therefore as essentially providing a *conceptual* way of integrating the many-agent problem into the theory of distortions and welfare, our result on optimal tariffs also has direct *policy* relevance. For example, if there are two income classes, rich and poor, in an open economy with monopoly power in trade, we can definitely assert now that, if an optimal tariff is always in place, redistribtuion from the rich to the poor will not lead to paradoxical results.

References

Aumann, R. J. and Peleg, B. A note on Gale's example. *Journal of Mathematical Economics* 2 (August 1974), 209–211.

Baldwin, Robert E. Equilibrium in international trade: A diagrammatic analysis. *Quarterly Journal of Economics* 62 (November 1948), 748–762.

Bhagwati, Jagdish N. Immiserizing growth: A geometrical note. *Review of Economic Studies* 25 (June 1958), 201–205.

Bhagwati, Jagdish N. 1968a. Gains from trade once again. *Oxford Economic Papers* 20 (July 1968), 137–148.

Bhagwati, Jagdish N. 1968b. Distortions and immiserizing growth: A generalization. *Review of Economic Studies* 35 (October 1968), 481–485.

Bhagwati, Jagdish N. The generalized theory of distortions and welfare. In his et al., eds., *Trade, Balance of Payments and Growth.* Amsterdam: North Holland, 1971.

Bhagwati, Jagdish N. Immiserizing growth and negative shadow factor prices: A comment on Aumann and Peleg. Mimeo., May 1982.

Bhagwati, Jagdish N., Brecher, Richard A., and Hatta, Tatsuo 1982a. The generalized theory of transfers and welfare (II): Exogenous (policy-imposed) and endogenous (transfer-induced) distortions. Mimeo., July 1982.

Bhagwati, Jagdish N., Brecher, Richard A., and Hatta, Tatsuo. 1982b. The paradoxes of immiserizing growth and donor-enriching (recipient-immiserizing) transfers: A tale of two literatures. Paper No. 15, International Economics Research Center, Columbia University, November 1982.

Brecher, Richard A., and Bhagwati, Jagdish N. Foreign ownership and the theory of trade and welfare. *Journal of Political Economy* 89 (June 1981), 497–511.

Brecher, Richard A., and Bhagwati, Jagdish N. Immiserizing transfers from abroad. *Journal of International Economics* 13 (November 1982), 353–364.

Chipman, John S. The Theory of Exploitative Trade and Investment Policies. In Louis E. DiMarco, ed., *International Economics and Development*, New York: Academic Press, 1972.

Chipman, John S. The transfer problem once again. In G. Horwich and Paul Samuelson, eds., *Trade, Stability and Macroeconomics: Essays in Honor of Lloyd A. Metzler*. New York: Academic Press, 1974.

Diamond, Peter A. Tax incidence in a two-good model. *Journal of Public Economics* 9 (June 1978), 283–299.

Dixit, Avinash, and Norman, V. *The Theory of International Trade*. Cambridge: Cambridge University Press, 1980.

Gale, David. Exchange equilibrium and Coalitions: An example. *Journal of Mathematical Economics* 1 (March 1974), 63–66.

Hatta, Tatsuo. 1973a. Compensation rules in multiple-consumer economies. The Johns Hopkins University. Mimeo., 1973.

Hatta, Tatsuo. 1973b. A theory of piecemeal policy recommendations. Unpublished doctoral dissertation. The Johns Hopkins University, 1973.

Hatta, Tatsuo. A recommendation for a better tariff structure. *Econometrica* 45 (November 1977), 1859–1869.

Hatta, Tatsuo, and Fukushima, Takashi. The welfare effect of tariff rate reductions in a many country world. *Journal of International Economics* 9 (November 1979), 503–511.

Johnson, Harry G. Income distribution, the offer curve and the effects of tariffs. *Manchester School of Economics* 28 (September 1960), 223–242.

Johnson, Harry G. The possibility of income losses from increased efficiency or factor accumulation in the presence of tariffs. *Economic Journal* 77 (March 1967), 151–154.

Jones, Ronald. The transfer problem revisited. *Economica* 37 (May 1970), 178–184.

Jones, Ronald. Presumption and the transfer problem. *Journal of International Economics* 5 (1975), 263–374. Reprinted in his *International Trade: Essays in Theory*. Amsterdam: North Holland, 1979.

Kemp, Murray C. Some issues in the analysis of trade gains. *Oxford Economic Papers* 20 (July 1968), 149–161.

Komiya, Ryotaro, and Shizuki, T. Transfer payments and income distribution. *Manchester School of Economics* 35 (September 1967), 245–255.

Leonard, Daniel, and Manning, Richard. Advantageous reallocations: A constructive example. Mimeo., 1982. *Journal of International Economics*, forthcoming.

Leontief, Wassily. Note on the pure theory of capital transfer. In *Explorations in Economics: Notes and Essays Contributed in Honor of F. W. Taussig.* New York: McGraw-Hill, 1936.

Samuelson, Paul A. *Foundations of Economic Analysis.* Cambridge: Harvard University Press, 1947.

Samuelson, Paul A. The transfer problem and transport costs: The terms of trade when impediments are absent. *Economic Journal* 62 (June 1952), 278–304.

Samuelson, Paul A. The transfer problem and transport costs, II: Analysis of effects of trade impediments. *Economic Journal* 64 (June 1954) 264–289.

Samuelson, Paul A. On the trail of conventional beliefs about the transfer problem. In J. Bhagwati et al., eds., *Trade, Balance of Payments and Growth.* Amsterdam: North Holland, 1971, 327–354.

Scitovsky, Tibor. A reconsideration of the theory of tariffs. *Review of Economic Studies* 9, no. 2 (1942), 89–110.

Vanek, Jaroslav. *General Equilibrium of International Discrimination: The Case of Customs Unions.* Cambridge: Harvard University Press, 1965.

Yano, Makoto. Welfare aspects in transfer problem: On the Validity of the "Neo-Orthodox" Presumptions. Mimeo., December 1981 (rev. 1982). *Journal of International Economics*, forthcoming.

Postscript

In section 1, we assumed (for the sake of concreteness) that $x^\beta < 0$, and stated that this assumption was made "without loss of generality." To elucidate that statement, this postscript explicitly considers the case in which $x^\beta > 0$, so that country β exports good Y. We are grateful to Murray Kemp for suggesting that we clarify this matter.

By Walras's law,

$$q\tilde{x}^\beta(q) + \tilde{y}^\beta(q) = 0,$$

where $\tilde{y}^\beta(q)$ is the uncompensated import-demand function of country β for good Y. Differentiation of this equation yields

$$x^\beta + q\tilde{x}_q^\beta + \tilde{y}_q^\beta = 0.$$

Since the marginal propensities to consume in each country sum to unity, we also have

$$\frac{qx_u^\gamma}{e_u^\gamma} + \frac{y_u^\gamma}{e_u^\gamma} = 1,$$

where $y^\gamma(q, u^\gamma)$ is the compensated import-demand function of country γ for good Y.

Substituting these last two equations into (12), rearranging terms, and recalling that $e_u^\gamma = 1$ initially, we obtain

$$\frac{du^\alpha}{dT} = \frac{[x_q^\alpha + x_q^\gamma - (\tilde{y}_q^\beta + x^\beta)(1/q) + x^\beta(1 - y_u^\gamma)(1/q)]}{\Delta}$$

$$= \frac{[x_q^\alpha + x_q^\gamma - \tilde{y}_q^\beta(1/q) - x^\beta y_u^\gamma(1/q)]}{\Delta}.$$

Thus, when $x^\beta > 0$, $du^\alpha/dT > 0$ only if *either* $y_u^\gamma < 0$ *or* $\tilde{y}_q^\beta < 0$. By similar reasoning, $du^\gamma/dT < 0$ only if *either* $y_u^\alpha < 0$ *or* $\tilde{y}_q^\beta < 0$, where $y^\alpha(q, u^\alpha)$ is the compensated import-demand function of country α for good Y. In other words, a welfare paradox for one country participating in the transfer implies that *either* the other participating country exhibits inferiority in consuming the nonparticipant country's export good *or* the offer curve of the nonparticipant is inelastic (such that the export supply of this country falls as its terms of trade improve).

When stated in this general way, the necessary conditions for a paradox do not depend on the sign of x^β.

IX
Foreign Investment

Introduction to Part IX

The final part reprints two major papers in the evolving theory of multi-national firms, namely, of direct foreign investment.

Markusen (chapter 28) and Helpman (chapter 29) model in rather similar fashion. Multiplant operations are considered by Markusen in the context of economies resulting therefrom, in consequence of "joint inputs" whose productivity can be obtained in different plants, regardless of the number of plants operated, much like public goods. Helpman also considers the notion that firm-specific assets relating to marketing, management skills, and product-specific R & D can be used in plants abroad even while they are employed at home. Both their analyses are akin to the new theories of international trade built in the imperfectly competitive mold.

In contrast, new theories of direct foreign investment that reflect rather the other major revolution in trade theory, that is the political economy theory of DUP activities, have also arisen, and the student ought to turn to them equally for new approaches in this burgeoning field.

Of particular interest is the theory of *quid pro quo* foreign investment where, say, Japanese foreign investment occurs in the United States because the investor is trying to coopt U.S. capitalists and/or labor and/or Congress into ceasing protectionist pressure. Thus a first-period loss is accepted by undertaking the foreign investment, but as a result the probability of keeping the U.S. market open in the second period is favorably affected. The *quid pro quo* to rewarding U.S. capitalists, U.S. labor, and/or U.S. government (which looks favorably upon such influx of foreign investment as creating jobs), admittedly at immediate loss in shifting part of the production to a higher-cost production source, is simply the favorable effect on reducing protectionist pressures. Such *quid pro quo* foreign investment has been explored in Bhagwati (*Journal of Policy Modelling*, 1985) and Bhagwati, Brecher, Dinopoulos, and Srinivasan (*Journal of Development Economics*, 1987).

28

Multinationals, Multi-Plant Economies, and the Gains from Trade

James R. Markusen

For many years there has existed a debate as to the allocative and distributive effects of multinational corporations. There is little general agreement as to these effects and, indeed, formal trade theory has largely failed to provide a rationale as to why these corporations exist at all. The empirical evidence sheds some light on this very basic question insofar as it suggests that the level of multinational activity in a particular industry is related to the importance of "intangibles" in that industry's overall operation (Caves 1980). These "intangibles" involve activities not directly related to the physical production of goods such as R & D, advertising, marketing, and distribution.[1]

Intangibles in turn seem to be closely related to the concept of economies of multiplant operation (Scherer et al. 1975; Scherer 1980). By "economies of multi-plant operation" we will mean technical or pecuniary advantages possessed by a single owner of two or more production facilities over an industry in which there are independent (even if joint-profit maximizing) owners of the same production facilities. The great body of research on Canada in particular seems to repeatedly emphasize economies of multiplant operation in explaining the incidence across industries of United States multinationals operating in Canada (Eastman and Stykolt 1967; Caves et al. 1980).

These stylized facts suggest two alternative avenues for developing a satisfactory theory of the multinational enterprise (MNE). One is based on strategic considerations such as using R & D, marketing investments, and foreign branch plants to pre-empt foreign competition. This is the approach taken by Magee (1977) and Horstmann and Markusen (1987). The second

This paper was originally published in *Journal of International Economics* 16, no. 3/4 (May 1984): 205–224. The present version omits sections 5 and 6 of the original article.

approach is to examine aspects of technology which by themselves (i.e., quite apart from strategic behaviour) imply the superior efficiency of multi-plant production. This second approach is used in this paper to develop a technology-based theory of MNE. The model is then used to address issues relating to market power, technical efficiency, the pattern of trade, and world income distribution.

In attempting to meet these objectives, a satisfactory model should meet five conditions: (1) The model should provide a rationale as to why a firm wishes to engage in direct rather than in portfolio investment. (2) The model should not rely on factor movements or factor price differences insofar as the MNE literature stresses that the MNE often provides for much of its needs from local factor markets. Both requirements imply that the general equilibrium literature on factor movements is of little use and that a theory of the firm approach may be more useful.[2] (3) The model should explain why multi-plant operation is superior to price collusion among independent producers. (4) The model must justify the fact that the MNE, by definition, chooses to carry on at least one type of activity in each of several countries rather than supply all countries from a single production facility. (5) The model should allow for positive economic profits since alternative distributions of profits may have important implications for the gains from trade. This suggests that a monopoly/duopoly model in which firms produce a single homogeneous good may provide a richer treatment than the more recent monopolistic competition models (Krugman 1979; Helpman 1981).

It seems that these requirements simply cannot be met by any model that relies on the assumptions of either constant returns in production or increasing returns of the usual neoclassical variety. In the former case, there is no role for the individual enterprise and hence direct foreign investment cannot be distinguished from portfolio investment. In the latter case, there will be a tendency for the firm to centralize rather than to geographically diversify production. Similarly, superior technical knowledge combined with an incentive to jump a tariff barrier is not an entirely satisfying basis for a theory. While differences in know-how may imply strategic considerations (Magee 1977; Horstmann and Markusen 1987), there is no purely technical reason why branch-plant production is superior to simply selling or licensing the superior technology.

The notion of multi-plant economies is thus appealing from a theoretical as well as an empirical point of view. The problem is that to the best of my knowledge, no one has precisely specified this notion in formal algebraic notation. To do so will be the first task of this paper.

1. Economies of Multi-Plant Operation

Sources of multi-plant economies are often found in firm-specific as opposed to plant-specific activities. These firm-specific activities include things like R & D, advertising, marketing, distribution, and management services, as noted above (Scherer et al. 1975; Scherer 1980). One characteristic of these activities that I wish to capture here is that they often involve a "public goods" or "jointness" aspect with respect to the firm's various production facilities. R & D expenditures on designing better products and/or production processes provide an interesting example. Once an innovation is made, it can be incorporated into any number of additional plants without reducing the marginal product of that innovation in existing plants.[3] The efficiency advantage of the multi-plant firm as modelled below lies in its ability to avoid the duplication in R & D and other activities which is necessarily involved in single-plant operation.[4]

We should also note that the MNE often tends to centralize these firm-specific activities (corporate headquarters); that is, R & D, marketing, finance, etc. are often centralized in a particular location while production activities are geographically dispersed. It is easy to think of reasons as to why this might be the case. The total output of two scientists working independently may, for example, be less than their output working cooperatively in the same location. Similarly, communication among different managerial and technical departments is more efficient in a centralized location. The model presented below will attempt to capture this "centralization" aspect as well as the "public-goods" or "jointness" aspect mentioned above.

The model consists of two goods (X and Y) and two countries (m and h). Superscripts m and h will denote countries throughout the model, with m denoting the MNE's home country and h denoting the host country in the MNE version of the problem. Other features of the model are as follows:

1. X and Y are each produced from labour and sector-specific capital. Total endowments of all factors are fixed.
2. Countries m and h have identical factor endowments, identical technology, and identical, homothetic community utility functions.
3. Y is produced with constant returns to scale by a competitive industry.
4. The output of X is the product of the outputs of two activities: activity C (for corporate or control) and activity F (for factory). C and F may be geographically separated in the production of X.
5. Capital which is sector specific to X is used in F but not in C, which uses only labour. F is characterized by constant returns (eliminating the possi-

bility of many domestic plants) and thus $X = C \cdot F$ is characterized by increasing returns.

6. Increasing returns in X are assumed to be weak relative to factor intensity effects such that the production set of each country is strictly convex. This ensures that a monopolist will maintain plants in both countries (i.e., become a MNE) rather than attempt to supply both countries from a single plant.[5]

7. For the multi-plant firm, the C activity has a "public goods" or "jointness" aspect in that additional geographic locations of F activities may be added to the firm without reducing the marginal product of C in existing F activities.

8. For the multi-plant firm, the C activity is also characterized by a "centralization" aspect in that for a fixed total allocation of labour to C activities, the output of C is maximized by undertaking C at a single location.

9. Equity ownership may cross international borders, but factors of production are immobile. There are no barriers to trade.

The C activity in producing X is intended to represent the R & D, marketing and managerial factors referred to above. F is intended to represent the physical transformation of inputs into outputs. Assumption 2 is made in order to neutralize the usual Heckscher-Ohlin, Ricardian, and demand bases for trade. The reason for this is that I wish to show clearly how multi-plant economies of scale can affect the pattern of trade and production. If we were to assume differences in factor endowments as well as the existence of scale economies, we would in general not be able to obtain any clear results or be able to tie results to one effect or the other. For the same reasons that we do not normally mix differences in technology (Ricardian trade models) with differences in factor endowments (Heckscher-Ohlin trade models) we will restrict the present analysis to a single basis for trade (scale economies).

The jointness and centralization aspects of C have been briefly discussed above. Only the results having to do with the volume and direction of trade depend on the centralization property as will be discussed from time to time. Gains from trade and welfare results will depend only on the jointness aspect.

Given the specifications 1–9 production functions for the single-plant and two-plant enterprises are given as follows:

$$X^i = C(L_c^i)F(L_f^i), \quad i = m, h, \tag{1}$$

$$X^m + X^h = C(L_c^m, L_c^h)[F(L_f^m) + F(L_f^h)]. \tag{2}$$

Given the sector-specific nature of capital, we can simply omit the capital arguments in the F functions which as a result are assumed to be characterized by $F'' < 0$.[6] The jointness aspect of the C activity is captured in (2) by $[F^m + F^h]$: changes in physical production (F) in one location do not affect the marginal product of C in the other location. F^m and F^h are also assumed to be independent in that there are no externality effects between geographically separated production facilities.

The centralization property of C is modelled by allowing the C isoquants to be concave to the origin in L^m and L^h space. While this is not in general sufficient to ensure that the MNE will centralize C (L_c^m or L_c^h equal to zero) due to the concavity of Y and F, it will be sufficient if $C(L_c^m, L_c^h) = \max(L_c^m, L_c^h)$; that is, running independent C activities is so inefficient that it is completely redundant. In what follows we will simply assume C is centralized at the MNE equilibrium. It must be emphasized that this assumption plays no role in the welfare analysis and simply serves to make the positive analysis of trade more interesting by introducing an asymmetry into the MNE equilibrium.[7]

In order to facilitate comparisons of eqs. (1) and (2), we will assume the following:

$$C(\bar{L}_c^m, 0) = C(0, \bar{L}_c^h) = C(\bar{L}_c^i), \quad \text{for} \quad \bar{L}_c^h = \bar{L}_c^m = \bar{L}_c^i. \tag{3}$$

Equation (3) states that if C is carried on in only one location by the MNE, the output of C activities is the same as the output from a single-plant operation given equal levels of L_c in the two cases. Equation (3) states, in other words, that the number of plants is irrelevant to the production function for C activities. In what follows, $C(L_c^m)$ will be used as shorthand for $C(L_c^m, 0)$ since we have assumed that centralization is optimal for the MNE and will arbitrarily assume that C is centralized in the home country.

2. The National Enterprise Equilibria

In this section we will derive reference solutions by assuming that there exists an independent monopoly (or duopoly) producer of X in each country. This formulation will be referred to as the national enterprise (NE) case. The list of NE equilibria is not comprehensive but rather is chosen to illustrate the possible trade-off between technical efficiency and market power when a MNE replaces two domestic firms.

It is assumed, as noted above, that all consumers including the monopolist have identical, homothetic utility functions and that the monopolist (or rather duopolist) in each country maximizes profits. With distributional and income effects thus removed, demand prices are simply a function of the relative outputs of X and Y (X/Y). If production takes place along the efficient production frontier of each country, the demand price ratio can be specified even more simply as just a function of X, since Y is uniquely related to X along the production frontier (Markusen 1981; Melvin and Warne 1973). Production must take place on the efficient production frontier even if the duopolists exercise monopsony power since there is only one factor mobile between sectors in this model. We will assume throughout the paper, however, that producers of X view factor prices as parametric.[8] This is of some help in simplifying the graphical comparison of the MNE and NE equilibria, as noted below. The formal analysis of section 4 will not rely on this assumption.

Let p denote the price of X in terms of Y. The autarky equilibrium conditions in which there is a single monopoly producer of X in each country are given very simply as follows (Melvin and Warne 1973; Markusen 1981):

$$p^i\left(1 - \frac{1}{\eta_x^i}\right) = MRT^i; \quad \eta_x^i = -\frac{p}{X}\frac{dX}{dp} > 0, \quad i = m, h, \tag{4}$$

where MRT^i is the marginal rate of transformation along country i's production frontier and η_x^i is the elasticity of demand for X in country i. Second-order conditions for (4) will be satisfied if η_x^i is more than one and is a decreasing function of X (or, more correctly, of X/Y). Melvin and Warne (1973) and Markusen (1981) show that these conditions will be satisfied for example by any CES utility function with an elasticity of substitution greater than one.

Given our assumptions of identical tastes, technology, and factor endowments, it should be apparent that the solutions to (4) must be identical for the two countries. Autarky outputs, commodity prices, elasticities of demand, and factor prices will be the same in the two countries. With p^i, η_x^i and MRT^i the same in each country, it must also be true that production takes place on the efficient world production frontier.

The equilibrium given by (4) is shown in figure 28.1 by point A. The production frontier $\overline{YX_n}$ can represent either the domestic or world production frontiers, with the latter being simply a radial blowup of the former. Similarly, U_a can represent either the world or the national community indifference curve given the symmetry in the solution. Factor prices are also equalized in the autarky equilibria.[9]

When trade is possible, the symmetry in the model implies that any type of symmetric behaviour on the part of the two duopolists results in (1) production on the world production frontier and (2) no trade (by virtue of the fact that outputs, commodity prices, etc., are equalized without trade). Interestingly enough, if the two duopolists engage in price collusion to

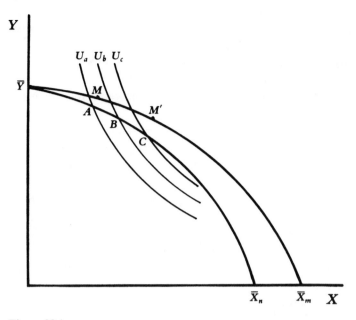

Figure 28.1

maximize joint profits or engage in a market-shares rivalry, exactly the same equilibrium will be reached as occurred with autarky production. There are no gains to be realized here from price collusion since the equilibrium condition is simply (4) with p^i and η^i_x equalized between countries.[10] But the two equations in (4) are already equalized at the autarky equilibrium. It is in turn fairly well known that a market-shares rivalry results in an outcome identical to price collusion in this type of model.

Cournot-Nash behaviour on the part of the duopolists does on the other hand produce a distinct equilibrium (Markusen 1981). Suppose the duopolist in country m now views X^h as parametric. Revenue and marginal revenue as viewed by the duopolist in m are now given by

$$R^m = p(X^m + \bar{X}^h)X^m;$$

$$MR^m = p + X^m \frac{dp}{dX} \tag{5}$$

$$MR^m = p + (X^m + X^h)\frac{dp}{dX}\left(\frac{X^m}{X^m + X^h}\right) = p\left(1 - \frac{\sigma^m}{\eta_x}\right), \quad \sigma^i = \frac{X^i}{X^m + X^h},$$

where σ^m represents m's market share and η_x continues to represent the world elasticity of demand for X. The Cournot-Nash equilibrium is thus given by

$$p\left(1 - \frac{\sigma^i}{\eta_x}\right) = MRT^i, \quad i = m, h. \tag{6}$$

As in the previous three cases, the solutions to (6) must be symmetric for m and h. Each country must have the same outputs, market share, consumption levels, factor prices, and so forth. Note, however, that there are gains from (potential) trade in the sense that welfare levels will be higher than in autarky. The symmetric equilibria in (6) must imply a market share of one-half for each duopolist. Thus, at the autarky equilibrium (point A in figure 28.1), each duopolist will now find that perceived marginal revenue exceeds marginal costs. The national or world equilibrium must now be at a point like B in figure 28.1 which, given our demand assumptions, constitutes an unambiguous improvement in welfare relative to A.[11] Further increases in production and welfare could be realized if the firms engaged in average-cost pricing to prevent entry (point C in figure 28.1).

We could of course also examine some nonsymmetric NE equilibria such as Stackelberg leader-follower behaviour. But the point here is simply to establish that competitive forms of duopoly behaviour (Cournot-Nash, average-cost pricing) create a situation in which it is unclear whether or not replacing an inefficient duopoly with an efficient monopoly will increase welfare. Since the properties of a Stackelberg equilibrium require a rather lengthy analysis, we do not therefore present this case here.

3. The Multinational Enterprise Equilibrium

Since it is not obvious that the MNE will produce efficiently, perhaps we should solve for the conditions that characterize the efficient world production frontier and compare them to the MNE's equilibrium conditions. It now makes little sense to talk about national production frontiers since the position of country h's production frontier will, for example, be determined by the level of C activities carried on in country m. A similar problem confronted Ethier (1979) in dealing with international externalities.

Assuming that it is optimal to centralize the C activity in country m, the conditions characterizing the efficient production frontier can be found by maximizing the output of X for a given level of Y production:

$$\max C(L_c^m)[F(L_f^m) + F(L_f^h)]$$

$$\text{s.t.} \quad \bar{Y} = G(\bar{L} - L_c^m - L_f^m) + G(\bar{L} - L_f^h), \tag{7}$$

$$\frac{G^{m'}}{C^{m'}(F^m + F^h)} = \frac{G^{m'}}{C^m F^{m'}} = \frac{G^{h'}}{C^m F^{h'}} = MRT, \tag{8}$$

where $\bar{L}$ denotes each economy's endowment of labour and $Y = G(L_y)$.

Let w^i denote the wage of labour in terms of Y. $w^i = G^{i'}$ follows from the assumption that factor markets and the Y industry are competitive ($G^{i'}$ equals the marginal product of labour in the production of Y). The MNE's programming problem and first-order conditions are given as follows:

$$\max pC(L_c^m)[F(L_f^m) + F(L_f^h)] - w^m(L_c^m + L_f^m) - w^h L_f^h, \quad p = p(X), \qquad (9)$$

$$p\left(1 - \frac{1}{\eta_x}\right) = \frac{G^{m'}}{C^{m'}(F^m + F^h)} = \frac{G^{m'}}{C^m F^{m'}} = \frac{G^{h'}}{C^m F^{h'}}, \quad \text{since } w^i = G^{i'}. \qquad (10)$$

Equation (10) satisfies the conditions given in (8) for the efficient use of inputs. Thus, the MNE equilibrium lies on the efficient MNE world production frontier. As shown in the next section, this MNE frontier will lie everywhere outside the NE frontier except as the Y axis ($\overline{YX}_m$ and $\overline{YX}_n$ in figure 28.1, respectively).

In the centralized equilibrium (10), the intra-country labour allocations cannot be the same. Suppose, for example, that $L_y^m = L_y^h$, then it must be the case that $L_f^m < L_f^h$, since some of L^m must be used in C. Such an allocation cannot satisfy (10) since $L_f^m < L_f^h$ implies $F^{m'} > F^{h'}$. A similar argument implies that L_f^m cannot equal L_f^h. In short, we must have the following:

$$\frac{G^{m'}}{C^m F^{m'}} = \frac{G^{h'}}{C^m F^{h'}}, \quad \text{iff } L_y^m < L_y^h, L_f^m < L_f^h, \text{ given } L_c^m > L_c^h = 0 \qquad (11)$$

The centralized equilibrium must imply that country m has less resources in both Y and F such that both $G^{m'}$ and $F^{m'}$ exceed $G^{h'}$ and $F^{h'}$. Country m has more total resources in X ($L_y^m < L_y^h$) but the distribution of these resources between C and F differs from that in country h. Since $G^{m'} > G^{h'}$, the wage rate must be higher in country m in terms of Y but also in terms of X since commodity prices are equalized. Conversely, both forms of capital must earn a lower return in country m. Each country has a relatively high price for the factors used intensively in its predominant activity (C for country m and G and F for country h).

The relationship between outputs in the two countries is not however so simple. Whether or not country m's production ratio (X/Y) differs from country h's ratio depends on the global properties of G and F. The fact that $(G^{m'}/F^{m'}) = (G^{h'}/F^{h'})$ from (10) does not imply that $(X^m/Y^m) = (X^h/Y^h)$ or alternative that $(G^m/F^m) = (G^h/F^h)$.

The implication of this dependence on the properties of G and F is that the direction and volume of trade cannot be fully predicted in the model. If the solution of (10) by pure chance involves $(X^m/Y^m) = (X^h/Y^h)$, as just noted, then trade will consist simply of a one-way profit repatriation of both commodities in the same production ratio. If the solution involves different production ratios, then identical, homothetic demand may imply two-way trade with m exporting Y, for example, if $(X^m/Y^m) < (X^h/Y^h)$.

These findings suggest that MNE activity as modelled above does affect the inter-sectoral allocation of economic activity in a country (i.e., $L_y^m < L_y^h$) and does therefore provide a basis for trade. It does not however offer a simple prediction as to the direction of trade. Nevertheless, there will always exist some trade (profit repatriation at a minimum) in the MNE equilibrium as opposed to the symmetric no-trade NE equilibria.

4. Comparing the MNE and NE Equilibria

Consider a fixed allocation of resources between the X and Y sectors for the NE version of the model. First-order conditions imply an optimal allocation of labour in X between the C and F activities. Denoting these labour allocations as $\bar{L}_j^i$, the maximum value of world X production given the fixed level of Y production is given by

$$\bar{X} = C(\bar{L}_c^m)F(\bar{L}_f^m) + C(\bar{L}_c^h)F(\bar{L}_f^h), \tag{12}$$

where $\bar{L}_i^m = \bar{L}_i^h$ by virtue of the symmetry of all of the NE equilibria.

The efficiency advantage of the MNE can easily be demonstrated by considering a simple (although not optimal) production plan. Specifically, the two-plant MNE enterprise could if it wished produce $\bar{X}$ from $\bar{L}_c^m$, $\bar{L}_f^m$, and $\bar{L}_f^h$ and still have $\bar{L}_c^h$ left over:

$$\bar{X} = C(\bar{L}_c^m)[F(\bar{L}_f^m) + F(\bar{L}_f^h)]. \tag{13}$$

Indeed, the MNE can do even better by optimally reallocating labour among the four X-sector activities so as to satisfy the MNE first-order conditions given in (10). Thus, producing $\bar{X}$ with $\bar{L}_c^h$ left over is the *minimum* improvement in productive efficiency that the MNE can realize.

In a sense, production by the MNE thus represents a technical improvement in the world production function for X. The efficient MNE world production frontier must lie everywhere outside the efficient NE world production frontier (except at $X = 0$). This is shown in figure 28.1, where $\overline{YX_m}$ represents the world MNE production frontier and $\overline{YX_n}$ represents the world *NE* production frontier.

An analysis of total world gains or losses from the MNE is straightforward. The process begins by noting that with a convex world production set, the value of the MNE equilibrium production bundle evaluated at a "price ratio" tangent to the production frontier at the MNE production point must exceed the value of any other feasible production bundle evaluated at the same price ratio [Kemp 1969; Markusen 1981). In our case, this "price ratio" is given by the MRT at the MNE equilibrium and therefore by $p_m(1 - 1/\eta_x)$, where subscript m denotes the MNE equilibrium value. The principle is illustrated in figure 28.1: at M, for example, the value of production evaluated at $(MRT)_m$ exceeds the value at that price ratio of all other feasible production bundles. Using subscript i to denote any arbitrary NE equilibrium allocation, this value relationship becomes

$$(Y_m^m + Y_m^h) + p_m\left(1 - \frac{1}{\eta_x}\right)(X_m^m + X_m^h)$$

$$\geq (Y_i^m + Y_i^h) + p_m\left(1 - \frac{1}{\eta_x}\right)(X_i^m + X_i^h). \tag{14}$$

Let C_{ij} denote the consumption of good j in allocation i. Aggregate market clearing requires that

$$(Y_i^m + Y_i^h) = (C_{iy}^m + C_{iy}^h), \quad (X_i^m + X_i^h) = (C_{ix}^m + C_{ix}^h). \tag{15}$$

Substituting (15) into (14) and rearranging, we have

$$[(C_{my}^m + C_{my}^h) + p_m(C_{mx}^m + C_{mx}^h)] \geq [(C_{iy}^m + C_{iy}^h) + p_m(C_{ix}^m + C_{ix}^h)]$$

$$+ \left(\frac{p_m}{\eta_x}\right)(X_m^m + X_m^h - X_i^m - X_i^h). \tag{16}$$

Equation (16) states, for example, that the value of MNE consumption will exceed the value of NE consumption (i.e., the MNE bundle will be revealed preferred) if the total output of X is higher in the MNE equilibrium relative to the NE equilibrium ($X_m^m + X_m^h > X_i^m + X_i^h$).

It is easy to show that the MNE production of X exceeds the combined autarky totals, implying from (16) that welfare is higher in the MNE equilibrium. If the NE autarky equilibrium is at point A in figure 28.1, then the MNE equilibrium must be at a point like M or M' in that diagram. M or M' must be "downhill" of the point on $\overline{YX}_m$ which lies on the same ray from the origin as point A. On such a ray, the MNE would face the same marginal revenue as the NE firms at A (since X/Y is the same) but a lower MRT (at equal X/Y, the MRT on $\overline{YX}_m$ is less than the MRT of $\overline{YX}_n$). Total X production at M or M' in figure 28.1 must exceed total production at A.

The relation between the MNE and Cournot-Nash equilibria (point B in figure 28.1) is ambiguous. Along the same ray from the origin as that through B, the MRT on $\overline{YX}_m$ is less than on $\overline{YX}_n$, but marginal revenue for the MNE is also less than the perceived marginal revenue of the

Cournot-Nash duopolies. Thus, the MNE may continue to achieve a gain in welfare over the NE equilibrium as shown by points M' and B in figure 28.1. On the other hand, the MNE and Cournot-Nash equilibria could be at points M and B, respectively, in figure 28.1, indicating a deterioration in welfare. Relative to the Cournot-Nash equilibrium, the MNE equilibrium enjoys greater productive efficiency at the expense of a higher degree of exercised market power. A more complete welfare analysis requires that we exploit profit and entry restrictions at the level of the individual countries, a subject to which we now turn.

Consider first the situation in the MNE's home country. A sufficient condition for country m to be better off with the MNE is that

$$C_{my}^m + p_m C_{mx}^m \geqq C_{iy}^m + p_m C_{ix}^m, \tag{17}$$

where subscript i again denotes some arbitrary NE equilibrium. The balance of payments constraint for country m is given by

$$C_{my}^m + p_m C_{mx}^m = Y_m^m + p_m X_m^m + \pi^*, \tag{18}$$

where π^* is profits repatriated from country h. Assuming that we are comparing the MNE equilibrium with a symmetric NE equilibrium with no trade, we will have $C_{ij}^m = X_{ij}^m$. Substituting this relationship and (18) into (17) gives us the sufficient condition for home country gains:

$$Y_m^m + p_m X_m^m + \pi^* \geqq Y_i^m + p_m X_i^m. \tag{19}$$

Now subtract from each side of (19) the value of the economy's factor endowment evaluated at the MNE equilibrium factor prices. This is given by

$$w_m \bar{L} + r_{my} \bar{K}_y + r_{mx} \bar{K}_x = w_m L_{jy}^m + w_m L_{jx}^m + r_{my} \bar{K}_y + r_{mx} \bar{K}_x, \tag{20}$$

where $\bar{K}_y$ and $\bar{K}_x$ are the endowments of sector-specific capital in Y and X and r_y and r_x their respective rental rates. $\bar{L}$ and w are the total endowment of labour and the wage rate, respectively. Subtracting (20) from (19), the latter becomes

$$[Y_m^m - w_m L_{my}^m - r_{my} \bar{K}_y] + [p_m X_m^m - w_m L_{mx}^m - r_{mx} \bar{K}_x] + \pi^*$$

$$\geqq [Y_i^m - w_m L_{iy}^m - r_{my} \bar{K}_y] + [p_m X_i^m - w_m L_{ix}^m - r_{mx} \bar{K}_x]. \tag{21}$$

Equation (21) expresses the gains from trade inequality in terms of industry profits evaluated at the MNE equilibrium. Sufficient conditions for (21) to hold and therefore for gains from trade to occur are that

$$\{Y_m^m - w_m L_{my}^m - r_{my} \bar{K}_y] \geqq [Y_i^m - w_m L_{iy}^m - r_{my} \bar{K}_y] \tag{22}$$

and

$$[p_m X_m^m - w_m L_{mx}^m - r_{mx}\bar{K}_x] + \pi^* \geq [p_m X_i^m - w_m L_{ix}^m - r_{mx}\bar{K}_x]. \tag{23}$$

Equation (22) can be rewritten as

$$[1 - w_m a_{lm} - r_{my}a_{km}] Y_m^m \geq [1 - w_m a_{li} - r_{my}a_{ki}] Y_i^m, \tag{24}$$

where a_{lm} and a_{li} are, for example, the unit labour requirements at the MNE and NE equilibria, respectively, for good Y. The left-hand side of (24) is thus unit revenue ($p_y = 1$) minus unit cost at the MNE equilibrium. This is zero due to the assumption of constant returns and perfect competition in Y. The right-hand side of (24) is unit revenue minus unit costs evaluated at the MNE prices but using the NE input coefficients. Since (a_{lm}, a_{km}) are the profit-maximizing input coefficients at prices (w_m, r_{my}), costs must be greater using unit inputs (a_{li}, a_{ki}) and thus the right-hand side of (24) is negative. Thus, the inequality shown in (24) and (22) does indeed hold.

The inequality in (24) is illustrated in figure 28.2, where $Y_m = Y_i = 1$ is the unit isoquant for Y. M and N are the efficient input combinations at the MNE and NE factor prices, respectively. Unit costs at the MNE equilibrium are just tangent to $Y = 1$, as shown. Unit costs using the NE

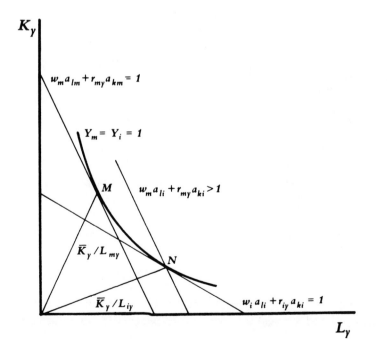

Figure 28.2

inputs (point N) but MNE factor prices are greater than one as shown in figure 28.2. The left-hand side of (24) thus equals zero, while the right-hand side is negative.

To demonstrate that (19) and (17) hold such that country m gains from the MNE now only requires us to show that (23) holds. The left-hand side of (23) is the MNE's total profits (domestic plus foreign repatriation), while the right-hand side is the profits from the NE output evaluated at the MNE prices. This inequality has a revealed preference interpretation similar to the one used above; that is, if (23) holds the MNE's profits are revealed preferred to its alternative NE profits. If this inequality did not hold, then the MNE would find it advantageous to drop one plant or alternatively to not have become a MNE in the first place. Thus, profit maximization plus freedom of entry or exit for MNE operation assures us that (23) does hold and thus (17) holds. If the MNE exists, the home country must gain.

Equations equivalent to (17)–(24) can be derived for the host country, the only difference being that π^* enters with a minus sign in (18), (19), (21), and (23). The analysis of (24) and figure 28.2 remains valid for the Y industry, and thus the host country equivalent of (22) holds. Gains from trade will therefore be realized if the host country equivalent of (23) holds. This is written as

$$[p_m X_m^h - w_m L_{mx}^h - r_{mx} \bar{K}_x] - \pi^* \geqq [p_m X_i^h - w_m L_{ix}^h - r_{mx} \bar{K}_x]. \tag{25}$$

The left-hand side of (25) is the profits earned by the MNE minus the profits repatriated and is assumed to be greater than or equal to zero. The right-hand side is the profits that would be earned by producing the NE output at the MNE prices. This is not necessarily negative, as will be discussed below. Thus, even though the MNE produces with greater technical efficiency, the fact that it repatriates profits which might otherwise have gone to host country entrepreneurs means that gains are not assured for the host country.

The possible trade-offs between efficiency and market power are shown in figures 28.3 and 28.4, where $\bar{Y}^h \bar{X}_n^h$ represents the NE transformation frontier for country h. $\bar{Y}^h \bar{X}_m^h$ gives the MNE frontier under the assumption that activity C is centralized in m and thus resources are freed for production in h. M denotes the MNE equilibrium and N the NE equilibrium in each diagram. The value of gross output measured in terms of Y is given by point G.

Since F is characterized by constant returns (as is Y), the marginal costs of producing X and Y equal average costs. Payments to domestic factor owners which equal total domestic income at the MNE equilibrium are therefore given in terms of Y by point F in each diagram (the slope of $\bar{Y}^h \bar{X}_m^h$

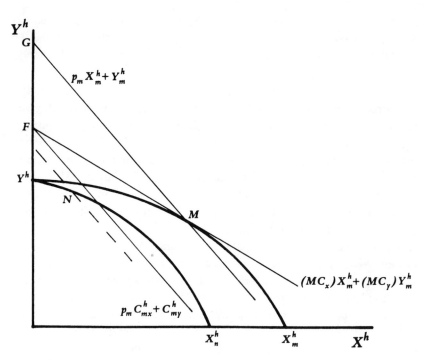

Figure 28.3

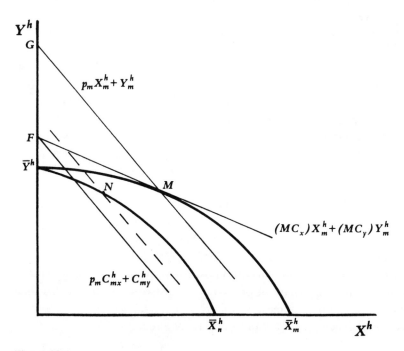

Figure 28.4

at M is the ratio of marginal costs). The budget line of domestic factor owners is constructed by drawing a line with slope p_m through point F. The distance between the price lines through G and F gives the MNE profits.

Using the revealed preference criteria employed above, the host country is assured of gains if the price line through F passes above N which gives national income (factor income plus profits of the domestic firm) at the NE equilibrium. (The dotted line in each diagram gives NE income at MNE prices.) As constructed, this does occur in figure 28.3 but not in figure 28.4. In the latter case, domestic gross income increases with the MNE, but repatriation leaves the host country worse off. The question now is whether or not the possibility illustrated in figure 28.4 can be ruled out by further considerations such as limit pricing.

Suppose that the entrants in the host country behave in a "Bertrand" fashion, viewing the MNE's prices as parametric in making their entry decision. Assume further that the MNE prices to prevent entry by these Bertrand firms; that is, the MNE must produce an output sufficiently large that at the resulting commodity and factor prices there is no profitable output that a single-plant entrant could produce. The right-hand side of (25) gives the profits that an entrant could earn at MNE prices by producing the NE output. If there is no profitable output that could be produced by a single-plant entrant at these prices, then this expression must be negative. This type of pricing to prevent entry by Bertrand firms thus implies that the inequality in (25) holds and that the host country is assured of gains.

Bertrand behaviour by entrants is not, of course, the only or the most reasonable form of entry behaviour. Unfortunately, it is also true that other forms of behaviour do not ensure that the right-hand side of (25) is non-positive. Suppose, for example, that entrants behave in a Cournot fashion, viewing the output of the MNE as fixed. The entrant then knows that if he enters, the price of X will fall as world production increases. With increasing returns to scale, he may therefore not find it profitable to enter even if the right-hand side of (25) is positive (e.g., if X_i^h is actually produced, price changes will lead to negative profits).

We can, however, offer one alternative sufficient condition for gains which looks at the problem from a somewhat different perspective. Suppose that country h taxes repatriated profits (in a non-distortionary manner) such that the left-hand side of (25) is positive. If the tax is set such that the revenue (country h's share of profits) is at least equal to the profits that would be earned by a domestic entrepreneur producing the NE output at MNE prices, then (25) holds and gains are assured.

Notes

Ideas contained in this paper were first presented at the Workshop on "Production and Trade in a World with Internationally Mobile Factors of Production" financed by the Bank of Sweden Tercentenary Foundation, and held at the Institute for International Economic Studies, University of Stockholm, 4–15 August 1980. The author would like to thank participants in the workshop for helpful comments and suggestions, and thank the Social Sciences and Humanities Research Council of Canada for financial support.

1. A few of the relevant works include McManus (1972), Buckley and Casson (1976), Dunning (1977), Kindleberger (1969, 1970), Caves (1971, 1974), Vernon (1971), Horst (1976), Hymer (1976), Gorecke (1976), and Parry (1980).

2. Recent analyses of general equilibrium theory of factor movements can be found, for example, in Jones (1967), Kemp (1969), Brecher and Díaz-Alejandro (1977), Bhagwati and Brecher (1980), and Markusen and Melvin (1979). These articles are not entirely satisfactory for the study of direct foreign investment since they provide no motivation as to why foreign investment might be concentrated in certain sectors, much less why it might direct rather than portfolio investment. Batra and Ramachandran (1980) have recently formalized the ideas of Caves (1971), who notes that international investment is often sector specific. Yet Batra and Ramachandran still do not come to grips with the issue of direct versus portfolio investment insofar as their model provides no motivation as to why a firm wishes to control a foreign subsidiary versus simply making a portfolio investment in the foreign industry. Like earlier works, the Batra and Ramachandran model continues to rely on perfect competition, constant returns, and physical factor flows generated by ex ante factor price differences.

3. Technological assumptions presented below ensure that there will be only a single plant in each country. Also, I should point out that the type of MNE modelled here would probably be termed a "horizontal" MNE in that production facilities in the two countries are concerned with producing only one good. On the other hand, countries will be partially specialized as to the activities they perform in the production of this good, and thus there is something of a "vertical" (or "hierarchical") dimension to this MNE as well. Caves (1980) notes that "a number of studies have established that the importance of intangible assets to an industry is an excellent predictor of horizontal direct investment."

4. We will assume throughout the paper that economies of multi-plant operation are such that independent firms have at best an imperfect ability to transfer "intangibles" among themselves. The idea is that to share fully in these economies, two independent firms would have to be fully integrated in everything but name (e.g., the two firms' engineers and managers would have to work together). Throughout the paper, the term joint-profit maximization will refer only to price collusion.

5. See Herberg and Kemp (1969) for an analysis of some local properties of the production frontier with increasing returns to scale. By assuming CES production functions, Markusen and Melvin (1981) are able to derive some global properties. Herberg and Kemp note that the production set must be nonconvex in a small

neighbourhood about $X = 0$, given Heckscher-Ohlin technology. This result does not necessarily hold for the specific-factors technology and we shall simply assume convexity of the production set over the relevant range of the production frontier.

6. See Jones (1971) and Neary (1978) for a discussion of sector-specific factors models.

7. Centralization of C could also be achieved by differences in factor endowments between countries m and h and differences in factor intensities between C and F activities. While such factor proportions effects may be empirically quite important, they are well understood from the existing literature. More to the point, one purpose of this paper is to suggest an entirely different basis for trade, as noted above.

8. The assumption that firms have no monopsony power may seem strained in a two-good model. However, none of the results to follow relies on the fact that there are only two goods. All results continue to hold if there are many competitive sectors such that we could more reasonably assume that the X sector is a small employer of labour. Recent general equilibrium models of monopsony include Feenstra (1980), McCulloch and Yellen (1980), and Markusen and Robson (1980).

9. The commodity price and factor price equalization property of autarky equilibrium breaks down if countries are of different size. With increasing returns to scale in X, the production frontier of the larger country will be flatter along any ray from the origin. This implies a lower autarky price ratio in the large country, and a world production bundle which is interior to the world production frontier (see Markusen and Melvin 1981; Markusen 1981).

10. This result will generally not hold if there are strongly increasing returns in X such that the production frontiers of m and h are convex (i.e., the production sets are nonconvex). In that case, the joint maximum will involve a nonsymmetric equilibrium in which countries specialize (see Melvin 1969; Kemp 1969; or Markusen and Melvin 1981).

11. I should be a bit careful in talking about "social welfare," since there are, of course, distributional differences between A and B in figure 28.1 (e.g., the monopolists are worse off at B). From either a revealed preference or a compensation principle approach, however, B is superior to A.

References

Batra, R. N., and R. Ramachandran. 1980. Multinational firms, and the theory of international trade and investment. *American Economic Review* 70, 278–290.

Bhagwati, Jagdish, and Richard A. Brecher. 1980. National welfare in an open economy in the presence of foreign owned factors of production. *Journal of International Economics* 10, 103–115.

Brecher, Richard A., and Carlos Díaz-Alejandro. 1977. Tariffs, foreign-capital and immiserizing growth. *Journal of International Economics* 7, 317–322.

Buckley, P. J., and M. Casson. 1976. *The Future of the Multinational Enterprise.* Macmillan, London.

Caves, Richard E. 1971. International corporations: The industrial economics of foreign investment. *Economica* 38, 1–27.

Caves, Richard E. 1974. Causes of direct investment: Foreign firms' shares in Canadian and U.K. manufacturing industries. *Review of Economics and Statistics* 56, 279–293.

Caves, Richard E. 1980. Investment and location policies of multinational companies. Harvard University Working Paper.

Caves, R. E., M. E. Porter, and M. Spence. 1980. *Competition in the Open Economy: A Model Applied to Canada.* Harvard University Press, Cambridge.

Dunning, J. H. 1977. The determinants of international production. *Oxford Economic Papers* 25, 289–330.

Eastman, H. C., and S. Stykolt. 1967. *The Tariff and Competition in Canada.* Macmillan, Toronto.

Ethier, Wilfred. 1979. Internationally decreasing costs and world trade. *Journal of International Economics* 9, 1–24.

Feenstra, R. C. 1980. Monopsony distortions in the open economy: A theoretical analysis. *Journal of International Economics* 10, 213–236.

Gorecke, Paul K. 1976. The determinants of entry by domestic and foreign enterprises in Canadian manufacturing. *Review of Economics and Statistics* 58, 485–488.

Helpman, Elhanan. 1981. International trade in the presence of product differentiation, economies of scale, and monopolistic competition. *Journal of International Economics* 11, 305–340.

Herberg, Horst, and Murray C. Kemp. 1969. Some implications of variable returns to scale. *Canadian Journal of Economics* 2, 403–415.

Horst, Thomas. 1976. American multinationals and the U.S. economy. *American Economic Review* 66, 149–154.

Horstmann, Ignatius, and James R. Markusen. 1987. Strategic investments and the development of multinationals. *International Economic Review*, forthcoming.

Hymer, Stephen H. 1976. *The International Operation of National Firms: A Study of Direct Foreign Investment.* MIT Press, Cambridge.

Jones, Ronald W. 1967. International capital movements and the theory of tariffs. *Quarterly Journal of Economics* 81, 1–38.

Jones, Ronald W. 1971. A three-factor model in theory, trade and history. In Jagdish N. Bhagwati et al., eds., *Trade, Balance of Payments and Growth: Papers in Honor of Charles P. Kindleberger.* North Holland, Amsterdam, 3–21.

Kemp, Murray C. 1969. *The Pure Theory of International Trade and Investment.* Prentice-Hall, Englewood Cliffs, N. J.

Kindleberger, Charles P. 1969. *American Business Abroad.* Yale University Press, New Haven.

Kindleberger, Charles P., ed. 1970. *The International Corporation.* MIT Press, Cambridge.

Krugman, Paul. 1979. Increasing returns, monopolistic competition and international trade. *Journal of International Economics* 9, 395–410.

Magee, Stephen P. 1977. Application of the dynamic limit pricing model to the price of technology and international technology transfer. In K. Brunner and A. Meltzer, eds., *Optimal Policies, Control Theory and Technology Exports*. North Holland, Amsterdam, 203–224.

McCulloch, R., and J. L. Yellen. 1980. Factor market monopsony and the allocation of resources. *Journal of International Economics* 10, 237–248.

McManus, J. C. 1972. The theory of the international firm. In G. Paquet, ed., *The Multinational Firm and the Nation State*. Collier-Macmillan, Don Mills, Ontario, 66–93.

Markusen, James R. 1981. Trade and the gains from trade with imperfect competition. *Journal of International Economics* 11, 531–551.

Markusen, James R. 1983. Factor movements and commodity trade as complements. *Journal of International Economics* 13, 341–356.

Markusen, James R., and James R. Melvin. 1979. Tariffs, capital mobility and foreign ownership. *Journal of International Economics* 9, 395–410.

Markusen, James R., and James R. Melvin. 1981. Trade, factor prices and the gains from trade with increasing returns to scale. *Canadian Journal of Economics* 14, 450–469.

Markusen, James R., and Arthur Robson. 1980. Simple general equilibrium with a monopsonized sector. *Canadian Journal of Economics* 13, 668–682.

Melvin, James R. 1969. Increasing returns to scale as a determinant of trade. *Canadian Journal of Economics* 2, 389–402.

Melvin, James R., and Robert Warne. 1973. Monopoly and the theory of international trade. *Journal of International Economics* 3, 117–134.

Neary, J. Peter. 1978. Short-run capital specificity and the pure theory of international trade. *Economic Journal* 88, 488–510.

Parry, Thomas G. 1980. *The Multinational Enterprise: International Investment and Host-Country Impacts*. Jai Press, Greenwich, Conn.

Scherer, F. M. 1980. *Industrial Market Structure and Economic Performance*. 2nd ed. Rand McNally, Chicago.

Scherer, F. M., et al. 1975. *The Economics of Multi-Plant Operation: An International Comparisons Study*. Harvard University Press, Cambridge.

Vernon, Raymond. 1971. *Sovereignty at Bay: The Multinational Spread of U.S. Enterprises*. Basic Books, New York.

29

A Simple Theory of International Trade with Multinational Corporations

Elhanan Helpman

The role of multinational corporations in the conduct of foreign trade has grown over time and has reached very large proportions. In the United States, for example, at the all-manufacturing level, multinational corporations accounted in 1970 for 62 percent of its exports ($22 billion out of $35 billion) and 34 percent of its imports ($10.5 billion out of $31 billion) (see U.S. Tariff Commission 1973, p. 322). It is therefore not surprising that the ramifications of their existence are of major concern to international trade experts. Nevertheless, there exists no well-articulated theory that explains the conditions for their emergence of predicts under these conditions a structure of trade that comes close to observed trade patterns.

Existing general equilibrium theories of international trade have been developed without explicit treatment of the multinational corporation. The discussion of direct foreign investment in Caves (1971) (and the work that followed from it) is an exception. There are many treatments of the multinational corporation in a partial equilibrium framework (see Caves 1982, chap. 2), but they shed only limited light on a central problem of trade theory, namely, the explanation of trade patterns. We are in need of a theory that describes conditions under which firms find it desirable to shift activities to foreign locations and that is able to predict the pattern of trade that emerges under these conditions. Foundations of such a theory are proposed in this paper with the following important features: (1) there are differentiated products, economies of scale, and monopolistic competition, and (2) there exist inputs (e.g., management, marketing, and R & D) that can serve product lines without being located in their plants.

In this paper the theory deals with single product firms. I deal with horizontal and vertical integration in Helpman (1985). Firms maximize

This paper was originally published in *Journal of Political Economy* 92, no. 3 (1984): 451–471. © 1984, The University of Chicago. All rights reserved.

profits and make, therefore, cost-minimizing location choices of product lines. This feature brings about the emergence of multinational corporations as a result of the tendency of factor rewards to differ across countries. Here the emphasis is on one source of pressure on relative factor rewards— differences in relative factor endowments. Transport costs and tariffs are assumed away, so that production facilities are not established in order to save transport costs or in order to produce behind tariff walls. Other reasons for multinationality, such as tax advantages of various forms, are also not considered.

Apart from describing in a general equilibrium system conditions under which firms choose to become multinational, the theory provides an explanation of trade patterns in which the multinational corporations play a central role. There is intersectoral, intra-industry, and intrafirm trade. The last trade component has become of major importance in recent years (see U.S. Tariff Commission 1973, chap. 3; Buckley and Pearce 1979).

In order to bring out as clearly as possible the value added of the theory, simplifying assumptions are used throughout. The next section provides a description of the basic model. The structure of an equilibrium in an integrated world economy is described in section 2. Then, in section 3, the features of the integrated world equilibrium are used in order to describe the relationship between factor endowments and trade patterns. The behavior of the volume of trade is analyzed in section 4 and the behavior of the shares of intra-industry and intrafirm trade is analyzed in section 5. The last section is devoted to concluding remarks.

1. The Basic Model

For the purpose of the current study I employ a two-sector modified version of the now standard model of international trade in differentiated products. Preferences are assumed to be identical everywhere and representable by a homothetic utility function $u(Y, U_x)$, where Y is the consumption level of a homogeneous product and $U_x = u_x(\cdot)$ is the subutility level attained in the consumption of differentiated products. The function $u_x(\cdot)$ depends on the specification of preferences for a differentiated product; they can be, for example, of the Dixit and Stiglitz (1977) type or of the Lancaster (1979) type (see Helpman 1984, sec. 8, for a description). In both cases a demand function facing a producer of a single variety can be derived; in the Dixit-Stiglitz case this demand function is of the constant elasticity type (assumed to be larger than one), while in the Lancaster case its elasticity depends on commodity prices and the number of varieties available to consumers (and this elasticity is always larger than one).

It is assumed that there are two factors of production: labor, L, and a general purpose input, H, whose special role in the production of differentiated products will be explained below. The homogeneous product is produced by means of a standard linear homogeneous production function with the associated unit cost function $c_Y(w_L, w_H)$, where w_i is the reward to factor i. A producer of the homogeneous product has to employ all inputs in the same location. In a competitive equilibrium the price of the homogeneous product, taken to be the numeraire, equals unit costs:

$$1 = c_Y(w_L, w_H). \tag{1}$$

The structure of production of differentiated products is more complicated. A firm that wants to produce a given variety has to hire the general purpose input H and adapt it at a cost in order to make it suitable for the production of this variety. Once adapted, the input becomes a firm-specific asset in the sense used by Williamson (1981), and it is tied to the entrepreneurial unit. However, this firm-specific input can serve many plants and it need not be located within a plant in order to serve its product line. In particular, it can serve plants that are located in different countries (see Hirsch 1976 for a similar assumption). Inputs that fit this description are management, distribution, and product-specific R & D. The importance of this type of asset in the operation of multinational corporations is described in Caves (1982, chap. 1). Clearly, in practice, combinations of inputs are required in order to generate such assets; here this aspect is simplified by assuming that only H can serve this purpose.

Let $l(x, h_x)$ be the quantity of labor required to produce x units of a variety of the differentiated product in a single plant when h_x units of H have been adapted for its particular use. A possible form for this function is $l = f_p + g_1(x, h_x)$, where $f_p > 0$ and $g_1(\cdot)$ is positively linear homogeneous. Here f_p generates a plant-specific fixed cost and the variable cost component exhibits constant returns to scale. More generally, I assume that $l(\cdot)$ is the inverse of an increasing-returns-to-scale production function in which h_x is essential for production. Let also $g(w_L, w_H, h_x)$ be the minimum costs required in order to adapt h_x to the desired variety, where $g(\cdot)$ is associated with a nondecreasing-returns-to-scale production function. Then the firm's single plant cost function is

$$C_X(w_L, w_H, x) = \min_{h_x} \; [w_L l(x, h_x) + g(w_L, w_H, h_x) + w_H h_x].$$

This function obviously has the standard properties of cost functions associated with increasing-returns-to-scale production functions. One can also define cost functions for larger numbers of plants. The point worth noting, however, is that the firm or corporation has fixed costs that are corporation specific but not plant specific (they consist of hiring h_X and adapting it), it has plant-specific fixed costs, and it has plant-specific variable costs. The assumption that $l(\cdot)$ is the inverse of an increasing-returns-to-scale production function implies that it pays to concentrate production in a single plant unless there are transportation costs or differences across location in product prices. Since impediments to trade are not considered in this paper, the single plant cost function described above is relevant for what follows. All varieties have the same cost structure.

It is assumed that there is Chamberlinian-type monopolistic competition in the differentiated product sector. Hence, as is well known, in this case firms equate marginal revenue to marginal costs and free entry brings about zero profits in every firm. In a symmetrical equilibrium these two conditions can be written as

$$px = C_X(w_L, w_H, x) \tag{2}$$

and

$$R(p, n) = \theta(w_L, w_H, x), \tag{3}$$

where p is the price of every variety of the differentiated product; $R(\cdot)$ is average revenue divided by marginal revenue, and it measures the degree of monopoly power (it is a constant under the Dixit-Stiglitz specification of preferences); n is the number of varieties available to consumers; and $\theta(\cdot)$ is average costs divided by marginal costs, using $C_X(\cdot)$, and it measures the degree of returns to scale in the production of differentiated products (see Helpman 1981).

The formal conditions of industry equilibrium (1)–(3) that were described above are identical to the conditions used in existing models of trade in differentiated products (see Helpman 1984). The important difference lies in the interpretation of the technology available to corporations in the differentiated product industry. As in most trade theory I will assume that factors of production do not move across national borders. However, because of the technology available in the differentiated product industry, the firm-specific asset h_X can serve product lines in plants that are located in countries other than the country in which h_X is located, and the specificity of h_X implies that arm's-length trade in its services is an inferior organizational form to an integrated firm (see Klein, Crawford, and Alchian 1978). This is precisely the feature that brings about the emergence of multinational corporations. We will call the country in which h_X and the entrepreneurial center are located the parent country of the corporation and the country in which the subsidiary is located the host country.

2. Equilibrium in an Integrated World Economy

As a first step toward the study of international trade between economies of the type described in the previous sections, I describe in this section the symmetrical equilibrium of an integrated world economy. The features of the integrated world economy will then be used to identify patterns of cross-country distributions of the world's endowment of labor and the H factor, which generate certain trade patterns and volumes of trade. This particular link provides valuable information because differences in factor endowments can be associated with differences in relative country size and differences in relative factor endowments, two variables that play a major role in empirical studies. We will study trade patterns and volumes of trade for a fixed-size world economy.

In a symmetrical equilibrium of an integrated world economy factor prices are the same everywhere, and all the corporations that operate in the sector that produces differentiated products have a similar structure; every corporation produces one variety, but there is no overlap in varieties produced by two different corporations; they employ the same quantity of the H factor and the same quantity of labor; they charge the same price for every variety and produce the same quantity of each one of them. Free entry into the industry brings profits down to zero. The number of corporations n is treated as a continuous variable. This is a reasonable approximation when n is a large number.

Apart from (1)–(3) the equilibrium conditions consist of equilibrium conditions in factor markets and in commodity markets. The equilibrium conditions in commodity markets depend on the specification of preferences, and we will not present them because no use is made of them in what follows (for an example, see Helpman 1981). It is only important to remember that the upper tier utility function $u(Y, U_x)$ is homothetic. The equilibrium conditions in factor markets are:

$$a_{LY}(w_L, w_H)y + A_{LX}(w_L, w_H, x)n = L, \tag{4}$$

$$a_{HY}(w_L, w_H)y + A_{HX}(w_L, w_H, x)n = H, \tag{5}$$

where $a_{iY}(w_L, w_H) = \partial c_Y(w_L, w_H)/\partial w_i$, $i = L, H$, is the cost-minimizing input of factor i per unit output of the homogeneous product; $A_{iX}(w_L, w_H, x) = \partial C_X(w_L, w_H, x)/\partial w_i$, $i = L, H$, is the cost-minimizing input of factor i in a representative corporation in the differentiated product industry, and L and H are the total quantities of labor and the H factor available. The quantity $A_{HX}(\cdot)$ consists of h_X plus any other quantity of H that might be required as an input in the process that coverts h_X into a firm-specific asset. Condition (4) ensures equilibrium in the labor market, and (5) ensures equilibrium in the H market. Conditions (1)–(5) plus an equilibrium condition in commodity markets (e.g., that the demand for Y equal its supply) determine the equilibrium values of factor rewards (w_L and w_H), the price of differentiated products (p), the output level of a single variety of the differentiated product (x), the output level of the homogeneous good (y), and the number of corporations in the differentiated product industry (n), which equals the number of varieties available to consumers.

For what follows I make the natural assumption that in this equilibrium the homogeneous product is labor intensive relative to the differentiated product; that is,

$$\frac{a_{LY}}{a_{HY}} > \frac{A_{LX}}{A_{HX}}.$$

Under this assumption the equilibrium distribution of employment across sectors can be described by means of figure 29.1. The vector $O\bar{E}$ represents the endowment of factors of production, the vector OQ represents employment in the differentiated product industry, while OQ' represents employment in the homogeneous good industry. The line BB' represents an equal factor cost line, its slope equals relative factor rewards. It is tangent to an isoquant of the homogeneous good at its intersection point with OQ'. At the intersection of BB' with OQ the equal factor cost line is also tangent to

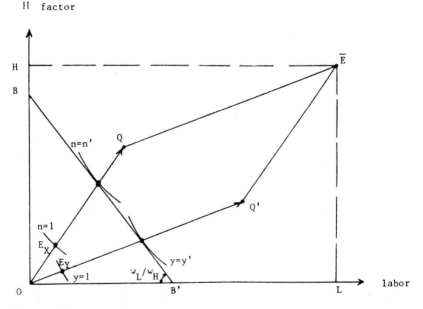

Figure 29.1

an isoquant, but one of a different nature. This isoquant can be recovered from the cost function by means of the set $\{(L_X, H_X)|\exists(w_L, w_H) > 0$ such that $(L_X, H_X) = [A_{LX}(w_L, w_H, x), A_{HX}(w_L, w_H, x)]\}$. This is the collection of inputs that makes possible the production level of a single corporation, and it can be represented by a regularly shaped isoquant, labeled $n = 1$ in figure 29.1. Now draw an entire family of isoquants by a radial expansion and contraction of this single corporation isoquant. Every isoquant in this family represents a different number of corporations, equally sloped on a ray from the origin. Thus, at the intersection of BB' with OQ there is an isoquant belonging to this family that is labeled $n = n'$. Because of its definition this isoquant is tangent to BB'.

Finally observe that using the single corporation isoquant we can calculate the number of corporations that can operate in equilibrium with inputs represented by a point on OQ by dividing the distance of the point from the origin by $\overline{OE_X}$. In a similar way the output of the homogeneous good that is obtained in equilibrium by an input combination represented by a point on OQ' can be calculated by dividing the distance of the point from the origin by $\overline{OE_Y}$. This completes the description of the integrated world equilibrium that is necessary for what follows.

3. The Pattern of Trade

In the standard Heckscher-Ohlin two-country, two-good, two-factor model in which there are no factor intensity reversals and preferences are homothetic and identical across countries, the set of endowment allocations can be divided into two subsets. In the interior of one subset there is factor price equalization and no specialization in production, and every country exports the good whose production makes relatively intensive use of the factor with which the country is relatively well endowed. In the interior of the other subset every country pays a lower reward to the factor of production with which it is relatively well endowed and a higher reward to the other factor of production, at least one country specializes in the production of the good which is a relatively heavy user of its cheaper factor of production, and the pattern of trade is the same as in the former subset. If figure 29.2 (which is a box-diagram reproduction of figure 29.1 with O_j representing the origin for country j) were to describe feasible allocations across countries for a standard Heckscher-Ohlin type economy, then the set with factor price equalization would be represented by O_1QO_2Q' and the other set by its complement.[1]

The pattern of trade that emerges in the present model is much richer than described above. It is useful to describe it by starting with intercountry factor allocations in the set O_1QO_2Q' of figure 29.2. Because of the symmetry

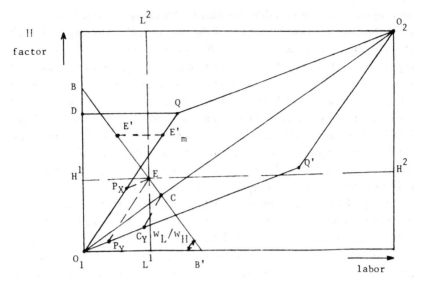

Figure 29.2

in structure it is sufficient of analyze endowment points above the diagonal O_1O_2; this way country 1 is the H-factor-rich country while country 2 is the labor-rich country. Allocations in this set were analyzed in Helpman (1981).

Take, for example, the factor endowment point E in figure 29.2. This point describes an allocation (L^1, H^1) of labor and the H factor to country 1 and an allocation (L^2, H^2) of labor and the H factor to country 2. It is straightforward to see that with this world structure there is an equilibrium with factor price equalization whose cross-country aggregation looks the same as the integrated world equilibrium described in the previous section. In this equilibrium corporations based in one country have no incentive to open subsidiaries in the other country in order to locate product lines there. Assuming that under these circumstances all operations of a corporation are concentrated in the parent country, the output level of the homogeneous product in country j and the number of corporations in the differentiated product industry in that country can be solved from the following factor market equilibrium conditions:

$$a_{LY}y^j + A_{LX}n^j = L^j, \tag{6}$$

$$a_{HY}y^j + A_{HX}n^j = H^j. \tag{7}$$

Here the input-output coefficients in the homogeneous product sector and labor and H-factor use per corporation in the differentiated product industry are taken from the equilibrium of the integrated world economy, because factor prices, product prices, and output per variety are the same in both cases. This is indeed an equilibrium if the solution (y^j, n^j) to (6)–(7) is nonnegative for $j = 1, 2$. But this is, of course, the case for every point in $O_1 Q O_2$, as is demonstrated by the broken-line parallelogram drawn from the particular E in figure 29.2.

Now observe that because profits are zero all income is factor income. Hence, by drawing through E a line BB' whose slope is w_L / w_H, we show the cross-country income distribution. Relative incomes can be read off as follows: Let C be the intersection point of BB' with the diagonal $O_1 O_2$. Then the relative income of country 1 is $\overline{O_1 C}$ divided by $\overline{CO_2}$. In fact, by a proper choice of units, $\overline{O_1 C}$ represents the income level of country 1 and $\overline{CO_2}$ represents the income level of country 2. Since both countries have the same spending pattern, country 1 consumes a proportion s^1 of the world's output y, where s^1 is its share in world income. Hence with a line through C parallel to $O_1 Q$ its comsumption of the homogeneous product can be represented by $\overline{O_1 C_Y}$, where C_Y is the intersection point of this line with $O_1 Q'$. Since production y^1 is represented by $\overline{O_1 P_Y}$, country 1 imports the homogeneous product. Finally, since trade is balanced, this means that country 1 is a net exporter of differentiated products.

I have shown that in the set of factor allocations $O_1 Q O_2$ the intersectoral pattern of trade is the same as in the Heckscher-Ohlin model. Here, however, there is also intra-industry trade in differentiated products. Country j produces n^j varieties of the differentiated product, and it exports them to its trading partner. Hence, the pattern of trade that emerges is the same as in the models of trade in differentiated products that were developed in recent years. To summarize, for factor endowments in the set $O_1 Q O_2$ free trade generates no incentive for the formation of multinational corporations. The structure of trade is the same as in recent models of trade in differentiated products; the intersectoral trade pattern is explained by differences in relative factor endowments while intra-industry trade is explained by monopolistic competition in differentiated products.

The theory proposed in this paper takes on interest because it can identify and analyze the implications of circumstances in which corporations find it profitable to establish subsidiaries abroad. This theory associates multinational corporations with the ability of firms to exploit cross-country differences in factor prices by shifting activities to the cheapest locations. Generally speaking, this theory can be applied to differences in factor prices that result from many different sources. However, in what follows it is applied to potential differences in factor rewards that arise from differences in relative factor endowments.

It is clear from conventional theory and from the previous discussion that factor endowment points above O_1QO_2 lead to unequal factor prices *if* firms have to employ all factor inputs in the same country. Suppose that under these circumstances the H factor is cheaper in country 1 and labor is cheaper in country 2. Now consider what happens when a corporation need not employ all labor and H at a single location; for simplicity also assume that no labor is used in the process that adapts h_x to the particular variety produced by the corporation. Clearly, under these circumstances corporations wish to choose country 1 as their parent country and they wish to open subsidiaries in country 2. These desires reduce the demand for labor in country 1 and increase it in country 2, and they increase the demand for the H factor in country 1 and reduce it in country 2. An equilibrium is attained when either factor prices are equalized or country 1 becomes the parent country of all corporations (with unequal factor prices all H producing differentiated products are located in the H-cheap country). When factor price equalization obtains, there are many equilibrium configurations with various degrees of foreign involvement of the corporations in the differentiated product industry, just as there are many configurations in the factor price equalization set O_1QO_2. In the latter case, factor price equalization is achieved without invoking the possibility that corporations can decentralize their activities geographically. In the case under current examination factor price equalization can be achieved *because* companies can decentralize their activities geographically. There are many ways in which the decentralization can be made consistent with equilibrium. The rule to be adopted below is to consider equilibria in which foreign labor employment is as small as possible, which amounts to considering equilibria with the smallest number of multinational corporations.[2]

Start by considering factor allocations that are in the set O_1DQ of figure 29.2. I argue that endowment points in this set lead to equilibria with factor price equalization and the emergence of multinational corporations (I maintain in the figure the assumption that labor is not used in the adaptation process). Clearly, for endowment points in this set there are no equilibria in which factor prices are equalized, and every firm employs its factors of production in a single location. Hence, multinational corporations have to emerge. The only question that remains, therefore, is whether their emergence brings about factor price equalization. Take, for example, the endowment point E' in figure 29.2. If all the resources of country 1 are employed in the production of differentiated products and its corporations employ in the foreign country the amount of labor $\overline{E'E'_m}$, where E'_m is the intersection point with O_1Q of a horizontal line drawn through E', then the aggregate world equilibrium corresponds to the equilibrium of the integrated world economy. In this discussion E' is the endowment point and E'_m is the employment point. The existence of international corporations enables the employment point to differ from the endowment point. The distance $\overline{O_1 E'_m}$ represents the number of corporations that are based in country 1 (n^1) and the distance $\overline{E'_m Q}$ represents the number of corporations that are based in country 2 (n^2) (the total number is the same as in the integrated world equilibrium). More precisely, since $y^1 = 0$ and $y^2 = y$, the number of corporations that are based in country j, n^j, and the employment of labor in country 2 by subsidiaries of country 1-based multinationals, L^f, are obtained from the following factor market-clearing conditions:

$$A_{LX} n^1 = L^1 + L^f, \quad a_{LY} y + A_{LX} n^2 = L^2 - L^f, \tag{8}$$

$$A_{HX} n^1 = H^1, \quad a_{HY} y + A_{HX} n^2 = H^2. \tag{9}$$

However, the number of varieties produced in country j does not equal n^j; the number of varieties produced in country 1 is smaller than n^1 and the number of varieties produced in country 2 is larger than n^2. The precise difference depends on the size of the labor force L^f employed by subsidiaries. In fact the number of varieties produced in country j, M^j, $j = 1$, 2, is

$$M^1 = n^1 - \frac{L^f}{A_{LX}}, \quad M^2 = n^2 + \frac{L^f}{A_{LX}}.$$

To summarize, we have seen that endowment points in the set $O_1 DQ$ lead to an equilibrium with factor price equalization and the emergence of multinational corporations. Under my assumption about locational tendencies of corporations, in this set country 1 specializes in the production of differentiated products and it serves as a base for the multinational corporations. Country 1 imports the homogeneous product, and there is intra-industry trade in differentiated products. Part of the intra-industry trade is carried out by multinationals. It is also easy to see that the set $O_1 DQ$ can be divided into two subsets such that in one subset country 1 is a *net exporter* of differentiated products and in the other subset country 1 is a *net importer* of differentiated products. Finally, there exists intrafirm trade whose nature is discussed below.

The existence of intrafirm trade is, of course, well documented in the empirical literature (see, e.g., U.S. Tariff Commission 1973, chap. 2; Buckley and Pearce 1979). This takes the form of imports of the parent firm from its subsidiaries as well as exports of the parent firm to its subsidiaries. Much of this trade stems from vertical integration with which one cannot deal satisfactorily by means of the framework employed in this study, but which can be dealt with in a proper extension (see Helpman 1985). However, there is one genuine component of intrafirm trade that is well represented by this model, namely, the invisible exports of the parent to its subsidiaries of services of the H input. Observe that because of the zero-profit condition (2) labor costs are lower than the revenue obtained from sales. This means that the multinational corporation is making "profits" in its subsidiary, because the subsidiary hires labor only in the host country. This means that the profits of the subsidiary are just sufficient to cover the costs of the H input, which is hired in the parent country. The difference between revenue and labor costs of all subsidiaries is $\mu px - w_L L^f$, where $\mu = L^f/A_{LX}$ is the number of multinational corporations. This can be considered to be either profits repatriated by the parent firms or payments by the subsidiaries for services rendered by the parent firms. From an economic point of view the second interpretation is the appropriate one. Hence, $\mu px - w_L L^f$ represents intrafirm trade.

In order to proceed with the analysis of trade patterns, figure 29.3 reproduces the basic features of figure 29.2 and contains a further division of the set above $O_1 Q O_2$. Now consider endowment points in the parallelogram $O_2 QDF$. Following the discussion of endowment points in the set $O_1 DQ$ it is clear that endowment points in $O_2 QDF$ lead to equilibria with factor price equalization and multinational corporations that are homo-

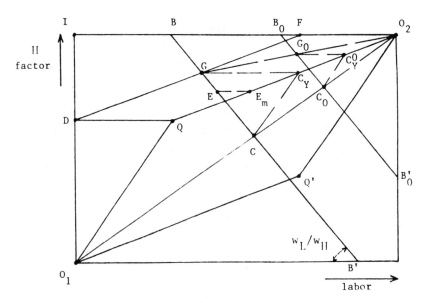

Figure 29.3

morphic to the integrated world economy equilibrium. Thus, if E is the endowment point, then E_m is a feasible employment point when the techniques of production of the integrated world equilibrium are used, and $\overline{EE_m}$ represents labor employment of country 1-based multinationals in country 2. It is also clear from figure 29.3 that endowment points in the set DIF can have no equilibria with factor price equalization, for in order to use the integrated world equilibrium production techniques, country 1 has to employ in country 2 a quantity of labor larger than total employment required in the differentiated product industry. This cannot take place, because only in this sector can corporations shift activities to other countries. Hence, for endowment points in the set DIF, all corporations that produce differentiated products are based in country 1 and all product lines are located in country 2.[3] Country 1 exports services of the H input and imports all the differentiated products from country 2. It may import or export the homogeneous product.

Returning to endowment points in the set O_2QDF, observe that there are two possible patterns of trade depending on the location of the endowment point. For the endowment point E and the employment point E_m, country 1 imports the homogeneous product as well as varieties of the differentiated product that are produced by its subsidiaries, and it exports the other varieties as well as services of the H input. The only part of this assertion that requires elaboration is that country 1 imports the homogeneous product. This can be seen as follows. Let BB' be the equal cost line that passes through E. Then its intersection point with the diagonal O_1O_2, that is, point C, represents each country's income level. Draw through C a line parallel to O_1Q, and let C_Y be its intersection point with O_2Q. Then $\overline{O_2C_Y}$ represents the consumption level of the homogeneous product in country 2, while $\overline{O_2E_m}$ represents the output level of the homogeneous product in country 2. Hence, country 2 exports the homogeneous product and country 1 imports it. It is clear from figure 29.3 that the same pattern of trade emerges for all endowment points on BB' that belong to O_2QDF.

Now consider endowment points in O_2QDF that lie on B_0B_0'. For the distribution of income represented by this line, the consumption of the homogeneous product is represented by $\overline{O_2C_Y^0}$ (constructed in the same way as above). It is clear, however, that only at endowment points below G_0 does country 2 export the homogeneous product, while at endowment points above G_0 country 1 exports the homogeneous product. At point G_0 (as well as at point G) there is no trade in the homogeneous product. Generally, at endowment points that are in O_2QDF, but below GO_2, the pattern of trade is as the one described for point E. On the other hand, at endowment points that belong to O_2QDF, but are above GO_2, country 1 exports the homogeneous product as well as services of the H input and some varieties, while country 2 exports only varieties that are produced by subsidiaries of country 1-based multinationals. A further division into subsets in which country 1 is a net exporter or a net importer of differentiated products is also possible.

We have identified five sets of endowment distributions relevant for the study of trade patterns $(O_1 QO_2, O_1 DQ, O_2 QDG, O_2 GF,$ and $DIF)$. In four of them the equilibrium requires the existence of multinational corporations. Overall, they represent a rich collection of trade patterns with features that seem to fit reality better than those provided by existing trade theories.

4. The Volume of Trade

I have described in the previous section possible trade patterns and how they are related to the distribution of the world's endowment of factors of production. As is clear from the partition of the endowment set into subsets in which certain patterns of trade obtain (see figure 29.3), the pattern of trade depends on two factors: (1) relative country size in terms of GNP and (2) the difference in relative factor endowments. For example, if country 1 is relatively small and has a relatively high endowment of the H factor, then the endowment point is in $O_1 DQ$, there exist multinational corporations that are based in country 1, country 1 exports differentiated products and invisible H services to its subsidiaries, and it imports differentiated products and the homogeneous good. Differences in relative factor endowments and the relative size of countries are observable economic variables of major interest. I provide, therefore, in this section a description of the effects that these two variables have on the volume of trade. These findings are summarized by figure 29.4 in which the arrows indicate directions in which the volume of trade increases.

Start by considering endowment points in the set $O_1 QO_2$. In this region there are no multinational corporations. The volume of trade is defined in the usual way as the sum of exports, where the summation is over countries and sectors. Because of balanced trade, this is equal in a two-country world to twice the exports of one of the countries. In this set country 1 exports only differentiated products, so that the volume of trade is

$$V = 2pxs^2 M^1, \quad \text{for } E \in O_1 QO_2, \tag{10a}$$

where M^1 is the number of varieties produced in country 1 and s^2 is the share of country 2 in world income. Hence, for fixed relative country size the volume of trade increases with the number of varieties produced in the H-factor-rich country, and for a fixed number of varieties produced in

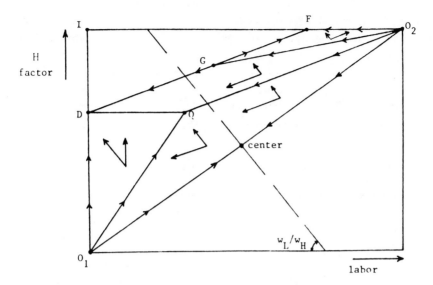

Figure 29.4

country 1 the volume of trade increases with the relative size of country 2. Since M^1 is fixed on lines parallel to O_2Q, the arrows inside the set O_1QO_2 and on O_2Q in figure 29.4 describe directions in which the volume of trade increases.

On the diagonal O_1O_2 we have $M^1 = s^1M$, where $M = n$ is the number of varieties produced in the world economy. Upon substitution into (10a) this yields

$$V = 2pxMs^1s^2, \quad \text{for } E \in O_1O_2, \tag{10b}$$

implying that the volume of trade is largest when the countries are of equal size and is smaller the more unequal the size of countries. This is also described by the arrows in figure 29.4.

On the line O_1Q we have $pxM^1 = s^1Z$, where Z is world income and spending and $M^1 = n^1$. Hence, upon substitution into (10a),

$$V = 2Zs^1s^2, \quad \text{for } E \in O_1Q, \tag{10c}$$

and the volume of trade rises the more equitable is the world's distribution of income. In figure 29.4 country 1 is of smaller size than country 2 at endowment points on O_1Q (which is, of course, not always the case); therefore the volume of trade increases in the northeastern direction as indicated by the arrows. The behavior of the volume of trade in the set O_1QO_2 described above is a generalization of propositions 5 and 6 in Helpman (1981).

For endowment points in O_1DQ country 2 exports the homogeneous good and M^2 varieties of the differentiated product. Some of the varieties it exports are produced by country 2-based firms while μ of them are produced by subsidiaries of country 1-based multinational corporations. The same trade pattern exists in O_2QDG, except that in this set all the varieties exported by country 2 are produced by country 1-based multinationals (i.e., $M^2 = \mu$). This means that the volume of trade can be represented as follows:

$$V = 2(y^2 - Y^2 + pxs^1M^2), \quad \text{for } E \in (O_1DQ) \cup (O_2QDG). \tag{11}$$

For endowment points in O_1DQ the homogeneous product is produced only in country 2, so that $y^2 = y$. Also, since $Y^2 = s^2y = (1 - s^1)y$, upon substitution into (11) we obtain

$$V = 2s^1(y + pxM^2), \quad \text{for } E \in O_1DQ. \tag{12}$$

This means that when the relative country size is given the volume of trade increases with the number of varieties produced in country 2, whereas when the number of varieties produced in country 2 is given, the volume of trade increases with the relative size of country 1, as shown in figure 29.4.

At endowment points in the set O_2QDG all the varieties exported by country 2 are produced by subsidiaries of country 1-based multinationals; that is, $M^2 = \mu$. Also $Y^2 = s^2y$ and $s^2Z = y^2 + w_L\mu A_{LX}$, where $Z = pxn + y$. Combining these with (11), we obtain

$$V = 2[(1 - s^1)pxn + px\mu(s^1 - \theta_{LX})], \quad \text{for } E \in O_2QDG, \tag{13a}$$

where θ_{LX} is the share of labor costs in the production of differentiated products. Hence, when the relative country size is given the volume of trade increases with the widening of the difference in relative factor endowments (with μ) if and only if the share of country 1 in world income exceeds the share of labor costs in the differentiated product industry. The arrows in O_2QDG that indicate the increase in the volume of trade in the northwestern direction (see figure 29.4) are drawn on the assumption $s^1 > \theta_{LX}$ (which always holds for endowment points close to O_2). It is also clear from (13a) that given μ, the volume of trade decreases as the relative size of country 1 increases. However, μ is constant on lines parallel to O_2Q. Therefore, the volume of trade increases in the southwestern direction, as indicated by the arrows drawn in region O_2QDG and on DG. Finally, on O_2G we have $M^2 = \mu$, $y^2 = Y^2 = s^2y$, and $s^2Z = y^2 + w_L\mu A_{LX}$, which yield upon substitution into (11):

$$V = \frac{2s^1s^2px(Z - y)}{w_LA_{LX}}, \quad \text{for } E \in O_2G, \tag{13b}$$

implying that the volume of trade declines the more unequal countries are in relative size. This is indicated by the arrows drawn on O_2G.

It remains to consider endowments in O_2GF. In this region country 2 exports only differentiated products produced by subsidiaries of country 1-based multinationals, and the volume of trade is

$$V = 2pxs^1\mu, \quad \text{for } E \in O_2GF, \tag{14}$$

implying that for given μ the volume of trade rises with the relative size of country 1 and that for given relative country size it rises with μ. On O_2F μ is proportional to s^2, which makes the volume of trade larger the closer the endowment is to F (because on O_2F, $s^1 > s^2$). These features are also represented by arrows in figure 29.4.

In summary, figure 29.4 represents a fairly detailed description of the relationship between factor endowments and the volume of trade. It shows that in some sense the larger the difference in relative factor endowments the larger is the volume of trade. On the other hand, relative country size has an ambiguous effect on the volume of trade.

5. Intraindustry and Intrafirm Trade

In this section I investigate the dependence of the shares of intraindustry and intrafirm trade on cross-country differences in relative factor endowments. In all cases, except for region O_1QO_2, the investigation is restricted to fixed relative sizes of the two countries.

The volume of intraindustry trade is defined as the total volume of trade minus the sum over all sectors of the absolute value of the difference between imports and exports. In the current model this reduces to

$$V_{i-i} = 2px \min(s^1M^2, s^2M^1). \tag{15}$$

The definition of the volume of intrafirm trade is more complicated. Exports of the parent firms of services of the H factor are undoubtedly part of this volume of trade. The problem arises with the treatment of the finished differentiated products. If parent firms serve as importers of the finished products manufactured by their subsidiaries, then this appears in the data as intrafirm trade, and similarly if subsidiaries serve as importers of the differentiated products manufactured by parent firms. In some cases the treatment of these flows of goods as intrafirm trade has no economic justification because it is more the consequence of bookkeeping practices than a true economic calculus. In the present model there is no natural choice—much depends on the implicit assumptions about the marketing technology. I choose, therefore, to define intrafirm trade as trade in the services of the H factor. Hence,

$$V_{i-f} = px\mu - w_L L^f = a\mu, \tag{16}$$

where $a = w_H A_{HX} > 0$.

For endowment points in $O_1 Q O_2$ we have $s^1 M^2 < s^2 M^1$ so that, using (10a) and (15), we calculate the share of intra-industry trade to be

$$S_{i-i} = \frac{s^1 M^2}{s^2 M^1} = \frac{s^1 n^2}{s^2 n^1}, \quad \text{for } E \in O_1 Q O_2. \tag{17}$$

This is shown in Helpman (1981, proposition 4) to be a declining function of the difference in relative factor endowments. The share of intrafirm trade is zero at endowment points that belong to $O_1 Q O_2$ because in this region there are no multinational corporations.

Using (12), we obtain

$$S_{i-i} = \frac{px \min(s^1 M^2, s^2 M^1)}{s^1(y + pxM^2)}, \quad \text{for } E \in O_1 DQ. \tag{18}$$

Since one can show that $M^1/M^2 > s^1/s^2$ on $O_1 Q$, then for a given relative country size the share of intra-industry trade rises with the difference in relative factor endowments as we start moving the endowment allocation along an equal income line from a point on $O_1 Q$ in the northwestern direction. If country 1 is small enough, however, this share reaches a maximum and declines with further redistributions that increase the gap in relative factor endowments. This means that with the emergence of multinational corporations the share of intra-industry trade may be positively or negatively related to differences in relative factor endowments. Using (16), the share of intrafirm trade in $O_1 DQ$ can be represented by

$$S_{i-f} = \frac{a(\mu/2)}{s^2 pxM^1 + a\mu}, \quad \text{for } E \in O_1 DQ, \tag{19}$$

where $s^2 pxM^1 + a\mu$ is the volume of exports from country 1. Therefore, for given relative country size a widening of the difference in the H to L ratio between country 1 and country 2 increases the share of intrafirm trade (because it increases μ and reduces M^1).

For an endowment point in $O_2 QDG$, we have $M^2 = \mu$, so that (15), (16), and (13a) imply:

$$S_{i-i} = \frac{px \min(s^1 \mu, s^2 M^1)}{(1 - s^1)pxM + px\mu(s^1 - \theta_{LX})}, \quad \text{for } E \in O_2 QDG, \tag{20}$$

$$S_{i-f} = \frac{a(\mu/2)}{(1 - s^1)pxM + px\mu(s^1 - \theta_{LX})}, \quad \text{for } E \in O_2 QDG. \tag{21}$$

Assume $s^1 > \theta_{LX}$ in this region. Then, for a given relative country size, starting from $O_2 Q$, the share of intra-industry trade rises with increases in the difference between the H to L ratio in country 1 and country 2, and it may reach a maximum and decline afterward. This pattern is similar to that in $O_1 DQ$. The share of intrafirm trade, on the other hand, is larger the larger the difference in relative factor endowments (given relative country size).

In region $O_2 GF$, country 2 exports only differentiated products. Therefore, because of balanced trade, at endowment points that belong to it $s^1 \mu > s^2 M^1$. Using this relationship as well as (14), (15), and (16), we find that on lines in $O_2 GF$ that represent constant relative country size, the share of intra-industry trade declines with increasing differences in relative factor endowments and the share of intrafirm trade is constant.

The broad picture that emerges from this analysis is that for a given relative country size, the share of intrafirm trade is larger, the larger the difference in relative factor endowments, but that in the presence of multinational corporations no clear-cut relationship exists between the share of intra-industry trade and differences in relative factor endowments.

6. Concluding Comments

I have developed in this paper a general equilibrium theory of international trade in which multinational corporations play an essential role. This theory can identify and analyze the implications of circumstances in which corporations find it profitable to become multinational. These corporations are well-defined economic entities, they possess firm-specific assets, they engage in monopolistic competition, and they play an active role in foreign trade. The theory explains the simultaneous existence of intersectoral trade, intra-industry trade, and intrafirm trade. Despite the relative richness of the theory it needs further extensions and elaborations in order to deal with the wide range of problems that are at the heart of international economics. An extension of the current theory to horizontally as well as vertically integrated corporations is presented in Helpman (1985). This extension generates more realistic patterns of resource allocation, without altering the fundamental properties of trade patterns that were derived in the current study. In particular, integrated multinational corporations end up having production facilities in parent as well as in host countries, and the existence of vertical integration brings about intrafirm trade both in H services and in intermediate inputs. This realism is achieved at a substantial cost in terms of the complexity of the theory of the firm. Nevertheless, I believe the benefit-cost ratio to be larger than one. The current theory can also explain cross-country penetration of multinational corporations as a result of impediments to trade (e.g., transport costs or tariffs). This is evident from the fact that the establishment of a new plant for the same variety requires additional fixed costs but saves the costs associated with trade impediments and does not require the hiring of new H factors. Hence, for sufficiently high impediments, cross-country penetration is expected.

Notes

I wish to thank Richard Caves for insightful discussions during my work on this project, as well as my wife Ruth for patiently listening to long lectures on the subject of this paper. Helpful comments on a previous version were provided by Eitan Berglas, Torsten Persson, Lars Svensson, and José Scheinkman. This is a revised and much simplified version of Harvard Institute of Economic Research Discussion Paper no. 961. The first version was written when I was a visiting professor in the Department of Economics at Harvard University.

1. See Dixit and Norman (1980, chap. 4), who also deal with a case in which there is factor intensity reversal.

2. This choice can be justified as a long-run equilibrium of a dynamic adjustment process in which it is costly to shift plants abroad.

3. This is necessarily so when production is homothetic. It seems that the reverse pattern of specialization is possible in the absence of homotheticity.

References

Buckley, Peter J., and Pearce, Robert D. Overseas production and exporting by the world's largest enterprises: A study in sourcing policy. *J. Internal. Bus. Studies* 10 (Spring/Summer 1979): 9–20.

Caves, Richard E. International corporations: The industrial economics of foreign investment. *Economica* 38 (February 1971): 1–27.

Caves, Richard E. *Multinational Enterprise and Economic Analysis*. Cambridge: Cambridge Univ. Press, 1982.

Dixit, Avinash K., and Norman, Victor. *Theory of International Trade*. Cambridge: Cambridge Univ. Press, 1980.

Dixit, Avinash K., and Stiglitz, Joseph E. Monopolistic competition and optimum product diversity. *A.E.R.* 67 (September 1977): 297–308.

Helpman, Elhanan. International trade in the presence of product differentiation, economies of scale and monopolistic competition: A Chamberlin-Heckscher-Ohlin approach. *J. Internat. Econ.* 11 (August 1981): 305–340.

Helpman, Elhanan. Increasing returns, imperfect markets, and trade theory. In *Handbook of International Economics*, vol. 1, edited by Ronald W. Jones and Peter B. Kenen. Amsterdam: North Holland, 1985.

Helpman, Elhanan. Multinational corporations and trade structure. *Rev. Econ. Stud.* 52 (July 1985): 443–457.

Hirsch, Seev. An international trade and investment theory of the firm. *Oxford Econ. Papers* 28 (July 1976): 258–270.

Klein, Benjamin, Crawford, Robert G., and Alchian, Armen A. Vertical integration, appropriable rents, and the competitive contracting process. *J. Law and Econ.* 21 (October 1978): 297–326.

Lancaster, Kelvin. *Variety, Equity, and Efficiency.* New York: Columbia Univ. Press. 1979.

U.S. Tariff Commission. *Implications of Multinational Firms for World Trade and Investment and for U.S. Trade and Labor.* Washington: Government Printing Office, 1973.

Williamson, Oliver E. The modern corporation: Origins, evolution, attributes. *J. Econ. Literature* 19 (December 1981): 1537–1568.

Index